D0714822

PERSONNEL PSYCHOLOGY AND HUMAN RESOURCE MANAGEMENT

PERSONNEL PSYCHOLOGY AND HUMAN RESOURCE MANAGEMENT

A Reader for Students and Practitioners

Edited by

Ivan T. Robertson
and
Cary L. Cooper

*University of Manchester
Institute of Science & Technology, UK*

JOHN WILEY & SONS, LTD
Chichester · New York · Weinheim · Brisbane · Singapore · Toronto

Copyright © 2001 by John Wiley & Sons, Ltd,
Baffins Lane, Chichester,
West Sussex PO19 1UD, England

National   01243 779777
International (+44) 1243 779777
e-mail (for orders and customer service enquiries): cs-books@wiley.co.uk
Visit our Home Page on http://www.wiley.co.uk
or http://www.wiley.com

All Rights Reserved. No part of this publication may be reproduced, stored in a retrieval
system, or transmitted, in any form or by any means, electronic, mechanical,
photocopying, recording, scanning or otherwise, except under the terms of the Copyright,
Designs and Patents Act 1988 or under the terms of a licence issued by the Copyright
Licensing Agency Ltd, 90 Tottenham Court Road, London W1P 9HE, UK, without the
permission in writing of the Publisher.

Other Wiley Editorial Offices

John Wiley & Sons, Inc., 605 Third Avenue,
New York, NY 10158-0012, USA

Wiley-VCH Verlag GmbH, Pappelallee 3,
D-69469 Weinheim, Germany

John Wiley & Sons Australia Ltd, 33 Park Road, Milton,
Queensland 4064, Australia

John Wiley & Sons (Asia) Pte Ltd, 2 Clementi Loop #02-01,
Jin Xing Distripark, Singapore 129809

John Wiley & Sons (Canada) Ltd, 22 Worcester Road,
Rexdale, Ontario M9W 1L1, Canada

Library of Congress Cataloguing-in-Publication Data

Personnel psychology and human resource management : a reader for students and
practitioners / edited by Cary L. Cooper and Ivan T. Robertson.
     p. cm.—(Key issues in industrial & organizational psychology)
   Includes bibliographical references and index.
   ISBN 0-471-49557-3
   1. Personnel management. 2. Psychology, Industrial. I. Cooper, Cary L. II. Robertson,
Ivan, 1946- III. Series.
HF5549 .P45263 2001
658.3'—dc21

2001017596

British Library Cataloguing in Publication Data
A catalogue record for this book is available from the British Library

ISBN 0-471-49557-3

Typeset in 10/12pt Plantin by Dorwyn Ltd, Rowlands Castle, Hants
Printed and bound in Great Britain by Antony Rowe Ltd, Chippenham, Wilts
This book is printed on acid-free paper responsibly manufactured from sustainable forestry,
in which at least two trees are planted for each one used for paper production.

CONTENTS

ABOUT THE SERIES

Each book in this exciting series draws together the most authoritative and important recent developments on a topic of central importance to industrial and organizational psychology. Selected from volumes of the International Review of Industrial and Organizational Psychology, these collections provide students and practitioners with the ideal tool for:

- Essays, dissertations and new projects
- Quickly updating an area of knowledge for the busy professional
- Source material for lecture courses and seminars
- Beginning research students
- Keeping the consultancy library relevant

Key Issues in Industrial and Organizational Psychology
Edited by Ivan T. Robertson and Cary L. Cooper

Current books published in this series are—

Organizational Psychology and Development
A Reader for Students and Practitioners
Edited by Cary L. Cooper and Ivan T. Robertson

Personnel Psychology and Human Resource Management
A Reader for Students and Practitioners
Edited by Ivan T. Robertson and Cary L. Cooper

Well-Being in Organizations
A Reader for Students and Practitioners
Edited by Cary L. Cooper and Ivan T. Robertson

ABOUT THE EDITORS

Cary L. Cooper
Ivan T. Robertson

Manchester School of Management, University of Manchester Institute of Science and Technology, PO Box 88, Manchester M60 1QD, UK.

Cary L. Cooper received his BS and MBA degrees from the University of California, Los Angeles, his PhD from the University of Leeds, UK, and holds honorary doctorates from Heriot-Watt University and Wolverhampton University. He is currently BUPA Professor of Organizational Psychology and Deputy Vice Chancellor of UMIST. Professor Cooper was Founding and current President of the *British Academy of Management* and is a Fellow of the British Psychological Society, Royal Society of Arts, Royal Society of Medicine and Royal Society of Health. He is also Founding Editor of the *Journal of Organizational Behavior* and co-editor of *Stress Medicine*, serves on the editorial board of a number of other scholarly journals, and is the author of over 90 books and 400 journal articles.

Ivan Robertson is Professor of Work and Organizational Psychology in the Manchester School of Management, UMIST, and Pro-Vice-Chancellor of UMIST. He is a Fellow of the British Academy of Management, and the British Psychological Society, and is a Chartered Psychologist. Professor Robertson's career includes several years experience working as an applied psychologist on a wide range of projects for a variety of different organizations. With Professor Cooper he founded Robertson Cooper Ltd (www.robertsoncooper.com), a business psychology firm which offers consultancy advice and products to clients. Professor Robertson's research and teaching interests focus on individual differences and organizational factors related to human performance. His other publications include 25 books and over 150 scientific articles and conference papers.

CONTRIBUTORS

Catriona Allan — *Institute of Work Psychology, The University of Sheffield, Sheffield S10 2TN, UK*

Caroline Baldry — *Psychology Department, Goldsmith's College, The University of London, New Cross, London SE14 6NW, UK*

Paul M. Brewerton — *Department of Psychology, University of Surrey, Guildford, Surrey GU2 5XH, UK*

Michael Campion — *Department of Organizational Behavior and HRM, Purdue University, 1310 Krannert Building, West Fayette, Indiana 47907, USA*

Thomas R. Caretta — *Aircrew Selection Research Branch, Department of the Air Force, Armstrong Laboratory (AFMC), 7909 Lindbergh Drive, Brooks Air Force Base, Texas 78235, USA*

Clive Fletcher — *Psychology Department, Goldsmith's College, The University of London, New Cross, London SE14 6NW, UK*

Gary Johns — *Department of Management, Concordia University, Montreal, Quebec H3G 1M8, Canada*

Richard J. Klimoski — *Department of Psychology (MS3F5), George Mason University, Fairfax, Virginia 22030–4444, USA*

Filip Lievens — *Department of Personnel Management, Work and Organizational Psychology, University of Ghent, Dunantlaan 2, 9000 Ghent, Belgium*

Carl Maertz — *Department of Organizational Behavior and HRM, Purdue University, 1310 Krannert Building, West Fayette, Indiana 47907, USA*

John P. Meyer — *Department of Psychology, The University of Western Ontario, London, Ontario N6A 5C2, Canada*

Lynne Millward — *Department of Psychology, University of Surrey, Guildford, Surrey GU2 5XH, UK*

Sue Newell   *Nottingham Business School, Nottingham Trent University, Burton Street, Nottingham NG1 4BU, UK*

Malcolm Ree   *Aircrew Selection Research Branch, Department of the Air Force, Armstrong Laboratory (AFMC), 7909 Lindbergh Drive, Brooks Air Force Base, Texas 78235, USA*

Jesús F. Salgado   *Depto Psicologia Social y Basica, Universidad de Santiago de Compostela, 15706 Santiago de Compostela, Spain*

Carole Tansley   *Nottingham Business School, Nottingham Trent University, Burton Street, Nottingham NG1 4BU, UK*

Peter Warr   *Institute of Work Psychology, The University of Sheffield, Sheffield S10 2TN, UK*

INTRODUCTION

I/O psychology has its origins in attempts to make better decisions about how to deal with people at work. In particular personnel selection, training and other key personnel practices have always been of central interest to I/O psychologists. This remains true in the 21st century, despite the significant growth in the influence and expertise of specialist personnel, or human resource practitioners and researchers. This volume covers a number of key topics at the interface of human resource (HR) management and I/O psychology. Although attempts to identify clear boundaries between HR management and I/O psychology are unproductive and futile, it is worth noting the distinctive expertise and point of view that I/O psychologists bring to HR issues. In general terms the essence of this is an approach to research which is driven by the hypothetico-deductive method. This approach includes the application of strong measurement techniques and the empirical testing of ideas, principles and theories. The contributions of I/O psychologists to personnel and HR issues are reflected in three main areas of organizational life: performance; attachment and well being. Topics concerned with well-being are the subject of another volume in this collection (Well-being in Organizations). Performance and attachment issues specifically related to teams or groups and organization-wide matters are also dealt with in another volume (Organizational Psychology and Development).

This volume concentrates on topics at the individual level. The chapters included explore the research in a range of topics. The chapters are written by leading scholars with international reputations in their fields, from Australia, Belgium, Canada, Spain, the UK and the USA. The book is divided into two broad sections: Personnel Psychology and Human Resource Management. As noted above the dividing lines between these fields are not firm and many researchers and practitioners from either field work in similar areas. The subdivision adopted below is merely a convenient way of grouping the chapters into related themes and does not reflect a firm distinction between the fields.

The chapters under the Personnel Psychology heading focus on selection and assessment, beginning with two chapters that provide an overview of research on personnel selection methods and their usage. The other three chapters look at more specific aspects of selection and assessment: assessment centres; multiple source (360 degree) feedback systems and cognitive ability testing. All of the chapters in this section provide a good indication of the way in which psychologists in this field have employed the empirical approach to personnel issues mentioned above. Taken together these five chapters provide an up to date and comprehensive view of the status of research in personnel selection and assessment.

The chapters under the Human Resource Management heading look at a wider set of issues related to attachment and performance in organizations. The first chapter in this section provides a thorough review of learning strategies and occupational training and together with the first chapter in the first section provides an indication of the state of the art in the two main approaches to delivering effective individual performance at work: selection and training. Chapters on absence, turnover, commitment and psychological contracts cover the major issues relating to attachment to organizations.

All of the topics are thoroughly reviewed, drawing on material from the leading volumes of the International Review of Industrial and Organizational Psychology. We hope that this compendium of quality reviews will help to improve research and practice in I/O psychology. In the end, we must attempt to move in the direction of understanding the simple truth of John Ruskin's comments about work in 1852: 'In order that people may be happy in their work, these three things are needed: they must be fit for it; they must not do too much of it; and they must have a sense of success in it.'

Part I

PERSONNEL PSYCHOLOGY

Chapter 1

PERSONNEL SELECTION METHODS

Jesús F. Salgado
Universidad de Santiago de Compostela

INTRODUCTION

This review considers the literature that appeared from 1991 to Autumn 1997. I have also included some materials published before 1991 which may be relevant to this review and were not previously cited in reviews of personnel selection methods in IRIOP, as well as some new materials currently under publication.

In these last six years, a number of topics appear specially relevant in the personnel selection field. First, more attention has been given to the theoretical aspects concerning the validity of predictors of job performance. Second, interviews based on a behavioral and structured format (e.g., situational, behavior description, behavioral structured interviews) have been the subject of a great deal of investigation. Third, personality measures have received a lot of interest from researchers in personnel selection and appear to be predictors of job performance against previous beliefs. Fourth, advances in methodology have also been of interest (e.g., improvements in meta-analysis and utility analysis). In addition to these issues, this review covers traditional topics of personnel selection methods: abilities, biodata, assessment centers, simulations, references and job analysis.

In order to find the literature for this review I used three strategies. First, I conducted several computer-aided searches in the PsycLit data base, using the main concepts as entry words (e.g., personnel selection, ability, personality, job performance) and cross-intersecting between them. Second, I conducted hand-made searches in the most relevant journals which cover the personnel selection area (e.g., *Journal of Applied Psychology*, *Personnel Psychology*, *Journal of Occupational and Organizational Psychology*). Third, I wrote to over one hundred researchers asking for relevant articles.

Several publications must also be remarked upon in this introduction. Dunnette and Hough (1990–1994) have edited the second edition of the

Personnel Selection Methods by Jesús F. Salgado taken from IRIOP 1999 v14, Edited by Cary L. Cooper and Ivan T. Robertson: © 1999 John Wiley & Sons, Ltd

'Bible' of Industrial and Organizational Psychology. Smith and Robertson (1993) have published the third edition of the personnel selection 'Bible' in Great Britain. Anderson and Herriot (1997) have edited an *International Handbook of Selection and Assessment* with contributors from 20 American, Asian and European countries. Other relevant books were edited or published by Cook (1993), Murphy (1996), Rumsay, Walker and Harris (1994), Schmitt and Borman (1993), and Schuler, Farr and Smith (1993). Also, a new journal has been published since 1993: the *International Journal of Selection and Assessment* (Neil Anderson, Editor). Furthermore, two commemorations must be noted. In 1992 the American Psychological Association celebrated its Centennial, and the *Journal of Applied Psychology* (*JAP*) published several articles related to the date (Austin & Villanova, 1992; Harrel, 1992; Katzell & Austin, 1992; Landy, 1992). The Society of Industrial and Organizational Psychology (APA's Division 14) celebrated its golden anniversary in 1996. To commemorate this date *JAP* published five articles on the history of applied psychology (Benjamin, 1997; Farr & Tesluk, 1997; Koppes, 1997; Landy, 1997; Van de Watter, 1997).

Finally, I must acknowledge to being a little biased in my review. The number of articles, book chapters, congress presentations, and so on, was so large, that I had to be somewhat selective, and to be selective in this field is very difficult and risky. Because of the fact that American literature on personnel selection is more well known than the European contributions, I tended to show the current European research whenever possible. I made this choice taking into account the fact that American literature is very well covered in the *Annual Review* chapters on personnel selection. Thus, I thought that showing the European contributions could open doors for possible cooperation between researchers from both continents.

PERFORMANCE AND JOB ANALYSIS ISSUES

Four advances were particularly relevant on performance topics and job analysis in the years that this review covers. One was the contribution made by J.P. Campbell (1994; Campbell, McCloy, Oppler & Sager, 1993; Campbell, Gasser & Oswald, 1996), who outlined a multidimensional theory of job performance. The second advance was the suggestion made by Borman and Motowidlo (1993) that job performance must be distinguished as task performance and contextual performance. The third advance was the result of work done by C. Viswesvaran (1993), who sustained that a general factor of job performance was responsible for most of the covariation among job performance dimensions. Furthermore, research was focused on investigating psychometric characteristics of job performance ratings (Salgado & Moscoso, 1996; Viswesvaran, Ones & Schmidt, 1996). An extended and comprehensive review of performance evaluation in work setting was written by Arvey and Murphy (1998) as an *Annual Review* chapter. The fourth remarkable advance was related to the development of a prototype to build an Occupational Information Network (O*NET; Peterson, Mumford, Borman, 1995).

Job Performance

Based on the findings of Project A, Campbell (1994; Campbell et al., 1993) has developed a conception of job performance characterized as a multidimensional construct. The theory is based mainly on four notions: '(1) the assumption of a general job performance factor cannot represent the best fit; (2) the notion of an ultimate criterion has no meaning; (3) the subjective versus objective distinction is false; and (4) there is a critically important distinction to be made between performance and the results of performance' (Campbell et al., 1993, p.38). To Campbell, performance is the same as behavior, and only includes actions or behaviors relevant to the organization's goals. Performance is not the consequence of action, it is the action itself. Therefore, it is necessary to distinguish between performance and consequences of performance (e.g., effectiveness, productivity or utility). Campbell et al. (1993) suggested that job performance is composed of eight factors, common to all jobs, but with different relevance for each one. The factors are: (1) job-specific task proficiency; (2) non-job-specific task proficiency; (3) written and oral communication task proficiency; (4) demonstration of effort; (5) maintenance of personal discipline; (6) facilitation of peer and team performance; (7) supervision/leadership; and (8) management/administration. Furthermore, according to Campbell et al. (1993) there are three determinants of individual differences in performance: (a) Declarative Knowledge (i.e., knowledge about facts and things); (b) Procedural Knowledge and Skill (i.e. cognitive skill, interpersonal skill); and (c) Motivation (i.e., combined choice effect to expend effort, choice of effort level to be expended, and choice to persist in the expenditure of that level of effort). A confirmatory factor analysis has given empirical support to his model (McCloy, Campbell & Cudeck, 1994).

A second relevant advance with regards to job performance is the suggestion made by Borman and Motowidlo (1993) to distinguish job performance as two different clusters of behaviors. They suggest that job performance includes both in-role behaviors as well as extra-role behaviors. The first behaviors assess task performance and the second behaviors assess what they call 'contextual' performance. The contextual performance construct is closely related to other constructs known as prosocial organizational behavior (Brief & Motowidlo, 1986), organizational citizenship (Munene, 1995; Organ, 1988), organizational spontaneity (George & Brief, 1992) and personal initiative (Frese, Fay, Hilburger et al., 1997). Borman and Motowidlo suggest that task performance is the incumbent proficiency when performing technical or services activities while contextual performance is the contribution made by the incumbent beyond the explicit job requirements (e.g., extra effort, cooperativeness, etc.). Borman and Motowidlo have also suggested that typical measures of job performance include not only task proficiency but also contextual proficiency. However, these two dimensions of job performance are not related to the same predictors. Task proficiency should be related to predictors of knowledge and aptitude (e.g., cognitive ability tests, job knowledge tests) while contextual performance should be related to motivational predictors (e.g., personality factors). Borman and Motowidlo (1997) have provided a taxonomy of contextual performance which is composed of five categories: (1) persisting with enthusiasm and extra effort where necessary to complete one's task activities successfully; (2) volunteering to carry out task activities that are not formally part of one's job; (3) helping and cooperation with others; (4) following organizational rules and procedures; (5) endorsing, supporting, and defending organizational objectives. According to Motowidlo, Borman and Schmit (1997), contextual and task performance are different in three ways. First, task activities vary across jobs whereas contextual activities are more general across jobs. Second, task activities are role-prescribed whereas contextual activities tend to be extra-role behaviors. Third, cognitive ability is a probable antecedent of task performance while personality and motivational variables are more probable antecedents of contextual performance.

Several studies supported the hypothesized differences between task performance and contextual performance. For example, Motowidlo and Van Scotter (1994) found that task and contextual performance contributed independently to overall performance. They also found that task proficiency was better predicted using cognitive ability while personality dimensions predicted contextual performance. Van Scotter and Motowidlo (1996) have made an effort to refine the construct of contextual performance by dividing it into two elements: interpersonal facilitation and job dedication. Interpersonal facilitation is the set of behaviors that contribute to organizational goal accomplishment (e.g., altruism, helping coworkers, acts that improve moral, cooperation, removing barriers). Job dedication consists of self-disciplined behaviors (e.g., following rules, working hard, taking initiative to problem-solving). Van Scotter and Motowidlo hypothesized that interpersonal facilitation was related to agreeableness, extraversion, high social confidence and positive affectivity. They also suggested that job dedication covaried with motivational and volitional traits such as conscientiousness, generalized expectancy of task success and goal orientation. Van Scotter and Motowidlo found that task performance correlated with experience, job knowledge, conscientiousness and expectancy of task success. Interpersonal facilitation correlated with experience, job knowledge, conscientiousness, expectancy of task success, extraversion, agreeableness and positive affectivity. However, the motivational elements defined as job dedication were associated with task performance and correlated with predictors such as experience, job knowledge and conscientiousness. Based on these findings, Van Scotter and Motowidlo suggested that the definitions of task performance and interpersonal facilitation should be revised in order to include the motivational elements of job dedication.

A different view of job performance was suggested by Viswesvaran (1993). In his research, Viswesvaran (1993) found that 13 job content areas represented comprehensively the job performance domain. The dimensions were: (1) overall job performance; (2) job productivity; (3) quality; (4) problem-solving and leadership; (5) communication skills; (6) administrative skills; (7) effort; (8) interpersonal skills; (9) job knowledge; (10) compliance and acceptance of authority; (11) absenteeism; (12) accidents; and (13) tenure. Psychometric meta-analysis was used to develop the correlation matrix between these content areas, and a confirmatory factor analysis was used to obtain the latent structure of job performance. Confirmatory analysis was conducted on two matrices, one with the intercorrelations between the organizational record-based dimensions (e.g., absenteeism, accidents) and another with the intercorrelations between ratings of the different dimensions of job performance. For each matrix, there was a general factor underlying most performance measures, although this general factor does not fully explain the relationship among performance ratings.

Viswesvaran, Ones and Schmidt (1996) have carried out the most comprehensive meta-analysis on the reliability of job performance ratings up to date. Using the ten dimensions of job performance ratings found by Viswesvaran, they compared the interrater and intrarater reliabilities of the ratings. For overall job performance, the most significant results showed that interrater reliability of supervisory rating was 0.52 (sample size weighted) and 0.68 (frequency weighted), the interrater peer rating reliabilities were 0.42 and 0.44, respectively. The stability coefficients for supervisory ratings of overall job performance were 0.81 (sample size weighted) and 0.84 (frequency weighted). The alpha reliabilities for supervisory ratings were 0.86 and 0.84 (sample size and frequency weighted respectively). For peer ratings the alpha coefficients were 0.85 and 0.81 (sample size and frequency weighted respectively). Viswesvaran, Ones and Schmidt (1996) also found that 20% to 30% of rating variance of job performance dimensions of the average rater was specific to the rater. In connection with the criterion reliability, Salgado and Moscoso (1996) also carried out a study on interrater reliability of job performance ratings in validity studies of personnel selection, using setting (civilian versus military) and criterion composition (single versus composite) as moderators of reliability. They conducted three meta-analyses in which interrater reliability (frequency weighted) was estimated for civilian composite criteria, military composite criteria and a single civilian criterion. The average reliabilities were 0.64, 0.53 and 0.40 respectively. These results therefore suggest that the setting (civilian vs military) and the criterion composition (single vs composite) are relevant moderators of interrater reliability of job performance ratings.

An interesting experimental study was carried out by Sanchez and De La Torre (1996) to check the relation between rating and behavioral accuracy in performance appraisal. They found that the relationship between behavioral and rating accuracy was confined to dimensional judgments of strengths and weaknesses. Sanchez and De La Torre suggested that judgments were related to behavioral memories depending on how relevant and easily accessible these memories were.

Job Analysis

An important advance in job analysis was carried out by Peterson et al. (1995), who developed a prototype to build a database of occupational information (O*NET). This prototype incorporates comprehensive information of both worker and work attributes, while the current Dictionary of Occupational Titles is based only on task descriptions. In the O*NET, jobs will be described showing (a) worker requirements, (b) worker characteristics, (c) experience requirements, (d) occupational requirements, (e) labor market characteristics, and (f) occupation-specific requirements. In order to measure the variables used in the descriptions of jobs, nine questionnaires were developed: (1) skills; (2) knowledge; (3) training, education, licensure and experience; (4) generalized work activities; (5) work context; (6) organizational context; (7) abilities; (8) occupational values; and (9) work styles.

Goldstein, Zedeck and Schneider (1993) explored job analysis as a prerequisite for establishing content validity of personnel selection procedures. Goldstein, Zedeck and Schneider concluded that the job analysis-content validity process could be questionable if attention was not paid to the series of processes and judgments involved in establishing content validity. Connected with this last point, Arthur, Doverspike and Barrett (1996) presented a method for determining the Relative Content Contribution (RCC) of each test in a battery, using a content-validity approach. The method uses job analysis information (e.g., KSAOs) to estimate the specific weights to be given to the tests. The RCC weight for each single test is a function of (a) importance of the work behavior, (b) time spent performing the work behavior, (c) consequence of error or cost associated with an error in the performance of the work behavior, and (d) time-to-proficiency. Arthur, Doverspike and Barrett presented the formulas to calculate RCC index and an illustrative case. Sanchez and Fraser (1992) examined the issue of which task scales to retain in task analysis. They examined interrater reliability, convergence among task scales and measurement of task importance. Sanchez and Fraser selected four typical task dimensions: (1) relative time spent; (2) difficulty in learning the task; (3) criticality or consequences of error; and (4) overall importance. The conclusions suggested that the choice of scales for task analysis has to be made considering that (a) the interrater reliability was over 0.60, (b) criticality and importance were highly redundant scales, (c) ratings of time spent, difficulty in learning and importance or criticality provided independent information, and (d) there was no clearly superior algorithm in order to make a composite.

Two other advances which must be mentioned are those concerned with job analysis and the 'Big Five' personality dimensions. In France, Rolland and Mogenet (1994) developed the 'Description in 5 Dimensions (D5D)' system, a computerized job analysis system based on the five factor model of personality. The D5D system provides a personality-related job profile based on ipsative scores. Also, applicant personality may be assessed with the D5D and a profile computed. With the D5D, different profile comparisons can be made using graphical presentation (e.g., job profile–applicant profile; group profile–applicant profile). The second advance was carried out by Raymark, Schmit and Guion (1997), who developed the Personality-Related Position Requirements Form (PPRF), a job analysis questionnaire to identify relevant personality traits for job performance. They noted that typical inventories of job analysis did not include items from which to generate hypotheses concerning personality variables that would be relevant for a job. For these reasons, the PPRF is based on the Big Five personality taxonomy and it is composed of 12 subdimensions. The first results indicated that the PPRF was a highly reliable instrument. Internal consistency reliabilities were mostly in the eighties and interrater reliability ranged from 0.85 to 0.97. Raymark, Schmit and Guion suggested that PPRF could be potentially useful to identify personality variables to be measured as predictors but PPRF could also be useful to develop criterion measures related to the personality dimensions associated with job behaviors.

COGNITIVE ABILITY

Abilities have been the most prominent predictors in personnel selection since the first decade of this century. However, Landy, Shankster and Kohler (1994) pointed out that I/O psychologists are currently doing little research in the development and validation of new cognitive ability tests beyond the classic ones. According to Landy, Shankster and Kohler (1994), there is slow progress as a result in the area.

Two principal lines of work may be distinguished in this topic which are related to personnel selection. One is that of psychometric-g proponents, who essentially suggest that specific abilities do not add incremental validity beyond g (e.g. Olea & Ree, 1994; Ree, Earles & Teachout, 1994; Schmidt, 1994). The second line is associated with the proponents of multiple abilities (e.g., Ackerman & Kanfer, 1993; Ackerman & Goff, 1995).

In connection with the first line of research, Carretta, Ree and their colleagues are carrying out a program on this topic, with emphasis on construct validity and criterion validity. The results of Carretta and Ree's research program show a strong support for g validity (see Ree & Carretta, 1997, 1998). Ree and Carretta (1994a) have shown that the Armed Services Vocational Aptitude Battery (ASVAB) has a hierarchical structure, including a higher order factor for g and the three lower order factors of speed (NO, CS), verbal/math (AR, WK, PC, MK), and technical knowledge (GS, AS, MC, EM). All ten tests load on g. The percentage of total variance accounted for by these factors was 63.8% for g, 6.2% for speed, 2.4% for verbal/math and 7.7% for technical knowledge. Stauffer, Ree and Carretta (1996), using hierarchic confirmatory factor analysis, showed that a battery containing 10 traditional paper-and-pencil aptitude tests (ASVAB) and a second battery of 25 cognitive-component-based tests (based on Kyllonen's 1993, 1994 work) appear to measure the same factor which they identified as g. In this study, the correlation between the higher order factors from the two batteries was 0.994, indicating that both measured g. Also, Carretta, Perry and Ree (1996) showed the validity of several cognitive-components-based tests for predicting aircraft pilot performance.

The Air Force Officer Qualifying Test (AFOQT) has been validated for the selection of pilots and navigators, as well as many other jobs within the Air Forces (Carretta & Ree, 1995; 1996; Olea & Ree, 1994). For pilot and navigator training, the criteria included passing–failing training, average flying, performance rankings, composites of specific check side performances, and day and night celestial navigational tests. Olea and Ree (1994) showed that the major source of validity for the AFOQT came from its measurement of g. They also showed that the incremental validity of the AFOQT subtest beyond g was approximately 0.02 (0.462 vs 0.482 for the summed composite criterion) for navigators across five individual training criteria and a summed composite of five training criteria. The incremental validity of non-g portions of the AFOQT for predicting pilot training success was about 0.08 (0.314 vs 0.398) for the summed composite criterion.

Ackerman and his colleagues (Ackerman & Goff, 1995; Ackerman & Heggestad, 1997) have developed a theory of intelligence that endeavours to integrate literature regarding the relations among personality, interest and intellectual development. The theory is known as PPIK. It is made up of four components: Intelligence-as-process, Personality, Interest and Intelligence as knowledge. In this theory, the construct of intelligence as typical performance is basic (Ackerman, 1994). According to Ackerman, one reason why intelligence tests do not show a correlation higher than 0.5 or 0.6 for academic performance or job performance is that intelligence is measured with a 'maximal' paradigm while academic and occupational performance takes place in a 'typical' environment (Ackerman & Goff, 1995). A measure of intelligence as typical performance should be more highly correlated with crystalized abilities (e.g., knowledge) and intelligence as maximal performance with fluid abilities (e.g., abstract reasoning). Some results appear to support this last prediction (Ackerman & Goff, 1995; Ackerman, Kanfer & Goff, 1995; Goff & Ackerman, 1992). Ackerman and Goff (1995) and Ackerman and Heggestad (1997) provided a set of extensive meta-analyses of the correlations between cognitive abilities, personality dimensions and career interests. Ackerman and Kanfer (1993) designed the Aptitude Assessment Battery (AAB), which is a cognitive test battery. The AAB contains nine ability tests and an 18-item measure of motivational skills. This battery was used for the selection of air traffic controllers and demonstrated its validity.

A relevant study was conducted by Levine, Spector, Menon, Narayanon and Canon-Bowers (1996). In a meta-analysis of craft jobs in the utility industry (e.g., electrical assembly, telephone technicians, mechanical jobs), they found that cognitive ability tests (e.g., tests of verbal ability, numerical ability, reasoning ability and memory tests) showed a corrected average validity of 0.43 ($k = 149$, $n = 12504$) for predicting job performance, with some validity variation across job families. Using training criteria, the corrected average validity was 0.67 ($k = 52$, $n = 5872$), a remarkably higher value than that found for job performance. Taken together these two findings confirmed Hunter and Hunter's (1984) results, which found that the average corrected validity of cognitive ability tests was 0.45 for performance ratings and 0.54 for training success.

An interesting result was found by Pettersen and Tziner (1995). They used two specific intelligence tests (Otis and Beta) to predict job performance in a manufacturing enterprise. They found that the predictive validity of both tests was stable over time. Another finding was that job complexity affected the predictive validity, with a higher validity when job complexity increased. Pettersen and Tziner suggested that the intelligence tests were a strong predictor, particularly with complex jobs. Pettersen and Tziner's findings contradicted the proposition of Hulin, Henry and Noon (1990), who proposed that validity varied as a function of time on the job. Contrary to Hulin, Henry and Noon (1990), Pettersen and Tziner's results suggest that predictive validity of intelligence is stable and does not change significantly as a function of time, as long as the job content remains the same. Salgado (1998a) found that cognitive ability tests were predictors of training proficiency in four samples of pilot trainees. He also found that all observed variability in 15 validity coefficients was accounted for by sampling error variance. Schuler, Moser, Diemand and Funke (1995) found that grades at the end of an apprenticeship training in a financial organization were predicted by cognitive abilities tests ($r = 0.55$; validity corrected for attenuation). Bartram and Baxter (1996) found that MICROPAT, a computer-based test battery, predicted flying grading and a pass–fail training criterion in a civilian pilot sample.

In summary, research carried out in the 1990s on cognitive abilities shows that they continue to be one of the best (if not the best) predictors of job performance and training performance. A future line of research will be to check Borman and Motowidlo's (1993) suggestion that cognitive abilities predict task performance and not contextual performance. Some recent studies indicate that this last suggestion may be correct but more research seems necessary.

PHYSICAL AND PSYCHOMOTOR ABILITIES

Not much literature on physical and psychomotor abilities has been published in the past few years, although some relevant contributions must be commented upon. J. Hogan (1991a) comprehensively reviewed the literature on physical aptitudes and integrated knowledge from different disciplines, including personnel selection, differential psychology, industrial engineering, biomechanics, work physiology and law. Hogan's review is probably the best review of physical aptitudes up to date. J. Hogan (1991b) also carried out several studies on the structure of physical requirements of occupational tasks. Her results showed that three components—muscular strength, cardio-vascular endurance and movement quality—described those requirements. This three-component structure was found in both job analysis and test performance data and it appeared to be independent of jobs, raters or incumbents' performance levels. J. Hogan, Arneson and Petersons (1992) developed and validated a physical performance test battery to select high-pressure cleaning workers. The battery included two types of predictor measures: ability tests and work sample simulations. J. Hogan and Quigley (1994) examined the effects of training and nontraining preparation on physical ability test-taking. Their results showed that preparation was capable of maximizing selection opportunities of qualified applicants for physically demanding jobs. Also they found that preparation could reduce adverse impact. Arvey, Landon, Nutting and Maxwell (1992) showed that eight physical ability tests used for police officers' selection were related to two constructs: strength and endurance. Blakley, Quiñones, Crawford and Jago (1994) reported the results of a meta-analysis of six studies in which isometric strength tests were used as selection procedures. They found that isometric strength tests were valid predictors of supervisory ratings of physical performance ($rho = 0.32$) and performance on work simulations ($rho = 0.55$).

With regard to psychomotor abilities, Carretta and Ree (1994) and Ree and Carretta (1994b) showed that the BAT, a psychomotor test battery, added a small incremental validity beyond the validity of cognitive tests. They suggested that this small incremental validity was due to the commonality of measurement. They also found that the psychomotor scores were g saturated. In a meta-analysis of validity studies carried out in Spain using psychomotor tests as predictors, Salgado (1994a) found a corrected average of 0.42. Salgado (1995) found that a psychomotor test (Rotary Pursuit Test) predicted the performance in a practical driving examination. Using cumulative techniques he found a validity of 0.26 (uncorrected for unreliability and range restriction). He also found that there was no variability across four samples of drivers. Levine et al. (1996), in a meta-analysis of craft jobs in the utility industry (e.g., electrical assembly, telephone technician, mechanical jobs), found a corrected average validity of 0.34 ($k = 147$, $n = 12677$) for predicting job performance, with some validity variation in job families. For example, electrical assembly jobs and mechanical jobs were best predicted (0.49 and 0.42 respectively). Using training criteria, the corrected average validity was 0.35 ($k = 41$, $n = 3042$), a similar value to the one found for job performance. In the case of training criteria, newly created electrical assembly and mechanical jobs presented the best validities (0.58 and 0.60 respectively).

In summary, recent evidence indicates that physical and psychomotor ability tests can be useful tools in physically demanding jobs. Also, some findings suggest that psychomotor adds little variance over cognitive ability tests. This may not be the case for physical ability tests. However, the current data are not conclusive.

JOB KNOWLEDGE TESTS

Under this rubric, three types of measures can be included: job knowledge tests (Hunter & Hunter, 1984), tacit knowledge tests (Sternberg, Wagner, Williams & Horvath, 1995), and situational judgment tests (Pulakos & Schmitt, 1996). In connection with job knowledge and tacit knowledge constructs, an interesting debate took place between Schmidt and Hunter (1993) and Sternberg and Wagner (1993). According to Schmidt and Hunter (1993) tacit knowledge is not a new construct. It is just changing the name of job knowledge which is a broader construct.

Dye, Reck and McDaniel (1993) examined the validity of written job knowledge tests as predictors of job performance and training success. Their database consisted of 502 validity coefficients and a total sample of 363 528 persons. They found a corrected mean validity of 0.45 for job performance and 0.47 for training success. Dye, Reck and McDaniel also found that validity was moderated by job-test similarity and job complexity. For the first moderator, results showed that validity was almost double (*rho* = 0.62 and *rho* = 0.76 for job performance and training success respectively) for high job-test similarity what it was for low job-test similarity (*rho* = 0.35 and *rho* = 0.46 for job performance and training success respectively). For the second moderator results showed that validity was greater for jobs of high complexity than for jobs of low complexity. For example, against a job performance criterion the corrected validities were 0.57 versus 0.39 respectively, for high and low complexity jobs. As regards training success, validities were 0.57 versus 0.46 for high and low job complexity respectively. Dye, Reck and McDaniel suggested to employers that when job knowledge tests were to be used, it was better to make them as job-specific as possible. They also suggested that job knowledge tests were better for high complexity jobs (jobs that demanded greater levels of knowledge and required greater judgment and synthesis of job knowledge). Borman, Hanson, Oppler et al. (1993) showed that job knowledge mediated in relations between cognitive ability and job performance ratings. This mediated effect was demonstrated previously by Hunter (1986). In connection with this last point, Pulakos, Schmitt and Chan (1996) found that job knowledge, assessed with a 117-item measure, had direct and indirect effects on performance ratings made by supervisors. The job knowledge test had a direct effect of 0.11 and an indirect effect of 0.04 on job performance.

The second line of research (i.e., practical intelligence) is associated with Sternberg, Wagner and their colleagues (Sternberg, 1997; Sternberg & Wagner, 1993; Sternberg et al., 1995; Wagner, 1994; Wagner & Sternberg, 1990). These authors suggested distinguishing between academic intelligence (as measured with intelligence test scores) and practical intelligence or common sense. In addition to the distinction between academic and practical kinds of intelligence, Sternberg and Wagner made a similar distinction between two types of knowledge: formal academic knowledge and tacit knowledge. The first is knowledge sampled by the ability tests. Tacit knowledge is action-oriented knowledge, acquired without direct help from others, that allows individuals to achieve goals they personally value. Tacit knowledge has three characteristics: (1) it is procedural in nature; (2) it is relevant to the attainment of goals people value; (3) it is acquired with little help from others. Tacit knowledge is typically measured with instruments containing a set of work-related situations, each having between 5 and 20 response items. Each situation poses a problem for the participant to solve by rating the various response items. Sternberg and Wagner also suggest that work problems are often (a) unformulated or in need of reformulation, (b) of personal interest, (c) lacking in information necessary for solution, (d) related to everyday experience, (e) poorly defined, (f) characterized by multiple 'correct' solutions, each with liabilities as well as assets, and (g) characterized by multiple methods for picking a problem solution. According to Sternberg (1997; Sternberg et al., 1995), the correlations between tacit knowledge and job criteria typically ranged from 0.2 to 0.4. However, a problem with these last studies is that the samples were of a small size and restricted range. Furthermore, Sue-Chan, Latham and Evans (1997) found that a tacit knowledge test for nurses had no incremental validity beyond g for predicting the first year and second year grade-point average.

The third type of job knowledge measures commented upon here are the situational judgment tests. Motowidlo and Tippins (1993), using a situational inventory which they named as low-fidelity simulation, found an overall validity of 0.28. Sanchez and Fraser (1993) developed and validated the Corporate Social Style Inventory (CSSI), a measure of customer service skills. The CSSI consisted of multiple-choice items that presented individuals with hypothetical situations and asked respondents how they would handle each situation. The results of eight studies indicated that CSSI had an acceptable test–retest reliability and showed criterion validity as well as incremental validity over cognitive ability to predict job-performance ratings. Pulakos and Schmitt (1996) found that a situational judgment test (SJT), a practical intelligence test, was a valid predictor of job performance. They also found that the correlation between cognitive ability measures and the SJT was very small ($r = 0.13$, $r = 0.07$ and $r = 0.17$). Moreover, the SJT showed incremental validity beyond the cognitive ability tests. Pulakos, Schmitt and Chan (1996) tested a model of supervisory performance ratings that included measures of cognitive ability, practical intelligence, job knowledge, task proficiency, achievement orientation, and performance ratings. They suggested that cognitive ability and practical intelligence were different constructs and that both had influenced performance ratings through job knowledge. In addition, the model proposed that practical intelligence directly influenced performance ratings. The results supported the model and showed that practical intelligence had a direct effect of 0.128 and an indirect effect of 0.024. Cognitive ability had an indirect effect of 0.124. McDaniel, Finnegan, Morgeson, Campion and Braveman (1997) examined the criterion validity of situational judgment (SJ) tests. They found that the corrected validity was 0.56. Furthermore, McDaniel et al. (1997) reported that SI tests had an average corrected correlation of 0.53 with general mental ability tests. This correlation reached 0.68 when the SI tests were based on a job analysis and fell to 0.29 when the tests were not based on a job analysis. These findings have important consequences for the constructs of situational judgment, tacit knowledge and practical intelligence. An important percentage of their predictive capacity can be due to the correlation with general mental ability, contradicting the opinion of 'street smart' supporters (e.g., Sternberg et al., 1995; Wagner, 1994) and giving support to Schmidt and Hunter's (1993) position.

PERSONALITY

Personality and personality measures have received considerable interest in the past six years, in part due to the consolidation of the Five Factor Model of personality as a paradigm of the area. Barrick and Mount (1991), in a large-sample meta-analysis of the Big Five dimensions, found that the validity of conscientiousness construct was 0.13 (0.22 corrected for criterion reliability and range restriction) and generalized across occupations and criteria. Tett, Jackson and Rothstein (1991), using studies in which the choice of personality measures was based on a job analysis or guided by hypotheses, found that confirmatory strategies moderated the validity of the Big Five. Hough (1992, 1997a) found that seven personality factors were needed to cover the personality domain in a more comprehensive fashion, and she also found that neuroticism, dependability and achievement (both facets of conscientiousness) generalized validity across occupations and criteria. More recently, Mount and Barrick (1995) suggested that previous meta-analyses may have understated the true validity of conscientiousness and affirmed that values of 0.18 (0.32 corrected for criterion reliability, range restriction and imperfect construct measurement) for overall job proficiency and 0.17 (0.30 corrected for criterion reliability, range restriction and imperfect construct measurement) for training proficiency criterion were probably closer to the true validity. All these meta-analyses were carried out using studies conducted with American samples. In order to know if validity generalization of the Big Five has geographical boundaries, Salgado (1997a, b, 1998b) conducted some meta-analyses using only European studies. He found that two factors generalized validity across occupations and criteria: conscientiousness and emotional stability. As a whole, all these meta-analyses suggest that two personality dimensions, conscientiousness and emotional stability (neuroticism) are valid predictors for all jobs and criteria. Recently, Barrick and Mount (1996) confirmed this suggestion in two samples in which conscientiousness and emotional stability were valid predictors of supervisory ratings and voluntary turnover in the two samples.

A number of articles provided evidence of criterion-related validity for some of the most popular Big Five-based questionnaires. For example, Piedmont and Weistein (1994) found validity evidence for concientiousness as it is assessed with the NEO-PI-R (Costa and McCrae, 1992) and Salgado and Rumbo (1997) found that a composite of the Big Five, assessed with the NEO-FFI (Costa and McCrae, 1992), was a valid predictor for financial service managers. Costa (1996) made a summary of reliability and validity of the NEO-PI-R and discussed its use in industrial and organizational psychology. Costa, McCrae and Kay (1995) also presented a NEO-PI-R-based profiler to be used in job analysis. Barrick and Mount (1993; Barrick, Mount & Strauss, 1993; Mount & Barrick, 1995) found evidence for the PCI (Barrick and Mount, 1996). Hogan and Hogan (1995) published the second edition of the manual for the Hogan Personality Inventory (HPI) that included a large list of studies in which the HPI was used and the corresponding validity found. In the European context, several researchers have presented empirical evidence supporting work-oriented personality questionnaires based on the five factor model. Bartram (1993) presented validity evidence for the ICES, Rolland and Magenet (1994) developed the

'Description in Five Dimensions' questionnaire and Salgado (1996a) showed construct-validity evidence of the IP/5F (Salgado, 1994b).

Two additional lines of evidence in favor of personality measures as predictors of work behavior were presented by Robertson and his associates and Day and Bedeian (1991, 1995). Robertson and Kinder (1993; see also Salgado, 1996b) found that personality predicted a large number of job competencies and validity was generalized across occupations. Nyfield, Gibbons, Baron and Robertson (1995) found that the Big Five dimensions which were assessed using the scales of the Occupational Personality Questionnaire (OPQ; Saville, Holdsworth, Nyfield et al., 1984) predicted managerial competencies across three different countries: USA, UK and Turkey. Saville, Sik, Nyfield et al. (1996) also presented a demonstration of the OPQ validity to predict job competencies in UK managers. Day and Bedeian (1991, 1995) observed interactions between personality factors (conscientiousness and agreeableness) and psychological climate dimensions to predict job performance, job satisfaction and tenure.

A number of articles checked the validity of complex personality variables such as integrity and customer service orientation. Ones, Viswesvaran and Schmidt (1993), in a large meta-analysis of integrity tests, found a validity value of 0.42 for predicting job performance and a value of 0.38 for predicting training proficiency. In two samples of prisoners previously employed in upper-level positions of authority, Collins and Schmidt (1993) found that the best single predictor that differentiated between offenders and nonoffenders was a personality-based integrity test. Ones (1993), using meta-analytic techniques, demonstrated that integrity measures were composed of conscientiousness, agreeableness and neuroticism, and that the correlation between integrity and cognitive ability was practically null. Murphy and Lee (1994) showed that conscientiousness explained a small percentage of integrity test validity. Sackett and Wanek (1996) presented the fourth report in a series of reviews of the use of integrity, checking the literature on criterion validity, construct validity (including the Big Five, cognitive ability, moral reasoning and social desirability), applicant reactions and legal effects. Hogan and Brinkmeyer (1997) investigated whether overt and personality-based integrity tests had the same psychological meaning. In a large applicant sample ($n = 2168$), they showed that overt and personality-based integrity tests were made up of four themes: (1) punitive attitudes; (2) admissions of illegal drug use; (3) reliability; and (4) theft admissions. Correlating the HPI, punitive attitudes, admissions of illegal drug use, theft admissions and the Abbreviated Reid Report, Hogan and Brinkmeyer (1997) also found that punitive attitudes and theft admission components correlated with prudence (conscientiousness) adjustment (emotional stability) and likeability (agreeableness). However, there were correlations with no practical significance between illegal drug use component and HPI scales. As a whole, the Abbreviated Reid Report correlated with prudence ($r = 0.50$), adjustment ($r = 0.44$), likeability ($r = 0.26$), ambition ($r = 0.28$) and school success ($r = 0.26$). These findings are a solid indication of the psychological meaning of an overt integrity test.

Frei and McDaniel (1997) carried out a meta-analysis of service-oriented questionnaires. The criterion validity was based on 41 coefficients with a total sample size of 6945. The mean validity corrected for criterion unreliability and range restriction was 0.50 (observed $r = 0.24$). They found strong relationships between the Big Five and customer service orientation measures. Emotional stability correlated 0.63 ($n = 15479$), agreeableness correlated 0.61 ($n = 14786$) and conscientiousness correlated 0.42 ($n = 95057$). They also found that customer service measures correlated with sales orientation ($r = 0.31$, $n = 2101$) but did not correlate with cognitive ability ($r = 0.06$, $n = 753$). Furnham (1995) found that the Customer Service Questionnaire (CSQ; Saville & Holdsworth, 1992) predicted job performance in an air company. Furthermore, Furnham and Coveney (1996) reported that CSQ correlated primarily with conscientiousness and neuroticism as measured by the NEO-PI-R. Ones and Viswesvaran (1996b) indicated that service-orientation measures were based on emotional stability, agreeableness and conscientiousness, and they also found a large correlation between customer service scales and integrity tests.

Taking together the meta-analyses of the Big Five validity (e.g., Barrick & Mount, 1991; Hough, 1992, 1997b; Salgado, 1997a,b, 1998b; Tett, Jackson & Rothstein, 1991) with the findings of the integrity tests meta-analysis (e.g., Ones, Viswesvaran & Schmidt, 1993) and with the findings of service-orientation measures (e.g., Frei & McDaniel, 1997), as well as the results of research carried out to analyze the constructs underlined on integrity and customer-service measures (e.g. Frei & McDaniel, 1997; Ones, 1993; Ones and Viswesvaran, 1996b), a conclusion reached might be that a composite of the Big Five dimensions tapped the most important aspects of all occupations in the industrialized countries. This hypothesis was tested by Salgado and Rumbo (1997) who found that a composite of the Big Five predicted job performance ($r = 0.51$) and job motivation ($r = 0.41$) in financial managers.

Two additional questions of great interest connected with personality measures are the use of broad or narrow measures as well as the role of social desirability in personality questionnaires and its effects on validity. Recently, Ones and Viswesvaran (1996a), J. Hogan and Roberts (1996) and Schneider, Hough and Dunnette (1996) participated in an excellent debate over the use of broad or narrow personality measures. Ones and Viswesvaran (1996a) have maintained that broad measures like the Big Five should be preferred from a theoretical point of view, because the five dimensions are supported by considerable empirical evidence. Furthermore, the Big Five are a very useful taxonomy to accumulate knowledge. Against this position, Schneider, Hough and Dunnette (1996) presented the relative merits of more narrow personality measures. They argued that narrower personality traits retain specificity that could add substantially to criterion validity. Furthermore, an increasing use of narrower traits and job performance constructs would also enhance the explanation of job behavior. In an intermediate position, Hogan and Roberts (1996) maintained that the nature of the criterion dictates what personality predictors are most appropriate and, therefore, that we must focus attention on the need to match the breadth predictors with the criteria. According to Hogan and Roberts, the question is not broad versus narrow traits but also broad versus broader conceptualizations of personality measurement. With regard to this point, Borman and Motowidlo (1997) and Borman, Hanson and Hedge (1997) suggest that personality predicts contextual performance more than task performance. Salgado, Rumbo, Santamaria and Rodriguez (1995) carried out a study partially connected with the narrow versus broad personality measures question. They checked if narrow personality measures were better predictors of job performance than broad measures. Using the 16PF as personality measure, two composites were formed, one with primary factors and a second integrating primary factors into the Big Five personality dimensions. The results showed that the multiple correlation using the Big Five was significant ($p < 0.025$) while the multiple correlation using the 16 primary factors was not significant ($p > 0.27$).

In connection with the effects of social desirability on validity, Christiansen, Goffin, Johnson and Rothstein (1994) found that motivational distortion of answers in the 16PF had no effect on validity. Ones, Viswesvaran and Reiss (1996) found that social desirability did not predict school success, task performance, counterproductive behaviors or job performance. They reported that social desirability correlated significantly with conscientiousness and emotional stability, but it did not attenuate their criterion-related validity. Ones, Viswesvaran and Reiss (1996) have also suggested that the practice of correcting personality scores for social desirability may affect the reliability (and validity) of tests. Ones, Viswesvaran and Korbin (1995) have recommended that those who may want to use personality variables in personnel selection should compile specific norms with applicant samples as an alternative to the correcting method. Confirming Ones, Viswesvaran and Reiss's (1996) results, Barrick and Mount (1996) found that self-deception and impression management, two aspects of social desirability (Paulhus, 1984), had no influence on the validity in two semi-truck driver samples. Hough (1997b), who examined research on intentional distortion of personality constructs, found that applicants' distortion was higher than that of incumbents. However, intentional distortion could be minimized if applicants were warned about the consequences that existed if they distorted their responses.

Several papers revised or described the Five Factor Model (FFM) of personality and its connection with occupational psychology. R. Hogan (1997) described his socioanalytic theory of personality and relations with the

FFM. In synthesis, Hogan's theory maintains that people are motivated by a desire for status and social approval, and that work is a great source of status and social approval. Furthermore, according to Hogan, there are individual differences in people's ability to acquire status and social approval, and these differences are related to their reputation in everyday life and their performance appraisals at work. In this paper, Hogan also suggests possible hypothetical linkages between personality dimensions and job criteria, and he shows findings supporting those hypotheses. Hogan, Hogan and Roberts (1996), in a highlighted article, have summarized the most frequent questions on the use of personality in personnel selection (e.g.: Is personality a valid predictor of performance? Do personality measures invade privacy? Are personality measures easily faked? What is the best way to use personality measures for pre-employment selection?). For each question examined, Hogan, Hogan and Roberts have given suggested responses based on first-rate research. Their main conclusions show that personality, as it is measured using well-constructed instruments, is a valid predictor of job performance in virtually all occupations, Furthermore, personality measures should be used together with other predictors (e.g., ability tests, job knowledge tests). Hough (1997b, Hough and Schneider, 1996; Schneider & Hough, 1995) has made very comprehensive reviews of the field of personality at work, considering different aspects connected with the usefulness of personality constructs for predicting job criteria (e.g., personality constructs, predictive validity, faking, and adverse impact).

Finally, Ones and Viswesvaran (1997) have developed a theory of conscientiousness at work, according to which highly conscientious individuals show greater productivity than less conscientious individuals because they: (1) spend more time on tasks they are assigned; (2) acquire greater job knowledge; (3) set goals autonomously and persist in following them; (4) go beyond role requirements in the workplace; and (5) avoid counterproductive behaviors.

INTERVIEW

The employment interview has received considerable interest in recent years and both meta-analytic and single studies have been conducted on interview validity and moderators of validity. Based on a series of meta-analyses, the interview is currently considered as one of the best predictors of job performance and training proficiency (Schmidt & Hunter, 1997a).

Several meta-analyses assessed different aspects related to criterion-validity of interview. Marchese and Muchinsky (1993) found an average observed validity of 0.27, a similar value to the one found by Wiesner and Cronshaw (1988) a few years earlier. They also found that interview validity correlated with some study characteristics. For example, validity correlated with structure ($r = 0.45$), length of the interview (-0.29) and applicant gender ($r = -0.27$). McDaniel, Whetzel, Schmidt and Maurer (1994) presented one of the most comprehensive meta-analyses of interview validity. Using job performance as the criterion, they found an average observed validity of 0.20 ($n = 25\ 444$). For training performance the average observed validity was 0.23. However, several characteristics modified interview validity: content, structure and criterion purpose. For interview content, three types of interviews were considered: situational, job-related (e.g., behavior description, job-analysis based) and psychological. Observed validities were 0.27, 0.21 and 0.15 respectively (0.50, 0.39 and 0.29 when corrected for criterion unreliability and range restriction). For interview structure, structured interviews showed an average observed validity of 0.24 (0.44 when corrected for unreliability and range restriction) compared to 0.18 for unstructured interviews (0.33 when corrected for unreliability and range restriction). If the criterion purpose was administrative, average validity was 0.19 (0.36 corrected) and when the purpose was research, the average validity reached 0.25 (0.47 corrected). Huffcutt and Arthur (1994) carried out a meta-analysis of 114 studies in which criterion validity was related to four levels of interview structures. The results showed that the structure level was a powerful moderator of interview validity, ranging from 0.20 for the lowest structure level to 0.56 for the highest structure level. Salgado and Moscoso (1995) found that behavioral structured interviews (e.g., behavior description, situational, multimodal, job-analysis based) showed an average interrater reliability equal to 0.75 (Median = 0.78, Sd = 0.12) and an observed validity of 0.28 ($k = 25$, $n = 2121$). Comparing validities from studies using concurrent versus predictive designs, the results showed that the design type was a relevant moderator (0.38 vs 0.24) for concurrent and predictive respectively). In a meta-analysis of 120 studies ($n = 18\ 158$), Huffcutt and Woehr (1997) checked the relationship between criterion-validity and interview factors and found that: (1) training should be provided to interviewers independently of interview type; (2) all interviewees should be interviewed by the same individual or the same interview panel, especially in the case of less structured interviews; and (3) using a panel of interviewers did not improve validity.

In a single study, Campion, Campion and Hudson (1994) found that past-oriented questions (i.e., behavior description) were better predictors of job performance than future-oriented (situational) questions (0.51 vs 0.39). They also found that past questions showed incremental validity beyond future questions (but not vice versa) and both question types had incremental validity beyond a battery of nine cognitive ability tests.

Landy, Shansker and Kohler (1994), in their chapter on personnel selection in the *Annual Review*, stated some very relevant questions: Exactly what is being measured in the interview? Are we measuring general intelligence, motivation, personality, individual skills and abilities, knowledge or experience? In other words, Landy, Shansker and Kohler inquired as to which constructs are assessed in the interview. Some articles have focused on studying the construct validity of behavioral structured interviews (e.g., situational interview, behavior description). Hunter and Hirsh (1987) and Schmidt (1988) had suggested that these interview types correlate highly with cognitive ability while conventional interviews correlate with social skills. Huffcutt, Roth and McDaniel (1996) found a corrected mean correlation of 0.40 between interview and cognitive ability. However, this value was moderated by structure level and the correlation decreased as the structure level increased (0.50 and 0.35 for low and high structure, respectively; both values corrected). Interestingly, the situational interview correlated more with cognitive ability than the behavior description interview (0.32 vs 0.18, both values corrected). Sue-Chan, Latham and Evans (1997) tested the hypothesis that the situational interview (SI) and the patterned behavioral description interview (PBDI) were related to cognitive ability and tacit knowledge. Their results did not support the hypothesis for both interview types. The two interviews correlated with a self-efficacy measure ($r = 0.56$ and $r = 0.55$ for SI and PBDI respectively) but they did not correlate with cognitive ability. However, the small sample size of the study ($n = 28$) precludes a negative conclusion regarding the relationship between cognitive ability and SI and PBDI. Schuler et al., (1995) found that situational questions included in the multimodal interview correlated 0.19 ($n = 307$) with cognitive ability. Finally, Harris (1998) reviewed the evidence regarding the construct validity of the structured interview and his main conclusions are that the structured interview may be measuring tacit knowledge, Knowledge, Skills and Abilities (KSAs) or person–organization fit. However, more research is needed as Harris's conclusions are mainly research hypotheses based on indirect findings and not on specific studies on the relationship between the structured interview and these other constructs.

In connection with the adverse impact of employment interview, Huffcutt and Roth (1998), using meta-analysis, found that the interview did not appear to have much negative impact on minorities ($d = 0.25$) and high-structure interviews (behavior description and situational) had a lower impact than low-structure interviews. This last result was supported by the findings of a study by Latham and Skarlicki (1996), who showed that the SI and the PBDI were resistant to the interviewer bias in minimizing in-group favoritism while the conventional structured interview (CSI) showed an in-group favoritism. According to Latham and Skarlicki, an explanation for these results would be the fact that the SI and the PBDI focus explicitly on the applicant's behavior while CSI does not always do so. Furthermore, CSI may have elicited less information than the SI and the PBDI.

The effects of the anchoring heuristic on SI, PBDI and CSI were investigated by Kataoka, Latham and Whyte (1997). This heuristic refers to the estimation process (e.g., rating the quality of an interviewee's responses) made by selecting an anchor, from which by adjustment a final estimate will be arrived at. They found that SI was more robust to the anchoring effects than PBDI and CSI.

Schuler and his associates (1992, 1997; Schuler & Moser, 1995; Schuler et al., 1995) conducted a series of studies on the multimodal interview (MI), a structured interview developed to improve the criterion and the construct validity of conventional interviews. The multimodal interview consisted of several parts, including candidate's self-presentation, autobiographical questions, realistic job previews, situational questions and candidate questions. In a large sample consisting of bank apprentices, they found that the MI predicted job performance (observed $r = 0.23$, $n = 584$) as well as sales and service potential (observed $r = 0.27$, $n = 435$) and showed incremental validity in addition to a cognitive ability test. They also found that the MI predicted vocational success 4.5 years later. In a sample of 153 engineers and chemists, they found that the MI correlated with performance ($r = 0.51$). With regard to the MI construct validity, Schuler (1992) reported relations between different parts of MI and emotional stability, extraversion, need for achievement, and a service orientation measure. The correlation between the total MI and cognitive ability was 0.21 ($n = 307$).

Anderson, Silvester, Cunningham-Snell and Haddleton (1997) carried out a study on recruiter and candidate decision-making. Using a semi-structured interview, Anderson et al. found that recruiter ratings were dependent upon candidate eye contact, and three personality characteristics (weak–strong, boring–interesting and dominant–submissive). Furthermore, the candidate's intentions to accept depended upon the attractiveness of the job and the prestige of the organization. Furthermore, recruiter ratings of candidates and candidates' ratings of recruiters showed correlations close to zero. These findings partially contradict previous studies (see Dipboye, 1992).

Two qualitative reviews were published in these recent years. In an extended review, Anderson (1992) distinguished two theoretical perspectives: (a) objectivist (psychometric), and (b) subjectivist (based on the social perception approach). He reached the conclusion that future research could be focused on: (1) the impression management of the interviewer; (2) interviewer decision-making and information processing dysfunctions; and (3) the effects of different distributions of situational power on the interview processes and results. In the second qualitative review, Campion, Palmer and Campion (1997) have identified 15 structural interview components which are grouped into two categories: content and process. Campion, Palmer and Campion have suggested that the interview structure is more complex than was previously thought and any interview could be enhanced by using at least some of the 15 components. They also concluded that there is no good rationale for using completely unstructured interviews and suggested that more research be carried out by studying the relationship between structure and user reactions.

Despite this amount of positive information in favor of structured be-havioral interviews, organizations do not rely very much upon highly structured interviews (Dipboye, 1997). Dipboye (1997) suggested six reasons to explain this underutilization: (1) these interviews may harm the ability to recruit applicants; (2) the interviewers may prefer an unstructured format because this format provides them with more autonomy; (3) unstructured interviews allow a better person–organization fit than structured interviews because this procedure emphasizes a good fit to the KASOs (knowledge, skills, attitudes and other factors) in the job; (4) unstructured interviews may be seen as fairer by interviewers and applicants; (5) unstructured interviews offer advantages to interviewers seeking power and influence; and (6) unstructured interviews may serve the symbolic function of conveying the central values of the organizational culture.

BIODATA

The importance of biographical data as predictors of job performance has been largely recognized in recent years, although they continue to be infrequently used (see Shackleton & Newell, 1997). Also, more attention has been requested for the constructs being measured by biodata (Schmidt, Ones & Hunter, 1992). A book edited by Stokes, Munford and Owens (1994) was intended to cover all aspects connected with biodata (e.g., item development, scoring, validation, generalizability and legal issues). Hough and Paullin (1994) found three different approaches in their review of scale development methods: (1) empirical keying; (2) based on factor analysis; and (3) based on theoretical or logic assumptions. In a similar fashion, Mael (1994) discussed approaches to biographical data.

Altink (1991) developed and validated a biodata instrument for hiring intermediaries in the Netherlands. The results showed a moderate predictive validity ($r = 0.40$, uncorrected) and the estimates of economic utility in several selection scenarios indicated that the biodata could yield considerable pay-offs. Bliesener (1996) carried out a comprehensive meta-analysis of criterion validity of biodata. In the study, only articles using biodata which contained just biographical items and no other types of predictors (e.g., personality scales) were included. The overall predictive validity (uncorrected) was 0.30 ($k = 165$, $n = 106\ 302$). Several methodological moderators showed an effect on validity. For example, double cross-validation produced a value of 0.50 while external validation or cross-validation showed 0.24 and 0.28 respectively. Also concurrent designs (0.35) showed higher validity than predictive designs (0.29) or predictive with selection designs (0.21). In addition, some situational factors were shown to be moderators. Criterion type, job and gender were situational moderators. Objective performance showed an observed validity equal to 0.53, for performance ratings validity was 0.32 and for training success it was 0.36. In the case of jobs, validity ranged from 0.23 for sales personnel to 0.46 for clerks. Interestingly, feminine samples showed higher validity than masculine samples (0.51 vs 0.27). Therefore, Bliesener's findings show a strong support for considering biodata as a valid predictor for personnel selection. Furthermore, it must be taken into account that Bliesener does not correct validity for unreliability or range restriction. If these corrections were made validity would be remarkably higher.

Mael and Ashforth (1995) found that a biodata inventory composed of four factors (rugged, solid citizen, team group and achievement orientation) predicted organizational identification and attrition in six periods ranging from 6 to 24 months. Mael, Connerley and Morath (1996) examined the invasiveness attributes of biodata items and noted that the areas that generated most invasiveness perception were sexuality or intimacy, religious behavior and items related to physical and mental health.

Several papers are related to fakability of biodata. Backer and Colquitt (1992), using a biodata with items that assessed school activities and ability as well as motivation and interests, found that the biodata was fakable in practice although less extensively than is possible. Douglas, McDaniel and Snell (1996) carried out a study on the effects of situationally-induced faking on the reliability and validity of a biodata which assessed conscientiousness and agreeableness. Subjects were told to either fake well or respond honestly. Douglas, McDaniel and Snell found that both construct and criterion validity of biodata decreased when subjects faked. Extending these last findings, Graham, McDaniel, Douglas and Snell (1997) found that the item attributes that predicted the item validity for honest respondents were not the same attributes that predicted the item validity for the faking respondent. Therefore, Douglas, McDaniel and Snell (1996) and Graham et al. (1997) reached different results than Backer and Colquitt (1992). An explanation for the divergence could be the different nature of items in the biodata. While Douglas, McDaniel and Snell's and Graham et al.'s biodata assessed personality attributes, Backer and Colquitt's biodata assessed information less fakable as well as less socially desirable (e.g., What kinds of activities were you involved in during high school? Athletics? Social clubs? Honor societies?)

A very interesting study was carried out by Brown and Campion (1994) on biodata phenomenology. Using biographical information such as is reported in résumés and applicant blanks, they examined how recruiters interpreted the information. Typically, this information is on work experience, education, activities and other life history information. Brown and Campion found that recruiters perceived and used these biodata as indicators of basic abilities (e.g., language, math and physical) as well as noncognitive characteristics (e.g., motivation). Language and math abilities were inferred from education-related items, physical abilities were seen in sport-related items, leadership and interpersonal attributes were considered in items associated with having held authority positions and items indicating activities of a social nature. Two additional relevant findings were that recruiters showed a moderate to high interrater reliability (ranging from 0.62 to 0.76) and that biodata were interpreted differently for different jobs.

In synthesis, the recent evidence on biodata indicates that: (1) they have a substantial and generalizable criterion validity; (2) the construct validity is well established; and (3) biodata are fakable, especially if personality attributes are assessed by the items.

ASSESSMENT CENTER

Historically, most of the literature on Assessment Centers (AC) has been published in the USA, although there is currently a growing body of AC research in Europe, especially in Germany, Great Britain and the Netherlands. Previous findings supported the criterion and content validity of ACs as well as a very small adverse impact (Baron & Janman, 1996; Thornton, 1992) but the question remains as to what constructs are assessed by ACs. An essential document on ACs was published by the International Personnel Management Association: *Guidelines and Ethical Considerations for Assessment Center Operations* (Task Force on Assessment Center Guidelines, 1989). These guidelines describe 10 essential elements which an AC must possess in order to be considered an AC: (1) the AC must be based on a job analysis; (2) behavioral observations by the assessor must be classified into some meaningful and relevant categories (e.g., dimensions, attributes, aptitudes, etc.); (3) techniques (exercises) must be designed to provide information for evaluating dimensions; (4) multiple assessment techniques must be used; (5) assessment techniques must include sufficient job-related simulations in order to allow multiple opportunities to observe each candidate's behavior related to each dimension; (6) multiple assessors must observe the performance of each assessee; (7) assessors must receive training prior to participating in an AC; (8) assessors must systematically record specific behavioral observations at the time of their occurrence; (9) assessors must prepare a report of each participant's performance in each exercise; and (10) the integration of behaviors must be based on a pooling of information or through a statistical integration process. In connection with the Guidelines, Spychalski, Quiñones, Gaugler, and Pohley (1997) conducted a survey on the AC practices in the USA in 1990. They found that managers indicated a close adherence to the Guidelines' recommendations in connection with center design and assessor training, but a large section of the recommendations were not followed.

A number of articles were concerned with the construct validity of ACs. Scholz and Schuler (1993) carried out a meta-analytic study of 51 single studies and 66 samples ($n = 22\ 106$) on the construct validity of ACs. They found that overall assessment rating correlated 0.43 with general intelligence

(n = 17 373), 0.15 with emotional stability (n = 909), 0.14 with extraversion (n = 1328), 0.30 with dominance (n = 909), 0.40 with achievement motivation (n = 613), 0.41 with social competence (n = 572), and 0.32 with self-confidence (n = 601). Anderson, Payne, Ferguson and Smith (1994) factor analyzed the overall dimension ratings and psychometric self-report scores. The results showed two factors. Factor I consisted of the ratings of dimensions and Factor II contained the psychometric self-reports. According to Anderson et al., their results indicated an unequivocal clustering by method of assessment. These results have consistently been found in factor analyses of AC ratings (Borman, Hanson & Hedge 1997). Ryan, Daum, Bauman et al. (1995) studied the rating accuracy of common assessment center dimensions in a group-discussion exercise under three types of conditions: direct, indirect and controlled observation. Direct observation was defined as directly observing an assessment center exercise, indirect observation was operationalized as observing the exercise through videotape without the ability to control the rate of observation (i.e., no pausing or rewinding), and controlled observation consisted of observing videotapes with pausing and rewinding. The rating accuracy was not differentially affected by the observing conditions. Schneider and Schmitt (1992) examined whether or not variance in ratings of assessee performance was explained by form or by content method factors. Two exercise forms (leaderless group discussion vs role playing) and two exercise contents (cooperative vs competitive) were manipulated. The results showed that form accounted for 16% of method's variances while content exercise had no effect. Shore, Shore and Thornton (1992) examined the construct validity of peer and self-evaluations of performance dimensions in an AC, using a nomological network. They found strong evidence supporting the construct validity of peer evaluations but very little for self-evaluations of performance dimensions. Another relevant finding of Shore, Shore and Thornton (1992) was that the dimension observability moderated construct validity, showing that the most observable dimensions had more construct validity. Shore, Shore and Thornton suggested that peer and self-evaluations would be more useful if they were focused on dimensions in which people had greater behavioral information on which to base the evaluation. Harris, Backer and Smith (1993) tested whether two different methods of AC scoring affected the cross-situational consistency of ratings and they found that dimension ratings correlated higher with different dimensions within the same exercise than the same dimension across exercises. Harris, Backer and Smith suggested that candidates in typical AC exercises might have insufficient behavioral opportunities, which could result in limited cross-cultural consistency. Kleinmann (1993) carried out a study partially connected with this last suggestion. Kleinmann hypothesized that if dimensions were transparent for participants they would perform better than in conditions lacking in transparency, and the results supported this hypothesis. Kleinmann also found that transparency enhanced the convergent construct validity. Additional evidence for transparency was obtained by Kleinmann, Kuptsch and Köller (1996). In an experimental situation, they found that the construct validity of an AC was higher when the administrator made the dimensions transparent by explaining the aim and function of the AC at the beginning of each AC. Therefore, putting together Harris, Backer and Smith's (1993), Shore, Shore and Thornton's (1992) and Kleinmann's (1993, Kleinmann, Kuptsch & Köller 1996) findings for increasing transparency, the participants can more clearly show behaviors connected with the dimensions. In the same way raters can obtain greater and clearer behavioral information on which to base their ratings.

Some articles examined the predictive validity of ACs. Wiersma, Van Leest, Nienhuis and Maas (1991) found a correlation equal to 0.48 between overall assessment ratings (OAR) and supervisor ratings of management potential. Schuler, Moser and Funke (1994) investigated the moderating effect of the rater–ratee acquaintance on the predictive validity of predictors in an assessment center. Rater–ratee acquaintance varied between 1 month and 30 years. The (uncorrected) validity of the AC was 0.37. This validity fell to 0.09 when the rater–ratee acquaintance was less than or equal to 2 years, but reached 0.50 when the rater–ratee acquaintance was greater than 2 years. Jansen and Stoop (1994) showed that the validity of the overall assessment center rating was 0.55 (corrected for range restriction) to predict present salary. Henderson, Anderson and Rick (1995) redesigned and validated an established AC to assess six competency dimensions which could be important in the future business career of graduates. Goffin, Rothstein and Johnston (1996) found that an AC for managers from forestry product organizations predicted performance and promotionability and that three personality traits (dominance, achievement and exhibition) showed incremental validity over AC performance prediction. Finally, an interesting study was carried out by Chan (1996). The study investigated criterion and construct validity simultaneously. Chan designed an AC for predicting job performance ratings and promotion potential of police sergeants. In addition, he examined the construct validity of an AC using multitrait-multimethod and factor analysis strategies. The results showed that the AC ratings predicted promotability but were not predictors of supervisory ratings. Furthermore, as in prior studies, the internal construct validity (based on factor analysis of the AC ratings) was found to be very low and the nomological network approach indicated no evidence of external construct validity (based on the correlation with other instruments). However, the very small sample size precluded strong conclusions.

In summary, empirical evidence continues to support the criterion validity of ACs and some steps have been taken in order to determine what constructs are assessed in an AC. However, we are far from establishing clearly the internal validity of ACs. Perhaps because of the reasons mentioned above the number of articles published in these years has decreased (Borman, Hanson & Hedge, 1997).

REFERENCES

Together with the interview, references are a very common part of selection systems. For example, Shackleton and Newell (1997) show that references to recruit managers were used in a percentage that ranged from 67% to 100% in companies in Australia, the European Community, and North America. Milkowich and Boudreau (1994) suggest that virtually every organization uses reference checks. With regard to this selection method, job candidates are usually asked to provide the name and telephone number of a personal reference and when this person is contacted two types of information are requested: (1) past job behavior (e.g., task performance); and (2) personal characteristics (e.g., personality traits). Also, the applicants are frequently categorized using rating scales. In this sense, references may be considered as a type of job performance rating and reliability should be similar to that of typical job performance ratings. However, this point has not been checked in the last few years. Furthermore, research on both references' validity and content is very small. Classic reviews of references' reports (e.g., references, letter of reference, letter of recommendation, reference check and reference statement) indicate that their criterion validity is very small, ranging from 0.14 (Reilly & Chao, 1982) to 0.19 (Muchinsky, 1979) or 0.26 (Hunter & Hunter, 1984) for predicting job performance ratings.

Recent research on references was carried out by Aamondt, Bryan and Whitcomb (1993), who examined the criterion validity of Peres and Garcia's (1962) adjective categories used in providing references. Aamondt, Bryan and Whitcomb (1993) found that the adjectives associated with mental agility were predictors of graduate school grade point average (GPA) ($r = 0.32$). Loher, Hazer, Tsai, Tilton & James (1997) suggested that previous research on references was atheoretical and proposed a conceptual framework for the reference letter process. According to Loher et al., the reference process seems to include two communication stages: the message to the writer and the message to the reader. One of Loher et al.'s study objectives was to determine what characteristics of the reference letter were related more to the reader's decision with regard to the acceptance or rejection of candidates. They considered 11 characteristics. Acceptance was related to lack of negative information and letter length.

A study somewhat related to the references was conducted by Mount, Barrick and Strauss (1994). In this study they examined the validity of personality ratings made by supervisors, peers, clients and subjects for predicting job performance. The raters assessed employees' personality using adjective descriptors of the Big Five personality dimensions. The validity coefficients of personality ratings made by supervisors were 0.23, 0.37, 0.28, 0.48, and 0.64, respectively for emotional stability, extraversion, openness, agreeableness and conscientiousness. Validity coefficients for clients were 0.13, 0.38, 0.21, 0.42 and 0.42. For peers, validities were 0.11, 0.34, 0.33, 0.17 and 0.37. Taking into account that the references provide information on the past work behavior of applicants, typically given by their past supervisors or peers, Mount, Barrick and Strauss's method is an excellent means of obtaining references. In this sense, Mount, Barrick and Strauss's results have confirmed the findings by Nash and Carroll (1970) on the suitability of supervisors for giving references. Furthermore, the validity coefficients found by Mount, Barrick and Strauss (1994) are greater than those typically found for personality dimensions (e.g. Barrick & Mount, 1991; Hough, 1992; Salgado, 1997a). An interesting conclusion derived from Mount, Barrick and Strauss's study is that if referees are asked for information on the personality of employees, references may have better predictive validity.

OTHER PREDICTORS

Some research was carried out with new predictors which were not commented on in previous reviews regarding personnel selection methods (e.g., video-technology, virtual reality technology). Also, some research was focused on predictors often used in applied settings but not included in the latest reviews on selection (e.g., drugs test, grades).

Video-technology is being used more and more in personnel selection, both in research and assessment contexts (Dalessio, 1994; Smiderle, Perry & Cronshaw, 1994; Van Leest & Meltzer, 1995; Weekly & Jones, 1997). In general, the results are supportive of the criterion validity of video-based tests. For example Dalessio, in a sample of insurance agents, found a validity of 0.13 ($n = 667$) for predicting turnover. Smiderle, Perry and Cronshaw (1994) did not find criterion validity evidence in a sample of metropolitan transit operators. McHenry and Schmitt (1994) reported two validity studies carried out by Wilson Learning, Inc., using the Wilson Learning Customer Service Skills Assessment, a video-based test for hiring customer service workers. The validities found in the two concurrent studies were 0.34 ($n = 60$) and 0.40 ($n = 126$). Pulakos and Schmitt (1996), using a video test developed as an alternative measure to the Verbal Ability Test of the AFOQT, found a validity of 0.15 ($n = 467$). The correlation between the Verbal Ability Test of the AFOQT and the video-based test was 0.39. Weekly and Jones (1997), in a first study, found that the validity of a video-based situational test was 0.22 ($n = 787$) and 0.33 ($n = 684$) for predicting job performance ratings. They also found that the video-based test accounted for 2.5% of the variance beyond cognitive ability and experience. In a second study, Weekly and Jones (1997) found validities of 0.35 ($n = 412$) and 0.24 ($n = 148$) for a video-based test. In this study, the correlation between cognitive ability and the video test was 0.27 ($n = 412$) and 0.15 ($n = 148$), and the incremental validity beyond cognitive ability was 5.7%. Probably in the future new ability tests and simulations will be developed using this technology in order to obtain more face validity and a greater acceptance by the assessee. Despite these supportive findings, two big problems within this technology are (1) the costs of developing video-based situational tests, which are estimated at $1500 per finished minute (Weekly & Jones, 1997), and (2) this technology does not seem greatly to improve the validity of classical predictors (e.g., cognitive ability test, structured interview), although it may add a small validity percentage over cognitive ability test validity.

A new technology, Virtual Reality Technology (VRT), has been suggested by Pierce and Aguinis (1997) as an alternative technology to conventional methodologies and video-based technology. VRT is a computer-simulated, multisensory environment in which the perceiver feels as if he himself is present in an environment generated by a computer. VRT may be used either as a predictor or a criterion, although there are no published studies on VRT validity. Pierce and Aguinis (1997) suggest that VR technology could enhance the internal and external validity. However, VRT has a big problem: it is terribly expensive. Currently, the costs of high resolution, full-color, head-mounted displays are in the $50 000 to $80 000 range.

A second group of predictors used very much by companies are drugs and alcohol tests and grades (Harris & Trusty, 1997; Roth, BeVier, Switzer and Schippman (1996). With regard to drugs and alcohol tests, in general, the findings indicated a very small relation ($r = 0.04$) with absenteeism and turnover and little or no additional validity over cognitive ability tests (Harris & Heft, 1993). With regard to grades, a couple of meta-analyses were focused on the relationship between grades point average (GPA) and job performance and salary. The criterion validity of grades for predicting job performance ratings was studied by Roth et al. (1996). These researchers found that the observed correlation between grades and job performance was 0.16 ($n = 13\ 984$) and 0.32 corrected by criterion reliability and range restriction. The grades validity was moderated by variables as years between GPA and performance, type of organization, education level, source of publication and source of performance information. For their part, Roth and Clarke (1998) meta-analyzed the relationship between grades and salary. They found that the observed correlation between GPA and starting salary was 0.13 (corrected for range restriction = 0.18; $n = 1238$), and the correlation between GPA and the current salary was 0.18 (corrected for range restriction = 0.25; $n = 9759$).

APPLICANT REACTIONS AND ATTITUDES

Because the selection process is a two-way decision-making process in which the decision made by an applicant may be as relevant as the one made by the organization, growing attention has been focused on applicant's reactions and attitudes in connection with predictors, the justice of the process and the process itself.

Rynes (1993) examined the selection process from the applicant's perspective, considering the effects that the characteristics of selection techniques could have on applicants' reactions (e.g., perceptions of invasiveness, invalidity and lack of relationship to job content, faking, and attempts to manipulate selection outcomes). Rynes and Connerley (1993) studied the attitudes and beliefs of applicants in connection with 13 alternative selection procedures. The main characteristic that affected the attitudes was the apparent content validity of the procedure, with the best scores for simulations, written exams and references and at the same time contrasting with ability tests. They also found that the applicant attitudes can be predicted from three characteristics: (1) faith in the evaluation system; (2) perception of the employer's need to know; and (3) beliefs about likely self-performance. Connerley and Rynes (1996) examined the perceptions of differences in staffing between Total Quality Management (TQM) companies and non-TQM companies on a sample of 145 engineer applicants. Connerley and Rynes found that the number of companies that described themselves as 'quality employers' was percentually small (18%). for this reason they needed to create a third category of companies: inferred-TQM firms. Secondly, they found that by comparing non-TQM companies with explicit-TQM firms, these last selected employees on a basis of their technical knowledge, skills and abilities. If the comparison was between non-TQM and inferred-TQM, the latter used more applicant information and emphasized social aspects of work. Thirdly, the TQM status per se had very little influence on the applicants' general perceptions, suggesting a small impact on applicant attraction. Smither, Reilly, Millsap, Pearlman and Stoffey (1993) found that the applicants' reactions to assessment could be of practical importance because of influences on the organizations' attractiveness to candidates.

A number of articles are related to test-taking motivation (TTM), which is defined by Arvey, Strickland, Drauden and Martin (1990) as positive or negative attitudes toward taking tests. Arvey et al. (1990) have suggested that TTM could affect test validity. According to their results, applicants showed higher TTM and made a greater effort to answer correctly than actual employees. Arvey et al. have also found that individual differences and performance factors are related to TTM (e.g., cognitive ability, race, sex and age). Interestingly, subjects higher in cognitive ability showed higher TTM. In a study partially related to TTM, Schmit and Ryan (1993) found that the type of situation in which the assessment process was carried out might modify the structure of personality self-report measures. They showed that the structure of a personality questionnaire could be different if the assessment process was identified as a personnel assessment process or as an anonymous assessment research. Schmit and Ryan found that in the personnel assessment situation, the individuals responded by using an 'ideal employee' as a reference frame while in an anonymous assessment situation the reference frame could be 'the description of a stranger'. Salgado, Remeseiro and Iglesias (1996) examined the relations between TTM, Big Five personality dimensions and motivational distortion. They found that positive TTM was related to extraversion, openness and conscientiousness while negative TTM was related to neuroticism and agreeableness. Neither positive TTM nor negative TTM was related to motivational distortion.

Gilliland (1993) examined the bases of selection reactions using organizational justice theories as a framework. He suggested four procedural justice dimensions that were applicable to selection procedures: job relatedness, opportunity to demonstrate one's abilities, interpersonal treatment and propriety of questions. Gilliland (1994) also found that job relatedness was a relevant determinant in perceptions of selection process fairness. Steiner and Gilliland (1996) conducted a research in which fairness in the most used predictors was assessed in France and the United States. The findings revealed not many cross-cultural differences in the perceived validity and justice of the instruments. Interviews, work sample tests, and résumés were perceived favorably in France and the United States. In both countries the participants in the study rated graphology negatively.

Putting together all the findings previously described, it seems clear that applicants' attitudes and perceptions on recruitment and selection methods can have a strong impact on the success or failure of selection programs. Therefore, in the future more research should be devoted to these topics.

UTILITY ANALYSIS

The utility analysis (UA) literature may be classified into two groups of articles. A first group involves estimating the parameters included in the classic utility models (e.g., SDy) and developments of new UA models. The second group is concerned primarily with the observed lack of interest in UA that managers appear to show. The latter is an important concern because, as Borman, Hanson, and Hedge (1997) note, the main objective of UA is to report the value of Human Resources Management systems (HRM) to managers.

Boudreau (1991) summarized and critically reviewed the UA literature and research. He suggested that UA should focus on the role of UA information in managerial decision processes. Boudreau, Sturman and Judge (1997) further proposed a model whereby they have suggested that: (1) new interventions are usually combined with existing ones; (2) predictor information is often used in ways that diverge from a top-down selection system; (3) the performance is multi-dimensional and multiple aspects or dimensions must be included. Russell, Colella and Bobko (1993) modified the Brogden–Cronbach–Gleser selection utility model to include strategic needs of decision-makers. These strategic needs vary within and between firms. Russell, Colella and Bobko also suggested that utility should be periodically estimated due to the fact that many relevant variables for the model can change over time (e.g., performance, validity, costs and strategic needs). Roth (1993, 1994a) considered the application of the fractile method and four group decision-making techniques with the Schmidt–Hunter estimation SDy procedure. The four techniques were: delphi, nominal group, consensus groups, and social judgment analysis. Roth suggested that the group methods of judgment could increase managers' accuracy and confidence in their SDy estimates. Raju, Cabrera and Lezotte (1997) have developed a UA model for assessing the utility of organizational interventions to be used when employee performance is considered dichotomous (e.g., successful vs unsuccessful employees). This model is based on logistic regression. Roth and Bobko (1998) recently noted that most UA applications in organizational interventions have considered only one outcome, the value of job performance in currency units. They have suggested using the Multi-Attribute Utility (MAU) as an alternative because it allows managers to incorporate multiple criteria when making analytic decisions (e.g., legal effects, workforce diversity, multiple decision-makers). In the article, Roth and Bobko outline the steps to implementing an MAU analysis.

Several articles are concerned with the acceptance of UA by managers, a big problem in the implementation of utility programs in human resource interventions. Latham and Whyte (1994) experimentally examined experienced managers' reactions to UA estimates. The managers reported much higher levels of commitment to an HRM decision when they were presented with just validity information rather than when presented with validity information and utility information. Latham and Whyte suggested that managers appeared to be incredulous about UA estimates and they also appeared to be negatively influenced by utility information. Whyte and Latham (1997) replicated the results of the prior research, even though an expert was used to induce positive attitudes to UA. Cronshaw (1997), who participated as the UA expert in Whyte and Latham's (1997) study, suggested that subjects might have reacted negatively against the expert's recommendation because they could have interpreted the expert's message as a high-pressure or coercive communication. Cronshaw (1997) recently recommended that practitioners must inform their clients that UA is a way of identifying those projects that will maximize the whole gains of the firm, instead of trying to 'sell' organizational interventions (e.g., selection tests). Hazer and Highhouse (1997) investigated the effect of three methods for estimating SDy as well as three characteristics of utility information on managers' reactions to UA in the context of a resource allocation scenario. They found that managers perceived UA as most credible and were most likely to use it when the 40% procedure was used to calculate SDy instead of the global procedure (Schmidt, Hunter, McKenzie & Muldrow, 1979) or the CREPID method (Cascio & Ramos, 1986). Hazer and Highhouse suggested that the 40% method was preferred because it represented the effortless way of arriving at an SDy estimate. They also found that the way in which the final dollar estimate was framed (utility estimate presented as a cost from not acting vs as a profit from acting), as well as HR intervention (training vs selection) and the comprehension of utility information, did not have any effect on managers' reactions. Roth, Segars and Wright (1997) developed a theory on why managers accept or do not accept UA decisions. The bases of the acceptance theory are the theory of reasoned action and the technology acceptance model.

METHODOLOGICAL ADVANCES

In the years that this review covers, some relevant methodological advances have occurred. Cooper and Hedges (1994) edited an exhaustive handbook on meta-analysis in which 43 authors of information science, statistics, psychology, education and social policy analysis participated (e.g. Cooper, Hedges, Hunter, Lipsey, Olkin, Rosenthal and Schmidt). Several procedures were developed that improved the estimates of validity generalization methods. Schmidt, Law, Hunter et al. (1993) presented three refinements of psychometric meta-analysis which had implications for the validity general-ization procedures. The three refinements were: (1) a more accurate pro-cedure for correcting residual SD for range restriction to estimated SDrho; (2) using r mean instead of study-observed rs in the formula for sampling error variance; and (3) removal of the non-Pearson rs (e.g., biserial correlations). The cumulative addition of all three refinements decreased the mean SDrho estimate by 29%. The accuracy of these three refinements was checked by Law, Schmidt and Hunter (1994a, b). Aguinis and Pierce (1998a) recently proposed a three-step procedure for testing moderator variable hypotheses meta-analytically. The procedure is based on the Hedges and Olkin (1995) meta-analysis method, but it incorporates correction for artifacts (as in Hunter and Schmidt's method). The three steps are: (1) correcting study-level effect size across-study variability due artifacts; (2) testing the overall homogeneity of effect size after the artifactual sources of variance have been removed; and (3) testing the effects of hypothesized moderator variables.

Johnson, Mullen and Salas (1995) compared the meta-analytic methods developed by Hedges and Olkin (1985), Rosenthal (1991) and Hunter and Schmidt (1990). They concluded that both Hedges and Olkin's method and Rosenthal's method yielded very similar results but Hunter and Schmidt's methods produced incorrect results. Johnson, Mullen and Salas found that Hunter and Schmidt's methods showed a mean correlation similar to the other methods. However, according to Johnson, Mullen and Salas's results, Hunter and Schmidt's method did not decrease the standard error of the mean correlation when increasing the number of studies. Schmidt and Hunter (1997b) have demonstrated that Johnson, Mullen and Salas's findings are based on the use of an erroneous formula for the standard error of the mean correlation. When the correct formula is used the results of Hunter and Schmidt's method are similar to the other meta-analysis procedures.

Various methodological articles are connected with range restriction and its effects. Ree, Carretta, Earles and Albert (1994) have shown that range restriction can have dramatic consequences on predictive validity. It is possible that, under some circumstances, range restriction can change the validity sign. This happens with indirect range restriction. They have suggested using Lawley's (1943) multivariate correction for range restriction, and have demonstrated that a multivariate correction does not yield the same results as a series of univariate corrections. Lawley's correction results in corrected validities that are closer to the population parameters as compared to correction several correlations one at a time. Aguinis and Whitehead (1997) examined the effects of indirect range restriction (IRR) on sampling variance in validity. They found that IRR increased the sampling error variance of validity to values as high as 8.5% which was larger than the analytically-derived expected values. Salgado (1997c), on the basis of the formulas developed by Bobko and Rieck (1980), developed a computer program to estimate the standard error of validity corrected for range restriction (based on selection ratio or on SD/sd) as well as validity corrected for unreliability in criterion and predictor. Sackett and Ostgaard (1994) showed that standard deviations from national norms could be used to calculate range restriction corrections, although a job-specific applicant pool had a slightly smaller standard deviation.

Research on differential prediction has received substantial attention in the last few years, and several articles are connected with the use of moderated multiple regression (MMR) to estimate moderating effects. For example, Stone-Romero and Anderson (1994) found that MMR emerged as more powerful than the subgroup-based correlation coefficients for detecting moderating effects. Aguinis, Pierce and Stone-Romero (1994; Aguinis & Pierce, 1998b) have developed a computer program for estimating the statistical power of moderated multiple regression to detect dichotomous moderator variables. Aguinis and Stone-Romero (1997) have shown that the power degree of MMR to detect moderating effects was affected by the main and interactive effects of: (1) predictor variable range restriction; (2) total sample size; (3) sample size for two moderator variable-based subgroups; (4) predictor variable intercorrelation; and (5) magnitude of the moderating effect. Aguinis and Pierce (1998c) have investigated the effects of the violation of homogeneity assumption of within-subgroup error variance on MMR-based conclusions. They found that heterogeneity of within-subgroup error variance led to very low statistical power and they suggested using alternative parametric methods in lieu of MMR when the homogeneity of within-subgroup error variance assumption is violated. In summary, this research shows that the typical differential prediction test lacks sufficient statistical power to detect gender and ethnicity-based effects. In this sense, Linn (1994) recommended that prediction differential should continue to be a topic on the validation research agenda.

Top-down selection model versus selection using banding has been the central issue of some articles. According to the top-down model, applicants are ranked on the basis of their observed test scores and the applicants with the highest scores are selected (SIOP, 1987). This selection model produces the highest validity and utility (Schmidt, 1991). However, it could produce an adverse impact (Sackett & Wilks, 1994). As an alternative to this method, test score banding was suggested (Cascio, Outtz, Zedeck & Goldstein, 1991). Using a banding method, the differences in test scores may be ignored and all applicants within a band are considered as if they have the same test score. In order to determine the width of the band the standard error of measurement (SEM) is used, or more specifically $C \times SEM \times 2\frac{1}{2}$, where C is the point of the normal curve that corresponds with the level of confidence desired in conclusions. Thus, all scores that are not significantly statistically different from the top score are included in the band and the rest are excluded. Cascio et al. (1991) admitted that banding resulted in some loss in utility, but they suggested that the sliding band procedure reconciled economic and social objectives. For example, it could reduce adverse impact or could increase work diversity (see also Cascio, Goldstein, Outtz & Zedeck, 1995; Zedeck, Outtz, Cascio & Goldstein, 1991). Schmidt (1991; Schmidt and Hunter, 1995) indicated that banding was logically flawed because there was a contradiction between the statistical rationale and the operational procedures used in banding methods. Murphy (1994) showed that test reliability had effects on banding. He found that highly reliable tests produced relatively narrow bands, while unreliable tests could produce very broad bands. Murphy, Osten and Myors (1995) examined the effects of several parameters on the proportions hired from higher and lower-scoring groups. Their most remarkable finding showed that the selection outcomes were more affected by the proportion of lower-scoring group members in the applicant pool than by the particular banding strategy used. Aguinis, Cortina and Goldberg (1997) developed a procedure for making bands using criterion data when available.

A group of articles is related to missing data techniques and their effects on the validity of selection procedures. Roth and his colleagues (1994b; Roth, Campion & Jones, 1996; Roth & Switzer, 1995; Switzer, Roth & Switzer, 1998), using both empirical data sets and Monte Carlo simulations, reviewed and discussed several techniques to deal with missing data: (1) listwise deletion; (2) pairwise deletion; (3) mean substitution technique; (4) regression substitution with variance correction; (5) regression substitution without variance correction; (6) hot deck imputation; (7) hot deck 'distance' imputation; and (8) random substitution. They found that the choice of the missing data technique influenced research findings. Using as criteria for decision-making the dispersion around true scores and the overestimation and underestimation of true values of various statistics, they recommended using pairwise deletion as first choice, because it preserved more information which might allow researchers to find significant validity coefficients (Roth, Campion & Jones, 1996; Roth & Switzer, 1995). Roth and colleagues also recommended avoiding mean substitution because it was only marginally better than substituting random numbers for the missing values (Switzer, Roth & Switzer, 1998).

An additional methodological advance is concerned with establishing validity in small sample settings. Bartram (1997a, b) developed a Selection Validation Index (SVI) designed to overcome the problems associated with the use of very small samples (e.g., $n = 10$) in validity studies. Using computer simulations, Bartram has shown that the SVI produces estimates similar to those obtained using correlation coefficients with large sample sizes after correction for range restriction in the predictor.

CONCLUSIONS

Personnel selection methods are enjoying an exceptionally good time. Meta-analytic investigations have shown that the majority of classic instruments in the area are good predictors of job performance. A summary of the meta-analytic results found in the last six years is shown in Table 1.1. In this table are included the meta-analyses which were carried out in the years covered by this review. Indeed, the findings of meta-analyses differ with respect to single studies, and the possible differences should be taken into account by readers. In fact, I suggest that one should read the specific section of each predictor before reading the table. Generally, there is only one meta-analysis for each predictor, but in some cases there may be several. For example, several meta-analyses were published on integrity test validity during this period. I have included the Ones, Viswesvaran and Schmidt (1993) meta-analysis because it is based on the larger database. Another case is emotional stability. Three American meta-analyses reach different conclusions, two concluding validity generalization, but one of these is based on a very small sample. For this reason I have included in the table the results of a European meta-analysis.

As can be seen in the table, we currently know that ability tests (e.g., cognitive, psychomotor, physical), job knowledge tests, situational judgment tests, personality tests (e.g., conscientiousness, emotional stability, integrity, service orientation), interviews (structured and unstructured), biodata, and assessment centers all have criterion validity ranging from medium to high (both for training success and for job performance ratings). Furthermore, if cognitive ability tests are combined with a second predictor, the multiple correlation reaches 0.68 with service orientation tests, 0.60 with integrity tests, and 0.58 with situational judgment tests. Schmidt and Hunter (1997a), in their revision of 85 years of research in personnel selection, have shown that

Table 1.1 Average validity of personnel selection methods (corrected for criterion unreliability and range restriction)

Predictor	P-CA	VAL(R)	MR	R^2	VAL(T)	MR	R^2	Source of validity
Cognitive ability	—	0.43	—	—	0.67	—	—	Levine et al. (1996)
Psychomotor ability	—	0.34	—	—	0.35	—	—	Levine et al. (1996)
Physical ability	0.00[a]	0.32	0.54	0.29	0.55[b]	0.87	0.75	Blakley et al. (1994)
Job knowledge	—	0.45	—	—	0.47	—	—	Dye Reck & McDaniel, (1993)
Situational judgment test	0.53[c]	0.56	0.58	0.34	—	—	—	McDaniel et al. (1997)
Conscientiousness	0.02[d]	0.32	0.53	0.28	0.30	0.73	0.53	Mount & Barrick (1995)
Emotional stability	0.06[d]	0.18	0.46	0.21	0.27	0.71	0.50	Salgado (1997b)
Integrity	0.02[e]	0.42	0.60	0.35	0.38	0.76	0.58	Ones, Viswesvaran & Schmidt (1993)
Service orientation	-0.06[f]	0.50	0.68	0.46	—	—	—	Frei & McDaniel (1997)
Interview (structured)	0.35[g]	0.44	0.53	0.28	0.34	0.70	0.46	McDaniel et al. (1994)
Interview (unstructured)	0.50[g]	0.33	0.45	0.20	0.36	0.67	0.45	McDaniel et al. (1994)
Biodata	0.48[i]	—	—	—	0.46[i]	—	—	Bliesener (1996)
Assessment center	0.43[h]	0.37[l]	0.48	0.23	—	—	—	Schuler, Moser & Funke (1994)
Grade point average	0.55[h]	0.32	0.44	0.20	—	—	—	Roth et al. (1996)

P-CA = correlation between cognitive ability and the predictor. VAL(R) = corrected validity for performance rating; MR = multiple correlation using cognitive ability and each predictor as second independent variable; R^2 = Square multiple correlation; VAL(T) = corrected validity for training; [a] = assumed; [b] = criterion was work sample rating; [c] = McDaniel et al. (1997); [d] = Ackerman & Goff (1995); [e] = Ones (1993); [f] = Frei & McDaniel (1997); [g] = Huffcutt, Roth & McDaniel (1996); [h] = Scholz & Schuler (1993); [i] = based on Bliesener (1996) and corrected for criterion unreliability and range restriction.; [k] = based on Schuler et al. (1995); [l] = I have used this value found by Schuler, Moser & Funke (1994), albeit uncorrected, because it is the same value (corrected) as found by Glauger et al. (1987), the meta-analysis with more up-to-date studies.

the multiple correlation using general mental ability and integrity or general mental ability and structured employment interviews reached 0.65 and 0.63 using general mental ability and work sample tests (when job performance ratings were criteria). Therefore, we can claim that the predictive phase in our science is well consolidated.

However, we must get beyond this predictive phase and move towards an explanatory phase. We need a comprehensive theory of personnel selection, and future efforts should be made in that direction. In this direction, a necessary step is to clarify what we want to explain (i.e., job performance, extra-role behavior). In other words, we need a work behavior theory in which performance constructs are well defined and assessed.

Meta-analysis is one of the best (perhaps the best) methods to advance in this direction, the theoretical account of work behavior. However, meta-analysis needs supplementary methods (e.g., experimental studies, structural equation methods) and new and innovative studies and propositions. Also, we must develop a consensus about certain key aspects. For example, consensus and clarification must be developed into job performance rating reliability. Recent studies have shown that rater reliability ranges from 0.40 to 0.65, but this is a very large interval for a consolidated science. Think for a moment about the employment interview. Today all of us accept its predictive validity. Several meta-analyses conducted with over 100 studies have shown a very similar observed validity, ranging from 0.24 to 0.28. However, when validity is corrected for unreliability the values range from 0.44 to 0.62, which is a very large interval for reaching sound conclusions on the predictive power of the interview.

Another point that must be considered in these conclusions is the similarities and differences found between American and non-American research conclusions. The majority of published meta-analyses only included validity coefficients found in the USA and did not include validities found in other countries (e.g., European countries). Because of cross-cultural characteristics (e.g., social, cultural, legislative differences), differences in validity from America to other countries might exist, and therefore, the international validity generalization of the American findings might not have a firm basis. In this sense, Shackleton and Newell (1997) summarized data suggesting that there were different practices of assessment in North America and the European Community. For example, well-known personality questionnaires in America (e.g., HPI, MMPI, NEO-PI-R) are virtually unused for personnel selection in Europe (Salgado, 1997a). Therefore, a summary conclusion about the non-North American work on selection may be useful. With regard to cognitive ability tests, European single studies reach similar results to the North American ones, showing that cognitive ability tests are good predictors of job performance, training proficiency and academic grades (see Bartram & Baxter, 1996; Schuler et al., 1995; Salgado, 1998b). With regard to psychomotor ability tests, a meta-analysis carried out in Spain

(Salgado, 1994a) showed a similar validity to the one found in the United States of America, for example the validity found by Levine et al. (1996). In the case of personality dimensions, the findings were similar for conscientiousness, due to the fact that in the USA and Europe this dimensionshowed validity generalization. However, emotional stability showed validity generalization in Europe but the North American findings were contradictory. In the USA, Barrick and Mount (1991) found that emotional stability did not generalize validity, but Hough (1992) and Tett, Jackson and Rothstein (1991) found evidence of validity generalization. In the personality field, there was a lot of confluence between European and North American researchers, mostly due to the use of the Five Factor Model of personality in both continents. With respect to the personnel interview, in Germany, Schuler and his colleagues (1992, 1995, 1997) developed the multimodal interview, which is a structured interview, and found evidence of predictive validity for this interview type (with coefficients similar to those of BD and situational interviews).

In addition to these confluent findings, some specific themes and results found in the European studies were: (1) the study of the construct validity of the assessment centers based on a large-scale meta-analysis (Schuler, Moser & Funke, 1994); (2) the study of the construct validity of biodata, using meta-analysis (Bliesener, 1996); (3) the effects of transparency conditions on assessment center ratings (Kleinmann, 1993; Kleinmann, Kuptsch & Köller, 1996); (4) the effects of rating acquaintance on validity coefficients; (5) several questionnaires based on the Big Five personality dimensions were developed in the European countries (e.g., France, Great Britain; Italy, the Netherlands, Spain).

Finally, as an agenda for the future, I suggest that more research should be devoted in the next few years to several themes. With regards to predictors, research should be focused on: (1) the criterion and construct validity of references and the different themes included in the references (e.g., past behavior; personality); (2) the criterion validity of video-based technology (e.g., meta-analysis of validity for job performance and training); (3) studies on the criterion validity of virtual reality technology for predicting performance and training; (4) the construct validity of interviews, not only cognitive ability but also job knowledge, personality, experience and grades; (5) studying the relation between grades and the 'Big Five'; (6) developing new cognitive ability tests using recent theoretical approaches (e.g., Ackerman's theory, Kyllonen's theory, Sternberg's theory) and new technologies (e.g., computer, video and virtual reality). With regard to criteria, research should be carried out on (1) task and contextual performance and their components; (2) the relationship between the Borman and Motowidlo two-factor performance model, the Campbell eight-factor performance model and the Viswesvaran one-factor performance model. The integration of the three models could result in the work behavior theory that the personnel selection field needs. In connection with the organizational use of personnel selection instruments, future research should show why more valid predictors (e.g., cognitive ability tests, integrity tests, personality tests, behavioral interview or biodata) are not always widely used and how to encourage their greater use. The organizational justice approach and the total quality management approach could be relevant ones to clarify this issue. If we know the reason for what candidates and professionals think about personnel selection methods, appropriate strategies might be developed in order to overcome this problem to some extent. Also, useful strategies should be developed to facilitate the adoption of organizational utility programs, and more research should be carried out on this topic.

ACKNOWLEDGMENT

I am grateful to all researchers who kindly provided me with published and unpublished articles for carrying out this review. I specially acknowledge H. Aguinis, P. Bobko, W. Borman, M.M. Harris, Joyce and Robert Hogan, A.I. Huffcutt, K.R. Murphy, M. Ree, I.T. Robertson, J.P. Rolland, P.L. Roth, F.L. Schmidt and D.I. Steiner. Their comments have greatly improved a previous version of this review. This research was partially supported by XUGA (Spain) grant n° 21104B97.

REFERENCES

Aamodt, M.G., Bryan, D.A. & Whitcomb, A.J. (1993). Predicting performance with letters of recommendation. *Public Personnel Management*, 22, 81–90.

Ackerman, P.L. (1994). Intelligence, attention and learning. Maximal and typical performance. In D.K. Detterman (Ed.), *Current Topics in Human Intelligence*. Vol. 4: *Theories of Intelligence* (pp 1–27). Norwood, NJ: Ablex.

Ackerman, P.L. & Goff, M. (1995). Intelligence, personality, and interest: Historical review and a model for adult intellect. Department of Psychology, University of Minnesota. Unpublished manuscript.

Ackerman, P.L. & Heggestad, E.D. (1997). Intelligence, personality and interests: Evidence for overlapping traits. *Psychological Bulletin*, 121, 219–245.

Ackerman, P.L. & Kanfer, R. (1993). Integrating laboratory and field study for improving selection: Development of a battery for predicting air traffic controller success. *Journal of Applied Psychology*, 78, 413–432.

Ackerman, P.L., Kanfer, R. & Goff, M. (1995). Cognitive and non-cognitive determinants and consequences of complex skill acquisition. *Journal of Experimental Psychology: Applied*, 1, 270–305.

Aguinis, H., Cortina, J.M. & Goldberg, E. (1998). A new procedure for computing equivalence bands in personnel selection. *Human Performance*, 11, 351–365.

Aguinis, H. & Pierce, C.A. (1998a). Testing moderator variable hypotheses meta-analytically. *Journal of Management*, 24, 577–592.

Aguinis, H. & Pierce, C.A. (1998b). Statistical power computations for detecting dichotomous moderator variables with moderated multiple regression. *Educational and Psychological Measurement*, 58, 668–676.

Aguinis, H. & Pierce, C.A. (1998c). Heterogeneity of error variance and the assessment of moderating effects of categorical variables: A conceptual review. *Organizational Research Methods*, 1, 296–314.

Aguinis, H., Pierce, C.A. & Stone-Romero, E.F. (1994). Estimating the power to detect dichotomous moderators with moderated multiple regression. *Educational and Psychological Measurement* 54, 690–692.

Aguinis, H. & Stone-Romero, E.F. (1997). Methodological artifacts in moderated multiple regression and their effects on statistical power. *Journal of Applied Psychology*, 82, 192–206.

Aguinis, H. & Whitehead, R. (1997). Sampling variance in the correlation coefficient under indirect range restriction: Implications for validity generalization. *Journal of Applied Psychology*, 82, 528–538.

Altink, W.M.M. (1991). Construction and validation of a biodata selection instrument. *European Work and Organizational Psychologist*, 1, 245–270.

Anderson, N. (1992). Eight decades of employment interview research: A retrospective meta-review and prospective commentary. *European Work and Organizational Psychologist*, 2, 1–32.

Anderson, N. & Herriot, P. (Eds) (1997). *International Handbook of Selection and Assessment*. London, UK: Wiley.

Anderson, N., Payne, T., Ferguson, E. & Smith, T. (1994). Assessor decision making, information processing and assessor decision strategies in a British assessment centre. *Personnel Review*, 23, 52–62.

Anderson, N., Silvester, J., Cunningham-Snell, N. & Haddleton, E. (1997). Interviews of the selection interview: Recruiter and candidate decision making in graduate employment interview. Manuscript submitted for publication.

Arthur, W., Doverspike, D. & Barrett, G.V. (1996). Development of a job analysis-based procedure for weighting and combining content-related tests into a single test battery score. *Personnel Psychology*, 49, 971–985.

Arvey, R.D., Landon, T.E., Nutting, S.M. & Maxwell, S.E. (1992). Development of physical ability tests for police officers: A construct validation approach. *Journal of Applied Psychology*, 77, 996–1009.

Arvey, R.D. & Murphy, K.R. (1998). Performance evaluation in work settings. *Annual Review of Psychology*, 49, 141–168.

Arvey, R.D., Strickland, W., Dauden, G. & Martin, C. (1990). Motivational components of test taking. *Personnel Psychology*, 43, 695–716.

Austin, J.T. & Villanova, P. (1992). The criterion problem: 1917–1992. *Journal of Applied Psychology*, 77, 836–874.

Backer, T.E. & Colquitt, A.L. (1992). Potential versus actual faking of a biodata form: An analysis along several dimensions of item type. *Personnel Psychology*, 45, 389–406.

Baron, H. & Janman, K. (1996). Fairness in the assessment centre. In C.L. Cooper and I.T. Robertson (Eds), *International Review of Industrial and Organizational Psychology*, Vol. 11 (pp 61–113). London, UK: Wiley.

Barrick. M.R. & Mount, M.K. (1991). The Big Five personality dimensions and job performance: a meta-analysis. *Personnel Psychology*, 44, 1–26.

Barrick, M.R. & Mount, M.K. (1993). Autonomy as a moderator of relationships between the big five personality dimensions and job performance. *Journal of Applied Psychology*, 78, 111–118.

Barrick, M.R. & Mount, M.K. (1996). Effects of impression management and self-deception on the predictive validity of personality constructs. *Journal of Applied Psychology*, 81, 261–272.

Barrick, M., Mount, M.K. & Strauss (1993). Conscientiousness and performance of sales representatives: Test of the mediating effects of goal setting. *Journal of Applied Psychology*, 78, 715–722.

Bartram, D. (1993). Validation of the ICES personality inventory. *European Review of Applied Psychology*, **43**, 207–218.

Bartram, D. (1997a). The Selection Validity Index (SVI): Measuring predictive validity without correlations. *Presentation at the British Psychological Society Occupational Psychology Conference*, Blackpool, UK.

Bartram, D. (1997b). The selection Validity Index (SVI): Measuring predictive validity without correlations. Department of Psychology, University of Hull, Hull, UK. Unpublished paper.

Bartram, D. & Baxter, P. (1996). Validation of the Cathay Pacific Airways pilot selection program. *International Journal of Aviation Psychology*, **6**, 149–169.

Benjamin, L.T. (1997). Organized industrial psychology before Division 14: The ACP and the AAAP (1930–1945). *Journal of Applied Psychology*, **82**, 459–466.

Blakley, B.R., Quiñones, M.A., Crawford, M.S. & Jago, I.A. (1994). The validity of isometric strength tests. *Personnel Psychology*, **47**, 247–274.

Bliesener, T. (1996). Methodological moderators in validating biographical data in personnel selection. *Journal of Occupational and Organizational Psychology*, **69**, 107–120.

Bobko, P. & Rieck, A. (1980). Large sample estimators for standard errors of functions of correlation coefficients. *Applied Psychological Measurement*, **4**, 385–398.

Borman, W.C., Hanson, M.A. & Hedge, J.W. (1997). Personnel selection. *Annual Review of Psychology*, **48**, 299–337.

Borman, W.C., Hanson, M.A., Oppler, S.H., Pulakos, E.D. & White, L.A. (1993). Role of early supervisory experience in supervisor performance. *Journal of Applied Psychology*, **78**, 443–449.

Borman, W.C. & Motowidlo, S.J. (1993). Expanding the criterion domain to include elements of contextual performance. In N.E. Schmitt and W.C. Borman (Eds), *Personnel Selection in Organizations*. (pp. 71–98). San Francisco, CA: Jossey-Bass.

Borman, W.C. & Motowidlo, S.J. (1997). Task performance and contextual performance: The meaning for personnel selection research. *Human Performance*, **10**, 99–109.

Boudreau, J.W. (1991). Utility analysis for decisions in human resource management. In M.D. Dunnette and L.H. Hough (Eds), *Handbook of Industrial and Organizational Psychology*. Vol 2 (pp. 621–752). Palo Alto, CA: Consulting Psychologists Press.

Boudreau, J.W., Sturman, M.C. & Judge, T.A. (1997). Utility analysis: What are the black boxes, and do they affect decisions? In N. Anderson & P. Herriot (Eds), *International Handbook of Selection and Assessment* (pp. 303–322). London, UK: Wiley.

Brief, A.P. & Motowidlo, S.J. (1986). Prosocial organizational behavior. *Academy of Management Review*, **11**, 710–725.

Brown, B.K. & Campion, M.K. (1994). Biodata phenomenology: Recruiters' perceptions and use of biographical information in resume screening. *Journal of Applied Psychology*, **79**, 897–908.

Campbell, J.P. (1994). Alternative models of job performance and their implications for selection and classification. In M.G. Rumsey, C.B. Walker & J.H. Harris (Eds), *Personnel Selection and Classification*. (pp. 33–51). Hillsdale, NJ: Erlbaum.

Campbell, J.P., Gasser, M.B. & Oswald, F.L. (1996). The substantive nature of job performance variability. In K.R. Murphy (Ed.), *Individual Differences and Behavior in Organizations* (pp. 258–299). San Francisco, CA: Jossey-Bass.

Campbell, J.P., McCloy, R.A., Oppler, S.H. & Sager, C.E. (1993). A theory of performance. In N.E. Schmitt and W.C. Borman (Eds), *Personnel Selection in Organizations* (pp. 35–70). San Francisco, CA: Jossey-Bass.

Campion, M.A., Campion, J.E. & Hudson, J.P. (1994). Structured interviewing: A note on incremental validity and alternative question types. *Journal of Applied Psychology*, **79**, 998–1002.

Campion, M.A., Palmer, D.K. & Campion, J.E. (1997). A review of structure in the selection interview. *Personnel Psychology*, **50**, 655–702.

Carretta, T.R., Perry, D.C. Jr & Ree, M.J. (1996). Prediction of situational awareness in F-15 pilots. *International Journal of Aviation Psychology*, **6**, 21–41.

Carretta, T.R. & Ree, M.J. (1994). Pilot candidate selection method (PCSM): Sources of validity. *International Journal of Aviation Psychology*, **4**, 103–117.

Carretta, T.R. & Ree, M.J. (1995). Air force officer qualifying test validity for predicting pilot training performance. *Journal of Business and Psychology*, **9**, 379–388.

Carretta, T.R. & Ree, M.J. (1996). Factor structure of the Air Force Qualifying Test: Analysis and comparison. *Military Psychology*, **8**, 29–42.

Cascio, W.F., Goldstein, I.L., Outtz, J. & Zedeck, S. (1995). Twenty issues and answers about sliding bands. *Human Performance*, **8**, 227–242.

Cascio, W., Outtz, J., Zedeck, S. & Goldstein, I.L. (1991). Statistical implications of six methods of test score use in personnel selection. *Human Performance*, **4**, 233–264.

Cascio, W.F. & Ramos, R.A. (1986). Development of a new method for assessing job performance in behavioral/economic terms. *Journal of Applied Psychology*, **71**, 20–28.

Chan, D. (1996). Criterion and construct validation of an assessment centre. *Journal of Occupational and Organizational Psychology*, **69**, 167–181.

Christiansen, N.D., Goffin, R.D., Johnson, N.G. & Rothstein, M.G. (1994). Correcting the 16PF for faking: Effects on criterion-related validity and individual hiring decisions. *Personnel Psychology*, **47**, 847–860.

Collins, J.M. & Schmidt, F.L. (1993). Personality, integrity, and white collar crime: A construct validity study. *Personnel Psychology*, **46**, 295–311.

Connerley, M.L. & Rynes, S.L. (1996) Does total quality management affect applicant perceptions of recruitment and selection processes? *Journal of Quality Management*, **1**, 207–225.

Cook, M. (1993). *Personnel Selection and Productivity*, 2nd edn. London, UK: Wiley.

Cooper, H. & Hedges, L.V. (Eds) (1994). *The Handbook of Research Synthesis*. New York: Russell Sage Foundation.

Costa, P.T., Jr (1996). Work and personality: Use of the NEO-PI-R in Industrial/ Organisational Psychology. *Applied Psychology: An International Review*, **45**, 225–242.

Costa, P. Jr & McCrae, R.R. (1992). *The Revised NEO Personality Inventory (NEO-PI-R) and NEO Five-Factor Inventory (NEO-FFI) Professional Manual*. Odessa, FL: Psychological Assessment Resources.

Costa, P.T. Jr, McCrae, R.R. & Kay, G.G. (1995). Persons, places and personality: Career assessment using the revised NEO Personality Inventory. *Journal of Career Assessment*, **3**, 123–139.

Cronshaw, S.F. (1997). Lo! The stimulus speaks: The insider's view on Whyte and Latham's the futility of utility analysis. *Personnel Psychology*, **50**, 611–615.

Dalessio, A.T. (1994). Predicting insurance agent turnover using a video-based situational judgment test. *Journal of Business and Psychology*, **9**, 23–32.

Day, D.V. & Bedeian, A.G. (1991). Predicting job performance across organizations: The interaction of work orientation and psychological climate. *Journal of Management*, **17**, 589–600.

Day, D.V. & Bedeian, A.G. (1995). Personality similarity and work-related outcomes among African-American nursing personnel: A test of the supplementary model of person–environment congruence. *Journal of Vocational Behavior*, **46**, 55–70.

Dipboye, R.L. (1992). *Selection Interviews: Process Perspectives*. Cincinnati, OH: South-Western Publishing Co.

Dipboye, R.L. (1997). Structured selection interviews: Why do they work? Why are they underutilized? In Anderson, N. & Herriot, P. (Eds), *International Handbook of Selection and Assessment* (pp. 455–473). London, UK: Wiley.

Douglas, E.F., McDaniel, M.A. & Snell, A.F. (1996). The validity of non-cognitive measures decays when applicants fake. *Academy of Management Proceedings*, Cincinnati, OH.

Dunnette, M.D. & Hough, L.H. (Eds) (1990–1994). *Handbook of Industrial and Organizational Psychology.* Vols 1–4. Palo Alto, CA: Consulting Psychologists Press.

Dye, D.A., Reck, M. & McDaniel, M.A. (1993). The validity of job knowledge measures. *International Journal of Selection and Assessment,* 1, 153–157.

Farr, J.L. & Tesluk, P.E. (1997). Bruce V. Moore: First president of Division 14. *Journal of Applied Psychology,* 82, 478–485.

Frei, R.L. & McDaniel, M.A. (1997). Validity of customer service measures in personnel selection: A review of criterion and construct evidence. *Human Performance,* 11, 1–27.

Frese, M., Fay, D., Hilburger, T., Leng, K. & Tag, A. (1997). The concept of personal initiative: operationalization, reliability and validity in two German samples. *Journal of Occupational and Organizational Psychology,* 70, 1359–1361.

Furnham, A. (1995). The validity of Customer Service Questionnaire (CSQ). *International Journal of Selection and Assessment,* 2, 157–165.

Furnham, A. & Coveney, R. (1996). Personality and customer service. *Psychological Reports,* 79, 675–681.

George, J.M. & Brief, A.P. (1992). Feeling good–doing good: A conceptual analysis of the mood at work–organizational spontaneity relationship. *Psychological Bulletin,* 112, 310–329.

Gilliland, S.W. (1993). The perceived fairness of selection systems: An organizational justice perspective. *Academy of Management Review,* 18, 691–701.

Gilliland, S.W. (1994). Effects of procedural and distributive justice on reactions to a selection system. *Journal of Applied Psychology,* 79, 691–701.

Glauger, B.B., Rosenthal, D.B., Thorton, G.C. & Benson, C. (1987). Meta-analysis of assessment center validity. *Journal of Applied Psychology,* 72, 493–511.

Goff, M. & Ackerman, P.L. (1992). Personality–intelligence relations: Assessing typical intellectual engagement. *Journal of Educational Psychology,* 84, 537–552.

Goffin, R.D., Rothstein, M.G. & Johnston, N.G. (1996). Personality testing and the assessment center: Incremental validity for managerial selection. *Journal of Applied Psychology,* 81, 746–756.

Goldstein, I.L., Zedeck, S. & Schneider, B. (1993). An exploration of the job analysis-content validity process. In N. Schmitt & W.C. Borman (Eds), *Personnel Selection in Organizations* (pp. 3–34). San Francisco, CA: Jossey-Bass.

Graham, K.E., McDaniel, M.A., Douglas, E.F. & Snell, A.F. (1997). Biodata validity decay and score inflation with faking: Do item attributes explain variance across items? *Paper presented at the 12th Annual Conference of the Society of Industrial and Organizational Psychology,* St. Louis, MI, April.

Harrel, T.W. (1992). Some history of the army general classification test. *Journal of Applied Psychology,* 77, 875–878.

Harris, M.M. (1998). The structured interview: What constructs are being measured? In R. Eder & M.M. Harris (Eds), *The Employment Interview: Theory, Research and Practice,* 2nd edn. Thousand Oaks, CA: Sage Publications.

Harris, M.M., Backer, A.S. & Smith, D.E. (1993). Does the assessment center scoring method affect the cross-situational consistency of ratings? *Journal of Applied Psychology,* 78, 675–679.

Harris, M.M. & Heft, L.L. (1993). Preemployment urinalysis drug testing: A critical review of psychometric and legal issues and effects on applicants. *Human Resources Management Review,* 3, 271–291.

Harris, M.M. & Trusty, M.L. (1997). Drug and alcohol programs in the workplace: A review of recent literature. In C.L. Cooper and I.T. Robertson (Eds), *International Review of Industrial and Organizational Psychology,* Vol. 12 (pp. 289–315). London, UK: Wiley.

Hazer, J.T. & Highhouse, S. (1997). Factors influencing managers' reactions to utility analysis: Effects of SDy method, information frame, and focal intervention. *Journal of Applied Psychology,* 82, 104–112.

Hedges, L.V. & Olkin, I. (1985). *Statistical Methods for Meta-analysis*. Orlando, FL: Academic Press.

Henderson, F., Anderson, N. & Rick, S. (1995). Future competency profiling. Validating and redesigning the ICL graduate assessment centre. *Personnel Review*, **24**, 19–31.

Hogan, J. (1991a). Physical abilities. In M.D. Dunnette & L.H. Hough (Eds), *Handbook of Industrial and Organizational Psychology*. Vol. 2. (pp. 753–831). Palo Alto, CA: Consulting Psychologists Press.

Hogan, J. (1991b). Structure of physical performance in occupational tasks. *Journal of Applied Psychology*, **76**, 495–507.

Hogan, J.C., Arneson, S. & Petersons, A.V. (1992). Validation of physical ability tests for high pressure cleaning occupations. Special Issue: Test validity yearbook: I. *Journal of Business and Psychology*, **7**, 119–135.

Hogan, J. & Brinkmeyer, K. (1997). Bridging the gap between overt and personality-based integrity tests. *Personnel Psychology*, **50**, 587–600.

Hogan, J. & Quigley, A. (1994). Effects of preparing for physical ability tests. *Public Personnel Management*, **23**, 85–104.

Hogan, J. & Roberts, B.W. (1996). Issues and nonissues in the fidelity/bandwidth tradeoff. *Journal of Organizational Behavior*, **17**, 627–637.

Hogan, R. (1997). Personality and I/O psychology. *Paper presented at the 105th Annual Convention of the American Psychological Association*, Chicago, IL: August.

Hogan, R. & Hogan, J. (1995). *Manual for the Hogan Personality Inventory*. Tulsa, OK: Hogan Assessment Systems.

Hogan, R., Hogan, J. & Roberts, B.W. (1996). Personality measurement and employment decisions. Questions and answers. *American Psychologist*, **51**, 469–477.

Hough, L.M. (1992). The 'Big Five' personality variables-construct confusion: Description versus prediction. *Human Performance*, **5**, 139–155.

Hough, L.M. (1997a). The millennium for personality psychology: New horizons or good old daze. *Applied Psychology: An International Review*, **47**, 233–261.

Hough, L.M. (1998). Personality at work: Issues and evidence. In M. Hakel (Ed.), *Beyond Multiple Choice: Evaluating Alternatives to Traditional Testing for Selection* (pp. 131–166). Hillsdale, NJ: Erlbaum.

Hough, L.M. & Paullin (1994). Construct oriented scale construction: The rational approach. In Stokes, G., Mumford, M. & Owens (Eds) (1994). *Biodata Handbook: Theory, Research and Use of Biographical Information in Selection and Performance Prediction* (pp. 109–145). Palo Alto, CA: Consulting Psychologists Press.

Hough, L.M. & Schneider, R.J. (1996). Personality traits, taxonomies, and applications in organizations. In K.R. Murphy (Ed.), *Individual Differences and Behavior in Organizations* (pp. 31–88). San Francisco, CA: Jossey-Bass.

Huffcutt, A.I. & Arthur Jr W. (1994). Hunter and Hunter (1984) revisited: Interview validity for entry-level jobs. *Journal of Applied Psychology*, **79**, 184–190.

Huffcutt, A.I. & Roth, P.L. (1998). Racial group differences in employment interview evaluations. Submitted for publication.

Huffcutt, A.I., Roth, P.L. & McDaniel, M.A. (1996). A meta-analytic investigation of cognitive ability in employment interview evaluations: Moderating characteristics and implications for incremental validity. *Journal of Applied Psychology*, **81**, 459–474.

Huffcutt, A.I. & Woehr, D.J. (1997). Further analysis of employment interview validity: A quantitative evaluation of interviewer-related structuring methods. Submitted for publication.

Hulin, C.L., Henry, R.A. & Noon, S.L. (1990). Adding a dimension: Time as a factor in generalizability of predictive relationships. *Psychological Bulletin*, **107**, 328–340.

Hunter, J.E. (1986). Cognitive ability, cognitive aptitudes, job knowledge, and job performance. *Journal of Vocational Behavior*, **29**, 340–362.

Hunter, J.E. & Hirsh, H.R. (1987). Applications of meta-analysis. In C.L. Cooper & I.T. Robertson (Eds), *International Review of Industrial and Organizational Psychology*, Vol. 2 (pp. 321–357). Chichester: Wiley.

Hunter, J.E. & Hunter, R.F. (1984). Validity and utility of alternate predictors of job performance. *psychological Bulletin*, **96**, 72–98.

Hunter, J.E. & Schmidt, F.L. (1990). *Methods of Meta-analysis: Correcting Error and Bias in Research Findings*. Newbury Park, CA: Sage.

Jansen, P. & Stoop, B. (1994). Assessment centre graduate selection: Decision processes, validity, and evaluation by candidates. *International Journal of Selection and Assessment*, **2**, 193–208.

Johnson, B.T., Mullen, B. & Salas, E. (1995). Comparison of three meta-analytic approaches. *Journal of Applied Psychology*, **80**, 94–106.

Kataoka, H.C., Latham, G.P. & Whyte, G. (1997). The relative resistance of the situational, patterned behavior, and conventional structured interviews to anchoring effects. *Human Performance*, **10**, 47–63.

Katzell, R.A. & Austin, J.T. (1992). From then to now: The development of industrial-organizational psychology in the United States. *Journal of Applied Psychology*, **77**, 803–835.

Kleinmann, M. (1993). Are rating dimensions in assessment centers transparent for participants? Consequences for criterion and construct validity. *Journal of Applied Psychology*, **78**, 988–993.

Kleinmann, M., Kuptsch, C. & Köller, O. (1996). Transparency: A necessary requirement for the construct validity of assessment centres. *Applied Psychology: An International Review*, **45**, 67–84.

Koppes, L.L. (1997). American female pioneers of industrial and organizational psychology during the early years. *Journal of Applied Psychology*, **82**, 500–515.

Kyllonen, P.C. (1993). Aptitude testing inspired by information processing: A test of the four-sources model. *Journal of General Psychology*, **120**, 375–405.

Kyllonen, P.C. (1994). Cognitive abilities testing: An agenda for the 1990s. In M.G. Rumsey, C.B. Walker & J.H. Harris (Eds), *Personnel Selection and Classification*. Hillsdale, NJ: Lawrence Erlbaum.

Landy, F.J. (1992). Hugo Münsterberg: Victim or visionary? *Journal of Applied Psychology*, **77**, 787–802.

Landy, F.J. (1997). Early influences on the development of industrial and organizational psychology. *Journal of Applied Psychology*, **82**, 467–477.

Landy, F.J., Shankster, L. & Kohler, S.S. (1994). Personnel selection and placement. *Annual Review of Psychology*, **46**, 261–296.

Latham, G.P. & Skarlicki, D.P. (1996). The effectiveness of situational, patterned behaviour, and conventional structured interviews in minimizing in-group favouritism of Canadian francophone managers. *Applied Psychology: An International Review*, **45**, 177–184.

Latham, G.P. & Whyte, G. (1994). The futility of utility analysis. *Personnel Psychology*, **47**, 31–46.

Law, K.S., Schmidt, F.L. & Hunter, J.E. (1994a). Nonlinearity of range restriction corrections in meta-analysis: Test of an improved procedure. *Journal of Applied Psychology*, **79**, 425–438.

Law, K.S., Schmidt, F.L. & Hunter, J.E. (1994b). A test of two refinements in procedures for meta-analysis. *Journal of Applied Psychology*, **79**, 978–986.

Lawley, D.N. (1943). A note on Karl Pearson's selection formulae. *Proceedings of the Royal Society of Edinburgh*, **62**, 28–30.

Levine, E.L., Spector, P.E., Menon, P.E., Narayanon, L. & Cannon-Bowers, J. (1996). Validity generalization for cognitive, psychomotor, and perceptual tests for craft jobs in the utility industry. *Human Performance*, **9**, 1–22.

Linn, R.L. (1994). Fair test use: Research and policy. In Rumsey, M.G., Walker, C.B. & Harris, J.H. (Eds), *Personnel Selection and Classification* (pp. 363–375). Hillsdale, NJ: Erlbaum.

Loher, B.T., Hazer, J.T., Tsai, A., Tilton, K. & James, J. (1997). Letters of reference: A process approach. *Journal of Business and Psychology*, **11**, 339–355.

Mael, F.A. (1994). If past behavior really predicts future, so should biodatas. In M. Rumsey, C. Walker & J. Harris (Eds), *Personnel Selection and Classification* (pp. 273–292). Hillsdale, NJ: Erlbaum.

Mael, F.A. & Ashforth, B.E. (1995). Loyal from day one: Biodata, organizational identification, and turnover among newcomers. *Personnel Psychology*, **48**, 309–334.

Mael, F.A., Connerley, M. & Morath, R.A. (1996). None of your business: Parameters of biodata invasiveness. *Personnel Psychology*, **49**, 613–650.

Marchese, M.C. & Muchinsky, P.M. (1993). The validity of the employment interview: A meta-analysis. *International Journal of Selection and Assessment*, **1**, 18–26.

McCloy, R.A., Campbell, J.P. & Cudeck, R. (1994). A confirmatory test of a model of performance determinants. *Journal of Applied Psychology*, **79**, 493–505.

McDaniel, M.A., Finnegan, E.B., Morgeson, F.P., Campion, M.A. & Braveman, E.P. (1997). Predicting job performance from common sense. *Paper presented at the 12th annual SIOP Conference*, April, St Louis.

McDaniel, M.A., Whetzel, D.L., Schmidt, F.L. & Maurer, S. (1994). The validity of employment interviews: A comprehensive review and meta-analysis. *Journal of Applied Psychology*, **79**, 599–616.

McHenry, J.J. & Schmitt, N. (1994). Multimedia testing. In Rumsey, M.G., Walker, C.B. & Harris, J.H. (Eds) (1994). *Personnel Selection and Classification* (pp. 193–232). Hillsdale, NJ: Erlbaum.

Milkovich, G.T. & Boudreau, J.W. (1994). *Human Resource Management*, 7th edn. Homewood, IL: Richard D. Irwin.

Motowidlo, S.J. & Van Scotter, J.R. (1994). Evidence that task performance should be distinguished from contextual performance. *Journal of Applied Psychology*, **79**, 475–480.

Motowidlo, S.J., Borman, W.C. & Schmit, M.J. (1997). A theory of individual differences in task and contextual performance. *Human Performance*, **10**, 71–83.

Motowidlo, S.J. & Tippins, N. (1993). Further studies of the low-fidelity simulation in the form of a situational inventory. *Journal of Occupational and Organizational Psychology*, **66**, 337–344.

Mount, M.K. & Barrick, M. (1995). The Big Five personality dimensions. Implications for research and practice in human resource management. *Research in Personnel and Human Resources Management*, **13**, 153–200.

Mount, M.K., Barrick, M. & Strauss, J.P. (1994). Validity of observer ratings of the Big Five personality factors. *Journal of Applied Psychology*, **79**, 272–280.

Muchinsky, P.M. (1979). The use of reference reports in personnel selection: A review and evaluation. *Journal of Occupational Psychology*, **52**, 287–297.

Munene, J.C. (1995). Not-on-seat: An investigation of some correlates of organizational citizenship behavior in Nigeria. *Applied Psychology: An International Review*, **44**, 111–122.

Murphy, K.R. (1994). Potential effects of banding as a function of test reliability. *Personnel Psychology*, **47**, 477–496.

Murphy, K.R. (Ed.) (1996). *Individual Differences and Behavior in Organizations*. San Francisco, CA: Jossey-Bass.

Murphy, K.R. & Lee, S.L. (1994). Does conscientiousness explain relationship between integrity and job performance? *International Journal of Selection and Assessment*, **2**, 226–233.

Murphy, K.R., Osten, K. & Myors, B. (1995). Modeling the effects of banding in personnel selection. *Personnel Psychology*, **48**, 61–84.

Nash, A.N. & Corroll, S.J. (1970). A hard look at the reference check: Its modest worth can be improved. *Business Horizons*, **13**, 43–49.

Nyfield, C., Gibbons, P.J., Baron, H. & Robertson, I. (1995, May). The cross-cultural validity of management assessment methods. Paper presented at the *10th Annual SIOP Conference*, Orlando, FL.

Olea, M.M. & Ree, M.J. (1994). Predicting pilot and navigator criteria: Not much more than g. *Journal of Applied Psychology*, **79**, 845–851.

Ones, D.S. (1993). *The construct of integrity tests*. Unpublished doctoral dissertation, University of Iowa, Iowa City.

Ones, D.S. & Viswesvaran, C. (1996a). Bandwidth-fidelity dilemma in personality measurement for personnel selection. *Journal of Organizational Behavior*, **17**, 609–626.

Ones, D.S. & Viswesvaran, C. (1996b). What do pre-employment customer service scales measure? Exploration in construct validity and implications for personnel selection. Unpublished manuscript.

Ones, D.S. & Viswesvaran, C. (1997). *Empirical and theoretical considerations in using conscientiousness measures in personnel selection*. Paper presented at the fifth European Congress of Psychology, Dublin, Ireland. July 6–11.

Ones, D.S., Viswesvaran, C. & Korbin, W.P. (1995). Meta-analyses of fakability estimates: Between-subject versus within-subject designs. Paper presented in F.L. Schmidt (Chair), *Response Distortion and Social Desirability in Personality Testing and Personnel Selection*. Symposium conducted at the tenth annual meeting of the Society of Industrial and Organizational Psychology, Orlando, FL.

Ones, D.S., Viswesvaran, C. & Reiss, A.D. (1996). Role of social desirability in personality testing for personnel selection: The red herring. *Journal of Applied Psychology*, **81**, 660–679.

Ones, D.S., Viswesvaran, C. & Schmidt, F.L. (1993). Comprehensive meta-analysis of integrity test validities: Findings and implications for personnel selection and theories of job performance [Monograph]. *Journal of Applied Psychology*, **78**, 679–703.

Organ, D. (1988). *Organizational Citizenship Behavior: The Good Soldier Syndrome*. Lexington, MA: Lexington Books.

Paulhus, D.L. (1984). Two-component models of social desirable responding. *Journal of Personality and Social Psychology*, **46**, 598–609.

Peres, S.H. & Garcia, J.R. (1962). Validity and dimensions of descriptive adjectives used in reference letters for engineering applicants. *Personnel Psychology*, **15**, 279–286.

Peterson, N.G., Mumford, M.D., Borman, W.C., Jeanneret, P. Richard & Fleishman, E.A. (1995). *Occupational Information Network (O*Net) Content Model. Vols I and II*. Salt Lake, UT: Utah Department of Employment Security.

Pettersen, N. & Tziner, A. (1995). The cognitive ability test as a predictor of job performance: Is its validity affected by complexity and tenure within the organization? *International Journal of Selection and Assessment*, **3**, 237–241.

Piedmont, R.L. & Weinstein, H.P. (1994). Predicting supervisory ratings of job performance using the NEO Personality Inventory. *Journal of Psychology*, **128**, 255–265.

Pierce, C.A. & Aguinis, H.A. (1997). Using virtual reality technology in organizational behavior research. *Journal of Organizational Behavior*, **18**, 407–410.

Pulakos, E.D. & Schmitt, N. (1996). An evaluation of two strategies for reducing adverse impact and their effects on criterion-related validity. *Human Performance*, **9**, 241–258.

Pulakos, E.D., Schmitt, N. & Chan, D. (1996). Models of job performance ratings: An examination of ratee race, ratee gender, and rater level effects. *Human Performance*, **9**, 103–119.

Raju, N.S., Cabrera, E.F. & Lezotte, D.V. (1997). Utility analysis when employee performance is classified into two categories. Manuscript submitted for publication.

Raymark, P.H., Schmit, M.J. & Guion, R.M. (1997). Identifying potentially useful personality constructs for employee selection. *Personnel Psychology*, 50, 723–736.

Ree, M.J. & Carretta, T.R. (1994a). Factor analysis of ASVAB: Confirming a Vernon-like model. *Educational and Psychological Measurement*, 54, 459–463.

Ree, M.J. & Carretta, T.R. (1994b). The correlation of general cognitive ability and psychomotor tracking tests. *International Journal of Selection and Assessment*, 2, 209–216.

Ree, M.J. & Carretta, T.R. (1997). What makes an aptitude test valid? In R. Dillon (Ed.), *Handbook of Testing* (pp. 65–81). Westport, CT: Greenwood Press.

Ree, M.J. & Carretta, T.R. (1998). General cognitive ability and occupational performance. In C.L. Cooper and I.T. Robertson (Eds), *International Review of Industrial and Organizational Psychology*, Vol. 13 (pp. 159–184). London, UK: Wiley.

Ree, M.J., Carretta, T.R., Earles, J.A. & Albert, W. (1994). Sign changes when correction for range restriction: A note on Pearson's and Lawley's selection formulas. *Journal of Applied Psychology*, 79, 298–301.

Ree, M.J., Earles, J.A. & Teachout, M.S. (1994). Predicting job performance: Not much more than g. *Journal of Applied Psychology*, 79, 518–524.

Reilly, R.R. & Chao, G.T. (1982). Validity and fairness of some alternative employee selection procedures. *Personnel Psychology*, 35, 1–62.

Robertson, I.T. & Kinder (1993). Personality and Job Competences: The criterion-related validity of some personality variables. *Journal of Occupational and Organizational Psychology*, 66, 225–244.

Rolland, J.P. & Mogenet, J.L. (1994). *Manuel d'application. Système D5D d'aide à l'évaluation des personnes. [User manual. D5D system of help for people assessment]*. Paris, France: Les Editions du Centre de Psychologie Appliquée.

Rosenthal, R. (1991). *Meta-analytic Procedures for Social Research*. Beverly Hills, CA: Sage.

Roth, P.L. (1993). Research trends in judgment and their implications for the Schmidt–Hunter global estimation procedure. *Organizational Behavior and Human Decision Processes*, 54, 299–319.

Roth, P.L. (1994a). Group approaches to the Schmidt–Hunter global estimation procedure. *Organizational Behavior and Human Decision Processes*, 59, 428–451.

Roth, P.L. (1994b). Missing data: A conceptual review for applied psychologists. *Personnel Psychology*, 47, 537–559.

Roth, P.L., BeVier, C.A., Switzer III, F.S. & Schippmann, J.S. (1996). Meta-analyzing the relationship between grades and job performance. *Journal of Applied Psychology*, 81, 548–556.

Roth, P.L. & Bobko, P. (1998). A research agenda for multi-attribute utility analysis in human resource management. *Human Resource Management*, in press.

Roth, P.L., Campion, J.E. & Jones, S.D. (1996). The impact of four missing data techniques on validity estimates in human resource management. *Journal of Business and Psychology*, 11, 101–112.

Roth, P.L. & Clarke, R.L. (1998). Meta-analyzing the relationship between grades and salary. Manuscript submitted for publication.

Roth, P.L., Segars, A.H. & Wright, P.M. (1997). The acceptance of utility analysis: designing a model. Manuscript submitted for publication.

Roth, P.L. & Switzer III, F.S. (1995). A Monte Carlo analysis of missing data techniques in a HRM setting. *Journal of Management*, 21, 1003–1023.

Rumsey, M.G., Walker, C.B. & Harris, J.H. (Eds) (1994). *Personnel Selection and Classification*. Hillsdale, NJ: Erlbaum.

Russell, C.J., Colella, A. & Bobko, P. (1993). Expanding the context of utility: the strategic impact of personnel selection. *Personnel Psychology*, 46, 781–801.

Ryan, A., Daum, D., Bauman, T., Grisez, M., Mattimore, K., Nalodka, T. & McCormick, S. (1995). Direct, indirect, and controlled observation and rating accuracy. *Journal of Applied Psychology*, **80**, 664–670.

Rynes, S.L. (1993). Who's selecting whom? Effects of selection practices on applicant attitudes and behavior. In N. Schmitt & W. Borman (Eds), *Personnel Selection in Organizations* (pp. 240–274). San Francisco, CA: Jossey-Bass.

Rynes, S.L. & Connerley, M.L. (1993). Applicant reactions to alternative selection procedures. *Journal of Business and Psychology*, 7, 261–277.

Sackett, P.R. & Ostgaard, D.J. (1994). Job-specific applicant pools and national norms for cognitive ability tests: implications for range restriction corrections in validation research. *Journal of Applied Psychology*, **79**, 680–684.

Sackett, P.R. & Wanek, J.E. (1996). New developments in the use of measures of honesty, integrity, conscientiousness, dependability, trustworthiness, and reliability for personnel selection. *Personnel Psychology*, **49**, 787–830.

Sackett, P.R. & Wilks, S.L. (1994). Within-group norming and other forms of score adjustment in psychological testing. *American Psychologist*, **49**, 929–954.

Salgado, J.F. (1994a). Validez de los tests de habilidades psicomotoras: Meta-análisis de los estudios publicados en España (1942–1990) [Validity of psychomotor ability tests: Meta-analysis of studies published in Spain (1942–1990)]. *Revista de Psicologia Social Aplicada*, **4**, 25–42.

Salgado, J.F. (1994b). Manual técnico del Inventario de Personalidad de Cinco Factores (IP/5F). [Technical manual of the Five Factor Personality Inventory (IP/5F)]. Manuscrito no publicado. Universidad de Santiago de Compostela, Santiago de Compostela, Spain.

Salgado, J.F. (1995). Situational specificity and within-setting validity variability. *Journal of Occupational and Organizational Psychology*, **68**, 123–132.

Salgado, J.F. (1996a). Análisis exploratorio y confirmatorio del IP/5F [Exploratory and confirmatory analysis of IP/5F]. *Psicológica*, **17**, 353–366.

Salgado, J.F. (1996b). Personality and job competences: A comment on the Robertson and Kinder (1993) study. *Journal of Occupational and Organizational Psychology*, **69**, 373–375.

Salgado, J.F. (1997a). The five factor model of personality and job performance in the European Community. *Journal of Applied Psychology*, **82**, 30–43.

Salgado, J.F. (1997b). Validity generalization of personality measures in Europe. Paper presented in the Symposium *Role of Personality in Industrial and Organizational Psychology: An International View*, conducted in the Fifth European Congress of Psychology. Dublin, Ireland, 6–11 July, 1997.

Salgado (1997c). VALCOR—A program to estimate standard error of corrected validity. *Behavior Research Methods, Instruments and Computers*, **29**, 464–467.

Salgado, J.F. (1998a). A contribution to the study of cognitive tests in personnel selection: The within-setting variability of validity. *European Review of Applied Psychology*, in press.

Salgado, J.F. (1998b). Big Five personality dimensions and job performance: A European Perspective. *Human Performance*, **11**, 273–288.

Salgado, J.F. & Moscoso, S. (1995). Validez de la entrevista conductual estructurada [Validity of structured behavioral interview]. *Revista de Psicoloía del Trabajo y las Organizaciones*, **11**, 9–24.

Salgado, J.F. & Moscoso, S. (1996). Meta-analysis of interrater reliability of job performance ratings in validity studies of personnel selection. *Perceptual and Motor Skills*, **83**, 1195–1201.

Salgado, J.F., Remeseiro, C. & Iglesias, M. (1996). Personality and test taking motivation. *Psicothema*, **8**, 553–562.

Salgado, J.F. & Rumbo, A. (1997). Personality and job performance in financial services managers. *International Journal of Selection and Assessment*, **5**, 91–100.

Salgado, J.F., Rumbo, A., Santamaria, G. & Rodriguez, M. (1995). El 16PF, el modelo de cinco factores y el rendimiento en el trabajo [The 16PF, five factor model and job performance]. *Revista de Psicología Social Aplicada*, 5, 81–94.

Sanchez, J.I. & Fraser, S.L. (1992). On the choice of scales for task analysis. *Journal of Applied Psychology*, 77, 545–553.

Sanchez, J.I. & Fraser, S.L. (1993). *Development and Validation of the Corporate Social Style Inventory: A Measure of Customer Service Skills.* Cambridge, MA: Marketing Science Institute.

Sanchez, J.I. & De La Torre, F. (1996). A second look at the relationship between rating and behavioral accuracy in performance appraisal. *Journal of Applied Psychology*, 81, 3–10.

Saville, P. & Holdsworth, R. (1992). *Customer Service Questionnaire.* Esher, UK: Saville & Holdsworth Ltd.

Saville, P., Holdsworth, R., Nyfield, G., Cramp, L. & Mabey, W. (1984). *The Occupational Personality Questionnaire (OPQ).* London: Saville & Holdsworth (UK) Ltd.

Saville, P., Sik, G., Nyfield, G., Hackston, J. & MacIver, R. (1996). A demonstration of the validity of the Occupational Personality Questionnaire (OPQ) in the measurement of job competencies across time and in separate organisations. *Applied Psychology: An International Review*, 45, 243–262.

Schmidt, F.L. (1988). The problem of group differences in ability test scores in employment selection. *Journal of Vocational Behavior*, 33, 272–292.

Schmidt, F.L. (1991). Why all banding procedures in personnel selection are logically flawed. *Human Performance*, 4, 265–278.

Schmidt, F.L. (1994). The future of personnel selection in the US Army. In Rumsey, M.G., Walker, C.B. & Harris, J.H. (Eds), *Personnel Selection and Classification* (pp. 33–51). Hillsdale, NJ: Erlbaum.

Schmidt, F.L. & Hunter, J.E. (1993). Tacit knowledge, practical intelligence, general mental ability, and job knowledge. *Current Directions of Psychological Science*, 2, 8–9.

Schmidt, F.L. & Hunter, J.E. (1995). The fatal internal contradiction in banding: Its statistical rationale is logically inconsistent with its operational procedures. *Human Performance*, 8, 203–214.

Schmidt, F.L. & Hunter, J.E. (1997a). *The validity and utility of selection methods in personnel psychology: Practical and theoretical implications of 85 years of research findings.* University of Iowa, Iowa City, unpublished manuscript.

Schmidt, F.L. & Hunter, J.E. (1997b). Comparison of three meta-analysis methods revisited: An error in Johnson, Mullen and Salas (1995). *Journal of Applied Psychology*, under review.

Schmidt, F.L., Hunter, J.E., McKenzie, R.C. & Muldrow, T.W. (1979). Impact of valid selection procedures on workforce productivity. *Journal of Applied Psychology*, 64, 609–626.

Schmidt, F.L., Law, K.S., Hunter, J.E., Rothstein, H.R., Pearlman, K. & McDaniel, M. (1993). Refinements in validity generalization methods: Implications for the situational specificity hypothesis. *Journal of Applied Psychology*, 78, 3–12.

Schmidt, F.L., Ones, D.S. & Hunter, J.E. (1992). Personnel selection. *Annual Review of Psychology*, 43, 671–710.

Schmit, M.J. & Ryan, A.M. (1993). The Big Five in personnel selection: factor structure in applicant and nonapplicant populations. *Journal of Applied Psychology*, 78, 966–974.

Schmitt, N. & Borman, W.C. (Eds) (1993). *Personnel Selection in Organizations.* San Francisco, CA: Jossey-Bass.

Schneider, J.R. & Schmitt, N. (1992). An exercise design approach to understanding assessment center dimensions and exercise constructs. *Journal of Applied Psychology*, 77, 32–41.

Schneider, R.J. & Hough, L.M. (1995). Personality and industrial/organizational psychology. In C.L. Cooper & I.T. Robertson (Eds), *International Review of Industrial and Organizational Psychology*, Vol. 10 (pp. 75–130). London, UK: Wiley.

Schneider, R.J., Hough, L.M. & Dunnette, M.D. (1996). Broadsided by broad traits, or how to sink science in five dimensions or less. *Journal of Organizational Behavior*, 17, 639–655.

Scholz, G. & Schuler, H. (1993). Das nomologische netzwek des assessment centers: eine metaanlyse [The nomological network of the assessment center: A meta-analysis]. *Zeitschrift für Arbeits- und Organisationspsychologie*, 37, 73–85.

Schuler, H. (1992). Das multimodale einstellungsinterview. [The multimodal employment interview]. *Diagnostica*, 38, 281–300.

Schuler, H. (1997). Validity of multimodal interview. *Paper presented at the 8th European Congress of Work and Organizational Psychology*, 2nd–5th April, Verona, Italy.

Schuler, H., Farr, J. & Smith, M. (Eds) (1993). *Personnel Selection and Assessment: Individual and Organizational Perspectives*. Hillsdale, NJ: Erlbaum.

Schuler, H. & Moser, K. (1995). Die validität des multimodalen interviews. [Validity of multimodal interviews]. *Zeitschrift für Arbets und Organisationspsychologie*, 39, 2–12.

Schuler, H., Moser, K., Diemand, A. & Funke, U. (1995). Validität eines einstellungsinterviews zur prognose des ausbildungserfolgs. [Validity of an employment interview for the prediction of training success]. *Zeitschrift für Pädagogische Psychologie*, 9, 45–54.

Schuler, H., Moser, K. & Funke, U. (1994). The moderating effect of rater–ratee-acquaintance on the validity of an assessment center. *Paper presented at 23rd International Congress of Applied Psychology*, Madrid, Spain.

Shackleton, V. & Newell, S. (1997). International assessment and selection. In N. Anderson & P. Herriot (Eds), *International Handbook of Selection and Assessment*. Chichester, UK: Wiley.

Shore, T.H., Shore, L.M. & Thornton III, G.C. (1992). Construct validity of self- and peer evaluations of performance dimensions in an assessment center. *Journal of Applied Psychology*, 27, 42–54.

Smiderle, D., Perry, B.A. & Cronshaw, S.F. (1994). Evaluation of video-based assessment in transit operator selection. *Journal of Business and Psychology*, 9, 3–22.

Smith, M. & Robertson, I.T. (1993). *The Theory and Practice of Systematic Personnel Selection*. Basingstoke, UK: McMillan.

Smither, J.M., Reilly, R.R., Millsap, R.E., Pearlman, K. & Stoffey, R.W. (1993). Applicants' reactions to selection procedures. *Personnel Psychology*, 46, 49–76.

Society for Industrial and Organizational Psychology (1987). *Principles for the Validation and Use of Personnel Selection Procedures*, (3rd edn.). College Park, MD: Author.

Spychalski, A.C., Quiñones, M.A., Gaugler, B.B. & Pohley, K. (1997). A survey of assessment center practices in organizations in the United States. *Personnel Psychology*, 50, 71–90.

Stauffer, J.M., Ree, M.J. & Carretta, T.R. (1996). Cognitive-components tests are not much more than g: An extension of Kyllonen's analyses. *Journal of General Psychology*, 123, 193–205.

Steiner, D.D. & Gilliland, S.W. (1996). Fairness reactions to personnel selection techniques in France and the United States. *Journal of Applied Psychology*, 81, 134–141.

Sternberg, R.J. (1997). Tacit knowledge and job success. In N. Anderson and P. Herriot (Eds), *International Handbook of Selection and Assessment* (pp. 201–213). London, UK: Wiley.

Sternberg, R.J. & Wagner, R.K. (1993). The g-ocentric view of intelligence and job performance is wrong. *Current Directions in Psychological Science*, 2, 1–5.

Sternberg, R.J., Wagner, R.K., Williams, W.M. & Horvath, J.A. (1995). Testing common sense. *American psychologist*, **50**, 912–927.

Stokes, G., Munford, M. & Owens (Eds) (1994). *Biodata Handbook: Theory, Research and Use of Biographical Information in Selection and Performance Prediction*. Palo Alto, CA: Consulting Psychologists Press.

Stone-Romero, E.F. & Anderson, L.E. (1994). Relative power of moderated multiple regression and the comparison of subgroup correlation coefficients for detecting moderating effects. *Journal of Applied Psychology*, **79**, 354–359.

Sue-Chan, C., Latham, G.P. & Evans, M.G. (1997). The construct validity of the situational and patterned behavior description interviews: Cognitive ability, tacit knowledge and self-efficacy as correlated. Joseph L. Rotman Faculty of Management, University of Toronto, Toronto: Canada. Unpublished manuscript.

Switzer III, F.S., Roth, P.L. & Switzer III, D. (1998). A Monte Carlo analysis of systematically missing data in HRM settings. *Journal of Management*, (in press).

Task Force On Assessment Center Guidelines (1989). Guidelines and ethical considerations for assessment center operations. *Public Personnel Management*, **18**, 457–470.

Tett, R.P., Jackson, D.N. & Rothstein, M. (1991). Personality measures as predictors of job performance: A meta-analytic review. *Personnel Psychology*, **44**, 703–742.

Thornton, G.C. (1992). *Assessment Centers in Human Resource Management*. Reading, MA: Addison-Wesley.

Van de Watter, T.J. (1997). Psychology's entrepreneurs and the marketing of industrial psychology. *Journal of Applied Psychology*, **82**, 486–499.

Van Leest, P.F. & Meltzer, P.H. (1995). Videotesting of social, leadership and commercial competencies. *Paper presented at the 7th EAWOP Congres*, Györ, Hungary.

Van Scotter, J.R. & Motowidlo, S.J. (1996). Interpersonal facilitation and job dedication as separate facets of contextual performance. *Journal of Applied Psychology*, **81**, 525–531.

Viswesvaran, C. (1993). Modeling job performance: Is there a general factor? Unpublished doctoral dissertation, Iowa City: University of Iowa.

Viswesvaran, C., Ones, D.S. & Schmidt, F.L. (1996). Comparative analysis of the reliability of job performance ratings. *Journal of Applied Psychology*, **81**, 557–574.

Wagner, R.K. (1994). Practical intelligence. *European Journal of Psychological Assessment*, **10**, 162–169.

Wagner, R.K. & Sternberg, R.J. (1990). Street smarts. In K.E. Clark & M.B. Clark (Eds), *Measures of Leadership* (pp. 493–504). West Orange, NJ: Leadership Library of America.

Weekly, J.A. & Jones, C. (1997). Video-based situational testing. *Personnel Psychology*, **50**, 25–50.

Whyte, G. & Latham, G. (1997). The futility of utility analysis revisited: When even an expert fails. *Personnel Psychology*, **50**, 601–610.

Wiersma, U.J., Van Leest, P.F., Nienhuis, T. & Maas, R. (1991). Validiteit van een Nederlands assessment center. [Validity of a Dutch assessment center]. *Gedrag en Organisatie*, **6**, 474–482.

Wiesner, W.H. & Cronshaw, S.F. (1988). A meta-analytic investigation of the impact of the validity format and degree of structure on the validity of the employment interview. *Journal of Occupational Psychology*, **61**, 275–290.

Zedeck, S., Outtz, J., Cascio, W.F. & Goldstein, I.L. (1991). Why do 'testing experts' have such limited vision?. *Human Performance*, **4**, 297–308.

Chapter 2

INTERNATIONAL USES OF SELECTION METHODS

Sue Newell
Royal Holloway, University of London, UK
and
Carole Tansley
Nottingham Trent University, UK

INTRODUCTION

Organisations are increasingly global enterprises spanning many countries and even continents. With the rise of such global organisations there are increasing problems of managing within an international context. One such problem is that of actually selecting individuals who will be competent to work in international settings. For example, there are problems of selecting individuals who can manage people from very diverse cultural backgrounds and/or selecting people who are competent and willing to travel and work internationally. This problem of selecting the 'international manager' has been discussed elsewhere (Sparrow, 1999). Here we focus rather on the problems associated with the empirically established fact that there is significant variation in selection practices across nations. This has both theoretical and practical significance. Theoretically, exploring these differences can help to develop our understanding of selection and assessment. Practically, this is important because it suggests that selection specialists need to tailor practice to the specific national context, for what works and is well accepted by candidates in one country, may be less acceptable in another. This is an important consideration for organisations that span national boundaries and/or recruit from an international pool.

However, this demand for the configuration or tailoring of selection methods to the particular national context is in opposition to current ideas about integrating and standardising processes (including HR processes) across global organisations, ideas which are facilitated by organisational-wide integration programmes such as Enterprise Resource Planning (ERP). ERP is about providing integrated ways of working supported by an integrated set of

International Uses of Selection Methods by Sue Newell and Carole Tansley taken from IRIOP 2001 v16, Edited by Cary L. Cooper and Ivan T. Robertson: © 2001 John Wiley & Sons, Ltd

computer systems. There is therefore a tension between demands for integration and standardisation and demands for autonomy and context-specific adaptation of organisational processes. This tension, between the need to modify practices (here selection practices) to 'fit' the particular national context and the strategy of adopting standard practices across a globally dispersed organisation in order to facilitate integration, is explored in more detail later in this chapter.

Specifically, in this chapter we will begin by looking at some problems in the empirical research base, comparing selection method use across countries, and then turn to consider what these national differences in selection practice actually are. We will then explore the reasons for these national differences. Essentially, there are two perspectives here. On the one hand, these differences could be seen to be the result of technical lag, with some countries, for a variety of reasons, lagging behind in terms of the adoption of 'best practice' selection methods. On the other hand, these differences could be considered to be the outcome of embedded national predispositions, such that what is considered to be 'best practice' in one national context is likely to be quite different in another. The implications of these different explanations of the observed differences will be considered. In the last section, we will focus upon exploring in more depth the previously mentioned tension between standardisation and unique tailoring of selection methods to the particular national context.

RESEARCHING INTERNATIONAL DIFFERENCES IN SELECTION METHOD USE

There is empirical research available which allows us to make comparisons about the differential use of selection methods across countries. However, before actually looking at this, it is important to recognise that there are problems with this research which means that these comparisons need to be treated somewhat cautiously. In particular, there is a problem because much of the previous research has been survey based. Fletcher (1994) rightly points out the problems with survey-based research. As an example, one of the authors in previous survey-based research identified that a similar proportion of firms used 'personality measures' in selection in the UK compared to firms in France (Shackleton & Newell, 1991). Sometime after this research had been published, a French student conducted a study using interviews to explore why and how various selection tools were actually being used in France and the UK. What he found was that in France many companies using 'personality measures' were actually using projective techniques (like the Thematic Apperception Test), rather than normative, objective personality questionnaires (like the OPQ or Myers–Briggs) which were dominant in the UK. Thus, while the survey had suggested similarity in the use of this method use of ('personality measures') in these two countries, the more in-depth research revealed fundamental differences.

It is likely that similar variability would be found in the use of other selection methods used in different countries. For example, what constitutes an assessment centre, may very well have national variation. This suggests that selection tools and techniques have what can be described as 'interpretative flexibility' (Bijker, Hughes & Pinch, 1987). Interpretative flexibility suggests that there is not a single, fixed way of using a particular technology (in this case a selection method). Rather, its use will be influenced by the predispositions and attitudes of those involved in implementing and using the technology. Thus, while the same 'method' (for example an assessment centre) may be used in two contexts (here national contexts) it will actually look and feel very different. The use of selection methods can therefore be described as equivocal because the user needs to engage in a sense-making process (Weick, 1990), choosing when and why, but also more fundamentally how a particular tool will be used. This 'interpretative flexibility' tends to be obscured in survey evidence of national differences. This needs to be borne in mind as we turn to consider the research, which explores national differences in selection practices.

Another related problem with previous research comparing selection method use across countries is that there are some contradictions in the findings. These can be at least partly explained as resulting from the use of different research methods. Thus, while the survey has been the dominant research method used, there have been other approaches (e.g. surveys— Shackleton & Newell, 1991 vs observations—Bruchon-Schweitser, 1996). The research has also focused on different groups (e.g. consultants—Clark, 1993 vs managers—McCulloch, 1993), which likewise may account for some of the contradictions in findings. In particular, research that does not go beyond broad measures of usage is unlikely to demonstrate differences as it is often in the detail of usage that these differences emerge. So, for example, Smith and Abrahamsen (1992) argue that: 'The overwhelming conclusion must be that the pattern of selection is very similar in all countries'. However, as Shackleton and Newell (1994) point out, this conclusion was only possible because they ignored the frequency of use of different methods and the detail about how the methods were used. Once these more detailed issues are considered, differences in patterns of usage do emerge, as shown below.

INTERNATIONAL DIFFERENCES IN SELECTION METHOD USE

Before turning to consider these differences, it is worth noting that there is clearly considerable variability within a particular national context in the selection methods used. For example, Di Milia, Smith and Brown (1994), looking at management selection in Australia, report differences between manufacturing, retail and government sectors compared to the business sector. The latter made significantly greater use of cognitive testing and assessment centres than the two former sectors. Gowing and Slivinski (1994) similarly demonstrate that different methods of selection are used for different types of employee within North America. Moreover, there is even variability in the way a particular method is used within a national context. For example, Lievens and Goemaere (1999) interviewed representatives from a sample of Dutch companies that used assessment centres and found a large variability in practice. 'Interpretative flexibility' (Bijker, Hughes & Pinch, 1987) is not constrained to national 'sense-making'. Thus, variability exists even within a particular national context. However, evidence suggests that there is even greater variability in the use of selection methods across countries.

There have been a number of studies and reviews of the research that have focused on national comparisons in selection practices. Much of this research has concentrated on only a limited number of countries and most of the work has been done on comparisons across Europe. This has demonstrated that the use of interviews and application forms is very common throughout companies in Europe (Shackleton & Newell, 1994). These methods are also very common in North America (Rowe, Williams & Day, 1994) and Australia (Di Milia, Smith & Brown, 1994). However, given the interpretative flexibility of selection method use, referred to above, it is clear that even though the same method may be common across many countries, it may actually be used in very different ways. So, for example, even though the interview is almost ubiquitous in selection, its style and format can be quite different. Thus, in a comparison of management selection in British, German, Italian, Belgian and French companies, Shackleton and Newell (1994) found:

- German companies were unlikely to use more than one interview while French companies virtually always used more than one interview.
- Italian companies rarely used panel interviews while they were much more common in Germany.
- In Italy a representative from the Personnel/HR department is very rarely present during the interview while in German and Belgian companies a representative is very typically present.
- German and Italian companies used one-to-one interviews less often than Belgian companies.

Comparing the results from this European study with surveys conducted in North America also suggests differences, particularly in terms of the use of structured interviews. For example, Gowing and Slivinski (1994) found that 82% of the respondents in their survey of North American organisations structured their oral interviews. This is a higher percentage than is typically found in surveys of European companies. In terms of other less common methods of selection, there is also variability in use. So for example, in terms of Assessment Centres, these will rarely include psychometric tests in Germany while these will be common in a British Assessment Centre (Mabey & Thompson, 1993; Shackleton & Newell, 1994).

Moreover, there are also some established differences in the actual methods that are used. Thus, for example, in a comparison of five European countries, Shackleton and Newell (1994) conclude: 'The regression analysis shows that it is country rather than company size, or other company variables such as number of managers recruited, which is the dominant influence on the selection methods used' (p. 101). Similarly, in one of the most recent studies, Ryan, McFarland, Baron and Page (1999), comparing the use of 11 different selection methods across 22 countries, concluded: 'National differences accounted for a substantial portion of the variance in the use of fixed interview questions, as well as sizeable portions of variance in using multiple methods of verification, testing and number of interviews. This confirms previous research indicating variability across nations in selection practices' (p. 371).

Some established differences include:

- While a significant minority of French companies (including French companies operating outside France) use graphology to assess the personality of potential recruits, this method is very rarely used elsewhere, at least in Europe (Shackleton & Newell, 1991; Clark, 1993; McCulloch, 1993; Levy-Leboyer, 1994; Ryan et al., 1999). Bruchon-Schweitser (1996) also found that astrology and graphology are still used by some French companies while these methods are almost unheard of outside France.
- Situational tests and assessment centres are used more often in the UK, Germany and the Netherlands than in France and Belgium (Shackleton & Newell, 1994; Levy-Leboyer, 1994; Ryan et al., 1999), while assessment centres are not used at all in Spain (Schuler et al., 1996).
- There is a greater use of tests in France and Belgium than in the UK and Germany (Levy-Leboyer, 1994).
- There is a somewhat greater use of references by British companies, at least as compared to France, Germany and Belgium (Shackleton & Newell, 1994; Clark, 1993; McCulloch, 1993).
- In Greece selection methods are very primitive and simple compared to methods used in other European countries, at least those that are members of the European Community (Tsannetou, 1996).
- In the US drug testing and honesty (or integrity) testing are becoming popular but these selection methods are very rare elsewhere (Shackleton & Newell, 1994).
- In China, Wang (1997) reports that selection decisions rely heavily on personal and economic information and that there is little emphasis on

assessing whether the candidate has the competencies to perform the job tasks.
- Italian companies make little use of any method except the interview (Shackleton & Newell, 1994).

This is not an exhaustive list of national trends in selection method use, but it does illustrate the variability that has been observed by empirical research.

Taken together this evidence suggests that more valid and reliable methods are commoner in some countries (e.g. the UK, Germany, North America) than others (e.g. China, Greece, Spain). However, it should be noted that there is a difference between the potential of a method to produce a valid result and its use in practice. For example, Di Milia and Gorodecki (1997) showed through looking at practice in a major Australian company, that although structured interviews may have the potential to produce high levels of validity, in practice this was often not achieved because the interviews were not undertaken as required. Similarly, in terms of the use of psychometric tests, research has demonstrated their inappropriate use in a number of countries:

- Mardberg (1996) reports on fairly extensive misuse of tests in Sweden.
- In New Zealand Smith and George (1992) report on the problem of indiscriminate use of personality tests.
- Rees (1996) notes the problem of inappropriate test use in the UK.
- Engelhart (1996) identified that tests are often used badly in France.
- O'Gorman (1996), looking at selection methods in Australia, identified a lack of training and unprofessional use of selection tests.

Moreover, even though there are variations across nations in terms of the use of more valid and reliable selection methods, the research findings also suggest that in virtually all countries there remains a heavy reliance on those methods of selection and assessment which are not the most valid. In other words, the methods used are not the most valid in terms of accurately measuring individual differences and so deciding on how suitable a person is for a particular job (Di Milia, Smith & Brown, 1994; Rowe, Williams & Day, 1994; Shackleton & Newell, 1994).

Therefore in virtually all countries, 'best practice' in the use of selection methods, at least as advocated by academic research from a criterion-related validity perspective, may be the exception rather than the rule. Nevertheless, taken together the evidence appears to suggest that there are national differences in the selection methods used. Moreover, given what was said in the introduction about the problem of using survey instruments to identify these differences, the evidence probably underestimates the variability that exists. Thus, while obviously there will be variability in selection practice at the level of the firm, it is also clear that there are national differences that need to be explained.

EXPLAINING NATIONAL DIFFERENCES IN SELECTION METHOD USE

The explanation for national differences in selection can only be tentative, as to date there has been very little systematic research exploring this issue. Rather, there has been a tendency for authors to speculate on reasons for differences once these differences have been observed. As Ryan et al. (1999) note: 'none of these studies has focused on why one might expect variability across nations in selection practices' (p. 360). This is not peculiar to the study of national differences in selection methods since demonstrations of differences in the ways in which particular technologies are unbundled, modified and (re)designed across nations are relatively rare (Swan, Newell & Robertson, 2000). We will draw on these previous speculations about the reasons for national differences in selection method use in this section, but will consider these explanations in the context of broader theorising about national differences in the diffusion and adoption of new ideas (in this case ideas about selection methods that can improve the effectiveness of selection decisions).

It is possible that the observed national differences in the use of selection methods are the result of national differences in task environments (Miles & Snow, 1978). And of course it is clear that the kind of selection methods used will be affected by the task environment. So, for example, the methods used to select a secretary are likely to be quite different to the methods used to select a university lecturer (e.g. giving a university lecturer a speed typing test may not be considered to be appropriate while for a secretary this would be deemed quite appropriate—even though, ironically, a lecturer may spend a majority of his/her time in front of a PC, typing!). However, the evidence on national differences suggests that there are cross-national differences in organisational practices related to the use of selection methods even when recruiting for similar tasks. Therefore managers will be selected using different methods in Italy compared to the UK even when controlling for organisational size (Shackleton & Newell, 1994). This suggests that there is a societal effect (Sorge, 1991) that needs to be used to explain the variation in selection practices across countries. A societal effect implies that differences in institutional networks, regulatory environments, economic factors and national culture are related to differences in selection method use. Each of these will be explored in turn in the next section.

SOCIETAL EFFECTS

It was suggested above that cross-national differences in selection method use could not be explained solely as a result of systematic differences in task environments. Rather, at least some cross-national differences in the adoption of organisational forms and practices may be more adequately explained in terms of the extent to which these forms and practices are close to wider differences in societal regimes, norms and practices and are articulated through institutions in the organisational environment. A 'societal effects' approach then predicts that those methods that are closer to societal norms and practices and which are articulated within prevailing institutions may be more widely diffused regardless of their 'fit' with local task contingencies (i.e. the job being recruited into) (Sorge, 1991). In the next section we look at some of these societal effects, focusing on differences in institutional networks, in the regulatory environment, in economic factors, and in national cultures. These are considered in more detail next.

Institutional Networks

Individuals within companies are unlikely to invent entirely new methods of selection and assessment. Rather, when changes are introduced to the methods used to select personnel, we are looking at a process of innovation. That is, the company will be introducing selection methods that have been developed and used elsewhere. There is a whole literature on the diffusion and adoption of new ideas that is relevant to understanding this process of innovation (Rogers, 1995). Exploring national differences in innovation processes (that is in the diffusion and adoption of new ideas) can, in turn, help to explain the national differences in selection method use that we have observed.

The innovation process must begin with an individual becoming aware of a new idea (in this case about a particular selection method). They must then be persuaded that this new idea is relevant and useful within their own context and persuade others within their company of this. A decision to adopt can then be made, which will lead to the implementation and use of the new method. Ideally, there will also be an evaluation of the success of the new method and changes introduced if the evaluation is not positive. Thus, in order to adopt a new selection method, an individual within a company has first to become aware that the new method exists, and then they must be convinced or persuaded that this method will improve the current selection process. This individual must then persuade others in the company so that a decision is made to adopt and implement the new method. In implementing the new selection method, it is likely to be modified to fit the particular organisational context of use, since as we have seen, selection methods (like other technologies) have a high degree of interpretative flexibility. This is why the literature on the adoption of new technologies talks about appropriation rather than simply implementation. Appropriation implies that the technologies are modified to suit the particular organisational context of use, rather than simply 'plugged in' and 'switched on'.

Institutional networks are important as they influence the diffusion of knowledge across a community of users. These networks typically have national boundaries. For example, educational institutions, a source of new ideas for many, typically draw both students and staff from a particular national context. One such network that may play a central role in this process of knowledge diffusion is that provided by a professional association. A professional association is an obvious arena for dominant professional norms and ideas about best practice to be developed and communicated. Many practitioners join professional associations precisely to learn about the latest 'best practice' in their particular domain as well as to enhance their career status (Lynch, 1989). Professional associations in the HR and organisational psychology domain have essentially three types of members. Firstly, there are members who work as practitioners in HR departments. Secondly, there are academics who teach and research in the related areas. Finally, there are members who work as suppliers of HR products and services, including selection methods (consultants and specialist selection advisers). Professional associations thus provide links between central suppliers of new ideas about 'best practice' in selection methods and their users. These networks will be important in influencing the diffusion and adoption of HR tools and practices (including selection methods) (Rogers, 1995; Swan & Newell, 1995). Differences between countries in the development and activities of professional associations may therefore account for some of the observed differences in selection method use across countries.

For example, Eleftheriou and Robertson (1999) report that human resource management in Greece is very underdeveloped with the main professional association (the Greek Personnel Managers' Association) having only 300 members in 1992 (Ball, 1992). In conjunction with this, the evidence shows that Greek firms tend to use subjective and intuitive methods (e.g. interviews, CV and personnel recommendations) and believe that these methods are more effective than, for instance, psychological tests (Kantas, Kalogera & Nikolaou, 1997). Even in North America, where arguably there is the most active research in the area, Rowe, Williams and Day (1994) concluded that many practitioners were not using 'state-of-the art' selection methods that were high in validity and reliability. One reason they gave for this was that there was a lack of awareness about valid assessment tools and technology due to a 'general dearth of specialised education and training in personnel departments' (p. 77). They quote Thacker and Cattaneo (1993) who found only a very small proportion of employees in personnel departments were graduates (28%). They argue that this, and other evidence they considered, suggests 'questionable professional competence' (p. 77).

In a similar vein, in attempting to understand differences in use of selection methods across Europe, Shackleton and Newell (1994) speculate that this might be related to 'the long-standing differences between countries in their intellectual and scientific traditions' (p. 101). This, they suggest, manifests itself in differential approaches to and teaching of psychology and management studies across European countries. For example, in Britain and

Germany psychology is more heavily influenced by the natural scientific tradition than in France and Italy. Moreover, in general in Germany and Britain the influence of occupational psychologists may be more significant than in France and Italy. This, they suggest, may help to explain the use of less 'scientific' methods in the latter countries compared to the former. Together this evidence suggests that individuals in different countries will be exposed to rather different ideas about 'best practice' in selection and that this in turn will influence the use of particular selection methods.

Regulatory Environment

Arvey and Faley (1988) demonstrate how the US legal/regulatory environment has played a significant role in shaping the selection practices of American firms. As organisational boundaries increasingly cut across national boundaries, then the effect of regulatory environments will similarly cross these borders. Nevertheless, regulation continues to operate at the national level. For example, Rowe, Williams and Day (1994) consider that the legal pressures in North America mean that the goal of selection is as much about meeting the standards for equal opportunity and human rights as it is about providing a reliable and productive workforce. They argue, that because of the threat of litigation, employers often use less threatening devices such as application blanks and interviews rather than psychological tests. While the North American regulatory environment has thus clearly influenced test use, the opposite is the case in Italy. For example, Shackleton and Newell (1994) argue that in Italy there is no recognised code of practice guiding recruitment and selection and therefore interview questions tend to be more searching than in countries where regulation is stronger, for example in Germany.

Economic Factors

The use of more sophisticated selection methods can clearly be expensive. For example, an assessment centre will typically involve considerable resources in terms of time of line managers and personnel representatives (and perhaps outside consultants) and money (e.g. to provide facilities for the centre and to purchase test materials). Countries where resources are more scarce, are therefore more likely to be inhibited for financial reasons from using these more sophisticated methods. In support of this, Eleftheriou and Robertson (1999) found that although the Greek firms in their sample tended to use more subjective and intuitive selection methods, they were in fact aware that other methods were available that were potentially more valid. When asked what methods they would use if there were no budgetary constraints, respondents were more likely to suggest they would use the more valid methods compared to the actual use of the less valid methods.

National Culture

Shackleton and Newell (1994) conclude that 'habit, tradition and culture determine the choice of selection method much more than do the relative predictive validities of the techniques' (p. 91). From a general perspective, the edited book by Tim Clark (1996) compared human resource management practice across seven European countries and demonstrated the divergence of practice. Clark (1996) argues that research should seek to understand the distinctive features of national culture and to consider how this influences the 'special understanding' of HRM in each nation. However, there are relatively few direct comparisons of these 'special understandings', especially in relation to selection practices. In one of the few empirical studies considering the link between national culture and selection method use, Ryan et al. (1999) did indeed find differences between countries high and low on uncertainty avoidance and between countries high and low on power distance (Hofstede, 1991). For example, countries high on uncertainty avoidance used more types of test, conducted more interviews and did more thorough audits of their processes. However, contrary to predictions, companies in countries high on uncertainty avoidance used overall fewer selection methods and verified backgrounds of candidates less. They explain the contradictory findings as being the result of the uncertainty avoidance manifesting itself in relation to avoiding the use of uncertain methods of selection (i.e. sticking to proven methods only—tests) and avoiding uncertain information sources (i.e. uncertain background information obtained from references), rather than in relation to avoiding uncertainty about the candidate.

Baron, Ryan and Page (1998) considered three dimensions of culture described by Trompenaars and Hampden-Turner (1993) and looked at how these were related to differences in selection method use in 14 countries. Their suggestions include:

1. Universalism versus Particularism: universalist cultures tend to look for universal, rational, objective rules and solutions while particularist cultures emphasise relationships (which may mean bending rules if this is important to save a personal relationship). China is an extremely particularist culture and they argue this explains why Wang (1997) found that companies in China relied on economic and personal information rather than task-specific information. In such a culture the emphasis is on getting to know the individual rather than trying to acquire objective verifiable information, as would be the case in a universalistic culture. In contrast, from their own survey, Switzerland and Canada (both high on universalism) have a preference for structured interviews, while France, Greece and Italy (all high on particularism) all rely much more on unstructured interviews.

2. Neutral versus Emotional: neutral cultures are ones where the expression of emotion is either hidden or denied. Emotional cultures are the opposite. Baron, Ryan and Page (1998) use anecdotal experience to suggest that this manifests itself in differences in interview style and emphasis. For example, in emotional cultures as present in Southern European countries, they are likely to rely heavily on one interview and be more influenced by the affective content of what is said. On the other hand, in neutral cultures like China and Britain, the emphasis would be on assessing the candidates' intellectual skills, and they would emphasise interviewer training to ensure the interviewer is not 'falsely persuaded' by idiosyncratic issues such as personal liking.

3. Achievement versus Ascription: achievement cultures focus on what an individual has done and what s/he has achieved, while ascriptive cultures focus on position and title (regardless of how these were acquired). Therefore in selection, achievement cultures would assess the candidates in terms of college grades and individual experience while in ascriptive cultures family background and place of study would be more important. In conjunction with this hypothesis Baron, Ryan and Page (1998) found that more achievement-oriented countries, such as Australia, New Zealand and Canada were more likely to follow up references and to use cognitive ability tests. In contrast, in high ascriptive cultures, for example Poland, more emphasis was placed on family connections, while in Japan, having attended the 'correct' school and university is of paramount importance.

Variations in national culture, therefore, appear to be related to the differences between countries in use of selection methods. There are probably other reasons for the observed differences in selection method use across countries. What is needed now is research that more directly focuses on understanding the sources of national variability. This is important because these sources of variability have implications for the relevance of these national differences, as will be discussed in the next section.

IMPLICATIONS OF NATIONAL DIFFERENCES IN SELECTION METHOD USE

If the best explanation for the observed national differences in selection method use is simply the result of a lack of diffusion of 'best practice' methods, then the implication is that these differences will dissolve as knowledge becomes more widely available. Therefore structured interviews, which have demonstrably higher predictive validity than unstructured interviews (Heffcutt & Arthur, 1994; McDaniel, Whetsel, Schmidt & Maurer, 1994) are not used in one country because knowledge about their efficacy has simply not diffused there yet and/or resources are limited so that it is too expensive to use this new method. The explanation for variability here is essentially a technical lag one. Globalisation and the rise of multinationals should then gradually erode these differences (Iles 1994). Similarly, as globalisation leads to a harmonisation of regulatory codes, then differences resulting from regulation differences will gradually evaporate.

On the other hand, if the observed differences are related to embedded differences in institutional networks and national cultures, the challenge is much greater because it suggests that selection method use will always need to be configured and adapted for the particular national context. Further, it suggests that even when the same method is actually used, the performance and interpretation of both candidates and assessors will be influenced by national predispositions (see conclusions section below). From this perspective then, structured interviews may not have been adopted so widely in a particular country, not because practitioners are unaware of them and the evidence of their higher predictive validity, but because this method is antithetical to beliefs about the interpersonal judgement ability of selection specialists. This is more of a challenge because, as will be discussed next, it contradicts the current trend, which is pushing towards the integration and standardisation of HR processes, including employee resourcing.

THE GLOBAL INTEGRATION OF HR PROCESSES: CONTRADICTIONS IN CURRENT THINKING

The conclusion that national predispositions and institutional networks at least partly explain national differences in selection method use suggests that there may be problems if attempts are made to implement standardised selection practices. These difficulties would go beyond those of establishing equivalence of test and interview materials (Ryan et al., 1999). Yet, ironically, this standardisation appears to be precisely what many companies are attempting to achieve as they implement company-wide systems such as Enterprise Resource Planning. This will be discussed next.

Increasingly, organisations are becoming globally distributed, with operations in several countries. This global dispersion has often been achieved through acquisition or merger so that a company develops a presence in a new country by acquiring or merging with an existing organisation in that country. This has created problems since in order to benefit from this growth there will need to be some rationalisation and integration of the organisational processes. This is because if two business units in two different countries are enacting the same process very differently then it may be more difficult to achieve collaboration and rationalisation. The result of this problem is that there is currently a strong push within organisations to integrate processes across their global operation. This is typically being achieved under the banner of Enterprise Resource Planning (ERP). ERP is typically supported by the implementation of an IT system which supports this integrated process across the dispersed organisation.

The first stage in an ERP project would be to map the processes and identify the 'best' process for a particular activity. The idea is that there will be multiple ways of achieving a particular task within the global organisation, but that to achieve integration a single process should be agreed that will allow integration of that particular activity across the globally dispersed organisation. While in the past the focus has been on integrating the line activities of an organisation (e.g. the supply chain or the design manufacturing process), there is now increasing attention paid to integrating HR processes. In line with this ERP, IT suppliers have developed systems to support integrated HR processes (e.g. SAP, Peoplesoft).

Selection method choice and design will be a significant element of the employee-resourcing HR process. Initial mapping and critical analysis of this process should lead to the identification of the selection methods that are most suited to the particular task demands of various job types. Taken to its logical conclusion, the outcome would be the specification of a set of skills and/or competences for a particular job (in whichever country) and the corresponding specification of which selection methods to use and how to use them. This assumes the key is to find the fit between the task environment and the selection methods that are most appropriate. However, this approach does not take into account the societal effects which, as we have seen, influence the type, design and use of selection methods. The potential outcome is the specification of a selection method that does not suit all the national contexts in which it is to be applied. For example, a French company may specify graphology as an appropriate method to use to assess the personality of its senior executives. However, while this may be well received by its potential French recruits, it may significantly disenchant those from other nationalities who may not see this method as legitimate or appropriate. For example, Steiner and Gilliland (1996) found graphology as a selection method was considered more acceptable by a group of French students than by a group of American students. On the other hand, suggesting to a French or Italian applicant that they have to participate in a variety of assessment centre exercises may appear as 'bizarre, unnecessary or privacy-invading' (Shackleton & Newell, 1994, p. 102). More pragmatically, introducing methods into a country which are not 'typical' is likely to require additional training for administrators and enhanced guidelines and practice for candidates (Challendar, 1998).

Therefore, while understanding that variability in selection method use across nations may help HR practitioners to determine the most appropriate selection strategy in a given country (Ryan et al., 1999), the current stress within ERP on integrating processes suggests an opposite and contradictory pressure on these practitioners. One response to achieve this standardisation may be to identify those selection methods which do exhibit less variability (e.g. the use of educational qualifications and interviews) and stick to these in the standardised process, avoiding those methods that exhibit high levels of variability (e.g. the use of structured interviews or graphology). This would be fine as long as those methods which were more universal were also those of higher validity. Unfortunately, the evidence suggests almost the opposite, with more valid methods actually having a far lower rate of cross-national penetration. For example, Hodgkinson and Payne (1998), comparing the methods used in French, Dutch and British companies to select graduates, conclude: 'while the more sophisticated techniques are being used to some extent in all three countries, some extremely poor methods (in terms of their known psychometric efficacy) are still widespread' (p. 362).

CONCLUSIONS

Adopting a cross-cultural perspective implies carrying out research which focuses on comparing national selection processes. Research adopting this approach has clearly demonstrated differences between countries in terms of the selection methods that are used (in terms of what methods are used, when they are used and how they are used). However, more important perhaps now is to adopt an intercultural perspective (Usunier, 1992), which considers the interactions between individuals from different national/cultural backgrounds in the context of a particular selection process. This is because, given the globalisation of many companies, a manager is increasingly likely to be involved in recruiting and selecting someone from a different national background and because individuals will be exposed to selection processes (and selection methods) in different countries. The question posed from this intercultural perspective is whether this interaction results in unfair discrimination and bias in the selection process (Scullion, 1994). This research question has been underexplored to date but in this concluding section we consider the limited research that has been published on the subject as well as giving some of our own speculations.

In terms of problems associated with individuals being exposed to selection processes in many different countries, the issues relate to candidate reactions and candidate performance. Candidates, faced with unfamiliar selection methods, may perform more poorly than do candidates who are familiar and comfortable with such methods. Moreover, candidate reactions to selection methods have been shown to be important in terms of their performance and in terms of their subsequent attitude to the organisation (Iles & Robertson, 1994). This was demonstrated clearly in a study by Mabey, Clark and Daniels (1996). They undertook a longitudinal study of graduates as they moved into the job market. They found that whether graduates registered satisfaction and commitment over the first 5 years of their careers was influenced by their views of the company formed during the selection process. So candidates faced with a selection method they do not perceive as fair or valid are unlikely to be fully motivated. This in turn may affect their performance negatively so that they are judged not to be competent on the skills being assessed. Moreover, exposed in one company to selection methods that are not seen as valid or fair, and in another where they are seen as fair, a candidate may, if faced with two job offers, opt for the latter.

One solution to this problem of a potentially poor candidate response in a situation of international selection, then, is to introduce common 'best practice' methods across countries. The technical lag explanation of national differences in selection method use would predict that this was not only possible but also probably inevitable in the long term. Moreover, the current trend towards integration and standardisation through introducing ERP systems suggests that many companies are actually attempting to achieve this, at least within their own global organisational context. However, this ignores the interpretative flexibility of selection methods that has been referred to earlier. Just because the same selection method is actually used, does not mean that the information gained from using this method will be the same in two different countries, and the interpretation of this information is even more likely to vary.

Part of the problem here relates to differences in attributional processes. Thus, in terms of managers involved in selecting individuals from different national and cultural backgrounds to their own, there will be an issue related to the attributional processes used by both assessors and assessed during a selection process. There is growing evidence that attributional patterns are in part culturally determined (Smith & Bond, 1993). For example, in collectivist cultures it is more acceptable to put collective goals before personal goals and to attribute success to group rather than individual performance (Al-Sahrani & Kaplowits, 1993). But during a selection interview this may lead to very different cultural responses to a question asked about achievement, which will in turn be differently interpreted depending on the cultural background of the interviewer. Thus, an individual from a collectivist culture, asked about their relative contribution to a group project may stress the collective input and involvement of the group. An individual from an individualistic culture, on the other hand, may stress their personal efforts, underemphasising the contributions of other group members. The interpretation of these responses will, in turn, reflect the cultural background of the interviewer. Thus, the interviewer from the collectivist culture may interpret the first response much more positively than the second, while the opposite would be the case for an interviewer from an individualistic culture. This may well lead to unfair discrimination if, for example, the latter interviewer infers a lack of motivation on the part of a candidate because s/he, coming from a collectivist culture, has attributed some personal success to a group rather than to him/herself as an individual (Sylvester & Chapman, 1996). In this instance, it is not differences in the selection method *per se* which are the problem. Rather, the problem arises from differences in the interpretation of the information derived from the same method. This is caused by cultural predispositions, which are difficult to overcome.

This research on how national differences in attributional processes bias interpersonal interactions is perhaps the best example to date of adopting an intercultural approach. What is now needed is more in-depth analysis of the interactions during the selection process between candidates and assessors from different national/cultural backgrounds when different selection methods are used. Understanding these micro processes will have real benefit both practically and theoretically.

REFERENCES

Al-Sahrani, S. S. & Kaplowits, S. A. (1993). Attributional biases in individualistic and collectivist cultures: A comparison of Americans with Saudis. *Social Psychology Quarterly*, **56**, 223–233.

Arvey, R. D. & Faley, R. H. (1988). *Fairness in Selecting Employees*. Reading, MA: Addison-Wesley.

Ball, G. (1992). Personnel management in Greece: The spartan profession. *Personnel Management*, Sept., 40–44.

Baron, H., Ryan, A. M. & Page, R. (1998). Results of an international recruitment and selection survey. Paper presented at the 24th International Congress of Applied Psychology, San Francisco, USA, August.

Bijker, W. E., Hughes, T. & Pinch, T. J. (Eds) (1987) *The Social Construction of Technological Systems*. London: MIT Press.

Bruchon-Schweitser, M. (1996). Some French studies in selection and assessment. In M. Smith & V. Sutherland (Eds), *International Review of Professional Issues in Selection and Assessment*, Vol. 2. New York: Wiley.

Challendar, J. (1998). Globally implementing cognitive and biodata tests. Presented at 13th annual conference of the Society for Industrial and Organisational Psychology, Dallas, TX.

Clark, T. (1993). Selection methods used by executive search consultancies in four European countries: A survey and critique. *International Journal of Selection and Assessment*, **1**, 41–49.

Clark, T. (Ed.) (1996). *European Human Resource Management: An Introduction to Comparative Theory and Practice*. Oxford: Blackwell.

Di Milia, L. & Gorodecki, M. (1997). Some factors explaining the reliability of a structured interview system at a worksite. *International Journal of Selection and Assessment*, **5**(4), 193–199.

Di Milia, L., Smith, P. A. & Brown, D. F. (1994). Management selection in Australia: A comparion with British and French findings. *International Journal of Selection and Assessment*, **2**(2), 80–90.

Eleftheriou, A. & Robertson, I. (1999). A survey of management selection practices in Greece. *International Journal of Selection and Assessment*, **7**(4), 203–208.

Englehart, D. (1996). The usage of psychometric tests in France. In M. Smith & V. Sutherland (Eds), *International Review of Professional Issues in Selection and Assessment*, Vol. 1. New York: Wiley.

Fletcher, C. (1994). Questionnaire surveys of organisational assessment practices: A critique of their methodology and validity, and a query about their future relevance. *International Journal of Selection and Assessment*, **2**, 172–175.

Funke, U. (1996). German studies in selection. In M. Smith & V. Sutherland (Eds), *International Review of Professional Issues in Selection and Assessment*, Vol. 2. New York: Wiley.

Gowing, M. K. & Slivinski, L. W. (1994). A review of North American selection procedures: Canada and the United States of America. *International Journal of Selection and Assessment*, 2(2), 103–114.

Heffeutt, A. I. & Arthur, W. (1994). Hunter and Hunter (1984) revisited: Interview validity and entry level jobs. *Journal of Applied Psychology*, 79, 184–190.

Hodgkinson, G. & Payne, R. (1998). Graduate selection in three European countries. *Journal of Occupational and Organisational Psychology*, 71(4), 359–365.

Hofstede, G. (1991). *Cultures and Organisation: Software of the Mind*. London: McGraw-Hill.

Iles, P. (1994). Diversity in selection practice: Culture, context and congruence. *International Journal of Selection and Assessment*, 2(2), 115–117.

Iles, P. & Robertson, I. (1994). The impact of personnel selection techniques on candidates. In N. Anderson & P. Herriot (Eds), *Handbook of Assessment and Selection in Organisations*. Chichester: John Wiley.

Kantas, A., Kalogera, S. & Nikolaou, I. (1997). Managerial practices and perceptions in the Greek private sector. In R. Pepermans, A. Buelens, C. J. Vinkenburg & P. Jansen (Eds), *Managerial Behaviour and Practices: European Research Issues*. Leuven: Amersfoort, Acco.

Levy-Leboyer, C. (1994). Selection and assessment in Europe. In H. C. Triandis, M. D. Dunnette & L. M. Hough (Eds), *Handbook of Industrial and Organizational Psychology*, Vol. 4. Palo Alto, CA: Consulting Psychologists Press.

Lievens, F. & Goemaere, H. (1999). A different look at assessment centres: Views of assessment centre users. *International Journal of Selection and Assessment*, 7(4), 215–219.

Lynch, J. (1989). Looking overseas for new members. *Association Management*, May, 110–115.

Mabey, W. & Thompson, B. W. (1993). Implementing a European Development and Assessment Centre. Paper presented at the EAWOP conference, Alicante, Spain.

Mabey, C., Clark, T. & Daniels, K. (1996). A 6 year longitudinal study of graduate expectations: The implications for company recruitment and selection strategies. *International Journal of Selection and Assessment*, 4(3), 139–150.

Mardberg, B. (1996). Improper use of tests in Sweden. *International Journal of Selection and Assessment*, 4(3), 155–158.

McCulloch, S. (1993). Recent trends in international assessment. *International Journal of Selection and Assessment*, 1, 59–61.

McDaniel, M. A., Whetsel, D. L., Schmidt, F. L. & Maurer, S. D. (1994). The validity of the employment interview: A comprehensive review and meta-analysis. *Journal of Applied Psychology*, 79, 599–616.

Miles, R. E. & Snow, C. C. (1978). *Organisational Structure, Strategy and Process*. New York: McGraw-Hill.

O'Gorman, J. G. (1996). Selection and assessment in Australia. In M. Smith & V. Sutherland (Eds), *International Review of Professional Issues in Selection and Assessment*, Vol. 1. New York: Wiley.

Rees, C. (1996). Psychometrics: Topical misunderstandings amongst test users. *International Journal of Selection and Assessment*, 4(1), 44–48.

Rogers, E. (1995). *Diffusion of Innovations*, 3rd edn. New York: Free Press.

Rowe, P. M., Williams, M. C. & Day, A. L. (1994). Selection procedures in North America. *International Journal of Selection and Assessment*, 2(2), 74–79.

Ryan, A. M., McFarland, L., Baron, H. & Page, R. (1999). An international look at selection practices: Nation and culture as explanations for variability in practice. *Personnel Psychology*, 52(2), 359–391.

Scullion, H. (1994). Creating international managers: Recruitment and development issues. In P. S. Kirkbridge (Ed.), *Human Resource Management in Europe: Perspectives for the 1990s*. London: Routledge.

Shackleton, V. & Newell, S. (1991). Management selection: A comparative survey of methods used in top British and French companies. *Journal of Occupational Psychology*, **64**, 23–36.

Shackleton, V. & Newell, S. (1994). European management selection methods: A comparison of five countries. *International Journal of Selection and Assessment*, **2**, 91–102.

Smith, M. & Abrahamsen, M. (1992). Patterns of selection in six countries. *The Psychologist*, **5**, 205–207.

Smith & Bond (1993). *Social Psychology Across Cultures: Analysis and Perspectives*. London: Harvester Wheatsheaf.

Smith, M. & George, D. (1992). Selection methods. In C. L. Cooper & I. T. Robertson (Eds), *International Review of Industrial and Organizational Psychology*, Vol. 7. Chichester: Wiley.

Sorge, A. (1991). Strategic fit and societal effects: Interpreting cross-national comparisons of technology, organisation and human resources. *Organization Studies*, **12**(2), 161–190.

Sparrow, P. (1999). Abroad minded. *People Management*, **5**(10), 40–44.

Steiner, D. D. & Gilliland, S. W. (1996). Fairness reactions to personnel selection techniques in France and the US. *Journal of Applied Psychology*, **81**(2), 134–141.

Swan, J. & Newell, S. (1995). The role of professional associations in technology diffusion. *Organisation Studies*, **16**(5), 847–874.

Swan, J., Newell, S. & Robertson, M. (2000). The diffusion, design and social shaping of production management information systems in Europe. *Journal of Information Technology and People*, **31**, 27–45.

Sylvester, J. & Chapman, A. (1996). Unfair discrimination in the selection interview: An attributional account. *International Journal of Selection and Assessment*, **4**(2), 63–70.

Thacker, J. W. & Catteneo, R. J. (1993). Survey of personnel practices in Canadian organisations: A summary report to respondents. Working paper series no. W92–04. Windsor, Ontario: University of Windsor.

Trompenaars, F. & Hampden-Turner, C. (1993). *Riding the Waves of Culture*. London: Nicholas Brealey.

Tsannetou, I. (1996). Greek studies in selection and assessment. In M. Smith & V. Sutherland (Eds), *International Review of Professional Issues in Selection and Assessment*, Vol. 2. New York: Wiley.

Usunier, J.-C. (1992). *Marketing across Cultures*. London: Prentice-Hall.

Wang, S. (1997). Integrated personnel selection, appraisal and decisions: A Chinese approach. In N. Anderson & P. Herriot (Eds), *International Handbook of Assessment and Selection*. Chichester: Wiley.

Weick, K. E. (1990) Technology as equivoque: Sensemaking in new technologies. In P. S. Goodman, L. S. Sproull & Associates, *Technology and Organisations*. Oxford: Jossey-Bass.

Chapter 3

UNDERSTANDING THE ASSESSMENT CENTRE PROCESS: WHERE ARE WE NOW?

Filip Lievens
Ghent University, Belgium
and
Richard J. Klimoski
George Mason University, USA

INTRODUCTION

Assessment centers have become widespread in Western Europe, Northern America, and Australia (Newell & Shackleton, 1994). The Task Force on Assessment Center Guidelines (1989) defined assessment centers as 'a standardized evaluation of behavior based on multiple inputs. Multiple trained observers and techniques are used. Judgments about behaviors are made, in major part, from specifically developed assessment simulations. These judgments are pooled in a meeting among the assessors or by a statistical integration process' (p. 460).

Originally, the assessment center method was considered to be an alternative measurement instrument to estimate predictor–criterion relationships. The vast majority of research also dealt with criterion–related validity and demonstrated that assessment centers were predictive for a variety of criteria of managerial effectiveness. Yet through the years the original conceptualization of assessment centers has changed dramatically (Howard, 1997). Three changes seem most noteworthy. First, whereas the output of assessment centers is still important, much more attention has been paid to assessment center 'processes'. This is most strongly reflected in the research on the construct validity of assessment centers. A second change is that the application of assessment centers has moved beyond selection/placement/promotion purposes. Recent surveys (e.g., Spychalski, Quinones, Gaugler, & Pohley, 1997) show that assessment centers are increasingly used for developmental purposes. As noted by Kudisch, Ladd, and Dobbins (1997) the goals of these developmental assessment centers vary from identification of participants' training needs, to formulation of personalized developmental recommendations and action plans, to skill development on the basis of immediate feedback and on-site practice. A third change is that nowadays multiple stakeholders are involved in assessment centers. These stakeholders include assessees, assessors, assessment center users, and the organization.

This chapter aims to provide a contribution relative to two of these changes. More specifically, we aim to provide a better understanding of the individual and collective processes and factors that affect the quality of assessor decisions. Hereby we primarily focus on the factors and forces which affect the capacity of assessment centers to provide construct valid estimates of individual attributes. This would seem to be most central to developmental assessment centers because such applications, by definition, need to produce 'true' and valid assessments of an assessee's strengths and weaknesses on the various dimensions. Moreover, developmental assessment centers assume that participants accept and act upon the feedback built around these assessments in the belief of their intrinsic validity (Thornton, Larsh, Layer, & Kaman, 1999). Thus, the quality of assessor decisions is at the core of acceptance of feedback and the motivation to thereby pursue developmental training activities. That said, it is also our view that the quality of assessor decisions in terms of construct measurement is also important for other applications (e.g., selection) as it gets to the heart of the method. In reviewing the recent literature, we will start with a relatively simple scheme adopted from the performance appraisal literature. Whereas we will treat it as a useful device for organizing the studies of interest, we will go on to argue that a more complex view will be needed as a roadmap for future research—research that will lead to a deeper understanding of the assessment center method.

The basis for our insight into the processes and factors affecting the quality of assessor decisions in assessment centers stems from our review of the literature published between 1990 and 1999. We conducted this search for relevant studies using a number of computerized databases (i.e., PsycLit, the Social Science Citation Index, Current Contents, and Dissertations Abstracts International). Additionally, we scrutinized reference lists from studies to find other published and unpublished studies. We did not only look for studies conducted in the US, but also searched for studies conducted in other countries.

We will use Landy and Farr's (1980, p. 73) component model of performance rating as a framework for organizing the studies. This framework is comprised of five classes of variables: (1) the roles (e.g., raters and ratees); (2) the rating context (e.g., rating purpose); (3) the rating vehicle (e.g., rating instrument); (4) the rating process; and (5) the results (e.g., rating information and actions based upon it). The structural relationship between these variables are as follows. Roles, context, and vehicle are expected to influence the rating process, which, in turn, should affect the results. Although this model was originally proposed in the broader field of performance rating, we feel it has heuristic value, making the various components easily transferable to (developmental) assessment centers. For instance, in this application 'roles' refer to assessors, assessees, and role-players, and 'results' refer to the ratings of assessees' strengths and weaknesses, the developmental feedback formulated, and the action plans (including any training and developmental assignments) suggested. The remainder structures the studies considered in terms of these five components. This will take the form of an elaboration of the Landy and Farr (1980) framework as portrayed in Figure 3.1.

Note that throughout this chapter we make reference to the notion of the 'quality' of assessment center judgements. Quality is operationalized or indexed in various ways in the studies under review. In most of these studies 'quality' is a shorthand way of referring to the degree of convergent and discriminant validity present in dimension ratings. To this end, authors examined patterns found in the multitrait–multimethod matrix, exploratory or confirmatory factor analysis, and correlations with external criteria. In other studies quality of assessor ratings was operationalized as dimensional accuracy, lack of bias in ratings, and even as positive reactions to assessment center (trait) ratings. Finally, whereas the traditional application of assessment centers has often relied on the strength of the correlation of overall ratings with job performance, we will view this evidence as reassuring but not definitive when assessment center results are used as the source of developmental feedback.

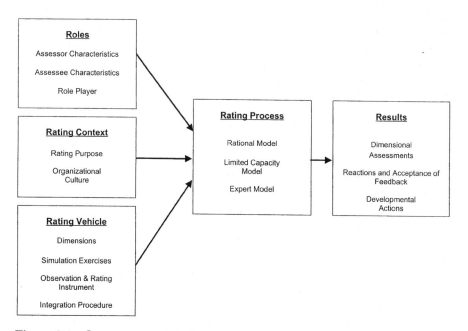

Figure 3.1 Component model of assessment centers

ROLES

Assessor Characteristics

Between 1990 and 1999 a first group of studies examined assessor characteristics as these may affect the assessment center rating process and, eventually, the quality of assessor ratings and decisions. Assessor characteristics refer to personal attributes (i.e., demographic and personality characteristics), assessor type, assessor source, and assessor training.

With respect to demographic characteristics of assessors, Lowry (1993) conducted a comprehensive study investigating the effects of age, race, education, rank, tenure, prior assessment center experience, managerial experience, and experience with the target job. Only assessor age and assessor rank exerted significant effects on the ratings. However, these two assessor characteristics accounted for less than 2% of the variance in ratings.

Other studies concentrated solely on the effects of assessor gender. Most of these studies found that ratings of male and female assessors did not differ significantly from each other (Binning, Adorno, & Williams, 1995; Weijerman & Born, 1995). Shore, Tashchian and Adams (1997), however, reported that in a role-play on four dimensions female assessors gave significantly higher ratings to both men and women assessees than did male assessors. In two other role-play exercises no effect of assessor gender was found. It is also possible that the gender of the assessee and the gender of the assessor interact to produce differences in assessment results. An earlier study (Walsh, Weinberg, & Fairfield, 1987) reported such a significant assessee–assessor gender interaction. In this case all-male assessor groups rated female candidates for a professional sales position significantly higher than male candidates. Yet two recent studies failed to replicate this interaction effect (Shore, Tashchian & Adams, 1997; Weijerman & Born, 1995).

Bartels and Doverspike (1997a) focused on the personality characteristics of assessors (measured by the 16 PF) and how they impacted on leniency in assessment center ratings. They found assessors high on intelligence, sensitivity, and poise to be more lenient.

Another variable studied was the type of assessor. Sagie and Magnezy (1997) compared ratings of psychologist assessors and managerial assessors in terms of convergent and discriminant validity. A confirmatory factor analysis of the ratings of psychologists revealed that the factors represented all five predetermined dimensions. Ratings of managers, however, yielded only two dimension factors. Lievens (1999) found that managerial assessors distinguished somewhat less among dimensions than industrial and organizational psychology students. Yet managers provided significantly more accurate ratings than these students. In this study accuracy was determined by the extent to which ratings were consistent with the values and norms espoused by the organization.

Several studies compared assessor ratings, self-ratings, and peer ratings to each other. Shore, Shore, and Thornton (1992) concluded that construct-related evidence in assessor ratings was stronger for peer ratings than for self-ratings. Shore, Tetrick, and Shore (1998) examined whether assessor, peer, and self-ratings were based on the same types of information when making overall assessments of managerial potential. They found support for the hypothesis that self-assessments of managerial potential were based to a greater extent on information not generated in the assessment center itself. Yet a counterintuitive finding was that assessor ratings and peer ratings (instead of self-ratings) were most dissimilar. Results of other studies (Clapham, 1998; Shechtman, 1998) reported more dissimilarity between assessor and self-ratings. In another study Nowack (1997) found that participant self-ratings were significantly associated with overall assessor ratings but not with overall job performance ratings.

A last assessor factor studied was the training given to assessors. Maher (1995) focused on the effects of different lengths of assessor training. Two days of assessor training increased accuracy more than one day. Yet adding a third day made no significant improvement. In other words, beyond a threshold level, additional assessor training was not useful. Lievens (1999) compared different training types (i.e., data-driven assessor training, schema-driven assessor training, and control training). The data-driven assessor training taught assessors to strictly distinguish various rating phases (e.g., observation, classification, and evaluation) from each other and to proceed to another phase only when the previous one was finished. Alternatively, schema-driven assessor training taught raters to use a specific performance theory as a mental scheme to 'scan' the behavioral stream for relevant incidents and to place these incidents—as they were observed—in one of the performance categories. Results showed that the data-driven and schema-driven assessor training approaches outperformed the control training in terms of interrater reliability, dimension differentiation, and differential accuracy. The schema-driven assessor training resulted in the largest values on all three dependent variables. In a similar study Schleicher, Day, Mayes, and Riggio (1999) compared frame-of-reference training, which conceptually builds on schema-driven principles, to no assessor training. Frame-of-reference training resulted in ratings with significantly higher interrater reliability, discriminant validity, and criterion-related validity.

Assessee Characteristics

In this section we discuss studies that investigated whether characteristics of assessees impact on assessor ratings. Personal characteristics such as race, gender or age were most frequently studied. Additionally, this research stream examined effects of assessee performance variability and assessee coaching. The remainder discusses the results of these studies.

Hoffman and Thornton (1997) summarized earlier studies on assessee race effects and concluded that these studies were almost evenly split between studies showing no significant rating differences and studies showing whites receiving higher ratings on average than other ethnic groups, usually less than one standard deviation. Recent studies confirmed this picture. Schmitt (1993) analyzed data from the selection of school administrators and found rating differences between black and white candidates (over one half of a standard deviation). However, Bobrow and Leonards (1997) found no such differences. Whereas these studies focused on black–white differences, Ramos (1992) reported that assessors scored Hispanics up to half a standard deviation lower than whites in the AT&T assessment centers on some criteria but their validity against a promotion criterion was as high as for whites. In a South African assessment center Kriek, Hurst, and Charoux (1994) did not find significant differential validity in predicting performance among whites, blacks and colored male supervisors.

Goldstein, Yusko, Braverman, Smith, and Chung (1998) provided a possible explanation for these mixed results regarding assessee race effects. The degree to which subgroup (black–white) mean differences occurred in assessor ratings was found to be a function of the type of exercise rated. Moreover, Goldstein et at. (1998) reported that the subgroup differences varied by the cognitive component of the exercise. In other words, race effects were more apparent in ratings, if an assessment center consisted of more exercises with a cognitive component (e.g., in-basket). Similarly, Sackett (1998) concluded that ratings of oral exercises included in an assessment center for lawyers displayed smaller subgroup differences than ratings of written exercises. Contrary to these conclusions, Rotenberry, Barrett, and Doverspike (1999) demonstrated that the underlying structure of in-basket ratings of 3399 safety personnel was invariant between races. The lesson learned from these studies is that it may be preferable to inspect the ratings made in the specific assessment center exercises (instead of the overall assessment center ratings) for race effects. Along these lines, Baron and Janman (1996) signaled the dearth of research about possible race effects in ratings of fact-findings, presentations, group exercises, or role-plays.

The gender of assessees should not affect the ratings of assessors. In other words, assessor ratings should reflect that men and women perform equally well in assessment centers and that assessment centers are equally valid predictors of future performance for men and women. Research by Weijerman and Born (1995) confirmed this assumption, as ratings of managerial potential of 77 Dutch civil servants were not biased by the gender of the candidates. Bobrow and Leonards (1997) and Rotenberry, Barrett and Doverspike (1999) reported similar results.

Nevertheless, in other studies ratings were prone to subtle gender bias, favoring women candidates. For instance, in Schmitt (1993) ratings indicated small performance differences in favor of female candidates. Neubauer (1990) found women received slightly higher ratings in a German high school career assessment center. In another study (Shore, 1992) 375 men and 61 women were assessed on their intellectual ability, performance-related and interpersonally related skills, and overall management potential. Although there were no significant differences between men and women in overall management potential ratings or in long-term job advancement, women obtained consistently higher ratings on performance-related skills.

Related to the above, Halpert, Wilson, and Hickman (1993) investigated whether people provided significantly different ratings to the videotaped assessment center performance of either a pregnant woman or a non-pregnant woman. Ratings of 2239 undergraduates revealed that the pregnant woman was consistently rated lower and that male undergraduates assigned significantly lower ratings than females.

With respect to the effects of assessee age on ratings, the results are again equivocal. Bobrow and Leonards (1997) analyzed ratings from an operational assessment center and found very small differences between candidates younger than 40 and candidates 40 and older. However, after controlling for education, years of service, and gender Clapham and Fulford (1997) reported negative correlations between candidate age and assessment center ratings. In particular, candidates younger than 40 received significantly higher ratings than candidates older than 40.

Morrow, McElroy, Stamper, and Wilson (1990) developed eight simulated assessment center candidates which varied on physical attractiveness (high vs. low), age (less than 40 years of age vs. more than 40 years of age), and gender (male vs. female). This experimental study revealed a main effect of physical attractiveness in the promotion ratings of 40 personnel professionals, but it explained only 2% of variance. Neither assessee age nor assessee gender significantly affected the promotion ratings.

Fletcher and Kerslake (1993) and Fletcher, Lovatt, and Baldry (1997) found that about 45% of participants reported stress and anxiety during the assessment center. A related question is whether this increased stress and anxiety of some candidates also results in lower assessor ratings. Fletcher, Lovatt and Baldry (1997) tackled this problem, using established measures of state, trait, and test anxiety. They did not report on a relationship between increased anxiety and lower assessment center ratings.

Gaugler and Rudolph (1992) investigated contrast effects in assessment centers. They examined both the effects of between assessee variability and within assessee variability. Regarding between assessee variability, a poor candidate in a generally 'good' group was rated significantly lower than a poor candidate in a generally 'poor' group. Regarding within assessee variability, a low assessee's performance was rated lower when the assessee's prior performance had been dissimilar (i.e., high) than when the assessee's prior performance had been similar (i.e., low). Finally, ratings of assessees displaying performance variation were more accurate than those obtained without performance variation. Assessee performance variability was also the focus of the study of Kuptsch, Kleinmann, and Köller (1998). Contrary to their expectations, they found that people who perceived their own behavior as more changeable or 'chameleon-like', were rated more consistently than participants who described themselves as more consistent.

A final line of research examined the effects of assessee coaching on assessor ratings. Earlier studies concluded that coaching (e.g., a formal training course or prior experiences) might lead to higher ratings in in-baskets (Brannick, Michaels, & Baker, 1989; Brostoff & Meyer, 1984; Gill, 1982), role-plays (Moses & Ritchie, 1976), leaderless group discussions (Kurecka, Austin, Johnson, & Mendoza, 1982; Petty, 1974), and business plan presentations (Dulewicz & Fletcher, 1982). There is a paucity of recent research in this area and, hence, only a snapshot of the possible coaching tactics (e.g., casual tips, (in)correct grapevine information, behaviorally specific feedback, self-study of workbooks, or comprehensive behavior modeling programs) have been addressed so far. In one exception Mayes, Belloli, Riggio, and Aguirre (1997) used a pretest-posttest design for examining the effects of two different management courses on assessment center ratings. Whereas the first course used lectures and discussions to teach various organizational behavior domains, the other course taught the same areas with a strong emphasis on experiential activities and skills. The conclusion was that both courses resulted in significantly better dimensional ratings in a role-play, higher overall ratings in an oral presentation, and one higher dimensional in-basket rating. The skills course emerged as significantly more effective than the traditional course in terms of higher role-play and in-basket ratings.

In addition to this lack of research on assessee coaching, we were not able to trace studies on whether assessor ratings are affected by assessee deception or impression management.

Role-player

As noted by Zedeck (1986) role-players are important factors in the assessment center. Trained role players are often used to increase standardization and to evoke dimension-related behavior from assessees. Unfortunately, little is known about their 'role' in the assessment center process. One exception is the unpublished dissertation of Tan (1996), who compared the effects of different types of role-players (i.e., active vs. passive). When role-players performed an active role (i.e., sought to elicit dimension-related behavior), assessor staff ratings showed somewhat higher convergent and discriminant validity. For passive role-players these validities were very low.

VEHICLE

This section deals with the vehicles which are used in assessment centers to obtain ratings. Logically, studies with respect to the dimensions, the various observation and rating instruments, and the integration procedures are discussed. We also include studies about the assessment center exercises because these exercises serve as vehicles to elicit job-relevant information upon which ratings are based. Although guidelines exist with regard to the design of these vital assessment center components (Task Force on Assessment Center Guidelines, 1989), several survey studies (Boyle, Fullerton, & Wood, 1995; Lievens & Goemaere, 1999; Lowry, 1996; Spychalski et al., 1997; Van Dam, Altink, & Kok, 1992) showed that their implementation across organizations differed considerably. In this section we review whether such procedural variations influence the rating process and the quality of assessor ratings.

Dimensions

Howard (1997) noted that '[assessment center] dimensions have always been muddled collections of traits (e.g., energy), learned skills (planning), readily demonstrable behaviors (oral communication), basic abilities (mental abilily), attitudes (social objectivity), motives (need for achievement), or knowledge (industry knowledge), and other attributes or behaviors' (p. 22). Studies have been conducted on the effects of varying the number, the distinctiveness, the nature, and the observability of these dimensions in terms of the quality of measurement in assessment centers.

A first group of studies varied the number and the level of abstraction of the dimensions rated. The general assumption is that asking assessors to rate a large number of dimensions (e.g., more than 4 or 5) per exercise overburdens the cognitive capabilities of the assessors. Maher (1990) confirmed this and showed that assessors' accuracy diminished when a larger number of dimensions was rated (see Gaugler & Thornton, 1989, for a similar previous study). Campbell (1991) compared the effectiveness of three general performance dimensions (i.e., inteilectual/communication skills, interpersonal skills, and administrative skills) and 14 specific dimensions on various aspects of rating quality. The results partially supported the hypothesis that categorization accuracy, rating accuracy, and interrater reliability would be significantly greater for the general dimensions than for the specific dimensions. The general dimensions also showed substantially greater evidence of convergent validity than the specific dimensions. No effect on discriminant validity was found. Campbell (1991) concluded that the use of general dimensions showed promise as a method of reducing the number of dimensions. In similar vein, Kolk, Born, Bleichrodt, and Van der Flier (1998) made a plea to group assessment center dimensions in three broad dimensions. They also found empirical evidence that 'feeling', 'thinking', and 'power' were useful labels of these meta-dimensions.

Kleinmann, Exler, Kuptsch, and Köller (1995) varied the distinctiveness of dimensions. Assessors were expected to have more difficulties distinguishing between dimensions, which were 'naturally' related to one another. With respect to this, correlations among dimensions might be split up in true (valid) and invalid correlations (see Cooper, 1981; Murphy, Jako, & Anhalt, 1993, for the distinction between 'true' and 'illusory', halo). Kleinmann et al. (1995) found higher discriminant validity when assessors rated assessees on conceptually distinct dimensions. With interchangeable dimensions, assessors provided interdependent ratings, which did not differ meaningfully from each other.

Another group of studies experimented with other types of dimensions/ constructs. Russell and Domm (1995), for example, explored the effectiveness of an assessment center in which assessors rated candidates on seven role requirements of the target position. For example, they defined the dimension initiative as 'the degree to which behaviors influence events to achieve goals by originating action rather than merely responding to events as required on the job of store manager' (p. 30). Nonetheless, there was little evidence that these task-dimensions were actually measured. Joyce, Thayer, and Pond (1994) compared the traditional dimensions to a set of constructs based on the functional structure of managerial work (e.g., internal contacts, performance management, etc.). Within-exercise ratings on these task-oriented dimensions also exhibited weak evidence of convergent and discriminant validity.

Next, many studies attempted to improve the definition and operationalization of dimensions. These studies were prompted by the fact that the behavioral domain of dimensions is often undefined or ill-defined (Kauffman, Jex, Love, & Libkuman 1993). In fact, different meanings are frequently associated with the same dimension and definitions of dimensions are not always clearly related to the behaviors elicited by the exercises.

Additionally, the interpretation of dimension constructs often changes from one exercise to another (Kauffman et al., 1993, Reilly, Henry, & Smither, 1990). For example, leadership in a group discussion (i.e., meeting leadership) would likely differ from leadership in a role-play with a subordinate (i.e., individual leadership). We will deal with the body of research on dimension definition and operationalization in the context of behavioral checklists.

Another group of studies looked at the impact of the observability of the dimensions (Reilly, Henry, & Smither, 1990). These studies were based on the principle of aggregation (Epstein, 1979), which states that the sum of a set of measurements is more stable than any single measurement from the set. Analogous to testing, exercise ratings of a dimension can be viewed as 'single items'. When an exercise elicits few items (read behaviors) relevant to a dimension, the representativeness of the assessee behavior for the construct domain is insufficient to obtain a consistent measure of the dimension (Kleinmann & Köller 1997).

Empirical studies reveal mixed support for this principle in the context of assessment centers. On the one hand, prior research showed that wide variations exist in the opportunity to display dimension-related behaviors across exercises (Donahue, Truxillo, Cornwell, & Gerrity, 1997; Reilly, Henry, & Smither 1990). For instance, in the Reilly, Henry, and Smither (1990) study the number of behaviors varied from 4 behaviors for one dimension to 32 behaviors for another dimension. Further, Reilly and colleagues discovered that the opportunity for assessors to observe dimension-related behavior (indicated by the number of items in a behavioral checklist) was related to the ratings on these dimensions. This relatively strong curvilinear relationship suggested that the correlation between observed behavior and ratings was a function of the number of behavioral checklist items up to certain point (i.e., 12 items), beyond which the relationship remained stable. Finally, Shore, Shore, and Thornton (1992) concluded that construct-related evidence in assessor ratings was stronger for more observable dimensions than for dimensions requiring more inferential processes on the part of assessors.

On the other hand, prior research also raised doubt on the effects of observability on the quality of assessor ratings. Kleinmann et al. (1995) experimentally manipulated the observability of dimensions (a priori rated by expert assessors) and found no differences between highly observable dimensions and poorly observable dimensions in terms of construct validity. In similar vein, Campbell (1991) did not report higher rating accuracy when relevant behaviors were displayed with high frequency than when they were displayed with low frequency.

A final set of studies took a closer look at the dimensions rated in assessment centers. In a sophisticated study Guldin and Schuler (1997) chose dimensions which systematically varied concerning their conceptual proximity to the trait concept. They discovered that between 34% and 55% of the true score variance was related to cross-situational relative interindividual differences. Dimensions such as activity and communication skills were most likely to be classified as trait-like. In similar vein, Tett (1998, 1999) called for careful consideration of the nature of the traits used in assessment centers and the process by which these traits find expression in behavior. He proposed the principle of trait activation, which holds that the behavioral expression of a trait requires arousal by trait-relevant situational cues (i.e., assessment center exercises). On the basis of this interactionist approach, Tett (1998, 1999) hypothesized that cross-exercise consistency in assessor ratings can be expected only when exercises shared trait-expressive opportunities. Results based on responses to two versions of an in-basket exercise ($n = 61, 63$) supported this trait activation hypothesis.

Simulation Exercises

Generally, assessment center exercises may be divided into three groups: individual exercises (e.g., in-basket, planning exercise, case analysis), one-to-one exercises (e.g., roleplay, fact-finding, presentation), and group exercises (e.g., leaderless group discussion). These exercises are developed to represent the most important elements of the target job (see Ahmed, Payne, & Whiddett, 1997, for a procedure to develop assessment center exercises). Because job demands and tasks are quite diverse, assessees often perform in different types of exercises, which may result in a weak consistency of ratings across exercises (i.e., low convergent validity). Researchers have explored several characteristics of assessment center exercises as possible determinants of this weak across-exercise consistency in assessor ratings. These characteristics include exercise form, exercise content, and exercise instructions.

Schneider and Schmitt (1992) experimentally manipulated the effects of exercise content and exercise form. Variance due to the form of the exercise (e.g., role-play vs. group discussion) emerged as the most important exercise factor to bolster different ratings across exercises. More specifically, exercise form explained 16% of the exercise variance in ratings. The effect of exercise content (competitive vs. cooperative) was negligible.

Highhouse and Harris (1993) examined the nature of the exercises in the typical assessment center and their effects on ratings. First, assessee behaviors were extracted from assessor report forms. Grouping similar behaviors into clusters yielded a list of 25 so-called performance constructs (e.g., maintains composure, generates enthusiasm, asks questions, etc.) used by assessors. Then, experienced assessors were asked to use these performance constructs to describe the ideal assessment center candidate in each exercise. Highhouse and Harris (1993) concluded that assessors perceived the exercise situations to be generally unrelated in terms of the behaviors required for successful performance. They also discovered some evidence for the hypothesis that assessees would be rated more consistently in exercises that were perceived to be more similar. For example, ratings of candidates in the simulated phone-call and fact-finding exercises were relatively consistent, and assessors also saw these exercises as more similar. Further, assessors perceived the group discussion and scheduling exercises to be quite different situations, and ratings of candidate performance in these exercises appeared to be less consistent. However, the relationship between perceived similarity in exercise content and actual consistency in assessee performance ratings across these exercises was not confirmed in other exercises.

Besides the usual exercise instructions Kleinmann and his colleagues (Kleinmann, 1993; Kleinmann, Kuptsch, & Köller, 1996; Kleinmann, 1997) made the dimensions rated transparent to assessees. Assessees were also informed which behaviors were relevant per dimension. Because in this case assessees oriented themselves more towards the given dimensions and demonstrated more clearly and consistently the accompanying behaviors, the quality of assessor ratings improved. Specifically, assessors were better able to provide distinct ratings (within exercises) and consistent ratings (across exercises). Nonetheless, Kleinmann (1997) discovered that divulging dimensions resulted in lower criterion-related validity for the transparent group. Smith-Jentsch (1996) also reported negative side-effects of transparent dimensions. Skill transparency was found to reduce the convergence between dimension ratings in a situational exercise and personality inventory scores, and the correlation between dimension ratings and self-reported performance one year later.

Observation and Rating Instrument

In the original AT&T assessment centers assessors took notes while observing candidates and afterwards used this information to rate the candidates. However, over the years several alternatives have been suggested to improve the quality of ratings. Behavioral checklists constitute one of the most popular options (Boyle, Fullerton & Wood, 1995; Spychalski et al., 1997). An advantage of behavioral checklists is that assessors are not required to categorize behavior. Instead, they can concentrate their efforts on the observation of relevant behaviors. As argued by Reilly, Henry, and Smither (1990), the checklists may further reduce cognitive demands by serving as retrieval cues to guide the recall of behaviors observed. However, according to Joyce, Thayer, and Pond (1994) a drawback of behavioral checklists may be that they re-define a dimension from one exercise to another. In this way the increased behavioral focus and specificity of behavioral checklists may contribute to the low correlations among dimension ratings across exercises.

The research evidence with regard to the effectiveness of behavioral checklists is mixed. Reilly, Henry, and Smithers (1990) reported positive findings because ratings made via behavioral checklists demonstrated higher convergent and somewhat higher discriminant validity than ratings without the use of behavioral checklists. In other studies behavioral checklists only enhanced discriminant validity (Donahue et al., 1997) or had virtually no effects (Fritzsche, Brannick, & Fisher-Hazucha, 1994; Schneider & Schmitt, 1992). Hennessy, Mabey, and Warr (1998) compared three observation procedures: traditional note taking, use of a behavioral checklist, and behavioral coding. The methods were found to yield similar outcomes in terms of accuracy of judgement, accuracy of written evidence, correlation between dimension ratings, and attitude toward the method employed, with a slight preference for behavioral coding.

Recent studies have also examined more specific aspects related to behavioral checklists. For example, Binning, Adorno, and Kroeck (1997) found that the discriminant validity of behavioral checklists increased only when the items were ordered in naturally occurring clusters. The discriminant validity of a randomly ordered checklist was low. Another specific aspect pertains to the number of items per dimension in checklists. With respect to this, Hauenstein (1994) argued to list only the key behaviors. Reilly, Henry, and Smither (1990) supported this 'key behavior' approach and determined that the optimal number of statements per dimension varied between 6 and 12. Lebreton, Gniatczyk, and Migetz (1999) also supported the use of shorter checklists. They demonstrated that checklists with fewer dimensions and behavioral items (e.g., 2 dimensions comprised of 14 behaviors instead of 6 dimensions made up of 45 behaviors) are to be preferred in light of predictive and construct validity.

Besides behavioral checklists, videotaping of assessees has also been used to assist assessors in their task and to improve the quality of their assessments. In particular, Ryan, Daum, Bauman and colleagues (1995) hypothesized that giving assessors the opportunity to rewind and pause videotaped assessment center exercises would improve the information processing capacities of assessors. Nonetheless, they concluded that the impact of the use of videotaping assessees on ratings was minimal. In particular, rewinding and pausing the videotape had some beneficial effects on the behavioral accuracy of assessors but did not increase rating accuracy.

With respect to rating procedures Harris, Becker, and Smith (1993) and Kleinmann, Andres, Fedtke, Godbersen, and Köller (1994) examined whether a variant of the behavior reporting method, the within-dimension method, showed higher convergent and discriminant validity. In the traditional behavior reporting method 'evaluation is postponed until the completion of all exercises, at which time the assessors share their observations and rate the candidates on a series of dimensions' (Sackett & Dreher, 1982, p. 402). According to the within-dimension rating method candidates are rated on each dimension upon completion of each exercise. Contrary to earlier findings (Silverman, Dalessio, Woods, & Johnson, 1986), both studies (Harris, Becker, & Smith 1993; Kleinmann et al., 1994) reported no beneficial effects for the within-dimension method.

Finally, the rotation scheme of assessors through the various exercises has been found to influence the quality of ratings. A first rotation scheme issue relates to the ratio of assessors to assessees. Lievens (in press) used generalizability analysis to examine the effects of reducing or increasing the number of assessors per assessee. Reducing the number of manager assessors from 3 to 1 had a serious impact on the generalizability coefficient as it dropped from 0.81 to 0.60. A second issue deals with the fact that in operational assessment centers, each assessor does not rate each candidate in every exercise. For example, a candidate might be rated by one assessor in an in-basket, and by a second assessor in a role-play exercise. Even if the candidate's behavior was consistent across exercises, very dissimilar ratings could result from low inter-rater agreement between assessors. Research by Adams and Osburn (1998) confirmed this expectation. This study also demonstrated that it is important to identify a rotation scheme, which minimizes rater inconsistencies. Andres and Kleinmann (1993) developed such a rotation system for reducing information overload, contrast effects, halo effects, and sympathy effects. No studies have empirically demonstrated the superiority of this rotation scheme.

Integration Procedure

At the end of the assessment center assessors typically meet to discuss observations and ratings. Survey studies show that this formal assessor discussion is almost always held. For instance, the survey of Spychalski et al. (1997) of US assessment center practices indicated that 84.1% of the organizations held a consensus discussion to integrate ratings. In Boyle, Fullerton, and Woods'

(1995) survey of UK assessment center practices this percentage reached 96%.

Despite this popularity, we traced only a couple of studies (conducted between 1990 and 1999) on the effects of the integration procedure. Firstly, studies examined the superiority of mechanically derived versus consensus-derived integration procedures in terms of predictiveness. Pynes and Bernardin (1992) found no difference in terms of predictive validity between mechanically derived and consensus-derived integration procedures. Lebreton, Binning, and Hesson-McInnis (1998), however, showed that clinical judgements were superior to statistically combined ratings. Secondly, Anderson, Payne, Ferguson, and Smith (1994) inspected how assessors integrated the information from various sources in the consensus discussion. They concluded that assessors relied more on information elicited first-hand (i.e., observational data in assessment center exercises) than on biodata or psychometric test scores.

This paucity of studies illustrates that Zedeck's (1986) point that 'group dynamics seems to be totally ignored within the assessment center literature' (p. 290) is still valid. Therefore, future studies could, among other things, investigate how personal characteristics (age, sex, status, education, and experience of the group members), group characteristics (size), and group dynamics (the development of norms, conformity, polarization) influence the integrative discussion.

CONTEXT

The assessment center rating process does not take place in a vacuum. The rating purpose and the organizational culture are among the factors which could affect the rating process and the quality of assessor ratings.

With respect to rating purpose, assessors may evaluate candidates differently, depending on whether their ratings will serve a selection purpose (i.e., 'yes/no' decision) or a developmental purpose (i.e., identification of strengths and weaknesses). A related concept is the processing objective (Lichtenstein & Srull, 1987). Assessors will process the incoming information differently if they are given an evaluative goal or an observational goal. To the best of our knowledge no studies in the assessment center field have experimentally manipulated these variables.

Another relevant contextual factor is the culture of the organization. Staufenbiel and Kleinmann (1999) tested the hypothesis that assessors do not judge assessees exclusively on the basis of the prescribed dimensions but also take into account the fit of the applicants into the culture of the organization. This study examined the so-called 'subtle criterion contamination' thesis (Klimoski & Brickner, 1987). This thesis posits that assessors' implicit constructs mimic the policy factors implicitly or explicitly defined by the organization. In their study Staufenbiel and Kleinmann gave student assessors information about the job and the dominant organizational leadership culture (competitive vs. cooperative). Afterwards, assessors watched four hypothetical candidates displaying either competitive or cooperative behaviors. Results predominantly showed that applicants demonstrating behavior in line with the organizational culture were rated more favorably.

Bartels and Doverspike (1997b) investigated whether differences in organizational level (i.e., upper and middle) and business stream (i.e., chemical, corporate, distributions, and research) moderated criterion-related validity. Assessment center performance validities did not increase when disaggregated according to either level or business stream.

RATING PROCESS

In this section we take a closer look at the rating process in assessment centers in terms of three divergent perspectives. In particular, the sparse research on the rating process in assessment centers is grouped along three conceptual models (Lord & Maher, 1990; Thornton, 1992): the rational model, the limited-capacity model, and the expert model.

Rational Model

A rational model of the rating process (Abelson, 1981; Bobrow & Norman, 1975; Borman, 1978; Rumelhart & Ortony, 1977) assumes people are able to attend to detailed behavior, to classify these many specific pieces of factual information into distinct categories, and to form relatively objective and accurate judgements. A rational model is also known as a data-driven, behavior-driven, or bottom-up model.

Most textbooks on assessment center practice (e.g., Ballantyne & Povah, 1995; Jansen & de Jongh, 1997; Woodruffe, 1993) adhere to this rational model. This model trains assessors to proceed carefully through the following rating phases. First, assessors observe verbal and nonverbal behavior of candidates. Most assessors observe ongoing behavior ('direct observation'), although in the US assessors also frequently observe videotaped performances of candidates ('indirect observation') (Bray & Byham, 1991). When observing, assessors are expected to record clear behavioral descriptions instead of vague nonbehavioral interpretations. After taking notes, assessors classify behaviors according to dimensions. This requires that assessors possess a thorough understanding of the dimensions and their definitions. Finally, assessors rate candidates on multiple job-related dimensions.

Thornton (1992) argues that these systematic and standardized practices lead to data-driven and accurate judgements. Several reasons underlie this argument. Firstly, in assessment centers the goal of accuracy (Neuberg, 1989) is stressed so that assessors are to devote time and energy to the distinct processes of observing, recording, and classifying behavior. Secondly, assessors are accountable for their ratings (Tetlock, 1983) as they have to justify their ratings to fellow assessors, to candidates, and to the organization. Thirdly, more careful and complex decision-making occurs when people know that their ratings and decisions may have important implications for the future (e.g., career) of the person being judged (Freund, Kruglanski, & Shpitzajzen, 1985). To date virtually no studies have manipulated the effects of these conditions (e.g., goal of accuracy, etc.). An exception is the study of Mero and Motowidlo (1995), who demonstrated that accountability promoted rating accuracy in an assessment center-related context.

Limited Capacity Model

This model posits that assessors possess limited information processing capacities and, therefore, are not always able to meet the cognitive demands of the assessment center process (Reilly, Henry, & Smither, 1990). One source of cognitive overload is that the behavioral information is presented to assessors at a very fast rate in the various exercises which often last over 30 minutes. Cognitive overload may also come from the many inferential leaps assessors must make in order to provide dimensional ratings. The determination of relevance, dimensionality, and relative weight of behaviors are among the inferences typically required of assessors. In particular, the assignment of individually observed behaviors to dimensions is an unstructured inference process where assessors judgementally review their notes. Additionally, they have to formulate a numerical rating for each dimension by intuitively averaging and weighing the relevant behaviors, as the performance levels often remain undefined and implicit.

Over the last decade this limited-capacity model has received considerable research attention as many studies tried to reduce the cognitive overload on the part of assessors. Examples included limiting the number of dimensions rated, using behavioral checklists, using video technology, or increasing the ratio of assessors to assessees. As discussed in previous sections, these studies were generally effective in reducing assessor cognitive overload as inferred by improvements in the quality of ratings.

Expert Model

The basic notion of this model is that professional assessors possess and use well-established cognitive structures when rating assessors. For expert assessors these organizing prior-knowledge frameworks, which develop by abstracting from previous assessment center experiences and training, are helpful because they guide attention, categorization, integration, and recall processes (Cantor & Mischel, 1977; Fiske & Taylor, 1991; Srull & Wyer, 1980, 1989; Zedeck,

1986). Conversely, novice assessors (e.g., students) are not expected to possess such well-established cognitive structures when rating.

Several of the studies described above supported this expert model of the assessment center rating process. An example included the finding of higher discriminant validity for psychologist assessors than for managerial assessors (Sagie & Magnezy, 1997). Another example was that assessors receiving frame-of-reference training were better able to use the dimensions differentially (Lievens, 1999; Schleicher et al., 1999). In light of the notion of the expert model this was not unexpected because frame-of-reference training provided assessors with a mental framework regarding both the assignment of behaviors by dimension and the correct effectiveness level of each behavior (in line with the organization's norms and values). Accordingly, assessors were expected to place relevant incidents—as they occurred—in the appropriate mental category. Yet use of prior-knowledge frameworks might also exert additional effects. Schuler, Moser, & Funke (1994, see also Moser, Schuler, and Funke, 1999), for example, examined how assessor–assessee acquaintance influenced assessment center validities. When assessor–assessee acquaintance was less than or equal to two years, the criterion-related validity was 0.09. This value increased dramatically to 0.50 when assessor–assessee acquaintance was greater than two years.

RESULTS

In developmental assessment centers the results of the rating process primarily refer to the (final or within-exercise) ratings on the various dimensions. These dimensional ratings are expected to provide a detailed and valid portrayal of managerial strengths and weaknesses. Additionally, the results also refer to the developmental feedback, training activities, and action plans suggested to participants.

An examination of the quality of these results in developmental assessment centers should comprise three criteria (Thornton et al., 1999, Carrick & Williams, 1998). A first criterion pertains to the quality of the dimensional ratings, namely these dimensional ratings should be valid indicants of managerial abilities. This refers to the construct validity issue in assessment centers. If the dimensions are not valid indicants of managerial abilities, the developmental feedback and action plans could be faulty or even detrimental (Fleenor, 1996; Joyce, Thayer, & Pond, 1994; Shore, Thornton, & Shore, 1990). The following example by Kudisch, Ladd, and Dobbins (1997) succinctly highlights this. 'Telling a candidate that he or she needs to improve his or her overall leadership skills may be inappropriate if the underlying construct being measured is dealing with a subordinate in a one-on-one situation (i.e., tapping individual leadership as opposed to group leadership)' (p. 131).

The second and third critera refer to the developmental feedback and developmental activities suggested to participants. In fact, participants should accept the developmental feedback provided. The literature on performance feedback (Ashford, 1986) shows that this is not as straightforward as it may seem at first sight. In addition, participants should act upon the feedback. This may imply that participants follow developmental recommendations, further develop their skills, and apply these skills on the job. The remainder of this section reviews research with respect to these three criteria and the factors affecting them.

Distinct Dimensional Assessment as Basis for Developmental Feedback

Internal validation strategy

To examine whether assessor ratings on the dimensions are valid indicants of managerial abilities the majority of studies used the multitrait–multimethod matrix (Campbell & Fiske, 1959). In these studies the dimensional ratings which assessors make after completion of each exercise (i.e., within-exercise dimension ratings) were cast as a multitrait–multimethod matrix in which assessment center dimensions served as traits and assessment center exercises as methods.

The general conclusion from earlier research (e.g., Sackett & Dreher, 1982; see Jones, 1992; Kauffman et al., 1993; Klimoski & Brickner, 1987, for reviews) was that assessment center ratings did not measure the constructs they were purported to measure. Whereas assessor ratings on the same dimensions across exercises were found to correlate lowly (i.e., low convergent validity), assessor ratings on different dimensions in a single exercise were found to correlate highly (i.e., low discriminant validity). Between 1990 and 1999 a first line of studies sought to examine the lack of convergent and discriminant validity of assessment centers in other settings. Generally, the troubling findings were replicated in British (Crawley, Pinder, & Herriot, 1990; Henderson, Anderson, & Smith, 1995; McCredie & Shackleton, 1994), Australian (Carless & Allwood, 1997), Dutch (Van der Velde, Born, & Hofkes, 1994), Belgian (Lievens & Van Keer, 1999), German (Kleinmann & Köller, 1997), French (Rolland, 1999), and Singaporean assessment centers (Chan, 1996). Three studies also examined the convergent and discriminant validity of assessor ratings in developmental assessment centers. The expectation was that the quality of construct measurement would improve in developmental assessment centers because they require a detailed assessment of participants' strengths and weaknesses. However, Joyce, Thayer, and Pond (1994) and Fleenor (1996) found that the disappointing results were also generalizable to developmental assessment centers. Kudisch, Ladd, and Dobbins (1997) revealed somewhat more construct-related evidence for developmental assessment centers. In this study both exercise factors and dimension factors provided the best representation of ratings in a developmental assessment center. Unfortunately, none of these studies experimentally manipulated assessment center purpose to examine the effect on the convergent and discriminant validity of the ratings.

Along these lines, a second stream of studies aimed to single out factors which might improve the quality of construct measurement in assessment centers. Lievens (1998) reviewed 21 studies which manipulated specific variables to determine their impact on assessment center convergent and discriminant validity. The rationale behind many of these design and procedural interventions was that they help assessors to deal with their complex task. This review study showed that dimension factors (number, conceptual distinctiveness, and transparency), assessor factors (type of assessor and type of assessor training), and exercise factors (exercise form and use of role-players) were found to slightly improve construct validity. Conversely, the studies regarding the impact of different observation, evaluation, and integration procedures yielded mixed results.

A third stream of studies used more powerful statistical techniques such as confirmatory factor analysis to examine construct validity (see Donahue et al., 1997; Harris, Becker, & Smith, 1993; Kudisch, Ladd, & Dobbins, 1997; Schneider & Schmitt, 1992; Van der Velde, Born, & Hofkes, 1994). Confirmatory factor analysis explains the multitrait–multimethod matrix in terms of underlying constructs, rather than observed variables. In factor analytic terms the question is: Do the factors underlying the ratings represent dimensions or exercises? Factors defined by multiple measures of the same trait reflect construct validity of the measures, whereas factors based on different trait measures with the same instrument indicate method effects. Additionally, separate variance estimates of dimensions, exercises, and error are available. The general conclusion was that in most of the samples the 'Exercise-only' model produced a good fit of the data (Schneider & Schmitt, 1992; Van der Velde, Born, & Hofke, 1994), although adding one or more dimension factors to this model often resulted in an even better fit. A trend that deserved attention was the finding that the latter were often dimensions which could be observed more easily (e.g., oral communication). In some samples the model 'Exercises and Dimensions' provided the best representation of assessment center ratings (Donahue et al., 1997; Kudisch, Ladd, & Dobbins, 1997). However, loadings on exercise factors were generally higher than loadings on dimension factors. Recently, alternative ways of modeling multitrait–multimethod data have also been proposed. More specifically, because of estimation problems inherent in the traditional confirmatory factor analysis approach, Sagie and Magnezy (1997), Kleinmann and Köller (1997), and Lievens and Van Keer (1999) modeled method (i.e., exercise) effects as correlated uniqueness (Marsh, 1989) instead of separate method factors. They showed that this procedure was less prone to ill-defined solutions and improper estimates. Kleinmann and

Köller (1997) and Lievens and Van Keer (1999) also found that the general confirmatory factor analysis approach was frequently plagued by inadmissible solutions.

A crucial question is whether the construct validity findings represent assessor biases or true relationships. The former interpretation hinges on both the limited-capacity and the expert models described above. For instance, the lack of discriminant validity may be explained by the fact that assessors often fail to meet the heavy cognitive demands of the assessment center procedure, resulting among other things in the inability to differentiate between the various dimensions. Otherwise, ecologically valid, schema-based processing on the part of assessors may also be responsible for the dimension overlap (Zedeck, 1986). According to the latter interpretation, assessors are not to blame for the low convergent and discriminant validities found. Instead, these findings are simply due to candidates' real performance differences across situations (Neidig & Neidig, 1984). For example, certain individuals may perform better in one-to-one exercises than in group situations, diminishing the convergence of ratings across exercises. These performance differences have been labeled as true 'exercise effects'. Low discriminant validity may then result from the fact that some candidates exhibit no performance variation on the dimensions. Recently, two studies tried to disentangle these rival interpretations. Lance, Newbolt, Gatewood, and Smith (1995) reported on several studies in which they correlated latent exercise factors and external correlates. In general, hypothesized relationships between the exercise factors and the external correlates were found, supporting the explanation that the exercise factors capture true variance instead of error. Lievens (in press) showed that assessor ratings were relatively veridical. When assessors rated videotaped candidates whose performances varied across dimensions, assessors were reasonably able to differentiate among the various dimensions. When assessors rated a videotaped candidate without clear performance fluctuations across dimensions, distinctions about dimensions were more blurred. Clearly, these two studies demonstrate that the troubling construct validity findings might reflect more true variance than previously thought and therefore shed a more positive light on assessment center construct validity.

External validation strategy

To examine whether developmental assessment centers yield distinct trait assessments some studies have used external criteria. These studies have linked final dimension ratings in a nomological net (Cronbach & Meehl, 1955) with personality questionnaires and cognitive ability measures.

Using this nomological network approach Shore, Thornton, and Shore (1990) hypothesized that final ratings on the dimensions were construct valid if the correlations between dimension scores and scores on conceptually related measures were higher than correlations between dimension scores and scores on conceptually unrelated measures. Per assessment center dimension, they classified psychological measures (e.g., measures of personality and cognitive ability) as either conceptually related or unrelated to that dimension. Conforming to their hypotheses, cognitive ability measures related more strongly to the performance-like dimensions (i.e., candidates' proficiency in performing their tasks) than to the interpersonal-style dimensions (i.e., candidates' style of behavior toward other people in work situations). Furthermore, convergent validity was found for all three interpersonal-style dimensions, and for three of six performance-like dimensions. Discriminant validity was established for two of the interpersonal-style dimensions, and for one of the performance-style dimensions. Recently, these results were confirmed by one study (Thornton, Tziner, Dahan, Clevenger, & Meir, 1997) but disconfirmed by two other studies (Chan, 1996; Fleenor, 1996). In these latter two studies the final dimension ratings failed to demonstrate most of the expected relationships with conceptually similar personality dimensions. Furthermore, the average correlations between final dimension ratings and conceptually dissimilar personality dimensions were equal or even higher than with conceptually related personality dimensions.

Scholz and Schuler (1993) conducted a meta-analysis ($n = 22\ 106$) of studies in which assessment center scores (e.g., overall assessment rating, dimensional scores, etc.) were correlated with an array of external measures such as cognitive ability measures or personality inventories. Their meta-analysis included 51 studies and 66 independent samples. Intelligence correlated 0.33 with the overall assessment rating, which increased to 0.43 when corrected for unreliability. Besides intelligence, the overall assessment center rating tended also to correlate 0.23 (corrected for unreliability) with dominance, 0.30 with achievement motivation, 0.31 with social competence, and 0.26 with self-confidence. Examining the utility and validity of selection devices generally, Schmidt and Hunter (1998) summarized 85 years of research findings. They reported that assessment center ratings did have a corrected correlation with external criteria of job success of 0.37. However, consistent with Scholz and Schuler (1993), they also pointed out the high correlation of assessment centers with general mental ability, which they estimated to be around 0.50. Because of this, when combined with a measure of general mental ability as part of a predictor battery, Schmidt and Hunter would expect an assessment center to account for very little additional variance, hence calling its utility into question. Recently, Fleenor (1996) found that the personality trait 'exhibition' was significantly correlated with all 10 assessment center dimensions, the trait 'aggression' with 7 and the trait 'dominance' with 5 dimensions. Apparently, participants who were 'good actors' and highly competitive were rated significantly higher in the assessment center. Moser, Diemand, and Schuler (1996) correlated ratings of 58 candidates on a self-monitoring questionnaire to their ratings in an assessment center, which was designed to provide recommendations for promotion to supervisory positions.

No relationship ($r = 0.02$) was found between high scores on the inconsistency scale of the self-monitoring questionnaire and higher assessment center ratings (for similar results, see Arthur & Tubre, 1999). However, the social skills scale showed significant correlations ($r = 26$) with assessee ratings. Furnham, Crump, and Whelan (1997) validated the NEO Personality Inventory using assessor ratings. A clear pattern emerged with conscientiousness and extraversion having strongest and most frequent correlations with assessor ratings. Other research does not lend support to the link between assessment centers and personality. Goffin, Rothstein, and Johnston (1996) reported a marked lack of correlation between personality and assessment center scores because both personality and dimensional assessment center scores had significant incremental validity over one another. Goffin, Rothstein, and Johnston (1996) concluded that 'personality and assessment centers sample different domains which in turn predict relatively different aspects of job performance' (p. 753).

A limitation of the majority of the aforementioned studies is that they did not relate ratings of developmental assessment centers to external criteria. Probably this explains why these studies used personality and cognitive ability as external criteria of the final dimension ratings measured. However, in assessment centers conducted for developmental purposes other constructs might serve as more relevant criteria. Examples include motivation-based constructs (Jones, 1997), extra-role performance, or general occupational interests.

Reactions and Acceptance of Developmental Feedback

As noted above, dimensional ratings serve as basis for the developmental feedback provided to participants in most applications of the assessment center method, but they are the *raison d'être* for the developmental assessment center. The quality of these assessor descriptions provided at the end of developmental assessment centers might be examined by looking at participants' acceptance and reactions of the feedback. If participants do not understand the feedback or do not accept it, it is unlikely that they will react positively and initiate in developmental activities (Thornton et al. 1999). Positive reactions are often found but these appear to be linked to the job-relatedness/face validity of the assessment center exercises (Iles & Mabey, 1993; Kluger & Rothstein, 1993; Kravitz, Stinson, & Chavez, 1996; Macan, Avedon, Paese, & Smith, 1994; Rynes & Connerly, 1993; Sichler, 1991; Smither, Reilly, Millsap, Pearlman, & Stoffey, 1993). Relatively few studies have addressed how participants react to the developmental feedback, and in particular, the role that the quality of the ratings plays.

In one noteworthy exception, a comprehensive study by Harris, Paese, and Greising (1999) used organizational justice theory as a framework to investigate which variables were related to feedback reactions in a developmental assessment center. Participants' feedback reactions were measured by three criteria: procedural fairness, distributive fairness, and perceived utility of the feedback. Results showed that variables related to assessment center exercises (perceived content validity, perceived feedback validity, and affect) with the exception of fakeability were generally related to all three measures of participants' feedback reactions. Not unexpectedly, participant reactions were also predicted by feedback process variables (i.e., participation, specificity of feedback, and personableness of the assessor). Met expectations, operationalized as the degree of difference between the expected rating and the actual rating, were related to both procedural and distributive fairness, but not to perceived utility of feedback. These results mesh well with studies by Burd and Ryan (1993) and Kudisch and Ladd (1997). They showed that acceptance of developmental feedback was related among other things to exercise realism, feedback favorability, and perceived assessor expertise. Other studies (Baisden & Robertson, 1993; Kudisch & Ladd, 1997) investigated whether specific personality characteristics of participants predicted feedback acceptance. However, no clear pattern emerged.

Besides the factors affecting feedback acceptance and reactions, another issue is which feedback type participants prefer. Thornton et al. (1999) distinguished between attribute feedback (i.e., organized around the dimensions) and exercise feedback (i.e., organized around the simulation exercises). Results indicated favorable reactions to both feedback types and no real differences in the extent to which participants perceived the attribute-based feedback or exercise-based feedback as accurate and useful.

Developmental Actions as a Result of the Feedback

A third and last criterion for examining the quality of assessor decisions in developmental assessment centers consists of looking at whether participants actually acted upon the developmental feedback and engaged in subsequent developmental activities. Research results are mixed. Engelbrecht and Fischer (1995) discovered that 41 managers who received feedback after an assessment center experience and who engaged in subsequent developmental activities were rated higher on six performance dimensions than a comparable group of 35 managers who had not gone through the assessment process. The effects of this developmental assessment center were still measurable three months later. Unfortunately, it was unlikely that in this study managers were randomly assigned to 'conditions'. Hence, it may be that those who went though the center differed in their orientation to self-development to begin with. Other studies demonstrated the limited effectiveness of developmental assessment centers. For instance, Jones and Whitmore (1995) pointed out the lack of differences in career advancement between managers who went through a developmental assessment center and a naturally occurring control sample. Acceptance of developmental feedback was also not related to promotion, and following recommended developmental activities was related to eventual promotion for only two of seven performance dimensions (i.e., career motivation and working with others). Mitchell and Maurer (1998) built on these disappointing findings and tried to explain which factors were related to participation in subsequent training and developmental activities. They showed that individuals who received lower ratings engaged in higher amounts of subsequent training. Perceived time constraints interfered with learning and developmental activities. Social support for development and managers' self-efficacy for development were related to on-the-job development constructs. Other perceived context factors and individual differences did not moderate the relationship between feedback and training/developmental activities.

CONCLUSIONS AND DISCUSSION

What Have We learned?

From our review, it seems clear that the 'quality' of assessment center decisions (i.e., dimensional/trait ratings) can be measured and indexed. And when quality has been measured, it has been found, to vary considerably—some centers have it, others do not. Moreover, the quality of the output of assessment centers appears to be linked to major assessment center 'design' parameters. The most profound insights from our review, however, are not solely associated with 'design' features of the assessment centers. Our review has also convinced us that we must have a deeper understanding of the nature of the assessor as a social information processor.

Assessment center design issues

Most notably, the nature and number of the dimensions seem to affect the quality of judgements made by center staff. In general, having to rate fewer conceptually independent dimensions, which can be clearly operationalized (and which have a real opportunity to reveal themselves in the exercises), results in higher quality. It also seems to help, if there is reasonable variability in the trait of interest and variability in the population of participants to be assessed, as relative judgements are always easier to make.

It has also been found that the nature of the exercises exerts considerable impact on judgement quality. Aspects of form, content, and the instructions given to participants make it easier to infer the existence of the traits being assessed. In similar vein, thoroughly trained role-players appear to help assessors observe relevant behaviors in exercises. It also seems likely that the order in which assessors see participants relative to exercises and the assignments given to assessors (e.g., the assignment to specialize on a particular dimension across exercises and participants) have major consequences for the ability of assessors to estimate a participant's strengths and weaknesses.

To put it simply, unless the exercises provide an opportunity to observe enough behaviors and to do so under (assessor) favorable conditions, it is very difficult to infer traits or dispositions. In this regard, most exercises appear to have been selected or designed more for their face (content) validity, than for their capacity to expose behavior that would reveal the level of specific traits possessed by the participant.

On a related matter, we might put forth as a thesis that the emphasis on exercises reflecting job content has another unintended effect. It would seem to highlight the capacity of individuals to perform well on job-relevant tasks. On the 'plus' side, as pointed out by Klimoski and Brickner (1987), this may help to account for the criterion-related validity of assessment centers. Simply restated, assuming the content validity of the exercises, assessors are focused on estimating (predicting) likely future job performance of the candidates. However, on the 'minus' side, this may actually interfere with their major task, which is (arguably) the estimation of scores on traits or dimensions. Given the aforementioned difficulty of trait estimation from behavior elicited by exercises we feel that this negative influence is quite likely. It is also problematic because performance is usually an imperfect indicator of key traits. In particular, the ecological validity of dimensions or traits *vis-à-vis* performance is rarely even considered in center design. Moreover, as we and others (e.g., Joyce, Thayer, & Pond, 1994) have noted, the particular mix of dimensions to be estimated usually varies by exercise, and performance on various exercises will be driven by different combinations of traits as well.

Social judgement design issues

Based on the performance-appraisal literature (Murphy & Cleveland, 1995), when poor quality ratings are encountered, it is reasonable to examine at least three factors. The first is the opportunity to observe. As described above, we do think that this is part of the story. The time with a given candidate and/or the circumstances surrounding the observations (e.g., the exercises and their opportunity to elicit dimension-related behaviors) do seem important.

A second relates to motivation, in this case, the motivation to provide quality judgements. Whereas it is possible that assessment center staff are not motivated, this may only be true in a nuanced sense. In the first place, assessors are typically a select and dedicated group. Most volunteer for the assignment. More telling, the structure of the typical assessment center would seem to emphasize accountability. For instance, as we reported, most centers make use of an integration session wherein assessors have to offer and justify their point of view regarding each participant's scores. Similarly, assessors frequently have to provide (face to face) feedback to participants. Such conditions of accountability are known to produce motivated behavior (Frink & Klimoski, 1998; Lerner & Tetlock, 1998; Mero & Motowidlo, 1995). The existence of these and other realities (e.g., most centers are 'high visibility' operations) leads us to believe that poor quality ratings are not caused by simple lack of effort. But, as will be detailed below, it may just be that effort is still part of the story if it is being allocated toward the wrong goals (e.g., estimating potential vs. dimensional accuracy).

If we have addressed the role of observation and motivation, what remains? In our opinion, the key may reside in a better understanding of a third factor, namely the capability of the assessor to make quality judgements. In the performance-appraisal literature, capability is usually thought of as an amalgam of skill and capacity. In fact, we feel that both skill and capacity are implicated in the issue of the quality of assessment center judgements. Quite clearly, most operational centers place a high premium on the training given to assessment center staff members. This is laudatory, as training is a very direct way to increase skill. However, notwithstanding some recent research examples (Lievens, 1999; Schleicher et al., 1999), training programs built around models of social information processing are still lacking in operational centers. Indeed, it is our position that assessment centers, their design (including assessor training), and their administration would profit from a better integration of current thinking in person perception, social information processing, interpersonal judgements, and decision-making. But even with this said, current models of social cognition, even once identified as useful, would still need to be translated into implications for assessment centers.

What Do We Need to Know?

The framework that we used as a heuristic for this review was derived from the performance-rating literature. To its credit, this included a consideration of the rating process. Moreover, we pointed out that when it comes to current thinking about the performance-rating process, the field has moved towards the so-called 'expert' model perspective, implicating such phenomena as cognitive structures, decisional heuristics, case-based reasoning, and the notion of cognitive resources. In characterizing the work on assessment centers in the last decade, it should seem clear that a substantial portion of the problem of dimensional assessment accuracy may indeed be better understood in terms of what we have learned about performance-related information processing. But it is not sufficient. Consistent with some of the suggestions of Murphy and Cleveland (1995), assessment center research should be guided by a realization that we are not just trying to model 'information' processing. In fact, in trying to unravel the puzzle of assessment center rating quality, we are essentially dealing with 'social' information, gathered in social or interpersonal settings. As such, findings from the literature on social cognition and social perception must be integrated into our thinking, into our research, and ultimately into our design solutions for assessment centers.

Although we could never do justice to the extensive social cognition domain in this chapter, we will try to highlight certain concepts and theories that have been found useful in characterizing the way people process social information. Much of the material below derives from Fiske's (1993) very useful and contemporary summary. In summarizing this material, we will, in effect, be implying a more sophisticated framework than the one at the start. Accordingly, we also hope that we will offer some guidance regarding the research needed to establish what could be thought of as 'contextualized' models of social information processing for the assessment center venue. Finally, we hope to integrate into our treatment some of the findings touched upon earlier in a manner designed to illustrate the potential of this more 'social' perspective. In this regard, the following represents our nominations of 'best bets' for future research.

Social judgement accuracy

The literature confirms that we have a propensity for and some skill in perceiving and judging others. In fact, it has been argued that we are generally pretty good at it. For example, we are quite accurate at judging dominance and warmth, with minimal opportunity to observe and to interact with someone. In fact, some might argue that the traits represented in the so-called Five Factor Model actually reflect the way that we generally perceive and describe people.

Given this, why do we not get higher quality judgements in the assessment center? One possibility is that the qualities used in the general case differ from those typically sought in assessment centers. Given the existing and natural tendencies to perceive and process people in a certain way, it may be that the assessment center dimensions represent some kind of an 'over-lay' task, that frequently comes into conflict with these tendencies. Whereas prior attempts to use other types of dimensions in assessment centers were generally unsuccessful (Joyce, Thayer, & Pond, 1994; Russell & Domm, 1995), it may be worthwhile examining the implications of selecting and using a set of dimensions with special regard to the generalized tendencies of people for trait accuracy.

The role of expectancies

Our expectancies regarding someone strongly affect our perceptions and cognitions. More to the point, we attend to and process expectancy-congruent and expectancy-incongruent information differently. To date, we know little about the effects of assessment center expectancies for levels of trait information that staff think they will encounter as a function of a specific simulation (see Highhouse & Harris, 1993, for an exception) or as a function of a specific individual being observed. As noted earlier, we do know that access to prior information about a candidate counts (Moser, Schuler, & Funke, 1999; Schuler, Moser, & Funke, 1994) but we do not know why and how these affect the judgement process.

The role of cognitive structures

Beliefs about traits and trait structures influence how interpersonal information is assembled and used but we know little of how typical trait structures link to behaviors and performance. For example, Reeder, Prior, and Wojciszke (cited in Fiske, 1993) distinguish among frequency-based traits (talkativeness), morality traits (honesty), capacity traits (ability), and those that implicate attitudes or values (work ethic) and point out the problematic inference from and behavior for each of these types. In light of the wide range of trait types used in operational centers (Howard, 1997), this aspect deserves to be studied. As already described, Tett's (1998, 1999) trait activation model may be useful here.

Similarly, stereotypes and prototypes (exemplars) are other structures that appear to affect attention, expectancies, and cognition in assessment centers. Particularly relevant is the potential role of cognitive structures called scripts (standard narrative structures and plausible causal sequences). In this regard, it is quite likely that behavioral conformance on the part of candidates to script-like structures and especially deviations from scripts plays an important part in the inference process of assessors. Here we know very little. We know even less about the manner in which assessors match their observations to the exemplars (or scripts) that they hold.

Finally, regarding structures for meaning-making, there is a great deal of evidence that social perceivers often use narrative reasoning. Here, in trying to make sense of social information, we construct brief 'stories' for ourselves in order to deal with inconsistent social information or to account for unexpected/atypical behavior on the part of someone. Given the demands of staff to communicate their impressions to one another, it is quite likely that, over time, they too would develop useful prototype narratives to 'explain' anomalies or inconsistencies in the performance of candidates about whom they have already developed an impression (e.g., he/she was tired, was in a high-performing group, etc.). In this regard, we really have very little information about how, when, and why staff make causal attributions.

In sum, we believe that cognitive structures are implicated in such things as attention, person perception, information processing, memory, and rating. Accordingly, they are an important mechanism to understand the conditions for rating quality.

Controlled vs. automatic processes

The literature on human cognition has highlighted that we operate at different awareness levels when it comes to information processing. Sometimes we are rather oblivious as to what stimuli we are attending to and how we are processing them. In other instances, we are most deliberate in our approach to attention, perception, and thinking. This is especially likely to be true in interpersonal relations and in the processing of social information. Generally speaking, automaticity implies cognitive efficiency. Hence, it is often the 'default' or natural approach to a complex and demanding world.

Current thinking has elaborated upon this dichotomy and offers a continuum with several noteworthy stages (Fiske, 1993). For instance, preconscious automaticity occurs without much awareness at all. We are not consciously attending to stimuli or to our processing of the stimulus. Also we do not start or stop such processing. Post-conscious automaticity implies that we are cognizant of the stimulus but not of its effects on us. Research on the dynamics of priming shows that aspects of an ambiguous stimulus (e.g., behavior of a participant in an assessment center) can activate structures in memory. Just which structures (e.g., trait associations) are activated appears to depend on their accessibility. Accessibility, in turn, can be a function of activation frequency or recency of use (or both). There is also evidence that accessibility of structures of information is related to salience. That is, because certain actions or features of an assessee often stand out (e.g., different gender, more talkative, extreme performance), they are likely to trigger structures and thereby affect inferences.

Goal-dependent automaticity is triggered by motivated effort. We are aware of the stimulus, but not necessarily of all of its effects on processing. In this regard, inferring traits appears to occur rather spontaneously (and effortlessly). Further, there is some evidence that we tend to infer dispositions very fast. We have a similar tendency to make categorical judgements regarding other people, based on stereotypes. When we form impressions, we realize that this is occurring, but we are usually not conscious of just what cues them and in what combinations they are having their effects. While this is fairly automatic, it can be controlled. This is often done via assessor training. Despite a tradition for careful training of assessors with the goal of turning them into experts, the record reveals that such traditional training still results in a relatively poor capacity to make valid dimensional judgements. One idea that we have already shared in this regard is that traditional training may have inadvertently confounded the notion of skill at assessing performance with that of assessing traits. One solution would be to design developmental centers differently (e.g., having the exercises elicit trait-revealing behaviors better). However, it may be that training needs to be different as well so that assessors master the distinction between valid performance structures and valid trait structures and the appropriate use for inferring the latter from the former.

Note also that some automatic processes start as controlled processes. This is what happens as a person develops skill and proficiency through practice and experience. But here the speed up is with regard to our processing of information generally and it is not target specific (e.g., as when a candidate seems to match a prototype completely). In an ideal scenario, social judgements and social categorizations are both fast and valid. This is the hallmark of the expert.

At the other end of the continuum is what Fiske (1993) refers to as fully intentional thinking. Here we are aware of our attempts at the deliberate control of attentional processes and are rather self-conscious about the way we go about processing what we see, what we think, and what we do. When thinking intentionally, we might also deliberately invoke the use of certain meta-cognitive strategies (plans, feedback seeking, etc.). In most settings where we are trying to learn a new skill or procedure this is probably what is occurring. Conversely, in instances where we are drawn into automatic processing, but where it may not be advisable, the challenge might be to find ways to enforce more deliberate cognition. Because of forces promoting automaticity (e.g., self-confidence, routineness) there are continuing risks for errors. Thus, in practice, we sometimes see the use of procedural checklists (e.g., as in a pre-flight inspection of an aircraft). Encouraging the use of checklists by assessors as described earlier in this chapter would seem to fall into this notion as well. Apart from its training value and capacity to shape valid cognitive structures, such checklists serve to raise the observation/rating process to a conscious level of awareness.

This more elaborate notion of automaticity can be used to guide assessment center research, particularly regarding the features of center design and administration that might promote or retard the formation and use of appropriate structures and the valid (and speedy) processing of social information. Specifically, we would recommend that research focuses on the motivational forces that might produce or reduce diligent processing.

Motivated cognition

Current research on social perception has highlighted that motivation is important. It is not just the level of motivation that is relevant, it is the goal that is behind it that counts. Moreover, the motivation and the underlying goals seem to have a profound effect on the strategies used in the service of social perception, impression formation, and judgements. In the end it may be that a better understanding of these strategies holds the clues for valid social information processing and trait inference in the assessment center. Fiske (1993) points out that there are two primary motives operating in social/interpersonal settings. One is the desire for accuracy and open-mindedness in the service of making valid assessments of others. The other is tied to seeking closure. This is basically an action orientation. For instance, a decision must be made or a result turned in. Generally, the motive for accuracy would imply the withholding of judgements or the willingness to revise judgements. In contrast, when action must be taken, we tend to adopt a confirmatory strategy.

Our thesis is that, despite policies to the contrary, in operational settings there appear to be forces that promote confirmation. In our analysis, the 'costs' for being wrong may frequently outweigh the 'costs' for being 'indecisive'. The literature on social cognition implicates such factors as complex and inconsistent stimuli, time pressure, an obligation to report (simple stories) to others, emotional arousal on the part of the perceiver, and the existence of well-established cognitive structures (performance prototypes). We suggest that some of these be considered in future research.

Social interaction as the basis for inference

As noted earlier, assessment centers make use of a variety of measurement techniques. However, a distinctive feature is the use of simulations that involve the interaction of groups of individuals. As noted, the observations from such interactions frequently carry the weight of inference.

Social judgement theory and social cognition models recognize that making (trait) inferences from limited observations of social interaction is not easy but they also offer perspectives and models for doing so. An example is the work on attribution theory (e.g., Ross & Nesbitt, 1991). In particular, it should be possible to translate descriptive and predictive studies of how observers make dispositional (trait) attributions into prescriptions for center design. For example, it may well be that a better basis for inference is to be able to observe the same target individual in both the same group and a different group over time.

Social interaction as accountability

We have noted that accountability theory would have some use in characterizing the forces that are operating on assessors relative to both the amount and the direction of their motivation. More must be done to carefully analyze the implications of center design, policy, and practice on such forces. In particular, very little work has been done on the normative structure of assessor teams and on the dynamics of the integration session (see Klimoski, Friedman, & Weldon, 1980, for an exception). Similarly, more must be done to understand the motivational properties of different arrangements of the feedback given. Clearly, facing the prospect of a meeting with a participant personally afterwards to provide feedback should have different consequences for the cognitive and affective process controlling the quality of assessor ratings.

The portrayal of the complexities of judgement and human information processing in a diagram or figure is always difficult. Thus, it is with some trepidute that we offer Figure 3.2. In this figure the rectangles may be considered as antecedents of the individual and collective processes (see the two circles in Figure 3.2) in assessment centers. The ovals are then the dependent variables of interest. We feel that Figure 3.2 is one attempt to represent some of the key factors discussed in this chapter. Moreover, it is our way of 'translating' what we have learned from the social cognition literature into the assessment center context. As such, it should be viewed as a heuristic for guiding future research on the quality of assessor judgements. Using it would

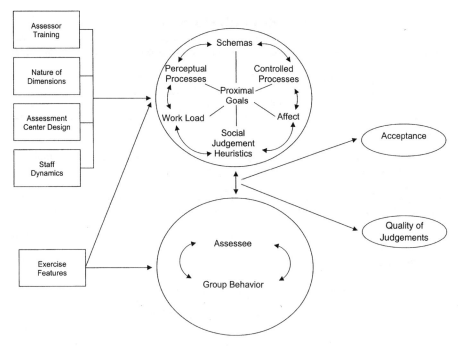

Figure 3.2 Assessment centers and the social judgement process

not only build on contemporary models of social judgement, but would also have the value of better informing practice relative to the most appropriate choice of center design features to be used in the future.

EPILOGUE

The last decade of research on assessment centers has been informative but it could have been even more so if investigators were more often working from a general plan of attack. In our opinion the next decade of research on the assessment center method would be far more informative if it were to be guided by findings and models from the social-cognition literature. It would serve to promote more systematic and programmatic efforts. It would also increase the likelihood that we will get closer to solving the 'puzzle' of assessment centers (Klimoski & Brickner, 1987).

ACKNOWLEDGEMENTS

Filip Lievens is a post-doctoral Research Fellow of the Fund of Scientific Research, Flanders. The authors would like to acknowledge Lisa Donahue for suggestions on an earlier version of this chapter.

REFERENCES

Abelson, R. P. (1981). Psychological status of the script concept. *American Psychologist*, **36**, 715–729.

Adams, K. A., & Osburn, H. G. (1998, April). *Reexamination of the exercise effect in assessment center ratings*. Paper presented at the Annual Conference of the Society for Industrial and Organizational Psychology, Dallas, TX.

Ahmed, Y., Payne, T., & Whiddett, S. (1997). A process for assessment exercise design: A model of best practice. *International Journal of Selection and Assessment*, **5**, 62–68.

Anderson, N., Payne, T., Ferguson, E., & Smith, T. (1994). Assessor decision making, information processing and assessor decision strategies in a British assessment centre. *Personnel Review*, **23**, 52–62.

Andres, J. & Kleinmann, M. (1993). Development of a rotation system for assessors' observations in the assessment center. [in German] *Zeitschrift für Arbeits- und Organisationspsychologie*, **37**, 19–25.

Arthur, W. E. & Tubre, T. C. (1999, May). *The assessment center construct-related validity paradox: A case of construct misspecification?* Paper presented at the Annual Conference of the Society for Industrial and Organizational Psychology, Atlanta, GA.

Ashford, S. (1986). Feedback-seeking in individual adaptation: A resource perspective. *Academy of Management Journal*, **29**, 465–487.

Baisden, H. E. & Robertson, L. (1993, March). *Predicting receptivity to feedback in a developmental assessment center*. Paper presented at the International Congress on the Assessment Center Method, Atlanta, GA.

Ballantyne, I. & and Povah, N. (1995). *Assessment and Development Centres*. Aldershot: Gower.

Baron, H. & Janman, K. (1996). Fairness in the assessment centre. *International Review of Industrial and Organizational Psychology*, **11**, 61–114.

Bartels, L. K. & Doverspike, D. (1997a). Assessing the assessor, the relationship of assessor personality to leniency in assessment center ratings. *Journal of Social Behavior and Personality*, **12**, 179–190.

Bartels, L. K. & Doverspike, D. (1997b). Effects of disaggregation on managerial assessment center validity. *Journal of Business and Psychology*, **12**, 45–53.

Binning, J. F., Adorno, A. J., & Kroeck, K. G. (1997, April). *Validity of behavior checklist and assessor judgmental ratings in an operational assessment center*. Paper presented at the Annual Conference of the Society for Industrial and Organizational Psychology, St. Louis, MO.

Binning, J. F., Adorno, A. J., & Williams, K. B. (1995, May). *Gender and race effects on behavior checklist and judgemental assessment center evaluations*. Paper presented at the Annual Conference of the Society for Industrial and Organizational Psychology, Orlando, FL.

Bobrow, D. G. & Norman, D. A. (1975). Some principles of memory schemata. In D. G. Bobrow & A. G. Collins (Eds), *Representation and Understanding: Studies in Cognitive Science* (pp. 131–150). New York: Academic Press.

Bobrow, W. & Leonards, J. S. (1997). Development and validation of an assessment center during organizational change. *Journal of Social Behavior and Personality*, **12**, 217–236.

Borman, W. C. (1978). Exploring the upper limits of reliability and validity in job performance ratings. *Journal of Applied Psychology*, **63**, 135–144.

Boyle, S., Fullerton, J. & Wood, R. (1995). Do assessment/development centres use optimum evaluation procedures? A survey of practice in UK organizations. *International Journal of Selection and Assessment*, **3**, 132–140.

Brannick, M. T., Michaels, C. E., & Baker, D. P. (1989). Construct validity of in-basket scores. *Journal of Applied Psychology*, 74, 957–963.

Bray, D. W. & Byham, W. C. (1991). Assessment centers and their derivates. *Journal of Continuing Higher Education*, 39, 8–11.

Brostoff, M. & Meyer, H. H. (1984). The effects of coaching on in-basket performance. *Journal of Assessment Center Technology*, 7, 17–21.

Burd, K. A. & Ryan, A. M. (1993, May). *Reactions to developmental feedback in an assessment center.* Paper presented at the Annual Conference of the Society for Industrial and Organizational Psychology, San Francisco, CA.

Campbell, D. T. & Fiske, D. W. (1959). Convergent and discriminant validation by the multitrait-multimethod matrix. *Psychological Bulletin*, 56, 81–105.

Campbell, W. J. (1991). *Comparison of the efficacy of general and specific performance dimensions in an operational assessment center.* Unpublished dissertation, Old Dominion University, VA.

Cantor, N. & Mischel, W. (1977). Traits as prototypes: Effects on recognition memory. *Journal of Personality and Social Psychology*, 35, 38–48.

Carless, S. A. & Allwood, V. E. (1997). Managerial assessment centres: What is being rated? *Australian Psychologist*, 32, 101–105.

Carrick, P. & Williams, R. (1998). Development centres: A review of assumptions. *Human Resource Management Journal*, 9, 77–92.

Chan, D. (1996). Criterion and construct validation of an assessment centre. *Journal of Occupational and Organizational Psychology*, 69, 167–181.

Clapham, M. M. (1998). A comparison of assessor and self dimension ratings in an advanced management assessment center. *Journal of Occupational and Organizational Psychology*, 71, 193–203.

Clapham, M. M. & Fulford, M. D. (1997). Age bias in assessment center ratings, *Journal of Managerial Issues*, 9, 373–387.

Cooper, W. H. (1981). Ubiquitous halo. *Psychological Bulletin*, 90, 218–244.

Crawley, B., Pinder, R., & Herriot, P. (1990). Assessment centre dimensions, personality and aptitudes. *Journal of Occupational Psychology*, 63, 211–216.

Cronbach, L. J. & Meehl, P. E. (1955). Construct validity in psychological tests. *Psychological Bulletin*, 62, 281–302.

Donahue, L. M., Truxillo, D. M., Cornwell, J. M., & Gerrity, M. J. (1997). Assessment center construct validity and behavioral checklists: some additional findings. *Journal of Social Behavior and Personality*, 12, 85–108.

Dulewicz, V. & Fletcher, C. (1982). The relationship between previous experience, intelligence and background characteristics of participants and their performance in an assessment centre. *Journal of Occupational Psychology*, 55, 197–207.

Engelbrecht, A. S. & Fischer, A. H. (1995). The managerial performance implications of a developmental assessment center process. *Human Relations*, 48, 387–404.

Epstein, S. (1979). The stability of behavior: I. On predicting most of the people much of the time. *Journal of Personality and Social Psychology*, 37, 1097–1126.

Fiske, S. T. (1993). Social cognition and social perception. *Annual Review of Psychology*, 44, 155–194.

Fiske, S. T. & Taylor, S. E. (1991). *Social Cognition.* Singapore: McGraw-Hill.

Fleenor, J. W. (1996). Constructs and developmental assessment centers: Further troubling empirical findings. *Journal of Business and Psychology*, 10, 319–333.

Fletcher, C. & Kerslake, C. (1993). Candidate anxiety and assessment centre performance. *Journal of Managerial Psychology*, 8, 19–23.

Fletcher, C., Lovatt C., & Baldry, C. (1997). A study of state, trait, and test anxiety, and their relationship to assessment center performance. *Journal of Social Behavior and Personality*, 12, 205–214.

Freund, T., Kruglanski, A. W., & Shpitzajzen, A. (1985). The freezing and unfreezing of impressional primacy: Effects of the need for structure and the fear of invalidity. *Personality and Social Psychology Bulletin*, 11, 479–487.

Frink, D. & Klimoski, R. J. (1998). Toward a theory of accountability in organizations and human resource management. In G. R. Ferris (Ed.), *Research in Personnel and Human Resource Management*, Vol. 16. Greenwich, CT: JAI press.

Fritzsche, B. A., Brannick, M. T., & Fisher-Hazucha, J. F. (1994, April). *The effects of using behavioral checklists on the predictive and construct validity of assessment center ratings.* Paper presented at the Annual Conference of the Society for Industrial and Organizational Psychology, Nashville, TN.

Furnham, A., Crump, J., & Whelan, J. (1997). Validating the NEO Personality Inventory using assessor's ratings. *Personality and Individual Differences*, 22, 669–675.

Gaugler, B. B. & Rudolph, A. S. (1992). The influence of assessee performance variation on assessors' judgments. *Personnel Psychology*, 45, 77–98.

Gaugler, B. B. & Thornton, G. C. (1989). Number of assessment center dimensions as a determinant of assessor accuracy, *Journal of Applied Psychology*, 74, 611–618.

Gill, R. W. T. (1982). A trainability concept for management potential and an empirical study of its relationship with intelligence for two managerial skills. *Journal of Occupational Psychology*, 52, 185–197.

Goffin, R. D., Rothstein, M. G., & Johnston, N. G. (1996). Personality testing and the assessment center: Incremental validity for managerial selection. *Journal of Applied Psychology*, 81, 746–756.

Goldstein, H. W. Yusko, K. P., Braverman, E. P., Smith, D. B., & Chung, B. (1998). The role of cognitive ability in the subgroup differences and incremental validity of assessment center exercises. *Personnel Psychology*, 51, 357–374.

Guldin, A. & Schuler, H. (1997). Consistency and specificity of assessment center criteria: A new approach for construct validation of assessment centers. [in German] *Diagnostica*, 73, 230–254.

Halpert, J. A., Wilson, M. L., & Hickman, J. L. (1993). Pregnancy as a source of bias in performance appraisals. *Journal of Organizational Behavior*, 14, 649–663.

Harris, M. M., Becker, A. S., & Smith, D. E. (1993). Does the assessment center scoring method affect the cross-situational consistency of ratings?, *Journal of Applied Psychology*, 78, 675–678.

Harris, M. M., Paese, M., & Greising, L. (1999, August). *Participant reactions to feedback from a developmental assessment center: An organizational justice theory approach.* Paper presented at the Academy of Management Meeting, Chicago, IL.

Hauenstein, P. C. (1994, April). *A key behavior approach for improving the utility of developmental assessment centers.* Paper presented at the Annual Conference of the Society for Industrial and Organizational Psychology, Nashville, TN.

Henderson, F., Anderson, N., & Smith, S. (1995). Future competency profiling: Validating and redesigning the ICL graduate assessment centre. *Personnel Review*, 24, 19–32.

Hennessy, J., Mabey, B., & Warr, P. (1998). Assessment centre observation procedures: An experimental comparison of traditional, checklist and coding methods. *International Journal of Selection and Assessment*, 6, 222–231.

Highhouse, S. & Harris, M. M. (1993). The measurement of assessment center, situations: Bem's template matching technique for examining exercise similarity. *Journal of Applied Social Psychology*, 23, 140–155.

Hoffman, C. C. & Thornton, G. C. III (1997). Examining selection utility where competing predictors differ in adverse impact. *Personnel Psychology*, 50, 455–470.

Howard, A. (1997). A reassessment of assessment centers, challenges for the 21st century. *Journal of Social Behavior and Personality*, 12, 13–52.

Iles, P. A. & Mabey, C. (1993). Managerial career development techniques: Effectiveness, acceptability and availability. *British Journal of Management*, 4, 103–118.

Jansen, P. G. W. & de Jongh, F. (1997). *Assessment Centers: a Practical Handbook.* Chicester: Wiley.

Jones, R. G. (1992). Construct validation of assessment center final dimension ratings: Definition and measurement issues. *Human Resource Management Review*, 2, 195–220.

Jones, R. G. (1997). A person perception explanation for validation evidence from assessment centers, *Journal of Social Behavior and Personality*, 12, 169–178.

Jones, R. G. & Whitmore, M. D. (1995). Evaluating developmental assessment centers as interventions. *Personnel Psychology*, 48, 377–388.

Joyce, L. W., Thayer, P. W., & Pond, S. B. (1994). Managerial functions: An alternative to traditional assessment center dimensions? *Personnel Psychology*, 47, 109–121.

Kauffman, J. R., Jex, S. M., Love, K. G., & Libkuman, T. M. (1993). The construct validity of assessment centre performance dimensions. *International Journal of Selection and Assessment*, 1, 213–223.

Kleinmann, M. (1993). Are rating dimensions in assessment centers transparent for participants? Consequences for criterion and construct validity. *Journal of Applied Psychology*, 78, 988–993.

Kleinmann, M. (1997). Transparency of the required dimensions: A moderator of assessment centers' construct and criterion validity. [In German] *Zeitschrift für Arbeits- und Organisationspsychologie*, 41, 171–181.

Kleinmann, M. & Köller, O. (1997). Construct validity of assessment centers: Appropriate use of confirmatory factor analysis and suitable construction principles. *Journal of Social Behavior and Personality*, 12, 65–84.

Kleinmann, M., Exler, C., Kuptsch, C., & Köller, O. (1995). Independence and observability of dimensions as moderators of construct validity in the assessment center. [In German] *Zeitschrift für Arbeits- und Organisationspsychologie*, 39, 22–28.

Kleinmann, M., Kuptsch, C., & Köller, O. (1996). Transparency: A necessary requirement for the construct validity of assessment centres. *Applied Psychology: An international Review*, 45, 67–84.

Kleinmann, M., Andres, J., Fedtke, C., Godbersen, F., & Köller, O. (1994). The influence of different rating procedures on the construct validity of assessment center methods. [In German] *Zeitschrift für Experimentelle und Angewandte Psychologie*, 41, 184–210.

Klimoski, R. J. & Brickner, M. (1987). Why do assessment centers work? The puzzle of assessment center validity. *Personnel Psychology*, 40, 243–260.

Klimoski, R. J., Friedman, B. A., & Weldon, E. (1980). Leader influence in the assessment of performance. *Personnel Psychology*, 33, 389–401.

Kluger, A. N. & Rothstein, H. R. (1993). The influence of selection test type on applicant reactions to employment testing. *Journal of Business and Psychology*, 8, 3–25.

Kolk, N. J., Born, M., Bleichrodt, N., & Flier, H., van der (1998, August). *A triarchic approach to assessment center dimensions: Empirical evidence for the Feeling-Thinking-Power model for AC dimensions.* Paper presented at the International Congress of Applied Psychology, San Francisco, CA.

Kravitz, D. A., Stinson, V., & Chavez, T. L. (1996). Evaluations of tests used for making selection and promotion decisions. *International Journal of Selection and Assessment*, 4, 24–34.

Kriek, H. J., Hurst, D. N., & Charoux, J. A. E. (1994). The assessment centre: Testing the fairness hypotheses. *Journal of Industrial Psychology*, 20, 21–25.

Kudisch, J. D. & Ladd, R. T. (1997, April). *Factors related to participants' acceptance of developmental assessment center feedback.* Paper presented at the Annual Conference of the Society for Industrial and Organizational Psychology, St. Louis, MO.

Kudisch, J. D., Ladd, R. T., & Dobbins, G. H. (1997). New evidence on the construct validity of diagnostic assessment centers: The findings may not be so troubling after all. *Journal of Social Behavior and Personality*, 12, 129–144.

Kuptsch, C., Kleinmann, M., & Kölller, O. (1998). The chameleon effect in assessment centers: The influence of cross-situational behavioral consistency on the convergent validity of assessment centers. *Journal of Social Behavior and Personality*, **13**, 102–116.

Kurecka, P. M., Austin, J. M., Johnson, W., & Mendoza, J. L. (1982). Full and errant coaching effects on assigned role leaderless group discussion performance. *Personnel Psychology*, **35**, 805–812.

Lance, C. E., Newbolt, W. H., Gatewood, R. D., & Smith, D. E. (1995, May). *Assessment center exercise factors represent cross-situational specificity, not method bias.* Paper presented at the Annual Conference of the Society for Industrial and Organizational Psychology, Orlando, FL.

Landy, F. J. & Farr, J. L. (1980). Performance rating. *Psychological Bulletin*, **87**, 72–107.

Lebreton, J. M., Binning, J. F., & Hesson-McInnis, M. S. (1998, August). *The effects of measurement structure on the validity of assessment center dimensions: The clinical-statistical debate revisited.* Paper presented at the Annual Meeting of the Academy of Management, San Diego, CA.

Lebreton, J. M., Gniatczyk, L. A., & Migetz, D. Z. (1999, May). *The relationship between behavior checklist ratings and judgmental ratings in an operational assessment center: An application of structural equation modeling.* Paper presented at the Annual Conference of the Society for Industrial and Organizational Psychology, Atlanta, GA.

Lerner, J. S. & Tetlock, T. E. (1998). Accounting for the effects of accountability. *Psychological Bulletin*, **125**, 255–275.

Lichtenstein, M. & Srull, T. K. (1987). Processing objectives as a determinant of the relationship between recall and judgement. *Journal of Experimental Social Psychology*, **23**, 93–118.

Lievens, F. (1998). Factors which improve the construct validity of assessment centers: A review. *International Journal of Selection and Assessment*, **6**, 141–152.

Lievens, F. (1999, May). *The effects of type of assessor training on the construct validity and accuracy of assessment center ratings.* Paper presented at the European Congress of Work and Organizational Psychology, Espoo- Helsinki, Finland.

Lievens, F. (in press). 'Assessors and use of assessment center dimensions: A fresh look at a troubling issue'. *Journal of Organizational Behavior.*

Lievens, F. & Goemaere, H. (1999). A different look at assessment centers: Views of assessment center users. *International Journal of Selection and Assessment*, **7**, 215–219.

Lievens, F. & and Van Keer, E. (1999, May). *Modeling method effects in assessment centers: An application of the correlated uniqueness approach.* Paper presented at the Annual Conference of the Society for Industrial and Organizational Psychology, Atlanta, GA.

Lord, R. G., & Maher, K. J. (1990). Alternative information-processing models and their implications for theory, research, and practice. *Academy of Management Review*, **15**, 9–28.

Lowry, P. E. (1993). The assessment center: An examination of the effects of assessor characteristics on assessor scores. *Public Personnel Management*, **22**, 487–501.

Lowry, P. E. (1996). A survey of the assessment center process in the public sector. *Public Personnel Management*, **25**, 307–321.

Macan, T. H., Avedon, M. J., Paese, M., & Smith, D. E. (1994). The effects of applicants' reactions to cognitive ability tests and an assessment center. *Personnel Psychology*, **47**, 715–738.

Maher, P. T. (1990, March). *How many dimensions are enough?* Paper presented at the International Congress on the Assessment Center Method, Orange, CA.

Maher, P. T. (1995, May). *An analysis of the impact of the length of assessor training on assessor competency.* Paper presented at the International Congress on the Assessment Center Method, Kansas City.

Marsh, H. W. (1989). Confirmatory factor analyses of multitrait–multimethod data: Many problems and a few solutions. *Applied Psychological Measurement*, **13**, 335–361.

Mayes, B. T., Belloli, C. A., Riggio, R. E., & Aguirre, M. (1997). Assessment centers for course evaluations: A demonstration. *Journal of Social Behavior and Personality*, **12**, 303–320.

McCredie, H. & Shackleton, V. (1994). The development and interim validation of a dimensions-based senior management assessment centre. *Human Resource Management Journal*, **5**, 91–101.

Mero, N. P. and Motowidlo, S. J. (1995). Effects of rater accountability on the accuracy and the favorability of performance ratings. *Journal of Applied Psychology*, **80**, 517–524.

Mitchell, D. R. D., & Maurer, T. J. (1998, August). *Assessment center feedback in relation to subsequent human resource development activity.* Paper presented at the Annual Meeting of the Academy of Management, San Diego, CA.

Morrow, P. C., McElroy, J. C, Stamper, B. G., & Wilson, M. A. (1990). The effects of physical attractiveness and other demographic characteristics on promotion decisions. *Journal of Management*, **16**, 723–736.

Moser, K., Diemand, A., & Schuler, H. (1996). Inconsistency and social skills as two components of self-monitoring. [In German] *Diagnostica*, **42**, 268–283.

Moser, K., Schuler, H., & Funke, U. (1999). The moderating effect of raters' opportunities to observe ratees' job performance on the validity of an assessment centre. *International Journal of Selection and Assessment*, **7**, 133–141.

Moses, J. L. & Ritchie, R. J. (1976). Supervisory relationships training: A behavioral evaluation of a behavior modeling program. *Personnel Psychology*, **29**, 337–343.

Murphy, K. R. & Cleveland, J. N. (1995). *Understanding Performance Appraisal*, Thousand Oaks, CA: Sage.

Murphy, K. R., Jako, R. A., & Anhalt, R. L. (1993). The nature and consequences of halo error: A critical analysis. *Journal of Applied Psychology*, **78**, 218–225.

Neidig, R. D., & Neidig, P. J. (1984). Multiple assessment center exercises and job relatedness. *Journal of Applied Psychology*, **69**, 182–186.

Neubauer, R. (1990). Women in the career assessment center—a victory? [In German] *Zeitschrift für Arbeits- und Organisationspsychologie*, **34**, 29–36.

Neuberg, S. L. (1989). The goal of forming accurate impressions during social interactions: Attenuating the impact of negative expectancies. *Journal of Personality and Social Psychology*, **56**, 374–386.

Newell, S. & Shackleton, V. (1994). Guest Editorial: International differences in selection methods. *International Journal of Selection and Assessment*, **2**, 71–73.

Nowack, K. M., (1997). Congruence between self-other ratings and assessment center performance., *Journal of Social Behavior and Personality*, **12**, 145–166.

Petty, M. M. (1974). A multivariate analysis of the effects of experience and training upon performance in a leaderless group discussion. *Personnel Psychology*, **27**, 271–282.

Pynes, J., & Bernardin, H. J. (1992). Mechanical vs consensus-derived assessment center ratings: A comparison of job performance validities. *Public Personnel Management*, **21**, 17–28.

Ramos, R. A. (1992). Testing and assessment of Hispanics for occupational and management positions: A developmental needs analysis. In K. F. Geisinger (Ed.), *Psychological Testing of Hispanics* (pp. 173–194). Washington, DC: American Psychological Association.

Reilly, R. R., Henry, S., & Smither, J. W. (1990). An examination of the effects of using behavior checklists on the construct validity of assessment center dimensions. *Personnel Psychology*, **43**, 71–84.

Rolland, J. P. (1999). Construct validity of in-basket dimensions. *European Review of Applied Psychology*, **49**, 251–259.

Ross L., & Nesbitt, R. F. (1991). *The Person and the Situation. Perspectives of Social Psychology.* New York: McGraw Hill.

Rotenberry, P. F., Barrett, G. V., & Doverspike, D. (1999, May). *Determination of systematic bias for an objectively scored in-basket assessment.* Paper presented at the Annual Conference of the Society for Industrial and Organizational Psychology, Atlanta, GA.

Rumelhart, D. E. & Ortony, A. (1977). The representation of knowledge in memory. In R. C. Anderson, R. J. Spiro, and W. E. Montague (Eds), *Schooling and the Acquisition of Knowledge* (pp. 99–136). Hillsdale, NJ: Erlbaum.

Russell, C. J. & Domm, D. R. (1995). Two field tests of an explanation of assessment centre validity. *Journal of Occupational and Organizational Psychology,* **68**, 25–47.

Ryan, A. M., Daum, D., Bauman, T., Grisez, M., Mattimore, K., Nalodka, T., & McCormick, S. (1995). Direct, indirect, and controlled observation and rating accuracy. *Journal of Applied Psychology,* **80**, 664–670.

Rynes, S. L. & Connerly, M. L. (1993). Applicant reactions to alternative selection procedures. *Journal of Business and Psychology,* 7, 261–278.

Sackett, P. R. (1998). Performance assessment in education and professional certification: Lessons for personnel selection?. In M. D. Hakel (Ed.), *Beyond Multiple Choice* (pp. 113–129). Mahwah, NJ: Erlbaum.

Sackett, P. R. & Dreher, G. F. (1982). Constructs and assessment center dimensions: Some troubling empirical findings. *Journal of Applied Psychology,* **67**, 401–410.

Sagie, A. & Magnezy, R. (1997). Assessor type, number of distinguishable dimension categories' and assessment centre construct validity. *Journal of Occupational and Organizational Psychology,* **70**, 103-108.

Schleicher, D. J., Day, D. V., Mayes, B. T., & Riggio, R. E. (1999, May). *A new frame for frame-of-reference training: Enhancing the construct validity of assessment centers.* Paper presented at the Annual Conference of the Society for Industrial and Organizational Psychology, Atlanta, GA.

Schmidt, F. L. & Hunter J. E. (1998). The validity and utility of selection methods in personnel psychology: Practical and theoretical implications of 85 years of research findings. *Psychological Bulletin,* **124**, 262–274.

Schmitt, N. (1993). Group composition, gender, and race effects on assessment center ratings. In H. Schuler, J. L. Farr, & M. Smith (Eds.), *Personnel Selection and Assessment: Individual and Organizational Perspectives* (pp. 315–332). Hillsdale, NJ: Erlbaum.

Schneider, J. R. & Schmitt, N. (1992). An exercise design approach to understanding assessment center dimension and exercise constructs. *Journal of Applied Psychology,* 77, 32–41.

Scholz, G. & Schuler, H. (1993). The nomological network of the assessment center: A meta-analysis. [In German] *Zeitschrift für Arbeits- und Organisationspsychologie,* **37**, 73–85.

Schuler, H. Moser, K, & Funke, U. (1994, August). *The moderating effect of rater-ratee acquaintance on the validity of an assessment center.* Paper presented at the International Congress of Applied Psychology, Madrid, Spain.

Shechtman, Z. (1998). Agreement between lay participants and professional assessors: Support of a group assessment procedure for selection purposes. *Journal of Personnel Evaluation in Education,* **12**, 5–17.

Shore, T. H. (1992). Subtle gender bias in the assessment of managerial potential. *Sex Roles,* 27, 499–515.

Shore, T. H., Shore, L. M., & Thornton, G. C. III (1992). Construct validity of self- and peer evaluations of performance dimensions in an assessment center. *Journal of Applied Psychology,* 77, 42–54.

Shore, T. H., Taschian, A., & Adams, J. S. (1997). The role of gender in a developmental assessment center. *Journal of Social Behavior and Personality,* **12**, 191–203.

Shore, L. M., Tetrick, L. E., & Shore, T. H. (1998). A comparison of self-, peer, and assessor evaluations of managerial potential. *Journal of Social Behavior and Personality*, **13**, 85–101.

Shore, T. H., Thornton, G.C. III, & Shore, L.M. (1990). Construct validity of two categories of assessment center ratings. *Personnel Psychology*, **43**, 101–116.

Sichler, R. (1991). Experiences and activities with an assessment center procedure: An empirical contribution to the 'social validity' of test situations. [In German] *Zeitschrift für Arbeits- und Organisationspsychologie*, **33**, 139–145.

Silverman, W. H., Dalessio, A., Woods, S. B., & Johnson, R. L. (1986). Influence of assessment center methods on assessors' ratings. *Personnel Psychology*, **39**, 565–578.

Smither, J. W., Reilly, R. R., Millsap, R. E., Pearlman, K, & Stoffey, R. W. (1993). Applicant reactions to selection procedures. *Personnel Psychology*, **46**, 49–78.

Smith-Jentsch, K. A. (1996, April). *Should rating dimensions in situational exercises be made transparent for participants? Empirical tests of the impact on convergent and predictive validity.* Paper presented at the Annual Conference of the Society for Industrial and Organizational Psychology, San Diego, CA.

Spychalski, A. C., Quinones, M. A., Gaugler, B. B., & Pohley, K. A. (1997). A survey of assessment center practices in organizations in the United States. *Personnel Psychology*, **50**, 71–90.

Srull, T. K. & Wyer, R. S. (1980). Category accessibility and social perception: Some implications for the study of person memory and interpersonal judgment. *Journal of Personality and Social Psychology*, **38**, 841–856.

Srull, T. K. & Wyer, R. S. (1989). Person memory and judgment. *Psychological Review*, **96**, 58–83.

Staufenbiel, T. & Kleinmann M. (1999, May). *Does P-O fit influence the judgments in assessment centers?* Paper presented at the European Congress of Work and Organizational Psychology, Espoo- Helsinki, Finland.

Steiner, D. D. & Gilliland, S. W. (1996). Fairness reactions to personnel selection techniques in France and the United States. *Journal of Applied Psychology*, **81**, 134–147.

Tan, M. (1996). *The effects of role-player standardization on the construct validity of dimensions in assessment exercises.* [in Dutch] Unpublished doctoral dissertation, University of Amsterdam.

Task Force on Assessment Center Guidelines (1989). Guidelines and ethical considerations for assessment center operations. *Public Personnel Management*, **18**, 457–470.

Tetlock, P. E. (1983). Accountability and complexity of thought. *Journal of Personality and Social Psychology*, **45**, 74–83.

Tett, R. P. (1998, April). *Traits, situations. and managerial behavior: Test of a trait activation hypothesis.* Paper presented at the Annual Conference of the Society for Industrial and Organizational Psychology, Dallas, TX.

Tett, R. P. (1999, May). *Assessment center-validity: New perspectives on an old problem.* Paper presented at the Annual Conference of the Society for Industrial and Organizational Psychology, Atlanta, GA.

Thornton, G. C. III (1992). *Assessment centers in Human Resource Management.* Reading, MA: Addison-Wesley.

Thornton, G. C. III, Larsh, S. Layer, S., & Kaman, V. (1999, May). *Reactions to attribute-based feedback and exercise-based feedback in developmental assessment centers.* Paper presented at the Annual Conference of the Society for Industrial and Organizational Psychology, Atlanta, GA.

Thornton, G. C. III, Tziner, A., Dahan, M., Clevenger, J. P., & Meir, E. (1997). Construct validity of assessment center judgments. *Journal of Social Behavior and Personality*, **12**, 109–128.

Van Dam, K., Altink, W. M. M., & Kok, B. (1992). Assessment center practice: A summary of problems encountered. [In Dutch] *De Psycholoog*, 7, 509–514.

Van der Velde, E. G., Born, M. P., & Hofkes, K. (1994). Construct validity of an assessment center using confirmatory factor analysis. [In Dutch] *Gedrag en Organisatie*, 7, 18–26.

Walsh, J. P., Weinberg, R. M., & Fairfield, M. L. (1987). The effects of gender on assessment centre evaluations. *Journal of Occupational Psychology*, **60**, 305–309.

Weijerman, E. A. P., & Born, M. P. (1995). The relationship between gender and assessment center scores. [In Dutch] *Gedrag en Organisatie*, **8**, 284–292.

Woodruffe, C. (1993). *Assessment Centres: Identifying and Developing Competences*. London: Gower.

Zedeck, S. (1986). A process analysis of the assessment center method. *Research in Organizational Behavior*, **8**, 259–296.

Chapter 4

MULTI-SOURCE FEEDBACK SYSTEMS: A RESEARCH PERSPECTIVE

Clive Fletcher and Caroline Baldry
The University of London

INTRODUCTION

Multi-source, multi-rater (MSMR) assessment systems, sometimes referred to as 360 degree feedback systems, generally entail a process whereby a target manager is rated on various behavioural dimensions or competencies by one or more bosses, peers, subordinates and—sometimes—customers. The dimensions chosen usually focus on interpersonal attributes, and in particular on leadership and team working. The ratings are usually aggregated and compared against the target's self-rating in a written report; the process may be paper-based or completed via specifically designed software packages. In a few organisations, the target manager may meet those who have contributed to the feedback to assist in formulating a personal development plan; sessions of this kind are usually facilitated by an external consultant or by a representative of the HR department. Some of these feedback systems do not include ratings from all these groups; for example, they may simply use subordinates' ratings (termed upward feedback) as a supplement to the conventional process of downward appraisal by the boss. They also tend to differ in terms of whether they are oriented primarily towards the target manager's development, or whether they are an integral part of the on-going appraisal of individual performance. As we will see, this difference may have considerable implications in terms of the structure and likely outcomes of MS system use. At the time of writing, MS systems are quite often related to appraisal and rewards in the USA: London and Smither (1995) report that 50% of the consultancy companies and MSMR system providers they contacted said that at least some of their clients used the systems for administrative purposes (i.e. appraisal, performance related pay, etc.). This is less often the case in the UK, where the emphasis remains on developmental use, but a number of companies there are also moving in the direction of applying it in the context of annual appraisal and performance-related pay (Handy, Devine & Heath, 1996).

The history of MSMR feedback systems is still a relatively short one, especially outside North America. As Redman and Mathews (1997) point out, surveys on both sides of the Atlantic in the mid-1980s showed about 10% of US companies using these techniques compared to none at all in the UK (though there were isolated accounts of them there, e.g. Stinson & Stokes, 1980). By the early 1990s, a few companies in the UK had adopted upward feedback and one or two—mainly subsidiaries of US multi-nationals—were operating full MSMR processes (Redman & Snape, 1992). Indeed, research relating to feedback systems in organisations was addressed in this series some eight years ago by Jen Algera (1990). However, preceding the widespread use of MSMR systems now seen, the theory and research available related to unidimensional performance criteria generally received informally through the course of day-to-day work. He concluded that future research should focus upon (1) the influence of multidimensional feedback on goal setting for complex tasks; and (2) the effects of feedback on group behaviour. As will become apparent in this chapter, Algera's suggestions bear relevance to the process of MSMR feedback.

360 degree feedback systems have been spread quickly across a whole range of public and private sector organisations in the UK, though there is less evidence of their becoming equally popular in the rest of Europe just yet (Fletcher, 1997b). Mostly, the applications in the UK have been in the context of development; they take place as part of career review workshops, leadership training programmes, or as stand-alone development exercises. Though it got off to an earlier start in the US, there are indications of its wider use there also (Romano, 1994). Antonioni (1996) states that 'without question, 360 degree appraisals are taking hold in American business', and other accounts suggest it is being taken on board in public service organisations there too (Pollack & Pollack, 1996).

There is a growing literature offering advice on how to develop, structure and run 360 degree feedback systems (e.g. Ward, 1997; Clifford & Bennet, 1997), though little of this guidance is empirically based. Indeed, the very speed with which this HR practice has been taken up seems to have left research effort trailing in its wake. Such research base as there is on MSMR systems is at present quite diverse. There are relatively few studies that have been based on full MSMR processes operating in organisations, though the number is steadily increasing. There are, however, many more that have examined separately aspects of one or more elements that can be found in such systems—self-assessment, peer assessment and upward feedback in particular. But it is very likely that this topic will attract more research in the near future. This is partly because of the greater use of these methods, and partly because they represent such good opportunities to examine in a field setting a number of phenomena of considerable interest to work psychologists. These include the psychometric properties of ratings made by different groups and the factors that influence those ratings, the impact of this kind of feedback on behaviour, the extent of self–other congruence in assessment, and so on.

The present chapter will review this emerging area of research from a number of perspectives. It will examine the findings against the broader backdrop of research on performance appraisal and on assessment in general, and look at how conceptualisation of work in this field fits with the models of feedback and its effects that already exist in the literature. Although there are a number of unique features of the 360 degree feedback situation, many of the concerns found in discussions of conventional performance appraisal are still highly relevant; there is some danger of these being overlooked in the enthusiasm with which this new phenomenon is being applied, sold and researched. The chapter will also seek to draw out some of the practical implications of the studies done to date for the use of 360 degree feedback in organisations. First, though, it will examine the three main themes that can be found in the literature on or relating to MSMR systems:

- The psychometric properties of the ratings made by different sources (i.e. rater groups) and the extent to which rater and ratee attributes influence these
- The influence of system methodology and organisational factors on process and outcomes
- The influence of MSMR feedback on attitudes and indicators of performance.

Subsequently, the chapter goes on to consider in depth a particular issue that arises from research in this field, namely the way self-ratings relate to ratings made by others; specifically, the causes and consequences of self-awareness (defined here in terms of congruence between individuals' self-ratings and the ratings made of them by others) will be explored. The theoretical frameworks relevant to understanding and integrating research on 360 degree feedback are then described and discussed. Finally, the implications of the literature reviewed both for future research and for practical use of MSMR processes will be considered.

PSYCHOMETRIC PROPERTIES OF RATINGS MADE BY DIFFERENT RATER GROUPS

Self-ratings

Research into self-assessment dominates much of the research literature concerned with the viability of using alternative ratings sources for assessment of managerial performance (Harris & Schaubroeck, 1988). This research has indicated that there are a number of issues relating to the psychometric properties of self-ratings that are of concern. However, despite being more susceptible to certain forms of bias than other rating sources, they are viewed by many as an essential element in a developmental feedback programme. By asking individuals to formally evaluate aspects of their behaviour at work, rather than simply providing others' feedback to them, it has been suggested (Riggio & Cole, 1992) that individuals will be more accepting of others' criticisms of aspects of their behaviour. Riggio and Cole also outline a number of other benefits to including self-assessment in a feedback programme. They suggest that allowing employees to participate in their own appraisal may make them more aware of, and committed to, performance goals, and point out that self-assessments provide a unique perspective—the uniqueness being the situational constraints under which the job must be performed. Ashford (1989) supports the use of self-assessments, noting from previous research how self-assessments have been related to efficacy expectations and aspiration level, persistence, effort and subsequent performance (Bandura, 1982; Janoff-Bulman & Brickman, 1981; Brockner, 1979).

Reliability

Definable as the extent to which a measure is free from error, reliability can be considered in terms of temporal stability and internal consistency. Self-assessment susceptibility to error due to rating idiosyncrasies such as leniency is well documented. Nilsen and Campbell (1993) demonstrated that the magnitude of error in an individual's self-assessment remains constant both over time and behavioural dimensions and concluded that self-assessments, despite being prone to leniency, can still be reliable measures of behaviour.

Convergent validity

Self-ratings are generally found to be moderately, but significantly related to supervisor, peer and subordinate ratings (Pollack & Pollack, 1996). In a meta-analysis of research conducted over the previous 30 years, Harris and Schaubroeck (1988) found a moderate correlation between self- and supervisor ratings ($\rho = 0.35$) and self- and peer ratings ($\rho = 0.36$), across different rating formats and rating scales. (Harris and Schaubroeck (1988) used the Hunter, Schmidt and Jackson (1982) meta-analytic procedure to correct for unreliability and range restriction with sporadic information. See Hunter, Schmidt and Jackson (1982) for further reading.) Similarly, in a study of profile agreement between self- and subordinate ratings from an upward feedback programme, London and Wohlers (1991) found a moderate but significant correlation ($r = 0.24$). In an earlier study Wohlers and London (1989) had looked at factors influencing convergence of ratings from different sources, within the context of an assessment centre. They found a significant relationship between the average correlation for the self-assessment rating to averaged co-worker ratings ($r = 0.45$). However, the average agreement between self-rating to any single co-worker rating ($r = 0.25$) was not significant. They concluded from this that the quality of assessment produced by self-evaluations is reasonable, particularly when one considers the lack of agreement between co-workers and consequent discrepancies in feedback that they receive from others.

Predictive validity

Shrauger and Osberg (1981) found that self-assessments were as good as, if not better than a number of other predictors—including test scores, grades and external rater evaluations—in predicting academic performance, vocational choice and job performance. However, much of the early research assessing the efficacy of self-assessments for predicting subsequent performance produced inconsistent or disappointing results; Mabe and West (1982) report predictive validity for self-assessments as averaging 0.29 across a range of performance measures. Ashford (1989) suggests that this variability is a direct result of the differing methodologies employed to investigate the predictive validity of self-assessments. In a review of this literature, she notes how studies vary in their sample populations (from students to assemblers and managers), their motivation, their methodological sophistication and their definition of accuracy.

More recently, in a study of sales managers carried out in a large leisure organisation, Lane and Herriott (1990) found that self-ratings did predict future performance and that predictive power increased over time; validity coefficients after six months compared favourably with those over three months. They concluded that self-assessment has high predictive power, and even with hard performance data, validities can be much higher than the average coefficient reported by Mabe and West (1982).

Bias

Self-appraisal suffers from only one particular source of bias, in comparison to ratings from other sources—that of leniency; research in the 1980s into self-assessments was almost exclusively centred around investigation of this form of bias, focusing on the magnitude of leniency in comparison to ratings from other sources, and what individual and situational factors were correlated to this. From a meta-analysis of this research, Harris and Schaubroeck (1988) concluded that self-ratings averaged over half a standard deviation higher than supervisory ratings, and approximately a quarter of a standard deviation higher than peer ratings. Nilsen and Campbell (1993) estimate that self-assessments are on average 0.3 standard deviations higher than ratings provided by others. However, London and Wohlers (1991) found in a study of an upward feedback programme that, overall, that there was a significant level of agreement between self-ratings and ratings by subordinates. Lane and Herriott (1990) demonstrated that leniency bias in self-assessments was constant, both over time and behaviours. So, although a self-assessment may not be a true representation of the individual's behavioural competencies, this inaccuracy seems to remain constant for all self-assessments the individual carries out, over a range of rating formats. Reliability is measured in terms of temporal stability and internal consistency; as leniency error has been demonstrated to have both temporal stability and internal consistency, reliability and validity of self-assessments are not necessarily reduced.

Subordinate Ratings

Research into the psychometric properties of appraisals by subordinates dates back to the early seventies. Systems were introduced at this time in response to dissatisfaction with traditional top-down assessments, and because of the change in organisational structure—from hierarchical to flatter structures, with supervisors having a wider span of control over more autonomous work units. The change in organisational structure legitimised the involvement of subordinates in a number of ways. Subordinates observe, and are affected by, managerial behaviours and decisions in a way that is not always evident to co-workers at a different organisational level—especially leadership behaviours (London and Beatty, 1993). Subordinates nowadays typically have more contact with the manager than his or her supervisor, giving them the opportunity to not only observe different behaviours, but also to observe more of the manager's behaviour (Pollack & Pollack, 1996). Another reason which justifies subordinates' assessment of a manager is that in most organisations, subordinates generally outnumber peers and the superiors an individual works to, so they constitute the largest rating group. Perhaps as a result of these factors, studies looking at managers' acceptance of upward feedback have generally been favourable (Pollack & Pollack, 1996).

Reliability

Mount (1984) determined the reliability of individual subordinate ratings by looking at intrarater agreement (i.e. the level of correlation between subordinate ratings of a particular manager). The values ranged from 0.15–0.18, suggesting that the reliability of a single subordinate rating is actually quite low. However, when the responses are averaged, research has generally found them to be of acceptable reliability. For example, in a longitudinal study of an upward feedback programme, McEvoy and Beatty (1989) found that averaged subordinate ratings were significantly related at all four time points in a seven-year period. Further, London and Wohlers (1991) found that reliability of subordinate ratings was significantly and positively related to the number of subordinates that provided ratings.

Convergent validity

The validity of subordinate ratings has generally been established by researchers correlating the averaged subordinate rating to others' ratings—typically supervisors' evaluations of the manager. Although one would not expect a high degree of correlation (the role of the manager invariably dictates different behaviours towards subordinates than to his/her supervisor) there should be a certain degree of overlap. As cited in Pollack and Pollack (1996) research has found a moderate level of correlation between 'Boss' and subordinates' ratings ($r = 0.44$). Across these studies, subordinate ratings are in greater agreement with supervisor ratings than self-ratings of performance; superior and self-ratings show least agreement.

Rubin (1995) investigated the level of agreement found between subordinates and 'Boss' evaluations; although the overall evaluation of a manager by their subordinates and superiors is related, he concluded that it is arrived at by different routes. Behaviours that subordinates saw as important and critical to managerial effectiveness were not valued to the same extent by superiors. This had been found in earlier research (Mount, 1984) and was thought at that time to relate to subordinates' opportunity to observe certain behaviours. More recent work by Salam, Cox and Sims (1997) suggests that it may be in fact due to bases of power inherent in an individual's role within the organisation, with raters placing more importance on aspects of the manager's behaviour that affects them (and their own level of work performance) directly. The upshot of all this research highlights the importance of receiving ratings from various sources within the organisation.

Predictive validity

Very few longitudinal studies have been carried out which examine the predictive validity of subordinate ratings. Returning again to the study by McEvoy and Beatty (1989), as well as establishing the reliability of subordinate ratings, they also investigated their predictive validity. Comparing subordinate ratings to assessment centre ratings for the prediction of promotion of the manager, they found the initial subordinate ratings were significantly and positively related to promotion seven years later, although the assessment centre had greater predictive validity. They found that the initial subordinate rating also predicted subsequent subordinate ratings (despite changes in the individual subordinates who provided ratings), and was a better intermediate predictor of superiors' ratings than the assessment centre rating.

Finally, they also found that subordinates' ratings predicted supervisory ratings at all time points within a seven-year period. They concluded from this that subordinate ratings do have acceptable predictive validity.

Bias

Research has also looked at possible forms of bias. It has been suggested that subordinates may lack the ability or information needed to assess their supervisor; they may be overly lenient either because they fear retaliation or want to gain influence with their manager—or that ratings will be more favourable than they should be, because managers will focus on pleasing subordinates during the appraisal process (Pollack & Pollack, 1996). However, although these are common reasons given by organisations against their use of upward feedback, there appears to be little empirical evidence to support them. The sources of bias suggested should all result in subordinates providing overly favourable ratings of a manager, but research into the psychometric properties of subordinate ratings suggests otherwise. Of any rating group, they generally have the most frequent contact to provide ratings (i.e. enough information to assess the supervisor). Ability to provide ratings would be indicated by whether they can distinguish between managers' effectiveness (which they can), and as subordinates generally provide the least favourable ratings out of any rating group, one could presume that leniency is not an idiosyncratic rating error common in subordinate appraisal.

Peer Ratings

From a meta-analysis of previous research Viswesvaran, Schmidt and Ones (1997) state that peer ratings are one of the most common sources of ratings for appraisal of performance (the other being supervisor ratings). As with subordinate appraisal, peer evaluations provide another unique perspective on the manager's behaviour; one would presume that peers are more aware of the situational constraints surrounding a manager than other external raters, because of the comparative similarity between their roles. Perhaps as a function of this, there is evidence that in comparison to supervisor evaluations, peer ratings are more likely to differentiate effort from performance, and more likely to focus on task-relevant abilities and competencies (Klimoski & London, 1974; Tucker, Kline & Schmitt, 1967). Also, because ratings are usually collected from a number of peers, they are more defensible from a legal standpoint, than ratings by the superior alone (Pollack & Pollack, 1996).

Despite the reported (Viswesvaran, Schmidt & Ones, 1997) widespread use, relatively few studies have been carried out into employees' acceptance of peer appraisals; Cederblom and Lounsbury (1980) were the first to look at user acceptance of an existing programme. They surveyed 174 faculty members on a peer appraisal system that had been in use for six years, and found relatively low acceptance. But subsequent research contradicts this early study. McEvoy and Buller (1987) surveyed employees of a food processing plant, concluding 'employees seem guarded in their endorsement of peer evaluations but are substantially more favourable than suggested by previous research'. They found an overwhelming 84% of employees thought the process was beneficial and should be continued. Wexley and Klimoski (1984) concluded from a review of existing research literature that peer ratings are potentially the most accurate judgements of employee behaviour. To a certain degree this conclusion is supported by research into the psychometric properties of peer appraisals.

Reliability

In a comparison of peer and supervisory ratings of management performance, Viswesvaran, Schmidt and Ones (1997) found from their meta-analysis that when two raters were from the same organisational level (i.e. both peers or both superiors to the manager being appraised) the average interrater reliability estimate was 0.52. This supports previous research which found peer ratings to be of acceptable interrater reliability and temporal stability (DeNisi & Mitchell, 1978; Imada, 1982; Kane & Lawler, 1978; Lewin & Zwany, 1976; Love, 1981; Reilly & Chao, 1982; Schmitt, Gooding, Noe & Kirsch, 1984; Siegal, 1982).

Convergent validity

Peer ratings are often validated by correlating them to supervisor ratings; research generally finds them to be moderately but significantly related. The moderate level of the relationship suggests that peers do indeed have a unique and valuable perspective on co-workers' performance (Pollack & Pollack, 1996). In a meta-analysis, after correcting for measurement error and range restriction, Harris and Schaubroeck (1988) found that the relationship between peer and supervisor evaluation was $\rho = 0.62$; between self-evaluations and peer appraisal $\rho = 0.36$. They also found that self–peer correlations were lower for managerial/professional employees ($r = 0.31$) than for blue-collar/service employees ($r = 0.40$). Peer–supervisor correlations of managerial and blue-collar employees did not differ significantly ($r = 0.64$ and $r = 0.62$ respectively).

Research has examined in greater depth the degree of overlap between peer and supervisor ratings of a manager. Viswesvaran, Schmidt and Ones (1997) conducted a meta-analysis of previous research that had looked at convergence of peer and supervisor ratings for different behaviours and rating scales. Using three different models of latent job structure to interpret data presented in their meta-analysis, Viswesvaran, Schmidt and Ones (1997) concluded that rating content does not moderate peer–supervisor convergence.

Predictive validity

When peer ratings are correlated with outcome measures (e.g. promotions, turnover, etc.) research has generally found them to be valid predictors of performance (Pollack & Pollack, 1996). Furthermore, when compared to other kinds of predictors, peer evaluations, along with supervisor ratings, assessment centre ratings and work samples, are among the best predictors of performance.

Bias

Despite the seemingly sound psychometric properties of peer appraisals, it has been suggested that organisations are reluctant to include peers in the appraisal process, because of the various forms of bias ratings are susceptible to. Possibly the most commonly cited reason in the research literature (and most frequent explanation given by organisations) is that of friendship bias. Friendship bias is negatively correlated to user acceptance of peer appraisals— the more managers that see their ratings of their peers influenced by their friendship with them, the less favourable they are to the use of peer appraisal (McEvoy & Buller, 1987; McEvoy, 1990). However, much of this research is based on samples from organisations that do not actually have a peer appraisal programme in operation—in practice it remains to be established whether these fears are justified. It also remains to be established what influence friendship has on the favourability of feedback ratings. This is discussed in greater detail later in this chapter.

Although friendship bias is negatively correlated to user acceptance of peer appraisals, research has indicated that this does not reduce the reliability or validity of such appraisals. Other suggested forms of bias are subgroup effects, reliance on stereotypes in ratings and the possibility of retaliation in subsequent ratings (DeNisi & Mitchell, 1978). However, this could be true of ratings from any rating source; there is no evidence from research showing peer appraisals to be overly susceptible to these forms of bias when used for developmental purposes.

Internal and External Customers

A minority of systems invite ratings of managers from internal or external customers. To date, no research literature has been produced on the psychometric properties of this rating group, if only because sample sizes are so small.

In view of the lack of research, one can only speculate on the value of such ratings. They would be especially relevant to customer-facing roles, and it may be that this aspect of interpersonal relationships will grow in significance. Many organisations are enabling employees to become more autonomous, and with the evolution of technology, practices such as tele-working are increasing. The end result is that employees may actually have very little contact with their immediate superiors, subordinates or peers but an increased level of direct contact with internal/external customers. So, as well as being able to comment upon the timeliness and quality of product delivery, customers may also be able to provide insight into the processes underlying the individual's effectiveness.

SYSTEM METHODOLOGY AND ORGANISATIONAL FACTORS AND THEIR INFLUENCE ON MSMR FEEDBACK

In implementing a multi-source feedback programme to assist either the development or formal appraisal of employees, certain aspects of system methodology and organisational factors may influence both the ratings ascribed to an individual (either in their self-assessment, or others' assessment of them) and the individual's response to these ratings. Many of the elements suggested are not based on empirical evidence, but inferred from survey research that has been carried out either prior to introduction of feedback, or after the system has been used for the first time. Again, much of the available research is based on organisations in the US.

System Methodology

Purpose

The first thing to consider here is the purpose of the system. Pollack and Pollack (1996) state that research and practice indicate data collection and feedback processes are most efficient and effective when ratings are collected for developmental rather than evaluative purposes. In a survey of organisations using 360 degree feedback as part of the formal appraisal process, they found that although most managers feel subordinate ratings are valuable for their personal development, they are inappropriate for pay and promotion decisions. Further, high-level managers with long tenure and who rate themselves as better performers are not as open to subordinate feedback (even when used for developmental purposes) as lower level, less tenured, low-performing managers. This has obvious implications for the use of feedback to assist administrative decisions as well.

As well as influencing the attitudes of those who are the subject of feedback, earlier research indicated that the purpose of assessment may also affect the ratings that people provide (McEvoy & Buller, 1987). They carried out an attitude survey of participants of a peer appraisal programme; raters stated if their ratings were used for administrative purposes, they would be overly lenient in their ratings because of fear of reprisal. From a review of previous research, Pollack and Pollack (1996) concluded that peer ratings when used for evaluative purposes are more lenient, less reliable, less valid and contain more halo effect than when used for developmental purposes. They also note that there is some indication that peer appraisal when used for administrative purposes will reduce morale and cause rivalries within a work unit over time.

Confidentiality/anonymity

Another system feature of importance is whether it offers confidentiality or anonymity to the respondents. Many systems emphasise in their instructions to raters that responses will remain confidential. One aspect of this, in relation to self ratings, was demonstrated by Meyer (1980) who asked employees to evaluate their level of performance in comparison to others at the same grade in the organisation. When responses were kept in confidence, statistical analysis found that these self-evaluations were overly favourable in comparison to others' ratings of them. However, when employees were told that the ratings they ascribed themselves would be publicly announced to the other individuals they had been asked to compare themselves to, leniency bias was significantly reduced. However, it is the ratings made by colleagues that are likely to be most susceptible to the influence of whether or not they are individually identifiable by the target. To date, no research has been published which has directly compared feedback ratings from anonymous raters to named raters. However, given the findings of survey research into user acceptance of peer and upward appraisal systems as discussed by Pollack and Pollack (1996), one would expect named raters to be less candid in their responses, for fear of adverse reactions from the individual receiving feedback.

Choice of raters

Many organisations allow individuals to choose who provides feedback to them. This is done in part because it eases administration, but also because the individual is arguably the best person to judge who is most familiar with their work. In allowing individuals to choose who provides feedback to them, there is an issue of whether the individual will simply choose those colleagues they are friendly with. Friendship bias has been found to be prevalent in peer appraisal; in a survey of managers participating in peer appraisal, raters stated that being friends with the individual would influence their ratings (Wohlers and London, 1989). However, research indicates that friendship bias does not necessarily reduce the reliability and validity of appraisals (McEvoy & Beatty, 1989). Further, the impact of friendship bias on ratings has yet to be established; it is possible that friends are more candid in their ratings of one another (and so less likely to hold back negative feedback); also, friendship may result in greater contact with the individual enabling more, and more varied, behaviours to be observed. Alternatively, ratings from friends may be more susceptible to leniency; as they like the individual, they may be less likely to attend to negative aspects of the individual's behaviour.

Frequency timeliness of feedback

There is no firm evidence on which to base guidance on how frequently MSMR feedback should be provided when used for developmental purposes, which reflects the fact that the speed and stability of post-feedback attitude and behaviour change has not been researched. Nor has it been established whether certain individuals benefit more from more frequent feedback than others (i.e. low performers, or those who are new to the organisation and/or role). Ashford (1989), in her model of self-perception accuracy, suggests that the timeliness of feedback affects the strength of its message. Again, research has not yet determined the most effective timespan within which feedback should be delivered, though evidence in other contexts suggests that the more delay, the less impact (Ashford, 1989; Fedor, 1991; Fletcher & Kerslake, 1992). Since the nature of MSMR feedback is not event-specific, perhaps this variable is less important. That said, though, the high administrative workload and level of involvement required by all raters in an MSMR system when it is being done on a number of people in the same business unit at the same time is high. There is a danger that the process of gathering the feedback and then integrating it can become a rather protracted one—and the feedback thus delayed—unless IT methods of collecting and processing the data are used.

Averaging of responses and the nature of the feedback provided

Virtually all systems in operation average responses from sources where there are multiple raters. As well as protecting anonymity, this reduces the effects of bias resulting from idiosyncrasies of the raters. In taking this approach, the feedback loses the 'sensitivity' of the data, and is less likely to pick up whether the individual is very negatively/positively perceived by one of their co-workers. Indeed, averaging could conceal a bi-modal distribution of ratings, possibly resulting from different attitudes the target has to different groups of peers or subordinates. So, although averaging of responses enables the feedback recipient to interpret more easily the feedback received, it may conceal some important variations. This is a practical issue that has not been researched, and much the same is true in relation to other aspects of the nature of the feedback provided.

The majority of MSMR systems simply produce a report that is a summary of the feedback ratings raters have ascribed to the individual. Most reports differentiate between ratings provided by external raters, thereby enabling the individual to see how they are perceived by their boss, their peers and their subordinates. Smither, Wohlers and London (1995) made a comparison between individualised feedback—where the team leaders received ratings from their colleagues—and normative feedback—where the only information given was the average ratings for the team leaders as a group. Those receiving individualised feedback viewed it as more useful, were more willing to discuss it and were more satisfied with the process; they did not express any greater intention to change their behaviour than did the other group, though.

Other than the Smither, Wohlers and London study, there is little research on which form of feedback representation is most effective in terms of facilitating individual acceptance and motivation to change behaviour. Some MSMR systems now offer computer-produced narrative reports based on the feedback profile, rather like those that are widely available for personality questionnaire interpretation; is this really necessary, or even valid, with MSMR feedback? Another unanswered question is whether the feedback report simply goes to the individual and that ends the process or whether it is more effective to have some kind of post-feedback report discussion with the raters.

Organisational Factors

Harris and Schaubroeck (1988) found that the level of convergence between self and peer ratings was moderated by the target employee's standing within an organisation. They found that self–peer correlations were significantly lower for managerial and professional employees ($r = 0.31$) than for blue-collar service employees ($r = 0.40$). However, this effect was only noted between these specific rating groups; peer–supervisor correlations of managerial and blue-collar service employees did not differ significantly. Similarly, in her model of self-assessment accuracy, Ashford (1989) suggests that the higher up the organisational hierarchy an individual is, the less likely they are to receive very negative feedback from individuals who report to them. This may also indicate that self–other rating congruence will be lower at higher organisational levels when MSMR feedback is first introduced, because of the previous lack of opportunity to get frank feedback.

Yammarino and Dubinsky (1990) found evidence that in work settings categorised as 'supportive' (i.e. which foster interpersonal relations) self and others' ratings of leadership and performance were more likely to be related and in agreement than when in an unsupportive climate. Using Ashford's model of self-assessment accuracy (1989) individuals may attend to feedback more when the organisation may be going through a period of change (i.e. downsizing) though it may be that this is simply an increase in sensitisation to threat, and represents a defensive strategy which may reduce constructive responses to feedback. Organisations may find applying MSMR feedback more effective for those individuals who are going through a transitional period (i.e. recently promoted to managerial level, or recently joined the organisation). It has been suggested that participating in feedback will make the target individual more aware of individual and organisational goals.

ATTITUDES TO, AND OUTCOMES OF, MULTI-RATER FEEDBACK

There is potentially a great range of possible outcomes from the implementation of 360 degree feedback systems, some of which are more obvious than others. Impact may be observed in relation to:

- Attitudes to the feedback process itself
- Changes in ratings: these may be in terms of any or all of the following:
  how target managers subsequently assess themselves
  how others subsequently assess the target managers
  how much closer, if at all, the agreement is between rater/ratee assessments with repeated feedback exercises
- Generation of development plans and activity
- Altered attitudes to work (satisfaction, commitment, etc.)
- Objective measures of target managers' performance
- Organisational culture and norms

Although this list suggests consequences that go from individual affective responses to feedback delivery right through to organisational change, much of what can be said here is still at a somewhat hypothetical level. The actual amount of empirical evidence on the impact of 360 degree feedback is disappointingly small considering the extent of its use; widespread adoption seems to have reflected faith rather than proven validity. This is unfortunate, given that the evidence suggests that feedback interventions in general have a long history of producing negative effects on performance (Kluger & DeNisi, 1996). Traditional top-down performance appraisal is far from convincing in light of research on its capacity to motivate and enable performance improvement. Ever since classic early studies in the General Electric Company of America by Meyer, Kay and French (1965), numerous investigations have shown that appraisal feedback has somewhat mixed and often not very positive effects (e.g. Fletcher, 1994; Prince & Lawler, 1986). Is more success likely to be achieved using a 360 degree feedback system? There are some hopeful signs, but as will be seen, as yet it is difficult to say more than that.

Attitudes to Feedback

Not surprisingly, this is one of the areas that has had most research so far, though quite a lot of it relates to subordinate ratings of bosses (i.e. upward feedback) and, to a lesser extent, peer appraisal, rather than to genuine 360 degree systems. Also, one has to differentiate between studies that examine attitudes of employees to the prospective use of 360 degree feedback systems and those that tap attitudes of staff who have actually participated in them. Thus, McEvoy (1990) found that about two thirds of a sample of public sector managers in five organisations expressed favourable attitudes to the use of upward feedback for developmental purposes, but most of them were against it being given any substantial weighting in the formal appraisal context— despite the fact that the sample rated themselves as being above average performers! As McEvoy points out, though, perhaps the concern about using such processes for administrative purposes is a fear that is not always borne out in practice, as other investigators (Bernadin & Beatty, 1987) have not found a negative attitude from employees who have actually been involved in such applications. Nonetheless, this is a persistent theme in the research; Bettenhausen and Fedor (1997), in a study of a broad sample of 195 managers, found that peer and upward feedback were seen as more likely to produce positive outcomes and less likely to produce negative outcomes when used for developmental rather than administrative purposes. Bettenhausen and Fedor also report that the experience of participating in peer or upward feedback only had the effect of making it even less likely that negative outcomes would result from its use for development purposes.

In the UK, Redman and Matthews (1997) surveyed 211 managers from a variety of companies, very few of whom had any exposure to upward feedback. They found that their sample were 'relatively indifferent' towards its use, with the full range of responses being shown from enthusiastic support (a rather small group) to a more sceptical and apprehensive attitude. Interestingly, given that 360 degree feedback is often seen as a significant vehicle for bringing about change, the managers in this study were convinced that it neither would be useful in a time of change nor make organisations a better place to work in. More positively, if somewhat in contradiction, they did feel that their subordinates knew enough about their (i.e. the managers') jobs to make a realistic appraisal of them.

Although the earlier research on attitudes tended to focus mainly on overall favourability of response to 360 degree feedback or its component parts, later investigations have concentrated on identifying the influence of a range of variables on these attitudes. For example, Funderburg and Levy (1997) examined the influence of both individual and contextual factors on the attitudes of staff who were participating in multi-rater appraisal systems. They concluded that while personality factors such as high self-esteem and internal locus of control were related to attitude favourability, contextual factors were more important. Significant predictors among the latter were the perceived costs of feedback seeking, the individual's self-rating on Organisational Citizenship Behaviour and their supervisor's style—employees whose bosses were perceived as being more autocratic had more positive attitudes to multi-rater feedback, a finding that ran counter to the study's hypothesis, but which in retrospect seems reasonable enough. The findings from this research have to be treated with some caution, as the sample size (75) is small.

Maurer and Tarulli (1996) addressed some fairly fundamental aspects of feedback systems in their study, namely whether those involved believed recipients could improve on the basis of the feedback, whether they felt the dimensions they were assessed on were appropriate and whether the ratees felt the raters had adequately observed the behaviour they were rating. They found that the more participants (raters and those rated) believed the target managers could be developed, the more favourable their attitude to the feedback system and the greater their belief that the managers' own bosses should have access to the ratings. Unfortunately, the results presented do not tell us just what proportion of raters did *not* feel those they were providing feedback to could be developed. The extent to which (1) the assessment dimensions were seen as relevant and (2) the raters had adequate opportunities to observe ratees' behaviour was also related to positive attitudes.

How useful is research on participant attitudes in the context of 360 degree feedback? It is probably more valuable where it is based on respondents who have experience in actually participating in such feedback processes, and where it throws some light on the conditions that help generate positive attitudes (e.g. Maurer & Tarulli, 1996). However, whilst it may be true that, as Murphy and Cleveland (1997) assert, attitudes place a ceiling on the level of effectiveness appraisal systems can achieve, research on some attitude factors is perhaps more academically interesting than directly useful. It is not entirely clear how, for example, the fact that self-ratings on Organisational Citizenship Behaviour are associated with more positive attitudes can be practically applied. The speed and enthusiasm with which organisations have embraced 360 degree feedback does not suggest that they are overly concerned with finely tuned systems that cater for subtle attitudinal differences in either the raters or those receiving the feedback.

Changes in Ratings as a Result of Feedback

This is the other aspect of MSMR operation and impact that has attracted most research, though still not a great deal and once again much of the research is on upward feedback rather than full 360 degree processes. Changes in ratings here stand as a proxy measure of performance, the assumption being that ratings from colleagues that become more favourable on successive applications of MSMR procedures indicate performance improvement. However, there is another aspect of rating change that needs to be considered, and this is the impact on rater–ratee agreement (congruence) over time. This may be independent of whether raters have identified any improvement in the target; it is possible for greater congruence to result from the raters' assessments remaining the same on separate occasions while self-ratings move from a more lenient, less congruent level to a less lenient and more congruent one as a result of repeated feedback exercises. Such a measure can be thought of as reflecting the extent to which self-awareness is enhanced—something that may be thought of as a desirable end in itself (Fletcher, 1997a).

One of the earlier studies in this field was reported by London and Wohlers (1991), who examined the boss–subordinate relationship items in a feedback survey questionnaire for the same group of 39 target managers on two occasions. They found that there was a significant increase in agreement between self-ratings and subordinate ratings, from 0.28 on the first administration to 0.34 a year later; although this increase is not all that large, it should be noted that there were some changes in the subordinates contributing the ratings from time 1 to time 2. The main focus of this study was factors affecting boss-subordinate agreement, and it is not possible from the data presented to comment on precisely how this greater agreement was achieved—through changes in ratee self-assessment, raters' assessments or both.

Atwater, Roush and Fischthal (1995) looked at both changes in ratings and changes in congruence resulting from successive feedback episodes in a large sample of subjects. They found that, overall, raters' assessments of targets increased in favourability, and that targets' self-ratings increased in congruence. Atwater, Roush and Fischthal went on to group the ratees according to whether the feedback received was positive, neutral or negative, based on the initial level of congruence. They found that for targets who received negative feedback (i.e. their self-assessments were more favourable than the feedback ratings they received), their subsequent self-assessments went down, while the opposite was true for targets receiving positive feedback. Further, they report that for the first group, rater assessments made 18 weeks later were more favourable but there was no change in the ratings given to the second (positive feedback) group—perhaps because the targets in the latter saw no need to change their behaviour when they found that they were underestimating themselves. This is an interesting study, but some caution has to be exercised in generalising from it as the subjects were student leaders and their juniors in a Naval Academy, and the nature of the feedback process was not all that typical of what is encountered elsewhere (e.g. the time lapse between successive feedback episodes was rather shorter than is normally the case).

Rather more conventional was the upward feedback system Smither, London, Vasilopoulos, Reilly, Millsap and Salvemini (1995) based their research on. Using a Behavioural Observation Scale, the self- and subordinate ratings of a sample of junior to middle managers were taken on two occasions six months apart. Again, Smither et al. found that managers whose initial performance ratings from subordinates were moderate or low attracted significantly improved ratings on the second feedback application. Relating their findings to Korman's (1970, 1976) self-consistency theory, they noted some evidence that managers whose self-evaluations were initially low and whose favourability of feedback was also low did not show much improvement; whether this does indeed reflect lack of motivation to improve based on a desire to maintain consistency with self-image, or simply lack of ability to improve is open to question. One further finding of note here is that a sample of managers who did not complete self-ratings actually improved more than those who did—leading the authors to ask whether including self-ratings helps or hinders acceptance of feedback.

Other studies that have produced generally consistent findings include that of Hazucha, Hezlett and Schneider (1993), which reports finding increases in congruence two years after receiving MSMR feedback, though their original sample had suffered considerable attrition over this period (down from 198 to 48). The self–other correlation was 0.07 at time 1 and 0.32 at time 2, a significant difference. On a slightly different track, a research study by Salam, Cox and Sims (1997) that sought assessment ratings from various sources—but not in the context of a 360 degree feedback system as such—observed that managers who were seen as challenging the status quo and encouraging subordinates to act independently were rated lower by their bosses but higher by their subordinates. This points up one of the problems of using changes in ratings as an outcome measure for MSMR schemes—different rating groups may have very differing perspectives, or they may sample different aspects of the individual ratee's behaviour. Thus, Bernadin, Hagan & Kane (1995) found that with a one-year gap between feedback exercises, a group of managers showed higher ratings from peers and subordinates but not from bosses or customers. Aggregating ratings from various rater groups may obscure very real discrepancies between them, and give a misleading picture of the effects of feedback provision.

There are two other problems that are encountered with using changes in ratings as a measure of impact. The first is that so far, the majority of MSMR processes seem to have been run on a one-off basis, thus precluding any monitoring of this kind (London & Smither, 1995). But even where feedback exercises are repeated for the same managers, it can be argued that neither of the measures mentioned here afford proof of actual performance improvement. London and Smither (1995) suggest that self-evaluations may become more congruent with colleagues' ratings as ratees develop their own schemas relating to the performance domains represented in the feedback questionnaire. More favourable assessments from raters or greater congruence could also result from enhanced impression management tactics, such as ingratiation (Giacalone & Rosenfeld, 1989), rather than from any fundamental behaviour change. Whilst this possibility cannot be ruled out, it does not mean that even if this were true to some extent or in some cases, there is no positive outcome. Managers receiving 360 degree feedback are often warned that the feedback is not objective, it is about people's perceptions—but that since perceptions are often what influence and determine behaviour, they have to be taken seriously. That argument cuts both ways—if impression management tactics on the part of the ratee influence raters to make more positive assessments, then this presumably (if it is maintained) will have beneficial effects in terms of work relationships.

Other Outcome Measures

Given that most MSMR systems seem to be developmentally oriented, one might expect there to be more attention paid to assessing the extent to which feedback leads to the generation of development plans and activity. In fact, we could find very little in this domain. Holt, Noe and Cavanaugh (1995) report that preparation of written development plans following 360 degree feedback was dependent on a number of factors, such as the amount of support for development provided by the organisation. Hazucha, Hezlett and Schneider (1993) found, contrary to their hypothesis, that managers who received more favourable feedback ratings and higher self–other congruence on the first round of feedback did not put more effort into developmental activity. In fact, it was those who received less favourable ratings who reported putting more effort into development—a finding which has a degree of logic to it! Objective measures of performance change following MSMR applications are similarly hard to come by. Hazucha, Hezlett and Schneider (1993) also found skill increases as a result of feedback, but since years of research on conventional performance appraisal have produced so few examples of objective measures of performance change, it is perhaps unrealistic to expect that the literature on 360 degree feedback will somehow be miraculously different.

Finally, although multi-source feedback is sometimes cited as a major intervention method for bringing about altered attitudes to work and major shifts in organisational culture and norms (e.g. Timmreck, 1995), there is little or no direct evidence to demonstrate this as yet. It is suggested (Smither et al., 1995) that MSMR programmes may influence participants' schemas about leadership behaviour over time. In terms of behaviour change—as far as this can be identified through shifts in successive sets of feedback ratings—the picture is of consistent but rather modest degrees of change. Perhaps the fact that multi-source feedback takes place at all, and that it has been adopted so widely and so quickly, is an indicator of the very considerable shift in organisational culture that has already taken place—feedback systems are more a symptom or expression of change than a factor in its causation.

SELF-ASSESSMENT AND SELF-AWARENESS

One of the incidental results of the spread of MSMR systems and the research on them has been a renewed interest in self-assessment and the gathering of more data on its attributes and accuracy. Ever since reviews by Mabe and West (1982) and Shrauger and Osberg (1981) held out a more positive view about the potential value of self-assessment, research on this theme has continued in a rather fitful manner across a diverse range of situations (assessment centres, appraisal, selection and so on). As indicated in the section of psychometric qualities of self-ratings, the results have been mixed, which is perhaps not surprising given that diversity. It is not the intention in this part of the chapter to go over the same ground as the earlier section; rather, the focus here will be on the quality of self-assessment, and more specifically on the notion of self-awareness.

Quality of self-assessment can be thought of either in terms of criterion validity, where self-ratings are compared to some external measure, other than ratings, relating to the same behaviour (e.g. Lindeman, Sundvik & Rouhiainen, 1995), or in terms of the kind of congruence between self-ratings and colleagues' ratings discussed earlier in the section on attitudes and outcomes of multi-rater feedback. These two ways of conceptualising quality are by no means the same—it is possible, for example, that there could be a high degree of congruence and little or no external validity, or indeed high predictive validity for self-ratings but low congruence with ratings from others. The evidence on the validity of self-ratings was covered when the psychometric properties of different rating sources were discussed. Much of the research on that topic pre-dates the widespread use of MSMR systems, but the latter have—not surprisingly—yielded data on congruence. Thus, for the remainder of this section, that is the measure of accuracy that will be our concern.

Why should agreement between self-ratings and ratings from colleagues be of interest—after all, it has just been pointed out that congruence or the lack of it does not necessarily imply predictive validity? The reasons for believing it to be important operate on different levels. At the most immediate level, managers who go through multi-source feedback are usually very keen to see how their colleagues' assessments of them compare with their own ratings. On an organisational level, the desirability of congruence is that it seems to be associated with higher performance. A number of studies have emerged that support this view. For example, Bass and Yammarino (1991) examined convergence of self- and subordinate ratings on leadership qualities amongst naval staff and found that higher convergence was correlated with higher performance measures. Similarly, Furnham and Stringfield (1994), in a large study of nearly 400 Chinese and Caucasian airline employees found that the smaller the difference between target managers' and subordinates' ratings on leading and motivating staff, the higher were superiors' appraisal ratings of the targets.

This study was done in the context of ongoing HR processes rather than simply for research.

Findings such as these prompt the question as to why greater self–other agreement should be linked with performance. There are a number of possible answers. First, it could be that greater agreement in ratings signals smoother relationships with bosses, who then assess the target managers more highly; Wexley, Alexander, Greenwalt and Couch (1980) found that lower levels of rater disagreement were an indicator of good relationships between managers and their subordinates. If this is a significant reason for the performance link, it suggests the possibility that higher performance ratings might simply reflect target managers' impression management or their bosses' desire for a quiet life rather than signalling genuinely greater effectiveness in the job. Another, more positive, interpretation is that congruence between self- and other ratings indicates that target managers attend to feedback more, have an accurate assessment of their competence and where it needs to be developed, and perform better accordingly (Wohlers & London, 1989; Yammarino & Atwater, 1993; London & Smither, 1995). Although there are various studies that support this interpretation (e.g. McCauley & Lombardo, 1990; Stumpf & Colarelli, 1980), they are mainly indirect in the evidence they provide. Finally, the methodological issues that arise when trying to produce measures of levels of agreement (such as difference scores) between different rating sources are not to be dismissed lightly (Edwards, 1994); there is some danger of finding relationships between performance and other ratings that are essentially artefactual.

Another issue that arises when this work is considered is whether agreement between self- ratings and colleagues' ratings can be construed as representing accuracy of self-assessment. As has already been pointed out, since congruence may have no relationship with self-ratings' predictive validity, there is little reason to suppose that agreement does represent some objective indicator of accuracy. However, the approach taken by Wohlers and London (1989) is surely a valuable one; they use the term *self-awareness*, define it as the degree to which individuals understand their own strengths and weaknesses, and operationalise it as the degree to which individuals see themselves as others see them. As we have seen, self- awareness so defined does show relationships with performance measures. Finding that your self-ratings are discrepant with others' ratings of you is likely to identify a need for behaviour change; London and Smither (1995) state that disagreement with self-ratings is a way to calibrate the extent of change needed from the target manager's viewpoint. The picture may be complicated if the congruence level differs across rating groups, of course; a research question here is whether greater congruence with ratings from bosses is more closely linked to performance than congruence with other rater groups.

Correlates of Self-awareness

Many writers on the subject of multi-source feedback treat self-awareness as a variable of interest in its own right, and recent work has turned towards studying the correlates of self-awareness. Most research on self-assessment up until now has centred more on the situational factors explaining why people do not produce self-ratings that correlate with other measures rather than looking at the characteristics of those people who do. The current pattern of research looks at both individual and organisational influences; identifying what promotes self-awareness should have some benefits in terms of how multi-source feedback is designed and used (Nilsen and Campbell, 1993).

Organisational and situational characteristics that London and Wohlers (1991) studied included target manager level, line vs staff function, and the number of subordinates in the work group. They report that profile agreement (based on the correlation of self-ratings with the average of subordinate rater assessments) was higher—as hypothesised—for line units and where there was a higher number of subordinates; the organisational level of the target manager was not, though. London and Wohlers suggest that the jobs of line managers are usually more structured and uniform than those of managers in staff units (e.g. HR), with clearer performance standards and more opportunity for subordinates to observe their bosses in similar situations. The reason for expecting larger subordinate numbers to be related to greater profile agreement is simply that greater numbers will add reliability to the ratings.

Although little attention has been given to organisational influences so far, there are likely to be many more that impact on self-assessment and its relationship with ratings by others. For example, the extent to which performance standards are clear, known and observable is likely to be important; as Mabe and West (1982) noted, the nature of the self-assessment task has to be transparent to individuals if they are to achieve accuracy. Another factor likely to be important is the quality and style of management and associated level of trust within the organisation. Credibility of source of feedback is a key variable in its acceptance (Bastos & Fletcher, 1995) and if ratees attribute greater trustworthiness to the feedback they get from their own observations than to those of others, there is likely to be lower agreement and less impact from the introduction of 360 degree feedback systems.

Turning to the work on individual differences in self-awareness, it is the same group of investigators who are responsible for the greater part of the research so far. London and Wohlers (1991) demonstrated that female managers tend to have higher levels of profile agreement than male managers, a finding that fits with a good deal of research in other areas suggesting that female managers are more self-critical and self-aware (Fletcher, 1997a). One study, by VanVelsor, Taylor and Leslie (1993) did not find that female managers had a higher level of profile agreement than male managers.

However, this finding may have arisen from the atypical sample used in this study—almost three-quarters of the managers were women. Female managers were perceived by their subordinates to have a higher level of self-awareness than male managers; subordinates rated them significantly higher in self-awareness than they did male managers. Looking at age as a variable, London and Wohlers (1991) did not find any relationship with self-awareness. This is perhaps a little surprising, but not for the factors (negative stereotypes about older workers, declining job involvement with age, etc.) London and Wohlers based their hypothesis on, which led them to anticipate a negative correlation. If, as Mabe and West (1982) suggest, self-assessment is a skill to be acquired, then older workers may have had more opportunity to do so, in which case a positive relationship is to be expected. In this context, it is worth noting that Gordon (1991) reports that moderate to high improvements in self-assessment accuracy resulted from training programmes emphasising self-assessment.

A number of writers have linked self-awareness to ratee personality attributes (Wohlers & London, 1989; Roush & Atwater, 1992; Nilsen & Campbell, 1993; London & Smither, 1995; Herold, Parsons & Rensvold, 1996; Fletcher, 1997a). There is also a good deal of literature in the general field of self-assessment research that examines the influence of self-efficacy and other variables in the formulation of self-assessment and attributions for performance (e.g. Jussim, Coleman & Nassau, 1987; Silver, Mitchell & Gist, 1995). One way to look at the work in this area is to consider it in terms of differences in propensity to *seek* feedback and in *reacting* to feedback when it is received. That there are wide variations in the extent to which people look for feedback is well established (Ashford & Cummings, 1983). In general, it would seem likely that individuals who typically seek feedback would have a more positive attitude to MSMR systems—though paradoxically they may have less need of them and would be likely to show greater self-awareness as a result of their willingness to seek information on how they are performing. Herold, Parsons and Rensvold (1996) identified three dimensions relevant to preferred sources from which feedback is sought. They labelled these dimensions as (1) internal propensity—a preference for self-mediated feedback and lack of trust in external sources; (2) internal ability—the ability to self-assess; and (3) external propensity—preference for seeking external feedback. They went on to examine personality correlates of these three dimensions. Internal ability was associated with high levels of self- esteem, need for achievement, initiative and self-assurance. Internal propensity had a similar but slightly weaker pattern of correlations, but also showed a negative relationship with Public Self-Consciousness—the authors suggest that this might indicate a lack of concern about how one appears to other people. External propensity showed more or less the opposite correlations from internal propensity, and also a negative association with Tolerance of Ambiguity. These findings demonstrate some of the personality variables that seem to be important in feedback seeking, and—

by implication—in self-awareness. However, they also indicate that these per-sonality characteristics (self-esteem, need for achievement, initiative, toler-ance for ambiguity, public self-consciousness) can reflect different preferences in the source from which feedback is sought and attended to, which in turn suggests that the effectiveness of 360 degree systems may vary considerably according to the personality of the feedback recipient.

However, getting feedback and accepting it are not the same thing. Most people who seek feedback are probably going to use it positively, but there are also likely to be some whose main aim in finding out how they are seen by others is defensive; they are likely either to reject the feedback or to adopt impression management tactics to nullify it. What are the personality determi-nants of individual's reactions to feedback—whether they sought it or not—once it has been received? These will surely affect its use and hence the degree of self-awareness shown. It seems likely that many of the attributes found by Herold, Parsons and Rensvold (1996) are again important, but other variables may be influential too. London and Wohlers (1991) found that co-workers' ratings of target managers' use of a self-protection mechanism labelled as Denial (described as reacting negatively to feedback, never admitting mis-takes, not accepting responsibility for one's part in a group failure) were negatively correlated with self-awareness measures. Roush and Atwater (1992) report that self-assessment accuracy was higher in introvert and sens-ing types, as measured by the MBTI, in students at a military academy.

Other individual difference constructs suggested as being of relevance to feedback acceptance and/or self-assessment accuracy include intelligence, locus of control, need for achievement (Mabe & West, 1982), narcissism (Nilsen & Campbell, 1993), emotional stability, and conscientiousness (Fletcher, 1997a). London and Smither (1995) contend that self-image influ-ences how feedback is received and interpreted, with some people having a bias towards self-enhancement. This is undoubtedly true, and is supported by Nilsen and Campbell's (1993) finding, based on a series of studies, that over-rating tendency was a stable characteristic. However, it seems likely that some people are also more biased towards self-criticism and that this can influence how they react to feedback and their accuracy of self-perception (Fletcher, Taylor & Glanfield, 1996); within limits, being self-critical should increase openness to feedback and enhance accurate self-assessment.

Some Further Points on Self-assessment and Self-awareness

Much of this section has implicitly addressed research needed, for example to elucidate the self-awareness–performance link. There are, though, a number of other observations that can be made. First, the personality correlates of self-awareness and/or feedback seeking are, as is so often the case, posited as having a linear relationship. But this seems unlikely, because a curvilinear association would make more sense in many cases. Thus, individuals with moderately high self-esteem may react more positively to feedback and change their self- assessments to some extent in line with the feedback, while those low in self-esteem may be more defensive and be less inclined to accept critical feedback and change their fragile self-image. However, individuals very high— perhaps unrealistically so—in self-esteem may be just as impervious to feedback and as unlikely to change their self-assessment as those who are low in that quality. Future research on personality correlates would do well to take the possibility of curvilinear relationships into account.

On a different theme, the place and meaning of self-assessment within MSMR systems is maybe more open to question than people have thought. Virtually every provider of such feedback mechanisms included self-assessment by the target as part of the process. Despite this, some doubt may be raised as to how much benefit is derived from including self-ratings; Roberson, Torkel, Korsgaard, Klein, Diddams and Cayer (1993) found that in a conventional appraisal system, managers who completed a self-rating before the review meeting felt they had less influence over the subsequent discussion than a control group who did not self-appraise. Bearing more directly on MSMR operations, Smither, Wohlers and London (1995), in their study of an upward feedback programme, found that target managers who did not complete self-ratings improved more on subordinates' ratings over successive feedback exercises than those who did do self-assessment as part of the process. Smither and his colleagues conclude that it is not yet clear whether self-rating helps or hinders acceptance of such feedback.

As has been noted, self-assessments are typically more lenient, but an interesting question is raised by the contention of Meyer (1980) that much of the leniency of self-ratings observed in studies done purely for research disappears when self-ratings are collected for 'real life' purposes such as appraisal. Meyer suggested that knowing that one's self-assessments would be seen by others exerted a powerful moderating influence on them, a suggestion that was subsequently supported by Mabe and West (1982) in their meta-analysis. If this is the case, one might ask whether the self-assessments collected as part of 360 degree feedback exercises represent 'true' beliefs on the part of those giving them, or a self-assessment that has been consciously toned-down in order either to impression manage or to deflect potential conflict and/or personal disappointment. In other circumstances, such as when 360 degree feedback is an element of appraisal and is linked to pay, it is conceivable that self-ratings will be deliberately shifted to reflect a more positive self-view than the individual would normally espouse, because of the need to advance the case for increased reward.

It is likely, though, that self-ratings will continue to be used as part of the MSMR input, because most managers seem to want to include them as a way of checking their perceptions against those of their colleagues. And if they are not collected, it would preclude getting any measures of self-awareness or of subsequent change. Perhaps these reasons alone are sufficient justification for valuing self-assessments, even though they may not be necessary for the MSMR process to achieve its basic aims.

THEORETICAL MODELS

Early research into MSMR feedback systems had very little cohesive conceptual basis; it seems only recently that it has been recognised that there is a need for clear delineation of the interaction between subprocesses operating within a 360 degree feedback system from both an individual and an organisational perspective. Prior to the widespread use of MSMR systems, a number of models concerned with self-perception accuracy and responses to performance feedback were proposed. Concepts and components of these models have subsequently been elaborated upon to produce models specifically for the context of MSMR developmental feedback. In all models described, emphasis is placed on the feedback recipient, and the cognitive processes that underlie both individuals' responses to feedback and subsequent changes in attitudes and/or behaviour. This is done by the integration of research findings, from both MS feedback research and more broader research concerned with interpersonal interaction in the workplace, to encompass:

- The moderating effects of factors relating to characteristics of the feedback source
- System methodology and organisational factors
- The degree of influence of feedback on the relationship between self-perception to others' perceptions
- The potential impact feedback can have on subsequent behaviour, attitudes and performance

The first model to be outlined here is that proposed by Susan Ashford (1989) which describes the process of self-assessment accuracy. Perhaps underlying the popularity of MSMR systems now seen, she noted how accurate self-perception has significant benefits for both the individual and the organisation. From research into the psychometric properties of self-assessments, and the variety of errors made, she inferred a variety of subprocesses operating during the task of self-assessment, which influence the accuracy of the outcome. For individuals to have an accurate view of their performance at work, she suggested they must fulfil three self-assessment tasks: they must establish the environment-specific standards on which they should judge their performance; they must learn which particular feedback cues they should attend to, out of all those available; they must correctly interpret these cues.

Ashford then outlines three problems in trying to complete these tasks, which will give rise to an inaccurate self-perception—the information problem, the ego-defence problem, and the self-presentation problem. The information problem is concerned with the information that the individual uses to decide what is the most effective behavioural strategy to reach particular performance goals. As has been indicated by research into convergence of feedback ratings from different sources, an individual can receive conflicting information about what it takes to achieve certain performance goals. There are also a number of environmental and individual antecedents that further bias this decision. Environmental antecedents include the variation in amount of feedback individuals receive, the extent to which feedback is received if actively sought, and finally bias in feedback cues, as a result of the individual's role within the organisation. Individual antecedents encompass schemas held by the individual about themselves and their environment, and personality characteristics such as self-esteem, which dictate the amount of feedback the individual can/will attend to.

The second problem the individual may encounter in trying to decide the most appropriate behavioural strategy for attainment of performance goals, is that of ego-defence. She notes how feedback raises affective as well as cognitive responses, which will result in bias in the interpretation of feedback message. The third problem she suggests is that of pressure on the individual from the organisation to be self-sufficient (the self-presentation problem). She states that an individual who is overly reliant on feedback will not be perceived as self-sufficient. The manner in which the individual resolves these problems influences the extent to which they fulfil the three self-assessment tasks successfully, and so have an accurate self-perception.

Although Ashford raised many salient points which are undoubtedly implicated in the process of self-perception, the model fails to explain fully the interaction between certain components (i.e. individual characteristics and environmental factors) or which of the three 'problems' has most influence over the accuracy of self-perception.

Indeed some of the components (i.e. the 'problems') are not directly applicable to MSMR feedback—and responses to it. In an MSMR system, feedback content is specific and deemed by the organisation to be relevant to the attainment of performance goals; the feedback is also provided by individuals the organisation deems credible—hence, there is no 'information problem' as such. Similarly, for the 'presentation problem'—in implementing an MSMR feedback programme, organisations are removing the pressure for self-presentation—attending to feedback is seen as a positive attribute, rather than negative as she suggests.

Considering these issues, if one follows Ashford's model, one would expect a higher level of self-assessment accuracy than is often observed within

MSMR systems (i.e. with no information- or presentation-problem, the only threat to self-assessment accuracy is that caused by ego-defence mechanisms). Hence, one does question the validity of some of the concepts of the model. However, the value of this model cannot be overlooked; it provides a rationale to providing structured feedback to employees and demonstrates how feedback systems may contribute to improvement in performance, if the problems are as she describes. It also provides a good starting point for theorists concerned with the influence of feedback on self-perception within the context of MSMR feedback.

Many aspects of London's (1994) insight formation model, for example, relate to Ashford's work. He states that the aim of the model is to postulate the cognitive processes underlying insight formation which can 'then act as a guideline for the design of development feedback programmes'. He does this by breaking the process of insight formation down into four sequential elements: (1) receiving information about oneself and/or others (reflected feedback); (2) integrating and reconciling the information with other information (categorisation); (3) interpreting the information (attribution); (4) incorporating the outcome into perceptions of oneself and others (cognitive re-evaluation of self-concept which results in implications for development). He proposes similar antecedents to Ashford, namely receiving and seeking feedback cues, characteristics of feedback cues, and initial feedback interpretation. Consequences include changes in schemas (i.e. expectations and beliefs) about self and others, and changes in behaviour and expressed attitudes.

The basic premise of London's model is that people derive information about themselves and others, from what others say and do; an individual's self-concept is determined largely by interpersonal feedback. In part, then, it reflects a symbolic interactionist position. Interpersonal feedback may be formal (e.g. appraisal ratings) or informal (i.e. information sought deliberately or obtained in the course of events), and objective or subjective. London proposes that people integrate interpersonal feedback into their self-concept by judging its accuracy and realism; these reactions to feedback are determined by its favourability and level of objectivity. Once performance feedback is internalised, the individual interprets its content in relation to his/her current beliefs. London adds to Ashford's model by applying a concept from another model (Fedor, 1991)—that of categorisation and attribution. London states that the way the individual interprets information is determined by pre-existing schemas. Feedback that is consistent with these schemas is accepted automatically, whereas information that is inconsistent causes either re-interpretation of the information or alteration of the individual's frame of reference. London also stipulates a number of individual characteristics that determine, and potentially bias, the cognitive and motivational processes determining the attributions made (for example, self-esteem, internal/external locus of control and so on). The resultant attributions made about the information determine the impact on the individual's self-perception.

There is considerable overlap between the work of Ashford and London. They both emphasise the individual as an 'active' processor of information and note the moderating influence of personal and situational characteristics that determine the way feedback cues are interpreted. However, London's model is arguably more applicable to the ongoing development and refinement of self-perception that is assisted by participation in a developmental feedback programme, than self-perception as described by Ashford. Whereas a number of Ashford's concepts do not bear relevance within the context of multi-source feedback programmes, the concepts and components proposed by London can be applied to interpersonal insight both in and outside of the MSMR feedback programme. Further, there are a number of issues that this model addresses (i.e. what factors determine the acceptance of feedback) which have direct practical implications for the design of MSMR systems. However, there are a number of other issues, notably the dynamic nature of the interaction between the feedback recipient and feedback providers, which are not addressed by either Ashford or London. This, and other issues relating to feedback recipients' responses to feedback, are addressed by Fedor (1991).

Fedor's model traces the processes by, and in which, recipients receive and respond to information about their performance. Like Ashford, Fedor sees individuals as 'central processors' and active gatherers of feedback. He states that certain characteristics of the individual receiving feedback will influence all of the phases in the model, from perceptions of the source and message characteristics to their subsequent behavioural intentions. He proposes a number of individual characteristics that may moderate perceptions of feedback source and message; these include expectations (Ammons, 1956), frame of reference and locus of control (Baron, Cowan & Ganz, 1974), self-esteem (Shrauger & Rosenberg 1970; Weiss, 1977), social anxiety (Smith & Sarason, 1975), age (Meyer & Walker, 1961), need for achievement (Steers, 1975), self-monitoring behaviour (Snyder, 1974) and need for cognition (Cacioppo & Petty, 1982). However, Fedor does not specify which individual differences relate to various components of the process of recipient response to feedback that he proposes.

Fedor holds that individual characteristics will affect their perceptions of characteristics of the feedback source (i.e. superiors, self, co-workers or job) and the feedback message. Feedback source characteristics are those factors that relate to source credibility and power, whereas feedback message characteristics are those factors that relate to specificity of feedback, its timeliness and favourability. Fedor classifies feedback source characteristics into four types: (1) other individuals; (2) the task environment (i.e. the job itself); (3) oneself; (4) the organisation. In reviewing the research literature, Fedor notes the issue of what constitutes a credible feedback source; it has been suggested by some that the job itself is the only objective source of job-related feedback—all other sources provide feedback that has gone through some evaluation purpose. However, research into the psychometric properties of ratings from different sources indicate that even if there is an element of subjective bias in feedback, it can still have concurrent, discriminant and predictive validity for job performance, and so have credibility.

Characteristics of the feedback message include whether it is solicited, unsolicited or self-generated, whether it is received directly from the source or indirectly from off-hand comments or actions and whether the feedback message is public or private, explicit or implicit. Factors such as the timeliness of the feedback message also influence its interpretation, as does its level of ambiguity, degree of favourability, and perceived relevance. Fedor regards self-evaluations as a measure of the individual's expectations of the feedback they should receive; these expectations will affect how they perceive characteristics of feedback actually received. As research has found self-evaluations to be generally more lenient than evaluations provided by others, Fedor highlights the need for research to determine the relationship between characteristics of feedback to expectations of feedback, and resultant perception and impact of feedback received.

On receiving feedback, Fedor proposes that the individual's perceptions of the source and message characteristics, in combination with their own personal characteristics, will affect the way the feedback message is processed (i.e. how extensively the individual will think about and examine the feedback). He termed this processing of feedback the 'level of elaboration'. The level of elaboration occurs because of feedback recipients 'innate desire to determine their level of responsibility (i.e. internal or external causality) for performance and subsequent feedback received. This processing may not always occur—occasionally feedback simply evokes a habitual or automatic response (e.g. if feedback is consistent with expectancies). However, in most instances, processing of feedback will result in a response that will result in the formulation, modification or affirmation of attitudes and behaviour. Fedor emphasises in the model that responses to feedback are not linear and that there is an interaction; the initial beliefs formulated in the elaboration phase may cause the recipient's perceptions of the feedback source, and so perceptions of the feedback itself to change. These changes may then cause further processing of feedback, which can result in an alternative response.

The processing of feedback results in beliefs that will affect attitudes about the feedback message and source, as well as alternative responses to feedback. The final stage in an individual's reaction to feedback is the formulation, modification or reaffirmation of attitudes which, in combination with relevant subjective norms and perceived control, influence feedback recipients' final behavioural intentions.

Fedor's model is probably the most comprehensive of those described thus far, though there are characteristics of feedback source that it may overlook (Bastos & Fletcher, 1995). However, as the theory was not conceptualised specifically for feedback elicited from MSMR systems, factors moderating the nature of this feedback such as system methodology are not given consideration.

As with Ashford's model, because not conceptualised specifically for the context of MSMR feedback programmes, a number of the components in Fedor's model are not as salient (i.e. certain characteristics of the feedback message will remain constant for all feedback recipients).

There are also a number of areas where the model remains vague, highlighting the need for further research in this area. The model does succeed, however, in demonstrating how providing feedback can influence and benefit not just the individual receiving feedback—but also those that provided it, and ultimately the organisation as a whole.

The final model to be outlined is that of London and Smither (1995). Conceptualised specifically for the subprocesses and moderating factors at play within an MSMR developmental feedback programme, it encompasses many of the theoretical concepts described thus far. However, before this model is outlined we will briefly mention the work of Yammarino and Atwater (1993). Although they term their work on self-perception accuracy within the context of multi-source feedback programmes, a model, it reads more as a summary of a series of studies that have looked at the convergence of ratings from different sources, and the accuracy of self-ratings.

The model begins at the point where an individual's self-perception has developed and they are capable of providing a full self-assessment (i.e. through sufficient tenure and range of experiences in that position, the individual holds a perception of their capabilities for all behaviours described in the self-assessment questionnaire). From previous research, Yammarino and Atwater suggest a number of personality and biographic factors that relate to the level of accuracy of the individual's initial self-perception of ability; these were outlined in the previous section on self-awareness. On the basis of these characteristics, Yammarino and Atwater suggest the initial self-perception is influenced further by a number of cognitive factors. Leniency bias (Fox & Dinur, 1988), social desirability bias (Podsakoff & Organ, 1986), attributional bias (DeVadar, Bateson & Lord 1986), self-protection mechanisms, such as denial (Wohlers & London, 1989), self-presentation pressures (Ashford, 1989), self-concept maintenance (Atwater & Yammarino, 1992) and cognitive categorisations of role behaviour (Foti, 1990) are cognitive processes that constitute idiosyncratic rating error, which self-assessments have been found to be more prone to than ratings from other sources. However, Yammarino and Atwater do not specify in the model exactly why these forms of bias occur, or what personality characteristics or other factors are related to them.

They also posit a number of external factors that may moderate the individual's initial self-perception and subsequent self-assessment:

1. *Error*. Working from Ashford's model of self-assessment accuracy, Yammarino and Atwater take up the issue of the variability of feedback—

in making a self-assessment, individuals may base it, at least in part, on feedback that is actually irrelevant to the achievement of their performance goals.

2. *Social Environment.* According to image theory, our self-perception arises from our interactions with others. Yammarino and Atwater note how the social environment provides both interpersonal data (the individual comparing him/herself to others) and intrapersonal data (the individual comparing their previous behaviour to their current behaviour). An individual's self-assessment is dependent upon their interpretation of both kinds of data.

3. *Job Factors.* Yammarino and Atwater suggest that certain characteristics of an individual's job moderate their self-assessment. These include task specificity, role ambiguity, role clarity and certainty of task feedback.

In summary, then, Yammarino and Atwater state that an individual's initial self-perception of ability is determined by personality and biographical factors which are then modified by internal cognitive processes and external factors. This leads to refinement of the self-perception which is reflected in their self-assessment responses. These writers also incorporate research into determinants of 'others' ratings (as this indirectly influences the individual's revised self-perception). They note how 'others' ratings are also influenced by a variety of factors—some of which determine the initial perception and others which result in its modification. Many of the initial factors linked to the feedback recipient's initial self-perception also influence the other's perception of them (i.e. personality and biographical characteristics). However, they do not make clear in the model whether they mean characteristics of the rater, the ratee, or both. They also note how familiarity and nature of contact between the rater and the individual receiving feedback moderate others' ratings.

Little can be said about this model, other than that it identifies correlates of self–other congruence, and self-assessment accuracy, and provides direction for future research. It does not attempt to describe the interaction between the correlates identified, or how the interaction that does take place influences individual and organisational outcomes following participation in a feedback process. Greater understanding of the actual processes involved in MSMR systems is gleaned from the model proposed by London and Smither (1995).

Conceptualised from research carried out within the context of MSMR feedback programmes, London and Smither's model looks at (1) how such feedback helps individuals understand how they are viewed by others, and (2) how it enables individuals to identify areas for skill development and performance improvement. The model proposes that employees compare feedback from others to their self-perception. This comparison affects the individual's perceptions of their goal–performance discrepancy. The degree of discrepancy perceived is moderated by four factors: (1) the individual's self-image (the propensity for self-enhancement); (2) the individual's feedback-seeking behaviour (the propensity to seek others' opinions about oneself—both positive and negative); (3) the individual's self-monitoring behaviour (interpersonal sensitivity—the ability to read others' verbal and non-verbal social cues and adapt behaviour accordingly); (4) characteristics of the rating/feedback method which influence the individual's schemas of expected behaviours. London and Smither state that (1) the number of raters; (2) whether the feedback is about behaviours rewarded by the organisation; (3) the credibility and reliability of those providing feedback, in conjunction with the different performance standards that each feedback provider holds, will also influence the individual's perceptions of goal–performance discrepancies.

Feedback recipients' goal–performance discrepancies and schemas of expected behaviours affect their self-awareness and possible re-evaluation of their self-image. If re-evaluation is necessary, they respond to the feedback received by setting goals, establishing areas for skill development, changing behaviour and improving performance. The likelihood of the individual thinking that re-evaluation is necessary is dependent upon three factors: (1) the individual's task efficacy (the individual's belief in their ability to perform a particular task successfully); (2) the individual's impression management desires (the behaviours people exhibit and the process of self-disclosure to create and maintain desired impressions); (3) the individual's perception of expected behaviours (i.e. the clarity of performance standards). London and Smither go on to provide a number of research hypotheses, stipulating exactly the manner in which characteristics of the individual, the feedback programme and the organisation can moderate the efficacy of a 360 degree feedback programme, as measured by changes in attitude and behaviour.

London and Smither's model has drawn upon a number of theoretical perspectives and research carried out in the field to provide a detailed description of individual, methodological and organisational factors which determine feedback recipients' attitudes and changes in behaviour following participation in MSMR feedback. The model offers considerable direction for research, providing a number of hypotheses and suggestions for the quantification of impact (both individual and organisational) of MSMR feedback systems. Considering the impact that MSMR feedback systems are reported to have on individuals and organisations—both anecdotally, and to a lesser extent, empirically—and the fact that the use of developmental feedback is almost commonplace, there is a need to verify the processes and moderating factors outlined by this model. In doing so, guidelines for best practice will become clearer.

CONCLUSIONS: SOME IMPLICATIONS FOR RESEARCH AND PRACTICE

In the introduction to this chapter, we predicted that although there had been relatively little research on MSMR systems to date, this would change quickly because this is a very 'researchable' area. One question, then, is what the priorities for the research should be? One may agree with the logic and good sense of Funderburg and Levy (1997) when they call for more investigation of the components of organisation readiness for the introduction of 360 degree feedback, but the reality is that putting our efforts in this direction may be as futile as passengers on the *Titanic* counting rowing boats on the first day of their voyage. Organisations have already steamed ahead and, regardless of the hazards identified by academics, they are unlikely to slow down or put about. This being the case, it would seem wiser to turn our attention not so much to where or whether it should be applied, but *how*, and with what effects. With this in mind, three possible priority research areas are discussed below. A fourth, on self-awareness, has already been discussed earlier, though this is perhaps a research theme that has virtue quite apart from the subject of MSMR systems. Numerous other, more limited, topics where research is needed have been flagged up as the chapter has progressed. Most of whatever research is done will benefit from the elaboration of models such as that of London and Smither (1995) or the general feedback conceptualisation put forward by Kluger and DeNisi (1996), and should be conducted and integrated within the framework of such models.

MSMR Feedback—Impact and Outcome

A useful exercise is to consider some parallels between 360 degree feedback and other assessment processes, including psychological testing (Fletcher, 1997b). An obvious one is in relation to the impact on the person assessed. In the field of selection and assessment more generally, there is a growing body of work that evaluates the methods used in terms of the effects they have on the candidates and how the latter view them (Iles & Robertson, 1997). Research in this domain has demonstrated that assessment processes and their outcomes may have a variety of unintended negative effects on those being assessed—they may impact on such variables as motivation, self-esteem and intention to leave the organisation (Robertson, Iles, Gratton & Sharpley, 1991; Fletcher, 1991). As there is little doubt that MSMR feedback usually exerts a powerful impact on the recipients—indeed, that is one of the reasons for using it—the possible ill effects should perhaps be investigated too. What influence do varying degrees of favourability of feedback have on self-esteem, motivation, satisfaction and commitment of target managers, and are the different sources of the feedback a factor here? If, as seems likely, there are unwanted consequences of critical feedback, how can these be minimised in the way the feedback is delivered?

There is some research of relevance to these questions that already exists, for example in relation to self-esteem differences and reactions to feedback (e.g. Sweeney & Wells, 1990; London, 1995), but not done within the context of MSMR systems. However, the background work on conventional top-down appraisal still has something to offer here. In particular, it was noted in some of the earliest studies (Kay, Meyer & French, 1965) that two critical comments were typically as much as appraisees could take in a single appraisal episode without becoming defensive, and subsequent work has shown that a variety of other factors—such as the extent to which criticism is balanced with positive feedback, and the style in which it is conveyed—are also important in tolerance for criticism (Fletcher, 1994). It seems very possible that observations made in relation to how people reacted to feedback from the boss are still at least partly applicable in the MSMR situation, not least because the boss is included as one of the sources of feedback. One would hypothesise, on the basis of the appraisal literature, that feedback exercises that provided more than a threshold level of critical content would be likely to exert a demotivating effect. Just what that threshold level is, remains to be determined. But on a purely practical level, feedback that highlights a whole series of development needs for an individual may be confusing and off-putting. It is not the normal practice in development to try to remedy all weaknesses simultaneously—the conventional wisdom would be to prioritise and to focus efforts to improve on just a couple of important areas, because even this will often take a lot of time, effort and (sometimes) resources. Some interfacing between the raw feedback and the target manager is desirable—but not always provided—to make the most effective use of the information for the individual.

Another aspect of recipient reactions to MSMR feedback is that the different rating sources may disagree on some or all facets of the target's behaviour. As Salam, Cox and Sims (1997) demonstrated, what is a positive behaviour to one group may be seen in a very different light by another; for example, being protective of the work pressures on one's subordinates is likely to be seen more favourably by them than by one's boss in some cases. As yet, research has not looked at the way targets react to differences of this kind, especially where there may be no immediate obvious reason why they should arise. Does it lead to a tendency to dismiss the whole feedback exercise, or simply to ignore the more critical aspects?

Finally, as far as this research agenda item is concerned, the overall effectiveness of MSMR systems in producing constructive outcomes has still to be ascertained. No doubt more studies of changes in ratings will accrue, which is useful, but there is also a need for examination of other possible consequences of these interventions—changes in objective performance measures, indices of career development activity, attitudes to management and so on. There is certainly no shortage of hypotheses that can be put forward in relation to outcomes. For example, does the introduction of MSMR feedback have an effect on manager–subordinate communication in other spheres, such as the appraisal interview? Do subordinates report any more favourably on their appraisal experiences after their boss has been through one or more feedback exercises? There is no denying that some of this research will be difficult to do, because it implies longitudinal designs, control groups, and so on; nonetheless, organisations will be inclined to take notice of research if it can demonstrate how different approaches to MSMR systems are associated with differing outcomes and/or levels of effectiveness.

MSMR for Appraisal, or for Development?

Although most of the applications of MSMR systems have been for developmental purposes, there is a shift towards using them as a direct input to the annual appraisal or performance review process. While appraisal and development are obviously linked, there is a fundamental difference in focus, and there are many issues and implications that follow-on from the aims of the system (Fletcher, 1997b). For example:

- Is participation mandatory or optional? If it is an aspect of the appraisal process, participation is more likely to be mandatory
- If it is to be part of an appraisal process, is it to be linked to pay/rewards?
- Is it to be done annually or not? If it is part of appraisal, then it will be a regular exercise, while for developmental purposes it may be a one-off.
- Who decides who is to contribute to the assessment process? In the developmental setting, the target managers usually choose their own raters, but adopting this approach in an appraisal situation could clearly lead to problems.
- Who is responsible for follow-up action? In development, it is usually the ratee, but in appraisal it is more likely to be their boss.

This chapter is not the place to argue the pros and cons of either purpose for MSMR feedback, but whichever one the system is put to is likely to have implications for the research questions posed and for the findings obtained. The studies on attitudes referred to earlier (McEvoy, 1990; Bettenhausen & Fedor, 1997) suggest that rater and ratee reactions may differ a good deal according to the use made of the ratings. As most of the use so far has been for development, most of the research also relates to this. More studies are needed of outcomes of appraisal-oriented MSMR systems; as they are still less common, this is an area where research has an opportunity to lead widespread practice. A consistent theme of research on appraisal processes over a long period has been that direct pay links do little either for the quality of the interaction that takes place in the appraisal interview or for the likelihood of subsequent constructive outcomes occurring (Meyer, Kay & French, 1965; Fletcher, 1997b), though few studies have been so negative (Prince & Lawler, 1986). An important issue for research on MSMR systems, then, is the impact of linking them with pay.

Diversity and MSMR Feedback

The vast majority of studies on attitudes have been carried out in the US, and there are perhaps some dangers in generalising their lessons too freely elsewhere. For example, Earley (1986) demonstrated differences in feedback reactions between British and American workers, with the former showing a less constructive response to criticism. It is possible that findings from studies with more widely diverging cultural backgrounds than US and UK workers—for example cultures differing in terms of power distance or emphasis on group vs individual achievement (Hofstede, 1985, 1991)—will yield some interesting comparisons. Although Furnham and Stringfield (1994) found few differences between Chinese and caucasian airline employees in the ratings given, more evidence from a range of ethnic and culturally-diverse groups is needed here. One question is whether there are differences between such groups in terms of willingness to give critical comments or ratings of superiors.

Gender differences in self-ratings and in congruence were mentioned in the section on self-awareness, as was London and Wohlers' (1991) surprising finding that age did not relate to self- awareness. Age and experience do look likely to be important in the feedback given and how it is received; raters may be willing to make more allowances for less experienced staff, for example. It would thus seem worthwhile looking further at this. Likewise with gender; one of the questions here is whether rater–ratee gender match has any influence on ratings, given that males and females may operate and value different models of leadership (Alimo-Metcalfe, 1995; Bass, Avolio & Atwater, 1996).

The Future of Multi-source, Multi-level Feedback Systems

The speed of adoption of MSMR feedback almost inevitably means that we are learning about it as we go along, and that some of the applications are not as effective or sound as they could or should be. The first author of this chapter wrote a cautionary note in a journal for HR practitioners and got a rejoinder from one of that fraternity in the following issue to the effect that MSMR feedback was not 'rocket science' and that all we need to do is to turn it over to line management and let them get on with it. Well, it certainly is not rocket science, but there is a danger of a great deal of effort and resource being poured into systems that do not do what they say they do, and which perhaps mislead and even psychologically damage individuals in the process. For example, a pilot 360 degree feedback system in a major oil company, when studied, was found: (1) not to measure the competencies it purported to; (2) to have a massive level of redundancy amongst the questionnaire items, such that it seemed only to measure one construct; (3) not to correlate with other measures of performance used within the organisation (Fletcher, Baldry & Cunningham-Snell, 1998). Although MSMR feedback systems are not psychological tests, it seems reasonable to propose that they should be subject to some of the same checks in terms of the internal consistency, fairness and external criterion validity as are tests—and all the more so if they are to be used for administrative purposes. This does not mean, of course, that one should seek to find a high correlation of different rating sources, or that all of their ratings should correlate with other performance indicators. But the feedback questionnaire items should cluster as intended in terms of the competencies measured, and where there are other relevant measures of a similar nature (e.g. superiors' ratings given in a 360 degree feedback exercise and their ratings given to subordinates as part of the formal appraisal system) they should show some relationship to the MSMR ratings.

One factor that may ultimately limit the extent to which MSMR feedback is used is simply the time it takes. A line manager might be asked to complete half a dozen or more sets of ratings on peers within quite a short space of time. There are already some signs of this causing resistance in organisations where it is being done on a frequent basis, though it may be overcome to some extent if feedback questionnaires can be made somewhat shorter than is typically the case at present without losing their value as accurate representations of colleagues' feedback. Using computer-based systems will also probably help here. Research may have lagged behind practice on this topic, but in the future it can perhaps help organisations to identify how and where to get the most out of MSMR feedback. The analogy with psychometric tests comes to mind again when considering the future of these techniques. Just as psychometric testing confounded the predictions of those who thought it would be a short-lived 'fad', so 360 degree feedback is likely to be more than just flavour of the month and shows all the signs of being with us for a long time. It is extending, shifting in function, and is seen as an agent of change in organisations for whom continual development has become a necessity. Just how effective it becomes is likely to depend on the amount and quality of research done on it.

REFERENCES

Algera, J.A. (1990). Feedback systems in organizations. In C.L. Cooper & I.T. Robertson (Eds), *International Review of Industrial and Organizational Psychology 1990* (Vol. 5, pp. 169–194). Chichester: Wiley.

Alimo-Metcalfe, B. (1995). An investigation of male and female constructs of leadership and empowerment. *Women in Management Review*, 10(2), 3–8.

Ammons, R.B. (1956). Effects of knowledge of performance: A survey and tentative theoretical formulation. *Journal of General Psychology*, 54, 279–299.

Antonioni, D. (1996). Designing an effective 360-degree appraisal feedback process. *Organizational Dynamics*, 25(2), 24–38.

Ashford, S.J. (1989). Self-assessments in organizations: A literature review and integrative model. *Research in Organizational Behaviour*, 11, 133–174.

Ashford, S.J. & Cummings, L.L. (1983). Feedback as an individual difference—personal strategies of creating information. *Organizational Behaviour and Human Performance*, **32**(3), 370–398.

Atwater, L., Roush, P. & Fischthal, A. (1995). The influence of upward feedback on self-ratings and follower ratings of leadership. *Personnel Psychology*, **48**(1), 35–59.

Atwater, L.E. & Yammarino, F.J. (1992). Does self–other agreement on leadership perceptions moderate the validity of leadership and performance predictions? *Personnel Psychology*, **45**(1), 141–164.

Bandura, A. (1982). Self-efficacy mechanisms in human agency. *American Psychologist*, **37**, 122–147.

Baron, R.A., Cowan, G. & Ganz, R.I. (1974). Interaction of locus of control and type of performance feedback. *Journal of Applied Psychology*, **75**, 1–11.

Bass, B., Avolio, B.J. & Atwater, L. (1996). The transformation and transactional leadership of men and women. *Applied Psychology: An International Review*, **45**(1), 5–34.

Bass, B.M. & Yammarino, F.J. (1991). Congruence of self and others' ratings of naval officers for understanding successful performance. *Applied Psychology—An International Review*, **40**(4), 437–454.

Bastos, M.W. & Fletcher, C. (1995). Exploring the individual's perception of sources and credibility of feedback in the work environment. *International Journal of Selection and Assessment*, **3**(1), 29–40.

Bernardin, H.J. & Beatty, R.W. (1987). Can subordinate appraisals enhance managerial productivity? *Sloan Management Review*, **28**(4), 63–73.

Bernardin, H.J., Hagan, C. & Kane, J.S. (1995, May). The effects of a 360-degree appraisal system on managerial performance: No matter how cynical I get I can't keep up. In Tornow, W.W. (Chair), *Upward Feedback. The Ups and Downs of It*. Symposium conducted at the Tenth Annual Conference of the Society for Industrial and Organizational Psychology, Orlando, FL.

Bettenhausen, K.L. & Fedor, D.B. (1997). Peer and upward appraisals—a comparison of their benefits and problems. *Group and Organization Management*, **22**(2), 236–263.

Brockner, J. (1979). The effects of self-esteem, success-failure and self-consciousness on task performance. *Journal of Personality and Social Psychology*, **37**, 1732–1741.

Cacioppo, J.T. & Petty, R.E. (1982). The need for cognition. *Journal of Personality and Social Psychology*, **42**, 116–131.

Cederblom, D. & Lounsbury, J.W. (1980). An investigation of user acceptance of peer evaluations. *Personnel Psychology*, **33**, 567–579.

Clifford, L. & Bennett, H. (1997). Best practice in 360 degree feedback. *Selection & Development Review*, **13**(2), 6–9.

DeNisi, A.S. & Mitchell, J.L. (1978). An analysis of peer ratings as predictors and criterion measures and a proposed new application. *Academy of Management Review*, **3**, 369–374.

DeVadar, C.L., Bateson, A.G. & Lord, R.G. (1986). Attribution theory: A meta-analysis of attributional hypothesis. In Locke, E. (Ed.), *Generalizing from Laboratory to Field Settings*. Lexington, MA: Lexington Books.

Earley, P.C. (1986). Trust, perceived importance of praise and criticism and work performance—an examination of feedback in the United States and England. *Journal of Management*, **12**(4), 457–473.

Edwards, J.R. (1994). The study of congruence in organizational behaviour research: Critique and a proposed alternative. *Organization Behaviour and Human Decision Processes*, **58**, 51–100.

Fedor, D.B. (1991). Recipient responses to performance feedback: A proposed model and its implications. *Personnel and Human Resources Management*, **9**, 73–120.

Fletcher, C. (1991). Candidates' reactions to assessment centres and their outcomes: A longitudinal study. *Journal of Occupational Psychology*, **64**, 117–127.

Fletcher, C. (1994). The effects of performance review in appraisal: Evidence and implications. In C. Mabey & P. Iles (Eds), *Managing Learning*. London: Routledge/Open University.

Fletcher, C. (1997a). Self-awareness—A neglected attribute in selection and assessment? *International Journal of Selection and Assessment*, 5(3), 183–187.

Fletcher, C. (1997b). *Appraisal: Routes to Improved Performance*, 2nd edn. London: Institute of Personnel & Development.

Fletcher, C., Baldry, C. & Cunningham-Snell, N. (1998). The psychometric properties of 360 degree feedback: An empirical study and cautionary tale. *International Journal of Selection and Assessment* (in press).

Fletcher, C. & Kerslake, C. (1992). The impact of assessment centres and their outcomes on participants' self-assessments. *Human Relations*, **45**, 73–81.

Fletcher, C., Taylor, P. & Glanfield, K. (1996). Acceptance of personality questionnaire feedback—the role of individual difference variables and source of interpretation. *Personality and Individual Differences*, 20(2), 151–156.

Foti, R. (1990). The role of cognitive categories in supervisor versus self-ratings. Paper presented at the *Academy of Management Conference*, August, San Francisco.

Fox, S. & Dinur, Y. (1988). Validity of self-assessment—A field evaluation. *Personnel Psychology*, 41(3), 581–592.

Funderburg, S.A. & Levy, P.E. (1997). The influence of individual and contextual variables on 360-degree feedback system attitudes. *Group & Organization Management*, 22(2), 210–235.

Furnham, A. & Stringfield, P. (1994). Correlates of self and subordinate ratings of managerial practices as a correlate of supervisor evaluation. *Journal of Occupational and Organizational Psychology*, 67(1), 57–67.

Giacalone, R.A. & Rosenfeld, P. (1989). The effect of sex and impression management on future salary estimations. *Journal of General Psychology*, 116(2), 215–219.

Gordon, M.J. (1991). A review of the validity and accuracy of self-assessments in health professionals' training. *Academic Medicine*, **66**, 762–769.

Handy, L., Devine, M. & Heath, L. (1996). *Feedback: Unguided Missile or Powerful Weapon?* Report published by the Ashridge Management Research Group, Ashridge Management College.

Harris, M.M. & Schaubroeck, J. (1988). A meta-analysis of self-supervisor, self-peer and peer-supervisor ratings. *Personnel Psychology*, **41**, 43–62.

Hazucha, J.F., Hezlett, S.A. & Schneider, R.J. (1993). The impact of 360-degree feedback on management skills development. *Human Resource Management*, 32(2–3), 325–351.

Herold, D.M., Parsons, C.K. & Rensvold, R.B. (1996). Individual differences in the generation and processing of performance feedback. *Educational and Psychological Measurement*, 56(1), 5–25.

Hofstede, G. (1985). The interaction between national and organizational value systems. *Journal of Management Studies*, 22(4), 347–357.

Hofstede, G. (1991). *Cultures and Organizations*. Maidenhead: McGraw-Hill.

Holt, K., Noe, R.A. & Cavanaugh, M. (1995). Managers' developmental responses to 360-degree feedback. Unpublished manuscript.

Hunter, J.E., Schmidt, F.L. & Jackson, G.B. (1982). *Meta-analysis: Cumulating Research Findings Across Studies*. Beverley Hills, CA: Sage Publications.

Iles, P.A. & Robertson, I.T. (1997). The impact of personnel selection procedures on candidates. In N. Anderson & P. Herriot (Eds), *International Handbook of Selection and Assessment*. Chichester, UK: Wiley.

Imada, A.S. (1982). Social interaction, observation and stereotypes as determinants of differentiation in peer ratings. *Organizational Behavior and Human Performance*, **29**, 397–415.

Janoff-Bulman, R. & Brickman, P. (1981). Expectations and learning from failure. In N.T. Feather (Ed.). *Expectancy Incentive and Action*. Hillsdale, NJ: Erlbaum.

Jussim, L., Coleman, L. & Nassau, S. (1987). The influence of self-esteem on perceptions of performance and feedback. *Social Psychology Quarterly*, **50**(1), 95–99.

Kane, J.S., Bernardin, H.J., Villanova, P. & Peyrefitte, J. (1995). Stability of rater leniency—3 studies. *Academy of Management Journal*, **38**(4), 1036–1051.

Kane, J.S. & Lawler, E.E. (1978). Methods of peer assessment. *Psychological Bulletin*, **85**, 555–586.

Kay, E., Meyer, H.H. & French, J.R.P. Jr (1965). Effects of threat in a performance appraisal interview. *Journal of Applied Psychology*, **49**, 311–317.

Klimoski, R.J. & London, M. (1974). Role of the rater in performance appraisal. *Journal of Applied Psychology*, **59**, 445–451.

Kluger, A.N. & DeNisi, A. (1996). The effects of feedback interventions on performance—A historical review, a meta-analysis, and a preliminary feedback intervention theory. *Psychological Bulletin*, **119**(2), 254–284.

Korman, A.K. (1970). Toward a hypothesis of work behaviour. *Journal of Applied Psychology*, **54**, 31–41.

Korman, A.K. (1976). Hypothesis of work behaviour revisited and an extension. *Academy of Management Review*, **1**, 50–63.

Lane, J. & Herriott, P. (1990). Self-ratings, supervisor ratings, positions and performance. *Journal of Occupational Psychology*, **63**, 77–88.

Lewin, A.Y. & Zwany, A. (1976). Peer nominations: A model, literature critique and a paradigm for research. *Personnel Psychology*, **29**, 423–447.

Lindeman, M., Sundvik, L. & Rouhiainen, P. (1995). Underestimation or over-estimation of self–person variables and self-assessment accuracy in work settings. *Journal of Social Behaviour and Personality*, **10**(1), 123–134.

London, M. (1994). Interpersonal insight in organizations: cognitive models for human resource development. *Human Resource Management Review*, **4**(4), 311–332.

London, M. (1995). Giving feedback—Source-centred antecedents and consequences of constructive and destructive feedback. *Human Resource Management Review*, **5**(3), 159–188.

London, M. & Beatty, R.W. (1993). 360-degree feedback as a competitive advantage. *Human Resource Management*, **32**(2–3), 353–372.

London, M. & Smither, J.W. (1995). Can multi-source feedback change perceptions of goal accomplishment, self-evaluations and performance related outcomes? Theory-based applications and directions for research. *Personnel Psychology*, **48**, 803–839.

London, M. & Wohlers, A.J. (1991). Agreement between subordinate and self-ratings in upward feedback. *Personnel Psychology*, **44**(2), 375–390.

Love, K.G. (1981). Comparison of peer assessment methods: Reliability, validity, friendship bias and user reaction. *Journal of Applied Psychology*, **66**, 451–457.

Mabe, P.A. & West, S.G. (1982). Validity of self-evaluation of ability—A review and meta-analysis. *Journal of Applied Psychology*, **67**(3), 280–296.

Maurer, T.J. & Tarulli, B.A. (1996). Acceptance of peer/upward performance appraisal systems: Role of work context factors and beliefs about managers' development capability. *Human Resource Management*, **35**(2), 217–241.

McCauley, C. & Lombardo, M. (1990). Benchmarks: An instrument for diagnosing managerial strengths and weaknesses. In K.E. Clark & M.B. Clark (Eds), *Measures of Leadership*. West Orange, NJ: Leadership Library of America.

McEvoy, G.M. (1990). Public sector managers' reactions to appraisal by subordinates. *Public Personnel Management*, **19**(2), 201–212.

McEvoy, G.M. & Beatty, R.W. (1989). Assessment centers and subordinate appraisal of managers: A seven year longitudinal examination of predictive validity. *Personnel Psychology*, **42**(1), 37–52.

McEvoy, G.M. & Buller, P.F. (1987). User acceptance of peer appraisals in an industrial setting. *Personnel Psychology*, **40**, 785–797.

Meyer, H.H. (1980). Self appraisal of job performance. *Personnel Psychology*, **33**, 291–295.

Meyer, H.H., Kay, E. & French, J.R.P. (1965). Split roles in performance appraisal. *Harvard Business Review*, **43**, 123–129.

Meyer, H.H. & Walker, W.B. (1961). A study of factors relating to the effectiveness of a performance appraisal program. *Personnel Psychology*, **14**, 291–298.

Mount, M.K. (1984). Psychometric properties of subordinate ratings of managerial performance. *Personnel Psychology*, **37**, 687 702.

Murphy, K.R. & Cleveland, J.N. (1997). Understanding performance appraisal: Social, organizational and goal-based perspectives. *International Journal of Selection and Adjustment*, **5**(1), 80–84.

Nilsen, D. & Campbell, D.P. (1993). Self-observer rating discrepancies—Once an overrater, always an overrater? *Human Resource Management*, **32**(2–3), 265–281.

Podsakoff, P.M. & Organ, D.W. (1986). Self-reports in organizational research: Problems and perspectives. *Journal of Management*, **12**, 531–544.

Pollack, D.M. & Pollack, L.J. (1996). Using 360È feedback in performance appraisal. *Public Personnel Management*, **25**(4), 507–528.

Prince, J.B. & Lawler, E.E. (1986). Does salary discussion hurt the developmental performance-appraisal? *Organizational Behaviour and Human Decision Processes*, **37**(3), 357–375.

Redman, T. & Mathews, B.P. (1997). What do recruiters want in a public sector manager? *Public Personnel Management*, **26**(2), 245–256.

Redman, T. & Snape, E. (1992). Upward and onward—Can staff appraise their managers? *Personnel Review*, **21**(7), 32–46.

Reilly, R.R. & Chao, G.T. (1982). Validity and fairness of some alternative employee selection procedures. *Personnel Psychology*, **35**(1), 1–62.

Riggio, R.E. & Cole, E.J. (1992). Agreement between subordinate ratings of supervisor performance and effects on self and subordinate satisfaction. *Journal of Occupational and Organizational Psychology*, **65**, 151–158.

Robertson, L., Torkel, S., Korsgaard, A., Klein, D., Diddams, M. & Cayer, M. (1993). Self-appraisal and perceptions of the appraisal discussion—A field experiment. *Journal of Organizational Behaviour*, **14**(2), 129–142.

Robertson, I.T., Iles, P.A., Gratton, L. & Sharpley, D. (1991). The impact of personnel selection and assessment methods on candidates reactions. *Human Relations*, **44**(9), 963–982.

Romano, C. (1994). Conquering the fear of feedback. *HR Focus*, **71**(3), 9–19.

Roush, P.E. & Atwater, L. (1992). Using the MBTI to understand transformational leadership and self-perception accuracy. *Military Psychology*, **4**(1), 17–34.

Rubin, R. (1995). Upward appraisal: What do subordinates consider important in evaluating their supervisors? *Library and Information Science Research*, **17**(2), 151–161.

Salam, S., Cox, J.F. & Sims, H.P. (1997). In the eye of the beholder—How leadership relates to 360-degree performance ratings. *Group and Organization Management*, **22**(2), 185–209.

Schmitt, N., Gooding, R.Z., Noe, R.A. & Kirsch, M. (1984). Meta-analysis of validity studies published between 1964 and 1982 and the investigation of study characteristics. *Personnel Psychology*, **37**, 407–422.

Shrauger, J.S. & Osberg, T.M. (1981). The relative accuracy of self-predictions and judgements by others in psychological assessment. *Psychological Bulletin*, **90**(2), 322–351.

Shrauger, J.S. & Rosenberg, S.F. (1970). Self-esteem and the effects of success and failure feedback on performance. *Journal of Personality*, **38**, 404–417.

Siegal, L. (1982). Paired comparison evaluations of managerial effectiveness by peers and supervisors. *Personnel Psychology*, **35**, 843–852.

Silver, W.S., Mitchell, T.R. & Gist, M.E. (1995). Responses of successful and unsuccessful performance—The moderating effect of self-efficacy on the relationship between performance and attributions. *Organizational Behaviour and Human Decision Processes*, **62**(3), 286–299.

Smith, R.E. & Sarason, I.G. (1975). Social anxiety and evaluation of negative interpersonal feedback. *Journal of Consulting and Clinical Psychology*, **43**, 429.

Smither, J.W., London, M., Vasilopoulos, M.L., Reilly, M.R., Millsap, R.E. & Salvemini, N. (1995). An examination of the effects of an upward feedback program over time. *Personnel Psychology*, **48**(1), 1–34.

Smither, J.W., Wohlers, A.J. & London, M. (1995). A field-study of reactions to normative versus individualized upward feedback. *Group & Organization Management*, **20**(1), 61–89.

Snyder, M. (1974). The self-monitoring of expressive behaviour. *Journal of Personality and Social Psychology*, **30**, 526–537.

Steers, R.M. (1975). Task–goal attributes, n-achievement, and supervisory performance. *Organizational Behaviour and Human Performance*, **13**, 392–403.

Stinson, J. & Stokes, J. (1980). How to multi-appraise. *Management Today*, June, 43–53.

Stumpf, S.A. & Colarelli, S.M. (1980). Career exploration—development of dimensions and some preliminary findings. *Psychological Reports*, **47**(3), 979–988.

Sweeney, P.D. & Wells, L.E. (1990). Reactions to feedback about performance—A test of three competing models. *Journal of Applied Social Psychology*, **20**(10), 818–834.

Timmreck, C.W. (1995, May). Upward feedback in the trenches: Challenges and realities. In W.W. Tornow (Chair), *Upward Feedback: The Ups and Downs of It*. Symposium conducted at the Tenth Annual Conference of the Society for Industrial and Organizational Psychology, Orlando, FL.

Tucker, M.F., Kline, V.B. & Schmitt, J.R. (1967). Prediction of creativity and other performance measures from biographical information among pharmaceutical scientists. *Journal of Applied Psychology*, **51**, 131–138.

VanVelsor, E., Taylor, S. & Leslie, J.B. (1993). An examination of the relationships among self-perception accuracy, self-awareness, gender and leader effectiveness. *Human Resource Management*, **32**(2–3), 249–263.

Viswesvaran, C., Schmidt, F.L. & Ones, D.S. (1997). The moderating influence of rating content on peer–supervisor convergence: A meta-analytic review based on four job performance models. Unpublished paper. Presented at *5th European Congress of Psychology*, Dublin, Ireland, July 1997.

Ward, P. (1997). *360-Degree Feedback*. London: IPD.

Weiss, H.M. (1977). Subordinate imitation of supervisor behaviour. *Organizational Behaviour and Human Performance*, **28**, 356–378.

Wexley, K.N., Alexander, R., Greenwalt, J. & Couch, M. (1980). Attitudinal congruence and similarity as related to interpersonal evaluation in manager-subordinate dyads. *Academy of Management Journal*, **23**, 320–330.

Wexley, K.N. & Klimoski, R. (1984). Performance appraisal: An update. In K.M. Rowland & G.R. Ferris (Eds), *Research in Personnel and Human Resources Management*, (Vol. 2, pp. 35–79). Greenwich, CT: JAI Press.

Wohlers, A.J. & London, M. (1989). Ratings of managerial characteristics—Evaluation difficulty, co-worker agreement and self-awareness. *Personnel Psychology*, **42**(2), 235–261.

Yammarino, F.J. & Atwater, L.E. (1993). Understanding self-perception accuracy—Implications for human resource management. *Human Resource Management*, **32**(2–3), 231–247.

Yammarino, F.J. & Dubinsky, A.J. (1990). Salesperson performance and managerially controllable factors—An investigation of individual and work group effects. *Journal of Management*, **16**(1), 87–106.

Zammuto, R.F., London, M. & Rowland, K.M. (1982). Organization and rater differences in performance appraisals. *Personnel Psychology*, **35**, 643–658.

Chapter 5

GENERAL COGNITIVE ABILITY AND OCCUPATIONAL PERFORMANCE*

Malcolm James Ree and Thomas R. Carretta
Air Force Research Laboratory, Brooks Air Force Base, USA

There is no substitute for talent. Industry and all the virtues are of no avail.
(Aldous Huxley)

This chapter consists of two parts. The first concerns the nature of general cognitive ability, *g*. We begin by describing the history of the measurement and the factor structure of human ability and then the broad range of its psychological, social, and physical correlates. In response to critics (Murphy, 1996), we pay particular attention to evidence of the physiological correlates and substrata of human intelligence. Although *g* and physiological correlates are well documented, little of that research has appeared in the industrial/ organizational psychology literature. The second part of this chapter examines the nexus of relations between *g* and occupational performance. Evidence of predictive validity and fairness is presented, as well as research on the incremental validity of specific abilities. Path-analyses are reviewed that document the possible causal relations among *g*, job knowledge, and performance in training and on the job.

GENERAL COGNITIVE ABILITY

Sir Francis Galton (1869), the English polymath, conceived the concept of general cognitive ability, *g*, Charles Spearman (1930) made it more familiar to psychology in his two-factor theory of human abilities. According to the two-

---

* The views expressed are those of the authors and not necessarily those of the United States Government, the Department of Defense, or the United States Air Force.

General Cognitive Ability and Occupational Performance by Malcolm James Ree and Thomas R. Carretta taken from IRIOP 1998 v13, Edited by Cary L. Cooper and Ivan T. Robertson: © 1998 John Wiley & Sons, Ltd

factor theory, every measure of ability had two components, a general component (g) and a specific component (s).

> One part depends on an element—or factor which remains always the same in all
> the abilities of the same individual. The other part depends on a second factor
> which, even for the same individual, differs freely from one ability to another. (p.
> 342)

The general component was measured by all tests and the specific component
was unique to the test. Each test might have a different specific component.
Spearman also observed that s could be found in common across a limited
number of tests. Therefore, the two-factor theory allowed for a verbal factor
that was distinct from g but found in several verbal tests. Factors shared by
tests were called 'group factors'. Spearman (1927) identified 'logical', 'mechanical', 'psychological', 'arithmetical', and 'ability to appreciate music' as
group factors. Spearman (1937) noted that group factors could be either
narrow or broad and that s could not be measured without measuring g. As we
have written elsewhere (Ree & Carretta, 1996),

> To be accurate, we should call mathematics not M but
>
> $$g + M$$
>
> with g written large to indicate its contribution to the variance of the factor.
> (p. 113)

Despite Spearman's early assertion (1930) that g was beyond dispute,
controversy never abated. Thurstone (1938) proposed a multiple ability
theory that stood in contrast to Spearman's model. In the Thurstone
theory there was no general factor, only seven unrelated abilities that he
considered 'primary'. However, within months, Spearman (1938) re-
analyzed Thurstone's data, noting that g had been submerged through
rotation. Spearman demonstrated the existence of g in Thurstone's tests.
This was independently confirmed by Holzinger and Harmon (1938) and
finally by Thurstone and Thurstone (1941). Notwithstanding, theories of
multiple abilities held sway in psychology (Fleishman & Quaintance, 1984;
Gardner, 1983; Guilford, 1956, 1959; Sternberg, 1985). This was
especially true in psychometrics where these theories led to the development of several multiple ability tests such as the Differential Aptitude Test,
General Aptitude Test Battery, Armed Services Vocational Aptitude Battery, Air Force Officer Qualifying Test, Flanagan Aptitude Tests,
Flanagan Industrial Tests, and others. Despite the interest in multiple
abilities, other researchers studied g (Arvey, 1986; Gottfredson, 1986,
1997; Gustafsson, 1980, 1984, 1988; Jensen, 1980, 1993; Thorndike,
1986; Vernon, 1950, 1969).

STRUCTURE OF ABILITIES

Early Conceptualizations

The structure of abilities has long been a subject of speculation and study. Aristotle distinguished ability, called *dianoia*, from *orexis*, emotional and moral faculty. The study of human abilities then passed to religious philosophers. Later, the French secular philosopher Descartes conceived of ability as *res cogitans*, the thing that thinks.

Peiró and Munduate (1994) report an early Spanish treatise on ability and work by Juan Huarte in 1575 called *Examen de Ingenios*, later published in English as *The examination of men's wits: Discovering the great differences of wits among men and what sort of learning suites best with each genius*. However, scientific study of human abilities is frequently traced back to Binet and to the US Army Alpha test of World War I.

Spearman (1927), in his view of *g* and *s*, often depicted these two constructs with overlapping circles. A large circle depicted *g* and smaller ovals, radially arrayed, portrayed *s*. Jensen (1980) illustrates Spearman's theory as in Figure 5.1. In this figure, the specific abilities are unique to a test and the amount of overlap with *g* varies, as shown by the spatial overlap of the circle representing *g* and the ovals representing *s*.

In 1931 the 'Unitary Traits Committee' was formed with E.L. Thorndike as the chair. The goal of this committee was to explore the problem of one versus multiple intelligences. Because of World War II and Spearman's death in 1945 the final summary report was never published.

Hierarchical Models

Ability can be conceptualized as having many equal factors (Thurstone's Primary Mental Abilities) or as hierarchically organized. There has been a growing consensus over the past five decades that abilities have a hierarchical structure. Burt (1949) proposed a five-level hierarchy with *g* at its apex, with successively expanding levels below. These levels from higher to lower are 'General Intelligence', 'Relations', 'Association', 'Perception', and 'Sensation'. He suggested that the second level was made up of broad group factors based on form and content. The successive levels were more numerous and composed of more specialized narrower group factors.

Vernon proposed and demonstrated a hierarchical structure as early as 1950 and continued to refine the hierarchical concept. Figure 5.2 shows the Vernon model.

Vernon's (1950, 1969) model also has *g* at its apex and two broad factors of verbal-educational (v:ed) and spatial-mechanical or spatial-perceptual-practical (k:m) next. These subdivide into minor group factors that devolve to specific factors.

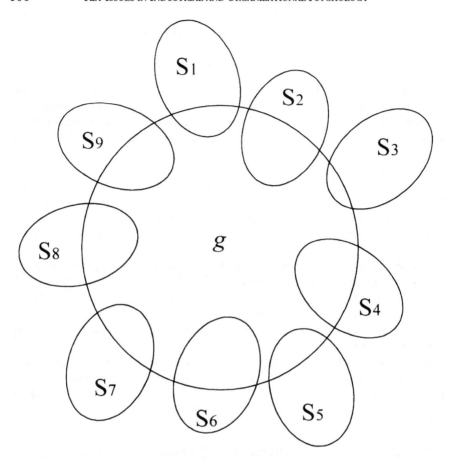

Figure 5.1   Representation of Spearman's two-factor theory of abilities, where every test measures a general factor common to all tests, g and a specific factor that is unique to each test, s_1 to s_9

Reproduced with permission from Jensen, A. R. (1980). *Bias in Mental Testing*. New York: Free Press

Cattell (1971) and Horn (1978) postulated a hierarchical model that does not include g. This model had two factors at its apogee, Gf or fluid ability and Gc or crystallized ability. However, Hakstian and Cattell (1978) tentatively added four others, Gv (visualization), Gps (perceptual speed), Gm (memory), and Gr (retrieval), but recognized the need for further confirmation in additional samples. Jager (1967) also proposed several higher-order factors but his model has not been influential.

Gustafsson (1988) has suggested a relationship between the Spearman-type g model and the Cattell–Horn synthesis. He suggests that Gc corresponds to v:ed, Gv to k:m, and Gf to g. Gustafsson (1980) partially supports his interpretation by finding the loading of Gf on g at 0.94.

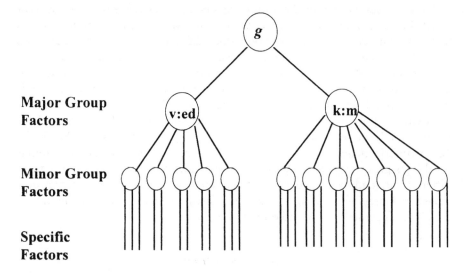

Figure 5.2   Representation of Vernon's hierarchical model of abilities

Hierarchical models imply higher-order sources of abilities and several specific lower-order sources. In cognitive ability, the highest-order factor (*g*) is usually found to account for more of the variance than all specific factors combined. It is important to residualize (Schmid & Leiman, 1957) and remove the effects of *g* to understand the nature of the lower-order factors. In representative multiple ability tests (Carretta & Ree, 1996; Ree & Carretta, 1994: Stauffer, Ree & Carretta, 1996) the largest proportion of variance accounted for by a residualized specific factor is about 8%. To put this in perspective, the amount of variance accounted for by *g* ranges from about 30 to 65% depending on the composition of the test battery. An informative review is provided elsewhere (Jensen, 1980, ch. 6).

Fairness and Similarity: Near Identity of Cognitive Structure

Several studies of cognitive factor similarity have been conducted. Comparing the factor structure of World War II US Army pilot selection tests for Blacks and Whites, Michael (1949) found virtually no differences. Humphreys and Taber (1973) also found no differences when they compared factor structures for high and low socio-economic status boys from Project Talent. Although the ethnicity of the participants in Project Talent was not specifically identified, they expected that the ethnic composition of the two groups would differ significantly.

Using 15 cognitive tests, DeFries, Vandenberg, McClearn et al. (1974) compared the structure of ability for Hawaiians of either European or Japanese ancestry. They found the same four factors and nearly identical factor loadings for the two groups.

These studies all examined common factors. Ree and Carretta (1995) investigated the comparative structure of ability across sex and ethnic groups using a hierarchical model. They observed only small differences on the verbal/math and speed factors. No significant differences were found for *g* on ability measures.

Carretta and Ree (1995) made comparisons of aptitude factor structures in large samples of young Americans. The factor model was hierarchical including *g* and five lower-order factors representing verbal, math, spatial, aircrew knowledge, and perceptual speed. The model showed good fit and little difference for both sexes and all five ethnic groups (White, Black, Hispanic, Asian-American, and Native-American). Correlations between factor loadings for the sex groups and for all pairs of groups indicated that there was no mean difference in loadings between males and females or among the ethnic groups. These and previous findings present a consistent picture of near identity of cognitive structure for sex and ethnic groups.

CORRELATES OF *g*

Psychological Correlates

There are many correlates of *g*. Brand (1987) presents an encompassing summary that includes four dozen characteristics with positive correlations with *g* and 19 that show negative correlations with *g*. Brand provides references for all examples listed below. Ree and Earles (1994) have divided these characteristics into several categories. These categories and examples for each category are:

- abilities (reaction time, analytic style, eminence)
- creativity/artistic (craftwork, musical ability)
- health and fitness (infant mortality, dietary preference, longevity)
- interests/choice (marital partner, sports participation, breadth and depth of interest)
- moral (delinquency (–), racial prejudice (–), values)
- ccupational (SES, occupational status, income)
- perceptual (myopia, field-independence, ability to perceive brief stimuli)
- personality (achievement motivation, altruism, dogmatism) (–)
- practical (social skills, practical knowledge) and other (motor skills)
- talking speed, accident proneness (–)

Physiological Correlates

Physiological correlates of *g* have long been postulated. Hart and Spearman (1914) and Spearman (1927) speculated about the possible physiological causes of *g*. Nominated were 'energy', 'plasticity', and 'the blood' among others. Thomson (1939) in a similar way speculated about 'sampling of mental bonds'. No empirical evidence was provided by Hart, Spearman, or Thomson.

Recently Murphy (1996) stated that little is known about the physiological, biochemical, or neural roots of cognitive ability. While not all is known, there exists a growing body of research in this area. We review several of these studies below, as almost none of them were published in journals traditionally read by industrial/organizational psychologists. Most industrial/organizational psychologists are unaware of the state of knowledge in this area.

Some physiological correlates of g have been identified. Jensen (1980) provided a brief summary. Below we update previously published summaries.

Brain structure

Brain size and g are positively correlated. Van Valen (1974) found a correlation of about 0.30. Broman, Nichols, Shaughnessy, and Kennedy (1987) found correlations of 0.1 to 0.2 for g and head perimeter, a relatively inefficient measure of brain size. With the advent of more advanced measurement devices, especially magnetic resonance imaging (MRI), evidence on the relationship of brain size and g has become firmer. Willerman, Schultz, Rutledge, and Bigler (1991) used MRI to demonstrate a correlation of 0.35 between g and brain size. Andreasen, Flaum, Swayze et al. (1993) found brain size–ability correlations of 0.40 and 0.44 for men and women respectively. They also found significant correlations for volumes of part of the brain such as the hippocampus and cerebellum. Other researchers have found similar values. For example, Wickett, Vernon, and Lee (1994) reported $r = 0.39$, Schultz, Gore, Sodhi, and Anderson (1993) reported an age-corrected $r = 0.43$, Egan, Wickett, and Vernon (1995) reported $r = 0.48$. Willerman and Schultz (1996) have noted that the accumulated evidence on the relationship of brain size to ability 'provides the first solid lead for understanding g at a biological level of analysis' (p. 16).

Brain myelination offers another possible physiological explanation of g. Schultz (1991) found a correlation ($r = 0.54$) between g and amount of brain myelination in young adults. The effect of myelin on conduction velocity is consistent with brighter people being speedier (Frearson, Eysenck & Barrett, 1990). Waxman (1992) suggested an alternative interpretation. The relationship might be a result of reduced 'noise' due to the effect of myelin on fidelity of transmission. Miller (1996) presents an instructive review.

Based on the work of Jouandet, Tramo, Herron et al. (1989) and Tramo, Loftus, Thomas et al. (1995), Willerman and Schultz (1996) suggest cortical surface area as a good index of ability. They cited Haug (1987) who conducted a small-scale postmortem study and found that cortical surface area was related to occupational prestige, a correlate of g. Willerman and Schultz speculated that regional (i.e. localized on the brain) surface areas would be even better predictors of ability. The review by Willerman and Schultz provides an excellent summary of the state of the art in understanding physiological substrata of g. An earlier review by Eysenck (1982) is also helpful.

Brain electrical potential

Correlations between various indices of brain electrical potentials and *g* have also been shown. Chalke and Ertl (1965) first presented data suggesting a relationship between average evoked potential (AEP) and measures of *g*. Their findings were supported by Ertl and Schafer (1969) who found correlations ranging from −0.10 to −0.35 for AEP and scores on the Wechsler Intelligence Scale for Children. A well-designed study by Shucard and Horn (1972) found similar correlations ranging from −0.15 to −0.32 between visual AEP and measures of fluid *g* and crystallized *g*.

Speed of neural processing

Reed and Jensen (1992) have demonstrated a correlation of 0.37 between speed of neural conductivity and measured intelligence. This relationship was found for an optic nerve leading to the brain. Faster neural conductive velocity was associated with higher *g*. Affirming replications are needed.

Brain glucose metabolism rate

Haier, Siegel, Nuechterlein et al. (1988) found a negative correlation between brain glucose metabolism and scores on the Ravens Advanced Progressive Matrices, a highly *g*-loaded test. Haier, Siegel, Tang et al. (1992) found support in brain glucose metabolism for their theory of brain efficiency and intelligence. However, Larson, Haier, LaCasse, and Hazen (1995) suggest the efficiency hypothesis may be dependent on task type and they urge caution.

Physical variables

Jensen (1993) observed that there are physical variables that correlate with *g* but for which the causal mechanism is unknown and hard to hypothesize. These included certain blood antigens, serum uric acid level, vital capacity (lung volume), facial features, basal metabolic rate in children, asthma and other allergies, presence or absence of the masa intermedia in the brain, ability to taste the chemical phenylthiocarbamide and the ability to curl the tongue. For example, Roseman and Buckley (1975) have found a negative correlation between serum level of IgA and *g* in adults. IgA is a blood antigen and the mechanism that relates it to ability is unknown.

Neural transmitters

It should be pointed out that research is absent on the relations of neural transmitters and *g*. There may be relations between such neural transmitters as dopamine or serotonin and *g*; however, such studies cannot be found in the literature. This is a complex area, but one that could expand our understanding.

SPECIFIC ABILITY, KNOWLEDGE, AND NONCOGNITIVE TRAITS

The measurement of specific abilities, knowledge, and noncognitive traits has often been proposed as crucial for understanding human characteristics and occupational performance. McClelland (1993), for example, suggested that under some circumstances noncognitive traits such as motivation may be better predictors of job performance than cognitive abilities. Sternberg and Wagner (1993) proposed the use of measures of tacit knowledge and practical intelligence in lieu of measures of 'academic intelligence'. They define tacit knowledge as 'the practical know how one needs for success on the job' (p. 2). Practical intelligence is defined as a more general form of tacit knowledge. Schmidt and Hunter (1993), in a review of Sternberg and Wagner, note that their concepts of tacit knowledge and practical intelligence are redundant with the well-established construct of job knowledge.

OCCUPATIONAL PERFORMANCE

There are several broad components to occupational performance. Possessing the knowledge, skills, and techniques is one broad component. Another is training and retraining for promotions or new jobs or just staying current with the changing demands of the 'same' job. The application of knowledge, skills, and techniques to achieve organizational goals comprises another component.

Training Measures

The first step in doing a job is to learn the knowledge and master the skills required. This begins in elementary school with reading, writing, and arithmetic. More specialized job knowledge is acquired in secondary school, college, formal job training, and on-the-job training. General cognitive ability is predictive of achievement in all these training settings.

Predictiveness of g

Jensen (1980, p. 319) provides the following estimates of the range of the validity of g for predicting academic success: elementary school—0.6 to 0.7, high school—0.5 to 0.6, college—0.4 to 0.5, and graduate school—0.3 to 0.4. He further observed that the apparent decrease in importance of g may be due to artifacts such as range restriction and selective assortment into educational track.

Thorndike (1986) presented an analysis of the predictiveness of g for six high school course grades. He found an average correlation of 0.532 for predicting these grades. This is consistent with Jensen (1980).

McNemar (1964), in his presidential address to the American Psychological Association, reported that g was the best predictor of school performance in 4096 studies conducted using the Differential Aptitude Tests. Brodnick and Ree (1995) reported that g was a better predictor of college performance than social class.

Roth and Campion (1992) showed the validity of a general ability composite for predicting training success in civilian occupations. Their participants were petroleum process technicians. The validity of the g-based composite was 0.50, corrected for range restriction.

Salgado (1995) used a general composite in the Spanish Air Force to predict training success and found biserial correlations of 0.38. His data were uncorrected for range restriction. Using cumulative techniques he demonstrated that there was no variability in the corrrelations across five classes of pilot trainees.

Jones (1988) computed the g-saturation of 10 subtests from a multiple aptitude battery as their loadings on an unrotated first principal component. She correlated these loadings with the average validity of the subtests for predicting training performance for 37 jobs and found a correlation of 0.76. She also computed the same correlation within four job families encompassing the 37 jobs. No differences were found between job families. Later Ree and Earles (1992) corrected the g loadings for unreliability and found the correlation to be 0.98. In a replication in a different sample across 150 jobs they found the same value (Ree & Earles, 1992).

Incrementing the predictiveness of g

Thorndike (1986) reported the comparative validity of specific ability composites vs measures of g for predicting training success in 35 technical schools for about 1900 enlisted US Army trainees. Specific abilities incremented g by about 0.03. Further, on cross-validation the multiple correlations for specific abilities most often shrunk below the bivariate correlation for g.

Using military samples, Ree and Earles (1991) showed that training performance was more a function of g than specific factors. A large scale study of 78 041 US Air Force enlisted personnel was conducted to determine if g predicted job training performance in about the same way regardless of the difficulty or the kind of the job. Based on Hull's theory (1928), it might be argued that g was useful for some jobs, but that specific abilities were compensatory or more important and thus, more valid for other jobs. Ree and Earles sought to evaluate Hull's hypothesis. Linear models were evaluated to test if the relationships of g to training performance criteria were the same for 82 jobs. This was done by first imposing the constraint that the regression coefficients for g be the same in each of the 82 equations, and then releasing the constraint and allowing the 82 regression coefficients to be estimated individually. Although there was statistical evidence that the relationship between g and the training criteria differed by job, these differences were so small as to be of no practical predictive consequence. The relationship between g and performance was nearly identical across jobs. Using a single prediction equation for all the jobs reduced the correlation less than 0.5%.

In practical personnel selection, sometimes specific ability tests are given to qualify applicants for jobs on the assumption that specific abilities are predictive or incrementally predictive. Such tests exist for US Air Force computer programmers and intelligence operatives. Besetsny, Earles, and Ree (1993) and Besetsny, Ree, and Earles (1993) investigated these two tests to determine if they measured something other than g and if their validity was incremental to g. The criterion was training performance. The samples were 3547 computer programming and 776 intelligence operative trainees. Two multiple regression equations were computed for each group of trainees. The first contained only g and the second contained g and specific abilities. The difference in R^2 between these two equations was tested to determine if specific abilities incremented g. For the two jobs, incremental validity gains for specific abilities beyond g were 0.00 and 0.02, respectively. These two tests contributed little or nothing beyond g although they were designed to measure specific abilities.

Thorndike (1986) reported World War II data on the incremental value of specific composites versus g for the prediction of passing/failing pilot training. Sample size was reported as 1000. He disclosed an increment of 0.05 (0.64 vs 0.59) for specifics above g. An examination of the content of the tests indicates that specific knowledge was tested (i.e. aviation information) that may have accounted for part of the increment.

In a similar vein, Olea and Ree (1994) conducted a study of the incremental validity of g and specific ability and specific knowledge in prediction of academic and work sample criteria for US Air Force pilot and navigator trainees. The measures were extracted from the Air Force Officer Qualifying Test (Carretta & Ree, 1996), a multiple aptitude battery that measures g and the lower-order factors of verbal, math, spatial, aircrew knowledge, and perceptual speed. The sample was approximately 5500 lieutenants, 4000 in pilot training and 1500 in navigator training. All were college graduates. Similar training performance criteria were available for the pilots and navigators. For the pilots, the criteria included academic grades, hands-on flying work samples (e.g. landings, loops, and rolls), passing/failing training, and an overall performance composite made by summing the other criteria. For the navigators, the criteria were academic grades, work samples of day and night celestial navigation, passing/failing training, and an overall performance composite made by summing the other criteria. As much as four years elapsed between ability testing and collection of the criteria.

Similar results were found for the pilot and navigator samples. The measure of g was the best predictor for all criteria. For the composite criterion, the broadest and most meaningful measure of performance, the validity corrected for range restriction was 0.40 for pilots and 0.49 for navigators. The non-g portions provided an average increase in predictive accuracy of 0.08 for pilots and 0.02 for navigators. Results suggested that the incremental validity found for pilots was due to specific knowledge about aviation (i.e. aviation controls, instruments, and principles) rather than specific cognitive abilities. The lack of incremental validity for specific knowledge for navigators may have occurred because there were no tests with content about navigation (i.e. estimation of course corrections).

Meta-analyses

A meta-analysis of 52 studies encompassing 5872 participants by Levine, Spector, Menon et al. (1996) found that the average true validity of g-saturated cognitive tests (see their Appendix 2) was 0.668 for training criteria. Hunter and Hunter (1984) have provided a broad meta-analysis of the predictiveness of g for training criteria. Their study included several hundred jobs across numerous job families as well as re-analyses of data from previous studies. They estimated the true validity of g as 0.54 for job-training criteria. These meta-analyses and other research reviewed demonstrate that g predicts training criteria well.

Dimensions of On-the-Job Performance

Sackett, Zedeck, and Fogli (1988) proposed a model of job performance that distinguishes typical from maximum performance. Sackett (personal correspondence, 20 Nov. 1996) suggests that typical performance is a combination of ability and conscientiousness.

Campbell, McHenry, and Wise (1990) proposed a multidimensional theory of job performance. They arrived at a model including eight dimensions that were deemed appropriately broad and generalizable across jobs. These eight are:

1. Job-specific task proficiency
2. Non-job-specific task proficiency
3. Written and oral communication task proficiency
4. Demonstrating effort
5. Maintaining personal discipline
6. Facilitating peer and team performance
7. Supervision/Leadership
8. Management/Administration.

Campbell, McCloy, Oppler, and Sager (1993) described these as the highest order factors that could be useful, discounting a general factor of job performance. They observed that not all the factors were relevant for all jobs.

> What the model asserts is that the eight components, or some subset of them, can describe the highest-order latent variables for every job in the occupational domain. Further, three of the factors—core task proficiency, demonstrated effort, and maintenance of personal discipline—are major performance components of *every* job. (pp. 48–49: emphasis in the original text)

In the first major test of the theory, Campbell, McHenry and Wise (1990) evaluated the model on nine entry-level enlisted jobs in the US Army. They found five factors to be appropriate for the jobs. These factors were core technical proficiency (job-specific task proficiency), general soldiering proficiency (non-job-specific task proficiency), effort and leadership (demonstrating effort), personal discipline (maintaining personal discipline), and physical fitness and military bearing. Campbell and colleagues tested a non-hierarchical model and found a good fit; however, they did not test a hierarchical model. Based on the correlations of the factors presented, we conducted a confirmatory factor analysis that disclosed two hierarchical factors that correlate 0.39. The first of these two factors is composed of Campbell, McHenry and Wise's lower-order factors of 'core technical proficiency' and 'general soldiering proficiency', and the second hierarchical factor is composed of their other three lower-order factors. These two higher-order factors are correlated, suggesting some common source.

Lance, Teachout, and Donnelly (1992) used hierarchical confirmatory factor analysis to model the latent structure of job performance. Basing this on a multidimensional conceptual model of performance in an electronics maintenance job, they confirmed four proficiency dimensions called 'maintenance', 'electronics systems maintenance', 'pickup, service, and delivery', and 'interpersonal proficiency'. The average correlations among the factors was 0.42 with a range of 0.13 to 0.83. An Eigenvalue analysis disclosed that a common first factor accounted for 59% of the variance. The range of loadings of these factors on the first common factors was from 0.3 to 0.6. The smallest value was for 'interpersonal proficiency', and the largest was for 'electronics systems maintenance'.

It should be noted that sometimes plans to create multidimensional criteria lead to unidimensional measures. For example, in Houck, Whitaker, and Kendall (1991) a job analysis disclosed eight performance dimensions for aircraft pilots. Despite the use of subject matter experts and trained psychologists in the writing of criterion items, a single performance factor accounted for 92% of the variance in performance ratings (see Carretta, Perry, & Ree, 1996).

Given these findings, it is reasonable to seek a common job performance factor and to ask if it has a hierarchical relationship to the other factors proposed by Campbell or found by Lance, Teachout, and Donnelly. Viswesvaran, Schmidt, and Ones (1996) conducted a broad-based meta-analysis of the factors of the criterion space of job performance. Cumulating results across 297 studies and across numerous measurement factors and sources, they found that job performance is arranged with a higher-order general factor. They suggested that the general job performance factor was both theoretically and practically important but awaits further research.

Nexus of OgB and Occupational Performance

Some of the earliest results on g and occupational performance were reported by Terman in his studies of gifted individuals. In a series of articles and books, Terman and his collaborators have demonstrated the relationship between ability measured in childhood at about age 11 and adult occupational attainment. Although numerous publications have resulted, much of the most relevant information is the 35-year follow-up (Terman & Oden, 1959). In this volume, they present occupational data for the gifted participants and show them to differ from the population at large. The educational attainment of the gifted group was very high, as was their occupational status. More than 85% of the male sample was in the professional-managerial job category. This exceeds the population proportion many times. On average, the gifted group had high incomes and numerous other signs of occupational accomplishment. Although Terman's work is very informative, it is descriptive rather than predictive or causal in nature. However, it is important because it helped to lay the foundation for later work on the relationship between g and occupational performance.

Predictiveness of g

The predictive validity of g varies systematically with the complexity of the job. This was demonstrated by Hunter (1983b) who analyzed data from the US Department of Labor. Hunter classified 515 occupations into categories according to complexity of data handling (low, medium, and high) and two categories of complexity of dealing with things: simple feeding/offbearing and complex set-up work. The validity of g rose as job complexity increased. The average corrected validities of g for the low, medium, and high data complexity jobs were 0.40, 0.51, and 0.58. For the low complexity feeding/offbearing jobs and complex set-up work jobs the corrected validities were 0.23 and 0.56. See Gottfredson (1997) for a more complete discussion.

An example of the predictiveness of g was presented by Vineburg and Taylor (1972) who used the g-saturated Armed Forces Qualification Test (AFQT). There were 1544 US Army enlistees in four jobs: armor, repair, supply, and cook. The range of experience was 30 days to 20 years and the job performance criteria were work samples. There was a significant correlation between ability and job performance. When the effects of experience and education were removed, the partial correlations between g as measured by the AFQT, and job performance for the four jobs were: armor 0.36, repair 0.32, supply 0.38, and cook 0.35. Vineburg and Taylor also reported the predictiveness of g for supervisory ratings and for the same jobs the validities were 0.26, 0.15, 0.11, and 0.15. These similar validities across dissimilar jobs caused Olea and Ree (1994) to observe 'From jelly rolls to aileron rolls, g predicts occupational criteria' (p. 848).

Roth and Campion (1992) showed the validity of a general ability composite for predicting job performance in the civilian occupation of petroleum process technician. The validity of the g-based composite was 0.37, corrected for range restriction.

Carretta, Perry, and Ree (1996) investigated job performance criteria for US Air Force pilots. The 171 pilots of the high performance F-15, the premier American air superiority aircraft, ranged from 193 to 2805 flying hours and from 1 to 22 years of job experience. The criterion was based on supervisory and peer ratings of job performance, specifically 'situational awareness'. This is a broad-based measure of knowledge of the moving aircraft and its relative position and potential with regard to all surrounding elements. Holding experience constant, g was found to be predictive of the criterion.

Clearly g predicts current performance but Chan (1996) points out another important prediction made by g. In a construct validation study of assessment centers involving members of the Singapore Police Force, scores from a highly g-loaded test predicted future promotions. Police officers who scored higher on the test were more likely to be promoted. He also reported correlations of the Raven's Progressive Matrices and 'initiative/creativity' and between the Raven's and the interpersonal style variable of 'problem confrontation'. Wilk, Desmarais, and Sackett (1995) demonstrated that g was a main cause of the 'gravitational hypothesis' of job mobility and promotion. They observed that 'individuals with higher cognitive ability move into jobs that require more cognitive ability and that individuals with lower cognitive ability move into jobs that require less cognitive ability' (p. 84).

Studying assessment center dimensions, Crawley, Pinder, and Herriot (1990) demonstrated that g was predictive of task-related dimensions. In their range-restricted sample, the highest correlation for g was with the task-based problem-solving dimension and the lowest correlation for g was with the assertiveness dimension.

Kalimo and Vouri (1991) investigated the relationship between g measures taken in childhood and the occupational health criteria of 'sense of competency' and physical and psychological health symptoms. They concluded that 'weak intellectual capacity', as measured in childhood, led to poor conditions and increased health problems.

If Chan (1996) and Kalimo and Vouri (1991) provide information about future occupational success, O'Toole (1990) and O'Toole and Stankov

(1992) provide eschatological predictions. O'Toole studied a sample of Australian military members and found that the Australian Army intelligence test was a good predictor of mortality by vehicular accident for men aged 20 to 44. The lower the test score the higher the probability of death by vehicular accident. O'Toole and Stankov (1992) added death by suicide and found similar results. For example, the mean intelligence score for those who met their deaths through suicide was about 0.25 standard deviations lower than comparable survivors, and a little more than 0.25 standard deviations lower for death by vehicular accident. Additionally, the survivors were different than the decedents on variables related to *g*. Survivors completed more years of schooling, obtained a greater number of academic degrees, were more likely to be employed in white-collar occupations, and rose to high rank in the military. O'Toole and Stankov asserted that 'The "theoretical" parts of driver examinations in most countries acts as primitive assessments of intelligence' (p. 715). Blasco (1994) pointed out that similar studies on the relation of ability to traffic accidents have been conducted in Spain and South America.

Although these results are compelling, none of these job performance studies investigated the incremental validity of specific abilities with respect to *g*.

Incrementing the predictiveness of g

McHenry, Hough, Toquam et al. (1990) presented the results of predicting the Campbell job performance model factors for nine US Army jobs. They found *g* to be the best predictor of the first two criterion factors, 'core technical proficiency' and 'general soldiering proficiency' with correlations of 0.63 and 0.65 corrected for range restriction. They had additional spatial, perceptual-psychomotor, temperament/personality, vocational interest, and job reward preference predictors. None added more than 0.02 in incremental validity. For the other job performance factors, temperament/personality was incremental to *g* or superior to *g* for prediction. This is consistent with Crawley, Pinder, and Herriot (1990). However, it should be noted that *g* was predictive of all job performance factors. It is interesting to note that the constructs that *g* predicts best are in the first higher-order factor and the constructs that personality predicts well are in the second higher-order factor in the re-analyzed Campbell model.

Ree, Earles, and Teachout (1994) investigated the relative predictiveness of specific abilities versus *g* for job performance. In a sample of 1036 enlisted members of the US Air Force in seven blue-collar jobs, they collected the job performance measures of hands-on work samples, job knowledge interviews, and a combination of the two called the 'Walk Through Performance Test'. The job knowledge interviews had both declarative and procedural knowledge content. The measures of *g* and specific abilities were extracted from a multiple aptitude battery and regressions compared the predictiveness of *g* and specific abilities for three criteria. Across the seven jobs the average validity of *g* was 0.40

for the hands-on work sample, 0.42 for the job knowledge interview, and 0.44 for the 'Walk Through Performance Test'. Adding the specific ability measures increased the validity an average of only 0.02. The results of Ree, Earles, and Teachout (1994) are very similar to those of McHenry et al. (1990).

Meta-analyses

Schmidt, Gooding, Noe, and Kirsch (1984) produced a 'bare bones' meta-analysis (McDaniel, Hirsh, Schmidt et al., 1986) of the predictive efficiency of g for job performance. Schmidt et al. found an average validity of 0.248. Using the meta-analytically derived default values in Raju, Burke, Normand, and Langlois (1991) we corrected this value for range restriction and predictor and criterion unreliability. The estimated true correlation was 0.512.

Hunter and Hunter (1984) meta-analyzed hundreds of studies of the relationship of g and job performance. They estimated a mean true correlation of 0.45 across job families covering a large portion of the American economy.

Building on the findings of McEvoy and Cascio (1987) on job separation and of Schmidt, Hunter, and Outerbridge (1986) on job performance, Barrick, Mount, and Strauss (1994) conducted a meta-analytic investigation of the relationship between g and involuntary job separation. Those with low job performance were more likely to be involuntarily separated. They found an indirect relationship between g and involuntary job separation moderated through job performance and supervisory ratings.

Path models

Hunter (1986) provided a major summary of research findings demonstrating that 'general cognitive ability has high validity predicting performance ratings and training success in all jobs' (p. 359). In addition to the validity of g, its causal role in job performance has been demonstrated. Hunter (1983a) reported path-analyses of meta-analytically cumulated correlations relating g, job knowledge, and job performance. In the 14 studies with 3264 participants he found that the major causal influence of g was on the acquisition of job knowledge. Job knowledge, in turn, had a major causal impact on work sample performance and supervisory ratings. No direct effect of ability on supervisory job performance ratings was reported; all effects were moderated. In Hunter's model (see Figure 5.3), job knowledge and work sample performance accounted for all of the relationship between ability and supervisory ratings. However, the total causal impact of g was considerable.

To extend Hunter (1983a), Schmidt, Hunter, and Outerbridge (1986) included experience on the job. They found that experience influenced job knowledge and work sample measures of job performance. These latter two directly influenced supervisory ratings. They found no direct linkage between g and experience. The causal impact of g was all indirect.

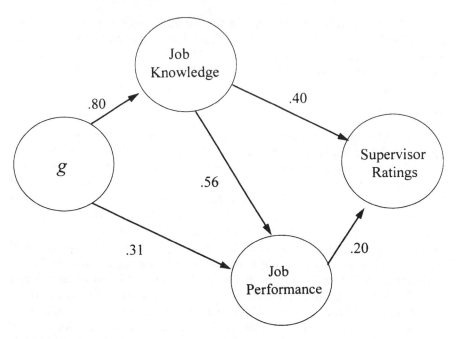

Figure 5.3 Hunter's (1986) model of determinants of job performance (reproduced by permission of the *Journal of Vocational Behaviour*)

Borman, White, Pulakos, and Oppler (1991) confirmed Hunter's (1983a) model in an additional sample of job incumbents. They went on to make it more parsimonious, showing sequential causal effects from ability to job knowledge to task proficiency to supervisory ratings. They found that the paths from ability to task proficiency and from job knowledge to supervisory ratings were unnecessary and attributed this to the uniformity of job experience of the participants. Borman, White, and Dorsey (1995) confirmed the Borman et al. (1991) parsimonious model on two additional peer and supervisory samples.

The previous studies were conducted with subordinate job incumbents. Borman, Hanson, Oppler et al. (1993) tested the model for supervisory job performance, again showing that ability influenced job knowledge. They also found a small but significant path between ability and experience (see Figure 5.4). They hypothesized that ability resulted in the individual having the opportunity to acquire supervisory job experience. Experience in turn led to increases in job knowledge, proficiency, and supervisory ratings.

Ree, Carretta, and Teachout (1995) and Ree, Carretta and Doub (1996) added the construct of prior job knowledge to occupational path models. Prior job knowledge was defined as job-relevant knowledge that applicants bring to training. In Ree, Carretta, and Teachout (1995), *g* had a strong causal influence on prior job knowledge. No direct path was found for *g* to either of two work sample performance factors, but indirect influence moderated through

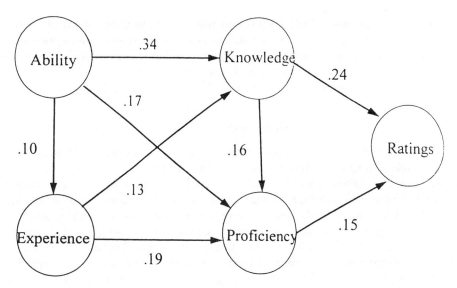

Figure 5.4 Borman et al.'s (1993) model of supervisory job performance (reproduced by permission of the *Journal of Applied Psychology*)

job knowledge was observed. This study also involved a set of three sequential training courses. The direct relationship between *g* and the first sequential training factor was large. It was almost zero for the second sequential training factor which builds on the knowledge of the first, and low positive for the third which introduces substantially new material. Most of the influence of *g* was exerted indirectly through the acquisition of job knowledge in the sequential training courses. The Ree, Carretta and Teachout (1995) model is shown in Figure 5.5.

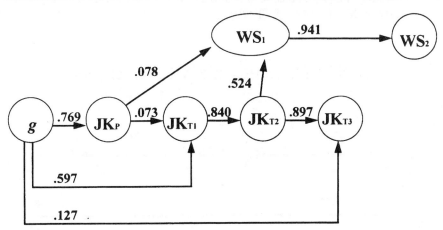

Figure 5.5 Ree, Carretta and Teachout's (1995) model of the influence of *g* and prior job knowledge on the acquisition of additional job knowledge and sequential training performance

Ree, Carretta, and Doub (1996) constructed a path model from the data from 83 studies and 42 399 participants to examine the roles of *g* and prior job knowledge in the acquisition of subsequent job knowledge. Results showed that *g* had a causal influence on both prior and subsequent job knowledge. Figure 5.6 shows the Ree, Carretta, and Doub (1996) model.

Answering Critiques

In a thoughtful critique, Murphy (1996) suggested that characterizing ability in a single index means that it is unitary. This is not necessarily the case. The fact that the relationship between, for example, two measures is (well) summarized by a single number does not imply that each measure is univariate. It implies and means that the two measures covary. Consider a typical multiple-aptitude battery. If you sum the subtests within a battery administered twice, the correlations of the sums will be almost 1.0. In fact, Dawes (1979) demonstrated that a simple composite of two uncorrelated variables will correlate with other weightings of the same two variables with a very high value.

Some have claimed that we have not given much effort to 'understand' the non-*g* portions of the aptitude tests. But we have not ignored their potential for prediction. In Earles and Ree (1991), Olea and Ree (1994), Ree, Carretta, and Teachout (1995), and Ree, Carretta, and Doub (1996) we have proposed explanations for the non-*g* portions of the tests.

Further, critics ask why we do not allow specifics to enter before *g* to determine if *g* adds to specifics. In Ree and Earles (1991) and Olea and Ree (1994), we observed that the distribution of validity for the specifics and *g* does not overlap. The predictive efficiency of the most valid specific ability was less than *g*. The same has been found by other investigators, notably in the large study by McHenry et al. (1990).

All 83 Electronics and Mechanical Jobs

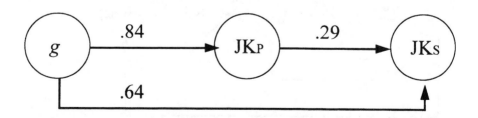

Figure 5.6 Ree, Carretta and Doub's (1996) model of influence of *g* and prior job knowledge on the aquisition of subsequent job knowledge

Individual differences in job performance are important to organizations. Campbell, Gasser, and Oswald (1996) reviewed the findings on the value of high and low job performance. They chose a conservative approach and estimated that the top 1% of workers produces a return 3.29 times as great as the lowest 1% of workers. Further, they estimated that the value may be from 3 to 10 times the return depending on the variability of job performance. Job performance makes a difference!

The validity of g as a predictor of occupation performance has been the subject of research for a long time. Gottfredson (1997) argued that 'no other measured trait, except perhaps conscientiousness . . . has such general utility across the sweep of jobs in the American economy'. Hattrup and Jackson (1996), summarizing the finding that specific abilities can be identified and measured, concluded that they 'have little value for building theories about ability–performance relationships (p. 532).

Occupational performance begins with learning the knowledge and skills required for the job and continues into on-the-job performance and beyond. We and other investigators have demonstrated that g predicts training performance, job performance, lifetime productivity, and finally, early mortality.

REFERENCES

Andreasen, N. C., Flaum, M., Swayze, V., O'Leary, D. S., Alliger, R., Cohen, G., Ehrhardt, J. & Yuh, T. C. (1993). Intelligence and brain structure in normal individuals. *American Journal of Psychiatry*, **150**, 130–134.

Arvey, R. D. (1986). General ability in employment: A discussion. *Journal of Vocational Behavior*, **29**, 415–420.

Barrick, M. R., Mount, M. K. & Strauss, J. P. (1994). Antecedents of involuntary turnover due to a reduction in force. *Personnel Psychology*, **47**, 515–535.

Besetsny, L. K., Earles, J. A. & Ree, M. J. (1993). Little incremental validity for a special test for Air Force intelligence operatives. *Educational and Psychological Measurement*, **53**, 993–997.

Besetsny, L. K., Ree, M. J. & Earles, J. A. (1993). Special tests for computer programmers? Not needed. *Educational and Psychological Measurement*, **53**, 507–511.

Blasco, R. D. (1994). Psychology and road safety. *Applied Psychology: An International Review*, **43**, 313–322.

Borman, W. C., Hanson, M. A., Oppler, S. H., Pulakos, E. D. & White, L. A. (1993). Role of early supervisory experience in supervisor performance. *Journal of Applied Psychology*, **78**, 443–449.

Borman, W. C., White, L. A. & Dorsey, D. W. (1995). Effects of ratee task performance and interpersonal factors on supervisor and peer performance ratings. *Journal of Applied Psychology*, **80**, 168–177.

Borman, W. C., White, L. A., Pulakos, E. D. & Oppler, S. H. (1991). Models of supervisory job performance ratings. *Journal of Applied Psychology*, **76**, 863–872.

Brand, C. (1987). The importance of general intelligence. In S. Modgil & C. Modgil (Eds), *Arthur Jensen: Consensus and Controversy* (pp. 251–265). New York: Falmer,

Brodnick, R. J. & Ree, M. J. (1995). A structural model of academic performance, socio-economic status, and Spearman's g. *Educational and Psychological Measurement*, **55**, 583–594.

Broman, S. H., Nichols, P. L., Shaughnessy, P. & Kennedy, W. (1987). *Retardation in Young Children*. Hillsdale, NJ: Lawrence Erlbaum.

Burt, C. (1949). The structure of the mind: A review of the results of factor analysis. *British Journal of Educational Psychology*, **19**, 100–111, 176–199.

Campbell, J. P., Gasser, M. B. & Oswald, F. L. (1996). The substantive nature of job performance variability. In K. R. Murphy (Ed.), *Individual Differences and Behavior in Organizations* (pp. 258–299). San Francisco: Jossey-Bass.

Campbell, J. P., McCloy, R. A., Oppler, S. H. & Sager, C. E. (1993). A theory of performance. In N. Schmidt, W. C. Borman & Associates (Eds), *Personnel Selection in Organizations* (pp. 35–70). San Franciso: Jossey-Bass.

Campbell, J. P., McHenry, J. J. & Wise, L. L. (1990). Modeling job performance in a population of jobs. Special Issue: Project A: The US Army Selection and Classification Project. *Personnel Psychology*, **43**, 313–333.

Carretta, T. R., Perry, D. C., Jr & Ree, M. J. (1996). Prediction of situational awareness in F-15 pilots. *International Journal of Aviation Psychology*, **6**, 21–41.

Carretta, T. R. & Ree, M. J. (1995). Near identity of cognitive structure in sex and ethnic groups. *Personality and Individual Differences*, **19**, 149–155.

Carretta, T. R. & Ree, M. J. (1996). Factor structure of the Air Force Office Qualifying Test: Analysis and comparison. *Military Psychology*, **8**, 29–42.

Cattell, R. B. (1971). *Abilities: Their Structure, Growth, and Action*. Boston: Houghton Mifflin.

Chalke, F. C. R. & Ertl, J. (1965). Evoked potentials and intelligence. *Life Sciences*, **4**, 1319–1322.

Chan, D. (1996). Criterion and construct validation of an assessment centre. *Journal of Occupational and Organizational Psychology*, **69**, 167–181.

Crawley, B., Pinder, R. & Herriot, P. (1990). Assessment centre dimensions, personality and aptitudes. *Journal of Occupational Psychology*, **63**, 211–216.

Dawes, R. (1979). The robust beauty of improper linear models. *American Psychologist*, **34**, 571–582.

DeFries, J. C., Vandenberg, S. G., McClearn, G. E., Kuse, A. R., Wilson, J. R., Ashton, G. C. & Johnson, R. C. (1974). Near identity of cognitive structure in two ethnic groups. *Science*, **183**, 338–339.

Earles, J. A. & Ree, M. J. (1991). *Air Force Officers Qualifying Test (AFOQT): Estimating the general ability component* (Al-TP-1991-0039). Armstrong Laboratory, Human Resources Directorate, Manpower and Personnel Research Division: Brooks AFB, TX.

Egan, V., Wickett, J. C. & Vernon, P. A. (1995). Brain size and intelligence: Erratum, addendum, and correction. *Personality and Individual Differences*, **19**, 113–16.

Ertl, J. & Schafer, E. W. P. (1969). Brain response correlates of psychometric intelligence. *Nature*, **223**, 421–422.

Eysenck, H. J. (1982). The psychophysiology of intelligence. In C. D. Spielberger & J. N. Butcher (Eds), *Advances in Personality Assessment* (Vol. 1, pp. 1–33). Hillsdale, NJ: Lawrence Erlbaum.

Fleishman, E. A. & Quaintance, M. K. (1984). *Taxonomies of Human Performance: The Description of Human Tasks*. Orlando, FL: Academic Press.

Frearson, W., Eysenck, H. J. & Barrett, P. T. (1990). The Fumereaux model of human problem solving: Its relationship to reaction time and intelligence. *Personality and Individual Differences*, **11**, 239–257.

Galton, F. (1869). *Hereditary Genius: An Inquiry into its Laws and Consequences*. London: Macmillan.

Gardner, H. (1983). *Frames of Mind: The Theory of Multiple Intelligence*. NY: Basic Books.

Gottfredson, L. S. (1986). Societal consequences of the *g* factor in employment. *Journal of Vocational Behavior*, **29**, 379–410.

Gottfredson, L. S. (1997). Why *g* matters: The complexity of everyday life. *Intelligence,* **24,** 79–132.

Guilford, J. P. (1956). The structure of intellect. *Psychological Bulletin,* **53,** 267–293.

Guilford, J. P. (1959). Three faces of intellect. *American Psychologist,* **14,** 469–479.

Gustafsson, J. E. (1980, April). *Testing hierarchical models of ability organization through covariance models.* Paper presented at the Annual Meeting of the American Educational Research Association, Boston.

Gustafsson, J. E. (1984). A unifying model for the structure of intellectual abilities. *Intelligence,* **8,** 179–203.

Gustafsson, J. E. (1988). Hierarchical models of individual differences in cognitive abilities. In R. J. Sternberg (Ed.), *Advances in the Psychology of Human Intelligence* (Vol. 4, pp. 35–71). Hillsdale, NJ: Lawrence Erlbaum.

Haier, R. J., Siegel, B. V., Nuechterlein, K. H., Hazlett, E., Wu, J. C., Pack, J., Browning, H. L. & Buchsbaum, M. S. (1988). Cortical glucose metabolic rate correlates of abstract reasoning and attention studied with positron emission tomography. *Intelligence,* **12,** 199–217.

Haier, R. J., Siegel, B., Tang, C., Able, L. & Buchsbaum, M. S. (1992). Intelligence and changes in regional cerebral glucose metabolic rate following learning. *Intelligence,* **16,** 415–426.

Hakstian, A. R. & Cattell, R. B. (1978). Higher-stratum ability structures on a basis of twenty primary abilities. *Journal of Educational Psychology,* **70,** 657–669.

Hart, B. & Spearman, C. (1914). Mental tests of dementia. *Journal of Abnormal Psychology,* **9,** 217–264.

Hattrup, K. & Jackson, S. E. (1996). Learning about individual differences by taking situations seriously. In K. R. Murphy (Ed.), *Individual Differences and Behavior in Organizations* (pp. 507–547). San Francisco: Josey-Bass.

Haug, H. (1987). Brain sizes, surfaces, and neuronal sizes of the cortex cerebri: A stereological investigation of man and his variability and a comparison with some species of mammals (primates, whales, marsupials, insectivores, and one elephant). *American Journal of Anatomy,* **180,** 126–142.

Holzinger, K. J. & Harmon, H. H. (1938). Comparison of two factorial analyses. *Psychometrika,* **3,** 45–60.

Horn, J. L. (1978). Human ability systems. In P. B. Baltes (Ed.), *Life-span Development and Behavior* (Vol. 1, 211–256). New York: Academic Press.

Houck, M. R., Whitaker, L. A. & Kendall, R. R. (1991). *Behavioral taxonomy for air combat F-15 defensive counter-air mission* (UDR-TR-91-147). Dayton, OH: University of Dayton Research Institute.

Hull, C. L. (1928). *Aptitude Testing.* Yonkers, NY: World Books.

Humphreys, L. G. & Taber, T. (1973). Ability factors as a function of advantaged and disadvantaged groups. *Journal of Educational Measurement,* **10,** 107–115.

Hunter, J. E. (1983a). A causal analysis of cognitive ability, job knowledge, job performance, and supervisor ratings. In F. Landy, S. Zedeck & J. Cleveland (Eds), *Performance Measurement and Theory.* Hillsdale, NJ: Lawrence Erlbaum.

Hunter, J. E. (1983b). *Overview of validity generalization for the U.S. Employment Service* (USES Test Research Report 43). Washington DC: US Department of Labor, Employment and Training Adminstration.

Hunter, J. E. (1986). Cognitive ability, cognitive aptitudes, job knowledge, and job performance. *Journal of Vocational Behavior,* **29,** 340–362.

Hunter, J. E. & Hunter, R. F. (1984). Validity and utility of alternative predictors of job performance. *Psychological Bulletin,* **96,** 72–98.

Jager, A. O. (1967). *Dimensionen der intelligenz.* [Dimensions of intelligence]. G. Göttingen: Hogrefe, Germany.

Jensen, A. R. (1980). *Bias in Mental Testing.* New York: Free Press.

Jensen, A. R. (1993). Spearman's *g*: Links between psychometrics and biology, *Annals of the New York Academy of Sciences*, **702**, 103–129.

Jones, G. E. (1988). Investigation of the efficacy of general ability versus specific abilities as predictors of occupational success. Unpublished master's thesis, Saint Mary's University of Texas, San Antonio, TX.

Jouandet, M. L., Tramo, M. J., Herron, D. M., Hermann, A., Loftus, W. C. & Gazzaniga, M. S. (1989). Brainprints: Computer-generated two-dimensional maps of the human cerebral cortex *in vivo*. *Journal of Cognitive Neuroscience*, **1**, 88–116.

Kalimo, R. & Vouri, J. (1991). Work factors and health: The predictive role of pre-employment experiences. *Journal of Occuaptional Psychology*, **64**, 97–115.

Lance, C. E., Teachout, M. S. & Donnelly, T. M. (1992). Specification of the criterion construct space: An application of hierarchical confirmatory factor analysis. *Journal of Applied Psychology*, **77**, 437–452.

Larson, G. E., Haier, R. J., LaCasse, L & Hazen, K. (1995). Evaluation of a 'mental effort' hypothesis for correlations between cortical metabolism and intelligence. *Intelligence*, **21**, 267–278.

Levine, E. L., Spector, P. E., Menon, S., Narayanan, L. & Cannon-Bowers, J. (1996). Validity generalization for cognitive, psychomotor, and perceptual tests for craft jobs in the utility industry. *Human Performance*, **9**, 1–22.

McClelland, D. C. (1993). Intelligence is not the best predictor of job performance. *Current Directions in Psychological Science*, **2**, 5–6.

McDaniel, M. A., Hirsh, H. R., Schmidt, F. L., Raju, N. S. & Hunter, J. E. (1986). Interpreting the results of meta-analytic research: A comment on Schmidt, Gooding, Noe, and Kirsch (1944). *Personnel Psychology*, **39**, 141–148.

McEvoy, G. M. & Cascio, W. F. (1987). Do good or poor performers leave? A meta-analysis of the relationship between performance and turnover. *Academy of Management Journal*, **30**, 744–762.

McHenry, J. J., Hough, L. M., Toquam, J. L., Hanson, M. A. & Ashworth, S. (1990). Project A validity results: The relationship between predictor and criterion domains. *Pesonnel Psychology*, **43**, 335–354.

McNemar, Q. (1964). Lost our intelligence? Why? *American Psychologist*, **19**, 871–882.

Michael, W. B. (1949). Factor analyses of tests and criteria: A comparative study of two AAF pilot populations. *Psychological Monographs*, **63**, 55–84.

Miller, E. M. (1996). Intelligence and brain myelination: A hypothesis. *Personality and Individual Differences*, **17**, 803–832.

Murphy, K. R. (1996). Individual differences and behavior in organizations: Much more than *g*. In K. R. Murphy (Ed.), *Individual differences and behavior in organizations* (pp. 3–30). San Francisco: Jossey-Bass.

Olea, M. M. & Ree, M. J. (1994). Predicting pilot and navigator criteria: Not much more than *g*. *Journal of Applied Psychology*, **79**, 845–851.

O'Toole, V. I. (1990). Intelligence and behavior and motor vehicle accident mortality. *Accident Analysis and Prevention*, **22**, 211–221.

O'Toole, V. I. & Stankov, L. (1992). Ultimate validity of psychological tests. *Personality and Individual Differences*, **13**, 699–716.

Peiró, J. M. & Munduate, L. (1994). Work and organizational psychology in Spain. *Applied Psychology: An International Reviews*, **43**, 231–274.

Raju, N. S., Burke, M. J., Normand, J. & Langlois, G. M. (1991). A new meta-analytic approach. *Journal of Applied Psychology*, **76**, 432–446.

Ree, M. J. & Carretta, T. R. (1994). Factor analysis of the ASVAB: Confirming a Vernon-like structure. *Educational and Psychological Measurement*, **54**, 459–463.

Ree, M. J. & Carretta (1995). Group differences in aptitude factor structure on the ASVAB. *Educational and Psychological Measurement*, **55**, 268–277.

Ree, M. J. & Carretta, T. R. (1996). Central role of *g* in military pilot selection. *International Journal of Aviation Psychology*, **6**, 111–123.

Ree, M. J., Carretta, T. R. & Doub, T. W. (1996). A test of three models of the role of *g* and prior job knowledge in the acquisition of subsequent job knowledge. Manuscript submitted for publication.

Ree, M. J., Carretta, T. R. & Teachout, M. S. (1995). Role of ability and prior job knowledge in complex training performance. *Journal of Applied Psychology*, **80**, 721–780.

Ree, M. J. & Earles, J. A. (1991). Predicting training success: Not much more than *g*. *Personnel Psychology*, **44**, 321–332.

Ree, M. J. & Earles, J. A. (1992). Intelligence is the best predictor of job performance. *Current Directions in Psychological Science*, **1**, 86–89.

Ree, M. J. & Earles, J. A. (1994). The ubiquitous predictiveness of *g*. In M. G. Rumsey, C. B. Walker & J. B. Harris (Eds), *Personnel Selection and Classification* (pp. 127–135), Hillsdale, NJ: Lawrence Erlbaum.

Ree, M. J., Earles, J. A. & Teachout, M. S. (1994). Predicting job performance: Not much more than *g*. *Journal of Applied Psychology*, **79**, 518–524.

Reed, T. E. & Jensen, A. R. (1992). Conduction velocity in a brain nerve pathway of normal adults correlates with intelligence level. *Intelligence*, **16**, 259–272.

Roseman, J. M. & Buckley, C. E. (1975, March). Inverse relationship between serum IgG concentrations and measures of intelligence in elderly persons. *Nature*, **254**, 55–56.

Roth, P. L. & Campion, J. E. (1992). An analysis of the predictive power of the panel interview and pre-employment tests. *Journal of Occupational and Organizational Psychology*, **65**, 51–60.

Sackett, P. R., Zedeck, S. & Fogli, L. (1988). Relations between measures of typical and maximum job performance. *Journal of Applied Psychology*, **73**, 482–486.

Salgado, J. F. (1995). Situational specificity and within-setting validity variability. *Journal of Occupational and Organizational Psychology*, **68**, 123–132.

Schmid, J. & Leiman, J. (1957). The development of hierarchical factor solutions. *Psychometrika*, **22**, 53–61.

Schmidt, F. L. & Hunter, J. E. (1993). Tacit knowledge, practical intelligence, general mental ability, and job knowledge. *Current Directions in Psychological Science*, **2**, 8–9.

Schmidt, F. L., Hunter, J. E. & Outerbridge, A. N. (1986). Impact of job experience and ability on job knowledge, work sample performance, and supervisory ratings of job performance. *Journal of Applied Psychology*, **71**, 432–439.

Schmidt, N., Gooding, R. Z., Noe, R. A. & Kirsch, M. (1984). Meta-analyses of validity studies published between 1964 and 1982 and the investigation of study characteristics. *Personnel Psychology*, **37**, 407–422.

Schultz, R. T. (1991). The relationship between intelligence and gray-white matter image contrast: An MRI study of healthy college students. Unpublished Doctoral Dissertation, University of Texas at Austin.

Schultz, R. T., Gore, J., Sodhi, V. & Anderson, A. L. (1993). Brain MRI correlates of IQ: Evidence from twin and singleton populations. *Behavior Genetics*, **23**, 565 (abstract).

Shucard, D. W. & Horn, J. L. (1972). Evoked cortical potentials and measurement of human abilities. *Journal of Comparative and Physiological Psychology*, **78**, 59–68.

Spearman, C. (1927). *The Abilities of Man: Their Nature and Measurement*. New York: Macmillan.

Spearman, C. (1930). 'G' and after—A school to end schools. In C. Murchison (Ed.), *Psychologies of 1930* (pp. 339–366), Worcester, MA: Clark University Press.

Spearman, C. (1937). *Psychology down the Ages* (Vol. II). London: Macmillan.

Spearman, C. (1938). Thurstone's work reworked. *Journal of Educational Psychology*, **39**, 1–16.

Stauffer, J. M., Ree, M. J. & Carretta, T. R. (1996). Cognitive components tests are not much more than *g*: An extension of Kyllonen's analyses. *Journal of General Psychology*, **123**, 193–205.

Sternberg, R. J. (1985). *Beyond IQ: A Triarchic Theory of Human Intelligence:* New York: Cambridge University Press.

Sternberg, R. J. & Wagner, R. K. (1993). The *g*-ocentric view of intelligence and job performance is wrong. *Current Directions in Psychological Science*, **2**, 1–5.

Terman, L. M. & Oden, M. H. (1959). The gifted group at mid-life: Thirty-five years' follow-up of the superior child. In L. M. Terman, Vol. V, *Genetic Studies of Genius.* Stanford, CA: Stanford University Press.

Thomson, G. (1939). *The Factorial Analysis of Human Ability.* London: University of London Press.

Thorndike, R. L. (1986). The role of general ability in prediction. *Journal of Vocational Behavior*, **29**, 322–339.

Thurstone, L. L. (1938). Primary mental abilities. *Psychometric Monographs No. 1.* Chicago: University of Chicago Press.

Thurstone, L. L. & Thurstone, T. G. (1941). Factorial studies of intelligence. *Psychometric Monographs No. 2.* Chicago: University of Chicago Press.

Tramo, M. J., Loftus, W. C., Thomas, C. E., Green, R. L., Mott, L. A. & Gazzaniga, M. S. (1995). Surface area of human cerebral cortex and its gross morphological subdivisions: *In vivo* measurements in monozygotic twins suggest differential hemispheric effects of genetic factors. *Journal of Cognitive Neuroscience*, **7**, 292–301.

Van Valen, L. (1974). Brain size and intelligence in man. *American Journal of Physical Anthropology*, **40**, 417–423.

Vernon, P. E. (1950). *The Structure of Human Abilities.* New York: Wiley.

Vernon, P. E. (1969). *Intelligence and Cultural Environment.* London: Methuen.

Vineburg, R. & Taylor, E. (1972). *Performance of four Army jobs by men at different aptitude (AFQT) levels: 3. The relationship of AFQT and job experience to job performance.* Human Resources Research Organization Technical Report 72–22. Washington DC: Department of the Army.

Viswesvaran, C., Schmidt, F. L. & Ones, D. S. (1996). *Modeling job performance: Is there a general factor?* Manuscript submitted for publication.

Waxman, S. G. (1992). Molecular organization and pathology of axons. In A. K. Asbury, G. M. McKhann & W. L. McDonald (Eds), *Diseases of the Nervous System: Clinical Neurobiology* (pp. 25–46). Philadelphia: Saunders.

Wickett, J. C., Vernon, P. A. & Lee, D. H. (1994). *In vitro* brain size, head perimeter, and intelligence in a sample of healthy adult females. *Personality and Individual Differences*, **16**, 831–838.

Wilk, S. L., Desmarais, L. B. & Sackett, P. R. (1995). Gravitation to jobs commensurate with ability: Longitudinal and cross-sectional tests. *Journal of Applied Psychology*, **80**, 79–85.

Willerman, L. & Schultz, R. T. (1996). The physical basis of psychometric *g* and primary abilities. Manuscript submitted for publication.

Willerman, L., Schultz, R. T., Rutledge, A. N. & Bigler, E. D. (1991). *In vivo* brain size and intelligence. *Intelligence*, **15**, 223–228.

Part II

HUMAN RESOURCE MANAGEMENT

Chapter 6

LEARNING STRATEGIES AND OCCUPATIONAL TRAINING

Peter Warr and Catriona Allan
University of Sheffield, UK

Research into training has always been a central part of industrial and organizational psychology. Processes and outcomes have been examined from several different perspectives, but the principal focus has traditionally been upon features of programme design or delivery. For example, attention has been directed to techniques of job analysis and the specification of criterion behaviours, the development of integrated instructional systems, the classification of learning tasks, applications of computers, behaviour modelling techniques, group-based training, and comparisons between specific methods of presentation.

More recently, attention has shifted to examine also the key characteristics of trainees: what features of a learner might influence the acquisition of new knowledge and skills? Research into personal characteristics has been undertaken for two reasons: to contribute to theoretical models of training, and to identify features of a learner which might receive practical attention in order to improve his or her performance. For example, if prior measures of motivation to learn are found to predict later learning achievement (Baldwin, Magjuka & Loher, 1991; Tannenbaum, Mathieu, Salas & Cannon-Bowers, 1991), then it may be feasible to enhance key components of this motivation, thereby increasing the effectiveness of an associated training intervention. In a similar way, activities to modify trainees' low self-efficacy (Eyring, Johnson & Francis, 1993) or high learning anxiety (Warr & Bunce, 1995) may serve to improve learning.

One individual factor which is widely believed to give rise to variations in learning success is the nature of the 'learning strategies' which a person applies. Such strategies have often been examined by educational psychologists in studies of school and college students, but they have received only limited attention from researchers into occupational training. This chapter aims to

---

Learning Strategies and Occupational Training by Peter Warr and Catriona Allan taken from IRIOP 1998 v13, Edited by Cary L. Cooper and Ivan T. Robertson: © 1998 John Wiley & Sons, Ltd

redress that imbalance. It will examine the notion of a learning strategy, identify the principal forms, consider procedures for measurement, review evidence for the importance of learning strategies and the degree to which their modification can increase learning, and consider issues requiring attention in industrial and organizational settings.

The topic is of special importance at the present time for several reasons. For example, research is increasingly directed at a better understanding of mental processes in the course of job activities, associated with the widespread shift from manual to cognitive work. As part of this trend, cognitive processes during learning are receiving more attention and becoming more accessible to investigators (Ford & Kraiger, 1995). Cognitive views of learning emphasize the selection, encoding and organization of material, and the extrapolation of concepts and findings from the cognitive laboratory into organizational settings holds considerable promise. More generally, training is of special importance in response to increasing demands for flexibility in conjunction with an ageing workforce in many developed countries (Goldstein & Gillam, 1990; Warr, 1994). Finally, associated with many companies' attempts to become 'learning organizations' (e.g. Pearn, Roderick & Mulrooney, 1995), there is a need to enhance people's competence as learners; how can they better learn how to learn? A deeper understanding of learning strategies would assist in that process.

THE NATURE OF LEARNING STRATEGIES

Terms such as 'strategy', 'style' and 'approach' are used somewhat inconsistently by different authors. Nevertheless, there is general agreement about principal terms and distinctions between them. Illustrative definitions of a learning strategy, set out in date order, are as follows:

> operations and procedures that the student may use to acquire, retain, and retrieve different kinds of knowledge and performance. (Rigney, 1978, p. 165)

> different competencies that researchers and practitioners have postulated as necessary, or helpful, for effective learning and retention of information for later use. (Weinstein & Underwood, 1985, p. 241)

> an effective strategy can be defined as a set of processes or steps that can facilitate the acquisition, storage, and/or utilization of information. (Dansereau, 1985, p. 210)

> the executive processes which choose, co-ordinate and apply skills. (Nisbet & Shucksmith, 1986, p. vii)

> behaviors and thoughts that a learner engages in during learning and that are intended to influence the learner's encoding process. (Weinstein & Mayer, 1986, p. 315)

behaviors of a learner that are intended to influence how the learner processes information. (Mayer, 1988, p. 11)

a sequence of procedures for accomplishing learning. (Schmeck, 1988a, p. 5)

combinations of cognitive (thinking) skills implemented when a situation is perceived as demanding learning. (Schmeck, 1988a, p. 17)

cognitive operations over and above the processes directly entailed in carrying out a task. (Pressley, Woloshyn, Lysynchuk, Martin, Wood & Willoughby, 1990, p. 3)

overt and covert information-processing activities used by learners at the time of encoding to facilitate the acquisition, storage, and subsequent retrieval of information to be learned. (Kardash & Amlund, 1991, p. 119)

particular, often used combinations of learning activities. (Vermunt, 1996, p. 25)

In general, researchers see learning strategies as illustrating active efforts by purposive individuals, in contrast to the (out-moded) view of learners as passive recipients of instruction. Learning strategies may be either intentional, being consciously selected and controlled, or they may be applied without conscious effort. The latter applications, being automatized and freeing mental capacity for other activity, may be specially effective. Individuals necessarily apply one or more strategies, since some procedures are inevitably required to learn new material, but differences are expected between people in the nature of the strategies they use.

Some strategies are specialized, being appropriate in only a narrow range of settings, whereas others may be valuable more generally. A continuum is thus present between narrow, content-specific, strategies and those which are broad and independent of content. For example, content-specific procedures have been created to develop students' knowledge about particular scientific theories (Dansereau, 1985). At the other end of the continuum are extremely general approaches, such as those devised to assist university students of all kinds (e.g. Vermunt, 1995). Attention here will be directed to those learning strategies which have potential in more than a single type of learning activity.

It is helpful to distinguish between two principal categories of learning strategy. These may be referred to as 'primary' and 'self-regulatory' strategies. Primary learning strategies are used in direct engagement with the material to be learned, influencing a learner's processes of selection, encoding, storage and retrieval. Such activities have also been labelled as 'cognitive' strategies (e.g. Pintrich, 1988; Pintrich & Garcia, 1991).

In contrast, 'self-regulatory' strategies (referred to as 'support' strategies by Dansereau, 1985, 'affective' strategies by Weinstein and Mayer, 1986, and 'resource management' strategies by Pintrich, Smith, Garcia and McKeachie, 1991, 1993) have their impact indirectly, influencing how learners maintain motivation, manage effort, ward off anxiety and monitor their progress. Self-regulatory strategies are important components in the models of action control proposed by Kuhl (1992) and Kanfer, Ackerman and Heggestad (1996). Those models emphasize the need for individuals to have available procedures to inhibit performance anxiety and other negative emotional distractions (referred to as procedures of 'emotion control') and procedures to maintain motivation and concentration in the face of difficulties ('motivation control'; see also Corno & Kanfer, 1993; Kanfer, 1996).

Self-regulation can be of two general kinds: affective strategies to control one's own emotions and motivation (illustrated above), and also processes to act more broadly upon the environment in which one is learning (Zimmerman & Martinez-Pons, 1990). The latter procedures (modifying the context rather than influencing current information processing) are best viewed as forms of study skill rather than learning strategy; this point will be developed later.

Research into learning strategies has mainly been undertaken by educational psychologists, whose focus has been on the processing of written textual material by students in school or university settings. Conceptualizations and measures have thus been restricted almost entirely to procedures for acquiring declarative knowledge from a written source. Such work is undoubtedly applicable to employee learning in many occupational settings, but it requires expansion to cover the acquisition of procedural skills through interaction with equipment or other people.

The framework presented in this review will retain the basic distinction between primary and self-regulatory strategies. However, in order to extend beyond educational researchers' concentration on the acquisition of information from written texts, we will propose two categories of primary strategies: those which are 'behavioural', as well as the more conventional 'cognitive' strategies.

Learning Strategies and Styles

Learning strategies should be distinguished from 'styles', although the two concepts undoubtedly shade into each other. A learning 'style' is usually viewed as more general and fixed across situations than is a strategy. For instance, Schmeck (1988a) thinks of a style as 'an inclination to use the same strategy in varied situations' (pp. 7–8) or a 'trait-like consistency' (p. 9). A style tends to be seen as reflecting a generally preferred learning strategy, in effect an aspect of an individual's personality with interconnected attitudes and motives. Although to some extent open to change, a style is generally considered to be less modifiable than a strategy.

Learning styles may be viewed as a subset of the broader category of 'cognitive styles'. The latter have been defined by Messick (1984, p. 61) as 'characteristic self-consistencies in information-processing that develop in congenial ways around personality trends'. Those wide-ranging self-consistencies affect information processing of all kinds, whereas learning styles are by definition restricted to activities associated with learning.

Styles have been viewed as covering predispositions or preferences of many different types. For instance, the learning style model of Dunn, Dunn and Price (1989) contains twenty different elements, representing (for example) concerns about noise level and temperature when studying, preferred time of day, preference for specific seating arrangements, and interest in collaborating with other people. The category of styles is thus broader than that of strategies, including both processes of information processing during actual learning activities and also preferences for a range of features of a learning context.

Investigators of university students' approaches to learning have emphasized the distinction between 'deep' and 'surface' processing (e.g. Biggs, 1993; Entwistle & Waterston, 1988; Murray-Harvey, 1994; Wilson, Smart & Watson, 1996). Students who approach learning in a 'deep' manner are said to exhibit an active concern for the underlying meaning of information, to make connections between apparently disparate ideas and facts, to evaluate critically the evidence which is available, and to have an interest in learning for learning's sake. A 'surface' approach is said to embody a preoccupation with memorization directed merely at reproduction of the material as presented, a reliance on tutors to determine task activity, and motives which are extrinsic, being directed only to the attainment of satisfactory outcomes in terms of qualifications or subsequent employment.

The learning styles which have received most attention from industrial/ organizational psychologists derive from Kolb's (e.g. 1984) four-feature model. This postulates two dimensions of functioning. The 'active–reflective' dimension ranges from a direct involvement in task activities to processes of detached observation; and 'abstract–concrete' ranges from dealing with theoretical ideas to working with physical objects. Dividing those dimensions into two and treating them as orthogonal yields four possibilities, labelled as concrete experience, reflective observation, abstract conceptualization, and active experimentation. It is argued that people tend to prefer one of the four styles relative to the others and that they apply their preferred style consistently in learning situations. Several applications of this broad approach have been reported, although a number of statistical and conceptual problems remain unresolved (Sims, Veres, Watson & Buckner, 1986; Hayes & Allinson, 1996; Willcoxson & Prosser, 1996). Significant associations with extraversion and other aspects of personality have been reported by Jackson and Lawty-Jones (1996).

Learning strategies are more focused and potentially more variable than styles, but a person's strategies in any one situation are likely to be influenced by his or her more general preferences. In some cases, specific strategies are viewed as elements within broader styles (e.g. Vermunt, 1995), and it is reasonable to expect some overlap in content between learning styles and learning strategies. For example, the deep and surface approaches to learning (usually viewed as styles) also occur in specific situations, and may be applied differentially in different settings. Features of the two approaches have thus been examined both as broad styles and also as more focused strategies. Illustrations will be cited later.

An associated difference is in terms of malleability or openness to change through training. Since learning styles are typically viewed as linked to deep-seated and long-standing features of personality, they are usually considered to be resistant to change. Their practical relevance is thought to be that procedures of instruction can helpfully be modified to match a person's preferred style. Conversely, the more focused learning strategies are considered to be open to adjustment; they can potentially be changed by training, in order to assist a person to learn more effectively in a particular setting. Styles are thus seen as largely fixed, whereas strategies are viewed as in principle modifiable through learning, despite some consistency within a person. Their practical value in education and training is thus seen to differ. Information about learning styles may be used to adjust procedures of instruction to suit the person, whereas information about learning strategies might be applied to modify the person's approach without necessarily changing the instruction.

Learning Strategies, Abilities and Study Skills

Less attention has been paid to the similarities and differences between learning strategies and abilities. In general, it seems clear that the category of learning strategies is conceptually distinct from that of mental abilities (which refer to maximum possible performance), although some empirical overlap is likely. Ability-linked differences are expected in respect of particular strategies, since some strategies require greater mental ability than others.

Educational researchers have also explored learners 'study skills' or 'study habits'. Investigations and applications have mainly been directed at school or college students, aiming to improve their general approach to work and their ability to pass examinations. The notion is a very broad one, covering note-taking, reading skills, time management, effective use of libraries, revision and test-taking procedures, as well as attitudes to and motives for studying (e.g. Williams, 1989). Information derived from self-report measures of study skills has been widely applied in the USA in counselling students in educational settings (e.g Weinstein & Underwood, 1985). Such information only rarely concerns the manner in which a person directly acquires new information and skills; that is the focus of learning strategies as examined here.

Recognizing that the concepts of study skill, learning style and learning strategy overlap in meaning and vary in use between writers, they may be characterized in the manner suggested in Table 6.1. This distinguishes between the *contexts* of learning (location, time, etc.) and the *activities* of learning (information processing about the subject-matter). In each case, learning procedures and learners' preferences may be relatively focused or relatively general. As indicated by the symbols in the table, study skills primarily concern

Table 6.1   Principal features of study skills, learning styles and learning strategies

	Study skills	Learning styles	Learning strategies
Concerned with learning contexts:			
● relatively focused procedures	★★★		
● relatively general preferences		★★★	
Concerned with learning activities:			
● relatively focused procedures	★★★		★★★
● relatively general preferences		★★★	

focused procedures with respect to both learning contexts and learning activities. Learning styles primarily concern relatively general preferences in both cases. And, as illustrated in the definitions cited previously, the term 'learning strategy' refers primarily to focused procedures applied in the course of learning itself.

Nevertheless, although study skills, learning strategies and learning styles are distinct, the concepts do shade into each other. For instance, despite the potential variability of learning strategies, they are also to some degree consistent across situations, reflecting in part an individual's personality, preferences and abilities; in that respect the content of some strategies is similar to that of some styles and some study skills.

It is assumed that there is no single 'best' strategy, but that the most effective procedure varies between different settings of learning (e.g. Levin, 1986). For example, strategies important in memorizing factual material are likely to differ from those useful in acquiring interpersonal skills. Research into principal types of learning strategy and available evidence about their effectiveness is presented in the following sections. First, however, we turn to examine conventional procedures of measurement.

THE MEASUREMENT OF LEARNING STRATEGIES

The questions of whether learning strategies can be identified and whether individuals can be trained to use them were raised initially in the 1970s, principally in school and university settings. Since then, a number of investigators have developed and applied multi-item questionnaires to obtain self-reports of learning strategies. These are typically completed immediately after an episode of learning, to characterize the approaches taken in that particular activity. Such episodes have sometimes covered an entire college course, but may in other cases be restricted to a briefer period of learning.

As indicated earlier, the content of particular styles and strategies can sometimes be similar. The key distinction is in terms of generality of focus. Measures of learning strategy are explicitly in relation to a particular learning activity. On the other hand, measures of learning style request cross-situational information in terms of what a person does during learning generally; they are not linked to a particular task.

Some investigators have sought to measure study skills, defined in terms of (for example) time management, work habits and attitudes toward school (see above). Inventories of this kind include the Survey of Study Habits and Attitudes (Brown & Holtzman, 1967) and the College Adjustment and Study Skills Inventory (Christensen, 1968). Consistent with the separation suggested in Table 6.1, those inventories will not be considered here.

The measurement of learning strategies has developed from two main theoretical positions: an information-processing perspective linked to quantitative experiments in cognitive psychology, and an interest in students' approaches to learning derived from qualitative analyses of interview reports of their own study processes. Within Europe the qualitative approach to learning strategies has until recently been the most common, whereas the cognitive psychological perspective has been more salient in North America. In practice, considerable commonality of content is found between the different inventories, despite their diversity of origin (Entwistle & Waterston, 1988; Christensen, Massey & Isaacs, 1991; Biggs, 1993; Cano-Garcia & Justicia-Justicia, 1994).

Five learning strategy questionnaires will be outlined in this section. Although devised for completion by school or college students, they are relevant here to exemplify the core concepts in this area, and to provide a basis for the taxonomy of learning strategies in employment settings which will be presented later. Sample items will be cited, but only for those scales which appear to meet the definitional criteria for a learning strategy (rather than being concerned with attitudes, study skills, etc.).

The Inventory of Learning Processes (ILP)

This 62-item self-report questionnaire was developed at Southern Illinois University, USA, in order to examine learning by American college students (Schmeck, 1983, 1988b). Despite its cross-situational (stylistic) perspective, it is included here, since it has been applied in relation to specific learning episodes and since its concern for elaborative processing has become important in later instruments. Four scales are included in the ILP, derived from factor analyses of pilot data based upon cognitive psychological theorizing. These are as follows.

- Deep processing: contains items which assess the extent to which students critically evaluate, conceptually organize, and compare and contrast the information they study. However, item wording in the questionnaire is directed at people's *ability* to process information in this way, so the scale should be viewed more as an aspect of learning self-efficacy than of style or strategy.

- Methodical study: covers study habits of planning one's work and systematic self-organization.
- Fact retention: concerns a person's ability to retain and recall information.
- Elaborative processing: addresses ways in which new material is mentally linked to other material, assuming that such a spread of processing encourages learning and retention. For example: 'I learn new words and ideas by associating them with words and ideas I already know.'

The four scales' internal reliability coefficients range between 0.58 and 0.82, and test–retest reliability is high (Schmeck, 1983). Responses were initially in true–false form, but a revised inventory, expanded to include aspects of self-concept and personality, now offers six disagree–agree alternatives (Schmeck, Geisler-Brenstein & Cercy, 1991). Items in the Inventory of Learning Processes would typically need modification before application in occupational settings, and they range broadly across what have been defined earlier as study skills, styles and strategies.

The Approaches to Studying Inventory (ASI)

Developed at the University of Lancaster, UK, the ASI has been widely used in research into student learning in British higher education institutions (e.g. Entwistle & Ramsden, 1983). The questionnaire incorporates themes taken from interviews with students about their approaches to learning, and has four main sets of items. These are described in terms of a meaning orientation, a reproducing orientation, an achieving orientation (concerned with motivation and goals), and several specific tendencies such as jumping to conclusions and excessive reliance on details. Only the first two groups of items fall within the domain of this chapter.

A 'meaning' orientation is viewed as taking a conceptually deep approach to the task, seeking to understand or mentally transform the material to be learned. On the other hand, 'reproducing' involves a surface approach, being concerned merely with specific facts and their storage without further interpretation. Later versions of the inventory contain four scales to tap each of those orientations, with responses on a five-point disagree–agree continuum. The eight scales in the short version (Richardson, 1990) are as follows (the first four representing a meaning orientation, and the second four covering reproduction):

- Taking a deep approach: items concern procedures actively to question and reflect on the material being learnt. For example: 'I usually set out to understand thoroughly the meaning of what I am asked to read.'

- Comprehension learning: covers a tendency to think widely around the topic. For example: 'Ideas in books often set me off on long chains of thought of my own, only tenuously related to what I was reading.'
- Relating ideas: concerned with making connections between different parts of a course. For example: 'I try to relate ideas in one subject to those in others, wherever possible.'
- Use of evidence: concerned to check through the evidence provided in support of conclusions. For instance: 'When I'm reading an article or research report, I generally examine the evidence carefully to decide whether the conclusion is justified.'
- Taking a surface approach: reflecting a preoccupation with memorization and avoiding deep reflection. For example: 'The best way for me to understand what technical terms mean is to remember the text-book definitions.'
- Improvidence: items emphasize a very cautious reliance on specific details and facts as provided. For instance: 'Tutors seem to want me to be more adventurous in making use of my own ideas.'
- Fear of failure: concerning pessimism and anxiety about academic outcomes.
- Syllabus boundness: involves relying on instructors to define the work to be done.

Despite their very different origins, the Approaches to Studying Questionnaire and the Inventory of Learning Processes have been found to have similar factor structures and considerable overlap (Entwistle & Waterston, 1988). The mental activities covered in both questionnaires are likely to be used in many situations of occupational learning.

The Learning and Study Strategies Inventory (LASSI)

The Learning and Study Strategies Inventory (LASSI) was developed by researchers in the Department of Educational Psychology at the University of Texas, Austin, USA. Several applications and modifications led to the creation of a 90-item instrument containing ten scales. Responses are on a five-point disagree–agree continuum, and mean scores are derived for each scale. Consistent with some uncertainty about labels in this area, the measure was originally described as a learning 'skills' inventory, but the title was later changed (Weinstein, Zimmerman & Palmer, 1988).

The final version of the questionnaire contains the following scales. The focus is a very broad one, extending beyond the limited activities during learning itself which are considered here to be 'strategies'. Examples of questionnaire items are again included only for those scales which appear to cover strategies as defined here.

- Concentration: deals with a student's tendency to maintain concentration despite distractions. For instance: 'I concentrate fully when studying.'
- Information-processing: despite its broad title (covering most of cognitive psychology), this scale addresses the mental elaboration of information and the making of connections with other material. For example: 'I try to find relationships between what I am learning and what I already know.' Scores are correlated 0.60 with the elaborative processing scale of the Inventory of Learning Processes (see above) (Weinstein, Zimmerman & Palmer, 1988, p. 35).
- Selecting the main idea: concerned with locating the key points and critical ideas in material to be learned. For instance: 'I have difficulty identifying the important points in my reading' (reverse-scored).
- Self-testing: covers checks made about the progress of learning. For instance: 'I stop periodically while reading and mentally go over or review what was said.'
- Anxiety: covers a tendency to worry about learning and being tested.
- Attitude: records feelings about and interest in the course being undertaken.
- Motivation: covers a student's willingness to work hard.
- Scheduling: measures use of time and the effectiveness of planning.
- Study aids: extends across a wide range of techniques and exercises.
- Test strategies: concerns the approach taken to taking tests and exams.

The Motivated Strategies for Learning Questionnaire (MSLQ)

The MSLQ was created by researchers at the US National Center for Research to Improve Postsecondary Teaching and Learning at the University of Michigan, USA. Under development since 1982, the questionnaire was designed to measure students' motivational orientations and their use of different strategies in a college course. The final version contains 81 items, each with a seven-point response continuum ranging from 'not at all true of me' to 'very true of me' (Pintrich et al., 1991, 1993).

There are two sections, spanning aspects of motivation and the use of different learning strategies. The motivation scales cover intrinsic and extrinsic goal orientation, perceived task value, perceived control of one's learning, self-efficacy for learning, and text anxiety. Consistent with the present focus, we will describe only the items concerned with reported learning strategies. Of these, 31 are identified as addressing 'cognitive and metacognitive' strategies and 19 are viewed in terms of 'resource management strategies' (referred to here as 'self-regulatory' strategies).

'Cognitive' learning strategies are tapped by these four scales:

- Rehearsal: covers students' use of basic strategies for reciting or naming items. For example: 'When I study for this class, I practise the material to myself over and over.'

- Elaboration: reflects procedures to help store information in long-term memory by building internal connections between items to be learned. For instance: 'When I study for this class, I pull together information from different sources, such as lectures, readings, and discussions.'
- Organization: measures students' use of strategies to prioritize and structure information. For example: 'I make simple charts, diagrams, or tables to help me organize course material.'
- Critical thinking: reflects students' attempts to analyse or question the assumptions inherent in course material. For example: 'I often find myself questioning things I hear or read in this course to decide if I find them convincing.'

A fifth scale covers 'metacognitive' activities, concerned with people's awareness, knowledge and control of their cognition. The coverage is broad, examining strategies for planning, monitoring and test-taking. For instance: 'I ask myself questions to make sure I understand the material I have been studying in this class.'

'Resource management' scales in the MSLQ are:

- Managing time and the study environment: reflects how a learner organizes his or her study schedules and working environments.
- Effort regulation: addresses students' regulation of their efforts and willingness to persist in the face of difficulties. For instance: 'Even when course materials are dull and uninteresting, I manage to keep working until I finish.'
- Peer learning: covers people's approach to working with other learners.
- Help-seeking: concerns requests made to peers and instructors. For example: 'I ask the instructor to clarify concepts I don't understand well.'

Development of the MSLQ included factor analyses, which broadly supported the structure adopted. Alpha coefficients of the scales' internal reliability range from 0.52 to 0.93.

The Inventory of Learning Styles in Higher Education (ILS)

This 120-item questionnaire was created in the Department of Educational Psychology at Tilburg University, The Netherlands. It aims to identify students' learning 'style', defined as a coordinating concept which brings together specific learning strategies in combination both with mental models of learning and with orientations to different possible outcomes (e.g. obtaining a qualification, being interested in new material, etc.) (Vermunt & Van Rijswijk, 1988; Vermunt, 1995). Only the scales to measure learning strategies will be described here.

Fifty-five items cover strategies of 'information-processing' and 'metacognitive regulation', with responses being made on a five-point continuum from 'I do this seldom or never' to 'I do this almost always'. Alpha coefficients of internal reliability vary between 0.48 and 0.89.

The three information-processing strategies cover:

- Deep processing (with subscales for relating and structuring and for critical processing). For instance: 'I try to see the connection between topics discussed in different chapters of a textbook'; 'I try to be critical of the interpretation of experts.'
- Step-wise processing (with subscales for memorizing and rehearsing and for analysing). For instance: 'I repeat the main parts of the subject-matter until I know them by heart'; 'I analyse the successive steps in an argument one by one.'
- Concrete processing. For instance: 'I pay particular attention to those parts of a course that have practical utility.'

The three regulation strategies are:

- Self-regulation (with subscales for self-regulation of learning processes and results and for self-regulation of learning content). For instance: 'To test my learning progress, I try to answer questions about the subject-matter which I make up myself'; 'In addition to the syllabus, I study other literature about the subject concerned.'
- External regulation (with subscales for external regulation of learning processes and for external regulation of learning results). For instance: 'I learn everything exactly as I find it in the textbooks'; 'I test my learning progress solely by completing the questions, tasks and exercises provided by the teacher or textbook.'
- Lack of regulation. For instance: 'I notice that it is difficult for me to determine whether I have mastered the subject-matter sufficiently.'

Other Inventories of Learning Strategies

A number of other instruments have been developed to measure learning strategies used in schools and colleges. These include the Self-regulated Learning Interview Schedule (Zimmerman & Martinez-Pons, 1986, 1988), the Learning Activities Questionnaire (Thomas & Bain, 1984), the Study Process Questionnaire (Biggs, 1987) and the Learning Strategies Survey (Kardash & Amlund, 1991). The content of all these measures is of potential relevance in occupational settings, but none of the instruments is immediately usable outside the educational context for which it was designed.

A TAXONOMY OF LEARNING STRATEGIES FOR
OCCUPATIONAL TRAINING

Considering the attention which learning strategies have received within the educational literature, there is a surprising absence of parallel research in the training field. Both educational and training programmes are designed with the intention of increasing students' or trainees' knowledge and understanding by means of some processes of instruction.

However, there may be differences between educational and occupational settings in the characteristics that individuals bring to the learning process and in the teaching/training methods adopted. Occupational training is likely to place a greater emphasis on procedural knowledge (about how to perform a particular practical skill) than is college education. The latter is certain to emphasize writing skills, both in note-taking during learning and as a medium through which progress is evaluated. Trainees in organizations are also likely to be older, to spend less time in learning than college students, and possibly to have different motivation and anxieties.

As is evident from the examples presented above, the content of many educational inventories is therefore inappropriate for use in the occupational field. Traditional questionnaires tend to range widely across non-strategy domains such as study methods or test-taking, their items refer to school or college activities, and they strongly emphasize procedures for selecting information from dense passages of text. They also tend to be rather long for organizational application. With these considerations in mind, an overall taxonomy is now proposed for application within the occupational training field.

This taxonomy was developed on the basis of a systematic review of published inventories in this area. The basic distinction was retained between 'primary' and 'support' strategies (see earlier). However, consistent with the need to expand beyond purely mental procedures, the category of primary strategies was itself divided into those which are 'cognitive' and those which are 'behavioural'. The latter include practical activities that may be of particular relevance to the interaction with materials and equipment that is required in many occupational training sessions; it represents a new addition to the previous frameworks.

The suggested taxonomy thus has three main components: cognitive and behavioural strategies (both of which are 'primary', being used in direct engagement with the material to be learned) and self-regulatory strategies, covering features sometimes referred to as 'support', 'affective' or 'resource management' strategies (see above). In order to remain within the time available for most organizational investigations, only those activities found to be of major significance in earlier research have been included. Three strategies in each of the three principal categories were considered to meet this criterion.

In determining which 'cognitive' learning strategies to select, emphasis was placed upon previous reviews of major learning activities (e.g. Weinstein &

Mayer, 1986; Pintrich et al., 1993). The principal cognitive procedures appear to be activities of rehearsal, elaboration and organization. The 'behavioural' strategies were partly based upon (unpublished) investigations in which individuals were asked to report their thought processes in the course of several practical learning tasks. On the basis of that information, suggestions in the literature and pilot applications of questionnaire items, it was concluded that the three principal behavioural learning strategies are seeking help from other people, seeking help from written material, and increasing knowledge through practical application.

'Self-regulatory' learning strategies are those control activities which do not directly affect the processes of learning. They include procedures for inhibiting anxiety about performance (referred to here as 'emotion control') and for maintaining motivation and concentration in the face of difficulties ('motivation control'). In addition, 'comprehension monitoring' is also important, as learners check their progress toward a goal and make necessary adjustments (e.g. Dansereau, 1985; Weinstein & Mayer, 1986; Pintrich et al., 1993; Kanfer, 1996; Kanfer, Ackerman & Heggestad, 1996). Indeed, regular monitoring of progress towards a target is a key component of expertise of all kinds (Ertmer & Newby, 1996).

This nine-category framework may be summarized as follows. In each case, an illustrative self-report item is cited.

1. *Cognitive learning strategies*

   (a) *Rehearsal*: procedures to repeat to oneself the material being learned. This does not involve reflecting about the meaning of the material, changing it, or seeing how it fits in with other material. Central is mental repetition (in some cases also copying) of information, usually in the form in which it was presented. An illustrative item, for completion after a learning episode, is: 'I learned things by going over them in my head until I felt I knew them.'

   (b) *Organization*: procedures to identify key issues, and to create mental structures which group and interrelate elements to be learned. This goes beyond rehearsal (1a) to impose some organization on the material; in certain cases, it involves preparing a written summary of the themes which have been selected and structured. An illustrative item is: 'I outlined in my mind the main points of the material and how they fitted together.'

   (c) *Elaboration*: procedures to examine implications, and to make mental connections between material to be learned and existing knowledge. This goes further than fitting different aspects together (1b), to seek to increase understanding by changing the way material is viewed in the context of other information. An illustrative item is: 'In order to understand something better, I thought about how it made sense in terms of what I already knew.'

2. *Behavioural learning strategies*

(a) *Interpersonal help-seeking*: procedures to obtain assistance from other people. This involves proactive behaviour to seek to increase understanding by asking for specific or general help, rather than receiving information from others merely through routine instruction. An illustrative item is: 'I checked with other people when I was not sure about some material.'

(b) *Seeking help from written material*: procedures to obtain information from written documents, manuals, computer programs and other non-social sources. This is the non-social analogue of 2a, involving self-generated efforts rather than routine learning activities. An illustrative item is: 'I filled in gaps in my knowledge by getting hold of some written material.'

(c) *Practical application*: procedures to increase one's knowledge by trying things out in practice. This involves seeking to increase understanding by carrying out a practical activity, rather than by talking with other people or looking up written material (2a and 2b). An illustrative item is: 'Rather than spend time reading or asking someone's advice, I tried to understand something by working it out in practice.'

3. *Self-regulatory strategies*

(a) *Emotion control*: procedures to ward of anxiety and prevent concentration failures caused by the intrusion of anxiety-linked thoughts. An illustrative item is: 'I tried not to worry about the possibility of doing worse than I wanted.'

(b) *Motivation control*: procedures to maintain motivation and attention despite a limited interest in the task. An illustrative item is: 'When my mind began to wander during a learning session, I made a special effort to keep concentrating.'

(c) *Comprehension monitoring*: procedures to assess the degree to which learning goals have been achieved and to modify behaviour if necessary. An illustrative item is: 'I asked myself questions about some material in order to test my understanding of it.'

This framework appears to be of potential value in examining a variety of occupational training activities. In the next two sections it will be used to review research findings about the relationships between individuals' use of the nine strategies and their performance in learning.

LEARNING STRATEGIES AND LEARNING SUCCESS: CROSS-SECTIONAL STUDIES

Given that some cognitive processes are essential in almost all learning, what evidence is there for the value of the nine principal strategies outlined above? Two kinds of investigation are possible. Cross-sectional studies can examine the relationship between the use of particular strategies and success in learning, without any intervention by a researcher. Alternatively, interventions might be made, modifying strategy use and examining the consequences of that modification. This section will review cross-sectional studies, and intervention research will be summarized in the following section.

Research of the first kind typically takes an overall measure of learning success, such as final course grade (perhaps standardized across several courses, in order to increase the size of a sample), and calculates the significance of the association between self-reported learning strategy and that criterion performance. We will first review such bivariate associations, and then examine other individual characteristics which may underlie the bivariate findings.

Cognitive Strategies and Success

Three main 'cognitive' strategies were outlined earlier: rehearsal, organization and elaboration. Findings in respect of the first of these have been ambiguous, but use of the other two is consistently associated with greater learning success.

Self-reported rehearsal has on several occasions been examined through the Motivated Strategies for Learning Questionnaire (see above). Two investigations of American college students by Pintrich et al. (1993) and Pintrich and Garcia (1993) both recorded correlations of only 0.05 with final course grade. However, an earlier study of the same design by Pintrich and Garcia (1991) found a significant association ($r = 0.31$). For American high-school students, the correlation of learning achievement with another index of rehearsal was 0.18 ($p < 0.01$) in research by Zimmerman and Martinez-Pons (1986), but that association was non-significant in a later study (Zimmerman & Martinez-Pons, 1990).

Use of the second cognitive strategy (organization) has been shown to be significantly associated with academic performance. Published correlations with reported organization of material are 0.31 (Zimmerman & Martinez-Pons, 1986), 0.17 (Pintrich et al., 1993) and 0.18 (Pintrich & Garcia, 1993). The difference in self-reported use of organization between high- and low-achieving school pupils was also significant in the study by Zimmerman and Martinez-Pons (1990).

A laboratory investigation with physics texts showed that specific processes of organization (identified through questions asked of participants in the course of their task) led to more effective learning and retention (Ferguson-Hessler & de Jong, 1990). Lonka, Lindblom-Ylänne and Maury (1994) studied high-school students' use of organizational strategies by directly scoring their work books. Greater organization (in terms of creating conceptual maps between key concepts) was significantly predictive of learning success, but only when the material to be learned was complex and required critical evaluation.

Positive findings have also been obtained in respect of the third cognitive strategy (elaboration). Using the Inventory of Learning Processes (above), Schmeck and Grove (1979) observed a significant difference between high- and low-achieving American college students, and Schmeck (1983) has summarized several other findings of that kind. In studies introduced above, Pintrich et al. (1993) and Pintrich and Garcia (1993) found significant correlations of mental elaboration with course grade of 0.22 and 0.18 respectively.

In practice, reported organization and elaboration tend to covary; for example, the intercorrelation was 0.52 in the study of Pintrich et al. (1993). Studies examining the combined effect of both those strategies together have produced results similar to findings for the individual strategies. In Pintrich and Garcia's (1991) study the correlation with course grade was 0.30, and Kardash and Amlund (1991) observed values of 0.31, 0.24, 0.38 and 0.25 in four other samples of American university students. The latter researchers also examined laboratory learning and recall of textual material as a function of reported organization and elaboration; the median correlation was 0.38.

Several investigators have obtained self-reports of strategy use combining both rehearsal and elaboration. For example, Thomas, Bol, Warkentin, Wilson, Strage, and Rohwer (1993) recorded a correlation with learning test score of 0.18 ($p < 0.05$) for American high-school students. The same level of association was found for 173 seventh-grade students by Pintrich and De Groot (1990), in respect of course grade and a measure combining all three mental strategies: rehearsal, elaboration and organization.

In an industrial study, Warr and Bunce (1995) examined through a single scale junior managers' reported rehearsal, elaboration and organization in a programme of open learning. It was found that the amount of use of the three strategies together was strongly associated with learning score at the end of the programme: $r = 0.46$.

Behavioural Strategies and Success

The principal behavioural strategies were identified above as interpersonal help-seeking, seeking help from written material, and practical application. In comparison with mental strategies, these have less often been examined by educational researchers, since their emphasis has been upon information-processing from textual material.

Some studies have investigated interpersonal help-seeking by school and college students, with mixed results. In the studies by Pintrich and Garcia (1991) and Pintrich et al. (1993) associations of course grade with general help-seeking were negligible (0.00 and 0.02). Zimmerman and Martinez-Pons (1986) obtained information about tenth-graders' assistance-seeking from peers, teachers and adults, and found significant correlations with learning achievement of 0.22, 0.27 and 0.22 respectively. In a later study, the difference between groups of high and low achievement was significant in respect of seeking help from peers and from adults only (Zimmerman & Martinez-Pons, 1990).

The help-seeking scale of the Motivated Strategies for Learning Questionnaire (used by Pintrich and colleagues) was also employed by Karabenick and Knapp (1991). They found a significant *negative* correlation with 396 college students' course grade (−0.19), and replicated that negative association with a second sample and a different measure of help-seeking ($r = -0.24$, $n = 386$). It was observed that help-seeking was significantly associated with a greater perceived need for help, so that those students most seeking help felt that they were in special need of assistance. It could thus be the case that more help-seeking may in practice reflect lower ability.

In respect of the second behavioural strategy, Zimmerman and Martinez-Pons (1986, 1990) examined schoolchildren's approaches to obtaining new information from written material, with inconsistent results. In their first study, the correlation of the use of written material with academic achievement was 0.37, but this difference between criterion groups was non-significant in a second study. There is now a particular need for investigations of this kind in occupational settings, where individuals often have the opportunity to seek assistance from their environment, both social and non-social.

An overall 12-item index of behavioural learning strategies was applied by Warr and Bunce (1995) in a study of open learning by managers. This index covered together the three aspects: interpersonal help-seeking, seeking help from written material, and practical application. Reported use of these strategies as a whole was found to be uncorrelated with managers' learning score. However, subsequent examination of the items has revealed three factors covering each of the behavioural strategies cited above (alpha reliabilities were 0.67, 0.84 and 0.89). Correlations with learning score at the end of the programme were found to be −0.09 (n.s.), 0.11 (n.s.) and 0.24 ($p < 0.01$) for interpersonal help-seeking, seeking help from written material and practical application respectively. In this setting, managers' activities to work through material in practical terms (the third behavioural strategy) were linked to more positive learning outcomes; note that the negative association with interpersonal help-seeking (although non-significant) is consistent with findings summarized above.

Self-regulatory Strategies and Success

The third set of strategies in the present framework covers emotion control, motivation control and comprehension monitoring. Emotion control, using procedures to ward off anxiety, appears not to have been examined on its own as a potential predictor of learning achievement in non-laboratory settings.

However, motivation control, using procedures to maintain interest in the task, has frequently been found to be associated with learning success

(Zimmerman & Martinez-Pons, 1986, 1990; Pintrich et al., 1993; Pintrich & Garcia, 1991, 1993). For instance, the association with course grade was 0.32 in the study by Pintrich et al. (1993). More generally, several laboratory investigations have pointed to the combined importance of emotion control and motivation control in both learning and task performance (Kuhl, 1984; Kanfer, 1996). For example, Kanfer (1996) observed a correlation of 0.42 between self-reported use of both forms of control (in a single scale) and final score on an experimental learning task.

Few studies have been published of the third self-regulatory strategy, comprehension monitoring, but evidence that is available suggests that the association of this factor alone with students' course grades is non-significant (Zimmerman & Martinez-Pons, 1986, 1990). However, an index apparently combining motivation control with comprehension monitoring has been found significantly to predict course grades ($r = 0.32$) (Pintrich & De Groot, 1990).

Factors influencing the potential value of comprehension monitoring have been illustrated by Winne (1995). He points out that, despite its importance, monitoring has psychological costs, requiring effort and interfering with learning activities. That is particularly the case for less able students, since they tend to make more errors in need of monitoring and correction, and since they are unlikely to have automated the necessary procedures. Overly frequent monitoring, or monitoring against vague or too extensive a set of criteria, can actually impair learning. The association between reported comprehension monitoring and learning success is thus likely to vary from situation to situation.

Learning Strategies, Ability and Motivation

Current evidence from correlational investigations into the self-reported use of learning strategies and learners' performance is summarized in Table 3.2. Results from school/college settings and from occupational settings are presented separately, and it is obvious that more research into strategies in occupational learning is required.

It appears appropriate to conclude from publications to date that self-reported learning strategies of organization, elaboration and motivation control are significantly associated with learning achievement; evidence comes mainly from school and college settings, but similar findings might be expected in occupational research. One study has indicated the importance of practical application in learning by employees, but we have been unable to locate any evidence about the relationship between emotion control and learning success in occupational settings. For the other strategies (rehearsal, interpersonal help-seeking, seeking help from written material and comprehension monitoring) results are conflicting, and additional research to reconcile inconsistencies is required. It seems likely that the value of a particular strategy in

Table 3.2 Summary of evidence currently available about the cross-sectional relationship between use of the principal learning strategies and success in learning

	Positive relationships between learning strategies and learning success	
	School or college settings	Occupational settings
1. Cognitive strategies		
(a) Rehearsal	Not sure	No evidence located
(b) Organization	Yes	No evidence located
(c) Elaboration	Yes	No evidence located
[1b plus 1c]	[Yes]	[Yes]
2. Behavioural strategies		
(a) Interpersonal help-seeking	Not sure	No
(b) Seeking help from written material	Not sure	No
(c) Practical application	No evidence located	Yes
3. Self-regulatory strategies		
(a) Emotion control	No evidence located	No evidence located
(b) Motivation control	Yes	No evidence located
[3a plus 3b]	[Yes]	[No evidence located]
(c) Comprehension monitoring	Not sure	No evidence located

Yes: the evidence suggests a significant association.
Not sure: the evidence is ambiguous, perhaps because the direction and strength of relationships depend on other factors.
No: the evidence suggests a non-significant association.

these cases will depend on the material to be learned (e.g. whether it involves discrete items or interconnected concepts) and the ability of the learners studied (e.g. whether or not they in fact need to seek assistance from outside sources).

The research summarized above leaves unclear the nature of causality. For example, it could be that learners who apply particular strategies are more able or more motivated (or both) than are other learners. Enhanced ability and/or motivation might thus be the primary cause of the better learning performance shown by users of specific strategies.

It is well established that cognitive ability is a strong predictor of learning success in a wide range of situations (e.g. Olea & Ree, 1994; Rothstein, Paunonen, Rush & King, 1994; Ackerman, Kanfer & Goff, 1995), and it is likely to have contributed to learning success in the studies cited above. However, only in Kanfer's (1996) study was ability-test information obtained to address that possibility directly. Instead, several investigators have asked about self-efficacy for learning, using items like 'I believe I will receive an excellent grade in this class' and 'I'm certain I can master the skills being taught in this class' (Pintrich et al., 1991). Reported learning ability of this kind is significantly associated with actual learning ability (e.g. Tannenbaum et al., 1991), as individuals consider their previous attainments in assessing their perceived competence. Treating learning self-efficacy of that kind as a proxy measure of actual ability, what is known about relationships with learning strategies and success?

Self-efficacy for learning is strongly predictive of course grade: 0.34, 0.41 and 0.53 in studies by Pintrich and De Groot (1990), Pintrich et al. (1993) and Pintrich and Garcia (1993) respectively. (This finding has also been reported for employees' learning success by Tannenbaum et al., 1991, and Warr and Bunce, 1995.) The three data-sets examined by Pintrich and colleagues reveal that learning self-efficacy is also significantly associated with the cognitive strategies of organization and elaboration (the average correlation is about 0.35). (The same finding from different measures has also been reported for students by Kardash and Amlund, 1991, Thomas et al., 1993, and Zimmerman & Martinez-Pons, 1990.) Given that learning self-efficacy and those two cognitive strategies covary significantly, it is possible that the greater learning success of high users of the two strategies (see above) derives primarily from their greater mental ability.

What about other learning strategies? Self-efficacy for learning is less strongly associated with mental rehearsal ($r = 0.10$ and 0.16 in studies by Pintrich et al., 1993, and Pintrich & Garcia, 1993). No information has been located about the relationship between self-efficacy and the three behavioural strategies, and evidence is limited about self-regulatory strategies. The two studies cited immediately above yielded correlations between learning self-efficacy and motivation control of 0.44 and 0.36, but no information about the relations of self-efficacy with emotion control or comprehension monitoring has been found.

In order to disentangle the effects on learning success of learning self-efficacy and the use of organization, elaboration and motivation control, it is desirable to carry out multiple regression analyses, controlling other variables in order to identify the independent effect of the strategies under examination. The appropriate test in this case would be first to enter learning self-efficacy and then to examine the effect of a specific learning strategy after the initial control. Analyses of this and similar kinds will be summarized shortly.

First, we should ask the parallel question about learner motivation. Is level of motivation predictive of learners' achievement, and is motivation level significantly associated with the use of particular strategies? The answer appears to be positive in both cases. A measure of perceived importance/value of the learning task was applied in research by Pintrich and De Groot (1990), Pintrich et al. (1993) and Pintrich and Garcia (1993). Correlations of this measure of motivation with course grade were 0.25, 0.22 and 0.19 respectively. Associations with the three cognitive strategies ranged from 0.12 to 0.63, and with the self-regulatory strategy of motivation control the range was between 0.25 and 0.47. More motivated students thus learn more successfully and also more extensively use several learning strategies. (Kanfer, Ackerman and Heggestad (1996) combined all nine strategies in the Motivated Strategies for Learning Questionnaire into a single score. This very general measure was found to be substantially correlated with students' measured need for achievement.) It is therefore possible that the observed associations between strategy use and learning achievement (reviewed above) are due to variations in learner motivation.

Four publications have been located which control for other variables in order to identify the independent effect of strategies on learning. In a study of seventh-grade students, Pintrich and De Groot (1990) examined together self-efficacy for learning, task motivation, text anxiety, an overall measure of the three cognitive strategies, and a broad index of self-regulation. In relation to average course grade, only learning self-efficacy and the broad index of self-regulation were independently significant. In this analysis the three cognitive strategies were no longer significantly associated with course grade after including other controls. However, as noted above, a precise test of the contribution of a learning strategy over and above either self-efficacy or motivation requires a separate examination of the strategy and each of the other factors on their own; and information is also needed about each of the three separate cognitive strategies singly.

The strategies of organization and elaboration were examined in a combined scale by Kardash and Amlund (1991), together with a test of verbal ability in a laboratory study of learning from prose. In addition to being significantly predicted by verbal ability, free recall scores were also independently correlated with cognitive strategy use over and above the effect of verbal ability. A similar finding was obtained in a study of training by 106 junior British managers. Warr and Bunce (1995) included in a multiple regression an overall measure of the three cognitive strategies and an overall measure of the three behavioural strategies, after control for learning self-efficacy, motivation, educational qualifications, age, job tenure, and learning anxiety. It was found that managers' use of the cognitive strategies during learning remained independently strongly predictive of learning score, despite those controls. (The other independently significant predictors were low age and high motivation.)

Kanfer (1996) described two studies in which self-reported use of emotion control and motivation control (together) was included in analyses with a measure of cognitive ability. In both cases, the two sets of variables were independently predictive of learning: the measured ability of air traffic control trainees significantly predicted their learning performance, and the self-regulatory strategies were found to have a significant effect over and above that association.

It is clearly very important to develop this form of research in occupational settings. As shown earlier, there is convincing evidence from correlational investigations (mainly by educational psychologists) that use of certain learning strategies is associated with more positive learning outcomes. However, it is not yet clear how far strategy use has a specific impact over and above learners' ability and motivation. The Kardash and Amlund (1991) and the Warr and Bunce (1995) findings suggest that cognitive strategies are influential in their own right, despite control of several other factors, although ability was measured only indirectly in the latter study. The Pintrich and De Groot (1990) results point to the primary importance of other processes rather than cognitive strategies, but the published analysis was too gross to be definitive and the findings from schoolchildren need to be replicated with adult learners. In respect of self-regulatory strategies, the Kanfer (1996) research shows that these can be independently important even after control for cognitive ability. On balance, learning strategies appear to be influential over and above motivation and ability, but more investigations of the kind illustrated above are still needed.

LEARNING STRATEGIES AND LEARNING SUCCESS: TRAINING INTERVENTIONS

It is important to carry out experimental interventions to examine the impact of attempts to change strategies through training. Such interventions address directly the question of causality, if comparisons with control or other groups are made. Although 'research on the effectiveness of strategy training for adults in the workplace is relatively sparse' (Corno & Kanfer, 1993, p. 321), the educational literature again provides some relevant evidence. The general picture is encouraging.

Most programmes have taught learning strategies in the context of learning from text. One of the first programmes available was the 'SQ3R' technique (Robinson, 1946, 1970), which was originally designed for service-people on short intensive courses during World War Two to improve their understanding and retention of ideas in text passages. (The technique is labelled in this way to summarize its concern for Surveying, Questioning, Reading, Reciting and Reviewing.) Teaching people to use this broad set of procedures has been shown in several studies to improve learning, but success depends on the provision of substantial instruction for students of lower ability (Dansereau, 1978; Caverly & Orlando, 1991).

Other comprehensive programmes provide training in a variety of activities over an extended time period, and have often been shown to be effective (Pressley et al., 1990). For example, in a university setting Vermunt (1995) applied a 'learning-to-learn' programme with three broad components. First was elicitation, feedback and interpretation of students' cognitive and self-regulatory strategies (and certain other perspectives and orientations); second was written advice about possible approaches to learning, with the intention of promoting personal reflection; and third were tutorials to examine key issues and effective study activities. It was found that students attending the programme achieved significantly better examination results and also reported a wider range of learning effects than did non-attenders.

Because of the breadth of these comprehensive programmes, it is difficult to determine the separate impact of the individual components. In this section, we will review evidence for the value of training individuals in each of the nine more specific strategies that are included in the present conceptual framework.

Training in Cognitive Strategies

Rehearsal strategies

Several studies have examined aspects of rehearsal in the form of summaries made during learning. It is clear that individuals taught to summarize explicitly what they have read perform better on text-recall measures than either students using their own strategies or those asked merely to read the material (e.g. Ross & DiVesta, 1976). Dansereau's (1978) 'paraphrase/imagery' strategy requires students to summarize the material in their own words and then form mental pictures of the concepts underlying the material. Both techniques have been found to lead to improved performance on a delayed essay test in comparison to a no-treatment control group.

Note-taking is probably the most common form of (fairly complex) rehearsal strategy in practical situations. This requires a learner to select certain issues as sufficiently important to be written down in a summary, and provides him or her with opportunities to review those selected themes at later times. Most studies indicate that note-taking aids learning, even in the absence of explicit instruction about the procedure (Caverly & Orlando, 1991), but the provision of training has itself been shown to yield significant benefits. For example, Carrier and Titus (1981) examined note-taking in a 20-minute lecture, making comparisons between students who had received prior training and two comparison groups. It was found that members of the trained group were significantly the most effective.

Training in both summarizing and note-taking can thus improve learning. In practice, those activities extend beyond rehearsal as defined above ('procedures to repeat to oneself the material being learned'), although reviewing a summary or notes is undoubtedly a form of rehearsal.

Other investigations have examined more specific processes in the laboratory, comparing the performance of individuals who carry out rehearsal against that of other learners. For instance, Dark and Loftus (1976) showed how repetition of material aids long-term memory storage, and Naka and Naoi (1995) demonstrated the effectiveness of repeatedly writing down the material which has to be learned. Driskell, Copper and Moran (1994) reported a meta-analysis of previous research findings about both mental and physical practice activities; learning and retention were clearly improved by rehearsal.

Organization strategies

Dansereau's training programme includes instruction in creating cognitive networks. This procedure requires students to transform the material to be learned into a diagram, representing key ideas as nodes and their interrelationship by links between the nodes. Dansereau, McDonald, Collins et al. (1979) and Holley, Dansereau, McDonald, Garland and Collins (1979) found that students given six hours of networking training performed significantly better than those who used their own strategies. The effects of training were particularly strong for students with low academic ability.

Comparisons between the three component activities within the overall programme (networking, paraphrase/imagery, and analysis of key concepts) were conducted by Dansereau et al. (1979). Students received twelve hours of overall strategy training, before receiving twelve hours training in one of the three specific activities. The results indicated that, relative to the other conditions, students trained in networking made the greatest gains throughout the learning.

A related approach has required students to identify within a text top-level structures that describe relationships among the main ideas. Several different structural taxonomies have been explored, such as grouping items according to their covariance in relation to fixed consequences (e.g. both a lack of power and a failure of steering in supertankers lead to oil spills) or by means of comparison (e.g. ground stations for supertankers are similar to control towers for aircraft) (Meyer, 1981). Weinstein and Mayer (1986) have summarized investigations in which students were trained to develop cognitive structures of this kind. For example, learners trained to recognize key forms of prose structure in a chemistry textbook performed significantly better than a control group on a recall post-test and in problem-solving. This gain was also found to transfer to test material in unfamiliar biology and physics textbooks.

In a review of research with college students, Caverly and Orlando (1991) concluded that procedures for networking and otherwise mentally structuring material were significantly effective, especially when the text to be learned was difficult and/or long. Instruction in the use of such strategies was found to be particularly helpful for lower-ability students; and providing opportunities to review the structural material (a form of rehearsal, above) was also beneficial.

Elaboration strategies

Elaboration techniques, such as creating connections between key words and images, have been successfully taught as a strategy to help children learn vocabulary (Beck, Perfetti & McKeown, 1982). Weinstein (1979, 1982) created a broad training programme to increase elaboration skills among school pupils. Instruction was provided in a range of procedures: using sentences as elaborators; using images as elaborators; forming analogies; drawing implications; creating relationships; and paraphrasing. Ninth-grade students were randomly assigned to one of three groups: training, control, or post-test only. The training course included five one-hour sessions, and post-tests consisted of two reading comprehension tasks, two trials of paired-associate learning and a one-trial free-recall task. The trained group significantly outperformed the other groups, both immediately and on a delayed post-test approximately one month later.

Training in Behavioural Strategies

Three main behavioural learning strategies were introduced above as interpersonal help-seeking, seeking help from written material and practical application. Consistent with the narrow focus of educational investigations on the processing of written text, these behavioural strategies have so far received little research attention.

One laboratory investigation bearing on practical application (the third behavioural strategy) has been located. Frese, Albrecht, Altmann et al. (1988) compared three different training programmes, one of which involved active experimentation to explore possible self-generated questions about a computer system. This form of practical learning proved to be significantly more effective than passive, purely cognitive processing.

A principal training requirement in this area is to improve people's procedures first to identify the presence of a need for action and then to select from possibly useful actions. Behavioural strategy training of those kinds appears very likely to enhance employees' learning.

Training in Self-regulation Strategies

Emotion control and motivation control

In contrast to training in the primary strategies (above), where research has almost all been in educational or laboratory settings, there has been some consideration of self-regulation strategies within the organizational literature. These training programmes typically involve instruction in the use of goal-setting, planning, self-monitoring and self-reinforcement, and have generally shown positive effects on the maintenance of job performance (Frayne & Latham, 1987; Gist, Stevens & Bavetta, 1991). However, such programmes take a very broad perspective, and their success may derive from enhancing motivation itself rather than through the learning strategies examined here.

A more focused approach was taken by Kanfer and Ackerman (1990). They examined the possible beneficial impact of emotion control strategies and motivation control strategies during laboratory-based training for US Air Force staff. Significant benefits followed the induction of an emotion control strategy, but these were found to vary according to learner ability. Lower-ability trainees were most assisted by training in emotion control, especially during the initial phase of skill learning, when attentional demands were particularly high. Contrary to expectations, no significant pattern was found for training in motivation control, perhaps because task demands were sufficiently high to sustain attention (i.e. not to require motivation control) even for higher-ability individuals (Kanfer & Ackerman, 1996, p. 165).

Dansereau's programme offers training in planning and scheduling, concentration management and monitoring. The concentration management technique includes elements of systematic desensitization, rational behaviour therapy and procedures based on positive self-talk. Trainees are instructed to use these techniques to establish and maintain an appropriate mood for studying. Collins, Dansereau, Garland, Holley and McDonald (1981) found that a combined concentration management strategy led to significantly better performance on text-processing in comparison to students using their own methods. Training was provided in three activities: self-initiated relaxation, which required participants to use a combination of relaxation techniques to maintain appropriate emotional states; self-coaching, which taught students to coach (talk to) themselves to create and maintain appropriate states; and a strategy which combined both relaxation and self-coaching. In comparison with a no-treatment control group, training in the combined strategy significantly improved performance.

In another programme to improve self-regulatory strategies, Weinstein and Underwood (1985) provided instruction in aspects of motivation, basic cognitive principles, methods to monitor one's understanding, procedures for using imaginal or verbal elaborations, and traditional study skills techniques such as note-taking. They showed that students made substantial improvements in their reading ability by the end of the course and that self-reported levels of anxiety were reduced. However, it is not possible from the research design to identify which of the several manipulated variables had a principal impact, and the training extended beyond merely learning strategies.

A number of other programmes have been devised to teach students strategies to help them cope with anxiety. Results have been generally positive (e.g. Goldfried, Linehan & Smith, 1978). However, this teaching is often embedded in other activities, so that it is again difficult to evaluate specific aspects of the instruction, such as applying the strategy of emotion control as identified here.

Comprehension monitoring

Studies reviewed by Weinstein and Mayer (1986) and in the book edited by Schunk and Zimmerman (1991) have provided training in order to improve comprehension monitoring when learning from text. Results typically show that a trained group performs better on a subsequent reading comprehension test than do other students. This difference has been maintained across several subsequent weeks. The evidence thus suggests that comprehension monitoring can be taught, and that benefits occur which are stable over time.

In practice, comprehension monitoring is likely to be accompanied by one or more of the 'primary' learning strategies (see the beginning of the chapter): a learner monitors achievements made through certain cognitive or behavioural strategies. Bielaczyc, Pirolli and Brown (1995) examined the impact of training to improve both comprehension monitoring and elaboration. Acquisition of computer-programming skill was significantly improved by this form of instruction.

Training in Learning Strategies: Overview

It is clear from this review that strategy training programmes can significantly affect the way that learners proceed through training. For example, Dansereau claims that there is a 30% to 40% improvement in performance for students trained in his comprehensive programme in comparison to students using their own learning methods. However investigations have mainly been in educational settings, and there is a great requirement for development of these ideas and procedures in occupational training.

A summary of the current position in respect of the nine principal strategies is set out in Table 3.3. It is clear that additional evidence is required in each case. In addition to expanding this database, research and practice in the area need to address a range of questions. For instance, training in content-independent learning strategies needs to be general enough to have fairly wide applicability, but specific enough for students to be able to easily see the relevance to their tasks. Achieving this balance can be difficult. There is also some debate as to whether adjunct training programmes, ancillary to the main learning activity as illustrated above, are more or less effective than strategy instruction that is built into training in a specific content area. This is an important question for organizations. On the one hand, if embedded programmes are found to be the more effective, content-specific trainers will usually need to alter their training programmes. On the other hand, if adjunct programmes are more effective, additional training activities must be devised to instruct employees in appropriate general strategies.

Issues of sequencing and the appropriate timing of training also require investigation. There is some evidence to suggest that it is beneficial first to train individuals in the primary strategies before providing training in the self-regulation strategies (Dansereau, 1985). Furthermore, the studies by Kanfer and Ackerman (1990, see above) suggest that emotion control training is specially valuable early in learning, whereas motivation control might be more important at later stages (see also Kanfer & Ackerman, 1996).

Table 3.3 Summary of evidence currently available about the effect of training people to use the principal learning strategies

	Significant impact of training in strategy use on learning success		
	School or college settings	Laboratory settings	Occupational settings
1. Cognitive strategies			
(a) Rehearsal	Yes	Yes	No evidence located
(b) Organization	Yes	No evidence located	No evidence located
(c) Elaboration	Yes	No evidence located	No evidence located
2. Behavioural strategies			
(a) Interpersonal help-seeking	No evidence located	No evidence located	No evidence located
(b) Seeking help from written material	No evidence located	No evidence located	No evidence located
(c) Practical application	No evidence located	Yes	No evidence located
3. Self-regulatory strategies			
(a) Emotion control	No evidence located	Yes	No evidence located
(b) Motivation control	No evidence located	Not sure	No evidence located
[3a plus 3b]	[Yes]	[No evidence located]	[No evidence located]
(c) Comprehension monitoring	Yes	No evidence located	No evidence located

Yes: the evidence suggests a significant association.

Also needed is more consideration of individual differences in relation to strategy training. In addition to variations in motivation, there have been several studies suggesting that the ability of trainees may interact with training to produce different outcomes (Snow, 1989; Caverly & Orlando, 1991). For example, Holley et al. (1979) found from comparisons between groups of students of high and low academic ability that a cognitive networking strategy tended to be more beneficial for low-ability learners. Veenman, Elshout and Busato (1994) observed that only low-intelligence individuals were aided by prompts designed to improve learning in physics experiments. And Kanfer and Ackerman (1990, see above) indicated that it is lower-ability individuals who benefit most from emotion control training early in a programme of learning.

An associated issue concerns individuals' customary levels of learning activity. It might be expected that people with little experience of learning would derive greater benefit from learning-to-learn training than would those with substantial previous experience. Consistent with that possible difference, Vermunt (1995) observed that a comprehensive programme (see above) produced larger effects for part-time than for full-time university students. It seems likely that instruction and guidance about key learning strategies would be of particular value for those employees who traditionally receive little training: individuals in lower-level jobs, those with longer tenure, those with fewer educational qualifications, older workers, part-time women employees, and workers in small establishments (Birdi, Gardner & Warr, 1997).

Another issue in need of organizational investigation concerns the transfer and retention of strategies which have been enhanced through training. There have been very few follow-up studies, and these have been restricted to only a single learning strategy as applied by college students or school pupils (e.g. Weinstein, 1979, 1982). As a result, we know that training to improve learning strategies can be effective in the short term, but we have very little knowledge about its long-term benefits.

LEARNING STRATEGIES AND INDUSTRIAL-ORGANIZATIONAL PSYCHOLOGY

The knowledge acquired about learning strategies now stands in need of application in business and public organizations. Principal types of strategies have been identified, similarities and differences with learning 'styles' have been clarified, and considerable evidence about the importance of learning strategies has been acquired in educational settings. However, very little research of this kind in employing organizations has been published.

It would now be valuable to include measures of strategies within studies of learner characteristics in occupational training. By identifying which strategies are associated with success in specific types of learning, it will be possible to attempt practical improvement through strategy-training and also to expand understanding of the processes of learning themselves. In developing this area of research, a number of issues now require attention.

First, it is important to examine the validity of self-report measures of strategy. How accurately do people describe their learning strategies subsequent to the activity? It is possible that some individuals are not aware of certain approaches which they previously adopted; others may choose to present themselves in what they consider to be a positive manner, biasing their reports accordingly.

There is a general need to undertake validity studies of self-report measures in this area. Possible criteria include think-aloud protocols, stimulated recall procedures, structured interviews or observed behaviours. For example, Zimmerman and Martinez-Pons (1988) found significant associations between students' reports of strategy use and teachers' ratings of that use. However, the application of certain learning strategies is not observable by other people, so that external ratings are unlikely to be accurate in all cases.

More generally, it may be the case that the validity of self-reports is greater when learning episodes are relatively brief (e.g. a single session) rather than being a course of study extended over several months. There is also a need for qualitative studies of learners' experiences and strategies in occupational settings, parallel to research already carried out in schools and colleges. Associated with new work to validate self-report measures, it would also be valuable to investigate in their own right the criterion indicators; how far do those measures themselves predict learning success?

Second, possible variations between learning situations need to be examined. It is expected that particular strategies will be differentially effective in different learning activities. For instance, it may be very appropriate to employ a rehearsal strategy when learning discrete facts, whereas organization and elaboration are likely to be needed when acquiring understanding of complex concepts. However, comparisons have rarely been undertaken. We need now to carry out inquiries in a range of domains, such as those requiring declarative knowledge, practical skills, social skills and personal skills, in order to develop profiles of appropriate learning strategies in each. One approach is in terms of different strategies within a 'MUD' taxonomy, distinguishing between facts which require *m*emorizing, concepts in need of *u*nderstanding and physical activities which need *d*oing (Downs, 1992). Levin (1986) has identified strategies likely to have different effects within a 'URA' framework of material requiring either *u*nderstanding, *r*emembering or *a*pplying.

Third, it is desirable to learn more about the operation of different learning strategies in combination. For instance, the use of elaboration does not necessarily exclude mental rehearsal; a learner may be active in both respects, even though they are conceptually distinct in that elaboration suggests a 'deep' approach whereas rehearsal is more 'surface'. It might thus be the case that in some circumstances a learning strategy of elaboration which is combined with rehearsal is more effective than either of those singly. The time is now ripe to examine the impact of specific combinations, rather than investigating single strategies on their own.

Fourth, the interrelationships between specific learning strategies and styles require study. For example, how far are people's stylistic differences in a deep or surface approach, across a range of situations, also visible in their patterns of strategy use in specific task activities? The issue here is somewhat like that concerning personality 'traits' and 'states'. The latter are more localized and variable than traits, but the two constructs overlap conceptually and tend to be significantly intercorrelated.

A fifth need is to identify how the value of a learning strategy depends upon a person's need for assistance or remedial action. For example, it was pointed out earlier that interpersonal help-seeking (the first behavioural strategy in the framework set out here) is sometimes *negatively* associated with learning success (e.g. Karabenick & Knapp, 1991). This negative association may arise from the fact that able learners do not need to make additional efforts of this kind, whereas those who are less competent require help from an external source. This pattern (in which greater strategy use derives at least in part from problems in learning) may extend to emotion control and motivation control; these self-regulatory strategies are only needed when a learner experiences high anxiety or low interest respectively. On the other hand, it could be that certain strategies are desirable for all people, so that their use will be associated with learning success irrespective of a person's need. At present, evidence about these alternative possibilities is very sparse.

A sixth requirement is to examine, in conjunction with strategies, other individual characteristics which are likely to affect learning success. As discussed earlier, key factors here are learners' motivation and ability. Motivation for learning has been shown to be significantly associated with reported use of cognitive strategies ($r = 0.38$; Warr & Bunce, 1995), and mental ability is likely to be correlated with use of more complex strategies. Given that particular strategies significantly predict learning success, what is their impact over and above the influence of motivation and ability? In effect, what is the 'incremental validity' of measures of learning strategy? Some investigations into that issue have been summarized above, but there is now a great need for their development.

A seventh need is for investigations into procedures to assist learners better to apply key strategies in occupational settings. Some progress has been made in 'developing skilled learners' by enhancing their use of strategies (e.g. Perry & Downs, 1985; see also the preceding section), but considerably more investigations are needed. Three types of investigation into strategy training are required:

1. Of particular importance are fresh studies which contrast different types of strategy induction. Three issues should be addressed here. First, when examining training in a particular strategy, how effective are different forms of that strategy? For instance, in teaching cognitive elaboration, what are the relative effects of image-based or verbal processes? Second, what are the consequences of focusing either on single strategies or on a range of different strategies together? Can one effectively teach people to use individual learning strategies, or does assistance in this area depend upon training in a combination of activities? A third issue of contrast concerns different sequences of instruction. As illustrated in the previous section, there have been suggestions that primary strategies should be taught before self-regulatory strategies,

and that emotion control strategies should be applied before motivation control strategies. These possibilities need examination in occupational settings.

2. In teaching people better to apply learning strategies, it is important to address the issue of possible 'aptitude–treatment interactions', the extent to which a given training procedure may be differentially effective for different types of learner. For instance, there is evidence from educational settings that instruction in learning strategies is more beneficial for individuals of lower rather than higher ability (Snow, 1989; see also the previous section). This possibility should be incorporated into the design of research into occupational training.

3. It is essential to explore the generalizability of learning about strategies; how far does instruction in strategy use transfer to new situations outside the original training setting? Stylistic preferences will exert some constraints here, but evidence reviewed earlier indicates that it is possible to induce people to modify at least some learning strategies. However, it is not yet clear how far they can learn to recognize which strategies would be most appropriate in specific new settings. That form of higher-order generalization, through development of a mental model to permit recognition of task similarities and differences, is essential if transfer of any type of learning is to occur (e.g. Ford & Kraiger, 1995). The development and application of such mental models and recognition processes now require investigation in the domain of this chapter.

Progress in these seven areas will bring practical rewards in the form of more effective training and learning in work settings. In addition, such progress will permit a deeper theoretical understanding of the psychological processes involved in a wide range of learning activities.

REFERENCES

Ackerman, P. L., Kanfer, R. & Goff, M. (1995). Cognitive and noncognitive determinants and consequences of complex skill acquisition. *Journal of Experimental Psychology: Applied*, **1**, 270–304.

Baldwin, T. T., Magjuka, R. J. & Loher, B. T. (1991). The perils of participation: Effects of choice of training on trainee motivation and learning. *Personnel Psychology*, **44**, 51–65.

Beck, I., Perfetti, C. & McKeown, J. (1982). The effects of long-term vocabulary instruction on lexical access in reading comprehension. *Journal of Educational Psychology*, **75**, 506–521.

Bielaczyc, K., Pirolli, P. L. & Brown, A. L. (1995). Training in self-explanation and self-regulation strategies: Investigating the effects of knowledge acquisition activities on problem solving. *Cognition and Instruction*, **13**, 221–252.

Biggs, J. B. (1987). *Student Approaches to Learning and Studying*. Hawthorn, Victoria: Australian Council for Educational Research.

Biggs, J. (1993). What do inventories of students' learning processes really measure? A theoretical review and clarification. *British Journal of Educational Psychology*, **63**, 3–19.

Birdi, K. S., Gardner, C. & Warr, P. B. (1997). Correlates and perceived outcomes of four types of employee development activity. *Journal of Applied Psychology*, in press.

Bjorklund, D. F., Ornstein, P. A. & Haig, J. R. (1977). Developmental differences in organization and recall: Training in the use of organizational techniques. *Developmental Psychology*, **13**, 175–183.

Brown, W. F. & Holtzman, W. H. (1967). *Survey of Study Habits and Attitudes*. New York: Psychological Corporation.

Cano-Garcia, F. & Justicia-Justicia, F. (1994). Learning strategies, styles and approaches: An analysis of their interrelationships. *Higher Education*, **27**, 239–260.

Carrier, C.A. & Titus, A. (1981). Effects of note-taking pretraining and test mode expectations on learning from lectures. *American Educational Research Journal*, **18**, 385–397.

Caverly, D. C. & Orlando, V. P. (1991). Textbook study strategies. In R. F. Flippo and D. C. Caverly (Eds), *Teaching Reading and Study Strategies at the College Level* (pp. 86–165). Newark, DE: International Reading Association.

Christensen, F. A. (1968). *College Adjustment and Study Skills Inventory*. Berea, OH: Personal Growth Press.

Christensen, C. A., Massey, D. R. & Isaacs, P. J. (1991). Cognitive strategies and study habits: An analysis of the measurement of tertiary students' learning. *British Journal of Educational Psychology*, **61**, 290–299.

Collins, K. W., Dansereau, D. F., Garland, J. C., Holley, C. D. & McDonald, B. A. (1981). Control of concentration during academic tasks. *Journal of Educational Psychology*, **73**, 122–128.

Corno, L. & Kanfer, R. (1993). The role of volition in learning and performance. In L. Darling-Hammond (Ed.), *Review of Research in Education* (Vol. 21, pp. 301–341). Itasca, IL: Peacock.

Dansereau, D. F. (1978). The development of a learning strategies curriculum. In H. R. O'Neil, Jr (Ed.), *Learning Strategies* (pp. 1–29). New York: Academic Press.

Dansereau, D. F. (1985). Learning strategy research. In J. W. Segal, S. F. Chipman & R. Glaser (Eds), *Thinking and Learning Skills* (Vol. 1, pp. 209–239). Hillsdale, NJ: Lawrence Erlbaum.

Dansereau, D. F., McDonald, B. A., Collins, K. W., Garland, J. C., Holley, C. D., Diekhoff, G. & Evans, S. H. (1979). Evaluation of a learning strategy system. In H. F. O'Neil, Jr & C. D. Spielberger (Eds), *Cognitive and Affective Learning Strategies* (pp. 3–43). New York: Academic Press.

Dark, V. J. & Loftus, G. R. (1976). The role of rehearsal in long-term memory performance. *Journal of Verbal Learning and Verbal Behavior*, **15**, 479–490.

Downs, S. (1992). Learning to learn. In S. Truelove (Ed.), *Handbook of Training and Development* (pp. 80–113). Oxford: Blackwell.

Driskell, J. E., Copper, C. & Moran, A. (1994). Does mental practice enhance performance? *Journal of Applied Psychology*, **79**, 481–492.

Dunn, R., Dunn, K. & Price, G. (1989). *The Learning Style Inventory*. Lawrence, KS: Price Systems.

Entwistle, N. J. & Ramsden, P. (1983). *Understanding Student Learning*. London: Croom Helm.

Entwistle, N. J. & Waterston, S. (1988). Approaches to studying and levels of processing in university students. *British Journal of Educational Psychology*, **58**, 258–265.

Ertmer, P. A. & Newby, T. J. (1996). The expert learner: Strategic, self-regulated, and reflective. *Instructional Science*, **24**, 1–24.

Eyring, J. D., Johnson, D. S. & Francis, D. J. (1993). A cross-level units-of-analysis approach to individual differences in skill acquisition. *Journal of Applied Psychology*, **78**, 805–814.

Ferguson-Hessler, M. G. M. & de Jong, T. (1990). Studying physics texts: Differences in study processes between good and poor performers. *Cognition and Instruction*, 7, 41–54.

Ford, J. K. & Kraiger, K. (1995). The application of cognitive constructs and principles to the instructional systems model of training: Implications for needs assessment, design and transfer. In C. L. Cooper & I. T. Robertson (Eds), *International Review of Industrial and Organizational Psychology* (Vol. 10, pp. 1–48). Chichester: Wiley.

Frayne, E. A. & Latham, G. P. (1987). Application of social learning theory to employee self-management of attendance. *Journal of Applied Psychology*, 72, 387–392.

Frese, M., Albrecht, K., Altmann, A., Lang, J., Papstein, P. V., Peyerl, R., Prümper, J., Schulte-Göcking, H., Wankmüller, I. & Wendel, R. (1988). The effects of an active development of the mental model in the training process: Experimental results in a word processing system. *Behaviour and Information Technology*, 7, 295–304.

Gist, M. E., Stevens, C. K. & Bavetta, A. G. (1991). Effects of self-efficacy and post-training intervention on the acquisition and maintenance of complex interpersonal skills. *Personnel Psychology*, 44, 837–861.

Goldfried, M. R., Linehan, M. M. & Smith, J. L. (1978). Reduction of test anxiety through cognitive restructuring. *Journal of Consulting and Clinical Psychology*, 46, 32–39.

Goldstein, I. & Gillam, P. (1990). Training system issues in the year 2000. *American Psychologist*, 45, 134–143.

Hayes, J. & Allinson, C. W. (1996). The implications of learning styles for training and development: A discussion of the matching hypothesis. *British Journal of Management*, 7, 63–73.

Holley, C. D., Dansereau, D. R., McDonald, B. A., Garland, J. C. & Collins, K. W. (1979). Evaluation of a hierarchical mapping technique as an aid to prose processing. *Contemporary Educational Psychology*, 4, 227–237.

Jackson, C. & Lawty-Jones, M. (1996). Explaining the overlap between personality and learning style. *Personality and Individual Differences*, 20, 293–300.

Kanfer, R. (1996). Self-regulatory and other non-ability determinants of skill acquisition. In J. A. Bargh & P. M. Gollwitzer (Eds), *The Psychology of Action: Linking Cognition and Motivation to Behavior* (pp. 403–423). New York: Guilford Press.

Kanfer, R. & Ackerman, P. L. (1990). *Ability and Metacognitive Determinants of Skill Acquisition and Transfer*. Minneapolis: University of Minnesota.

Kanfer, R. & Ackerman, P. L. (1996). A self-regulatory skills perspective to reducing cognitive interference. In I. G. Sarason, G. R. Pierce and B. R. Sarason (Eds), *Cognitive Interference: Theories, Methods, and Findings* (pp. 153–171). Mahwah, NJ: Lawrence Erlbaum.

Kanfer, R., Ackerman, P. L. & Heggestad, E. D. (1996). Motivational skills and self-regulation for learning: A trait perspective. *Learning and Individual Differences*, 8, 185–210.

Karabenick, S. A. & Knapp, J. R. (1991). Relationship of academic help seeking to the use of learning strategies and other instrumental achievement behaviors in college students. *Journal of Educational Psychology*, 83, 221–230.

Kardash, C. M. & Amlund, J. T. (1991). Self-reported learning strategies and learning from expository text. *Contemporary Educational Psychology*, 16, 117–138.

Kolb, D. A. (1984). *Experiential Learning*. Englewood Cliffs, NJ: Prentice-Hall.

Kuhl, J. (1984). Volitional aspects of achievement motivation and learned helplessness: Toward a comprehensive theory of action control. In B. A. Maher (Ed.), *Progress in Experimental Personality Research* (Vol. 13, pp. 99–171). New York: Academic Press.

Kuhl, J. (1992). A theory of self-regulation: Action versus state orientation, self-discrimination, and some applications. *Applied Psychology: An International Review*, 41, 97–129.

Levin, J. R. (1986). Four cognitive principles of learning-strategy instruction. *Educational Psychologist*, **21**, 3–17.

Lonka, K., Lindblom-Ylänne, S. & Maury, S. (1994). The effect of study strategies on learning from text. *Learning and Instruction*, **4**, 253–271.

Mayer, R. E. (1988). Learning strategies: An overview. In C. E. Weinstein, E. T. Goetz & P. A. Alexander (Eds), *Learning and Study Strategies* (pp. 11–21). San Diego: Academic Press.

Messick, S. (1984). The nature of cognitive styles: Problems and promise in educational practice. *Educational Psychologist*, **19**, 59–74.

Meyer, B. J. F. (1981). Basic research on prose comprehension: A critical review. In D. F. Fisher & C. W. Peters (Eds), *Comprehension and the Competent Reader* (pp. 8–35). New York: Praeger.

Murray-Harvey, R. (1994). Learning styles and approaches to learning: Distinguishing between concepts and instruments. *British Journal of Educational Psychology*, **64**, 373–388.

Naka, M. & Naoi, H. (1995). The effect of repeated writing on memory. *Memory and Cognition*, **23**, 201–212.

Nisbet, J. & Schucksmith, J. (1986). *Learning Strategies*. London: Routledge & Kegan Paul.

Olea, M. M. & Ree, M. J. (1994). Predicting pilot and navigator criteria: Not much more than *g*. *Journal of Applied Psychology*, **79**, 845–851.

Pearn, M., Roderick, C. & Mulrooney, C. (1995). *Learning Organizations In Practice*. London: McGraw-Hill.

Perry, P. & Downs, S. (1985). Skills, strategies and ways of learning: Can we help people to learn? *Programmed Learning and Educational Technology*, **22**, 177–181.

Pintrich, P. R. (1988). A process-oriented view of student motivation and cognition. In J. S. Stark & L. A. Mets (Eds), *Improving Teaching and Learning through Research* (pp. 65–79). San Francisco: Jossey-Bass.

Pintrich, P. R. & De Groot, E. V. (1990). Motivational and self-regulated learning components of classroom academic performance. *Journal of Educational Psychology*, **82**, 33–40.

Pintrich, P. R. & Garcia, T. (1991). Student goal orientation and self-regulation in the college classroom. In M. Maehr & P. R. Pintrich (Eds), *Advances in Motivation and Achievement* (Vol. 7, pp. 371–402). Greenwich, CT: JAI Press.

Pintrich, P. R. & Garcia, T. (1993). Intra-individual differences in students' motivation and self-regulated learning. *Zeitschrift für Pädagogische Psychologie*, **7**, 99–107.

Pintrich, P. R., Smith, D. A. F., Garcia, T. & McKeachie, W. J. (1991). *A Manual for the Use of the Motivated Strategies for Learning Questionnaire*. Ann Arbor, MI: School of Education, University of Michigan.

Pintrich, P. R., Smith, D. A. F., Garcia, T. & McKeachie, W. J. (1993). Reliability and predictive validity of the Motivated Strategies for Learning Questionnaire. (MSLQ). *Educational and Psychological Measurement*, **53**, 801–813.

Pressley, M., Woloshyn, V., Lysynchuk, L. M., Martin, V., Wood, E. & Willoughby, T. (1990). A primer of research on cognitive strategy instruction: The important issues and how to address them. *Educational Psychology Review*, **2**, 1–76.

Richardson, J. T. E. (1990). Reliability and replicability of the Approaches to Studying Questionnaire. *Studies in Higher Education*, **15**, 155–168.

Rigney, J. W. (1978). Learning strategies: A theoretical perspective. In H. F. O'Neill (Ed.), *Learning Strategies* (pp. 165–205). New York: Academic Press.

Robinson, F. P. (1946). *Effective Study*. New York: Harper.

Robinson, F. P. (1970). *Effective Study* (4th edn). New York: Harper & Row.

Ross, S. M. & DiVesta, F. J. (1976). Oral summary as a review strategy for enhancing recall of textual material. *Journal of Educational Psychology*, **68**, 689–695.

Rothstein, M. G., Paunonen, S. V., Rush, J. C. & King, G. A. (1994). Personality and cognitive ability predictors of performance in graduate business school. *Journal of Educational Psychology*, **86**, 516–530.

Schmeck, R. R. (1983). Learning styles of college students. In R.F. Dillon & R.R. Schmeck (Eds), *Individual Differences in Cognition* (Vol. 1, pp. 233–279). New York: Academic Press.

Schmeck, R. R. (1988a). An introduction to strategies and styles of learning. In R. R. Schmeck (Ed.), *Learning Strategies and Learning Styles* (pp. 3–19). New York: Plenum Press.

Schmeck, R. R. (1988b). Individual differences and learning strategies. In C. E. Weinstein, E. T. Goetz & P. A. Alexander (Eds), *Learning and Study Strategies* (pp. 171–191). San Diego: Academic Press.

Schmeck, R. R. & Grove, E. (1979). Academic achievement and individual differences in learning processes. *Applied Psychological Measurement*, **3**, 43–49.

Schmeck, R. R., Geisler-Brenstein, E. & Cercy, S. P. (1991). Self-concept and learning: The revised Inventory of Learning Processes. *Educational Psychology*, **11**, 343–362.

Schunk, D. & Zimmerman, B. (Eds) (1991). *Self-regulation of Learning and Performance*. Hillsdale, NJ: Lawrence Erlbaum.

Sims, R. R., Veres, J. G., Watson, P. & Buckner, K. E. (1986). The reliability and classification stability of the learning style inventory. *Educational and Psychological Measurement*, **46**, 753–760.

Snow, R. E. (1989). Aptitude–treatment interaction as a framework for research on individual differences in learning. In P. L. Ackerman, R. J. Sternberg & R. Glaser (Eds), *Learning and Individual Differences* (pp. 13–59). New York: Freeman.

Tannenbaum, S. I., Mathieu, J. E., Salas, E. & Cannon-Bowers, J. A. (1991). Meeting trainees' expectations: The influence of training fulfillment on the development of commitment, self-efficacy, and motivation. *Journal of Applied Psychology*, **76**, 759–769.

Thomas, J. W., Bol, L., Warkentin, R. W., Wilson, M., Strage, A. & Rohwer, W. D. (1993). Interrelationships among students' study activities, self-concept of academic ability, and achievement as a function of characteristics of high-school biology courses. *Applied Cognitive Psychology*, **7**, 499–532.

Thomas, P. R. & Bain, J. D. (1984). Contextual dependence of learning approaches: The effects of assessments. *Human Learning*, **3**, 227–240.

Veenman, M. V. J., Elshout, J. J. & Busato, V. V. (1994). Metacognitive mediation in learning with computer-based simulations. *Computers in Human Behavior*, **10**, 93–106.

Vermunt, J. D. (1995). Process-oriented instruction in learning and thinking strategies. *European Journal of Psychology of Education*, **10**, 325–49.

Vermunt, J. D. (1996). Metacognitive, cognitive and affective aspects of learning styles and strategies: A phenomenographic analysis. *Higher Education*, **31**, 25–50.

Vermunt, J. D. & van Rijswijk, F. A. W. M. (1988). Analysis and development of students' skill in self-regulated learning. *Higher Education*, **17**, 647–682.

Warr, P. B. (1994). Age and employment. In H. C. Triandis, M. D. Dunnette & L. M. Hough (Eds), *Handbook of Industrial and Organizational Psychology* (Vol. 4, pp. 484–550). Palo Alto, CA: Consulting Psychologists Press.

Warr, P. B. & Bunce, D. J. (1995). Trainee characteristics and the outcomes of open learning. *Personnel Psychology*, **48**, 347–375.

Weinstein, C. E. (1979). Elaboration skills as a learning strategy. In H.F. O'Neill (Ed.), *Learning Strategies* (pp. 31–55). New York: Academic Press.

Weinstein, C. E. (1982). Training students to use elaboration learning strategies. *Contemporary Educational Psychology*, **7**, 301–311.

Weinstein, C. E. & Mayer, R. E. (1986). The teaching of learning strategies. In M.C. Wittock (Ed.), *Handbook of Research on Teaching* (3rd edn, pp. 315–327). New York: Macmillan.

Weinstein, C. E. & Underwood, V. L. (1995). Learning strategies: The how of learning. In J. W. Segal, S. F. Chipman & R. Glaser (Eds), *Thinking and Learning Skills* (Vol. 1, pp. 241–258). Hillsdale, NJ: Lawrence Erlbaum.

Weinstein, C. E., Zimmerman, S. A. & Palmer, D. R. (1988). Assessing learning strategies: The design and development of the LASSI. In C. L. Weinstein, E. T. Goetz & P. A. Alexander (Eds), *Learning and Study Strategies* (pp. 25–39). San Diego: Academic Press.

Willcoxson, L. & Prosser, M. (1996). Kolb's Learning Style Inventory (1985): Review and further study of validity and reliability. *British Journal of Educational Psychology*, **66**, 247–257.

Williams, K. (1989). *Study Skills*. London: Macmillan.

Wilson, K. L., Smart, R. M. & Watson, R. J. (1996). Gender differences in approaches to learning in first year psychology students. *British Journal of Educational Psychology*, **66**, 59–71.

Winne, P. H. (1995). Inherent details in self-regulated learning. *Educational Psychologist*, **30**, 173–187.

Zimmerman, B. J. & Martinez-Pons, M. (1986). Development of a structured interview for assessing student use of self-regulated learning strategies. *American Educational Research Journal*, **23**, 614–628.

Zimmerman, B. J. & Martinez-Pons, M. (1988). Construct validation of a strategy model of student self-regulated learning. *Journal of Educational Psychology*, **80**, 284–290.

Zimmerman, B. J. & Martinez-Pons, M. (1990). Student differences in self-regulated learning: Relating grade, sex, and giftedness to self-efficacy and strategy use. *Journal of Educational Psychology*, **82**, 51–59.

Chapter 7

CONTEMPORARY RESEARCH ON ABSENCE FROM WORK: CORRELATES, CAUSES AND CONSEQUENCES

Gary Johns
Concordia University

The purpose of this chapter is to review the research literature on absence from work that has been published in the last 15 years or so. The review is meant to be fairly comprehensive in that it spans various correlates, causes, consequences, theoretical perspectives, and research methods used to study absenteeism. However, due to space limitations, it does not cover interventions used to manage attendance. This will be the subject of another paper.

The time span of 15 years is not arbitrary. Rather, it reflects the fact that it has been a good while since a more comprehensive review of this subject has been attempted. Earlier reviews include those by Porter and Steers (1973) and Muchinsky (1977). Subsequent reviews have been selective, focusing on particular theories or models of attendance (Brooke, 1986; Chadwick-Jones, Nicholson, & Brown, 1982; Mowday, Porter, & Steers, 1982; Steers & Rhodes, 1978), demographic correlates of absence (Nicholson, Brown, & Chadwick-Jones, 1977), job satisfaction and absence (Nicholson, Brown, & Chadwick-Jones, 1976), and absence management strategies (Rhodes & Steers, 1990). The reader is directed to these earlier qualitative reviews, all of which provide useful summaries of research in particular areas. In addition, since 1984, a number of meta-analyses have been conducted that provide quantitative summaries of particular correlates of absence. The conclusions of these meta-analyses will form part of the present review.

The chapter is organized around a loose series of informal 'models' that reflect various presumed correlates or causes of absence. In some cases, these models are espoused both by researchers and by lay people.

Contemporary Research on Absence from Work: Correlates, Causes and Consequences by Gary Johns taken from IRIOP 1997 v12, Edited by Cary L. Cooper and Ivan T. Robertson: © 1997 John Wiley & Sons, Ltd

PROCESS AND DECISION MODELS

Process and decision models are included in the same section because both attempt to 'decompose' the causes of at least some forms of absence. Process models are more macro models that attempt to integrate a number of causal factors and thus provide some order to the extreme diversity of absence research. Decision models are more micro models that probe the cognitions underlying absence or that attempt to understand how a series of individual absences unfolds. The term *decision* does not always refer to a deliberate act but rather to a set of cognitive or temporal parameters that influence attendance patterns. Both types of models are concerned with *how* absence and attendance occur.

Process Models

Steers and Rhodes (Rhodes & Steers, 1990; Steers & Rhodes, 1984) updated their original process model of absenteeism (Steers & Rhodes, 1978). The initial model contained 24 variables grouped into eight conceptual categories: Personal characteristics, values, job situation, job satisfaction, pressures to attend, attendance motivation, ability to attend, and attendance. Brooke (1986) developed a model that contained 16 variables, although he claimed some advantages in terms of breadth of coverage.

Rhodes and Steers (1990) review five studies that provided mostly partial tests of their model. Each of these tests confirms some aspects of the model and fails to support others. The theorists conclude that 'these studies provide some support for the Steers and Rhodes model as originally proposed' (p. 52). Earlier, Fichman (1984, p. 5) came to a less positive conclusion that the 'model to date has theoretical problems and lacks strong empirical support.' Using self-reported absence data, Brooke and Price (1989) found partial support for Brooke's (1986) model. Hendrix and Spencer (1989) obtained a poor fit between Brooke's model and their data and offered a revised model.

One appreciates the sequencing of variables and the interactions suggested by the process models in comparison to some economic models that consist of one well-stocked regression equation. Nevertheless, process models struggle to represent *breadth* when it is becoming clearer that *depth* is necessary to understand absence. Expecting a complex set of linkages, generally inferred from bivariate associations, to hold up in any given sample is too much to ask. Absence is a low base rate behavior, the occurrence of which is highly constrained by contextual factors. Mid-range models that capture the essence of this point will probably fare better than broad-based process models that serve as useful teaching devices but that are incapable of being confirmed in any given sample or replicated across samples.

Decision Models

Fichman (1988) applied a Cox proportional hazard rate event history model (Cox, 1972) to the absence and attendance spells of coal miners in order to understand how these behaviors unfolded over time. The unit of analysis was an attendance spell, and the hazard rate of going absent was framed as the strength of nonwork motives. Essentially, it is the 'timing of time allocation' that is being studied with this procedure. Fichman found that the hazard rate was affected by the type (voluntary, semi-voluntary, involuntary) of prior and subsequent absence exhibited. In a later study using the same technique, Fichman (1989) found positive duration dependence, the tendency for the hazard rate of absence to increase with the duration of an attendance spell. He contrasted this with lack of support for a random model or a habit model, which would predict negative duration dependence. Harrison and Hulin (1989) also used a Cox model to study the attendance patterns of white-collar employees. These patterns revealed strong temporal effects related to day of the week, month of the year, and number of absences taken previously. Demographic variables which are usually correlated with aggregated absence did not contribute to the model, and the authors surmise that the more basic psychological variables for which they are surrogates were already reflected in the temporal patterns.

Thus far, the event history technique has not captured the imagination of other absence researchers despite its clear advantage of framing absence as a time allocation problem. The extant examples have a rather closed system quality, since the basic data simply consist of attendance patterns. What this line of work needs is some theoretically driven independent variables that are measured repeatedly over a time span that corresponds to the collection of the absence data. Both work and nonwork measures would be very attractive given Fichman's position that this is essentially a problem of motivated time allocation between these two spheres. The following study illustrates a method for accomplishing this.

In a very inventive study, Hackett, Bycio, and Guion (1989) had nurses keep a daily diary in which they rated the occurrence of various potential causes of absence and recorded how much they would have liked to be absent. This idiographic-longitudinal design allows for the examination of decision processes that are common across respondents as well as those are unique to individuals. Hard-to-justify causes were more predictive of desire to be absent than actual absence, and a number of factors predicted absenteeism among the sample as a whole (e.g. tiredness, ill health, home responsibilities, and disrupted sleep). However, the most interesting result was the power of within-person regression analysis to explain the absence behavior of individual nurses, something that was masked by group-level analysis. This finding illustrates precisely what Johns and Nicholson (1982) meant when they argued that absence has different meanings for different people.

Martocchio and Judge (1994) used an experimental design and policy capturing techniques to also examine within-person decisions. Subjects responded to 96 scenarios in which potential causes of absence were systematically manipulated and rated each in terms of likelihood of missing work. Although most reported that they would miss due to illness, there were considerable differences among respondents in the extent to which other causes were expected to provoke absence, including counterintuitive signs. The authors interpreted these results as supporting Johns and Nicholson (1982) concerning the phenomenological uniqueness of absence events. The results regarding individual differences are impressive in light of the potential for experimental demand and social desirability in such a design.

It should be noted that neither of these within-person studies examined interactions among causes. However, a good case can be made that such interactions would uniquely influence decision processes. To extend Nicholson's (1977) examples, it is the concert pianist *with* the broken finger that is likely to be absent, not the pianist or the person with a broken finger.

Finally, Martocchio and Harrison (1993) developed a decision-making theory of absence that draws on the theory of reasoned action (Ajzen & Fishbein, 1980) and the theory of planned behavior (Ajzen, 1991). Key components include attitudes toward attendance, subjective norms favoring attendance, perceived control over one's behavior, and (more recently added by Harrison) perceptions of moral obligation to attend. In general, research shows that intentions to attend (attendance motivation) mediate the relationship between actual attendance and the independent contribution of attitudes toward attendance, norms, and moral obligation, although the importance of these constructs varies sensibly across samples (Harrison, 1995; Harrison & Bell, 1995; Martocchio, 1992). This research is important because it isolates various specific theoretical levers by which attendance might be improved. In particular, research shows that perceived control over obstacles to attendance (self-efficacy) can be enhanced with self-management training (Frayne & Latham, 1987; Latham & Frayne, 1989). It is also important because of its confirmation of social influences on absence, a point to be developed below.

All in all, the decision models seem to hold more promise than the process models. However, tests of decision models have a rather descriptive quality to them. Now that we have some ideas about *how* attendance decisions are made, we need to learn more about *why* they are made. In other words, decision variables need to be positioned as mediators of theoretically or practically relevant independent variables. The other models discussed here suggest some likely candidates.

THE WITHDRAWAL MODEL

The withdrawal model has been a dominant paradigm in absence research. Under this model, absence from work is thought to represent withdrawal from aversive work circumstances. Beyond this, the exact theoretical underpinnings for this model are generally unstated, and could range from operant learning theory (Skinner, 1974) to theories of person–environment fit (Edwards, 1991) or met expectations (Porter & Steers, 1973).

Job Satisfaction

The withdrawal model has most often been examined by correlating measures of job satisfaction with absenteeism. Earlier qualitative reviews of the connection between job satisfaction and absence were not in perfect agreement. For example, Muchinsky (1977) concluded that overall satisfaction and satisfaction with work content were negatively correlated with absenteeism but that other satisfaction facets were not. Reviewing the literature and offering new data from 16 organizations, Nicholson, Brown, and Chadwick-Jones (1976) concluded that 'at best it seems that job satisfaction and absence from work are tenuously related' (p. 734). This conclusion was strongly influenced by the results from their original data, for which they claimed various methodological improvements. Still, noting cross-site differences in associations, they speculated about moderators such as norms, sanctions, and supervisory practices that might influence the absence–satisfaction connection.

Since 1984, there have been at least five meta-analyses of the relationship between job satisfaction and absence from work (Farrell & Stamm, 1988; Hackett, 1989; Hackett & Guion, 1985; McShane, 1984; Scott & Taylor, 1985). A careful examination of the three earliest of these papers reveals a number of differences in sampling, methodology (e.g. reliability corrections made), results, and conclusions drawn. Hackett (1989) provides a succinct summary of these differences, the chief of which was the inclusion of 528 correlation coefficients by Nicholson (1975) in the Hackett and Guion (1985) analysis that were not included by McShane (1984) or Scott and Taylor (1985).

Hackett (1989) reanalyzed his massive data set, with methodological refinements, with and without the Nicholson data. He corrected for unreliability in both absence and satisfaction. In the comprehensive data set, the strongest sample-size–weighted mean correlations were −0.23 between overall satisfaction and time lost and −0.21 between satisfaction with work itself and frequency. The respective figures excluding the Nicholson coefficients were −0.23 and −0.27. Correlations for other facets of satisfaction were generally much lower.

A synthesis of the existing meta-analyses suggests that the following conclusions are fairly well established regarding the connection between job satisfaction and absence:

- Overall satisfaction and satisfaction with the content of the work itself are the best predictors of absenteeism. Correcting for attenuation in both variables, the population estimate for these correlations ranges from the low to the mid 20s.

- Frequency of absence is more highly correlated with job satisfaction than is time lost.
- The potential exists for moderators of the job satisfaction–absence relationship.

Given the proliferation of zero order correlations between satisfaction and absence, there has been relatively little systematic examination of potential moderators. However, gender warrants specific scrutiny. Hackett (1989) found that satisfaction–absenteeism relationships were stronger as the proportion of women in research samples increased. As will be seen below, this corresponds to other evidence that men and women differ substantially in terms of the dynamics of absenteeism.

In concluding this discussion of the relationship between job satisfaction and absenteeism, it should be emphasized that the withdrawal model assumes that the former variable causes the latter. However, in one study (Tharenou, 1993), absenteeism was more likely to influence subsequent job satisfaction than the reverse. This finding, which will be discussed in more detail under *The Consequences of Absenteeism*, is not conducive to the withdrawal model. Thus, not all of the variance in absenteeism that is 'accounted for' by correlation with satisfaction may be indicative of withdrawal.

Organizational Commitment

If job satisfaction reflects attitudes regarding one's immediate work environment, organizational commitment reflects attachment toward the larger organization. Although satisfaction and commitment tend to be positively related, there is much evidence that they are discriminable constructs (e.g. Brooke, Russell, & Price, 1988; Mathieu & Farr, 1991). While there have been fewer studies that correlate commitment with absence, the basic withdrawal paradigm is the same as that for job satisfaction—people will be more likely to withdraw from organizations to which they lack commitment. From the other side of the coin, the Steers and Rhodes (1978) attendance model classified commitment as a pressure to attend work.

There are three extant meta-analyses that summarize the empirical evidence on this hypothesis. Mathieu and Zajac (1990) reported a mean sample-size-weighted correlation corrected for attenuation of 0.10 between commitment and attendance. This estimate was based on 24 samples that used a wide variety of absence measures. They concluded that it was unlikely that this relationship was moderated. Using seven samples, Cohen (1991) found a mean weighted and corrected correlation of −0.11 between commitment and absence. Also, he concluded that career stage, indexed by tenure, moderated this relationship. Specifically, the correlation was −0.08 for samples with a mean tenure of 3 to 8 years and −0.24 for samples with a mean tenure of 9 or more years. However, this conclusion is based on only three and two samples respectively, the latter two including only 231 subjects. Farrell and Stamm (1988) reported a mean corrected correlation of –0.12 between commitment and time lost absence in eleven samples. This figure was substantially higher, –0.23, in six samples that measured frequency of absence. In turn, the frequency estimate was moderated by occupational status, with a correlation of –0.41 for higher status samples and –0.15 for lower status samples.

Trends in these results appear to be the following: In general, the relationship between organizational commitment and absence is very low. However, when frequency of absence is the criterion, the size of the relationship approaches those found for overall and work satisfaction. The moderator analyses by Cohen and by Farrell and Stamm suggest that commitment increases in importance as a correlate of absence as people's engagement with the organizational increases via tenure or elevated position. Indeed, Cohen's (1991) thesis is that concerns with the immediate task environment (including job satisfaction) dominate early career stages and that organizational commitment becomes more important in determining work behavior in later career stages.

Given their vintage, most of the studies reviewed in the meta-analyses would have used the Organizational Commitment Questionnaire (OCQ, Mowday, Steers, & Porter, 1979) or a similar measure. This measure is generally conceded to reflect affective attachment to the organization. However, Meyer and Allen's (1991) three-component conception of commitment argues for two additional bases for attachment, normative commitment and continuance commitment. Under normative commitment, people remain attached to the organization and its goals because of ideology or felt obligation. Under continuance commitment, attachment stems from having few employment alternatives or perceiving the cost of movement as high.

Hypotheses bearing on these three forms of commitment are quite interesting in light of the general withdrawal rubric. Straightforwardly, in the spirit of the three meta-analyses reviewed earlier, affective commitment is expected to be negatively related to absenteeism. Normative commitment, due to a feeling of obligation to the organization, might be expected to stimulate attendance and, importantly, to mitigate the deleterious effects of low job satisfaction. On the other hand, continuance commitment might be expected to *stimulate* absence, especially under conditions of felt inequity (cf. Johns & Nicholson, 1982). Feeling 'locked in' might stimulate reactance (Brehm, 1966), expressed in short episodes of escape, and feeling locked in and badly treated would only exacerbate the withdrawal response.

Thus far, evidence relevant to these hypotheses is sparse. Hackett, Bycio, and Hausdorf (1994) found a negative correlation between commitment and 'culpable' absence for a sample of bus drivers using the Allen and Meyer (1990) measure. However, this relationship did not hold up when age, tenure, and general job satisfaction were controlled. In this study, normative and continuance commitment were uncorrelated with absence, while an abbreviated version of the OCQ demonstrated a consistent negative relationship. Meyer, Allen, and Smith (1993) found that affective and normative commitment to both the organization and the occupation were negatively correlated with self-reported voluntary absence in a sample of registered nurses. Continuance commitment was unrelated to absence. Mayer and Schoorman (1992) found in a sample of financial institution employees that affective but not continuance commitment was negatively related to unexcused time lost. Gellatley (1995) found that affective commitment was negatively related to absence frequency and time lost for a sample of hospital employees. Suggestively, continuance commitment due to a felt sacrifice of quitting was *positively* correlated with frequency of absence. Although this study measured perceptions of organizational fairness, it did not examine the interaction between continuance commitment and fairness to test the 'worst scenario' (locked in, badly treated) hypothesis. In another nursing sample (Somers, 1995), it was found that affective commitment was negatively related to frequency of 'annexed' absences, those tied to a weekend or holiday period. The other two forms of commitment were unrelated to annexed absences or a straight frequency measure. Somers also found that affective commitment and continuance commitment interacted to predict annexed absence. The relationship between affective commitment and absence was strongest when continuance commitment was low. This result is in line with the thesis that attitudes will be most predictive of behavior when constraints against action are low (Johns, 1991). Finally, Randall, Fedor, and Longenecker (1990) found no significant main effects or interaction between the three forms of commitment in predicting a self-reported composite of tendency to avoid being absent or late. However, the OCQ did correlate 0.16 with this measure of 'presence'.

Blau and Boal (1987) presented a theory of how organizational commitment might interact with job involvement to affect absence. It is particularly interesting in its predictions about how different types of absence might derive from various combinations of commitment and involvement. For instance, absence for individuals high on both variables is expected to be centered on medical causes, while that for those low on both variables is expected to be more calculative. For present purposes, however, the more mundane prediction is that the former individuals will exhibit the least volume of absence and the latter will exhibit the greatest. Blau (1986) confirmed this interaction between commitment and involvement for unexcused absence among nurses. However, Mathieu and Kohler (1990a) found a rather different interaction between these two attitudes with regard to absences for 'personal reasons' among bus drivers. Although they also found that absence was lowest among high involvement-high commitment drivers, absence was greatest among those with low commitment and *high* involvement.

In these two studies, the commitment measure was identical (a short form of the OCQ) and the absence measures appear very similar. This suggests the possibility that work context was important. Indeed, Mathieu and Kohler (1990a) speculate that high involvement-low commitment drivers (Blau & Boal's [1987] 'lone wolves') might have been likely to substitute regular attendance with better paid overtime, a practice seen at the transit authority. However, this is surely the calculative response that Blau and Boal predict for low-low employees, not the career enhancing motive that they attribute to lone wolves.

Very occasionally, organizational commitment has been treated as a mediator of other causes of absence. For example, Brooke's (1986) model treated commitment as a mediator of distributive justice, job satisfaction, and job involvement. Brooke and Price (1989) failed to confirm this role, although Hendrix and Spencer (1989) found mediation of satisfaction and involvement. Zaccaro and Collins (1988) measured the attendance of college fraternity members at mandatory meetings. They found that commitment to the fraternity mediated the impact of rank (i.e. holding a leadership position) and perceptions of the fraternity's interaction process on unexcused absence at required meetings. Higher rank and more favorable perceptions were associated with reduced absence via elevated commitment.

Finally, in a very interesting twist on commitment research, Ostroff (1992) found that the organizational commitment of high school teachers, aggregated at the school level, was positively related to student attendance rates. This study controlled for a number of variables (e.g. student to teacher ratio) that might have spuriously produced the association.

Thus far, although the work on commitment suggests some interesting hypotheses regarding absence, it is fair to conclude that the empirical evidence is somewhat disappointing. One can't help having the feeling that researchers need to think much more about the *context* in which various forms of commitment might influence attendance. To take one example, normative commitment might be critical for the attendance of volunteer workers whereas continuance commitment might be irrelevant. In tentative support of this idea, Harrison (995) found that moral obligation was a critical factor in the attendance motivation of volunteer workers at a homeless shelter.

Part of the context of commitment may have to do with the exact bases upon which the various forms of commitment are developed among different employees. Using a social exchange perspective, Eisenberger and colleagues (Eisenberger, Huntington, Hutchison, & Sowa, 1986; Eisenberger, Fasolo, & Davis-LaMastro, 1990) argued that absenteeism is most likely to be low when employees feel that *the organization is committed to them*. In other words, perceived organizational support will make salient a reciprocity norm that stimulates prosocial behavior in the form of attendance. Indeed, in several samples, these authors report negative correlations between perceived organizational support and absenteeism (especially frequency) that are well above those revealed in the literature for organizational commitment. This suggests that it is not commitment *per se* but the *source* of commitment that shapes attendance behavior.

Absence and Other 'Withdrawal' Behaviors

One of the most interesting aspects of the withdrawal model concerns theoretical predictions about how absenteeism might be related to other work behaviors that also could reflect withdrawal. Although lateness, absence, and turnover have been the most commonly linked variables, Hanisch and Hulin (1990) extended the argument to retirement intentions and Wise (1993) to systematic reductions in degree of labour participation, such as working part time.

Rosse and Miller (1984) and Hulin (1991) have explicated several models that have been proposed to account for possible connections among withdrawal behaviors:

- *Independent forms.* The different behaviors have different antecedents, functions, and consequences, and should thus be studied independently.
- *Compensatory forms.* The various withdrawal behaviors serve the same function such that engaging in one decreases the likelihood of using another. Holding job satisfaction constant, withdrawal behaviors should be negatively correlated.
- *Alternate forms.* The various behaviors can substitute for each other under conditions of constraint. If quitting is precluded due to economic conditions, absenteeism may increase.
- *Spillover.* Withdrawal is nonspecific avoidance such that dissatisfaction will result in an increase in all forms, which will be positively correlated.
- *Progression.* People will tend to engage in progressively more salient forms of withdrawal. For instance one might progress from daydreaming to lateness to absence to turnover to early retirement.

These models have a seductively simple appearance. However, they can be quite complicated to test. For example, Rosse and Miller (1984) observe that progression of withdrawal could reflect various causal mechanisms, including objectively worsening conditions, gradual awareness of poor fit, or experimentation with increasingly irreversible behaviors. Hulin (1991) notes that the alternate forms model predicts negative relations between withdrawal behaviors when one alternative is constrained but little relationship under other circumstances.

In order to truly test these models, the functional relationship among several types of withdrawal behaviors would have to be studied over time. In addition, antecedents, consequences, and relevant moderators would have to be examined. In practice, most of the evidence regarding these models comes from cross-sectional correlations among withdrawal behaviors and examination of the extent to which they have similar affective antecedents. Rosse and Miller (1984) provided a detailed review of the evidence on these issues, concluding that absence, lateness, and turnover do tend to be positively correlated and that they do share some common affective antecedents. By far, the clearest evidence here is that for a positive correlation between absenteeism and turn-over. Mitra, Jenkins, and Gupta (1992) reported a mean corrected correlation of 0.33 for 33 such coefficients. This result was unmoderated by type of absence measure. Since turnover does share some job satisfaction antecedents with absence (Mowday, Porter, & Steers, 1982) they concluded support for the progression form of the withdrawal model.

Mitra, Jenkins, and Gupta's (1992) data and logic do support a withdrawal thesis and do appear to rule out the independent forms model and orthodox interpretations of the compensatory and alternate forms models that specify nega-tive relationships. Interestingly, the authors found that absenteeism-turnover cor-relations were highest when national unemployment was low. It is possible that the ready availability of jobs permits withdrawal-prone absentees the opportunity to convert their tendencies into turnover. Alternatively, it is possible that this result is a spurious function of the increased base rates that have been observed for absenteeism (Markham, 1985; Markham & McKee, 1991) and turnover (Carsten & Spector, 1987) under conditions of low unemployment. If so, the results are equally conducive to the spillover and progression models.

Whatever its exact causal mechanism, demonstrating progression requires a transitive chain of events in which an increased rate of variable *a* precedes the occurrence of or an increased rate of variable *b*. There is very little such research. Rosse and Miller (1984) reviewed five studies, three of which showed some evidence of progression from lateness to absence or absence to turnover. Subsequently, several additional studies have appeared. Farrell and Peterson (1984) found that increased absenteeism preceded turnover in small samples of newly hired nurses and accountants. Evidence that this was with-drawal, *per se*, stems from a concomitant decrease in organizational commit-ment. In a sample of newly hired hospital employees, Rosse (1988) found progression *within* classes of withdrawal (lateness and absence) as well as between lateness and absence and absence and quitting. In samples of news-paper workers and nurses, Larson and Fukami (1985) found that frequency of absence was highest among those who desired to leave the organization and who perceived high ease of movement. They interpreted this as support for progression, especially since alternative forms predicts that absence would be elevated under *low* perceived ease of movement. Dalton and Mesch (1992) found that utility workers who requested and received internal job transfers exhibited about half the absence of those who wanted a transfer but had not received it (cf. Dalton & Todor, 1993). This suggests alternate forms. Wise (1993), studying nurses, found that elevated absence preceded turnover but that it reduced the odds of employees systematically reducing their labor participation by adopting part-time or casual status. This suggests that both progression (absence to turnover) and alternate forms (absence for reduced work participation) were operating. This attention to systematically reduced participation is useful in thinking about how attendance will be influenced by new forms of employment such as job sharing.

In a very interesting study, Sheridan (1985) used catastrophe theory to study the performance, absence, and turnover of nurses over time. He concluded that increased absence preceded turnover, and that this relationship was discontinuous and nonlinear. In other words, turnover was preceded by a rapid, rather than gradual, buildup of absenteeism. This study makes the important point that nonlinearity may be an important missing ingredient in models of the association among behaviors thought to reflect withdrawal.

Sheridan's (1985) primary sample consisted of recent hires. Intuitively, one might assume that progression would be most clear in such a sample due to socialization and work role transition dynamics (Nicholson & West, 1988). Indeed, he found that his cusp catastrophe model accounted for 21% of the variance in turnover in recent hires and only 14% in a replication sample with between 7 and 60 months tenure. The role of tenure was also apparent in Kanfer, Crosby, and Brandt's (1988) study of operative employees. In this research, absence did not predict turnover for people with 2 to 5 months tenure or those with over 12 months tenure. However, between 6 and 12 months, leavers exhibited more absence than stayers. In concert, these two studies suggest that if progression of withdrawal exists, it may be most demonstrable at certain earlier stages in the job cycle. Notice, however, that sheer base rate considerations may make early turnover more predictable, giving the appearance of importance to tenure (cf. Bass & Ager, 1991). Also, the results of a study by Ferris and Rowland (1987) appear to run counter to this trend. They found that organizational tenure did not moderate the relationship between absence and turnover intentions in a sample of nurses. However, tenure with supervisor did serve as a moderator. For low-tenure subjects there was a *negative* relationship between absence and intentions, while for high-tenure subjects there was a *positive* relationship.

Hulin (1991) has been a proponent of the idea that it is often unwise to study particular withdrawal behaviors (such as absenteeism) in isolation. Rather, he argues that various behavioral manifestations of withdrawal are loosely coupled attempts at adaptation to dissatisfaction that are indicative of a latent withdrawal construct. Serving the same psychological function, they can thus be aggregated to obtain a more precise (and more psychometrically tractable) fix on this construct.

Hanisch and Hulin (1990, 1991) pursued this logic in two studies that showed that self-reported absenteeism was part of a larger work withdrawal construct. All of the data in these studies were self-reported, and the absence measure was verbally anchored rather than a report of days missed (see Johns, 1994b). Also, the inclusion of 'unfavorable job behaviors' may confound deviance with withdrawal. Nevertheless, the search for a more generalized withdrawal construct may have some real theoretical merit. In passing, it must be emphasized that this construct is only relevant to that portion of absenteeism that represents job withdrawal, a presumably small proportion when one recalls the meta-analytic results for satisfaction–absence correlations. Also, by its very nature, this approach runs counter to the decomposition of absence into various components that might have different functions and different predictors (e.g. Blau, 1985; Kohler & Mathieu, 1993).

DEMOGRAPHIC MODELS

The heading of this section obviously pushes the use of the term *models* to its limit. Although correlating demographic variables with absenteeism is common, this practice has seldom been guided by some articulated theory that suggests what one should expect to find. Thus, most of the existing knowledge is incidental, fragmented, and bivariate. Nevertheless, some developments have occurred on this front during the review period.

Age and Tenure

On the surface, the likely relationships between age and tenure and absentee-ism are not entirely obvious. Should young workers have better attendance because they are healthy or poorer attendance because of competing role demands? Should high tenure workers have better attendance because they enjoy the perks that come with seniority or poorer attendance because they can get away with absence? Two meta-analyses have clarified the functional relationships, although they cannot speak precisely to causes.

Correcting for unreliability in absence, Martocchio (1989) found a mean correlation between age and frequency of absence of −0.20 in 27 samples. The relationship was slightly more negative in physically demanding than undemanding jobs. However, gender was a much stronger moderator, revealing a corrected relationship of −0.27 for men and −0.03 for women. The corrected correlation between age and time lost was −0.11 in 29 samples. When samples were partitioned by gender, this figure fell to −0.07 for women. In fact, the confidence intervals for women's frequency and time lost both included zero.

Hackett (1990) also used meta-analysis to find a corrected correlation of −0.30 between age and frequency of absence in 25 samples, −0.07 between age and time lost in 37 samples, and −0.24 between age and attitudinal absence (number of absences of three days or less) in 20 samples. Controlling for tenure, these figures were −0.15, −0.01, and −0.23 respectively. Apparent relationships between *tenure* and absence were greatly reduced when age was controlled. This analysis is important, because as Hackett notes, it speaks against the idea that a negative association between age and absence is due to accrued perks or elevated satisfaction acquired with tenure. Hackett also found that age–satisfaction relationships were strongly reduced as the percentage of women in the sample increased. In 12 all-male samples, the corrected correlation between frequency and age was −0.37, while it was 0.02 in 4 all-female samples. A similar pattern existed for attitudinal absence.

In combination, these meta-analyses establish fairly firmly that younger men tend to exhibit higher levels of frequency and attitudinal absences, measures that are often thought to capture voluntariness. Women tend not to exhibit an age–absence association, and tenure is unconnected to absence when age is controlled. It should be emphasized that all of these findings were presaged in an excellent qualitative review and original analysis by Nicholson, Brown, and Chadwick-Jones (1977).

The negative relationship between age and absence frequency for men might be explained by habituation to work or elevated job satisfaction among older workers or more off-the-job distractions for younger workers. Obviously, some attention needs to be paid to mediating variables to better understand this relationship. Kohler and Mathieu (1993) found that the association between absence and a set of 'individual resource characteristics' that included age, tenure, and gender was partially mediated by a set of affective reactions to work. Unfortunately, this analysis was not fine-grained enough to speak specifically to age and absence. Older workers do tend to exhibit greater job satisfaction (Birdi, Warr, & Oswald, 1995) and organizational commitment (Mathieu & Zajac, 1990). Thus, scope exists for enhanced affect to be a mechanism for absence reduction among older workers. Finding mediators of the age–satisfaction relationship may suggest some important ways that organizations can manage absence among younger males.

In closing this section, the reader is reminded that the meta-analyses of age and absence have summarized linear relationships, although the possibility of nonlinear effects has long been recognized. The most typical expectation is that a U-shaped function might occur due to the susceptibility of older workers to illness. Although Nicholson, Brown, and Chadwick-Jones (1977) reviewed evidence and reported original data that revealed both U- and inverted U-shaped functions, little subsequent research has explored this issue.

Gender

The role that gender plays in absenteeism is extremely interesting, extremely confusing, and rather poorly researched.

Côté and Haccoun (1991) conducted a much needed meta-analysis of the relationship between gender and absenteeism. Correcting for unreliability in absenteeism, they concluded that the best population estimate of this relationship was $r = 0.24$, with women exhibiting more absence than men. This result was based on 29 data sets and did not differ much for frequency versus time lost. As noted earlier in this review, there is ample suggestion that the dynamics of absenteeism seem to differ for men and women, given the facts that age fails to predict women's absence, but that job satisfaction is more predictive of women's than men's absence.

Why are women absent more than men? The question is all the more interesting when it is recognized that women do not receive lower performance evaluations than men (Latham, Skarlicki, Irvine, & Siegel, 1993) except when they represent only a very small proportion of an employee group (Sackett, DuBois, & Noe, 1991). One often advocated theory is that the brunt of childcare responsibilities tends to fall on women and that nonwork demands thus prompt women's absence. Indeed, Goff, Mount, and Jamison (1990) found a correlation of 0.73 between gender and primary responsibility for childcare, with women assuming the major share. Kossek (1990) reviews similar evidence. A logical conclusion from this is that women should be more likely than men to exhibit elevated absence as family size increases. However, neither Zaccaro, Craig, and Quinn (1991) nor Scott and McClellan (1990) were able to demonstrate predicted interactions between gender and family size in accounting for absenteeism. In fact, the latter researchers found little evidence of gender interactions for a wide range of variables. In a study that went to some pains to measure kinship responsibility, Blegen, Mueller, and Price (1988) found it uncorrelated with one and two day absences.

Controlling for several relevant variables, Kossek (1990) determined that gender was not associated with reports of problems with childcare. However, women did have more negative attitudes about managing work and childcare arrangements. In turn, the latter variable was associated with more self-reported time taken off work due to childcare responsibilities. A mediated relationship (gender to attitudes to absence) can be inferred. It is possible that this refinement of the criterion variable is just what is needed to understand the relationship between gender and absence. However, as Johns (1994b) notes, asking about childcare responsibilities and resulting absenteeism in the same questionnaire is susceptible to problems of common method variance and self-generated validity.

A couple of studies have used household surveys to measure people's stated reasons for recent absences. Compared to using organizational records, this tactic might be assumed to increase the accuracy of reportage. Among 21 possible reasons for absence, Haccoun and Desgent (1993) discovered four gender differences. Women were more likely to report going absent due to a child's illness. Men were more likely to report going absent due to a spouse's illness, a professional appointment, or a family social function. These results are fairly similar to those of Nicholson and Payne (1987), who found three gender differences out of 12 possible reasons. Women were more likely to be absent due to both serious and minor domestic problems. Men were more likely to be absent due to personal business matters. It is worth noting that personal illness revealed no gender difference in either study.

Haccoun and Dupont (1987) used a clever design to explore gender differences in absenteeism. Specifically, they content analyzed interviews with hospital workers who had just returned from a scheduled day off or an unscheduled day off that was classified by the employer as a sickness absence. Fully 72% of the sample admitted to not being sick on the latter day. The focus of the interviews was on what activities were engaged in during the day off. Results revealed that women reported engaging in a greater range of activities on the day off, whether the day was scheduled or unscheduled. They also reported resting less than the men in either case. Instead, women appeared to be preoccupied with more purposive activities such as shopping and tending to family matters. In fact, gender and the type of day off interacted such that women were more likely to be tending to family matters on an absence day. In an echo of the household surveys, women did not report engaging in more health-related activities than men on their day off. Although this study would have been stronger as a within-subjects design, it does provide some suggestions about the role pressures that might induce greater absenteeism among women.

At least three studies have tested models that include a large number of potential causes of absenteeism separately for men and women. The general thinking is that there are complex structural differences and substantially different absence taking processes that are obscured by pooling data for both sexes. Using data from the Michigan Quality of Employment Survey, Leigh (1983) examined self-reported absence over a two-week period. He found that self-reported health status predicted absence for both men and women. However, the following variables were significantly related only to women's absence: Incidence of colds, sleep problems, smoking, overweight status, and the presence of young children in the family. VandenHeuvel and Wooden (1995) conducted a similar study using a large sample of mostly manufacturing employees from various Australian firms. Stressful life events, self-estimated health, and attitudes toward absence predicted self-reported absence for both men and women, although stressful events were more critical for women. Long commuting time and shift work were associated with absence for women but not men. The presence of dependants had little impact for either group.

A final study derived separate stress-related models for men and women using records-based absence data (Hendrix, Spenser, & Gibson, 1994). The women's model was more complex, revealing direct effects on absenteeism due to boredom, financial problems, somatic symptoms, and cold and flu episodes. Only cold and flu were directly implicated in men's absence. Both models revealed upstream effects for job stress and emotional exhaustion as mediators of job and/or family conditions.

If there is a trend in all of these results, it is subtle, suggesting that the causes of elevated absenteeism among women may be more syndromic than the result of some 'smoking pistol'. The occurrence of boredom, financial problems, commuting time, and shift work among the differentiating variables reminds us that even today it is uncommon to find gender-mixed samples that are equivalently matched on job status. Thus, some sampling bias may contribute to these differences, with women experiencing objectively less favorable job situations. However women often exhibit greater absence even when compared to men doing the same job, such as teaching (Alexanderson, Leijon, Åkerlind, Rydh, & Bjurulf, 1994; Scott & McClelland, 1990). Also, among factory employees, Johns (1978) found that women were absent more than men even when controlling for differences in job content and job satisfaction. Melamed, Ben-Avi, Luz, and Green (1995) found that women blue-collar workers were much more likely than men to exhibit sickness absence in response to objectively monotonous jobs. They suggested that women are more likely than men to use absence as a means of coping with stress. Alexanderson et al. (1994) found that women were especially likely to exhibit elevated absence when they were performing jobs numerically dominated by males (such as metal work), while there was some tendency for men to exhibit more absenteeism in women-dominated jobs (such as clerical and secretarial). One is reminded here of research which shows that token representation in work settings is associated with lower performance evaluations for women (Sackett, DuBois, & Noe, 1991).

The presence of dependants and family responsibilities figures in some studies but not others. This uneven trend, noted in earlier research, may suggest that it is not responsibilities *per se* that cause absence but how well one is equipped to deal with these responsibilities without taking a day off. In fact, Goff, Mount, and Jamison (1990) measured work–family conflict directly and found it uncorrelated with number of children under five. Thomas and Ganster (1995) found that flexible scheduling and supportive supervision increased feelings of employee control, which decreased work–family conflict and stress symptoms. Such context factors have probably confounded simple correlations between number of dependants and absenteeism.

Kossek (1990) queried respondents about their preferences for a variety of childcare options. Out of nine options, the only one that differentiated by gender was women's greater preference for job sharing and part-time work. Similarly, Scott and McClellan (1990) found that women wished to work fewer hours than men. This suggests that women may be more likely than men to need a 'safety valve' to give them time to achieve the purposive activities on a day off suggested by the Haccoun and Dupont (1987) study. Indeed, Ferris, Bergin, and Wayne (1988) found that gender interacted with ability to control anxiety to predict absence among teachers. This ability was negatively related to absence for women but not for men.

A final trend in the research reviewed above is the role of sex differences in conceptions of physical and mental health. Again, this role is subtle, because gender does not generally interact with a self-reported health status or generalized self-reports of taking days off due to illness *per se*. Nevertheless, women exhibit more generalized ill health (morbidity) than men, and they are more protective of their health in terms of physicians' visits, hospital visits, and prescription drug use (e.g. Rodin & Ickovics, 1990). As will be seen below, women seem prone to certain medical conditions which are implicated in work absence.

Given the increase in research on gender issues in organizational behavior and industrial/organizational psychology, the relative lack of attention to absenteeism is surprising. In addition, the high reliability of the gender–absence connection suggests that it is a window through which a better general understanding of absence might be achieved. One approach might be to probe the possibility that women and men share distinct absence cultures, separate normative views about the legitimacy of the behavior (Johns & Nicholson, 1982). Thomas and Thomas (1994) showed that US Navy enlisted personnel of both sexes exhibited equivalent absence from duty when pregnant women were removed from their samples. This shows that an attendance-oriented culture can erase gender differences. During roughly the same period, the expected gender difference was found for a sample of *civilian* US Navy employees (Rogers & Herting, 1993). This reflects a potential difference in absence cultures between the civilian and military contexts.

In doing research on gender and absenteeism it is wise to keep in mind the great changes that have occurred to women's employment in the past 20 years. There is every reason to believe that there might be strong cohort effects, and that research trends may change over time. For instance, the tendency for gender to moderate age and satisfaction effects may reflect career dynamics for women that are less applicable today than in the past.

THE MEDICAL MODEL

The medical model is the most paradoxical of all of the models discussed in this chapter. Previous reviews of the absence literature, focusing on the psychological and management literatures, could lead one to believe that sickness is an unlikely cause of work absence. That is, these reviews have had little to say about the possible medical causes of absence (except Brooke, 1986). It is possible that medically oriented research has been viewed as out of the scope of organizational behavior because it is thought to deal with unavoidable or involuntary behavior. On the other side of the coin, most medically oriented research has blithely ignored mainstream organizational behavior research, in the process sometimes connoting that virtually all absence is due to sickness. If the medical model is the model of choice for medically oriented researchers, it is also the most popular model people use to explain their own absence behavior to researchers (Chadwick-Jones, Nicholson, & Brown, 1982; Hackett, Bycio, & Guion, 1989; Nicholson & Payne, 1987; Xie & Johns, 1995).

None of this is to suggest that people's public or private attributions about the causes of their absence are especially accurate (Johns, 1994b). Rushmore and Youngblood (1979) found motivational correlates of records-based sickness absence. In a principal-components analysis of diary ratings and potential absence causes, Hackett, Bycio, and Guion (1989) found that tiredness, stress, and personal problems loaded on the same factor as ill health. Nicholson and Payne (1987) concluded that people underestimate their own tendency to take off work for minor medical problems. Taylor, Haynes,

Sackett, and Gibson (1981) found that work absenteeism rose dramatically among steelworkers who were diagnosed as hypertensive, a clear manifestation of the adoption of a sick role. Johnson and Ondrich (1990) found that the duration of post-injury absences from work was conditioned by economic incentives. All in all, these results suggest that much ostensible sickness absence has a strong psychological component, and that using strict medical criteria for separating voluntary from involuntary absence is probably a futile exercise.

A few words are in order about the studies cited in this section. There appears to have been a burgeoning interest in work absence among medical researchers in recent years. Traditionally, the criteria for evaluating medical treatments have been efficacy and safety. However, the medical establishment has also become interested in the economic consequences of ill health and its repair. Absenteeism is one such economic indicator. Because of the volume of research, due to space limitations, I have tried to be representative rather than exhaustive in presenting this material. Of necessity, most epidemiological research and most clinical trials use self-reported absence, and most of the research discussed here falls into these categories. Johns (1994b) reviews the psychometric properties of self-reports of absence.

Smoking and Drinking

During the review period, several studies have reaffirmed the earlier-established positive relationship between smoking and absence (Leigh, 1986; North, Syme, Feeney, Head, Shipley, & Marmot, 1993; Parkes, 1983, 1987). However, Parkes (1983) also found that frequency of absence was only elevated among 'stress smokers' who were experiencing high affective distress and unable to smoke in the hospital environment where the study was conducted. In the same vein, Manning, Osland, and Osland (1989) found elevated short-term absence among respondents who had recently ceased smoking. This was coupled with decreases in job satisfaction and self-appraised health. Taken together, the latter two studies suggest that there are some cases in which attendance gains due to improved health might be offset by absence due to stress when smoking cessation is enforced. Ault, Ekelund, Jackson, Saba, and Saurman (1991) argue that the association between smoking and absence is artifactual, and that it occurs because smokers tend to be younger, drink more alcohol, and hold lower status jobs. Given these provocative findings, I look forward to seeing studies of the impact of workplace smoking bans on absenteeism.

In common with much of the traditional research on smoking, research concerning alcohol consumption has also taken a rather mechanical approach. Thus, Marmot, North, Feeney, and Head (1993) review evidence confirming that problem drinking is associated with absenteeism. A more interesting question exists as to whether more moderate levels of consumption are associated with absence and whether abstinence holds any benefits. Among male civil servants, Marmot et al. (1993) found a U-shaped relationship between alcohol intake and short spells of absence (cf. Jenkins, 1986). Long spells increased with frequency of drinking but not alcohol consumption. Patterns were less pronounced for women, although nondrinkers exhibited higher absence rates.

Webb, Redman, Hennrikus, Kelman, Gibberd, and Sanson-Fisher (1994) present a careful review of research assessing the association between drinking and work injuries. They conclude that much of this research is flawed (e.g. no control group), and that the connection is inconclusive. Their own well-designed study found that problem drinking, but not consumption, was associated with injury-related absence. In fact, problem drinkers were almost three times as likely as non-problem drinkers to exhibit such absence. Rare for a medical study, this research also measured job satisfaction, finding that those with low levels were about twice as likely as others to exhibit absences due to injury.

Psychological Disorder

A fair amount of epidemiological research implicates psychological disorder as a cause of work absence. For example, a large-scale study of London-based civil servants found that psychological disorders (mainly neurosis) were the third most common 'medical' cause of long sickness spells among women and the fourth among men. For both sexes, such disorders were the second most prevalent cause of very long spells (Stansfeld, Feeney, Head, Canner, North, & Marmot, 1995). Jenkins (1985) had earlier reported how minor psychological disorders such as anxiety and depression accounted for the absence of British civil service executive officers. Both reports emphasize that there is good reason to believe that psychological disorders are likely to be under-reported as a cause of absence due to both poor recognition and stigma. Borgquist, Hansson, Nettlebladt, Nordström, and Lindelöw (1993) found that these 'hidden cases' not detected by general practitioners were particularly prone to absence, taking twice the sick leave of those diagnosed with psychological problems.

Using data from the Eastern Baltimore Mental Health Survey, Kouzis and Eaton (1994) found that major depression, panic disorder, and schizophrenia were causes of work absence. In a similar North Carolina survey, Broadhead, Blazer, George, and Tse (1990) also implicated major depression, although the effect was weak. Tollefson, Souetre, Thomander, and Potvin (1993) reported a positive relationship between severity of depression and work absence, and Skodol, Schwartz, Dohrenwend, Levav, and Shrout (1994) were able to implicate even minor depression as a contributor to work absence. In another large-scale study, Garrison and Eaton (1992) found that women who were secretaries were more likely to be depressed and more likely to have missed work in the previous three months than other employed women. However, they were unable to attribute the absenteeism directly to depression *per se* and suggested that both depression and absence might be part of a stress-related syndrome.

In a study conducted at First Chicago Corporation, Conti and Burton (1994) found that depression surpassed common chronic medical problems such as low back pain and heart disease in terms of average duration of absence. Depressed people were also most prone to recidivistic absence. In this study, women were more prone than men to be diagnosed with depression.

There is a strong relationship between self-reported physical illness and psychological disorder that is much less evidenced when objective physical health indicators are applied (Stansfeld, Smith, & Marmot, 1993). This suggests that self-reports of minor medical causes of absence are often camouflaging emotional distress.

In the US, the Americans with Disabilities Act of 1990 necessitates that employers provide reasonable accommodations for employees with mental health disabilities. Over the years, arbitrators have been fairly well disposed toward carefully documented cases of excessive absenteeism as grounds for dismissal. It will be interesting to see if employees begin to claim mental health problems as reasons for excessive absenteeism and ask for reasonable accommodation in terms of less demanding scheduling and so on (cf. Kaufmann, 1993).

Pain

Various lines of research have explored the connection between physical pain and absence. Migraine headaches have been particularly implicated. In the 1990 Kentucky Health Survey, 13% of household respondents reported serious headaches within the past year (Kryst & Scherl, 1994). Close to 50% of those with self-reported migraine symptoms said that they interfered with work or school attendance, while only a little more than 20% of other headache sufferers reported attendance problems. The American Migraine Study found that '50% of women [migraine sufferers] lost 3 or more days of work per year and that 31% lost 6 or more days per year. Among men, the corresponding values were 30% and 17%' (Lipton, Steward, & Von Korff, 1994, p. 218). In a large-scale study of young adults, Breslau and Davis (1993) found that 31% of migraine sufferers versus 19% of nonsufferers reported missing work in the last month.

Two points about this research deserve elaboration. First, population studies consistently show that women suffer more from migraine than men (Lipton, Steward, & Von Korff, 1994). Thus, this is one likely contributor to women's elevated absenteeism. In five of six studies summarized by Lissovoy and Lazarus (1994) women reported missing more work days due to migraine than men. Second, it is hard to separate the physical and psychological aspects of migraine. In their prospective study, Breslau and Davis (1993) found that migraine was associated with the subsequent occurrence of major depression and panic disorders, problems that are themselves implicated as causes of absenteeism.

Taylor and Burridge (1982) documented the trends in medical diagnosis for sickness absence in the British Post Office over the years, finding a marked increase in psychiatric problems and musculoskeletal difficulties such as low back pain. In relation to work attendance, low back pain has been determined to have a substantial psychological component. In a clinical study, Öhlund, Lindström, Areskoug, Eek, Peterson, and Nachemson (1994) found that self-assessments of back strength and general health were better predictors of long-term absence due to low back pain than physicians' judgments of behavioral signs. In another clinical study, Waddell, Newton, Henderson, Somerville, and Main (1993) found that there was minimal direct connection between biomedical low back pain and disability. Even controlling for biomedical severity of pain, subjective fear avoidance beliefs (beliefs that avoiding work will prevent pain) accounted for 26% of the variance in absenteeism. Depressive symptoms accounted for some additional variance.

Busch, Costa, Whitehead, and Heller (1988) found that severity of premenstrual and menstrual symptoms was related to frequency of absence, although nongynecological symptoms were much more likely to result in absence. Again, however, the role of cognitive factors is implicated. Among women with severe symptoms, attitudes toward menstruation and perceived consequences of absence are predictive of actual absence (Gruber & Wildman, 1987).

Self-efficacy regarding one's own ability to master pain may be a key mediating variable in predicting work attendance. In fact research shows that internal health locus of control is more likely than external health locus of control to be associated with reduced absence (Ivancevich, 1985; Johns, 1994c).

Since absentees often frame the reasons for their absence in medical terms, organizational behavior research would probably profit from incorporating some medical perspectives. On the other hand, the obvious psychological component to much 'sickness' absence suggests that medical approaches would profit from a more careful consideration of the work context.

THE STRESS MODEL

Spielberger and Reheiser (1994) have documented the tremendous increase in research concerning work-related stress. In the PsycLit database between 1978 and 1980, for example, there were fewer than 30 articles with the terms occupational stress, job stress, or work stress in their titles. In the period from 1990 to 1992 there were approximately 170 such articles, with steady growth during the interim. Given this trend, it is perhaps not surprising that a number of articles have appeared that attempt to link work stress with absenteeism.

From the outset, the stress literature has been mired in terminological confusion that is more sport than necessity (Kahn & Byosiere, 1992). In what follows, I use *stress* in the sense of a perception of failure to cope with job demands. Often called *strain*, this is frequently accompanied by feelings of tension and anxiety. *Stressors* are external factors thought to cause these psychological reactions.

I have intentionally separated the stress model from the medical model for the following reason. It is very common for the popular press, certain researchers, and certain institutions to impute negative medical consequences to work stress. However, this is as much social construction as it is research fact. The relationship between psychological stress and medical symptoms is complex, varied, and often far from consistent (Cohen & Williamson, 1991; Fried, Rowland, & Ferris, 1984; Kahn & Byosiere, 1992). It is certainly possible that medical symptomatology mediates the relationship between stress and some forms of absence. Alternatively, absence may be an independent reaction to stress or an alternative reaction that alleviates physiological responses. For these reasons, stress models of absence must be able to stand on their own merits rather than imputing universal (but usually untested) medical mediation.

The most common version of the stress model seems to be predicated on the following logic: Stress is bad, and elevated absence will prove it. This neoclassical twist on the withdrawal model casts absence as a dependent variable and justifies stress research to skeptical managers who may be looking for its bottom-line impact (Dwyer & Ganster, 1991). Although some research reveals little or no connection between stress or stressors and absence (e.g. Galloway, Panckhurst, Boswell, Boswell, & Green, 1984; McKee, Markham, & Scott, 1992; Rees & Cooper, 1990; Spector, Dwyer, & Jex, 1988), most of the work reviewed below does reveal a positive relationship.

A different viewpoint casts absence as an independent variable and suggests that it can be proactive and positively adaptive, at least for the individual absentee. *En extremus*, people who are absent more will exhibit *less* stress due to recuperative activities. No research has been designed to truly probe this viewpoint, although there are some hints in the results of the more conventional studies that it is worth pursuing.

In the stress literature, some of the most interesting research has concentrated on job designs that place employees at particular risk for stress and absenteeism. This work has generally been conducted under the guidance of Karasek's (1979) job demands and control model, in which high demands and low control are predicted to produce an extreme level of stress. Karasek (1990) used retrospective data to probe the reactions of white-collar workers toward job changes. He found that job reorganizations that involved increased control and that were initiated with employee participation resulted in lower self-reports of absenteeism, depression, and heart disease symptoms. In a sample of manufacturing employees, Dwyer and Ganster (1991) found that both perceived workload and 'objective' psychological demands (estimated by job analysis) interacted with perceived control to stimulate absence, generally supporting Karasek's expectations. Using all self-report data, Kristensen (1991) found that a high work pace and 'Taylorized' job design interacted to provoke the highest level of absenteeism among slaughterhouse workers. In a remarkable graphic (Figure 3), the author illustrates how absenteeism escalates with these job properties, with piecework-paid 'slaughtering of pigs, work with knife' topping the list. Finally, Melamed et al. (1995) found that both subjectively perceived monotony and objective monotony (indexed by repetition or passive underload) were positively correlated with both psychological distress and frequency of sickness absence among blue-collar workers.

This line of research is particularly relevant to the thesis that absenteeism can be used as a coping mechanism and is not simply a reaction to dissatisfaction. Constrained by a lack of control from engaging in alternative adjustment mechanisms, absenteeism becomes a viable alternative (cf. Johns, 1991). In fact, in the Dwyer and Ganster (1991) study, overall job satisfaction and satisfaction with the work itself were *positively* correlated with sick days taken. This theme is also echoed in studies of hospital workers by Arsenault and Dolan (1983) and Léonard, Van Ameringen, Dolan, and Arsenault (1987). In both studies, a composite of stressors said to be contextual or extrinsic to the job (e.g. role stressors, career ambiguity, and pay inequity) was positively correlated with absence frequency while a composite said to be content-oriented and intrinsic to the job (e.g. urgent decisions, responsibility, workload) was negatively correlated with frequency. Although a factor analysis is mentioned, the exact logic behind the intrinsic–extrinsic distinction is unclear. However, the research suggests that some kinds of potential stressors are associated with less absence. In a related vein, high psychological demands themselves were not associated with absence in the Dwyer and Ganster (1991) research. Only when coupled with low control did problems occur. In this study, the demands seem to reflect job content while degree of control is more reflective of job context. In a longitudinal study, George (1989) found that positive mood at work was negatively associated with absence. She interpreted her results as indicating that her subjects used absenteeism to control their mood states. Again, relevant to the proactivity thesis, *negative* mood was *not* correlated with absence.

A couple of studies have examined absenteeism and stress under the general rubric of person–environment fit as opposed to the 'one job absents all' thrust of the Karasek model. Using all self-reported data from nurses, Landeweerd and Boumans (1994) found that preference for work autonomy moderated the relationships between job design and absence. Nurses with little preference for autonomy tended to absent themselves from autonomous jobs, and those with a high preference tended to absent themselves from jobs in which tasks, rather than patients, were allocated. However, these interactions were not observed for 'health complaints' which addressed stress-related variables such as anxiety, depression, and irritability. In yet another study of nurses, Furnham and Walsh (1991) used measures of career congruence and career consistency to index person–environment fit (cf. Holland, 1973). Although both measures were negatively correlated with frustration, both were positively correlated with absenteeism, counter to the prediction that good fit would reduce absence. Frustration was uncorrelated with absence. The explanation for these results is unclear.

The person–environment fit approach suggests the more general question about whether certain personality characteristics moderate the relationship between stress or stressors and absence. Put another way, are certain types of people more or less likely to react to stress by absenting themselves? Arsenault and Dolan (1983) reported some tentative evidence that two types of personalities were likely to absent themselves when confronted with contextual stressors: high strivers with internal locus of control and low strivers with external local of control. They interpreted these types as engaging respectively in active versus passive avoidance.

Tang and Hammontree (1992) found that the personality trait of hardiness (Kobasa, 1979) moderated the relationship between work stress and self-reported absence among police officers. Most studies of hardiness have centered on its buffering effects in the conversion of stress into illness. Tang and Hammontree found no such effect. In addition, contrary to expectations, they found that the highest absence was exhibited by officers *high* in hardiness who were experiencing work stress. The authors' interpretation of this result is obscure. I think that it illustrates the adaptive, coping nature of absence—hardy officers might have used absence strategically in response to stress. Under my thesis, stress would be reduced after a period of absence by hardy officers. Although the study was longitudinal, this hypothesis was not tested.

Parkes (1983) found that student nurses who reported themselves to be 'stress smokers' were most likely to exhibit frequent absence in response to affective distress. Because smoking was prohibited on this job, she interpreted this interaction between smoking style and stress as indicative of the impairment of coping through smoking.

Like the Arsenault and Dolan (1983) research, other studies have reported relationships between absenteeism and variables that are commonly thought to be stressors without actually measuring stress *per se*. In other words, tests of actual mediated models (stressor → stress → absence) are rare. In a meta-analysis, Jackson and Schuler (1985) reported a mean corrected correlation of 0.47 between role ambiguity and tension or anxiety in 43 samples. Similarly, they reported corrected correlation of 0.43 between role conflict and these same variables in 23 samples. However, the corrected correlation between role ambiguity and absence was 0.13 (5 samples) and that between role conflict and absence was −0.02 (3 samples). In a subsequent well-designed study of nurses, Jamal (1984) found much higher correlations, 0.34 for ambiguity and 0.23 for conflict. Barling, MacEwen, Kelloway, and Higginbottom (1994) found that interrole conflict (i.e. work versus family) due to eldercare had direct effects on both psychological strain and self-reported partial absence (e.g. arriving late or leaving early).

Jackson and Schuler (1985) make the sensible point that one must clearly specify one's theory when making predictions about role relationships and absenteeism. For example, they note that role conflict that stems from work overload may actually discourage absence because things will only get worse if time off is taken. Similarly, they point out how inter-sender role conflict might affect the pattern rather than volume of absence or how attendance at work might relieve stress in the nonwork domain. Again, the importance of local context in the expression of the behavior is underlined.

In the work stress literature, some attention has been devoted to trying to sort out the effects of work stress from those due to nonwork factors. This is particularly relevant to absenteeism research. On one hand, stressful events off the job might be occasions for adaptive absence from work. On the other hand, attendance at work might serve as an escape from nonwork sources of stress. Tang and Hammontree (1992) found that work stress, but not general life stress, was associated with a lagged measure of absenteeism among police officers. Manning and Osland (1989) found that work stressors, life stressors, and life strain were positively correlated with several absence measures for the year preceding the stress survey but not for the year following the survey. Subjects were white-collar employees in a manufacturing concern. Among government employees, Hendrix, Spencer, and Gibson (1994) found that life stress influenced job stress and that both variables operated indirectly on absenteeism via a variety of emotional and medical mediators. Also, they concluded that there was a 'direct effect of absenteeism on job stress for females' (p. 121). At minimum, all three of these studies can be interpreted as ruling out the 'escape to work' hypothesis. Although he did not measure work stress separately, Baba (1990) found a weak positive association between life stress and absence among male professionals.

The results of the Manning and Osland and the Hendrix, Spencer, and Gibson studies raise the intriguing possibility that absence causes stress rather than *vice versa*. The most likely mechanisms by which this could occur would be a negative reaction to one's absence by the organization or increased work-load following absence. However, both of these scenarios seem highly contextual. It should be emphasized that neither of these studies was designed to determine causality. While the Manning and Osland study lacked two waves of stress data, the Hendrix, Spencer, and Gibson study used only a single wave of data for all variables.

It might be expected that absenteeism would be a particularly likely response to the extreme form of work stress known as burnout. Because of its negative qualities of depersonalization, reduced personal accomplishment, and emotional exhaustion (Maslach & Jackson, 1984), burnout would seem to prompt absence both in terms of withdrawal from aversion as well as more proactive motives. The evidence on this is mixed. Saxton, Phillips, and Blakeney (1991) found that emotional exhaustion was a key correlate of time lost among airline reservations personnel. They did not measure the other burnout dimensions. Among nurses, Firth and Britton (1989) found that emotional exhaustion, but not the other two dimensions, was positively correlated with time lost. Lawson and O'Brien (1994) determined that depersonalization was correlated with time lost in one period for developmental disabilities workers. Although the other dimensions were uncorrelated with absence, some burnout symptoms measured with activity sampling by observers were so.

Most psychological research has been concerned with chronic work stressors. However, Theorell, Leymann, Jodko, Konarski, and Norbeck (1994) report an excellent prospective longitudinal study with matched control groups of reactions to an acute stressor—'person under train' incidents among Stockholm subway drivers. Absence data were self-reported, but physiological measures were taken. Control drivers exhibited less absence than incident drivers at three weeks and from three months to one year after the incident. Drivers who were involved with seriously injured victims were absent more than those involved with mildly injured or dead victims.

Although the incorporation of a hard behavioral measure such as absenteeism has profited the stress literature, it is less certain that the study of absenteeism has been greatly illuminated by the introduction of a stress paradigm. Most of the research reviewed above framed absence as physical withdrawal. This neoclassical version of the withdrawal model evinces a certain literal-mindedness that preempts some of the more interesting questions about stress and absence. One of these questions concerns the conditions under which absenteeism represents a reasonable and sensible response to stress that benefits both the employee and the organization. As noted above, some incidental evidence points to this more positive, proactive view of absence as coping. What is needed is research targeted specifically at this issue, casting absence as a variable that is reciprocally related to stress (Edwards, 1992).

The association between personality and absenteeism has not been studied very extensively. Although main effects are possible, personality's role as a moderator of the stress–absence relationship might prove to be an especially fruitful venue for study. Just what kind of people are likely to respond to stress with *absence*, as opposed to some other work behavior? And for whom is absence a reasoned and proactive behavior versus passive withdrawal?

Finally, the kind of research that I would most like to see would link absence to the social construction of stress and its variation across occupational or organizational subcultures (cf. Barley & Knight, 1992; Meyerson, 1994). This would tie stress research to the work on absence cultures covered below. A key question has to do with the conditions under which absenteeism might be institutionalized as a *legitimate* reaction to stress. Meyerson (1994) found interesting cross-site differences in the extent to which hospital social workers saw role ambiguity as enabling versus constraining or normal versus abnormal. Similarly, the sites varied in the extent to which burnout was seen as normal versus pathological or individual versus social. These differences were linked to whether a medical model or a social work model dominated each site. In this case, one would expect to see absenteeism accepted as a legitimate response to stress in hospitals where ambiguity was viewed as constraining and abnormal and an illegitimate response where it was viewed as enabling and normal.

Barley and Knight (1992) have documented and analyzed how the nursing profession has embraced work stress as a salient feature of employment. Indeed, a disproportionate number of the studies reviewed in this section has used nursing samples, as nurses seem quite open to having their stressful work legitimated as such by researchers. In Hackett, Bycio, and Guion's (1989) study of nurses' absenteeism, subjects talked quite openly about taking 'mental health days' in response to work stress, although stress was found to load on the same factor as ill health, tiredness, and personal problems. One can imagine occupational cultures, such as the military, where stress is a less acceptable reason for absence. All of this deserves research attention.

SOCIAL AND CULTURAL MODELS

Most of the other models of absence around which this chapter is organized are essentially individual-level models. That is, individual differences in demographic background, work attitudes, stress reactions, and health are purported to explain variations in attendance patterns. The limitations of this viewpoint are apparent when it is recognized that absenteeism and attendance are, respectively, the violation and fulfillment of *social* expectations that one party has for another.

One of the first descriptions of the social shaping of attendance patterns is seen in the work of Hill and Trist (1955), who showed how novice coal miners came to calibrate their attendance with that of their veteran colleagues. This early insight went largely unheeded until the limitations of individual demographic and attitudinal approaches became apparent. This resulted in a call for more social approaches to the study of absence (Chadwick-Jones, Nicholson, & Brown, 1982; Johns, 1984; Johns & Nicholson, 1982; Marcus & Smith, 1985; Nicholson & Johns, 1985). Since this mostly theoretical work was published, there has been a gradual accumulation of empirical evidence bearing on social influences on absence and attendance. In fact, if a new approach to absence can be said to have emerged during the review period, this is it. As Johns (1984) notes, this approach allows for a range of social influence from subtle social cues about acceptable attendance behavior to full-blown, highly salient absence cultures with explicit norms and elaborate monitoring and enforcement mechanisms.

In what follows, I organize the reported research in an order that reflects increasing directness and confirmability of social influence on absence and attendance. That is, the order is meant to correspond to the extent to which alternative causes are less likely and 'black boxes' are replaced by explicit social mechanisms. Nevertheless, an ideal study would exhibit all of the features of this ascending hierarchy:

1. Between-unit differences in absenteeism.
2. Normative and other social correlates of absence.
3. Cross-level and multi-level effects in which attendance patterns at a higher level are mirrored in individual behavior.

Between-Unit Differences

A large amount of research has noted, usually in passing, great variations in absence rates or patterns between distinct social units. These units span nations (Prins & de Graaf, 1986; Steers & Rhodes, 1984), industries (Meissenheimer, 1990; Wooden, 1990), occupations (Akyeampong, 1992; Meissenheimer, 1990), organizations within the same industry (Parkes, 1983), plants or geographically replicated work units within the same organization (Johns, 1987; Mathieu & Kohler, 1990b), departments within plants (Johns, 1987), and supervisory groups within departments (Johns, 1994c; Markham & McKee, 1995a, b).

Between-unit differences such as these provide a particularly visible suggestion that social mechanisms in the realm of climate or culture are at work. Although some differences are so large as to rule out certain individual-level causes (e.g. variations in health between developed nations), unmeasured individual variables (or combinations thereof) could conceivably explain these differences. Also, differences between horizontal units of analysis (e.g. plants) can be confounded by differences in vertical levels of analysis (e.g. workgroups within plants). Thus, between-unit differences in absence must be supplemented with social process information that begins to identify appropriate causal mechanisms and the level at which they operate.

Norms and Other Social Mechanisms

The social process mechanism that has received the most attention thus far is a normative mechanism. This research is especially interesting in that it is representative of 'new wave' absence research in which subjects are actually queried about their own or others' attendance behavior, a rare event in traditional research. The general question explored is whether one's perception of normative expectations is correlated with one's own attendance behavior. The methods have been varied enough to ensure that results are not overly dictated by methodological choice.

Baba and Harris (1989) found a simple rating of peer absence was a robust predictor of the respondent's own frequency and time lost in a white-collar sample. Other studies have approached this issue by having people provide verbally anchored estimates of the extent to which they felt that there were subjective norms favoring attendance. This work has used Ajzen and Fishbein's (1980) theory of reasoned action as a point of departure, predicting that such norms combine with attitudes toward absence to influence attendance via intensions. Support for the role of normative expectations in influencing intentions (and for intentions influencing absence) has been reported for financial services employees (Martocchio, 1992), homeless shelter volunteers (Harrison, 1995), students, and fitness program participants (Harrison & Bell, 1995). Furthermore, Harrison has shown that generalized and internalized moral obligations to attend supplement the other reasoned action theoretical components in explaining intentions to attend work, school, or volunteer activities, but not exercise class (Harrison, 1995; Harrison & Bell, 1995).

Other studies have bypassed the expectations aspect of norms and attempted to measure attendance norms more directly by asking people how many days or sessions their work group peers tend to miss over a particular period of time. Gellatly (1995), Harrison and Shaffer (1994), and Johns (1994a) all found that this direct normative estimate was positively correlated with the respondents' actual absence. The latter two studies also revealed that people have a consistent tendency to provide self-reports of their own absence falling significantly below this perceived norm.

Is it possible that the perceived 'norms' in these studies are simply inflated (and thus self-serving) projections of employees' own attendance records? The evidence is unclear. Johns (1994a) found a correlation of only 0.13 between individual employees' group estimates and the groups' actual absence rates. Aggregating the estimates by group boosted the correlation to 0.31. Gellatly (1995) found that the perceived norm mediated the relationship between the work groups' previous year's absence frequency rate and the individual's next year's absence frequency. The product of a model that also included demographic and attitudinal variables, these results speak against the projection thesis.

Geurts, Buunk, and Schaufeli (1994) found that feelings of disadvantageous inequity vis-à-vis one's work colleagues were associated with more tolerant personal absence standards and elevated absence frequency. In one of the two Dutch plants studied, personal standards also mediated the relationship between perceived group absence norms and absenteeism. Both group norms and personal standards were measured with a series of questions probing tolerance of absence in various circumstances. This study highlights both the role of absence norms and the use of labor withdrawal to deal with perceived inequity (Johns & Nicholson, 1982).

Gale (1993) made clever use of Jackson's (1960) methodology to construct a *group* level measure of absence norm strength that reflected both the intensity of approval of the behavior and the degree of agreement within the group. This measure partially mitigates the projection problem, and it also incorporates the connotation of legitimacy that underlies some treatments of norms. Confirming the theoretical predictions of Nicholson and Johns (1985), Gale found that absence norms regarding time lost were strongest for cohesive work groups and those in which task interdependence was high. In turn, normative tolerance for absence was positively correlated with time lost at both the individual and group levels. This relationship did not hold for frequency of absence. In a similar vein, Haccoun and Jeanrie (1995) found that *personal* tolerance for absence was correlated with self-reported time lost.

Edwards and Whitston(1993) to some extent downplay the operation of norms in their combined qualitative and quantitative study of absence in four organizations. To them, norms are 'the extent to which workers discuss both their own absence and that of others' (p. 112). They found that 29% of their sample discussed taking time off with others and 59% discussed the absence of other workers, although there was a fair degree of cross-site and within-site variation in these figures. Responses to these single-item measures were uncorrelated with actual absence, and the authors take these gross percentages as evidence that norms were unimportant. Although the authors claim to measure work group norms, most of their inferences about the operation of norms pertain to individuals, occupations, or organizations. As suggested above and illustrated below, supervisory work groups are a likely focus for normative influence.

A few other studies have examined the role of group cohesiveness with regard to absence. Spink and Carron (1992) found that both task cohesiveness and social cohesiveness were negatively correlated with absence from adult exercise classes. However, the design compared extreme groups of high and low absentees and thus might have capitalized on inflated effect sizes. Zaccaro (1991) found that task cohesion, but not social cohesion, was negatively correlated with absence from scheduled meetings by military cadets. Newsome (1993) determined that work group social cohesion was negatively associated with the absence frequency of employees in three manufacturing firms. Drago and Wooden (1992) found that a general measure of cohesiveness interacted with job satisfaction to predict self-reported absence in a cross-national data set. Cohesion was associated with low absence when satisfaction was high and high absence when satisfaction was low. These results were interpreted in normative terms. In each of these studies, cohesiveness was measured with individual-level perceptions, although Zaccaro also adjusted for group-level effects.

A couple of studies have claimed individual-level support for Nicholson and Johns's (1985) theoretical arguments about the potential importance of absence cultures. Haccoun and Jeanrie (1995) used factor analysis to derive a measure of absence culture that included items concerning employees' perception of their boss's tolerance of absence, their own tolerance of their co-workers' absence, and their own trivialization of absence. The separate scales accounted for significant variance in the self-reported time lost of hospital employees. Deery, Erwin, Iverson, and Ambrose (in press) tested a large LISREL model of absence antecedents on Australian auto workers. They found that a measure of absence culture was correlated with frequency of noncertified one and two day absences but concluded that this influence was indirect, working through job motivation. The two-item measure is said to be from Ilgen and Hollenback (1977), although I am unable to verify its location in that article.

Each of the lines of research reviewed in this section has its weak points. Tests of the theory of reasoned action are vulnerable to common method variance between subjective norms and intentions. More direct measures of absence norms are vulnerable to projection and thus to reverse causation. Little theory has been invoked to explain exactly when and how cohesiveness influences attendance or to allow for the possibility that more cohesive groups could collude to exhibit elevated absence. Studies that measure absence culture solely at the individual level of analysis are prone to ecological fallacy. Nevertheless, in concert, the reviewed research suggests that individuals are sensitive to the social connotations of absence and others' expectations about this behavior.

Cross-Level and Multi-Level Effects

A few absence studies have employed cross-level or multi-level designs (Rousseau, 1985). The former designs explore the extent to which absenteeism (or related variables) at a higher level of analysis is systematically related to individual absence. The latter designs explore the extent to which individual effects are replicated at higher levels of analysis. In both cases, positive results imply social influence in which between-unit differences in absence are supplemented with systematic social effects within and between units.

Such designs vary in their capacity to uncover social or cultural influences on absence. A 'bare-bones' cross-level design might assign group-level absence data to individuals and examine its correlation with individual-level absence. The problem with such a design is the possibility of individual differences across groups masquerading as group-level effects. Thus, it is wise to control for individual correlates of absence in such analyses, although the complexity of absence causation renders unmeasured variables a real problem. At the other extreme, a really successful cross-level design would demonstrate cross-level effects on absence *and* uncover *socially* mediated effects that reveal some conscious awareness of a group's absence culture.

Mathieu and Kohler (1990b) assigned garage-level absence data to transit operators and examined its contribution to individual absence when controlling for several demographic and affective variables. They found that garage-level time lost predicted subsequent individual time lost; no such effect was observed for frequency. These results are impressive given the relative physical isolation of bus drivers from their peers, but the study did not measure any social mechanisms that might have corresponded to possible across-garage differences in culture.

Martocchio (1994) employed a rather different form of cross-level design to study the absenteeism of clerical employees in five separate units of a Fortune 500 firm. At the individual level, he measured perceived outcomes that might encourage absence (e.g. time with friends) and deter absence (e.g. demotion) (cf. Nicholson & Johns, 1985). Then, he aggregated these responses at the work-unit level and assigned them to individuals. Controlling for demographics, work attitudes, and the individual level outcomes, he found that unit-level outcomes (interpreted as unit culture) predicted paid frequency of absence. This study contains some exploration of the context of the absence cultures that the Mathieu and Kohler (1990b) study lacked. However, although within-unit agreement justified aggregating the costs and the benefits of absence, the conceptual reasons for this agreement are not perfectly clear. This is especially the case for the benefits, which included several items that would seem to be very personal matters (e.g. time with friends and family). As Martocchio notes, this study would have benefited from the inclusion of some clear group-level constructs.

Johns (1994c) used a cross-level design in which he assigned the absence rates of utility company work groups to individual employees after removing the individual's absence data from the group's. Controlling for a number of individual-level predictors, Johns found that group level time lost accounted for variance in individual time lost; no such effect was observed for frequency. He also found that perceptions of the salience of the group's absence culture (indexed by noticing peers' absence and knowing who was absent most and least) were negatively correlated with time lost at the individual and group levels, and he also found evidence of a cross-level effect. Thus, this study replicated the Mathieu and Kohler (1990b) study while providing some supporting evidence for social mechanisms underlying the differences between groups.

George (1990) studied the absence behavior of 26 work groups in a large department store. She found that the positive affective tone of the groups (their average positive affectivity) was negatively associated with their absence frequency rate. She interpreted this as a group-level effect, an interpretation that requires both theoretical and empirical support given the fact that affectivity is generally seen to be an individual difference variable. Part of this support was provided by the partial application of within-and-between analysis (Dansereau, Alutto, & Yammarino, 1984). Yammarino and Markham (1992) have criticized this application and disputed the contention that George's data reveal group-level effects. George and James (1993) countered that the data reveal both individual and group effects, given the limits of within-and-between analysis. This exchange is instructive, if only to remind the reader that the determination of the level of analysis at which effects operate can be difficult and contentious.

In a very enlightening study, Markham and McKee (1995a) used within-and-between analysis to probe the existence of absence cultures at the work group level of garment assembly plants. They found that employee-perceived managerial standards and personal standards for absenteeism covaried with absence frequency within and between groups such as to support genuine group-level effects (but not plant effects). That is, work groups differed collectively in their views of external and internal absence standards and their absence behavior followed suit. In turn, group absence rates were also associated with supervisors' personal standards for absence. The authors state that these data provide an illustration of the operation of what Nicholson and Johns (1985) described as absence culture salience. These results are all the more interesting when it is recognized that piecerate paid cut-and-sew operations would not seem to provide the most conducive atmosphere for collective pursuits. The authors implicated the gender mix of the work groups as contributing to these cultural differences, and they also replicated their basic findings in a longitudinal follow-up (Markham & McKee, 1995b).

Taken together, these cross-level and multi-level designs provide the best quantitative evidence for social influence on absenteeism and for the existence of absence cultures. This is because they combine the illustration of between-unit differences with some indications about the content of the culture. The latter point deserves refinement with further research. Of the studies reviewed in this section, only Johns (1994c) included an explicitly social referent (monitoring *each other*'s attendance) in his design. More attention to such mechanisms will illustrate *how* variables such as costs, benefits, mood, and perceived absence standards translate into attendance patterns at the group level. Such work could also profit from comparative studies of groups that are thought on *a priori* grounds to have distinctive absence cultures. For an example, see the following section.

The two sections that follow illustrate further models of absenteeism that are mostly (*The Conflict Model*) and partly (*The Deviance Model*) social in their essence.

THE CONFLICT MODEL

Research shows that absenteeism is the focus of much conflict between employers and employees. Thus, arbitration is common in such matters as the appropriateness of attendance policies, the classification of absences as to cause, and discharge resulting from excessive absenteeism (Clay & Stephens, 1994). Beneath the tip of this legal iceberg lies a rich body of mainly qualitative research that casts absenteeism as a manifestation of unorganized conflict between management and labor. It should be emphasized that the term *unorganized* means in comparison to organized strike activity (Hyman, 1975), not necessarily *dis*organized. Thus, absence could represent both individualized and more collective manifestations of conflict with the employer.

For the absence scholar, industrial relations research guided by the conflict model is especially useful in illustrating how the labor–management interface generates and maintains distinctive patterns of absence and attendance. In many cases, apparent anomalies become understandable when the industrial relations context is taken into account. Put another way, absence cultures are best understood when the *entire* ambient social system is accounted for. Thus, Nicholson (1985) illustrates how the local community culture and emergent labor–management relations led to the remarkable practice of a bus company sending around cars to pick up absentee bus drivers in the mornings. Similarly, Adler (1993) explains how seemingly draconian attendance policies and regimented work design actually reduced apparent conflict about absence at the General Motors–Toyota joint venture auto assembly plant in California.

Turnbull and Sapsford (1992) present an interesting analysis of absenteeism over the years among British dockworkers. The essence of their findings is that mechanization and a government-mandated move from casual to permanent employment changed the meaning of absence over time and the consequent relationship between strikes and absenteeism. Over time, absence changed from the assertion of one's freedom, to a behavior tolerated by employers, to a source of entrenched conflict. In the latter two periods, the relationships between absence and strikes shifted from negative to positive. Conceptual parallels to the 'progression of withdrawal' controversy are apparent. In fact, Australian data show that increases in absence precede increases in industrial disputes (Kenyan & Dawkins, 1989).

Paul Edwards and colleagues (Edwards & Scullion, 1982, 1984; Edwards & Whitston, 1993) have studied absenteeism extensively from a conflict perspective. For them, patterns of absence and associated attitudes are one indicator of how the larger issue of managerial control gets played out in contrasting organizational settings. For example, Edwards and Scullion (1984) contrast absenteeism practices in garment factories with those in engineering factories. They conclude that the high absenteeism in the clothing plants was a more individualized response to management control. In the engineering plants, strong collective organization among the employees enabled them to control the pace and level of work in such a way that absence was less common. This even extended to informal schedules as to who would miss work when. In later research, Edwards and Whitston (1993) extended these contrasts to British Rail, a hospital, and white-collar financial work, again illustrating how attempts at management control are accommodated and resisted via attendance patterns. In this study, rich case descriptions are supplemented with quantitative responses of employees to written vignettes of absence incidents.

However, since these responses were virtually uncorrelated with demographics, work attitudes, self-reported behavior, or aggregated records-based data, the validity of the vignette responses, said to measure a construct called considerateness, is uncertain.

Two very interesting papers have used the conflict model to (re)interpret past research and practice regarding absenteeism. Nichols (1994) takes a fresh look at the much-cited Tavistock work of Hill and Trist (1953, 1955). Although this research is often described as showing absence patterns as a form of social adaptation to work, Nichols argues that the research is excessively intrapsychic (i.e. psychoanalytic), adopts a managerial perspective that blames the victim (the sick or injured absentee), and downplays absence as a symptom of conflicting interests between employees and employers. Tansey and Hyman (1992) provide a compelling description of the public relations campaign against industrial absenteeism during World War II that was spearheaded by Eddie Rickenbacker of Eastern Airlines and the Warner and Swasey company of Cleveland. They argue that this campaign reflected a nineteenth-century moral vision of the unilateral prerogatives of management, and that it ignored the true causes of absenteeism. The authors present a clever content analysis of Warner and Swasey advocacy ads appearing in *Newsweek* between 1939 and 1945, many of which stressed worker deviance, appealed to fear, and drew close connections between factory absenteeism and lost lives on the front. The excesses of unions were a common theme.

The case studies that form the bulk of the research base for the conflict model represent especially striking examples of the workings of absence cultures because they illustrate the operation of social context. However, true to their method, they suffer from limited generalizability and a severe lack of parsimony. One useful way to proceed would be to supplement the traditional methods with more quantitative, micro-level investigations of ideas suggested by the case studies. For example, some views hold that grievance filing can serve as a substitute for other expressions of conflict, such as absenteeism, while other views (such as the deviance model) would suggest that absenteeism and grievances are complementary expressions of dissidence (Klaas, Heneman, & Olson, 1991). The first view suggests a negative relationship between grievance activity and absence, while the second suggests a positive relationship. Klaas (1989) reviews research that shows that both individual grievances and grievance rates are positively related to absenteeism. Refining the argument, Klaas, Heneman, and Olson (1991) found a positive relationship between absenteeism and the filing of policy grievances and a negative relationship between absenteeism and the filing of disciplinary grievances. They reason that feelings of generalized inequity prompt both absence and policy grievances but that disciplinary grievances can forestall other forms of conflictual behavior. This kind of work is important because it speaks to both the various meanings of absence and the detailed processes that presumably underpin the conflict model.

On a final note, the conflict model may find some interesting challenges in accounting for attitudes toward absence and for attendance patterns in emerging forms of work organizations. Some studies have reported an increase in absenteeism among semi-autonomous or self-managing teams or elevated absence in comparison with traditionally managed work groups (e.g. Cordery, Mueller, & Smith, 1991). Since these responses to reduced supervision were accompanied by *improved* work attitudes, the results seem to run counter to the basic tenets of the 'absence as conflict' thesis. Indeed, Barker's (1993) qualitative study of a successful conversion to self-management in an electronics firm illustrates how attendance standards can become a major source of conflict among team members and how teams can apply indigenous sanctions that are more controlling than those of traditional management. Thus, studying absence may be one concrete vehicle for understanding emerging patterns of industrial relations.

THE DEVIANCE MODEL

The deviance model is rather broad, encompassing both stronger and weaker forms (Johns, 1994a). In the weaker form, absenteeism is viewed as deviant because of its negative consequences for organizational effectiveness and its violation of legal or psychological work contracts. In its stronger form, absenteeism is viewed as a product of negative traits that result in malingering, laziness, or disloyalty. The deviance model is partly a social model because it is concerned with attributions made by observers of the behavior and with the absentee's own awareness of these attributions.

Do observers of absenteeism tend to make negative attributions about the behavior, and do actors exhibit a parallel awareness of this negative view? Runcie (1988) defines deviance as behavior that is at odds with a norm and describes absenteeism as a 'classic example of worker deviance' (p. 134). Robinson and Bennett (1995) define deviance as the voluntary violation of important norms that threaten the functioning of an organization. They used multidimensional scaling to construct a typology of deviant workplace behavior, finding that 'calling in sick when not' was an example of what they labeled production deviance. This is deviance with minor rather than serious consequences that tends to harm the organization more than specific individuals.

Punishment is a common response to deviant behavior, and Scott and Markham (1982) have documented the strong role of discipline and punishment in organizational attendance management programs. Deviance also produces conflict between actors and observers, and research shows that dismissal or punishment for excessive absenteeism is one of the most commonly arbitrated labor disputes (Clay & Stephens, 1994; Moore, Nichol, & McHugh, 1992; Scott & Taylor, 1983). Unfortunately for the thesis being pursued here, this research on the determinants of arbitration decisions has focused totally on the discipline procedures used by organizations rather than the behavior of the absentee. Thus, arbitrators' attributions about absence *per se* remain obscure.

What is less obscure is that managers and their subordinates often differ in their norms about typical or normal absence behavior, and this undoubtedly fuels the conflict that results in arbitration. Both Johns (1994a) and Markham and McKee (1995a) found that supervisors had more stringent expectations for attendance than their subordinates. Martocchio and Judge (1995) found related differences in opinions about severity of discipline for absence, some of which were associated with the demographic similarity of the parties. Xie and Johns (1995) found good normative agreement between these parties in a sample of manufacturing employees in the People's Republic of China and explained the agreement in cultural terms.

Absentees and potential absentees seem to be aware of the negative connotations of absence and marshal selective perception to disassociate themselves from the behavior. Hackett, Bycio, and Guion (1989) determined that guilt about taking time off motivated nurses to attend even when they wished not to do so. In a review of the self-report absence literature, Johns (1994b) found a consistent tendency for people to underreport their own absence behavior. In addition, people tend to see their own attendance behavior as superior to that of their work group peers or classmates (Harrison & Shaffer, 1994; Johns, 1994a; Xie & Johns, 1995). This self-serving bias is also accompanied by a group-serving bias that attributes more absence to one's general occupation than to one's work group peers (Johns, 1994a). Xie and Johns (1995) found that this phenomenon was particularly pronounced in China. Johns (1994a, b) presents the logic that this pattern of perceptions is mainly ego-protective while considering the possibility of more cognitive mechanisms.

None of the above should be taken to imply that people are incapable of viewing the absence of others with understanding, especially when it occurs in some context that makes salient situational constraints on attendance or fair motives for absence. Edwards and Whitston (1993) illustrate this both in their qualitative data and in quantitative responses to a variety of vignettes in which employees often provided 'considerate' responses to the absence exhibited by others. Also using vignettes, Judge and Martocchio (1995) found that supervisors who made more external attributions about absence causes and who valued fairness more rendered less severe disciplinary decisions. Again using vignettes, Conlon and Stone (1992) illustrated that managers were sensitive to the volume of absence (and, to some extent, its pattern) in rendering judgements about absentees. The within-subjects designs of these studies make them potentially vulnerable to demand characteristics in which subjects exhibit excessive rationality to discriminate among absentees. Nevertheless, the larger point being made here is that the deviance model often comprises a default model when contextual information is lacking, vague, or contradictory.

Since most people get to work most of the time, excessive absenteeism represents consistent, low consensus behavior, a pattern that invites dispositional attributions (Kelley, 1972). But is there any evidence for a dispositional link to absenteeism? During the review period, the renewed interest in disposition at work (Judge, 1992) has included some research on attendance.

A dispositional facet to behavior suggests some degree of temporal consistency as a minimum condition. Indeed, past absenteeism consistently figures as one of the best predictors of current absenteeism. Farrell and Stamm's (1988) meta-analysis estimated absence history to be correlated 0.71 with current time lost (10 samples) and 0.65 with current frequency (15 samples). Going further, there is also some evidence of cross-situational consistency in the behavior. Brenner (1968) found that high school absenteeism was positively related ($r = 0.30$) to absenteeism in employment following high school. Ivancevich (1985) determined that past work absence predicted subsequent absence even among employees who were assigned to new jobs that involved substantial training and new equipment and control systems. Although these results are consistent with a dispositional thesis, they do not rule out stable off-work demands or chronic health problems as causes of absence. Also, in a cohort study, Dalton and Mesch (1992) found that employees who asked for and received job transfers exhibited lower absence rates than those who had asked for but not received a transfer. This suggests that changes of situation do affect attendance.

Further evidence for a deviant dispositional input to absence would be evidenced by the correlation of absenteeism with a constellation of other 'counterproductive' behaviors or attitudes. Chen and Spector (1992) found that self-reported absence was positively related to self-reported anger, aggression, and hostility at work. Hogan and Hogan (1989) present some factor analytic results that suggest that, as criterion variables, absences, grievances, and compensation claims load on the same factor. Normand, Salyards, and Mahoney (1990) found that US Postal Service job applicants who tested positive for illicit drug use exhibited 59% more time lost after hiring than those who tested negative. Probably the most relevant data regarding the possible dispositional substrate to absenteeism comes from the evidence on so-called integrity, honesty, or reliability tests. Although such tests are controversial (Camara & Schneider, 1994), it appears that absenteeism is part of a broad composite of counterproductive behaviors that is predictable with both overt and personality-based integrity measures (Ones, Viswesvaran, & Schmidt, 1993). In a typical study, Borofsky and Smith (1993) used the Employee Reliability Inventory as a pre-employment screening device. A pre-post comparison showed a significant reduction in unauthorized time lost following the introduction of the inventory.

The linking of attendance to the integrity construct also raises questions about its status as an example of organizational citizenship behavior. Organ (1988) asserts that reasonable attendance at work is contractual, but that excellent attendance over long periods of time goes well beyond organizational expectations. He cites such attendance as an example of the conscientiousness dimension of organizational citizenship. Mayer and Schoorman (1992) found that unexcused time lost was negatively correlated with altruism and organization-specific citizenship behaviors.

A final study located firmly in the deviance domain was conducted by Sands and Miller (1991). They examined the relationship between lunar phases and absenteeism in an insurance company. Controlling for a number of temporal variables, they found, contrary to conventional expectations, a weak *decrease* in absence when the moon was full. So much for folk wisdom.

It is my impression that managers have a tendency to overuse the deviance model as an explanation for absence. In turn, this leads them to seek out and punish individual offenders while ignoring more proactive and more culturally oriented means of managing attendance. On the other hand, researchers have probably not paid enough attention to the deviant connotations of absence. As illustrated above, these connotations strongly shape how people view their own behavior and that of their work group and occupational peers. In turn, these views stimulate politics and conflict when employees try to justify their behavior to managers (cf. Fitzgibbons, 1992). More direct study of this process would be welcome.

THE ECONOMIC MODEL

Most commonly, the economic model treats absenteeism and attendance as problems of labor supply (Chelius, 1981). People who sell their time to employers forego leisure. As wage rates increase, it is increasingly attractive to substitute work for leisure (the substitution effect). But as income increases, it is increasingly attractive to take time off for consumatory purposes (the income effect). Unconstrained, people should attend only up to the point where their internal time value (marginal rate of substitution of income for leisure) is equal to the marginal wage (Dunn & Youngblood, 1986).

This basic formulation predicts that absence will increase with the length of the workweek (due to the decreasing marginal utility of attendance), increase as nonlabor income rises, and decrease as financial penalties for absence increase (Drago & Wooden, 1992). It is ambiguous concerning the correlation between wages and absence due to the competing forces of substitution versus income, although Allen (1981a) suggests that job choice mechanisms might work in favor of substitution.

In practice, much research in this area has simply examined the relationship between wages and absenteeism. A negative relationship has often been found, suggesting the domination of substitution effects (e.g. Allen, 1981b; Barmby & Treble, 1991; Chaudhury & Ng, 1992; Drago & Wooden, 1992; Kenyon & Dawkins, 1989). Similarly, higher wages are associated with lower durations of absence from work following injury (Johnson & Ondrich, 1990). However, such effects are often weak and not always consistently observed (e.g. Leigh, 1986, 1991). Put simply, typical economic data sets lack both the process and control variables required to fish successfully in these waters. Barmby, Orme, and Treble (1991) implicate the need for data on demand side absence control mechanisms, and Drago and Wooden (1992) show that higher sick leave entitlements are associated with higher self-reported absence. More basically, however, more precise measures of the value of time are required. Using individual level data and *direct* measures of the internal value of time, Dunn and Youngblood (1986) found that employees used absence to reduce their marginal rate of substitution and achieve optimal equilibrium. Using some of the same data, Youngblood (1984) earlier illustrated that time lost increased with the value of nonwork time whereas frequency of absence was weakly influenced by work attachment, indexed by job scope and job satisfaction. Such dedicated measurement answers questions that gross economic data cannot, and Youngblood and Dunn are to be commended.

Economists have also shown an interest in the impact of unionization on absence. Allen (1984) lays out the basic question: Does unionization decrease absenteeism by improving working conditions and providing 'voice', or does it increase absenteeism by protecting absentees from sanctions? Although these precise mechanisms have not been explored, the general trend is clear: Unionized employees tend to exhibit greater absence (Allen, 1984; Chaudhury & Ng, 1992; Leigh, 1981, 1984, 1985, 1986). Wilson and Peel show that the relationship between various 'voice' and participation mechanisms and absence is in fact quite complex. However, in their sample of engineering and metal working firms, profit-sharing and share ownership plans were unambiguously associated with reduced absence rates (Peel & Wilson, 1990; Wilson & Peel, 1991).

Another prediction made by the economic model is that absenteeism should decrease when unemployment rises. Two mechanisms could underpin this prediction (Leigh, 1985). One is that employees, aware of the deviant connotations of absence, are more likely to exhibit good attendance when layoffs are possible and prospects for other employment are slim. The other is that employers use hard times to divest themselves of high-absence employees. Controlling for a number of economic variables and surrogates, Leigh (1985) found support for a negative relationship between unemployment rates and absence rates at both the industry level and the national (US) level. Kenyon and Dawkins (1989) replicated this effect with Australian national data. Markham (1985) found similar results at the national (US), regional, and organizational levels. Markham and McKee (1991) found that local unemployment was negatively correlated with plant absence rates and that attendance improvements appeared to lead unemployment rates. That is, it was as if employees anticipated tough economic times with improved attendance. These authors also found an independent effect for plant staff size—as plants declined in size, attendance figures improved.

A final prediction of the economic model, alluded to briefly above, is that absenteeism will be responsive to the economic incentives and disincentives contained in absence control plans, sick day and disability provisions, and so on. Indeed, there is substantial evidence that the provision of liberal sick days results in more absence and that policy details are strong predictors of absence (Dalton & Mesch, 1991; Dalton & Perry, 1981; Drago & Wooden, 1992; Ehrenberg, Ehrenberg, Rees, & Ehrenberg, 1991; Ng, 1989).

A few economists have presented theoretical models that extend or complement the traditional labor–leisure perspective. Gafni and Peled (1984) attempt to account for the documented increase in absenteeism that follows the diagnosis of hypertension among people previously unaware of this medical problem. They argue that the increased absence is due to an increased demand for leisure in the face of a shortened life and the decreased value of retirement savings. Given the well developed psychology of the sick role (Levine & Kozloff, 1978), this economic explanation seems implausible. Both Barmby, Sessions, and Treble (1994) and Kahana and Weiss (1992) present models that attempt to account for absenteeism given asymmetric information about employee health. The latter paper further uses game theory to compare incentives for absence in labor-managed versus traditionally managed firms.

The economic model has good potential as a vehicle for thinking about how the value of work and nonwork time influences absence and how family economic circumstances might affect attendance patterns. Unfortunately, traditional economic studies often substitute a well-filled regression equation for careful theorizing and generate data bases that are filled with single-item measures, unnecessarily dichotomized variables, and self-reported absence measures (see Johns, 1994b). More careful measurement and theorizing that integrates the economic model with other models would be welcome. Youngblood's (1984) study is a good example. Drago and Wooden (1992) illustrate how disciplinary and normative perspectives complement the traditional labor–leisure approach.

THE CONSEQUENCES OF ABSENCE

The large majority of research on absenteeism has tended to cast the behavior as a dependent variable. However, over the years, a body of work has accumulated that frames the behavior as an independent variable and then examines its consequences.

Some of the first theoretical treatment of this issue was provided by Mowday, Porter, and Steers (1982), who speculated about the positive and negative consequences of absenteeism for individuals, work groups, and organizations. Although they were able to cite almost no research on these effects, their work does highlight the possibility for conflict between these levels of analysis. That is, what might be good for one party (reduced individual stress) might be bad for another party (reduced organizational productivity).

The most systematic and thorough treatment of the possible consequences of absence is provided by Goodman and Atkin (1984) who also extended the list of stakeholders to unions, the family, and society. They outline the theoretical rationale for various consequences and provide a research agenda for several.

Does absence lower job performance? Bycio (1992) provides an indirect answer to this question with a meta-analysis of 46 studies of the relationship between individual performance and absenteeism. He determined that both supervisory performance evaluations and nonrating measures of performance quality (e.g. cash imbalances) were negatively related to various forms of absenteeism. However, credibility intervals were wide, and artifacts did not explain all the variance across studies. This finding is open to questions of both direction of causality and causal mechanism, and Bycio does a good job of working through the possibilities. Chief among these is that irritated supervisors give high absentees low evaluations. Given the finding of a connection for nonrating data and some subsidiary analyses, he concludes that there is more to this association than supervisory annoyance. Indeed, respondents to a random telephone survey reported that supervisory wrath and threats to promotion were unlikely consequences of work absence (Haccoun & Desgent, 1993), and Baba (1990) found that perceptions of such consequences were uncorrelated with absence. Bycio also explains how employee disposition (the deviance model) or progression of withdrawal (from lowered performance to absence, cf. Sheridan, 1985) could account for his results.

Tharenou (1993) provides the clearest evidence that absence can result in lower job performance at the individual level. In a longitudinal study of electrical apprentices that included two full waves of data collection, she found that prior absence was associated with subsequent lower supervisory performance ratings and course grades. In addition, she presents some evidence that suggests the ratings were not contaminated by absence. Tharenou notes that further progress in this domain will probably require the fine-grained application of event history analysis (Fichman, 1988; Harrison & Hulin, 1989) to absence and performance data. Her finding that absenteeism led to reduced course grades corresponds to Gunn's (1993) cross-sectional findings of a strong positive association between class attendance and academic performance in introductory psychology classes and the Ehrenberg et al. (1991) finding that absenteeism in school districts was associated with lower district scores on standardized tests.

All of the studies reviewed by Bycio were individual-level studies, and virtually none of them was purpose-designed to probe the fine details of the absence–performance connection. Several group-level studies have done this. Moch and Fitzgibbons (1985) found that absenteeism decreased departmental production efficiency only when it could not be anticipated or when the production process was not highly automated. Under these conditions, absenteeism resulted in the production of substantial scrap. Goodman and Leyden (1991) found that absenteeism among underground coal mining crews reduced crew familiarity, which in turn resulted in lower productivity. In related research, Goodman and Garber (1988) found that unfamiliarity due to absence resulted in increased accident rates among miners.

These group-level studies are very important because they speak to the impact of absence on productivity in terms of the context of the social system and work design. It would be interesting to see this work extended to more complex models of how automation, interdependence, and other task and technology variables condition the influence of absence. It would also be fascinating to see this line of research extended to white-collar work and to forms of 'pseudo-absence' due to business travel or telecommuting. How do such absences affect social relationships and unit performance? How does 'electronic absence' differ from conventional absence?

Clegg (1983) provided an excellent critique of causality issues in research on work 'withdrawal' and considered the possibility that absenteeism might result in subsequent job dissatisfaction, a direction of causality contrary to the conventional withdrawal model. Clegg claimed to find such evidence, and this study is frequently cited as showing reverse causality. Unfortunately, it did not include two waves of satisfaction data. Clegg controlled for prior absence when testing the job satisfaction causes absence hypothesis, but not when testing the absence causes satisfaction hypothesis. This combination of factors means that reverse causality in this study may be spurious. However, Tharenou (1993) obtained two full waves of data and did indeed conclude that increased absenteeism led to a subsequent reduction in job satisfaction, rather than the other way around. As the author herself implies, the fact that the subjects were apprentice electricians, followed from the beginning of their apprenticeship, might especially favor reverse causality. For new recruits to a rather structured work training program, early absence may trigger a downward spiral of events that precipitates negative affect.

Performance and job satisfaction are variables that are of interest to both the organization and the individual. Is there any evidence regarding the consequences of absence that is more exclusively pertinent to the individual? Earlier, it was pointed out that evidence for the stress-reductive, adjustive properties of absence is very indirect and incidental. Other than that work, the only suggestive research is that in which people explain why they are typically absent. Medical reasons tend to dominate such explanations (Hackett, Bycio, & Guion, 1989; Nicholson & Payne, 1987; Xie & Johns, 1995), suggesting physical recuperation as a common consequence. However, the reader is reminded that there are documented cross-cultural and gender differences in stated reasons for absence (Haccoun & Desgent, 1993; Xie & Johns, 1995) and gender differences in activities pursued on days taken off (Haccoun & Dupont, 1987). This suggests that the personal consequences of absence will vary substantially across individuals (cf. Johns & Nicholson, 1982, the meanings of absence).

Given Goodman and Atkin's (1984) excellent outline of needed work, research on the consequences of absence is disappointing by virtue of its low volume. Behavior is shaped by its consequences for oneself and others, and lack of awareness of these consequences sets limits on our ability to understand behavior. Perhaps the growing emphasis on increased interdependence and teamwork will provide some impetus for focusing on absence's consequences.

CONCLUSION

What do we know about the correlates, causes, and consequences of absence that we didn't know 15 years ago? Because of its less than ideal psychometric properties, absenteeism has particularly profited from the advantages of meta-analytic summary. In the domains of job satisfaction and demographics, we now have a solid base of population estimates of effect sizes, a fact that both stimulates shifts in research emphasis (from job satisfaction to commitment) and challenges researchers to explain these effects (e.g. gender and absence). In the domains of performance and turnover, wide confidence intervals in estimated correlations with absence have inspired good theoretical thinking about likely moderators.

Fifteen years ago, because few had even asked, we knew very little about how people viewed their own absence behavior or that of others. Now, we know that people have a tendency to underestimate their own absence and hold inflated views of the absence of others. Managers and employees hold different standards about how much absence is acceptable, but managers are capable of applying reasonable attributional criteria to judgments about absence. Key variables from the theory of reasoned action account for variance in intentions to be absent. Within-person decision models show that the meanings of absence vary among individuals despite some more universal causal mechanisms.

Fifteen years ago, little was known about the social and cultural dynamics of absenteeism. In my opinion, the enhancement of knowledge on this front represents the greatest advance during the review period. Meaningful cross-group differences and normative mechanisms are now well established, and it is becoming clear that supervisory groups are often critical in shaping the attendance patterns of their members. The social perspective is important because it forces the researcher to attend to a factor that seems to be critically important in matters of absence and attendance—work context. In this domain, the conflict model provides some especially good examples. As noted at several points earlier, the social perspective also holds excellent promise as a partial explanatory mechanism for phenomena covered under the other models, including how gender affects absence and how absence is or is not legitimated as a response to stress or ill health.

Fifteen years ago, with the exception of some experimental tests of interventions, the standard study of absence passed out a questionnaire in the workplace and obtained absence data from personnel records. Although this is still true, it is important to remember that the advances noted above have stemmed from a remarkable diversity of methods, including the use of observation, interviews, diaries, vignettes, self-reports, supervisory reports, telephone surveys, household visits, within-person designs, content analysis, and meta-analysis. Absence is difficult to study, and one should use what works. This diversity (uncommon in many research areas) is to be commended.

Fifteen years ago, there were very few studies of work stress and absenteeism. Now, there are many, but they do little to enhance our general understanding of absence, either because they fail to probe rigorously the possible adjustive aspects of absence or because they fail to consider when absence might be the preferred reaction to stress over other responses.

Except for the micro-level studies of time valuation, the fruits of the economic model are generally unenlightening, often replicating effects seen in firm-level studies. This is unfortunate, because the economic model seems moderately well equipped to probe some aspects of a very important issue— the impact of nonwork factors on absence. The lack of information on these factors was decried 15 years ago (Johns & Nicholson, 1982), and this is still a serious omission from the absence research agenda.

The increasing interest in absenteeism by medical researchers holds promise if absenteeism is viewed as a psychologically mediated response to medical condition and not simply as an economic indicator of the cost of sickness or the efficacy of treatment. This requires that research in the medical domain incorporate more understanding of workplace psychology and behavior.

In my opinion, progress in the past 15 years has been due to creative anarchy in theory and method. In this sense, the lack of a dominant paradigm or model has been helpful. On certain terms and conditions, some organization of this anarchy might be welcome. However, two temptations should be avoided, both of which have to do with putting quantity before quality. At one extreme, I have already alluded to the fallacy of organizing empirically with a regression equation stocked with variables from more and more models. We already have evidence that knowledge accruing from this approach is literally noncumulative (e.g. Johns, 1978) and simply trying to account for more variance is a futile task in any event (Nicholson & Martocchio, 1995). At the other extreme, organizing theoretically with a grand process model has the limitations alluded to at the beginning of the chapter.

What is needed now are probably some small theories that cross-cut two or more of the models described above. For example, one can conceive of a theory that combines differential medical susceptibility, culture, and notions of deviance to explain in part why women are often absent more than men and when they might not be. A series of such small theories would better organize our understanding of absenteeism while still respecting the wide varieties of meanings that absence holds for individuals and groups.

AUTHOR NOTE

This research was supported by grant 94ER0506 from Quebec's Fonds pour la Formation de Chercheurs et l'Aide à la Recherche and grant 410-920202 from the Social Sciences and Humanities Research Council of Canada.

REFERENCES

Adler, P. S. (1993) The 'learning bureaucracy': New United Motor Manufacturing, Inc. *Research in Organizational Behavior*, **15**, 111–194.

Ajzen, I. (1991) The theory of planned behavior. *Organizational Behavior and Human Decision Processes*, **50**, 179–211.

Ajzen, I. & Fishbein, M. (1980) *Understanding Attitudes and Predicting Social Behavior*. Englewood Cliffs, NJ: Prentice-Hall.

Akyeampong, E. B. (1992, Spring) Absences from work revisited. *Statistics Canada Perspectives*, 44–53.

Alexanderson, K., Leijon, M., Åkerlind, I., Rydh, H., & Bjurulf, P. (1994) Epidemiology of sickness absence in a Swedish county in 1985, 1986 and 1987. *Scandinavian Journal of Social Medicine*, **22**, 27–34.

Allen, N. J. & Meyer, J. P. (1990) The measurement and antecedents of affective continuance, and normative commitment to the organization. *Journal of Occupational Psychology*, **63**, 1–18.

Allen, S. G. (1981a) Compensation, safety, and absenteeism: Evidence from the paper industry. *Industrial and Labor Relations Review*, **34**, 207–218.

Allen, S. G. (1981b) An empirical model of work attendance. *Review of Economics and Statistics*, **63**, 77–87.

Allen, S. G. (1984) Trade unions, absenteeism, and exit-voice. *Industrial and Labor Relations Review*, **37**, 331–345.

Arsenault, A. & Dolan, S. (1983) The role of personality, occupation and organization in understanding the relationship between job stress, performance and absenteeism. *Journal of Occupational Psychology*, **56**, 227–240.

Ault, R. W., Ekelund, R. B. Jr, Jackson, J. D., Saba, R. S., & Saurman, D. S. (1991) Smoking and absenteeism. *Applied Economics*, **23**, 743–754.

Baba, V. V. (1990) Methodological issues in modeling absence: A comparison of least squares and tobit analyses. *Journal of Applied Psychology*, **75**, 428–432.

Baba, V. V. & Harris, M. J. (1989) Stress and absence: A cross-cultural perspective. *Research in Personnel and Human Resources Management, Suppl. 1*, 317–337.

Barker, J. R. (1993) Tightening the iron cage: Concertive control in self-managing teams. *Administrative Science Quarterly*, **38**, 408–437.

Barley, S. R. & Knight, D. B. (1992) Toward a cultural theory of stress complaints. *Research in Organizational Behavior*, **14**, 1–48.

Barling, J., MacEwen, K. E., Kelloway, K., & Higginbottom, S. F. (1994) Predictors and outcomes of elder-care-based interrole conflict. *Psychology and Aging*, **9**, 391–397.

Barmby, T. A., Orme, C. D., & Treble, J. G. (1991) Worker absenteeism: An analysis using microdata. *Economic Journal*, **101**, 214–229.

Barmby, T., Sessions, J., & Treble, J. (1994) Absenteeism, efficiency wages and shirking. *Scandinavian Journal of Economics*, **96**, 561–566.

Barmby, T. A. & Treble, J. G. (1991) Absenteeism in a medium-sized manufacturing plant. *Applied Economics*, **23**, 161–166.

Bass, A. R. & Ager, J. (1991) Correcting point-biserial turnover correlations for comparative analysis. *Journal of Applied Psychology*, **76**, 595–598.

Birdi, K., Warr, P., & Oswald, A. (1995) Age differences in three components of employee well-being. *Applied Psychology: An International Review*, **44**, 345–373.

Blau, G. (1985) Relationship of extrinsic, intrinsic, and demographic predictors to various types of withdrawal behaviors. *Journal of Applied Psychology*, **70**, 442–450.

Blau, G. J. (1986) Job involvement and organizational commitment as interactive predictors of tardiness and absenteeism. *Journal of Management*, **12**, 577–584.

Blau, G. J. & Boal, K. B. (1987) Conceptualizing how job involvement and organizational commitment affect turnover and absenteeism. *Academy of Management Review*, **12**, 288–300.

Blegen, M. A., Mueller, C. W., & Price, J. L. (1988) Measurement of kinship responsibility for organizational research. *Journal of Applied Psychology*, **73**, 402–409.

Borgquist, L., Hansson, L., Nettelbladt, P., Nordström, G., & Lindelöw, G. (1993) Perceived health and high consumers of care: A study of mental health problems in a Swedish primary health care district. *Psychological Medicine*, **22**, 763–770.

Borofsky, G. L. & Smith, M. (1993) Reductions in turnover, accidents, and absenteeism: The contribution of a pre-employment screening inventory. *Journal of Clinical Psychology*, **49**, 109–116.

Brehm, J. W. (1966) *A Psychological Theory of Reactance*. New York: Academic Press.

Brenner, M. H. (1968) Use of high school data to predict work performance. *Journal of Applied Psychology*, **52**, 29–30.

Breslau, N. & Davis, G. C. (1993) Migraine, physical health and psychiatric disorder: A prospective epidemiologic study in young adults. *Journal of Psychiatric Research*, **27**, 211–221.

Broadhead, W. E., Blazer, D. G., George, L. K., & Tse, C. K. (1990) Depression, disability days, and days lost from work in a prospective epidemiologic survey. *Journal of the American Medical Association*, **264**, 2524–2528.

Brooke, P. P., Russell, D. W., & Price, J. L. (1988) Discriminant validation of measures of job satisfaction, job involvement, and organizational commitment. *Journal of Applied Psychology*, **73**, 139–145.

Brooke, P. P. Jr (1986) Beyond the Steers and Rhodes model of employee attendance. *Academy of Management Review*, **11**, 345–361.

Brooke, P. P. Jr. & Price, J. L. (1989) The determinants of employee absenteeism: An empirical test of a causal model. *Journal of Occupational Psychology*, **62**, 1–19.

Busch, C. M., Costa., P. T. J., Whitehead, W. E., & Heller, B. R. (1988) Severe perimenstrual symptoms: Prevalence and effects on absenteeism and health care seeking in a non-clinical sample. *Women & Health*, **14**, 59–74.

Bycio, P. (1992) Job performance and absenteeism: A review and meta-analysis. *Human Relations*, **45**, 193–220.

Camara, W. J. & Schneider, D. L. (1994) Integrity tests: Facts and unresolved issues. *American Psychologist*, **49**, 112–119.

Carsten, J. M. & Spector, P. E. (1987) Unemployment, job satisfaction, and employee turnover: A meta-analytic test of the Muchinsky model. *Journal of Applied Psychology*, **72**, 374–381.

Chadwick-Jones, J. K., Nicholson, N., & Brown, C. (1982) *Social Psychology of Absenteeism*. New York: Praeger.

Chaudhury, M. & Ng, I. (1992) Absenteeism predictors: Least squares, rank regression, and model selection results. *Canadian Journal of Economics*, **25**, 615–635.

Chelius, J. R. (1981) Understanding absenteeism: The potential contribution of economic theory. *Journal of Business Researh*, **9**, 409–418.

Chen, P. Y. & Spector, P. E. (1992) Relationships of work stressors with aggression, withdrawal, theft, and substance use: An exploratory study. *Journal of Occupational and Organizational Psychology*, **65**, 177–184.

Clay, J. M. & Stephens, E. C. (1994) An analysis of absenteeism arbitration cases: Factors used by arbitrators in making decisions. *International Journal of Conflict Management*, **5**, 130–142.

Clegg, C. W. (1983) Psychology of employee lateness, absence, and turnover: A methodological critique and an empirical study. *Journal of Applied Psychology*, **68**, 88–101.

Cohen, A. (1991) Career stage as a moderator of the relationships between organizational commitment and its outcomes: A meta-analysis. *Journal of Occupational Psychology*, **64**, 253–268.

Cohen, S. & Williamson, G. M. (1991) Stress and infectious disease in humans. *Psychological Bulletin*, **109**, 5–24.

Conlon, E. J. & Stone, T. H. (1992) Absence schema and managerial judgment. *Journal of Management*, **18**, 435–454.

Conti, D. J. & Burton, W. N. (1994) The economic impact of depression in a workplace. *Journal of Occupational Medicine*, **36**, 983–988.

Cordery, J. L., Mueller, W. S., & Smith, L. M. (1991) Attitudinal and behavioral effects of autonomous group working: A longitudinal field study. *Academy of Management Journal*, **34**, 464–476.

Côté, D. & Haccoun, R. R. (1991) L'absentéisme des femmes et des hommes: Une méta-analyse. *Canadian Journal of Administrative Sciences*, **8**, 130–139.

Cox, D. R. (1972) Regression models and life-tables. *Journal of the Royal Statistical Society, Series B*, **34**, 187–202.

Dalton, D. R. & Mesch, D. J. (1991) On the extent and reduction of avoidable absenteeism: An assessment of absence policy provisions. *Journal of Applied Psychology*, **76**, 810–817.

Dalton, D. R. & Mesch, D. J. (1992) The impact of employee-initiated transfer on absenteeism: A four-year cohort assessment. *Human Relations*, **45**, 291–304.

Dalton, D. R. & Perry, J. L. (1981) Absenteeism and the collective bargaining agreement: An empirical test. *Academy of Management Journal*, **24**, 425–431.

Dalton, D. R. & Todor, W. D. (1993) Turnover, transfer, and absenteeism: An interdependent perspective. *Journal of Management*, **19**, 193–219.

Dansereau, F., Alutto, J. A., & Yammarino, F. J. (1984) *Theory Testing in Organizational Behavior: The Varient Approach*. Englewood Cliffs, NJ: Prentice-Hall.

Deery, S. J., Erwin, P. J., Iverson, R. D., & Ambrose, M. L. (in press) The determinants of absenteeism: Evidence from Australian blue-collar employees. *International Journal of Human Resource Management*.

Drago, R. & Wooden, M. (1992) The determinants of labor absence: Economic factors and workgroup norms across countries. *Industrial and Labor Relations Review*, **45**, 764–778.

Dunn, L. F. & Youngblood, S. A. (1986) Absenteeism as a mechanism for approaching an optimal labor market equilibrium: An empirical study. *Review of Economics and Statistics*, **68**, 668–674.

Dwyer, D. J. & Ganster, D. C. (1991) The effects of job demands and control on employee attendance and satisfaction. *Journal of Organizational Behavior*, **12**, 595–608.

Edwards, J. R. (1991) Person–job fit: A conceptual integration, literature review, and methodological critique. *International Review of Industrial and Organizational Psychology*, **6**, 283–357.

Edwards, J. R. (1992) A cybernetic theory of stress, coping, and well-being in organizations. *Academy of Management Review*, **17**, 238–274.

Edwards, P. K. & Scullion, H. (1982) *The Social Organization of Industrial Conflict: Control and Resistance in the Workplace.* Oxford: Blackwell.

Edwards, P. & Scullion, H. (1984) The social organization of industrial conflict. *Sociological Review*, **32**, 547–571.

Edwards, P. & Whitston, C. (1993) *Attending to Work: The Management of Attendance and Shopfloor Order.* Oxford: Blackwell.

Ehrenberg, R. G., Ehrenberg, R. A., Rees, D. I., & Ehrenberg, E. L. (1991) School district leave policies, teacher absenteeism, and student achievement. *Journal of Human Resources*, **26**, 72–105.

Eisenberger, R., Fasolo, P., & Davis-LaMastro, V. (1990) Perceived organizational support and employee diligence, commitment, and innovation. *Journal of Applied Psychology*, **75**, 51–59.

Eisenberger, R., Huntington, R., Hutchison, S., & Sowa, D. (1986) Perceived organizational support. *Journal of Applied Psychology*, **71**, 500–507.

Farrell, D. & Peterson, J. C. (1984) Commitment, absenteeism, and turnover of new employees: A longitudinal study. *Human Relations*, **37**, 681–692.

Farrell, D. & Stamm, C. L. (1988) Meta-analysis of the correlates of employee absence. *Human Relations*, **41**, 211–227.

Ferris, G. R., Bergin, T. G., & Wayne, S. J. (1988) Personal characteristics, job performance, and absenteeism of public school teachers. *Journal of Applied Social Psychology*, **18**, 552–563.

Ferris, G. R. & Rowland, K. M. (1987) Tenure as a moderator of the absence–intent to leave relationship. *Human Relations*, **40**, 255–266.

Fichman, M. (1984) A theoretical approach to understanding employee absence. In P. S. Goodman & R. S. Atkin (eds), *Absenteeism: New Approaches to Understanding, Measuring, and Managing Employee Absence* (pp. 1–46). San Francisco: Jossey-Bass.

Fichman, M. (1988) Motivational consequences of absence and attendance: Proportional hazard estimation of a dynamic motivation model. *Journal of Applied Psychology*, **73**, 119–134.

Fichman, M. (1989) Attendance makes the heart grow fonder: A hazard rate approach to modeling attendance. *Journal of Applied Psychology*, **74**, 325–335.

Firth, H. & Britton, P. (1989) 'Burnout', absence and turnover amongst British nursing staff. *Journal of Occupational Psychology*, **62**, 55–59.

Fitzgibbons, D. E. (1992) A critical reexamination of employee absence: The impact of relational contracting, the negotiated order, and the employment relationship. *Research in Personnel and Human Resources Management*, **10**, 73–120.

Frayne, C. A. & Latham, G. P. (1987) Application of social learning theory to employee self-management of attendance. *Journal of Applied Psychology*, **72**, 387–392.

Fried, Y., Rowland, K. M., & Ferris, G. R. (1984) The physiological measurement of work stress: A critique. *Personnel Psychology*, **37**, 583–615.

Furnham, A. & Walsh, J. (1991) Consequences of person–environment incongruence: Absenteeism, frustration, and stress. *Journal of Social Psychology*, **13**, 187–204.

Gafni, A. & Peled, D. (1984) The effect of labelling on illness related absenteeism. *Journal of Health Economics*, **3**, 173–178.

Gale, E. K. (1993) *The effect of norms and significant others' attitudes on absenteeism.* Paper presented at the annual meeting of the Society for Industrial and Organizational Psychology, San Francisco.

Galloway, D., Panckhurst, F., Bosewll, K., Boswell, C., & Green, K. (1984) Mental health, absences from work, stress and satisfaction in a sample of New Zealand primary school teachers. *Australian and New Zealand Journal of Psychiatry*, **18**, 359–363.

Garrison, R. & Eaton, W. (1992) Secretaries, depression and absenteeism. *Women & Health*, 18(4), 53–76.

Gellatly, I. R. (1995) Individual and group determinants of employee absenteeism: Test of a causal model. *Journal of Organizational Behavior*, 16, 469–485.

George, J. M. (1989) Mood and absence. *Journal of Applied Psychology*, 74, 317–324.

George, J. M. (1990) Personality, affect, and behavior in groups. *Journal of Applied Psychology*, 75, 107–116.

George, J. M. & James, L. R. (1993) Personality, affect, the behavior in groups revisited: Comment on aggregation, levels of analysis, and a recent application of within and between analysis. *Journal of Applied Psychology*, 78, 798–804.

Geurts, S. A., Buunk, B. P., & Schaufeli, W. B. (1994) Social comparisons and absenteeism: A structural modeling approach. *Journal of Applied Social Psychology*, 24, 1871–1890.

Goff, S. J., Mount, M., K., & Jamison, R. L. (1990) Employer supported child care, work/family conflict, and absenteeism: A field study. *Personnel Psychology*, 43, 793–809.

Goodman, P. S. & Atkin, R. S. (1984) Effects of absenteeism on individuals and organizations. In P. S. Goodman & R. S. Atkin (eds), *Absenteeism: New Approaches to Understanding, Measuring, and Managing Employee Absence* (pp. 276–321). San Francisco: Jossey-Bass.

Goodman, P. S. & Garber, S. (1988) Absenteeism and accidents in a dangerous environment: Empirical analysis of underground coal mines. *Journal of Applied Psychology*, 73, 81–86.

Goodman, P. S. & Leyden, D. P. (1991) Familiarity and group productivity. *Journal of Applied Psychology*, 76, 578–586.

Gruber, V. A. & Wildman, B. G. (1987) The impact of dysmehorrhea on daily activities. *Behaviour Research and Therapy*, 25, 123–128.

Gunn, K. P. (1993) A correlation between attendance and grades in a first-year psychology class. *Canadian Psychology*, 34, 201–202.

Haccoun, R. R. & Desgent, C. (1993) Perceived reasons and consequences of work absence: A survey of French-speaking employees in Quebec. *International Journal of Psychology*, 28, 97–117.

Haccoun, R. R. & Dupont, S. (1987) Absence research: A critique of previous approaches and an example for a new direction. *Canadian Journal of Administrative Sciences*, 4, 143–156.

Haccoun, R. R. & Jeanrie, C. (1995) Self reports of work absence as a function of personal attitudes towards absence, and perceptions of the organization. *Applied Psychology: An International Review*, 44, 155–170.

Hackett, R. D. (1989) Work attitudes and employee absenteeism: A synthesis of the literature. *Journal of Occupational Psychology*, 62, 235–248.

Hackett, R. D. (1990) Age, tenure, and employee absenteeism. *Human Relations*, 43, 610–619.

Hackett, R. D., Bycio, P., & Guion, R. M. (1989) Absenteeism among hospital nurses: An idiographic-longitudinal analysis. *Academy of Management Journal*, 32, 424–453.

Hackett, R. D., Bycio, P., & Hausdorf, P. A. (1994) Further assessments of Meyer and Allen's (1991) three-component model of organizational commitment. *Journal of Applied Psychology*, 79, 15–23.

Hackett, R. D. & Guion, R. M. (1995) A reevaluation of the absenteeism–job satisfaction relationship. *Organizational Behavior and Human Decision Processes*, 35, 340–381.

Hanisch, K. A. & Hulin, C. L. (1990) Job attitudes and organizational withdrawal: An examination of retirement and other voluntary withdrawal behaviors. *Journal of Vocational Behavior*, 37, 60–78.

Hanisch, K. A. & Hulin, C. L. (1991) General attitudes and organizational with-drawal: An evaluation of a causal model. *Journal of Vocational Behavior*, **39**, 110–128.

Harrison, D. A. (1995) Volunteer motivation and attendance decisions: Competitive theory testing in multiple samples from a homeless shelter. *Journal of Applied Psychology*, **80**, 371–385.

Harrison, D. A. & Bell, M. P. (1995) *Social expectations and attendance decisions: Implications for absence control programs.* Paper presented at the annual meeting of the Academy of Management, Vancouver.

Harrison, D. A. & Hulin, C. L. (1989) Investigations of absenteeism: Using event history models to study the absence-taking process. *Journal of Applied Psychology*, **74**, 300–316.

Harrison, D. A. & Shaffer, M. A. (1994) Comparative examinations of self-reports and perceived absenteeism norms: Wading through Lake Wobegon. *Journal of Applied Psychology*, **79**, 240–251.

Hendrix, W. H. & Spencer, B. A. (1989) Development and test of a multivariate model of absenteeism. *Psychological Reports*, **64**, 923–938.

Hendrix, W. H., Spencer, B. A., & Gibson, G. S. (1994) Organizational and extra-organizational factors affecting stress, employee well-being, and absenteeism for males and females. *Journal of Business and Psychology*, **9**, 103–128.

Hill, J. M. M. & Trist, E. L. (1953) A consideration of industrial accidents as a means of withdrawal fro the work situation. *Human Relations*, **6**, 357–380.

Hill, J. M. M. & Trist, E. L. (1955) Changes in accidents and other absences with length of service. *Human Relations*, **8**, 121–152.

Hogan, J. & Hogan, R. (1989) How to measure employee reliability. *Journal of Applied Psychology*, **65**, 177–184.

Holland, J. L. (1973) *Making Vocational Choices: A Theory of Careers*. Englewood Cliffs, NJ: Prentice-Hall.

Hulin, C. (1991) Adaptation, persistence, and commitment in organizations. In M. D. Dunnette & L. M. Hough (eds), *Handbook of Industrial and Organizational Psychology* 2nd edn, Vol. 2 (pp. 445–505). Palo Alto, CA: Consulting Psychologists Press.

Hyman, R. (1975) *Industrial Relations: A Marxist Introduction*. London: Macmillan.

Ilgen, D. R. & Hollenback, J. H. (1977) The role of job satisfaction in absence behavior. *Organizational Behavior and Human Performance*, **19**, 148–161.

Ivancevich, J. M. (1985) Predicting absenteeism from prior absence and work attitudes. *Academy of Management Journal*, **28**, 219–228.

Jackson, J. (1960) Structural characteristics of norms In N. B. Henry (ed), *The Dynamics of Instructional Groups. Fifty-ninth Yearbook of the National Society for the Study of Education, Part II*. Chicago: University of Chicago Press.

Jackson, S. E. & Schuler, R. S. (1985) A meta-analysis and conceptual critique of research on role ambiguity and role conflict in work settings. *Organizational Behavior and Human Decision Processes*, **36**, 16–78.

Jamal, M. (1984) Job stress and job performance controversy: An empirical assessment. *Organizational Behavior and Human Performance*, **33**, 1–21.

Jenkins, R. (1985) Minor psychiatric morbidity in employed young men and women and its contribution to sickness absence. *British Journal of Industrial Medicine*, **42**, 147–154.

Jenkins, R. (1986) Sex differences in alcohol consumption and its associated morbidity in young civil servants. *British Journal of Addiction*, **81**, 525–535.

Johns, G. (1978) Attitudinal and nonattitudinal predictors of two forms of absence from work. *Organizational Behavior and Human Performance*, **22**, 431–444.

Johns, G. (1984) Unresolved issues in the study and management of abence from work. In P. S. Goodman & R. S. Atkin (eds), *Absenteeism: New Approaches to Understanding, Measuring, and Managing Employee Absence* (pp. 360–390). San Francisco: Jossey-Bass.

Johns, G. (1987, October) The great escape. *Psychology Today*, 30–33.

Johns, G. (1991) Substantive and methodological constraints on behavior and attitudes in organizational research. *Organizational Behavior and Human Decision Processes*, **49**, 80–104.

Johns, G. (1994a) Absenteeism estimates by employees and managers: Divergent perspectives and self-serving perceptions. *Journal of Applied Psychology*, **79**, 229–239.

Johns, G. (1994b) How often were you absent? A review of the use of self-reported absence data. *Journal of Applied Psychology*, **79**, 574–591.

Johns, G. (1994c) *Medical, ethical, and cultural constraints on work absence and attendance*. Presentation made at the International Congress of Applied Psychology, Madrid.

Johns, G. & Nicholson, N. (1982) The meanings of absence: New strategies for theory and research. *Research in Organizational Behavior*, **4**, 127–172.

Johnson, W. G. & Ondrich, J. (1990) The duration of post-injury absences from work. *Review of Economics and Statistics*, **72**, 578–586.

Judge, T. A. (1992) The dispositional perspective in human resources research. *Research in Personnel and Human Resources Management*, **10**, 31–72.

Judge, T. A. & Martocchio, J. J. (1995) The role of fairness orientation and supervisor attributions in absence disciplinary decisions. *Journal of Business and Psychology*, **10**, 115–137.

Kahana, N. & Weiss, A. (1992) Absenteeism: A comparison of incentives. *Journal of Comparative Economics*, **16**, 573–595.

Kahn, R. L. & Byosiere, P. (1992) Stress in organizations. In M. D. Dunnette & L. M. Hough (eds), *Handbook of Industrial and Organizational Psychology* 2nd edn, Vol. 3 (pp. 571–650). Palo Alto, CA: Consulting Psychologists Press.

Kanfer, R., Crosby, J. V., & Brandt, D. M. (1988) Investigating behavioral antecedents of turnover at three job tenure levels. *Journal of Applied Psychology*, **73**, 331–335.

Karasek, R. (1990) Lower health risk with increased job control among white collar workers. *Journal of Organizational Behavior*, **11**, 171–185.

Karasek, R. A. Jr (1979) Job demands, decision latitude, and mental strain: Implications for job redesign. *Administrative Science Quarterly*, **24**, 285–308.

Kaufmann, C. L. (1993) Reasonable accommodation to mental health disabilities at work: Legal constructs and practical applications. *Journal of Psychiatry & Law*, **21**, 153–174.

Kelley, H. H. (1972) Attribution in social interaction. E. E. Jones et al. (eds), *Attribution: Perceiving the Causes of Behavior* (pp. 1–26). Morristown, NJ: General Learning Press.

Kenyon, P. & Dawkins, P. (1989) A time series analysis of labour absence in Australia. *Review of Economics and Statistics*, **71**, 232–239.

Klass, B. S. (1989) Determinants of grievance activity and the grievance system's impact on employee behavior: An integrative perspective. *Academy of Management Review*, **14**, 445–458.

Klass, B. S., Heneman, H. G. III, & Olson, C. A. (1991) Effects of grievance activity on absenteeism. *Journal of Applied Psychology*, **76**, 818–824.

Kobasa, S. C. (1979) Stressful life events, personality, and health: An inquiry into hardiness. *Journal of Personality and Social Psychology*, **37**, 1–11.

Kohler, S. S. & Mathieu, J. E. (1993) Individual characteristics, work perceptions, and affective reactions influences on differentiated absence criteria. *Journal of Organizational Behavior*, **14**, 515–530.

Kossek, E. E. (1990) Diversity in child care assistance needs: Employee problems, preferences, and work-related outcomes. *Personnel Psychology*, **43**, 769–791.

Kouzis, A. C. & Eaton, W. W. (1994) Emotional disability days: Prevalence and predictors. *American Journal of Public Health*, **84**, 1304–1307.

Kristensen, T. S. (1991) Sickness absence and work strain among Danish slaughterhouse workers: An analysis of absence from work regarded as coping behaviour. *Social Science and Medicine*, **32**, 15–27.

Kryst, S. & Scherl, E. (1994) A population-based survey of the social and personal impact of headache. *Headache*, **34**, 344–350.

Landeweerd, J. A. & Boumans, N. P. G. (1994) The effect of work dimensions and need for autonomy on nurses' work satisfaction and health. *Journal of Occupational and Organizational Psychology*, **67**, 207–217.

Larson, E. W. & Fukami, C. V. (1985) Employee absenteeism: The role of ease of movement. *Academy of Management Journal*, **28**, 464–471.

Latham, G. P. & Frayne, C. A. (1989) Self-management training for increasing job attendance: A follow-up and a replication. *Journal of Applied Psychology*, **74**, 411–416.

Latham, G. P., Skarlicki, D., Irvine, D., & Siegel, J. P. (1993) The increasing importance of performance appraisals to employee effectiveness in employment settings in North America. *International Review of Industrial and Organizational Psychology*, **8**, 87–132.

Lawson, D. A. & O'Brien, R. M. (1994) Behavioral and self-report measures of staff burnout in development disabilities. *Journal of Organizational Behavior Management*, **14**(2), 37–54.

Leigh, J. P. (1981) The effects of union membership on absence from work due to illness. *Journal of Labor Research*, **2**, 329–336.

Leigh, J. P. (1983) Sex differences in absenteeism. *Industrial Relations*, **22**, 349–361.

Leigh, J. P. (1984) Unionization and absenteeism. *Applied Economics*, **16**, 147–157.

Leigh, J. P. (1985) The effects of unemployment and the business cycle on absenteeism. *Journal of Economics and Business*, **37**, 159–170.

Leigh, J. P. (1986) Correlates of absence from work due to illness. *Human Relations*, **39**, 81–100.

Leigh, J. P. (1991) Employee and job attributes as predictors of absenteeism in a national sample of workers: The importance of health and dangerous working conditions. *Social Science and Medicine*, **33**, 127–137.

Léonard, C., Van Ameringen, M.-R., Dolan, S. L., & Arsenault, A. (1987) Absentéisme et assiduité au travail. Deux moyens d'adaptation au stress? *Relations Industrielles*, **42**, 774–789.

Levine, S. & Kozloff, M. A. (1978) The sick role: Assessment and overview. *Annual Review of Sociology*, **4**, 317–343.

Lipton, R. B., Steward, W. F., & Von Korff, M. (1994) The burden of migraine: A review of cost to society. *PharmacoEconomics*, **6**, 215–221.

Lissovoy, G. & Lazarus, S. S. (1994) The economic cost of migraine. *Neurology*, **44**(Suppl. 4), S56–S62.

Manning, M. R. & Osland, J. S. (1989) The relationship between absenteeism and stress. *Work & Stress*, **3**, 223–235.

Manning, M. R., Osland, J. S., & Osland, A. (1989) Work-related consequences of smoking cessation. *Academy of Management Journal*, **32**, 606–621.

Marcus, P. M. & Smith, C. B. (1985) Absenteeism in an organizational context. *Work and Occupations*, **12**, 251–268.

Markham, S. E. (1985) An investigation of the relationship between unemployment and absenteeism: A multi-level approach. *Academy of Management Journal*, **28**, 228–234.

Markham, S. E. & McKee, G. H. (1991) Declining organizational size and increasing unemployment rates: Predicting employee absenteeism from within- and between-plant perspectives. *Academy of Management Journal*, **34**, 952–965.

Markham, S. E. & McKee, G. H. (1995a) Group absence behavior and standards: A multilevel analysis. *Academy of Management Journal*, **38**, 1174–1190.

Markham, S. E. & McKee, G. H. (1995b) *Finding leverage points for transforming absence culture: A longitudinal investigation into the importance of work groups.* Paper presented at the annual meeting of the Academy of Management, Vancouver.

Marmot, M. G., North, F., Feeney, A., & Head, J. (1993) Alcohol consumption and sickness absence: From the Whitehall II study. *Addiction*, **88**, 369–382.

Martocchio, J. J. (1989) Age-related differences in employee absenteeism: A meta-analysis. *Psychology and Aging*, **4**, 409–414.

Martocchio, J. J. (1992) The financial cost of absence decisions. *Journal of Management*, **18**, 133–152.

Martocchio, J. J. (1994) The effects of absence culture on individual absence. *Human Relations*, **47**, 243–262.

Martocchio, J. J. & Harrison, D. A. (1993) To be there or not to be there? Questions, theories, and methods in absenteeism research. *Research in Personnel and Human Resources Management*, **11**, 259–328.

Martocchio, J. J. & Judge, T. A. (1994) A policy-capturing approach to individuals' decisions to be absent. *Organizational Behavior and Human Decision Processes*, **57**, 358–386.

Martocchio, J. J. & Judge, T. A. (1995) When we don't see eye to eye: Discrepancies between supervisors and subordinates in absence disciplinary decisions. *Journal of Management*, **21**, 251–278.

Maslach, C. & Jackson, S. E. (1984) Burnout in organizational settings. In S. Oskamp (ed), *Applied Social Psychology Annual*, Vol. 5. Beverly Hills, CA: Sage.

Mathieu, J. E. & Farr, J. L. (1991) Further evidence for the discriminant validity of measures of organizational commitment, job involvement, and job satisfaction. *Journal of Applied Psychology*, **76**, 127–133.

Mathieu, J. E. & Kohler, S. S. (1990a) A test of the interactive effects of organizational commitment and job involvement on various types of absence. *Journal of Vocational Behavior*, **36**, 33–44.

Mathieu, J. E. & Kohler, S. S. (1990b) A cross-level examination of group absence influences on individual absence. *Journal of Applied Psychology*, **75**, 217–220.

Mathieu, J. E. & Zajac, D. M. (1990) A review and meta-analysis of the antecedents, correlates, and consequences of organizational commitment. *Psychological Bulletin*, **108**, 171–194.

Mayer, R. C. & Schoorman, F. D. (1992) Predicting participation and production outcomes through a two-dimensional model of organizational commitment. *Academy of Management Journal*, **35**, 671–684.

McKee, G. H., Markham, S. E., & Scott, K. D. (1992) Job stress and employee withdrawal from work. In J. C. Quick, L. R. Murphey, & J. J. Hurrell Jr (eds), *Work and Well-being: Assessments and Interventions for Occupational Mental Health.* Washington, DC: American Psychological Association.

McShane, S. L. (1984) Job satisfaction and absenteeism: A meta-analytic re-examination. *Canadian Journal of Administrative Sciences*, **1**, 61–77.

Meisenheimer, J. R. Jr (1990, August) Employee absences in 1989: A new look at data from the CPS. *Monthly Labor Review*, 28–33.

Melamed, S., Ben-Avi, I., Luz, J., & Green, M. S. (1995) Objective and subjective work monotony: Effects of job satisfaction, psychological distress, and absenteeism in blue-collar workers. *Journal of Applied Psychology*, **80**, 29–42.

Meyer, J. P. & Allen, N. J. (1991) A three-component conceptualization of organizational commitment. *Human Resource Management Review*, **1**, 61–98.

Meyer, J. P., Allen, N. J., & Smith, C. A. (1993) Commitment to organizations and occupations: Extension and test of a three-component conceptualization. *Journal of Applied Psychology*, **78**, 538–551.

Meyerson, D. E. (1994) Interpretations of stress in institutions: The cultural production of ambiguity and burnout. *Administrative Science Quarterly*, **39**, 628–653.

Mitra, A., Jenkins, G. D., Jr, & Gupta, N. (1992) A meta-analytic review of the relationship between absence and turnover. *Journal of Applied Psychology*, 77, 879–889.

Moch, M. K. & Fitzgibbons, D. E. (1985) The relationship between absenteeism and production efficiency: An empirical assessment. *Journal of Occuaptional Psychology*, 58, 39–47.

Moore, M. L., Nichol, V. W., & McHugh, P. P. (1992) Review of no-fault absenteeism cases taken to arbitration, 1980–1989: A rights and responsibilities analysis. *Employee Responsibilities and Rights Journal*, 5, 29–48.

Mowday, R. T., Porter, L. W., & Steers, R. M. (1982) *Employee–Organization Linkages: The Psychology of Commitment, Absenteeism, and Turnover.* New York: Academic Press.

Mowday, R. T., Steers, R. M., & Porter, L. W. (1979) The measurement of organizational commitment. *Journal of Vocational Behavior*, 14, 224–247.

Muchinsky, P. M. (1977) Employee absenteeism: A review of the literature. *Journal of Vocational Behavior*, 10, 316–340.

Newsome, S. (1993) *Predicting absence without work attitudes.* Paper presented at the annual meeting of the Canadian Psychological Association, Montreal.

Ng. I. (1989) The effect of vacation and sickleave policies on absenteeism. *Canadian Journal of Administrative Sciences*, 6(4), 18–27.

Nichols, T. (1994) Industrial accidents as a means of withdrawal from the workplace according to the Tavistock Institute of Human Relations: A re-examination of a classic study. *British Journal of Sociology*, 45, 387–406.

Nicholson, N. (1975) *Industrial absence as an indicant of employee motivation and job satisfaction.* Unpublished doctoral dissertation, University of Wales, Cardiff.

Nicholson, N. (1977) Absence behaviour and attendance motivation: A conceptual synthesis. *Journal of Management Studies*, 14, 231–252.

Nicholson, N. (1985) Absence and turnover: The absentee bus crews. In C. Clegg, N. Kemp, & K. Legge (eds), *Case Studies in Organizational Behaviour* (pp. 114–121). London: Harper & Row.

Nicholson, N., Brown, C. A., & Chadwick-Jones, J. K. (1976) Absence from work and job satisfaction. *Journal of Applied Psychology*, 61, 728–737.

Nicholson, N., Brown, C. A., & Chadwick-Jones, J. K. (1977) Absence from work and personal characteristics. *Journal of Applied Psychology*, 62, 319–327.

Nicholson, N. & Johns, G. (1985) The absence culture and the psychological contract—Who's in control of absence? *Academy of Management Review*, 10, 397–407.

Nicholson, N. & Martocchio, J. J. (1995) The management of absence: What do we know? What can we do? G. R. Ferris, S. D. Rosen, & D. T. Barnum (eds), *Handbook of Human Resources Management* (pp. 567–614). Oxford: Blackwell.

Nicholson, N. & Payne, R. (1987) Absence from work: Explanations and attributions. *Applied Psychology: An International Review*, 36, 121–132.

Nicholson, N. & West, M. A. (1988) *Managerial Job Change: Men and Women in Transition.* Cambridge: Cambridge University Press.

Normand, J., Salyards, S. D., & Mahoney, J. J. (1990) An evaluation of preemployment drug testing. *Journal of Applied Psychology*, 75, 629–639.

North, F., Syme, S. L., Feeney, A., Head, J., Shipley, M., & Marmot, M. G.(1993) Explaining socioeconomic differences in sickness absence: The Whitehall II study. *British Medical Journal*, 306, 361–366.

Öhlund, C., Lindström, I., Areskoug, B., Eek, C., Peterson, L.-E., & Nachemson, A. (1994) Pain behavior in industrial subacute low back pain. Part I. Reliability: Concurrent and predictive validity of pain behavior assessments. *Pain*, 58, 201–209.

Ones, D. S., Viswesvaran, C., & Schmidt, F. L. (1993) Comprehensive meta-analysis of integrity test validities: Findings and implications for personnel selection and theories of job performance. *Journal of Applied Psychology*, 78, 679–703.

Organ, D. W. (1988) *Organizational Citizenship Behavior: The Good Soldier Syndrome.* Lexington, MA: Lexington.

Ostroff, C. (1992) The relationship between satisfaction, attitudes, and performance: An organizational level analysis. *Journal of Applied Psychology*, 77, 963–974.

Parkes, K. R. (1983) Smoking as a moderator of the relationship between affective state and absence from work. *Journal of Applied Psychology*, **68**, 698–708.

Parkes, K. R. (1987) Relative weight, smoking, and mental health as predictors of sickness and absence from work. *Journal of Applied Psychology*, 72, 275–286.

Peel, M. J. & Wilson, N. (1990) Labour absenteeism: The impact of profit sharing, voice and participation. *International Journal of Manpower*, 11(7), 17–24.

Porter, L. W. & Steers, R. M. (1973) Organizational, work, and personal factors in employee turnover and absenteeism. *Psychological Bulletin*, 80, 151–176.

Prins, R. & de Graaf, A. (1986) Comparison of sickness absence in Belgian, German and Dutch firms. *British Journal of Industrial Medicine*, 43, 529–536.

Randall, D. M., Fedor, D. B., & Longenecker, C. O. (1990) The behavioral expression of organizational commitment. *Journal of Vocational Behavior*, 36, 210–224.

Rees, D. W. & Cooper, C. L. (1990) Occupational stress in health service employees. *Health Services Management Research*, 3, 163–172.

Rhodes, S. R. & Steers, R. M. (1990) *Managing Employee Absenteeism.* Reading, MA: Addison-Wesley.

Robinson, S. L. & Bennett, R. J. (1995) A typology of deviant workplace behaviors: A multidimensional scaling study. *Academy of Management Journal*, 38, 555–572.

Rodin, J. & Ickovics, J. R. (1990) Women's health: Review and research agenda as we approach the 21st century. *American Psychologist*, 45, 1018–1034.

Rogers, R. E. & Herting, S. R. (1993) Patterns of absenteeism among government employees. *Public Personnel Management*, 22, 215–235.

Rosse, J. G. (1988) Relations among lateness, absence, and turnover: Is there a progression of withdrawal? *Human Relations*, 41, 517–531.

Rosse, J. G. & Miller, H. E. (1984) Relationship between absenteeism and other employee behaviors. In P. S. Goodman and R. S. Atkin (eds), *Absenteeism: New Approaches to Understanding, Measuring, and Managing Absence* (pp. 194–228). San Francisco: Jossey-Bass.

Rousseau, D. M. (1985) Issues of level in organizational research: Multi-level and cross-level perspectives. *Research in Organizational Behavior*, 7, 1–37.

Runcie, J. F. (1988) 'Deviant behavior'. Achieving autonomy in a machine-paced environment. In M. O. Jones, M. D. Moore, & R. C. Snyder (eds), *Inside Organizations: Understanding the Human Dimension* (pp. 129-140). Newbury Park, CA: Sage.

Rushmore, C. H. & Youngblood, S. A. (1979) Medically-related absenteeism: Random or motivated behavior? *Journal of Occupational Medicine*, 21, 245–250.

Sackett, P. R., DuBois, C. L. Z., Noe, A. W. (1991) Tokenism in performance evaluation: The effects of work group representation on male–female and white–black differences in performance ratings. *Journal of Applied Psychology*, 76, 263–267.

Sands, J. M. & Miller, L. E. (1991) Effects of moon phase and other temporal variables on absenteeism. *Psychological Reports*, 69, 959–962.

Saxton, M. J., Phillips, J. S., & Blakeney, R. N. (1991) Antecedents and consequences of emotional exhaustion in the airline reservations service sector. *Human Relations*, 44, 583–595.

Scott, D. & Markham, S. (1982) Absenteeism control methods: A survey of practices and results. *Personnel Administrator*, 27, 73–84.

Scott, D. & Taylor, G. S. (1983) An analysis of absenteeism cases taken to arbitration: 1975–1981. *Arbitration Journal*, 38(3), 61–70.

Scott, K. D. & McClellan, E. L. (1990) Gender differences in absenteeism. *Public Personnel Management*, 19, 229–253.

Scott, K. D. & Taylor, G. S. (1985) An examination of conflicting findings on the relationship between job satisfaction and absenteeism: A meta-analysis. *Academy of Management Journal*, **28**, 599–612.

Sheridan, J. E. (1985) A catastrophe model of employee withdrawal leading to low job performance, high absenteeism, and job turnover during the first year of employment. *Academy of Management Journal*, **28**, 88–109.

Skinner, B. F. (1974) *About Behaviorism*. New York: Knopf.

Skodol, A. E., Schwartz, S., Dohrenwend, B. P., Levav, I., & Shrout, P. E. (1994) Minor depression in a cohort of young adults in Israel. *Archives of General Psychiatry*, **51**, 542–551.

Somers, M. J. (1995) Organizational commitment, turnover and absenteeism: An examination of direct and interaction effects. *Journal of Organizational Behavior*, **16**, 49–58.

Spector, P. E., Dwyer, D. J., & Jex, S. M. (1988) Relation of job stressors to affective, health, and performance outcomes: A comparison of multiple data sources. *Journal of Applied Psychology*, **73**, 11–19.

Spielberger, C. D. & Reheiser, E. C. (1994) The job stress survey: Measuring gender differences in occupational stress. *Journal of Social Behavior and Personality*, **9**, 199–218.

Spink, K. S. & Carron, A. V. (1992) Group cohesion and adherence in exercise classes. *Journal of Sport and Exercise Psychology*, **14**, 78–86.

Stansfeld, S., Feeney, A., Head, J., Canner, R., North, F., & Marmot, M. (1995) Sickness absence for psychiatric illness: The Whitehall II study. *Social Science and Medicine*, **40**, 189–197.

Stansfeld, S. A., Smith, G. D., & Marmot, M. (1993) Association between physical and psychological morbidity in the Whitehall II study. *Journal of Psychosomatic Research*, **37**, 227–238.

Steers, R. M. & Rhodes, S. R. (1978) Major influences on employee attendance: A process model. *Journal of Applied Psychology*, **63**, 391–407.

Steers, R. M. & Rhodes, S. R. (1984) Knowledge and speculation about absenteeism. In P. S. Goodman & R. S. Atkin (eds), *Absenteeism: New Approaches to Understanding, Measuring, and Managing Employee Absence* (pp. 229–275). San Francisco: Jossey-Bass.

Tang, T. L.-P. & Hammontree, M. L. (1992) The effects of hardiness, police stress, and life stress on police officers' illness and absenteeism. *Public Personnel Management*, **21**, 493–510.

Tansey, R. R. & Hyman, M. R. (1992) Public relations, advocacy ads, and the campaign against absenteeism during World War II. *Business & Professional Ethics Journal*, **11**(3 & 4), 129–164.

Taylor, D. W., Haynes, R. B., Sackett, D. L., & Gibson, E. S. (1981) Longterm follow-up of absenteeism among working men following the detection and treatment of their hypertension. *Clinical and Investigative Medicine*, **4**(3/4), 173–177.

Taylor, P. J. & Burridge, J. (1982) Trends in death, disablement, and sickness absence in the British Post Office since 1891. *British Journal of Industrial Medicine*, **39**, 1–10.

Tharenou, P. (1993) A test of reciprocal causality for absenteeism. *Journal of Organizational Behavior*, **14**, 269–290.

Theorell, T., Leymann, H., Jodko, M., Konarski, K., & Norbeck, H. E. (1994) 'Person under train' incidents from the subway driver's point of view—a prospective 1-year follow-up study: The design, and medical and psychiatric data. *Social Science and Medicine*, **38**, 471–475.

Thomas, L. T. & Ganster, D. C. (1995) Impact of family-supportive work variables on work–family conflict and strain: A control perspective. *Journal of Applied Psychology*, **80**, 6–15.

Thomas, P. J. & Thomas, M. D. (1994) Effects of sex, marital status, and parental status on absenteeism among navy enlisted personnel. *Military Psychology*, **6**, 95–108.

Tollefson, G. D., Souetre, E. J., Thomander, L., & Potvin, J. H. (1993) Comorbid anxious signs and symptoms in major depression: Impact on functional capacity and comparative treatment outcomes. *International Clinical Psychopharmacology*, **8**, 281–293.

Turnbull, P. & Sapsford, D. (1992) A sea of discontent: The tides of organised and 'unorganised' conflict on the docks. *Sociology*, **26**, 291–309.

VandenHeuvel, A. & Wooden, M. (1995) Do explanations of absenteeism differ for men and women? *Human Relations*, **48**, 1309–1330.

Waddell, G., Newton, M., Henderson, I., Somerville, D., & Main, C. J. (1993) A fear-avoidance beliefs questionnaire (FABQ) and the role of fear-avoidance beliefs in chronic low back pain and disability. *Pain*, **52**, 157–168.

Webb, G. R., Redman, S., Hennrikus, D. J., Kelman, G. R., Gibberd, R. W., & Sanson-Fisher, R. W. (1994) The relationships between high-risk and problem drinking and the occurrence of work injuries and related absences. *Journal of Studies on Alcohol*, **55**, 434–446.

Wilson, N. & Peel, M. J. (1991) The impact on absenteeism and quits of profit-sharing and other forms of employee participation. *Industrial and Labor Relations Review*, **44**, 454–468.

Wise, L. C. (1993) The erosion of nursing resources: Employee withdrawal behavior. *Research in Nursing & Health*, **16**, 67–75.

Wooden, M. (1990, December) The 'sickie': A public sector phenomenon? *Journal of Industrial Relations*, 560–576.

Xie, J. L. & Johns, G. (1995) *Perceptions of absence from work: The People's Republic of China versus Canada.* Manuscript under review.

Yammarino, F. J. & Markham, S. E. (1992) On the application of within and between analysis: Are absence and affect really group-based phenomena? *Journal of Applied Psychology*, **77**, 168–176.

Youngblood, S. A. (1984) Work, nonwork, and withdrawal. *Journal of Applied Psychology*, **69**, 106–117.

Zaccaro, S. J. (1991) Nonequivalent associations between forms of cohesiveness and group-related outcomes: Evidence for multidimensionality. *Journal of Social Psychology*, **13**, 387–399.

Zaccaro, S. J. & Collins, T. T. (1988) Excused and unexcused absenteeism in normative organizations. *Group & Organization Studies*, **13**(1), 81–99.

Zaccaro, S. J., Craig, B., & Quinn, J. (1991) Prior absenteeism, supervisory style, job satisfaction, and personal characteristics: An investigation of some mediated and moderated linkages to work absenteeism. *Organizational Behavior and Human Decision Processes*, **50**, 24–44.

Chapter 8

ORGANIZATIONAL COMMITMENT

John P. Meyer
University of Western Ontario

It has been more than 10 years since Griffin and Bateman (1986) reviewed the organizational commitment literature in Volume 1 of the *International Review of Industrial and Organizational Psychology*. In that chapter, commitment shared the spotlight with job satisfaction. Much has happened in the field since then. New approaches have been taken to the conceptualization and measurement of organizational commitment and advances have been made in the research designs and analytic techniques used to examine the development and consequences of commitment. Close to a dozen meta-analytic reviews focusing specifically on organizational commitment and its relations with other variables have been published. Finally, data are being collected in countries around the world, and interest in other forms of work-related commitment, and their interactions, is increasing.

To make the task of reviewing these developments more manageable, I will, like Griffin and Bateman, focus primarily on theory and research pertaining to organizational commitment. I will start by focusing on the results of recent meta-analytic investigations. Although the meta-analyses themselves were published within the time frame covered in this review (i.e. the 1990s), the studies included in these analyses were generally published much earlier. Consequently, the results of the meta-analyses provide a snapshot of the field as we entered the 1990s and serve to highlight the important substantive and methodological limitations that needed to be addressed. In subsequent sections of this review I will examine the progress that has been made in addressing these limitations, particularly as they pertain to the measurement of commitment and the investigation of its development and consequences. Although I will include the results of studies conducted outside North America and the UK in this discussion, I will not specifically address cross-cultural issues that arise from this research. Finally, I will conclude with some suggestions for the direction of commitment research in the future.

Organizational Commitment by John P. Meyer taken from IRIOP 1997 v12, Edited by Cary L. Cooper and Ivan T. Robertson: © 1997 John Wiley & Sons, Ltd

META-ANALYSES

The most comprehensive and widely cited meta-analytic review of the organizational commitment literature was that conducted by Mathieu and Zajac (1990). Mathieu and Zajac reported mean sample-weighted correlations, corrected for unreliability, between organizational commitment and 48 other work-related variables divided into three categories: antecedents (26), consequences (8), and correlates (14). I will organize my review of meta-analytic findings around these same three categories. Within each category, I will begin by summarizing the findings obtained by Mathieu and Zajac and then present the results of more recent analyses. The latter generally had a narrower focus and included more detailed assessments of moderator effects. Unless otherwise stated, all correlations reported in this section of the article are sample-weighted and corrected for attenuation due to unreliability.

Antecedents of Commitment

Among the variables Mathieu and Zajac (1990) classified as antecedents of commitment were those reflecting personal characteristics, job characteristics, group–leader relations, organizational characteristics, and role states. Of these, the strongest correlations were obtained for job characteristics, particularly job scope (enrichment), and group–leader relations (e.g. leader communication, participative leadership, task interdependence). Personal characteristics (with the exception of perceived personal competence) were generally found to have weak correlations with commitment. Sex was one of the personal characteristics found not to be related to commitment. Aven, Parker, and McEvoy (1993) confirmed this result in a more recent meta-analysis based on a larger set of studies. Few studies examined relations between commitment and organizational characteristics and those that did reported relatively weak correlations. Role states (ambiguity, conflict, overload) were not found to have meaningful links to commitment, although there was sufficient between-study variance to suggest that moderators might be operating.

Cohen and his colleagues conducted a series of meta-analyses to address more specific antecedent–commitment relations and potential moderating effects. For example, Cohen and Lowenberg (1990) reviewed the findings of studies conducted to test Becker's side-bet theory of commitment. According to Becker, commitment increases as employees make side-bets, or investments, that would be lost if they were to leave the organization. Cohen and Lowenberg found that the correlations between commitment and 11 side-bet variables (e.g. age, tenure, gender) were generally weak, and concluded that there is little evidence to support side-bet theory. They cautioned, however, that the side-bet and commitment measures used in the studies included in their analyses might not have been appropriate for testing side-bet theory (cf. Meyer & Allen, 1984).

Cohen (1992) tested for the moderating effect of occupation on the correlations between commitment and various personal and organizational antecedent variables. He found that commitment was more strongly related to personal characteristics (e.g. tenure, education, marital status, gender, motivation) for employees in blue-collar and non-professional white-collar occupations than for professionals. Correlations between commitment and organizational characteristics also varied across occupational groups, but the pattern was less consistent. For example, role ambiguity correlated more strongly with commitment among non-professionals, whereas autonomy and communication correlated more strongly with commitment among professionals. These latter findings suggest that, in general, the needs and preferences of members of these broad occupational groups differ, and that the commitment they experience varies as a function of whether these needs and preferences are satisfied at work.

In a related analysis, Cohen (1993a) examined the correlations between commitment and age and tenure within different career stages. He found that the correlation between age and commitment was stronger among younger employees (i.e. those under 30) than it was for the other age groups. In contrast, the correlation between tenure and commitment was greater among the more senior employees (i.e. those with more than nine years of experience). These findings suggest that the correlations involving age and tenure may not be linear, and might help to account for the relatively weak correlations reported by Mathieu and Zajac (1990).

Cohen and Gattiker (1994) used meta-analysis to examine the link between organizational commitment and rewards, operationalized as actual income and pay satisfaction. Across all studies, commitment was more strongly related to pay satisfaction than to actual income. These relations were moderated to some extent, however, by structural characteristics. Specifically, pay satisfaction correlated more strongly with commitment in the private versus public sector, and the correlation between actual income and commitment was greater for professional than for clerical employees.

Consequences of Commitment

Included in Mathieu and Zajac's (1990) 'consequence' category were job performance, perceived job alternatives, intention to search, intention to leave, attendance, lateness, and turnover. Not surprisingly, given the nature of the construct, the most widely investigated outcomes, and the ones with the strongest correlations with commitment (in order) were intention to search, intention to leave, and actual turnover. Correlations with the other outcome variables were disappointingly low, although there was some evidence to suggest that moderators might be operating. The only moderator variable considered by Mathieu and Zajac, however, was a methodological one. They found, in general, that relations between commitment and outcome measures were greater when an attitudinal rather than a calculative measure of commitment was used.

Randall (1990) also conducted a meta-analysis of studies examining the relations between commitment and various work outcomes. Her findings closely paralleled those of Mathieu and Zajac. In an examination of methodological moderator effects, Randall found that overall correlations tended to be slightly stronger (i) in studies using cross-sectional rather than longitudinal designs, (ii) for white-collar as opposed to blue-collar samples (a finding replicated by Cohen & Hudecek, 1993), (iii) when commitment was measured using the Organizational Commitment Questionnaire (OCQ: see Mowday, Steers, & Porter, 1979) rather than another instrument, and (iv) when objective or self-report measures of the outcome rather than supervisor ratings were used. These differences tended to be quite small, prompting Randall to conclude that the overall weak relations between commitment and behaviour cannot be explained from a methodological perspective.

Cohen (1991) examined the impact of career stage on the relation between commitment and various organizational outcomes. He found that, when age was used as the career indicator, the correlation between commitment and turnover (actual and intended) was greater among those in the early as opposed to middle or late career stages. He also found a moderating effect of career stage, defined in terms of tenure, on absenteeism and performance. In this case, the correlations were stronger for those in the late as opposed to early and middle career stages. Based on these findings, he concluded that organizations can benefit from the commitment of employees across career stages, but that the nature of the benefit (e.g. retention, performance) might differ. As for why age and tenure operated differently in moderating commitment–outcome relations, Cohen speculated that age, like turnover, has relevance not only for one's work, but for life in general. On the other hand, tenure, is a more work-specific variable, as are absenteeism and performance.

Finally, Cohen (1993b) tested for the interaction of two potential moderators of the correlation between commitment and turnover: time lapse between measures and career stage. He found evidence for such an interaction when career stage was defined in terms of age but not in terms of tenure. Although the strength of the correlation between commitment and turnover was stronger for younger employees when the interval between the measures was short, for older employees commitment predicted turnover better when the interval was longer. Cohen argued that this might be due to the fact that commitment is less stable in younger employees and, therefore, the longer the interval the more likely it is to change (along with the decision to stay or leave). In contrast, for older employees, commitment is likely to be more stable, but it might be more difficult for those with weak commitment to leave because of structural bonds, lack of alternatives, and so on. The longer the measurement interval, the more likely it is that uncommitted employees will find the means to overcome these obstacles.

Correlates of Commitment

Included in Mathieu and Zajac's (1990) category of 'correlates' of commitment were variables that, like commitment, reflect an employee's psychological reactions to work (e.g. motivation, job involvement, stress, union commitment, occupational commitment, job satisfaction). The causal connections between these variables and commitment are either unknown or the subject of debate. These variables showed some of the highest correlations with commitment of any included in the analyses. The magnitude of these correlations has raised concerns in the past about the potential for redundancy among the constructs themselves (e.g. Morrow, 1983). There is now considerable evidence, however, to suggest that construct redundancy is not a serious problem in the case of organizational commitment (e.g. Brooke, Russell, & Price, 1988; Meyer, Allen & Smith, 1993; Morrow, 1993; Mathieu & Farr, 1991; Randall & Cote, 1991; Reilly & Orsak, 1991). Nevertheless, the fact that organizational commitment is so strongly associated with these other reaction measures suggests a need to examine their connections more closely.

In a more recent meta-analysis, Wallace (1993) estimated the correlation between organizational commitment and professional commitment, a variable not included in Mathieu and Zajac's analysis. She reported a mean corrected correlation of 0.452, suggesting that commitment to an organization and a profession are not necessarily incompatible. This positive correlation does not rule out the possibility of differences in absolute levels of organizational and professional commitment, and does not preclude the possibility that conflicts might arise. Wallace also found evidence for moderator effects. Specifically, although positive in all cases, the magnitude of the correlation between professional and organizational commitment varied with degree of professionalization in an occupation and with position or rank in the employing organization. The correlations also varied depending on how professional commitment was conceptualized and measured (professional, occupational, or career commitment, or career salience). The latter finding is consistent with concerns recently expressed about the conceptualization and measurement of work commitments (see Morrow, 1993).

Summary and Implications

As noted earlier, these meta-analytic investigations serve two important purposes. First, they provide a summary of what we know about the relations between organizational commitment and other variables. The results of analyses involving antecedent variables, for example, suggest that commitment is more strongly related to characteristics of the job and work situation than to personal or structural characteristics. The analyses involving consequence variables indicate that, consistent with its historical roots (see Mowday, Porter, & Steers, 1982), commitment correlates most strongly with turnover (and related variables). Correlations with other outcome variables appear to be generally quite weak. The strongest correlations were obtained in analyses involving other 'reaction' measures. These correlations were not of sufficient magnitude, however, to suggest that organizational commitment is redundant with these other constructs (cf. Morrow, 1993).

It must be kept in mind that, although the variables included in these meta-analyses are commonly classified as antecedents, consequences, and correlates of commitment, the data used in these analyses were, for the most part, obtained in cross-sectional studies involving self-report measures. Thus, although the findings appear to reflect meaningful patterns with implications for how organizations might foster commitment in their employees and the consequences that might result, they must be interpreted with caution. At best, the results of these analyses help to place organizational commitment within a nomological network of work-related variables. The magnitudes of the correlations suggest that organizational commitment is meaningfully related to many of these variables, but the nature of the relations is as yet unclear.

A second, and arguably more important, contribution made by these meta-analyses is that they identified a number of limitations in commitment research that need to be addressed. Among the more frequently cited problems were (i) lack of clarity and consensus concerning the conceptualization and measurement of commitment, (ii) the atheoretical nature of antecedent research, including lack of attention to mediating mechanisms, (iii) the overly narrow focus of outcome research, with a general lack of attention to potential negative outcomes and to outcomes of more direct relevance to employees, (iv) the use of methods ill-suited to investigation of causal relations, and (v) the focus in both the antecedent and consequence research on main effects with a lack of systematic investigation of moderator effects. These concerns are, of course, not completely independent. In what follows, I will review recent developments in the commitment literature as they pertain to three broad issues, the conceptualization and measurement of organizational commitment, its development, and its consequences.

CONCEPTUALIZATION AND MEASUREMENT OF ORGANIZATIONAL COMMITMENT

Part of the difficulty in interpreting the results of studies (individual or meta-analytic) designed to examine the development and consequences of organizational commitment is the fact that commitment has been defined and measured in many different ways. Moreover, the definitions and measures used within a given study do not always correspond (cf. Meyer & Allen, 1984, 1991). Recent efforts to clarify the meaning of organizational commitment and to refine its measurement have taken two distinct directions. The first involved attempts to clarify the construct by illustrating that commitment can take different forms. That is, the nature of the commitment that defines the relationship between an employee and an organization can vary. The second involved making distinctions among specific entities within the organization to which employees become committed. These two approaches at classification are not incompatible. After discussing each individually, I will conclude this section with a discussion of how, in combination, the two approaches help to clarify our understanding of organizational commitment, how it develops, and its implications for individuals and organizations.

The Nature of the Commitment

Although there is a growing consensus that commitment is a multidimensional construct, various approaches have been taken to identify its dimensions. I will focus my discussion here on two of these approaches. In each case, I will describe the distinctions that have been made and, where relevant, will discuss the development and evaluation of measures. Unless it is relevant to the evaluation of measures, I will reserve discussion of research using these measures to address substantive issues (e.g. development and consequences) for subsequent sections.

Allen and Meyer (1990b, Meyer & Allen, 1991) developed a multidimensional model of commitment based on their observation that existing definitions of the construct reflected at least three distinct themes. Specifically, commitment has been viewed as an affective orientation toward the organization (e.g. Mowday, Porter, & Steers, 1982), a recognition of costs associated with leaving the organization (e.g. Becker, 1960), and a moral obligation to remain with the organization (e.g. Weiner, 1982). Common to these perspectives 'is the view that commitment is a psychological state that (a) characterizes the employee's relationship with the organization, and (b) has implications for the decision to continue membership in the organization' (Meyer & Allen, 1991, p. 67). Thus, regardless of the definition, committed employees are more likely to remain in the organization than are uncommitted employees. What differs is the nature of the psychological state being described.

Meyer and Allen (1991) argued that the psychological states reflected in these different definitions of commitment are not mutually exclusive, and that a clearer understanding of an employee's relationship with an organization can be gained by considering the strength of all three. In developing their model, therefore, they referred to these states as components, rather than types, of commitment and gave each an identifying label: affective (emotional attachment), continuance (cost-based), and normative (obligation). Finally, Meyer and Allen reasoned that the psychological states reflected in the three components of commitment would develop on the basis of quite different experiences (antecedents) and have potentially different implications for employees' behaviour (consequences), other than their tendency to remain in the organization.

Allen and Meyer (1990b) developed measures to be used in testing the three-component model. The Affective (ACS), Continuance (CCS), and Normative (NCS) Commitment Scales have been subjected to fairly extensive psychometric evaluation and have received considerable support (see Allen & Meyer, in press, for a review). For example, the three scales were found in both exploratory (Allen & Meyer, 1990b; McGee & Ford, 1987; Reilly & Orsak, 1991) and confirmatory (Dunham, Grube, & Castaneda, 1994; Hackett, Bycio, & Hausdorf, 1994; Meyer, Allen, & Gellatly, 1990; Moorman, Niehoff, & Organ, 1993; Shore & Tetrick, 1991; Somers, 1993; Vandenberghe, in press) factor analyses to measure distinguishable constructs. Moreover, studies that have examined the links between the three commitment scales and various antecedent and consequence measures (e.g. Allen & Meyer, 1990b; Bycio, Hackett, & Allen, 1995; Dunham, Grube, & Castaneda, 1994; Hackett, Bycio, & Hausdorf, 1994; Konovsky & Cropanzano, 1991; Meyer, Allen, & Smith, 1993; Randall, Fedor, & Longenecker, 1990; Shore & Wayne, 1993; Whitener & Walz, 1993) have generally found a pattern of correlations consistent with the predictions generated from the model. Finally, the three commitment constructs have been found in factor analyses to be distinguishable from related constructs including job satisfaction (Shore & Tetrick, 1991), career, job, and work values (Blau, Paul, & St. John, 1993); career commitment (Reilly & Orsak, 1991), occupational commitment (Meyer, Allen, & Smith, 1993), and perceived organizational support (Shore & Tetrick, 1991). Shore and Tetrick found that items from the ACS loaded on the same factor as items from the OCQ, which is consistent with the view that the OCQ measures primarily affective commitment (cf. Allen & Meyer, 1990b).

In spite of this supportive evidence, there have been findings that suggest the need for further refinement of the Allen and Meyer (1990b) measures. Most notably, the CCS has been found in some studies to comprise two related dimensions, one reflecting lack of alternatives, and the other high personal sacrifice (Hackett, Bycio, & Hausdorf, 1994; Meyer, Allen, & Gellatly, 1990, McGee & Ford, 1987; Sommers, 1993). The implications of this are unclear at this point. McGee and Ford found that the two subscales correlated in opposite directions with affective commitment and concluded that they measure somewhat different constructs. They advocated further development of the subscales. In contrast, others have found that the two dimensions/subscales are highly related and correlated similarly with other constructs (e.g. Hackett, Bycio, & Hausdorf, 1994; Meyer, Paunonen, Gellatly, Goffin, & Jackson, 1989). These findings, combined with evidence that the internal consistency of the full CCS is acceptable (Allen & Meyer, in press), suggest that there may be little to be gained by further development of the subscales. Nevertheless, users might be wise to evaluate the utility of using subscales on a case by case basis until this issue is resolved (Meyer, Allen, & Gellatly, 1990).

Studies have also revealed stronger than expected correlations between the ACS and NCS, suggesting that feelings of affective attachment and sense of obligation to an organization are not independent of one another (e.g. Hackett, Bycio, & Hausdorf, 1994). The two scales also tend to show similar patterns of correlation with antecedent and outcome measures; the correlations involving the ACS tend to be somewhat stronger than those involving the NCS, however (see Allen & Meyer, in press). A recent modification of the NCS did not correct these problems (Meyer, Allen, & Smith, 1993).

Finally, Vandenberg and Self (1993) found that the factor structure of the ACS and CCS was somewhat unstable during the early months of employment, and cautioned that the scales might not be appropriate for use with new employees. Meyer and Gardner (1994) conducted similar analysis, however, and found little evidence of instability. The difference in findings might be due to differences in the timing of measurement in the two studies; Vandenberg and Self obtained their measures after one day, one month and three months, whereas the measures examined by Meyer and Gardner were administered after one, six and 12 months. In light of these findings, researchers wanting to use the ACS and CCS to examine changes in commitment, and/or its correlations with other variables over time, should determine that the factor structure is indeed stable over the time frame examined.

O'Reilly and his colleagues (e.g. Caldwell, Chatman, & O'Reilly, 1990; O'Reilly & Chatman, 1986) took a somewhat different approach to categorizing the various forms of commitment. Like Meyer and Allen (1991), they argued that commitment reflects the 'psychological bond' that ties the employee to the organization, but that the nature of the bond can differ. Following from Kelman's (1958) work on attitude and behaviour change, they suggest that the psychological bond between an employee and an organization can take three distinct forms which they labelled compliance, identification, and internalization. Compliance occurs when employees adopt certain attitudes and behaviours in order to gain reward. Identification involves the acceptance of influence to maintain a satisfying relationship. Internalization occurs when the induced attitudes and behaviours are congruent with the employee's own values. O'Reilly and Chatman argued that an employee's psychological attachment to an organization can reflect varying combinations of each of these three psychological foundations.

O'Reilly and Chatman (1986) proposed that the behavioural consequences of the three forms of commitment might be quite different. To illustrate, they developed measures of compliance, identification, and internalization and examined their relations with several outcome measures (e.g. prosocial behaviour, turnover intention, and turnover). Identification and internalization were negatively related to turnover intention and turnover and positively related to prosocial behaviour. Moreover, in some analyses it was found that identification and internalization each accounted for unique variance in the outcome measures. Compliance showed the opposite pattern of relations and was also found to contribute uniquely to the prediction of turnover intention.

Although it served to sensitize researchers to the multidimensional nature of commitment, the impact of O'Reilly's classification system has been weakened somewhat by the fact that it has been difficult to distinguish identification and internalization (e.g. Caldwell, Chatman, & O'Reilly, 1990; O'Reilly, Chatman, & Caldwell, 1991; Sutton & Harrison, 1993; Vandenberg, Self, & Seo, 1994); the measures tend to correlate highly with one another and to show similar patterns of correlations with measures of other variables (for an exception, see Harris, Hirschfeld, Feild, & Mossholder, 1993). In fact, in their more recent research (Caldwell, Chatman, & O'Reilly, 1990; O'Reilly, Chatman, & Caldwell, 1991), O'Reilly and his colleagues combined the identification and internalization items to form a measure of what they called normative commitment. (Note that this construct corresponds more closely to affective commitment in Meyer and Allen's (1991) model and should not be confused with the latter's use of the term normative commitment.) Furthermore, although compliance (also referred to as instrumental commitment in more recent work) is clearly distinct from identification and internalization, one might question whether it can truly be considered commitment. For example, whereas commitment is generally assumed to reduce turnover (Mowday, Porter, & Steers, 1982), compliance has been found to correlate positively with employee turnover (O'Reilly & Chatman, 1986).

Before turning to a discussion of the focus of commitment, it should be noted that there have been several other attempts to identify and measure different forms of commitment, and to determine how these measures related to other (antecedent and consequence) variables (e.g., Jaros, Jermier, Koehler, & Sincich, 1993; Mayer & Schoorman, 1992; Penley & Gould, 1988). Space does not permit me to describe these different approaches in detail. It is important to note, however, that in some cases the same labels are used to describe quite different forms of commitment whereas, in other cases, different labels are used to describe very similar forms. Consumers of this research should, therefore, rely more on the construct definitions, or on the scale items, than on labels to determine what form of commitment is actually being measured.

The Focus of Commitment

Reichers (1985) noted that, in the organizational commitment literature, the 'organization' has typically been 'viewed as a monolithic, undifferentiated entity that elicits an identification and attachment on the part of the individual' (p. 469). She argued that, in reality, organizations comprise various 'coalitions and constituencies' (e.g. owners/managers; rank and file employees, customers/ clients), each with its own goals and values that might or might not be compatible with the goals of the organization per se. Therefore, organizational commitment can best be understood as a collection of multiple commitments. This raises the possibility that (i) employees can have varying commitment profiles, and (ii) conflict can exist among an employee's commitments.

Reichers (1986) provided some preliminary support for this multiple-constituency perspective. More recently, Becker (1992) provided additional support by demonstrating that employees' commitments to top management, immediate supervisor, and work group contributed significantly beyond commitment to the organization to the prediction of job satisfaction, intention to quit, and prosocial organizational behaviour. Based on a reanalysis of Becker's data, however, Hunt and Morgan (1994) suggested that commitment to specific constituencies might be better viewed as exerting their influence on these outcomes through their effects on overall commitment to the organization. Nevertheless, they also noted that this mediating effect might be strongest for constituencies that are psychologically closer to the organization (e.g. top management, supervisor), and that direct effects of commitment to constituencies might be expected for outcomes that are of more direct relevance to that constituency.

In another analysis of these data, Becker and Billings (1993) used cluster analysis to identify commitment profiles (i.e. differing patterns of commitment to the various constituencies within the organization). They found four dominant profiles: '(1) the Locally Committed (employees who are attached to their supervisor and work group), (2) the Globally Committed (employees who are attached to top management and the organization), (3) the Committed (employees who are attached to both local and global foci), and (4) the Uncommitted (employees who are attached to neither local nor global foci)' (p. 177). Employees who were committed to both local and global foci had the highest level of overall job satisfaction, were least likely to intend to leave, and demonstrated the highest levels of prosocial behaviour. The locally and globally committed employees did not differ from one another in terms of general attitudes and behaviour, falling between the committed and uncommitted in all cases. Interestingly, however, when attitudes and prosocial behaviour directed at the supervisor and work group were assessed, both were found to be higher among the locally committed than among the globally committed. Again, this suggests that the benefits of assessing commitments to specific constituencies are more likely to be realized in attempts to predict constituency-relevant behaviour.

Cohen (1993c) measured commitment to the organization, occupation, union, and job in a sample of 129 white-collar employees from three organizations. He hypothesized that behaviour of relevance to a particular constituency would be best predicted by commitment to that constituency. The findings provided some support for this hypothesis. For example, the best predictor of intention to leave the organization was organizational commitment, whereas job commitment was the best predictor of job withdrawal, and union commitment was the best predictor of perceived union success. Interestingly, there was also some evidence that prediction could be enhanced by considering commitments other than that to the most relevant constituency. For example, occupational commitment contributed *positively* to the prediction of both organizational and job withdrawal intention. Job commitment contributed positively to the prediction of union activity, and occupational commitment contributed negatively to the prediction of perceived union success. The latter findings indicate that there is a potential for both compatibility and conflict among commitments.

Lawler (1992) also noted that organizations are composed of multiple subgroups. He referred to these subgroups as 'nested collectives' because each subgroup is subsumed by a larger group (e.g. work teams are part of departments, which are part of divisions, and so on). Lawler further argued that the amount of affect employees have to invest in these collectives is fixed and, therefore, the more they invest in one, the less they will have to invest in others. Finally, he proposed that employees will be most committed to the collective that is seen to afford them the greatest opportunity for self control. Typically, this is the smaller, more proximal, group (e.g. a work team). Thus, employees are more likely to develop attachments to subgroups within the organization than to the organization itself.

Although Lawler's (1992) theory has yet to receive much empirical investigation, a recent study by Yoon, Baker, and Ko (1994) is relevant. They measured commitment to the organization as well as interpersonal attachments to persons with higher or lower positions in their local work unit (vertical attachment) and to co-workers (horizontal attachments) in a large sample of employees from 62 Korean organizations. They argued that, if a subgroup approach such as that advocated by Lawler is correct, organizational commitment should correlate positively with vertical attachments and negatively with horizontal attachments. Although they found that vertical attachments correlated more strongly with organizational commitment than did horizontal attachments, the correlation with horizontal attachments was also positive. The latter finding is more consistent with a 'cohesion approach' suggesting that attachment (commitment) to subunits within the organization enhances commitment to the larger collective (i.e. the organization).

In summary, although the multiple-constituency framework has not been tested extensively, preliminary evidence indicates that there may be some value in measuring commitments to more specific foci within the organization. Existing evidence, however, does not negate the value of measuring organizational commitment at a global level. Becker (1992) found fairly strong correlations between global commitment and job satisfaction, turnover intention, and prosocial organizational behaviour. Although significant, the increment in prediction contributed by commitment to specific foci was small. It should be kept in mind, however, that when we measure commitment to the organization as a whole, we are probably measuring employees' commitment to 'top management' (Reichers, 1986), or to a combination of top management and more local subgroups (Becker & Billings, 1993; Hunt & Morgan, 1994). If our intention is to use commitment as a means of understanding or predicting behaviour of relevance to the organization as a whole (or to top management specifically), it would seem that our purpose can be well served with global measures of organizational commitment. If, on the other hand, we are interested in behaviour of relevance to more specific constituencies (e.g. the work team), better understanding and prediction might be afforded by a measure of commitment to the relevant constituency (Cohen, 1993c).

An Integration of the Multidimensional Approaches

As illustrated above, commitment can be considered multidimensional both in its form and its focus. These two approaches to developing a multidimensional framework are not incompatible. Indeed, one can envision a two-dimensional matrix with different forms of commitment listed along one axis, and the different foci along the other. The various cells within this matrix then reflect the nature of the commitment an employee has toward each individual constituency of relevance to him or her. Note that this matrix should not be used to classify employees. Rather, each employee's commitment profile should reflect varying degrees of different forms of commitment to each of the different constituencies.

At this time, it is not clear how commitments within the various cells of this two-dimensional matrix might relate to one another. According to Lawler's (1992) nested-collectives theory, there might be some dependencies, particularly among the cells reflecting affective attachments. Moreover, following Lawler's logic, if strong affective attachments to nested subgroups within the organizations are accompanied by a lower level of attachment to the organization, an interesting situation is created. In order to maintain their membership in the smaller unit, employees must remain in the larger organization, in spite of relatively low levels of affective commitment. This 'need' to remain might reflect what Allen and Meyer (1990b; Meyer & Allen, 1991) called continuance commitment. Consequently, there may be dependencies across both focus and form of commitment. Although the findings of Yoon, Baker, and Ko (1994) did not provide strong support for Lawler's theory, they too suggested a complex set of relations among commitments.

Combining the two multidimensional perspectives creates a potentially very complex model of commitment that becomes virtually impossible to test, or use, in its entirety. Nevertheless, acknowledging the complex multidimensional structure of commitment should serve to raise awareness of the fact that, in trying to understand how employees' commitment develops and relates to behaviour, we must frame our research questions more precisely than we have in the past. That is, we must specify clearly the form of commitment, and the constituency to which it is directed.

DEVELOPMENT OF COMMITMENT

There continues to be a considerable amount of research conducted to investigate the development of commitment. Although the strategy of correlating commitment with variables presumed to be its antecedents is less common today than it was during the 1970s and 80s, studies of this type are still being conducted. Typically, however, the objective of these studies has been to illustrate that different components of commitment have different antecedents (see Allen and Meyer, in press, for a review of this research as it pertains to their three-component model). In this section I will focus on three relatively recent lines of research. First, I will describe the results of studies that have used path analytic or structural equation modelling procedures to examine the 'causal' connections presumed to exist between commitment and its antecedents. Next, I will discuss theory and research pertaining to the development process (i.e. the mechanisms through which various antecedent variables exert their influence on commitment). Finally, on a more practical note, I will review the results of recent research that sheds some light on the role played by organizational human resource management (HRM) policies and practices in the development of employees' commitment.

Causal Models

Among the concerns expressed by reviewers about the earlier antecedent literature were that (i) it was largely atheoretical, and (ii) the methods used were not appropriate for establishing causal direction. More recently, there has been an increase in the use of structural equation modelling procedures to examine the development of commitment. Although they still rely on correlational data, these procedures allow more confidence in inferences about causal connections than do simple bivariate correlations. Moreover, appropriate use of these procedures requires an *a priori* theoretical rationale for the ordering of variables.

My intent here is not to provide an exhaustive review of structural equation modelling studies, but rather to provide some illustrative examples. I will first describe a series of studies designed to establish causal ordering among antecedent variables identified in earlier research. I will then summarize the results of several studies of relevance to the long-standing debate over whether job satisfaction influences organizational commitment or commitment influences job satisfaction.

Causal ordering of antecedents

Mathieu and his colleagues (Mathieu, 1988, 1991; Mathieu & Hamel, 1989) conducted a series of studies to examine the causal ordering of antecedent variables. Although, in each of these studies, self-report data were collected on a single occasion, what distinguished them from earlier antecedent studies was the use of path analysis to test theory-based causal models. In these models, variables believed to be antecedent to commitment were ordered in terms of causal priority on the basis of Lewin's (1943) field theory. According to field theory, employees' reactions to their environment (e.g. commitment to the organization) should be primarily a function of their perceptions of, and reactions to, proximal elements in their environment or life space (e.g. work experiences and satisfaction). Environmental and personal characteristics are considered to be more distal causes that are likely to exert their influence on commitment indirectly through the more proximal causes.

Mathieu (1988) tested a model of the development process in a military training context. He measured variables from each of the four broad antecedent categories identified in previous work (i.e. personal characteristics, role states, job characteristics, and work experiences), and ordered them in accord with field theory predictions. For example, personal characteristics and role states were expected to exert their influence indirectly through perceptions of, and reactions to, the training experience (i.e. training characteristics and satisfaction with training, respectively). Although the original model was found to fit the data reasonably well, Mathieu found that a revised model fitted the data better. Training characteristics continued to have the strongest direct effect on commitment, but some of the variables expected initially to have only indirect effects (e.g. achievement motivation, role strain) were found to have direct effects as well. In a similar study conducted with a larger sample, Mathieu (1991) found that general job satisfaction, when measured in place of satisfaction with training, had the strongest direct effect on commitment, and that all other variables, with the exception of achievement motivation, had only indirect effects.

Mathieu and Hamel (1989) developed a causal model to be tested in a non-military context. Data were obtained from professionals and non-professionals in two government agencies and a state university. They found that, in general, the two most proximal causes of organizational commitment were job satisfaction and mental health. Job and personal characteristics (and their interaction), as well as role strain and organizational characteristics, were all found to exert their effects indirectly through the more proximal causes. The strength of some of the indirect effects was found to differ between professionals and non-professionals, however.

Mathieu and his colleagues speculated that some of their findings might have been unique to the samples they used (i.e. military and government). Moreover, there are no doubt other important antecedent variables and mediating and moderating effects that they did not consider. Nevertheless, their findings should provide some guidance for future research.

Job satisfaction and commitment

We know from the meta-analytic findings reviewed above that commitment and satisfaction are highly related, but there has been no consensus about whether, or how, the two variables are causally connected. The findings of earlier attempts to address this issue produced mixed results. Consequently, as structural equation modelling procedures have become more sophisticated, researchers have continued to revisit this issue.

Mathieu (1991) and Lance (1991) conducted cross-sectional studies that permitted them to test for both non-recursive and recursive effects. Both found evidence for an asymmetrical reciprocal relation. That is, satisfaction and commitment were found to exert effects on each other, but the effect of satisfaction on commitment was greater than the effect of commitment on satisfaction.

Farkas and Tetrick (1989) applied structural equation modelling procedures to longitudinal data and found evidence to suggest that the causal ordering of satisfaction and commitment reverses over time, perhaps reflecting either cyclical or reciprocal effects. Vandenberg and Lance (1992) also collected longitudinal data but tested only for causal effects within-time. Their findings provided the strongest support for a commitment–causes–satisfaction model.

It appears from the results of these studies that the relation between job satisfaction and commitment might be quite complex. It is not clear at this point whether we will ever be able to determine which, if either, is causally prior. From the standpoint of understanding how organizational commitment develops, this might not be a crucial issue. It might, however, be more important in the consideration of how satisfaction and commitment relate to behaviour. I will address this issue again in the discussion of the consequences of commitment.

The Development Process

Although the results of analyses designed to evaluate the causal ordering of antecedent variables are a significant advance over previous research, they still do not address the issue of how or why these variables are related to commitment. Relatively little attention has been given to explaining or investigating the mechanisms through which the various antecedent variables exert their influence on commitment. It appears that most studies have been conducted under the assumption that commitment develops on the principle of exchange; employees commit themselves to organizations that provide them with desired outcomes. Hence, commitment is generally expected (and found) to correlate positively with desirable work characteristics and conditions, and negatively with undesirable ones. Although it might well be the case that exchange principles operate in the development of commitment, the recent recognition that commitment can take different forms makes it evident that the picture is more complicated than this.

To illustrate, consider affective, continuance, and normative commitment as described by Meyer and Allen (1991). Each represents a relatively distinct psychological state and relates somewhat differently to behaviour, yet the development of each can be explained, in part, using the principle of exchange. That is, employees who encounter positive experiences at work can develop a desire to remain and contribute (affective commitment), or a sense of moral obligation to do so (normative commitment). Moreover, if employees recognize that leaving the organization would require them to give up some of the benefits they derive from membership, they might feel a need to remain (continuance commitment). Clearly, then, there is more to the development of commitment than simple exchange.

There is little evidence in the literature of a systematic attempt to examine the development process. Nevertheless, there are several lines of research that come closer to addressing what might be considered 'mechanisms' in the development process than has been the case in the past. I will briefly discuss five such mechanisms: person–job fit, met-expectations, causal attribution, organizational justice and support, and retrospective rationalization. In most cases, the research pertaining to these mechanisms has been concerned with the development of affective commitment. In some cases, however, there might also be implications for the development of other forms of commitment as I will illustrate.

Person–job fit

It has long been argued that employees will be more satisfied with their jobs to the extent that there is a good match between what the person is looking for in a job and what the job provides (cf. Dawis, 1992; Locke, 1976). It is only recently, however, that person–job fit has been examined as a factor in the development of commitment (e.g. Meglino, Ravlin, & Adkins, 1989; Vancouver & Schmitt, 1991; O'Reilly, Chatman, & Caldwell, 1991).

Tests of the person–job fit hypothesis have typically involved computing an index of fit and correlating it with an outcome measure of interest. Consistent with this practice, Meglino, Ravlin, and Adkins (1989) computed the rank order correlations between employees' values and those of supervisors and management, O'Reilly, Chatman, and Caldwell (1991) obtained correlations between employees' culture preference ratings and measures of perceived organizational culture, and Vancouver and Schmitt (1991) calculated the sum of squared differences (reflected) between subordinate and supervisor goals. In all three studies, these fit indices were found to correlate positively with commitment.

Whether these findings can be taken as evidence to support the person–job fit hypothesis is unclear in light of recent concerns raised by Edwards and his colleagues (e.g. Edwards, 1991, 1993, 1994; Edwards & Cooper, 1990) about the meaningfulness of the fit indices used in these studies. Edwards suggested an alternative set of procedures for testing the person–job fit hypothesis, but these have yet to be applied to test the hypothesis as it pertains to the development of commitment. This is an area where further research is needed.

A related line of research has been to examine the interaction of person and job (or organization) characteristics in the prediction of commitment (e.g.

Blau, 1987; Meyer, Irving, & Allen, in press). (See Edwards and Cooper [1990] for a discussion of the difference between person–job fit and person x situation interaction.) The findings have been mixed. Whereas Blau found no evidence of a person x situation interaction in the prediction of commitment, Meyer, Irving, and Allen did. The findings reported by Meyer, Irving, and Allen, however, were not completely consistent with prediction. Although they found that experiences that contributed to employees' comfort in the organization had a stronger influence on commitment among those who placed greater value on such experiences, the opposite was found to be true for competence-related experiences. That is, the effect of competence-bolstering experiences on commitment (both affective and normative) was greater for those who initially placed less importance on such experiences. Although this somewhat counterintuitive finding was found to replicate, Meyer, Irving, and Allen could only speculate on why it occurred. Again, in light of the inconsistent and somewhat unexpected results obtained to date, this is an area where additional research is needed (cf. Mathieu & Zajac, 1990).

Met-expectations

Related to the notion that employees will be more committed to organizations when they encounter a good fit is the hypothesis that commitment will be greater when employees' experiences on the job match their pre-entry expectations (e.g. Wanous, 1980). This 'met-expectations' hypothesis has been tested in several studies and, in a recent meta-analysis, Wanous, Poland, Premack, and Davis (1992) reported a corrected average correlation of 0.39 between indices of met expectations and commitment. As was the case with person–job fit, however, there are problems associated with the procedures that have commonly been used to test the met-expectations hypothesis (see Irving & Meyer, 1994, 1995). Consequently, this correlation must be interpreted with some caution.

Irving and Meyer (1994) tested the met-expectations hypothesis using analytic procedures similar to those recommended by Edwards (1991) for tests of the person–job fit hypothesis. They found only modest support for the hypothesis. Instead, their findings suggested that commitment was greater among employees who reported positive work experiences during the early months of employment regardless of what they initially expected. Major, Kozlowski, Chao, and Gardner (1995) found that unmet expectations did have a negative impact on commitment, but that this effect was ameliorated by positive relations with managers and coworkers. Clearly, it is premature to draw firm conclusions about the role that confirmation of expectations plays in the development of commitment. There appears to be considerable agreement, however, that the first year of employment is an important time for the development of commitment (e.g. Louis, 1980; Wanous, 1980) and, therefore, more research is needed to determine how expectations and experiences combine to shape commitment during this period. Care must be taken, however, to ensure that appropriate methods are used to examine these effects.

Causal attribution

There is considerable evidence to suggest that commitment is associated with positive work experiences. The person–job fit and met-expectations hypotheses suggest the possibility that the impact of these experiences might be moderated by individual differences in needs/values and expectations. Another potential moderator is the attribution employees make for these experiences (Meyer & Allen, 1991). That is, having positive experiences at work might be more likely to contribute to the development of an affective attachment to the organization if employees view the organization as having been responsible for those experiences than if they attribute their existence to other sources (e.g. union, profession, job).

Although this attribution hypothesis has not yet been evaluated systematically, on one direct test of the hypothesis, Meyer and Allen (1995) found some evidence for a moderating effect of attribution on the relations between work experiences and their affective reactions to their organizations, jobs, and immediate supervisors. Other evidence for the role played by attributions was provided by Koys (1988, 1991) who found that the impact of desirable HRM practices on commitment was greater when employees believed that they reflected the organization's concern for the employees rather than an attempt to satisfy legal requirements. Similarly, Mellor (1992) found that employees were less committed to their union when they were led to attribute the need for organizational downsizing to the union.

Additional research is needed to determine whether, and to what extent, attribution processes are involved in the development of commitment. Evidence in support of the attribution hypothesis would help to explain inconsistencies across studies in the magnitude of correlations between specific antecedent variables and commitment. It might also help us to understand when and how various experiences are likely to influence commitment to the different constituencies within and outside organizations.

Organizational justice and support

Although it is not entirely clear whether organizational justice and support can be considered process variables *per se*, it might be argued that employees evaluate their experiences at work in terms of whether they are fair and/or they reflect a concern on the part of the organization for the well-being of the employees. If so, perceptions of justice and support could be considered more proximal causes of commitment than, say, job characteristics or organizational policies and practices. If these more distal causes exert their influence on commitment by shaping perceptions of justice and support, the latter take on the role of mediating mechanisms. At any rate, both organizational justice and support are receiving increased attention in the commitment literature, and warrant some discussion.

Like commitment, organizational justice is now generally viewed as a multi-dimensional construct (see Greenberg, 1990, 1993). Perhaps most relevant to the present discussion is the distinction made between the fairness of outcomes received (distributive justice) and fairness of the procedures used in determining outcomes (procedural justice). Several studies have been conducted to examine the relative strength of these two forms of justice on organizational commitment. For example, Folger and Konovsky (1989) used measures of distributive and procedural justice concerning pay raises to predict employees' pay satisfaction and organizational commitment. They found that perceptions of distributive justice accounted for more variance in pay satisfaction than did procedural justice, whereas procedural justice perceptions accounted for more variance in commitment. Similar results were reported by Sweeney and McFarlin (1993) and Konovsky and Cropanzano (1991). Together the findings support the more general position advanced by Lind and Tyler (1988) that 'procedural justice has especially strong effects on attitudes about institutions or authorities, as opposed to attitudes about specific outcomes in question' (p. 179).

These findings suggest that employees' commitment to the organization might be shaped, at least in part, by their perceptions of how fairly they are treated by the organization. Additional evidence for this claim will be provided when I discuss the impact of HRM practices on commitment below. Whether justice perceptions themselves have a direct or indirect effect on commitment is not clear. One possibility suggested in the justice literature is that, by treating employees fairly, organizations communicate their commitment to employees (e.g. Folger & Konovsky, 1989). That is, the effect of justice perceptions on commitment might be mediated by perceptions of the organization's commitment to employees.

The idea that employees become committed to organizations that demonstrate commitment to them is consistent with an exchange theory perspective. To my knowledge, however, there has been no attempt to define or measure 'organizational commitment to employees.' A construct that comes close is organizational support (Eisenberger, Huntington, Hutchison, & Sowa, 1986). Eisenberger et al. developed a 17-item instrument, the Survey of Perceived Organizational Support (SPOS), to measure employees' 'global beliefs concerning the extent to which the organization values their contributions and cares about their well-being' (p. 501). The SPOS has been found in several studies (e.g. Eisenberger, Fasolo, & Davis-LaMastro, 1990; Guzzo, Noonan, & Elron, 1994; Shore & Tetrick, 1991; Shore & Wayne, 1993; Smith & Meyer, 1996) to correlate positively with measures of affective commitment (i.e. the OCQ and ACS). There is also some evidence that the SPOS correlates positively with normative commitment (Smith & Meyer, 1996), but not with continuance commitment (Shore & Wayne, 1993; Smith & Meyer, 1996).

These findings are potentially important, and suggest that organizations wanting to foster a greater affective (or normative) commitment in their employees might do so by first providing evidence of their commitment to employees. The SPOS measures employees' perceptions of two aspects of such commitment (valuing employees' contribution and concern for their well-being). There may be other aspects of commitment to employees, however, that are not tapped by the SPOS (e.g. providing job security). This would seem to be a construct deserving of further development.

Retrospective rationalization

The mechanisms discussed to this point might best be considered examples of prospective rationality. That is, commitment develops on the basis of an assessment of what benefits are being, or will be, derived from association with the organization. Another possibility that derives largely from research in the behavioral commitment literature, is that psychological (particularly affective) commitment develops in an effort to justify previous behaviours or decisions (e.g. Kiesler, 1971; Salancik, 1977). Kiesler and Salancik identified several conditions under which a behaviour, once initiated, will tend to be repeated. These include freedom of choice, irrevocability, explicitness, publicness, and importance. Commitment to remain in an organization, therefore, should be greater when the employee feels that he/she freely chose to work for the organization, the decision cannot be undone, others know about the decision, and so on. Moreover, to be consistent with their behaviour, employees might be expected to develop a positive reaction (affective commitment) to the organization. The latter is typically explained in terms of dissonance reduction or self-justification processes (e.g. Mowday Porter, & Steers, 1982).

Retrospective rationalization processes are difficult to study and most of the evidence provided to illustrate its role in the development of organizational commitment has come from findings obtained in laboratory research (see Salancik, 1977). One exception was a study by O'Reilly and Caldwell (1981). Two more recent studies were conducted to extend the findings of O'Reilly and Caldwell. Meyer, Bobocel, and Allen (1991), like O'Reilly and Caldwell, used proxy measures of the conditions assumed to bind employees to their decision. For example, number of job offers was used as one index of volition. Of the binding variables measured (volition, irrevocability, importance), only volition was found to be positively related to commitment. Although this could be taken as evidence of retrospective rationalization, Meyer, Bobocel, and Allen argued that it might also reflect prospective rationality (i.e. those who have more choice chose better jobs). Consistent with the latter explanation, the correlation between volition and affective commitment became non-significant when perceived quality of decision was controlled. Also of interest was the finding that irrevocability (e.g. difficulty of finding another job) was not related to affective commitment as expected. Rather, it was found to correlate positively with continuance commitment (i.e. perceived cost of leaving).

Kline and Peters (1991) measured the binding variables (volition, irrevocability, publicness) directly with self-report scales administered on the first day of employment. Consistent with the retrospective rationalization hypothesis, they found that commitment correlated positively with volition and publicness and negatively with revocability (presumably the inverse of irrevocability). Of course, the positive correlation with volition could reflect quality of choice. Moreover, although revocability, as measured, was assumed to be the inverse of irrevocability, this might not have been true. For example, a negative response to the item 'I am trying out this job to see if it works out' does not necessarily imply irrevocability. It could reflect anticipated satisfaction with the job/organization. Thus, Kline and Peter's findings cannot be taken as unequivocal support for the retrospective rationalization hypothesis.

At best, the findings concerning the impact of retrospective rationality processes in the development of commitment are mixed. Past experimental evidence suggests that these processes do operate and can help to explain attitude development. There is also evidence that these effects can occur in applied settings (Staw, 1974). It is not clear, however, whether these findings have relevance for organizations wanting to foster commitment in their employees. Ethical issues aside, it might be difficult to create the conditions necessary to include retrospective rationalization processes. Failure to do so could result in organizations increasing employees' continuance rather than their affective commitment as intended (Meyer, Bobocel, & Allen, 1991).

Organizational Policies and Practices

Another line of antecedent research of relatively recent origin is the investigation of the impact of HRM policies and practices on commitment. Unlike most of the earlier antecedent research that examined employees' perceptions of their immediate work context (e.g. job characteristics, work experiences), this research focuses on the policies and practices that serve, in part, to shape those perceptions. Although HRM policies and practices are likely to be more distal antecedents of commitment, one advantage of considering them is that they are under more direct control by the organization. Again, most research to date has focused on efforts designed to foster affective commitment. This is because (i) it is only recently that multidimensional models and measures of commitment have been developed, and (ii) affective commitment has arguably the most desirable consequences for an organization.

Recruitment and selection

There has not been a great deal of research examining the impact of recruitment and selection practices on commitment, although a number of studies have provided data of relevance to this issue. For example, Premack and Wanous (1985), in their meta-analyses of effects of realistic job previews (RJP), found a positive, albeit weak, effect on commitment. As noted earlier, Wanous et al. (1992) found that met expectations, one of the intended effects of RJPs, was positively related to commitment. Although the latter finding must be interpreted with some caution because of methodological weaknesses in the studies included in the meta-analysis (see Irving & Meyer, 1994, 1995), there is at least some indication that organizational recruitment practices might contribute to the early development of commitment. More research is needed to examine this influence.

Mowday, Porter, and Steers (1982) argued that employees entering an organization might differ in their propensity to become committed. They identified three broad categories of variables that, together, determine propensity: personal characteristics (e.g. desire to establish a career in an organization, self-efficacy), pre-entry expectations, and organizational choice variables (e.g. volition, irrevocability). The propensity hypothesis has been tested in two studies (Lee, Ashford, Walsh, & Mowday, 1992; Pierce & Dunham, 1987) and both reported that propensity, measured prior to entry, predicted subsequent commitment. Lee et al. (1992) also found some evidence to suggest that propensity might influence commitment by shaping the way employees perceive their early experiences; those with a higher propensity for commitment tended to view the same objective experiences more positively than those with lower propensity.

Unfortunately, it is difficult to assess the implications of these findings because the propensity construct, as defined and operationalized, is so complex. It is not clear what components of propensity (e.g. expectation, personal characteristics) are responsible for the correlation with subsequent commitment. Until these effects can be teased apart, we will not know whether it is possible to select for propensity, or if propensity is largely shaped during the recruitment and selection processes.

Socialization and training

One way in which organizations might hope to build on employees' initial propensity for commitment is through the socialization process. Investigation of the effects of socialization practices on commitment was facilitated by Van Maanen and Schein (1979) who devised a six-dimensional classification scheme, and Jones (1986) who developed a set of measures that could be used to determine where along these dimensions an organization's socialization practices fall. These measures have now been used in several studies and the evidence clearly indicates a link between perceived socialization experiences and commitment (e.g. Allen & Meyer, 1990a; Ashforth & Saks, 1996; Baker & Feldman, 1990; Jones, 1986; Mignerey, Robin, & Gordon, 1995).

The dimension that has consistently been found to have the strongest association with commitment is *Investiture versus Divestiture* (e.g. Allen & Meyer,

1990a; Ashforth & Saks, 1996; Jones, 1986). The investiture–divestiture dimension, as measured by Jones' (1986) instrument, reflects the 'degree to which newcomers receive positive [investiture] or negative [divestiture] support after entry from experienced organizational members' (p. 265). Commitment tends to be stronger when organizations use investiture tactics.

Instilling commitment is only one of several objectives organizations attempt to achieve through socialization. A somewhat disconcerting finding reported by Jones (1986), therefore, was that the socialization practices associated with higher levels of commitment tended to be negatively associated with employees' self-reported tendency to adapt an innovative role orientation. Moreover, commitment itself was found to correlate negatively with orientation toward innovation. These findings might be of particular concern to organizations wanting to foster both a high level of commitment and a willingness to innovate in their employees. More recent research has demonstrated that commitment and innovation are not strongly related, however, and that the socialization dimensions that have the strongest influence on these two outcomes are different (Allen & Meyer, 1990a; Ashforth & Saks, 1996). Nevertheless, these findings should sensitize researchers and practitioners to the fact that socialization practices are likely to have multiple effects, and that to focus exclusively on any one might be shortsighted.

Although these findings suggest some guiding principles for the design of socialization programs, there are limitations of the research that raise questions about the generalizability of these principles. For example, tests of Van Maanen and Schein's (1979) model have been conducted largely with highly educated newcomers (e.g. MBAs) during the first year of employment (Ashforth & Saks, 1996; for an exception, see Baker & Feldman, 1990). It is unclear to what extent these findings are representative of what would be found with other less educated, or more heterogeneous, samples, or for socialization conducted during later career stages. Moreover, research to date has focused largely on the *form* of socialization without concern for the *content*. It might well be that the message conveyed to employees during socialization will be more important in determining their commitment than the structural characteristics of the practices (cf. Ashforth & Saks, 1996). Chao, O'Leary-Kelly, Wolf, Klein, and Gardner (1994) recently developed a method of classifying socialization content that might be useful in testing this hypothesis. Finally, there has been little attempt to determine how these organization-initiated socialization practices interact with employees' own information-seeking strategies (see Morrison, 1993; Ostroff & Kozlowski, 1992).

Training is often an important part of the socialization process. Although commitment is not necessarily the intended, or at least most obvious, objective of training, it can nevertheless be influenced in the process. Gaertner and Nollen (1989) found that commitment was related to employees' perceptions of organizational efforts to provide them with training, but not to their actual training experiences. They suggest that the fact that actual training experiences did not predict commitment might have been due to the fact that the measure did not reflect frequency or content of training.

Tannenbaum, Mathieu, Salas, and Cannon-Bowers (1991) assessed the commitment of recruits immediately upon arrival at a US Naval Training Command for an 8-week socialization-type training process, and again following training. They found that, overall, organizational commitment increased following training. Moreover, with pre-training commitment controlled, post-training commitment was positively related to training fulfilment (the extent to which the training fulfilled trainees' expectations and desires), satisfaction with the training experience, and training performance. Thus, it would appear that successful training experiences can contribute to the development of affective commitment. Saks (1995) obtained similar results in a study conducted with a civilian sample (accountants).

Tannenbaum et al. (1991) also found some evidence that organizational commitment might have reciprocal effects on training success. They reported a strong positive correlation between commitment and employees' motivation for training, a variable that was found to be an important predictor of training satisfaction and performance. This finding was recently replicated in a large-scale study of government supervisory and management personnel (Facteau, Dobbins, Russell, Ladd, & Kudisch, 1995). Thus, although more research is necessary, particularly in the private sector, existing evidence suggests that commitment can be affected by training experiences and can, in turn, influence employees' motivation for training.

Promotion

Policies and practices concerning the movement of employees, particularly upward movement, once they are in the organization might also be expected to have an impact on their commitment. Gaertner and Nollen (1989) found that commitment was higher among employees who had been promoted, and was also related to employees' perceptions that the company had a policy of promoting from within. Such a policy might be perceived as an example of the company's commitment to the employee as discussed earlier.

Robertson, Iles, Gratton, and Sharpley (1991) examined the impact of a management development and tiering program used by a large financial services organization to evaluate employees in early and mid-career. They found that commitment and turnover intentions were strongly influenced by the outcome of early career assessments; those who received negative feedback became less committed and more likely to consider leaving the company. Reactions to assessments conducted in mid-career (early 30s), however, were affected more by the perceived adequacy of the procedures involved than by the outcome. Thus, different strategies might be needed to maintain commitment among those given failure feedback depending on career stage.

Schwarzwald, Koslowsky, & Shalit (1992) examined the effect of promotion decisions on the commitment of a group of Israeli employees who had declared their candidacy for promotion. Those who were promoted were subsequently more committed than those who were not. Those who were not promoted also perceived greater inequity than those who were promoted and tended to be absent more frequently following the decision. Schwarzwald, Koslowsky, and Shalit suggested that equity considerations might be the mediating factor in determining the attitudinal and behavioural outcomes of failure to be promoted.

Finally, Fletcher (1991) found that the commitment of managerial candidates who went through assessment centres changed little in pre-assessment, post-assessment, and follow-up surveys. Moreover, successful and unsuccessful candidates differed little in commitment either before or after the assessment. Performance in the assessment centre did, however, affect candidates in other ways (e.g. self-esteem). In light of the findings of the studies described above, it is possible that the absence of an effect on commitment in this study was due to perceptions that the assessments were fair.

Together, these findings suggest that a policy of promotion from within can have a beneficial effect on commitment. Among those who are considered for promotion, the outcome of the decision is likely to have an effect on commitment but, for some, the perception of fairness in the decision-making process might be even more important. This suggests that companies should communicate clearly how their decisions were made and why those who did not receive the promotion were passed over.

Compensation and benefits

Although relatively little attention has been given to examining the effects of the administration of salary and benefits on commitment, one compensation-relevant practice that has received some attention is the use of Employee Stock Ownership Plans (ESOP). ESOPs are increasing in popularity for several reasons, including the belief that employees who have a stake in the company will be more committed to it (Klein, 1987). Indeed, evidence for a link between organizational commitment and ESOPs (and related systems) has now been obtained in several studies (e.g. Buchko, 1992, 1993; Florkowski & Schuster, 1992); Klein, 1987; Klein & Hall, 1988; Tucker, Nock, & Toscano, 1989; Wetzel & Gallagher, 1990). Many of these studies also addressed the issue of why ESOPs are related to commitment.

Klein (1987) identified three models that have been used to explain the link between employee ownership and commitment. According to the first of these, the Intrinsic Satisfaction Model, commitment derives directly from ownership and should therefore be proportional to the amount of stock an employee holds. The Extrinsic Satisfaction Model proposes that commitment will be proportional to the degree of financial gain the employee realizes (or has the potential to realize) as a function of holding stock in the company. Finally, according to the Instrumental Satisfaction Model, employee ownership is believed to increase commitment because it increases the actual or perceived influence that employees have in decision-making within the organization. Using data from over 2800 ESOP participants from 37 different companies, Klein found some support for both the Extrinsic and Instrumental Satisfaction models, but not for the Intrinsic Satisfaction model.

More recent studies have provided mixed support for the Instrumental Satisfaction and Extrinsic Satisfaction models, and almost no support for the Intrinsic Satisfaction model. For example, Buchko (1993) found that financial value of the ESOP was indirectly related to commitment through its influence on overall satisfaction with the plan. In contrast, perceived influence resulting from ownership was found to be directly related to both satisfaction with the plan and commitment to the organization. In a quasi-experimental study, Tucker, Nock, and Toscano (1989) found that organizational commitment increased following the introduction of an ESOP in a small clothing store, but that perceived influence did not change. Interestingly, they found that the commitment of both participants and non-participants increased following the introduction of the ESOP, and they speculated that this might have been due to a general change in the climate of the organization. Finally, in a study designed to examine the influence of profit sharing on commitment, Florkowski and Schuster (1992) found that concerns about the financial implication of the plan (i.e. performance-reward contingency; pay equity) were related to support for the plan which, in turn, was an important determinant of organizational commitment. Perceived influence was not directly related to plan support as had been anticipated, but did relate to commitment indirectly through its influence on job satisfaction.

Together these findings suggest that the introduction of an ESOP alone is not sufficient to increase affective commitment. Employees will expect to benefit either financially or in terms of their ability to influence decisions, or both. If increasing commitment is an objective, it would appear that making the plan financially meaningful, and/or increasing employees' opportunity to participate in decision-making, should be an important part of the plan. With regard to financial meaningfulness, however, it must be kept in mind that too much emphasis on this factor could actually reduce affective commitment (cf. Caldwell, Chatman, & O'Reilly, 1990; Oliver, 1990) or lead to the development of other forms of commitment. For example, an ESOP that requires that employees stay for a fixed period of time in order to receive the organization's contribution to the plan can increase the cost of leaving the organization (i.e. continuance commitment).

Even less research has been conducted to examine the impact of benefits on commitment. Nevertheless, the administration of benefits might conceivably have implications for employee commitment. Consider, for example, the potential impact of organizations' efforts to respond to the increase in the number of dual-career families by providing family-responsive benefits (e.g. flexible hours; daycare assistance). Grover and Crooker (1995) used data collected in a national survey of over 1500 US workers to examine the relation between availability of family-responsive benefits and affective organizational commitment. They found a positive correlation between the availability of such benefits and commitment, even for those who would not benefit directly. They argued that organizations that offer such benefits are perceived by employees as showing greater caring and concern (organizational support) and as being fair in their dealings with employees.

It should be noted that the correlations obtained by Grover and Crooker (1995) were not large and that there may be limits to generalizability. For example, Grover and Crooker suggested that the introduction of family-responsive benefits should be consistent with the existing culture of the organization. If employees view these benefits as having been introduced in response to external pressure or as a token gesture, they may have less impact (cf. Koys, 1988, 1991). Moreover, Grover and Crooker's explanation for their findings assumes that a norm for need-based distribution of resources exists; if the norm is for equity-based distribution, the provision of benefits that meet the needs of a select group of employees might create some resentment.

Change management

Organizations in both the public and private sectors are coming under increasing pressures to change the way they operate. Many of these changes, and the way they are implemented, can be expected to have an influence on organizational commitment. To illustrate, consider the case of organizational downsizing. It has been estimated that approximately 90% of large organizations in North America reduced their workforce in recent years (Emshoff, 1994). Unfortunately, it appears that the anticipated economic and organizational gains expected from downsizing are often not realized (Cascio, 1993). This may be due, in part, to the fact that downsizing organizations sometimes have difficulty in retaining their most valued employees (cf. Mone, 1994).

A number of recent studies have been conducted to examine how the commitment of 'survivors' is affected by downsizing. A common thread running through much of this research has been the importance of procedural justice. Survivors were likely to have higher levels of post-layoff commitment when they felt that the downsizing was unavoidable and was implemented fairly (see Konovsky & Brockner, 1993). Among the factors found to influence perceptions of justice were the level of support provided to the victims (Brockner, Grover, Reed, DeWitt, & O'Malley, 1987), the fairness of decision-making in the past (Davy, Kinicki, & Scheck, 1991), and the adequacy of the explanation provided (Brockner, DeWitt, Grover, & Reed, 1990). Other factors that contributed to commitment in addition to, or in interaction with, justice were feelings of job security (Davy, Kinicki, & Scheck, 1991), perceptions of the intrinsic quality of jobs following the layoff (Brockner, Weisenfeld, Reed, Grover, & Martin, 1993), and pre-layoff commitment (Brockner, Tyler, & Cooper-Schneider, 1992). Interestingly, those with the strongest commitment prior to the layoff were the ones most adversely affected by perceived injustice in the downsizing process.

Summary

The investigation of the development of commitment has clearly progressed beyond efforts to correlate commitment with variables presumed to be its antecedents. Structural equation modelling analyses have helped to increase our confidence in the causal ordering of variables involved in the development of commitment. Many issues remain, however, including the appropriate time lag for detecting causal effects, and whether it is better to use cross-sectional or longitudinal designs to examine reciprocal effects (cf. Farkas & Tetrick, 1989; Mathieu, 1991).

There is much to be learned yet about the processes involved in the development of commitment. What we know has been learned almost incidentally. There has been little in the way of systematic investigation of process issues. What research has been done has focused primarily on the development of affect-based commitment. We need to know more about how the various forms of commitment, and commitments to different constituencies, develop in order to understand and predict how changes in the workplace are likely to influence employees' commitment profiles.

There appears to be evidence that organizations can, intentionally or unintentionally, influence their employees' commitment through their HRM practices. Before drawing firm conclusions about the influence of any particular HRM practice, however, it is important to keep in mind that most of the research has been correlational. A correlation between an HRM practice and commitment is difficult to interpret. Organizations are likely to adapt management practices that are compatible with one another and with general organizational objectives. Consequently, when examined individually, a particular practice might be related to commitment, not because it has an impact on commitment, but because it is associated with other HRM practices, or general business strategies, that do (Huselid, 1995). It is also important to note that HRM practices were often measured using surveys administered to employees. Employees' perceptions may or may not be accurate. More attention needs to be given in future research to examining the impact of actual practices.

CONSEQUENCES

The results of the meta-analyses described earlier revealed that, with the exception of turnover-related variables, correlations between organizational commitment and outcome measures were disappointingly weak. Based on these findings, Randall (1990) concluded that 'researchers do not have a very powerful scientific foundation upon which to base claims of the importance of OC as a research topic and as an organizationally desirable attitude' (p. 375). Perhaps in an attempt to solidify that foundation, investigators have continued to examine the links between commitment and organizationally relevant outcomes. There has also been some attempt to look for links with outcomes of greater relevance to the employees themselves.

Turnover Intention and Turnover

Even though the link between organizational commitment and turnover-related variables has been relatively well established, a considerable amount of attention continues to be given to this relationship. Rather than trying to provide a comprehensive review of this research, I will focus attention on some common themes. Specifically, I will review the findings of studies undertaken to (i) examine the relations between various components of commitment and turnover-related variables, (ii) identify potential moderators of the commitment-turnover relation and (iii) assess the relative contributions of commitment and other attitude variables (e.g. job satisfaction, job involvement) to the prediction of turnover intention and turnover. I will conclude with a discussion of a somewhat contentious issue concerning the redundancy of the commitment and turnover intention constructs.

Turnover and components of commitment

Several studies have examined the correlations between turnover, or turnover intention, and two or more of Allen and Meyer's (1990b) three components of commitment. Affective commitment has consistently been found to correlate negatively with turnover intention and/or actual turnover (e.g. Carson & Bedeian, 1994; Cropanzano, James, & Konovsky, 1993; Hackett, Bycio, & Hausdorf, 1994; Jenkins, 1993; Konovsky & Cropanzano, 1991; Meyer, Allen, & Smith, 1993; Somers, 1995; Whitener & Walz, 1993). Although it has received less attention, normative commitment has also been found to correlate negatively with turnover intention and turnover (Hackett, Bycio, & Hausdorf, 1994; Meyer, Allen, & Smith, 1993; Somers, 1995). The findings have been less consistent for continuance commitment; significant negative correlations were obtained in some studies (Hackett, Bycio, & Hausdorf, 1994; Whitener & Walz, 1993) but not in others (e.g. Cropanzano, James, & Konovsky, 1993; Konovsky & Cropanzano, 1991; Somers, 1995). Somers (1995) found that, although continuance commitment did not contribute independently to the prediction of turnover intention, it did moderate the effect of affective commitment. The link between affective commitment and turnover was weaker when continuance commitment was high; presumably those with low affective commitment were less inclined to leave when the perceived cost of doing so was high.

Components of commitment identified in other multidimensional models have also been linked to commitment. Vandenberg, Self, and Seo (1994) examined the contribution of the components of commitment identified by O'Reilly and Chatman (1986), identification, internalization, and compliance, to the prediction of turnover intention and turnover, relative to the OCQ. They found internalization and compliance had only modest correlations with turnover intention and turnover (those with compliance were opposite in direction) and that, when entered into a structural equation model along with the OCQ, only the latter had a significant effect on turnover intention. The effect of the OCQ on turnover was mediated by turnover intention and job search. In a preliminary analysis, Vandenberg, Self, and Seo found that identification was not distinguishable from the OCQ and therefore did not include it in the structural equation modelling analyses.

Jaros et al. (1993) included measures of affective, continuance, and moral commitment in competitive tests of several models of the turnover process. The measures of commitment paralleled, but were not the same as, those developed by Allen and Meyer (1990b). Jaros et al. found that, in the best fitting model, affective and continuance commitment contributed significantly and independently to the prediction of withdrawal tendency, which, in turn, predicted actual turnover; moral commitment did not contribute significantly to prediction.

Ben-Bakr, Al-Shammari, Jefri, & Prasad (1994) examined the relative strength of the correlation between turnover intention and commitment in a sample of employees in various occupations and organizations in Saudi Arabia. They found a significant negative correlation for overall commitment, but when the OCQ was divided into subscales to create value commitment and continuance commitment measures (see Angle & Perry, 1981), the value commitment scale was found to correlate more strongly with turnover intention than was the continuance commitment scale. (Note, continuance commitment operationalized this way is not the same as continuance commitment as defined by Allen and Meyer, 1990b.)

Finally, Mayer and Schoorman (1992) tested a two-dimensional model of organizational commitment and its link to turnover intention and turnover. Using measures of continuance and value commitment developed by Schechter (1985), they found that both forms of commitment correlated significantly with intent to stay, and negatively with turnover. Although the correlations with intent were of roughly equal magnitude, continuance commitment correlated more strongly with actual turnover.

In sum, although affect-based forms of commitment have been found consistently to relate to turnover intention and turnover, other forms of commitment (e.g. continuance and normative commitment) also appear to play a role in the turnover process, albeit somewhat less consistently. Of particular interest is the finding that different forms of commitment may interact to influence turnover decisions (Somers, 1995). Although it has been suggested that a fuller understanding of the consequences of commitment might be gained by examining the joint influences of the different components (Meyer & Allen, 1991), there has been little systematic effort to do so. Somers' findings suggest that this may be a fruitful avenue for future investigation.

Moderator effects

Meta-analyses of the relations between commitment and turnover-related variables suggested that there might be moderator effects operating. Several studies have since attempted to identify variables that might interact with commitment to influence turnover. For example, Jenkins (1993) tested for, and found, a moderating effect of individual differences in self-monitoring on the relation between affective commitment and turnover intention. The correlation between affective commitment and turnover intention was stronger for low self-monitors than for high self-monitors.

Blau and Boal (1987) outlined a conceptual model in which they argued that organizational commitment would interact with job involvement to influence turnover. Blau and Boal (1989) conducted a partial test of the model and found, as predicted, that the interaction contributed to prediction beyond the main effects of involvement and commitment (as well as demographic variables and withdrawal cognitions). The highest turnover was found among those with low involvement and commitment, and the lowest turnover was found for those with high involvement and commitment. The interaction effect was due primarily to the fact that commitment had a stronger effect on turnover when involvement was low than involvement did when commitment was low.

Huselid and Day (1991) conducted a similar test and were able to replicate Blau and Boal's (1989) findings when they used ordinary least squares (OLS) regression analyses, but not when they used logistic regression (LR) analysis, which is more appropriate for binary dependent variables. In the latter analyses, they found neither significant main or interaction effects. At a more general level, they questioned the meaningfulness of results of much of the turnover research because of its reliance on OLS analyses.

Martin and Hafer (1995) tested Blau and Boal's (1987) interaction model using turnover intention as the criterion variable. Moreover, they tested the model separately for part-time and full-time telemarketing employees. Consistent with Blau and Boal (1989), they found evidence to support the interaction hypothesis for the combined groups, and for full-time employees only. The pattern of results obtained for part-time employees, however, was slightly different from that for full-time employees. Rather than finding the lowest turnover intentions among those with high commitment and high involvement, as was the case for the full-time employees, they found the lowest intention in the low involvement, high commitment group for part-time employees.

In sum, it appears that commitment might interact with other individual difference variables to influence turnover intention and turnover. The investigation of these interaction effects, however, has not been extensive, nor particularly systematic. Although it is important to identify other variables that influence the effect of commitment or turnover, or other outcome variables, the investigation of these moderator effects should be guided by theory and conducted with appropriate procedures.

Comparative tests of effects

There has been considerable rhetoric over the last two decades about the relative magnitude of the effects of different work attitude variables, most notably organizational commitment and job satisfaction, on employee turnover. This issue has now been addressed in a number of studies using various methodologies. In some cases, the relative magnitudes of correlations with turnover, or turnover intention, were compared. These studies have produced mixed results, with some finding stronger correlations for commitment (e.g. Ben-Bakr et al., 1994), and others for satisfaction (e.g. Rosin & Korabik, 1991). Jenkins (1993) found that the relative strength of correlations with turnover intention differed for high and low self-monitors; commitment was more strongly correlated for low self-monitors, but the reverse was true for high self-monitors.

Another approach has been to include commitment and satisfaction together as predictors in regression or structural equation modelling analyses to assess the relative strength of their independent contributions to prediction. These studies have also yielded somewhat mixed results. For example, Shore, Newton, and Thorton (1990) evaluated several models of the relations between work attitudes and behavioural intentions using cross-sectional data obtained from university employees. They found that job satisfaction and organizational commitment were both related to turnover intentions, but that commitment was a better predictor than was job satisfaction. Similarly, in a national sample of accountants, Rahim and Afza (1993) found that organizational commitment and job satisfaction both made significant independent contributions to the prediction of propensity to leave the organization, but that the contribution made by commitment was greater. Mueller, Boyer, Price, and Iverson (1994) investigated the turnover process in smaller organizations (i.e. dental offices). They found that, although commitment was negatively related to turnover intention and turnover, job satisfaction was a more important mediator of the influence of work conditions on turnover intention. Finally, Shore and Martin (1989) compared the relative contribution of commitment and satisfaction to the prediction of turnover intention for professional and clerical employees. They found that commitment was a better predictor for the latter, but satisfaction was a better predictor for the former.

Tett and Meyer (1993) examined the relative strength of the contribution of job satisfaction and organizational commitment to the prediction of turnover intention and turnover by combining meta-analyses and structural equation modelling. Specifically, they used meta-analyses to develop a matrix of correlations among four variables, organizational commitment, job satisfaction, turnover intention, and turnover. These correlations were then used to evaluate the contribution of commitment and satisfaction to prediction using structural equation modelling procedures. Their findings suggested that job satisfaction and organizational commitment contributed independently to the prediction of turnover intention, but that the effect of job satisfaction was slightly stronger. Moreover, they found that the effect of job satisfaction on turnover was mediated completely by turnover intention, but that, in addition to its indirect effect, commitment also exerted a small direct effect on turnover.

It appears from these findings that job satisfaction and organizational commitment are both implicated in the turnover process. The relative magnitude of their contributions to the prediction of turnover is still unclear however. One reason for the confusion might be that, as noted earlier, it is not clear whether, or how, satisfaction and commitment influence each other. Another reason might be that investigators have not adequately recognized the complexity of the turnover process. Lee and Mitchell (1991) outlined what they described as an 'unfolding model' of turnover that includes four somewhat different decision paths. They noted that commitment and satisfaction are only relevant to the turnover decision in a limited set of conditions identified in these decision paths.

Commitment and turnover intention: the issue of construct redundancy

It has been argued that one reason why organizational commitment might be a better predictor of turnover intention than job satisfaction and other work attitudes is that the constructs of commitment and turnover intention are redundant (at least in part). Two studies conducted recently to address this issue empirically produced mixed results. Kong, Wertheimer, Serradel, & McGhan (1994) conducted a factor analysis of OCQ items and a five-item measure of turnover intention developed by Hunt, Osborn, and Martin (1981). They found that both sets of items loaded on a single factor and, therefore, questioned whether commitment and turnover intention are different constructs. In contrast, Mueller, Wallace, and Price (1992), using confirmatory factor analysis, demonstrated that organizational commitment and turnover intention were distinguishable constructs.

The Kong et al. (1994) findings appear to be an anomaly. Although there has been only one disconfirming factor analytic study, the magnitude of the correlations reported between measures of organizational commitment and turnover intention are typically not strong enough to warrant the claim that the constructs are identical (see Tett & Meyer, 1993). Nevertheless, the question of how we should interpret the correlation between commitment and turnover intention remains. The same question applies to the comparison of correlations (e.g. job satisfaction versus organizational commitment) as discussed above.

Concern over the construct redundancy issue has perhaps been most evident in criticisms levelled at measures of commitment. It is often claimed, for example, that the OCQ includes items that assess turnover intention (e.g. Blau, 1989; Davy, Kinicki, & Scheck, 1991; Farkas & Tetrick, 1989). Are these claims legitimate? A careful reading of OCQ items reveals that there are no items that measure 'intention to leave' *per se*. At best (or worst), it can be argued that there are items that tap into 'withdrawal cognitions.' Given that commitment reflects a propensity to continue a course of action, this does not seem unreasonable.

The distinction between commitment and turnover intention can perhaps be seen more clearly by considering the different forms that commitment itself can take. According to Meyer and Allen (1991), commitment has been described as a *desire*, a *need*, or an *obligation* to continue a course of action. None of these is synonymous with *intention* to continue. Rather, each can contribute to such an intention. Moreover, the absence of a desire, a need, or an obligation to remain does not imply an intention to leave. For example, an employee with a low desire to remain may nevertheless have a strong intention to remain because of a strong need or sense of obligation.

In sum, then, the correlation between commitment and turnover intention should best be considered a reflection of the association between a psychological state and a behavioural intention, and as suggesting that one might be used to predict the other. It does not reflect construct redundancy. Moreover, it should be kept in mind that the (presumed) problem does not exist when commitment is evaluated as a predictor of turnover which is, after all, what we are ultimately interested in predicting.

Absenteeism and Tardiness

Little has changed in the investigation of the relation between commitment and absenteeism other than the fact that studies are now being conducted to determine whether the strength and/or direction varies across different forms of commitment. For example, several investigators have examined the relation between absenteeism and two or more of Allen and Meyer's (1990b) three components of commitment. Gellatly (1995) correlated affective and continuance commitment measures obtained from nurses and food service workers in a chronic care hospital with indices of their absence frequency and total days absent over a 12-month period following the survey. Affective commitment correlated significantly in the negative direction with both indices; continuance commitment did not correlate significantly with either index. When included in a structural equation model with other individual- and group-level variables, affective commitment was still found to contribute significantly to the prediction of absence frequency.

Hackett, Bycio, and Hausdorf (1994) correlated affective, continuance, and normative commitment scores obtained from a sample of bus drivers with indices of culpable and non-culpable absence. The only significant correlation they found was between affective commitment and culpable absence. This correlation was not significant when age, tenure, and job satisfaction were controlled.

Somers (1995) examined the relations between absence (total and annexed) and affective, continuance, and normative commitment in a sample of nurses. He found that only affective commitment predicted absence, albeit modestly, and then only annexed absence. As was the case with turnover intention noted above, however, Somers also found a significant interaction effect of affective and continuance commitment. The link between affective commitment and absence was greater for those who were low in continuance commitment. The highest rate of absence was found among those with both low affective and continuance commitment. These employees may have been using absence as an escape, or as an opportunity to find alternative employment.

These findings suggest that, as was the case with turnover, affect-based measures of commitment show the strongest and most consistent relation to voluntary absence. There may, of course, be factors that moderate this relation, as was suggested by the meta-analyses reviewed earlier. Indeed, Mathieu and Kohler (1990) found some evidence for a moderating effect of job involvement. There is also some evidence that other forms of commitment may have an effect on commitment, but the findings are less consistent. This could reflect the operation of moderators. Alternatively, the lack of consistency across studies might simply reflect chance fluctuation around a relatively low true correlation. There have, as yet, been too few studies using non-affect-based measures of commitment to determine which of these two possibilities is most likely. Based on the findings of Somers (1995), it might be useful to look for interaction effects among the components of commitment in future research.

Turning to tardiness, recent research has generally confirmed that, even when significant, the correlation between commitment and lateness behaviour tends to be relatively weak (e.g. Blau, 1995). Blau (1994) argued that one explanation for this weak relation might be the inadequate conceptualization of the tardiness construct. He identified and measured three different forms of lateness behaviour: increasing chronic, stable periodic, and unavoidable. He found that affective commitment was most strongly related to chronic lateness, accounting for 17% of the variance in a sample of hospital employees and 14% of the variance in bank employees.

There have been too few studies to draw firm conclusions about the link between commitment and lateness behaviour. Future research should consider the distinctions in tardiness behaviour made by Blau (1994). One potential avenue for research would be to examine whether the different forms of lateness behaviour relate differently to different forms of commitment.

Another might be to determine whether lateness is better predicted by commitment to some organizational constituencies than others.

In-role Job Performance

The meta-analytic findings concerning the relation between organizational commitment and in-role job performance paralleled those obtained in earlier meta-analyses involving job satisfaction (e.g. Iaffaldano & Muchinsky, 1985); the corrected mean correlation is positive but relatively weak. This is not surprising given that there are many factors contributing to employees' performance, some of which might be unrelated to commitment or satisfaction (e.g. ability, resources). Consistent with these meta-analytic findings, significant correlations have been found between commitment and performance in some recent studies (e.g. Cropanzano, Jamer, & Konovsky, 1993; Johnston & Snizek, 1991; Saks, 1995) but not in others (e.g. Ganster & Dwyer, 1995; Schweiger & DeNisi, 1991).

Again, there are at least two explanations for the inconsistent findings. First, the inconsistency might simply reflect chance fluctuations around a weak true correlation. Alternatively, there might be meaningful moderators operating. For example, Brett, Cron, and Slocum (1995) found a moderating effect of financial requirements on the relation between organizational commitment and sales performance in two organizations. The link between commitment and performance was stronger when financial requirements were low. Because pay was based on performance, a high financial need would provide a powerful incentive for performance, and reduce the impact that commitment might have.

One way in which recent research has extended the meta-analytic findings is the demonstration that the strength, and even the direction, of the correlation can vary depending on the form of commitment being considered. For example, Meyer et al. (1989) found that the affective commitment of managers in a food service company was positively related to their district managers' ratings of performance and promotability, whereas their continuance commitment was negatively related to these ratings. A similar finding was reported by Cropanzano, James, and Konovsky (1993) with employees in a pathology laboratory.

Hackett, Bycio, and Hausdorf (1994) correlated measures of affective, continuance, and normative commitment with four indices of performance (commendations, complaints, accidents, in-service rating checklist) in a sample of bus drivers. When age, tenure, and satisfaction were controlled, the only significant correlations that remained were those between affective commitment and accident rate (negative), and between continuance commitment and the receipt of commendations (negative).

Angle and Lawson (1994) examined the relations between two forms of commitment, affective and continuance, and supervisor rating of performance among employees in a Fortune 500 manufacturing organization. They found that neither affective nor continuance commitment was related to the global measure of performance. When they examined correlations with facet measures of performance, however, they found that affective commitment was positively related to ratings of dependability and initiative, but not to organization/accomplishment or judgment. Continuance commitment was not significantly related to any of the facet measures. Angle and Lawson argued, therefore, that the link between commitment and performance might depend not only on the nature of the commitment measure, but also on the type of performance being measured. For example, affective commitment might be more strongly related to measures of performance that reflect motivation rather than ability. Consistent with the latter suggestion, in a sample of life insurance agents in Singapore, Leong, Randall, and Cote (1994) found that commitment influenced job performance through its effects on levels of exertion (working harder), and well-directed effort (working smarter).

Most studies of the commitment–performance relation have been conducted at the individual level of analysis. Ostroff (1992) examined the link using an organization-level analysis. The commitment of over 13,808 teachers in 298 schools was measured and averages were computed within school. These school averages were then related to various indices of school performance (e.g. student achievement and satisfaction). Ostroff found that commitment was related to most indices of performance in the predicted direction. Although there are problems with comparison, she noted that the magnitude of the correlations obtained in this study tended to be somewhat stronger than those obtained in studies using an individual level of analysis. One possible explanation for this finding is that commitment contributes to employees' tendency to engage in unique, and perhaps idiosyncratic, forms of behaviour that are not captured in measures of individual performance, but are nevertheless reflected in the performance of the overall unit to which they are directed.

Extra-role Performance and Organizational Citizenship

Unlike in-role performance that is highly regulated and has various non-motivational determinants, extra-role performance (Katz, 1964) and organizational citizenship behaviour (Organ, 1988) are, by definition, discretionary. Consequently, there is reason to suspect that employees' commitment to an organization would have a stronger and more consistent link to behaviour that falls outside the defined role than to in-role performance. Such has been found to be the case with job satisfaction (see Organ, 1988).

A number of studies have examined the link between commitment and various indices of extra-role performance and citizenship, and most have reported significant correlations (e.g. Aryee & Heng, 1990; Munene, 1995; Wittig-Berman & Lang, 1990). One exception was a study by Williams and

Anderson (1991) using O'Reilly and Chatman's (1986) measures of identification and internalization. In a recent meta-analytic investigation of the correlates of citizenship behaviour, Organ and Ryan (1995) found a corrected mean correlation of 0.316 with organizational commitment. This correlation is larger than that typically found in meta-analyses of the relation between commitment and in-role performance.

Like the investigation of other outcome measures, a recent development has been to consider relations between extra-role behaviour and different forms of commitment. For example, Meyer, Allen, and Smith (1993) found positive correlations between nurses' affective commitment and their self-reports of helping others and effective use of time; normative commitment was also found to be positively related to the use of time measure. Continuance commitment was not related to either measure. Meyer, Allen, and Smith also asked nurses to indicate how they believed they would to react to dissatisfying conditions at work. They found that affective and normative commitment were positively related to the tendency to seek change (voice) or accept the condition (loyalty), and negatively related to the tendency to passively withdraw (neglect). Continuance commitment was unrelated to voice and loyalty, but positively related to neglect.

In a structural equation modelling analysis of data obtained from employees in a national cable television company, Moorman, Neihoff, and Organ (1993) found evidence for a relation between affective commitment and citizenship behaviour (supervisor ratings), but this relation disappeared when perceptions of procedural justice were controlled. Positive zero-order correlations were obtained between affective commitment and measures of several components of OCB. Some positive correlations, albeit weaker, were also obtained for continuance commitment.

Shore and Wayne (1993) found that affective commitment correlated positively with several components (altruism, compliance, and favours) of organizational citizenship behaviour, as rated by supervisors of employees in a large multinational firm; continuance commitment correlated negatively with two components (altruism and compliance). When affective commitment and perceived organizational support were entered together in regression analyses to predict citizenship, affective commitment did not make a significant unique contribution, whereas perceived support did. When continuance commitment and perceived support were entered together, both made significant contributions, and the effect of continuance commitment continued to be negative.

Morrison (1994) took a somewhat different perspective to the study of citizenship behaviour. She argued, and found, that employees differ in what they personally define as in-role and extra-role (citizenship) behaviour. She also found that affective and normative commitment were related to perceived job breadth. That is, those with stronger affective and normative commitment were more likely to view what have traditionally been considered citizenship behaviours as components of their job. Relations with affective commitment were generally stronger and more consistent (across behaviour categories) than those involving normative commitment.

In another slightly different twist to examining the relation between commitment and citizenship behaviour, Shore, Barksdale, and Shore (1995) asked managers to estimate the affective and continuance commitment of their employees. They found that citizenship behaviour predicted perceived affective commitment, whereas side-bets (a composite of education, age, job tenure, and organization tenure) predicted perceived continuance commitment. Supervisor ratings of employees' affective commitment were positively related to their own judgments of managerial potential and promotability, and to their employees' ratings of leader reward behaviour. Supervisor ratings of continuance commitment were negatively related to judgments of potential and promotability as well as to the extent they fulfil employees' requests. Interestingly, citizenship was a better predictor of manager-rated affective commitment than was performance, perhaps because the discretionary nature of citizenship behaviour made it more informative.

Because citizenship behaviour is discretionary, it can be directed at different targets. Therefore, in addition to considering how citizenship behaviour might relate differently to different forms of commitment, it is also important to consider whether, and how, it relates to commitment to different constituencies within, or outside, the organization. Some evidence that prosocial organizational behaviour relates differently to commitment to different constituencies within the organization was provided by Becker and Billings (1993) in a study described earlier. In another study along these lines, Gregersen (1993) examined the relations between supervisor ratings of extra-role behaviour and a global measure of organizational commitment as well as several facet measures (i.e. commitment to supervisor, top management, co-workers and customers). He also tested for moderating effects of tenure. Gregersen found that extra-role behaviour was not related to any form of commitment for those who were in the company for less than two years, but that it was positively related to global commitment for those with two to eight years in the company, and to commitment to immediate supervisor for those with a tenure of two to eight, and more than eight, years. Extra-role behaviour was negatively related to commitment to top management for the more senior employees.

In sum, these findings suggest that commitment to the organization might exert its strongest effects on citizenship and extra-role behaviours. The effects, however, might be quite complex. Additional research is needed to determine what forms of behaviour are related to what forms of commitment, to what constituencies, and under what conditions.

Employee Health and Well-being

The overwhelming majority of studies examining the consequences of commitment have focused on outcomes of relevance to the employing organization. It is only recently that outcomes of immediate and more direct relevance to the employees themselves have been investigated. For example, Romzek (1989) examined the correlations between commitment and various indices of non-work and career satisfaction in a sample of public-service employees. She found that commitment to the organization correlated positively with these measures. Although her data cannot be taken as evidence that commitment to an organization will actually contribute to employees' life and career satisfaction, she pointed out that the findings contradict the claim made by some that committing oneself to an organization necessitates a sacrifice in these other areas (cf. Cohen & Kirchmeyer, 1995).

Begley and Czajka (1993) measured the commitment of hospital employees before and after a major divisional consolidation. They found that commitment served to buffer the impact of stress on a measure of displeasure (a combination of job dissatisfaction, intent to quit, and irritation). Job displeasure was positively associated with stress only when commitment was low.

Ostroff and Kozlowski (1992) surveyed recent university graduates within the first few months of their starting career-oriented employment in a broad range of organizations, and again five months later. They found a significant negative correlation between commitment and self-reported psychological and physical stress, and a significant positive correlation with adjustment to the work situation, at both times. Wittig-Berman and Lang (1990) correlated the commitment of employed MBA students with self- and other-reports of symptoms of stress and with self-reports of alienation. They found that commitment was negatively related to both stress and alienation.

Summary

The findings of research conducted since the publication of the meta-analytic reviews described earlier continue to demonstrate relatively modest correlations between commitment and the outcome variables it has been assumed to influence. On a more positive note, however, it is clear that affective commitment has modest correlations with a number of different behaviours. Thus, organizations might expect to reap small benefits in several different ways by having affectively committed employees. The strongest correlations tended to be found with behaviours over which employees have the greatest control (e.g. turnover, citizenship). The influence of discretion is nicely illustrated by Somer's (1995) finding that the correlation between affective commitment and turnover intention was stronger among employees with lower continuance commitment. Presumably those with higher levels of continuance commitment felt they had less freedom to leave.

If our primary objective is to predict specific behaviours, Randall (1990) was correct in suggesting that we could do a better job using reasoned action models (e.g. Ajzen & Fishbein, 1980). These models have been found to yield quite accurate prediction. Nevertheless, they have been characterized by Roznowski and Hulin (1992) as *idiot savants* in recognition of the fact that they do one thing, but only one thing, very well. Employers are arguably more interested in knowing that their employees will take the organization's interests into consideration across situations than they are in predicting any one type of behaviour. Morrison's (1994) finding that more committed employees define their jobs more broadly (i.e. citizenship behaviours are viewed as in-role) illustrates the value of commitment in this regard. Similarly, Ostroff's (1992) finding that the correlation between commitment and performance is greater when both are measured at a group level suggests that committed employees can contribute to organizational effectiveness in ways that are not necessarily reflected in measures of an individual's performance.

The findings also illustrate the importance of distinguishing among different forms of commitment, and among commitments to different constituencies, in the investigation of commitment–behaviour relations. Moreover, they suggest that commitment might interact with other personal and situational characteristics to influence behaviour, but it is not clear at this point what the most important moderators might be.

Research continues to focus primarily on the positive consequences of commitment in spite of reminders that there may be negative consequences as well (e.g. Randall, 1987). There have been only a few studies that examined the relation between commitment and behaviour that, arguably, might have negative implications for the organization or employee. For example, Somers and Casal (1994) found some evidence for an inverted-U shaped relation between affective commitment and whistle-blowing behaviour. Grover (1993) found that committed employees were less likely than uncommitted employees to indicate that they would mis-report their behaviour to authorities, although both committed and uncommitted employees said they would be more likely to mis-report if they felt there was a conflict between their organizational and professional roles. Finally, Wahn (1993) found a positive correlation between continuance commitment and self-reports of unethical conduct. There is clearly a need for more research examining the potential 'down side' of commitment.

Finally, a word of caution is in order. Most of the research reviewed in this section was correlational. Therefore, although it is tempting to conclude that (affective) commitment has the desirable consequences discussed above, we cannot rule out other interpretations of the findings. It is possible, for example, that commitment is a consequence rather than a cause of an 'outcome' variable. For example, Brown, Cron, and Leigh (1993) provided data to suggest that employees' sales performance exerted an influence on their work attitudes, including commitment, by enhancing their feelings of success. Another possibility is that commitment and the outcome variables of interest are related only because they have a common cause. For example, Schweiger and DeNisi (1991) reported a significant negative correlation between commitment and stress. It would be tempting to conclude that commitment reduces stress but, in this case, it is more likely that both stress and commitment were influenced by reactions to an ongoing merger.

CONCLUSIONS

There has been considerable change in the organizational commitment literature since Griffin and Bateman conducted their review in 1986. Although they noted at that time that commitment might take different forms, there has been a much more systematic attempt to examine the multidimensional nature of organizational commitment, both in form and focus, in the last 10 years. There have also been advances made in the methods used to study the development and consequences of commitment. In particular, researchers have moved away from a reliance on bivariate correlations and are taking advantage of developments in structural equation modelling techniques to investigate causal connections on both the antecedent and consequence sides. These procedures still rely on patterns of covariance to infer causality, however, and must be interpreted with caution. A few attempts have been made to use quasi-experimental procedures to examine the influence of organizational practices (e.g. merger, promotion) on commitment. We need more of this kind of research in the future.

Throughout this review I have suggested areas where additional research is needed to build on current developments. Among the most important of these, I think, is the study of process. Much of the research directed at understanding how commitment develops has rested on untested assumptions about underlying mechanisms. The need to examine process has been highlighted by the recognition that commitment can take different forms and that each develops in different ways. For example, without understanding process, we are less well equipped to predict which, if any, form of commitment is likely to be affected by changes in conditions at work. For example, will the introduction of an attractive benefit program contribute to employees' affective attachment to the company, make them feel obligated to reciprocate, or increase their perception of the economic costs of leaving? Preliminary evidence suggests that the answer depends on how the practice is perceived, but we need to know much more about how these perceptions are shaped and get translated into commitment.

Additional research is also needed to clarify further the distinctions that have been made among forms of commitment. Even in the more well-developed multidimensional models, there is disagreement about the number of dimensions and how they are related. There is also a need for additional research to determine how employees become committed to different constituencies within organizations, and how these commitments interact to shape behaviour. Finally, there is a need for more systematic investigation of (i) moderators of relations with antecedent and outcome variables, (ii) potential negative consequences of commitment, and consequences of greater relevance to employees, and (iii) the impact of specific organizational policies and practices on employees' commitment.

It goes without saying that, in addressing these substantive issues, care must be taken to ensure that appropriate methods are being used. New developments in analytic procedures have contributed to the advances in commitment research noted above. In light of these methodological developments, however, it might be necessary to go back and re-examine findings that we have perhaps taken for granted. The impact of person–job fit and met-expectations are examples. In the same vein, we must be sensitive to developments in the conceptualization and measurement of constructs included in our models of commitment. Absenteeism and tardiness are good examples here.

Another important issue that needs to be addressed involves both substantive and methodological considerations. The models of commitment discussed here have, for the most part, been developed and tested in Western countries. There is a need for more systematic research to determine whether these models apply elsewhere. Although studies have been conducted in non-Western countries, without systematic cross-cultural research, it is impossible to know whether any discrepancies in the findings reflect true cultural differences in constructs and/or the way they relate to one another, or are due to problems with the way the constructs are measured, including difficulties with translation.

Finally, a major challenge ahead will be to determine how the changes being experienced by organizations throughout the world (e.g. downsizing, mergers and acquisitions, re-engineering, globalization) affect the role played by organizational commitment. Two quite discrepant scenarios can be envisioned. On the one hand, it is possible that as organizations become more streamlined, and the need for flexibility and adaptability increases, having a committed workforce will become less important, and perhaps even a liability. On the other hand, as organizations become leaner, they rely more heavily on those who remain to fulfil their mission. These employees are also likely to be given much more responsibility for managing their own behaviour. As I noted earlier, it is under conditions where employees have greater discretion that global attitudes, including organizational commitment, are likely to exert their strongest effects.

Even if employee commitment to the organization itself becomes less of an issue in the future, it is unlikely that concerns over commitment in general will disappear. In the process of studying organizational commitment we have learned much about what commitment is, how it develops, and how it influences behaviour, that should generalize to other work-related (e.g. career, occupation, union) commitments. As we expand the study of commitment to these other contexts, we should not ignore what has been learned in the study of commitment to the organization.

ACKNOWLEDGEMENTS

Preparation of this chapter was supported by a grant from the Social Sciences and Humanities Research Council of Canada. I am grateful to Meridith Black and Julie McCarthy for their assistance in the literature search and preparation of the manuscript.

REFERENCES

Ajzen, I. & Fishbein, M. (1980) *Understanding Attitudes and Predicting Social Behavior.* Englewood Cliffs, NJ: Prentice-Hall.

Allen, N. J. & Meyer, J. P. (1990a) Organizational socialization tactics: A longitudinal analysis of links to newcomers' commitment and role orientation. *Academy of Management Journal,* **33**, 847–858.

Allen, N. J. & Meyer, J. P. (1990b) The measurement and antecedents of affective, continuance, and normative commitment to the organization. *Journal of Occupational Psychology,* **63**, 1–18.

Allen, N. J. & Meyer, J. P. (in press) Affective, continuance, and normative commitment to the organization: An examination of construct validity. *Journal of Vocational Behavior.*

Angle, H. L. & Lawson, M. B. (1994) Organizational commitment and employees' performance ratings: Both type of commitment and type of performance count. *Psychological Reports,* 1539–1551.

Angle, H. L. & Perry, J. L. (1981) An empirical assessment of organizational commitment and organizational effectiveness. *Administrative Science Quarterly,* **27**, 1–14.

Aryee, S. & Heng, L. J. (1990) A note on the applicability of an organizational commitment model. *Work and Occupations,* **17**, 229–239.

Ashforth, B. E. & Saks, A. M. (1996) Socialization tactics: Longitudinal effects on newcomer adjustment. *Academy of Management Journal,* **39**, 149–178.

Aven, F. F., Parker, B., & McEvoy, G. M. (1993) Gender and attitudinal commitment to organizations: A meta-analysis Special Issue: Loyalty in a multi-commitment world, *Journal of Business Research,* **26**, 63–73.

Baker III, H. E. & Feldman, D. C. (1990) Strategies of organizational socialization and their impact on newcomer adjustment. *Journal of Managerial Issues,* **2**, 198–212.

Becker, H. S. (1960) Notes on the concept of commitment. *American Journal of Sociology,* **66**, 32–42.

Becker, T. E. (1992) Foci and bases of commitment: Are they distinctions worth making? *Academy of Management Journal,* **35**, 232–244.

Becker, T. E. & Billings, R. S. (1993) Profiles of Commitment: An Empirical Test. *Journal of Organizational Behavior,* **14**, 177–190.

Begley, T. M. & Czajka, J. M. (1993) Panel analysis of the moderating effects of commitment on job satisfaction, intent to quit, and health following organizational change. *Journal of Applied Psychology,* **78**, 552–556.

Ben-Bakr, K. A., Al-Shammari, I. S., Jefri, O. A., & Prasad, J. N. (1994) Organizational commitment, satisfaction, and turnover in Saudi organizations: A predictive study. *Journal of Socio-Economics,* **23**, 449–456.

Blau, G. J. (1987) Using a person–environment fit model to predict job involvement and organizational commitment. *Journal of Vocational Behavior,* **30**, 240–257.

Blau, G. (1989) Testing the generalizability of a career commitment measure and its impact on employee turnover. *Journal of Vocational Behavior,* **35**, 88–103.

Blau, G. (1994) Developing and testing a taxonomy of lateness behavior. *Journal of Applied Psychology*, **79**, 959–970.

Blau, G. (1995) Influence of group lateness on individual lateness: A cross-level examination. *Academy of Management Journal*, **38**, 1483–1496.

Blau, G. & Boal, K. (1987) Conceptualizing how job involvement and organizational commitment affect turnover and absenteeism. *Academy of Management Review*, **12**, 288–300.

Blau, G. & Boal, K. (1989) Using job involvement and organizational commitment interactively to predict turnover. *Journal of Management*, **15**, 115–127.

Blau, G., Paul, A., & St. John, N. (1993) On developing a general index of work commitment. *Journal of Vocational Behavior*, **42**, 298–314.

Brett, J. E., Cron, W. L., & Slocum, J. W. (1995) Economic dependency on work: A moderator of the relationship between organizational commitment and performance. *Academy of Management Journal*, **38**, 261–271.

Brockner, J., DeWitt, R., Grover, S. L., & Reed, T. (1990) When it is especially important to explain why: Factors affecting the relationship between managers' explanations of a layoff and survivors' reaction to the layoff. *Journal of Experimental Social Psychology*, **26**, 389–407.

Brockner, J., Grover, S., Reed, T., DeWitt, R., & O'Malley, M. (1987) Survivors' reactions to layoffs: We get by with a little help from our friends. *Administrative Science Quarterly*, **32**, 526–542.

Brockner, J. B., Tyler, T. R., & Cooper-Schneider, R. (1992) The influence of prior commitment to an institution on reactions to perceived unfairness: The higher they are, the harder they fall. *Administrative Science Quarterly*, **37**, 241–261.

Brockner, J., Weisenfeld, B. M., Reed, T., Grover, S., & Martin, C. (1993) Interactive effect of job content and content on the reactions of layoff survivors. *Journal of Personality and Social Psychology*, **64**, 187–197.

Brooke, P. P., Russell, D. W., & Price, J. L. (1988) Discriminant validation of measures of job satisfaction, job involvement, and organizational commitment. *Journal of Applied Psychology*, **73**, 139–145.

Brown, S. P., Cron, W. L., & Leigh, T. W. (1993) Do feelings of success mediate sales performance–work attitude relationships? *Journal of the Academy of Marketing Science*, **21**, 91–100.

Buchko, A. A. (1992) Employee ownership, attitudes, and turnover: An empirical assessment. *Human Relations*, **45**, 711–733.

Buchko, A. A. (1993) The effects of employee ownership on employee attitudes: An integrated causal model and path analysis. *Journal of Management Studies*, **30**, 633–657.

Bycio, P., Hackett, R. D., & Allen J. S. (1995) Further assessments of Bass's (1985) conceptualization of transactional and transformational leadership. *Journal of Applied Psychology*, **80**, 468–478.

Caldwell, D. F., Chatman, J. A. & O'Reilly, C. A. (1990) Building organizational commitment: A multi-firm study. *Journal of Occupational Psychology*, **63**, 245–261.

Carson, K. D. & Bedeian, A. G. (1994) Career commitment: Construction of a measure and examination of its psychometric properties. *Journal of Vocational Behavior*, **44**, 237–262.

Cascio, W. F. (1993) Downsizing: What do we know? What have we learned? *Academy of Management Executive*, **7**, 95–104.

Chao, G. T., O'Leary-Kelly, A. M., Wolf, S., Klein, H. J., & Gardner, P. D. (1994) Organizational socialization: Its content and consequences. *Journal of Applied Psychology*, **79**, 730–743.

Cohen, A. (1991) Career stage as a moderator of the relationships between organizational commitment and its outcomes: A meta-analysis. *Journal of Occupational Psychology*, **64**, 253–268.

Cohen, A. (1992) Antecedents of organizational commitment across occupational groups: A meta-analysis. *Journal of Organizational Behavior*, **13**, 539–558.

Cohen, A (1993a) Age and tenure in relation to organizational commitment: A meta-analysis. *Basic and Applied Social Psychology*, **14**, 143–159.

Cohen, A. (1993b) On the discriminant validity of the Meyer and Allen (1984) measure of organizational commitment: How does it fit with the work commitment construct? In N. S. Bruning (ed.), *Proceedings of the Annual Meeting of the Administrative Science Association of Canada: Organizational Behaviour*, **14**, 82–91.

Cohen, A. (1993c) Work commitment in relation to withdrawal intentions and union effectiveness. *Journal of Business Research*, **26**, 75–90.

Cohen, A. & Gattiker, U. E. (1994) Rewards and organizational commitment across structural characteristics: A meta-analysis. *Journal of Business and Psychology*, **9**, 137–157.

Cohen, A., & Hudecek, N. (1993) Organizational commitment–turnover relationship across occupational groups: A meta-analysis. *Group and Organization Management*, **18**, 188–213.

Cohen, A. & Kirchmeyer, C. (1995) A multidimensional approach to the relation between organizational commitment and nonwork participation. *Journal of Vocational Behavior*, **46**, 189–202.

Cohen, A. & Lowenberg, G. (1990) A re-examination of the side-bet theory as applied to organizational commitment: A meta-analysis. *Human Relations*, **43**, 1015-1050.

Cropanzano, R., James, K., & Konovsky, M. A. (1993) Dispositional affectivity as a predictor of work attitude and job performance. *Journal of Organizational Behavior*, **14**, 595–606.

Davy, J. A., Kinicki, A. J., & Scheck, C. L. (1991) Developing and testing a model of survivor responses to layoffs. *Journal of Vocational Behavior*, **38**, 302–317.

Dawis, R. V. (1992) Person–environment fit and job satisfaction. In C. J. Cranny, P., C. Smith, and E. F. Stone (eds), *Job Satisfaction*, New York: Lexington Books.

Dunham, R.B., Grube, J. A., & Castaneda, M. B. (1994) Organizational commitment: The utility of an integrative definition. *Journal of Applied Psychology*, **79**, 370–380.

Edwards, J. R. (1991) Person–job fit: A conceptual integration, literature review, and methodological critique. In C. L. Cooper, and I. T. Robertson (eds), *International Review of Industrial and Organizational Psychology*, Vol. 6. New York: Wiley.

Edwards, J. R. (1993) Problems with the use of profile similarity indices in the study of congruence in organizational research. *Personnel Psychology*, **46**, 641–665.

Edwards, J. R. (1994) The study of congruence in organizational behavior research: Critique and a proposed alternative. *Journal of Organizational Behavior and Human Decision Processes*, **58**, 51–100.

Edwards, J. R. & Cooper, C. L. (1990) The person–environment fit approach to stress: Recurring problems and some suggested solutions. *Journal of Organizational Behavior*, **11**, 293–307.

Eisenberger, R., Fasolo, P., & Davis-LaMastro, V. (1990) Perceived organizational support and employee diligence, commitment, and innovatin. *Journal of Applied Psychology*, **75**, 51–59.

Eisenberger, R., Huntington, R., Hutchison, S., & Sowa, D. (1986) Perceived organizational support. *Journal of Applied Psychology*, **71**, 500–507.

Emshoff, J. R. (1994) How to increase employee loyalty while you downsize. *Business Horizons*, **37**, 49–57.

Facteau, J. D., Dobbins, G. H., Russell, J. E. A., Ladd, R. T., & Kudisch, J. D. (1995) The influence of general perceptions of the training environment on pretraining motivation and perceived training transfer. *Journal of Management*, **21**, 1–25.

Farkas, A. J. & Tetrick, L. E. (1989) A three-wave longitudinal analysis on the causal ordering of satisfaction and commitment on turnover decision. *Journal of Applied Psychology*, **74**, 855–868.

Fletcher, C. (1991) Candidates' reactions to assessment centres and their outcomes: A longitudinal study. *Journal of Occupational Psychology*, **64**, 117–127.

Florkowski, G. W. & Schuster, M. H. (1992) Support for profit sharing and organizational commitment: A path analysis. *Human Relations*, **45**, 507–523.

Folger, R. & Konovsky, M. A. (1989) Effects of procedural and distributive justice on reactions to pay raise decisions. *Academy of Management Journal*, **32**, 115–130.

Gaertner, K. N. & Nollen, S. D. (1989) Career experiences, perceptions of employment practices, and psychological commitment to the organization. *Human Relations*, **42**, 975–991.

Ganster, D. C. & Dwyer, D. J. (1995) The effects of under staffing on individual and group performance in professional and trade occupations. *Journal of Management*, **21**, 175–190.

Gellatly, I. R. (1995) Individual and group determinants of employee absenteeism: Test of a causal model. *Journal of Organizational Behavior*, **16**, 469–485.

Greenberg, J. (1990) Organizational justice: Yesterday, today and tomorrow. *Journal of Management*, **16**, 399–432.

Greenberg, J. (1993) Stealing in the name of justice: Informational and interpersonal moderators of theft reactions to underpayment inequity. *Organizational Behavior and Human Decision Processes*, **54**, 81–103.

Gregersen, H. B. (1993) Multiple commitments at work and extrarole behavior during three stages of organizational tenure. *Journal of Business Research*, **26**, 31–47.

Griffin, R. W. & Bateman, T. S. (1986) Job satisfaction and organizational commitment. In C. L. Cooper and I. Robertson (eds), *International Review of Industrial and Organizational Psychology*, Vol. 2. New York: Wiley.

Grover, S. L. (1993) Why professionals lie: The impact of professional role conflict on reporting accuracy. *Organizational Behavior and Human Decision Processes*, **55**, 251–272.

Grover, S. L. & Crooker, K. J. (1995) Who appreciates family-responsive human resource policies: The impact of family-friendly policies on the organizational attachment of parents and non-parents. *Personnel Psychology*, **48**, 271–288.

Guzzo, R. A., Noonan, K. A., & Elron, E. (1994) Expatriate managers and the psychological contract. *Journal of Applied Psychology*, 79, 617–626.

Hackett, R. D., Bycio, P., & Hausdorf, P. A. (1994) Further assessments of Meyer and Allen's (1991) three-component model of organizational commitment. *Journal of Applied Psychology*, 79, 15–23.

Harris, S. G., Hirschfeld, R. R., Feild, H. S. & Mossholder, K. W. (1993) Psychological attachment: Relationships with job characteristics, attitudes, and preferences for newcomer development. *Group and Organization Management*, **18**, 459–481.

Hunt, J. G., Osborn, R. N., & Martin, H. J. (1981) A multiple influence model of leadership. *Technical Report No. 520, US Army Research Institute for Behavioral and Social Sciences*, Alexandria, VA.

Hunt, S. D. & Morgan, R. M. (1994) Organizational commitment: One of many commitments or key mediating construct? *Academy of Management Journal*, **37**, 1568–1587.

Huselid, M. A. (1995) The impact of human resource management practices on turnover, productivity, and corporate financial performance. *Academy of Management Journal*, **38**, 635–672.

Huselid, M. A. & Day, N. E. (1991) Organizational commitment, job involvement, and turnover: A substantive and methodological analysis. *Journal of Applied Psychology*, **76**, 380–391.

Iaffaldano, M. T. & Muchinsky, P. M. (1985) Job satisfaction and performance: A meta-analysis. *Psychological Bulletin*, **97**, 251–273.

Irving, G. P. & Meyer, J. P. (1994) Reexamination of the met-expectations hypothesis: A longitidunal analysis. *Journal of Applied Psychology*, **79**, 937–949.

Irving, G. P. & Meyer, J. P. (1995) On using direct measures of met expectations: A methodological note. *Journal of Management*, 21, 1159–1175.

Jaros, S. J., Jermier, J. M. Koehler, J. W., & Sincich, T. (1993) Effects of continuance, affective, and moral commitment on the withdrawal process: An evaluation of eight structural equation models. *Academy of Management Journal*, 36, 951–995.

Jenkins, J. M. (1993) Self-monitoring and turnover: The impact of personality on intent to leave. *Journal of Organizational Behavior*, 14, 83–91.

Johnston III, G. P. & Snizek, W. (1991) Combining head and heart in complex organizations: A test of Etzioni's dual compliance structure hypothesis. *Human Relations*, 44, 1255–1272.

Jones, G. R. (1986) Socialization tactics, self-efficacy, and newcomers' adjustments to organizations. *Academy of Management Journal*, 29, 262–279.

Katz, D. (1964) The motivational basis of organizational behavior. *Behavioral Science*, 9, 131–146.

Kelman, H. C. (1958) Compliance, identification, and internalization: Three processes of attitude change. *Journal of Conflict Resolution*, 2, 51–60.

Kiesler, C. A (1971) *The Psychology of Commitment: Experiments Linking Behavior to Belief*. New York: Academic Press.

Klein, K. J. (1987) Employee stock ownership and employee attitudes: A test of three models. *Journal of Applied Psychology*, 72, 319–332.

Klein, K. J. & Hall, R. J. (1988) Correlates of employee satisfaction with stock ownership: Who likes an ESOP most? *Journal of Applied Psychology*, 73, 630–638.

Kline, C. J. & Peters, L. H. (1991) Behavioral commitment and tenure of new employees: A replication and extension. *Academy of Management Journal*, 34, 194–204.

Kong, S. X., Wertheimer, J. S., Serradell, J., & McGhan, W. F. (1994) Psychometric evaluation of measures of organizational commitment and intention to quit among pharmaceutical scientists. *Pharmaceutical Research*, 11, 171–180.

Konovsky, M. A. & Brockner, J. (1993) Managing victim and survivor layoff reactions: A procedural justice perspective. In R. Cropanzano (ed.), *Justice in the Workplace*. Hillsdale, NJ: Erlbaum.

Konovsky, M. A. & Cropanzano, R. (1991) Perceived fairness of employee drug testing as a predictor of employee attitudes and job performance. *Journal of Applied Psychology*, 76, 698–707.

Koys, D. J. (1988) Human resource management and a culture of respect: Effects on employee's organizational commitment. *Employee Responsibilities and Rights Journal*, 1, 57–68.

Koys, D. J. (1991) Fairness, legal compliance, and organizational commitment. *Employee Responsibilities and Rights Journal*, 4, 283–291.

Lance, C. E. (1991) Evaluation of a structural model relating job satisfaction, organizational commitment and precursors to voluntary turnover. *Multivariate Behavioral Research*, 26, 137–162.

Lawler, E. J. (1992) Affective attachment to nested groups: A choice process theory. *American Sociological Review*, 57, 327–339.

Lee, T. W., Ashford, S. J., Walsh, J. P., & Mowday, R. T. (1992) Commitment propensity, organizational commitment, and voluntary turnover: A longitudinal study of organizational entry processes. *Journal of Management*, 18, 15–32.

Lee, T. W. & Mitchell, T. R. (1991) The unfolding effects of organization commitment and anticipated job satisfaction on voluntary employee turnover. *Motivation and Emotion*, 15, 99–121.

Leong, S. M. Randall, D. M., & Cote, J. A. (1994) Exploring the organizational commitment-performance linkage in marketing: A study of life insurance salespeople. *Journal of Business Research*, 29, 57–63.

Lewin, K. (1943) Defining the 'field at a given time'. *Psychological Review*, 50, 292–310.

Lind, E. A. & Tyler, T. R. (1988) *The Social Psychology of Procedural Justice*. New York: Plenum Press.

Locke, E. A. (1976) The nature and consequences of job satisfaction. In M. D. Dunnette (ed.), *Handbook of Industrial and Organizational Psychology*, Chicago: Rand McNally.

Louis, M. R. (1980) Surprise and sense-making: What newcomers experience in entering unfamiliar organizational settings. *Administrative Science Quarterly*, 25, 226–251.

Major, D. A., Kozlowski, S. W. J., Chao, G. T., & Gardner, P. D. (1995) A longitudinal investigation of newcomer experiences, early socialization outcomes, and the moderating effects of role development factors. *Journal of Applied Psychology*, 80, 418–431.

Martin, T. N. & Hafer, J. C. (1995) The multiplicative interaction effects of job involvement and organizational commitment on the turnover intentions of full and part-time employees. *Journal of Vocational Behavior*, 46, 310–331.

Mathieu, J. E. (1988) A causal model of organizational commitment in a military training environment. *Journal of Vocational Behavior*, 34, 321–335.

Mathieu, J. E. (1991) A cross-level nonrecursive model of the antecedents of organizational commitment and satisfaction. *Journal of Applied Psychology*, 76, 607–618.

Mathieu, J. E. & Farr, J. L. (1991) Further evidence for the discriminant validity of measures of organizational commitment, job involvement, and job satisfaction. *Journal of Applied Psychology*, 76, 127–133.

Mathieu, J. E. & Hamel, K. (1989) A causal model of the antecedents of organizational commitment among professionals and nonprofessionals. *Journal of Vocational Behavior*, 34, 299–317.

Mathieu, J. E. & Kohler, S. S. (1990) A test of the interactive effects of organizational commitment and job involvement on various types of absence. *Journal of Vocational Behavior*, 36, 33–44.

Mathieu, J. E. & Zajac, D. M. (1990) A review and meta-analysis of the antecedents, correlates, and consequences of organizational commitment. *Psychological Bulletin*, 108, 171–194.

Mayer, R. C. & Schoorman, F. D. (1992) Predicting participation and production outcomes through a two-dimensional model of organizational commitment. *Academy of Management Journal*, 35, 671–684.

McGee, G. W. & Ford, R. C. (1987) Two (or more?) dimensions of organizational commitment: Reexamination of the Affective and Continuance Commitment Scales. *Journal of Applied Psychology*, 72, 638–642.

Meglino, B. M., Ravlin, E. C., & Adkins, C. L. (1989) A work values approach to corporate culture: A field test of the value congruence process and its relationship to individual outcomes. *Journal of Applied Psychology*, 74, 424–432.

Mellor, S. (1992) The influence of layoff severity on postlayoff union commitment among survivors: The moderating effect of the perceived legitimacy of a layoff account. *Personnel Psychology*, 45, 579–600.

Meyer, J. P. & Allen, N. J. (1984) Testing the 'side-bet theory' of organizational commitment: Some methodological considerations. *Journal of Applied Psychology*, 69, 372–378.

Meyer, J. P. & Allen, N. J. (1991) A three-component conceptualization of organizational commitment. *Human Resource Management Review*, 1, 61–89.

Meyer, J. P. & Allen, N. J. (1995, May) *Work characteristic and work attitude relations: Moderating effect of attributions*. Paper presented at the annual meeting of the Society of Industrial and Organizational Psychology, Orlando, Florida.

Meyer, J. P., Allen, N. J., & Gellatly, I. R. (1990) Affective and continuance commitment to the organization: Evaluation of measures and analysis of concurrent and time-lagged relations. *Journal of Applied Psychology*, 75, 710–720.

Meyer, J. P., Allen, N. J., & Smith, C. A. (1993) Commitment to organizations and occupations: Extension and test of a three-component conceptualization. *Journal of Applied Psychology*, **78**, 538–551.

Meyer, J. P., Bobocel, D. R., & Allen, N. J. (1991) Development of organizational commitment during the first year of employment: A longitudinal study of pre- and post-entry influences. *Journal of Management*, **17**, 717–733.

Meyer, J. P. & Gardner, R. C. (1994, March) *Assessment of change in organizational commitment during the first year of employment: An application of confirmatory factor analysis*. Paper presented at the Academy of Management, Research Methods Division, Conference on Causal Modelling, West Lafayette, Indiana.

Meyer, J. P., Irving, G. P. & Allen, N. J. (in press) Examination of the combined effects of work values and early work experiences on organizational commitment. *Journal of Organizational Behavior*.

Meyer, J. P., Paunonen, S. V., Gellatly, I. H., Goffin, R. D., & Jackson, D. N. (1989) Organizational commitment and job performance: It's the nature of the commitment that counts. *Journal of Applied Psychology*, **74**, 152–156.

Mignerey, J. T., Rubin, R. B., & Gordon, W. I. (1995) Organizational entry: An investigation of newcomer communication behavior and uncertainty. *Communication Research*, **22**, 54–85.

Mone, M. A. (1994) Relationships between self-concepts, aspirations, emotional responses, and intent to leave a downsizing organization. *Human Resource Management*, **33**, 281–298.

Moorman, R. H., Niehoff, B. P., & Organ, D. W. (1993) Treating employees fairly and organizational citizenship behavior: Sorting the effects of job satisfaction, organizational commitment, and procedural justice. *Employee Responsibilities and Rights Journal*, **6**, 209–225.

Morrison, E. W. (1993) Longitudinal study of the effects of information seeking on newcomer socialization. *Journal of Applied Psychology*, **78**, 173–183.

Morrison, E. W. (1994) Role definitions and organizational citizenship behavior: The importance of the employee's perspective. *Academy of Management Journal*, **37**, 1543–1567.

Morrow, P. C. (1983) Concept redundancy in organizational research: The case of work commitment. *Academy of Management Review*, **8**, 486–500.

Morrow, P. C. (1993) *The Theory and Measurement of Work Commitment*. Greenwich, CT: JAI Press.

Mowday, R. T., Porter, L. W., & Steers, R. M. (1982) *Employee–Organization Linkages: The Psychology of Commitment, Absenteeism, and Turnover*. New York: Academic Press.

Mowday, R. T., Steers, R. M. & Porter, L. W. (1979) The measurement of organizational commitment. *Journal of Vocational Behavior*, **14**, 224–247.

Mueller, C. W., Boyer, E. M., Price, J. L., & Iverson, R. D. (1994) Employee attachment and noncoercive conditions of work: The case of dental hygienists. *Work and Occupations*, **21**, 179–212.

Mueller, C. W., Wallace, J. E., & Price, J. L. (1992) Employee commitment: Resolving some issues. *Work and Occupations*, **19**, 211–236.

Munene, J. C. (1995) 'Not on seat': An investigation of some correlates of organizational citizenship behavior in Nigeria. *Applied Psychology: An International Review*, **44**, 111–222.

Oliver, N. (1990) Work rewards, work values, and organizational commitment in an employee-owned firm: Evidence from the UK. *Human Relations*, **43**, 513–526.

O'Reilly, C. A. & Caldwell, D. F. (1981) The commitment and job tenure of new employees: Some evidence of postdecisional justification. *Administrative Science Quarterly*, **26**, 597–616.

O'Reilly, C. A. & Chatman, J. (1986) Organizational commitment and psychological attachment: The effects of compliance, identification, and internalization on prosocial behavior. *Journal of Applied Psychology*, 71, 492–499.

O'Reilly, C. A., Chatman, J., & Caldwell, D. F. (1991) People and organizational culture: A profile comparison approach to assessing person-organization fit. *Academy of Management Journal*, 34, 487–516.

Organ, D. W. (1988) *Organizational Citizenship Behavior: The Good Soldier Syndrome.* Lexington, MA: Lexington Books.

Organ, D. W. & Ryan, K. (1995) A meta-analytic review of attitudinal and dispositional predictors of organizational citizenship behavior. *Personnel Psychology*, 48, 775–802.

Ostrof, C. (1992) The relationship between satisfaction, attitudes, and performance: An organizational level analysis. *Journal of Applied Psychology*, 77, 963–974.

Ostroff, C. & Kozlowski, S. W. J. (1992) Organizational socialization as a learning process: The role of information acquisition. *Personnel Psychology*, 45, 849–874.

Penley, L. E. & Gould, S. (1988) Etzioni's model of organizational involvement: A perspective for understanding commitment to organizations. *Journal of Organizational Behavior*, 9, 43–59.

Pierce, J. L. & Dunham, R. B. (1987) Organizational commitment: Pre-employment propensity and initial work experiences. *Journal of Management*, 13, 163–178.

Premack, S. L. & Wanous, J. P. (1985) A meta-analysis of realistic job preview experiments. *Journal of Applied Psychology*, 70, 706–719.

Rahim, M. A. & Afza, M. (1993) Leader power, commitment, saisfaction, compliance, and propensity to leave a job among US accountants. *Journal of Social Psychology*, 133, 611–625.

Randall, D. M. (1987) Commitment and the organization: The organization man revisited. *Academy of Management Review*, 12, 460–471.

Randall, D. M. (1990) The consequences of organizational commitment: Methodological investigation. *Journal of Organizational Behavior*, 11, 361–378.

Randall, D. M. & Cote, J. A. (1991) Interrelationships of work commitment constructs. *Work and Occupations*, 18, 194–211.

Randall, D. M., Fedor, D. B. & Longenecker, C. O. (1990) The behavioral expression of organizational commitment. *Journal of Vocational Behavior*, 36, 210–224.

Reichers, A. E. (1985) A review and reconceptualization of organizational commitment. *Academy of Management Review*, 10, 465–476.

Reichers, A. E. (1986) Conflict and organizational commitments', *Journal of Applied Psychology*, 71, 508–514.

Reilly, N. P. & Orsak, C. L. (1991) A career stage analysis of career and organizational commitment in nursing. *Journal of Vocational Behavior*, 39, 311–330.

Robertson, I. T., Iles, P. A., Gratton, L., & Sharpley, D. (1991) The impact of personnel selection and assessment methods on candidates. *Human Relations*, 44, 963–982.

Romzek, B. S. (1989) Personal consequences of employee commitment. *Academy of Management Journal*, 32, 649–661.

Rosin, H. M. & Korabik, K. (1991) Workplace variables, affective responses, and intention to leave among women managers. *Journal of Occupational Psychology*, 64, 317–330.

Roznowski, M. & Hulin, C. (1992) The scientific merit of valid measures of general constructs with special reference to job satisfaction and job withdrawal. In C. J. Cranny, P. C. Smith, and E. F. Stone (eds), *Job Satisfaction.* New York: Lexington Books.

Saks, A. M. (1995) Longitudinal field investigation of the moderating and mediating effects of self-efficacy on the relationship between training and newcomer adjustment. *Journal of Applied Psychology*, 80, 211–225.

Salancik, G. R. (1977) Commitment and the control of organizational behavior. In B. M. Staw and G. R. Salancik, (eds), *New Directions in Organizational Behavior*. Chicago: St. Clair Press.

Schechter, D. S. (1985) *Value and continuance commitment: A field test of a dual conceptualization of organizational commitment*. Unpublished Master's thesis, University of Maryland, College Park.

Schwarzwald, J., Koslowsky, M., & Shalit, B. (1992) A field study of employees' attitudes and behaviors after promotion decisions. *Journal of Applied Psychology*, 77, 511–514.

Schweiger, D. M. & DeNisi, A. S. (1991) Communication with employees following a merger: A longitudinal field experiment. *Academy of Management Journal*, 34, 110–135.

Shore, L. M., Barksdale, K., & Shore, T. H. (1995) Managerial perceptions of employee commitment to the organization. *Academy of Management Journal*, 38, 1593–1615.

Shore, L. M. & Martin, H. J. (1989) Job satisfaction and organizational commitment in relation to work performance and turnover intentions. *Human Relations*, 42, 625–638.

Shore, L. M., Newton, L. A., & Thorton III, G. C. (1990) Job and organizational attitudes in relation to employee behavioral intentions. *Journal of Organizational Behavior*, 11, 57–67.

Shore, L. M. & Tetrick, L. E. (1991) A construct validity study of the Survey of Perceived Organizational Support. *Journal of Appled Psychology*, 76, 637–643.

Shore, L. M. & Wayne, S. J. (1993) Commitment and employee behavior: Comparison of affective and continuance commitment with perceived organizational support. *Journal of Applied Psychology*, 78, 774–780.

Smith, C. A. & Meyer, J. P. (1996, April) *HRM practices and organizational commitment: Test of a mediation model*. Paper presented at the annual meeting of the Society for Industrial and Organizational Psychology, San Diego, CA.

Somers, M. J. (1993) A test of the relationship between affective and continuance commitment using non-recursive models. *Journal of Occupational and Organizational Psychology*, 66, 185–192.

Somers, M. J. (1995) Organizational commitment, turnover and absenteeism: An examination of direct and interaction effects. *Journal of Organizational Behavior*, 16, 49–58.

Somers, M. J. & Casal, J. C. (1994) Organizational commitment and whistle-blowing. *Group and Organization Management*, 19, 270–284.

Staw, B. M. (1974) Attitudinal and behavioral consequences of changing a major organizational reward: A natural field experiment. *Journal of Personality and Social Psychology*, 6, 742–751.

Sutton, C. D. & Harrison, A. W. (1993) Validity assessment of compliance, identification, and internalization as dimensions of organizational commitment. *Educational and Psychological Measurement*, 53, 217–223.

Sweeney, P. D. & McFarlin, D. B. (1993) Workers' evaluations of the 'ends' and the 'means': An examination of four models of distributive and procedural justice. *Organizational Behavior and Human Decision Processes*, 55, 23–40.

Tannenbaum, S. I., Mathieu, J. E., Salas, E., & Cannon-Bowers, J. A. (1991) Meeting trainees' expectations: The influence of training fulfilment on the development of commitment, self-efficacy, and motivation. *Journal of Applied Psychology*, 76, 759–769.

Tett, R. P. & Meyer, J. P. (1993) Job satisfaction, organizational commitment, turnover intention and turnover: Path analyses based on meta-analytic findings. *Personnel Psychology*, 46, 259–293.

Tucker, J., Nock, S. L., & Toscano, D. J. (1989) Employee ownership and perceptions at work. *Work and Occupations*, **16**, 26–42.

Vancouver, J. B. & Schmitt, N. W. (1991) An exploratory examination of person–organization fit: Organizational goal congruence. *Personnel Psychology*, **44**, 333–352.

Vandenberg, R. J. & Lance, C. E. (1992) Examining the causal order of job satisfaction and organizational commitment. *Journal of Management*, **18**, 153–167.

Vandenberg, R. J. & Self, R. M. (1993) Assessing newcomers' changing commitments to the organization during the first 6 months of work. *Journal of Applied Psychology*, **78**, 557–568.

Vandenberg, R. J., Self, R. M., & Seo, J. H. (1994) A critical examination of the internalization, identification, and compliance commitment measures. *Journal of Management*, **20**, 123–140.

Vandenberghe, C. (1996) Assessing organizational commitment in a Belgian context: Evidence for the three-dimensional model. *Applied Psychology: An International Review*, **45**, 371–386.

Van Maanen, J. & Schein, E. H. (1979) Toward a theory of organizational socialization. *Research in Organizational Behavior*, **1**, 209–264.

Wahn, J. (1993) Organizational dependence and the likelihood of complying with organization pressures to behave unethically. *Journal of Business Ethics*, **12**, 245–251.

Wallace, J. E. (1993) Professional and organizational commitment: Compatible or incompatible? *Journal of Vocational Behavior*, **42**, 333–349.

Wanous, J. P. (1980) *Organizational Entry*. Reading, MA: Addison-Wesley.

Wanous, J. P., Poland, T. D., Premack, S. L., & Davis, S. K. (1992) The effects of met expectations on newcomer attitudes and behaviors: A review and meta-analysis. *Journal of Applied Psychology*, **77**, 288–297.

Weiner, Y. (1982) Commitment in organizations: A normative view. *Academy of Management Review*, **7**, 418–428.

Wetzel, K. W. & Gallagher, D. G. (1990) A comparative analysis of organizational commitment among workers in the cooperative and private sectors. *Economic and Industrial Democracy*, **11**, 93–109.

Whitener, E. M. & Walz, P. M. (1993) Exchange theory determinants of affective and continuance commitment and turnover. *Journal of Vocational Behavior*, **42**, 265–281.

Williams, L. J. & Anderson, S. E. (1991) Job satisfaction and organizational commitment as predictors of organizational citizenship and in-role behaviors. *Journal of Management*, **17**, 601–617.

Wittig-Berman, U. & Lang, D. (1990) Organizational commitment and its outcomes: Differing effects of value commitment and continuance commitment on stress reactions, alienation and organization-serving behaviors. *Work and Stress*, **4**, 167–177.

Yoon, J., Baker, M. R., & Ko, J. W. (1994) Interpersonal attachment and organizational commitment: Subgroup hypothesis revisited', *Human Relations*, **47**, 329–351.

Chapter 9

25 YEARS OF VOLUNTARY TURNOVER RESEARCH: A REVIEW AND CRITIQUE

Carl P. Maertz, Jr and Michael A. Campion
Purdue University, USA

Although there have been literally thousands of studies including voluntary turnover as a variable of interest, there has been a scarcity of comprehensive narrative reviews on the topic. Several well-known reviews exist, but they concentrate primarily on summarizing empirical bivariate relationships (e.g. Cotton & Tuttle, 1986; Mobley, Griffeth, Hand & Meglino, 1979) or developing voluntary turnover models (e.g. Bluedorn, 1982; Lee & Mitchell, 1994; Muchinsky & Morrow, 1980; Price, 1977; Steers & Mowday, 1981). None of these reviews has attempted to cover all major areas of the individual turnover literature. The current chapter seeks to fill this gap, with the caveat that more space is generally devoted to studies not reviewed previously. A review of all major areas of voluntary turnover in one chapter allows researchers to have a broader perspective on the literature from which new interconnections and synergies can emerge. Also, this chapter should help clarify where incremental contributions can best be made and where relatively less research is needed.

The main organizing framework includes three sections: (a) Early Studies (1970s–middle 1980s), (b) Recent Studies (middle 1980s through present), and (c) Conclusions and Future Research. For reviews of studies prior to the 1970s, see Porter and Steers (1973) and Schuh (1967). The temporal division between the 'Early Studies' and 'Recent Studies' sections is not arbitrary. Different issues and subtopics have emerged since the middle 1980s, suggesting two main phases in the research. In the first two sections, we address major issues in voluntary turnover that came to prominence during each phase. In the final section, we suggest general directions for future turnover research.

25 Years of Voluntary Turnover Research: A Review and Critique by Carl P. Maertz, Jr and Michael A. Campion
taken from IRIOP 1998 v13, Edited by Cary L. Cooper and Ivan T. Robertson: © 1998 John Wiley & Sons, Ltd

However, before beginning the main body, we attempt to better clarify the meaning of voluntary turnover. The definition of voluntary turnover has often been assumed to be straightforward and clear in much of the organizational psychology literature. Multiple perspectives do exist, however. Individual turnover decisions that are voluntary is the intended content domain of this review, but even this requires further specification.

Defining Voluntary Turnover

The turnover criterion includes several different dimensions (Campion, 1991). The most obvious dimension of individual turnover, voluntariness, has typically been considered dichotomous (i.e. voluntary or involuntary). However, this dichotomization may fail to fully consider the complexity of reasons behind turnover decisions. For instance, some turnover reasons, such as quitting due to pregnancy, quitting due to the relocation of a spouse, or quitting to avoid expected involuntary termination, seem to have both voluntary and involuntary aspects. Ideally, research should accurately measure turnover voluntariness on a continuum.

However, there are many problems with turnover measurement (Campion, 1991). First, deficiencies exist in number and scope of turnover reasons typically collected in exit surveys and recorded in personnel files. Second, Campion (1991) pointed out that former employees and their supervisors may report multiple reasons for quitting. He found that agreement on all reasons among these two sources and personnel files was quite low (25%), even though agreement on at least one reason was higher (68%). This lack of agreement, along with the possibility of self-serving, retrospective biases affecting responses (e.g. Muchinsky & Tuttle, 1979), calls into question whether reasons can be reliably measured at all.

Lack of agreement also implies that voluntariness may depend on who you ask about the occurrence of turnover—employer or employee. Because most of the literature concerns psychological predictors and individual choice models, the employee perception would seem most important. However, different individuals can hold variant ideas on what constitutes a truly free-choice decision. Moreover, where surveying leavers is impossible, management's perspective on who initiated the termination may be the only information available to researchers.

Problems aside, future research must at minimum make explicit the criteria used for classifying cases as voluntary vs involuntary. In other words, researchers need to use relatively objective, verifiable criteria across studies. Toward this end, we define voluntary turnover here as: *instances wherein management agrees that the employee had the physical opportunity to continue employment with the company, at the time of termination.*

Voluntariness means that there was no impediment to continued employment from physical disability or from company management (i.e. employee had not been advised of involuntary termination). For example, voluntary reasons would include non-mandatory retirement, quitting for family reloca-tion, and quitting for a more secure job. All these reasons imply individual choice, even though the employee may feel as though the choice to stay is extremely costly. Future research should endeavor to collect multiple reasons for turnover from both employer and employee, to better ascertain voluntariness and to better approach a voluntariness continuum in the future.

EARLY STUDIES

In early research there was a primary concern with the bivariate empirical correlates of voluntary turnover (Porter & Steers, 1973). In the 1970s, multi-variate models of turnover antecedents and processes began to emerge, largely constructed from successful bivariate predictors. Multivariate models later came to dominate the literature in the late 1970s and early 1980s. But before discussing models which lead into more recent developments, we review liter-ature on organizational consequences, avoidability, and control of voluntary turnover.

Organizational Consequences

The negative consequences of voluntary turnover to the organization have been noted by researchers and practitioners alike. Probably the most obvious negative consequences of turnover are the added staffing and training costs associated with personnel loss (e.g. Mirvis & Lawler, 1977). Administrative costs usually increase with more cases of turnover (Dalton & Todor, 1982). Operational disruption may also occur (Staw, 1980), leading to lost capacity, production, and profits, especially in organizations where turnover rates are high or unpredictable. For instance, an employee with key skills and experi-ence can be particularly costly for the organization to lose. Excessive voluntary turnover may also result in other intangible costs (e.g. low morale).

In contrast, some feel that negative effects have been overemphasized (Dalton, Todor & Krackhardt, 1982). A certain amount of voluntary turnover may even be positive for the organization, the economy, the society, and the individual employee (Dalton & Todor, 1979). The economy and society de-rive benefit from turnover because it generally permits job movement. A bene-fit accrues particularly when turnover occurs in the primary labor market, allowing entrance to those in secondary labor markets (Muchinsky & Morrow, 1980). To the extent that voluntary turnover contributes to this sort of move-ment or improves person–job match, it can benefit society.

Dalton and his colleagues (e.g. Dalton & Todor, 1979; Dalton, Todor & Krackhardt, 1982) contend that there may be cases of functional turnover which bring financial and other benefits to the organization. For example, an organization saves in salary costs if a highly paid, long-tenured employee is replaced by a new hire (Campion, 1991; Dalton & Todor, 1982). Voluntary turnover can also be considered beneficial if the employee was a poor performer or if the resignation facilitated flexibility or creativity by bringing in 'new blood' (Campion, 1991; Dalton, Todor & Krackhardt, 1982; Muchinsky & Morrow, 1980).

Boudreau and Berger (1985) pointed out the need for a broader perspective on turnover consequences. Their organizational utility perspective considered quantity of movers, the quality of movers, and the costs to produce movement. They expanded traditional utility equations to include not only the replacement employee, but also multiple hiring cohorts, continuous retentions, and repeated acquisitions. Equations use average service values and costs to estimate utility under various rates, distributions, and conditions of turnover. In short, employee turnover may bring benefits to the organization, especially when the selection, training, and other replacement costs are low. These equations provide the most comprehensive model available to evaluate the organizational consequences of turnover. Follow-up research using these equations is scarce, perhaps because obtaining estimates for the many parameters is difficult. Nevertheless, more utility research would facilitate accurate assessment of organizational consequences.

Not all instances of quitting are of equal consequence to the organization. Thus, the major question seems to be, which employees would organizations most want to prevent from quitting? We can answer this question through research on turnover utility at the individual level, including the individual's performance, potential, compensation, and other values, along with these same quantities for the replacement employee. After the question, which turnover *should* be prevented, is adequately answered, two other questions become the central issues for management: Which voluntary turnover can be prevented by the organization, and what are the best methods to do this?

Avoidability and Organizational Control

Given the potentially important consequences of voluntary turnover, several researchers have emphasized the avoidability of turnover (Abelson, 1987; Campion, 1991). Dalton, Krackhardt and Porter (1981) suggested a 2 × 2 taxonomy for turnover including avoidability and voluntariness as dimensions. They suggested that those quitting for avoidable reasons are considerably different from both unavoidable leavers and stayers, and they proposed that failing to recognize this distinction may help to explain weak prediction of voluntary turnover. Typically, voluntary turnover that is controllable would be considered more negative by managers than unavoidable turnover (Dalton, Todor & Krackardt, 1982). Presumably, if there is nothing to be done about a person quitting, the occurrence and its consequences are of less concern.

Defining avoidability

Avoidability of an instance of turnover is a matter of perspective; the existing conceptualizations and measures define at least three distinct themes (Abelson, 1987; Campion, 1991; Dalton, Krackhardt & Porter, 1981). They include (a) whether the employee's stated reasons for leaving are organizational or non-work factors, (b) whether the employee believes the organization *would* offer an inducement that would make them stay, and (c) whether or not the organization *actually could* induce the employee to stay.

First, *organization-based reasons* have been thought to indicate avoidable turnover while non-organizational reasons indicate unavoidable turnover (Abelson, 1987; Dalton, Krackhardt & Porter, 1981). Type and origin of reasons are conceptually interesting distinctions but are not directly related to actual avoidability. Using subjective judgments of reasons, Abelson (1987) and Campion (1991) found that those reporting reasons for quitting, judged by management and researchers to be avoidable, had lower satisfaction and commitment than unavoidable leavers and stayers. This seems to confirm that negative attitudes are more associated with organizational reasons than non-work reasons (Dalton, Krackhardt & Porter, 1981).

While non-work reasons may be more difficult for management to learn about or address than organizational reasons, this conceptualization wrongly assumes that non-work reasons for quitting (e.g. family pressure, desire for career change, or desire to relocate) cannot be offset by any potential organizational inducement (Abelson, 1987). This is clearly untrue for certain individuals and situations. In addition, a reason classified as unavoidable for one individual and situation may seem very avoidable for another. Therefore, reasons cannot be judged as avoidable or unavoidable by a researcher naïve to the individual circumstances.

Secondly, *perceived avoidability* reflects whether the employee or supervisor believes the company would have been able to do something to make the employee stay. Campion's (1991) continuous measure directly measures level of avoidability as reported by university employees themselves and their supervisors. Although some items about the origin of reasons appeared in the continuous measure, the scales mainly reflect perceived avoidability from the employee's or the supervisor's point of view. He found that perceived avoidability was negatively associated with measures of voluntariness and satisfaction of the employee. Avoidability from the supervisor's perspective was related to lower employee job performance, perhaps suggesting that organizations may decide *not* to avoid the turnover of poor performers.

Although perceived avoidability has yielded some insights, measurement seems to involve some guesswork from respondents about what the organization *would do* realistically. Even though employees felt turnover was more avoidable on average than supervisors (Campion, 1991), both are unlikely to consider all the potential inducements the organization *actually could* offer. Thereby this measure of avoidability tends to confuse the expected with the possible. Thus, to accurately assess whether turnover is avoidable, the potential of management to offer inducements must be considered.

There is a third interactive perspective that we call *actual avoidability*, which necessarily involves both the individual's and management's input. This perspective assumes that nearly all quitting is potentially avoidable with enough inducement, except for the rare individual whose resolve to quit is unshakable at any price. Actual avoidability essentially reflects whether the organization currently possesses and is willing to offer necessary inducement to the employee, determined through some type of interaction. In short, this perspective changes the meaning of unavoidable turnover, from 'reported reasons originating outside the organization' or 'individual beliefs that the organization would not offer adequate inducement', to instead 'quitting that the organization chooses not to stop (or cannot stop) by way of negotiation and inducements'. Assuming some inducement could be offered, measures might include whether or not the organization will offer the necessary inducement (dichotomous) and the difference between the level of an inducement offered and the level requested by the leaver (continuous).

Methods of control

Even assuming that all voluntary turnover is avoidable given enough inducements, there has been very little research specifically on which inducements or methods to use. This may be because determining which turnover is most beneficial to stop has been difficult. Several findings do directly address interventions to control turnover. For instance, realistic job previews and job redesign were found in a meta-analysis to improve retention rates by an average of 9% and 17%, respectively (McEvoy & Cascio, 1985). Selection, socialization, rewards, training leaders, flexible scheduling, and career planning are other potential interventions for controlling turnover to test in future research (Mobley, 1982).

Conclusion

The questions of which turnover is avoidable and how to manage it have been considered but not answered. Turnover reasons and employee perceptions are imperfect substitutes for more direct measures of actual avoidability. Whether an instance of turnover is truly avoidable for the organization depends largely on what inducements management has at its disposal and how much it offers. Inherent in studying this concept of avoidability are the type and level of inducements needed for retention. Therefore, the areas of utility, avoidability, and control are necessarily linked and should not be studied separately as in the past, but rather as a unified area (i.e. management of voluntary turnover). Management also includes encouraging voluntary turnover, where it has positive utility for the organization. Research is badly needed on which inducements are most effective in preventing or facilitating turnover across various populations and situations.

Model Content

Presumably because understanding and controlling turnover requires some level of predictive success, many empirical studies during this early period attempted to identify bivariate predictors and correlates of voluntary turnover. For reviews of various individual predictors, see for example, Carsten and Spector (1987), Cotton and Tuttle (1986), McEvoy and Cascio (1985, 1987), Michaels and Spector (1982), Mobley et al. (1979), Muchinsky and Tuttle (1979), Porter and Steers (1973), and Schuh (1967). Because many existing reviews already focus on bivariate relationships. we will not specifically focus on them here. Instead, we review major antecedent categories found in voluntary turnover models. These categories equate to distinct types of psychological forces found in the literature that motivate quitting. They are summarized in Figure 9.1.

Withdrawal intentions and cognitions

Intention to quit has demonstrated the highest, most consistent bivariate relationship to turnover behavior, $r = 0.50$ (Steel & Ovalle, 1984). Tett and Meyer (1993) reported a meta-analytic correlation between multiple item measures of turnover intention and turnover of $r = 0.65$. Other withdrawal cognitions have received considerable attention as predictors as well. Thinking of searching, thinking of quitting, and intention to search have demonstrated consistent, positive correlations with turnover behavior, $rs = 0.30$–0.50 (Hom, Caranikas-Walker, Prussia & Griffeth, 1992; Tett & Meyer, 1993). Recently, Hom and Griffeth (1991) proposed that all these cognitions and intentions are part of a single withdrawal cognition syndrome, a proposition that should be tested in the future by confirmatory factor analyses. In summary, turnover intention is the best predictor and the proposed immediate psychological precursor of quitting (Steel & Ovalle, 1984).

Current affect and perceived alternatives

The main content elements of most models from this period can be linked to March and Simon's (1958) concepts of perceived ease of movement and desirability of movement, which are typically operationalized as work attitudes and perceived alternative opportunities, respectively. Work attitudes such as global satisfaction, facet satisfaction, and organizational commitment have

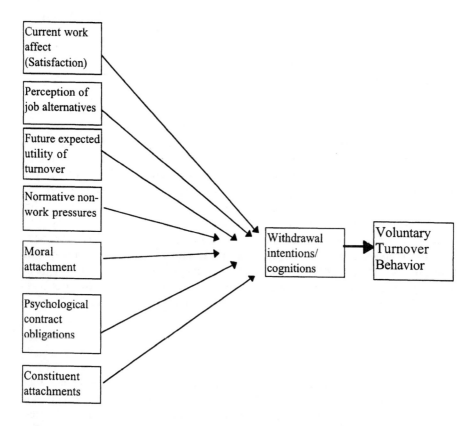

Figure 9.1   Major antecedent forces affecting voluntary turnover intentions and decisions

demonstrated moderate negative correlations with turnover (Cotton & Tuttle, 1986; Muchinsky & Tuttle, 1979; Tett & Meyer, 1993). Number, certainty, or quality of perceived alternative opportunities have demonstrated consistent positive relationships to turnover, although relatively small in magnitude. Steel and Griffeth (1989) and Hom et al. (1992) reported corrected correlations between perceived alternatives and turnover of $r = 0.13$ and $r = 0.14$, respectively. Forrest, Cummings & Johnson (1977) and Price (1977) integrated the psychological and economic perspectives by including both individual attitudes and labor market influences on turnover. Together with turnover intentions and cognitions, affect and alternatives have been the predominant antecedents to turnover in multivariate models (e.g. Bluedorn, 1982; Mobley, 1977; Muchinsky & Morrow, 1980; Price & Mueller, 1981; Steers & Mowday, 1981). However, other distinct antecedents may also impact voluntary turnover decisions.

Future expected utility of turnover

Forrest, Cummings and Johnson (1977) suggested that anticipated satisfaction was a relevant determinant of turnover, distinct from current affective responses based on past experiences. Mobley et al. (1979) included future evaluations in their model such that future prospects on the current job and those on an alternative job help determine turnover intention. This would include calculation of lost investments in current membership incurred by leaving (Becker, 1960) vs expected future gains from an alternative. Considering both current and alternative jobs, anticipated satisfaction becomes a future expected utility or valence–instrumentality–expectancy calculation (e.g. Vroom, 1964) regarding the choice to stay or leave.

Normative pressures

Hom, Katerberg and Hulin (1979) and Newman (1974) utilized the Fishbein (1967) model of reasoned action, attempting to predict turnover better than traditional attitude measures. In these models, normative beliefs were antecedents of behavioral intention to turnover. They found that by using normative measures, they explained a higher portion of variance in resignation than with attitude measures alone, a finding that has been replicated (Prestholdt, Lane & Matthews, 1987). In turnover models Fishbein's (1967) normative beliefs are perceived expectations of non-work referents regarding the employee's turnover behavior. Normative beliefs reflect psychological pressure to quit or stay caused by friends and family members, assuming the individual wants to meet their expectations. Normative and non-work influences have been included in other turnover models as well (e.g. Hom, Griffeth & Sellaro, 1984; Mobley et al., 1979). Normative commitment (Wiener, 1982) and work–family conflict (Greenhaus & Beutell, 1985) further exemplify normative pressures which have been linked to turnover.

Moral attachment

Hom, Katerberg and Hulin (1979) hypothesized effects for personal moral obligation in their model of reenlistment. A personal norm of loyalty is consistent with a component of Triandis' (1975) model of social behavior and with the protestant work ethic (Morrow, 1983). Moral commitment has been negatively linked with turnover as well (Jaros, Jermier, Koehler & Sincich, 1993). Moral attachment, as we call this category, is essentially a value of loyalty or general duty, causing one to persist at an organization. While normative forces depend on beliefs about how *others* feel and would react to one's quitting, moral attachment is an internalized individual value. Thus, it may be more stable across situations than normative pressures. Such moral attachment may be increasingly rare in today's turbulent work environment. Nevertheless, it should be studied further. Perhaps it can be thought of as a continuum, with the opposite anchor being the internalized value that *changing* jobs is a virtue.

The psychological antecedents just discussed can each be linked directly to behavioral intention through established models of individual behavior (i.e. Fishbein & Azjen, 1975; Triandis, 1975). However, there are other forces in the literature relevant to turnover decisions which do not appear in multivariate turnover models. These include psychological contract perception and attachment caused by relationships with constituents in the organization.

Psychological contract

Related to equity perceptions is the concept of the psychological contract with the organization (Rousseau & Parks, 1992). A psychological contract is a set of individual beliefs about reciprocal obligations in an employment relationship, not involving a third party observer (Rousseau, 1989). A psychological contract does require accepting a norm of reciprocity (e.g. Scholl, 1981) to some extent and recognizing obligations for both parties. There are two major types of perceived reciprocal obligations between employer and employee (Robinson, Kraatz & Rousseau, 1994). They may be formalized and transactional (e.g. salary, merit pay, advancement, in exchange for, giving notice, accepting transfers, and keeping company secrets), or they may be less tangible and relational (e.g. job security, training, and career development in exchange for loyalty, overtime, and extra-role behaviors).

Changes in obligations over time seem to be self-serving for the employee. From the employee perspective, their obligations decrease and employer obligations increase with tenure (Robinson, Kraatz & Rousseau, 1994). Employees may consider tenure itself to be an ongoing input toward fulfillment of their contract obligation. Further, clear failure to meet the employee's expectations under the contract can constitute a violation of the psychological contract, which either decreases the amount the employee feels he or she owes to the organization or invalidates the contract completely. Employer violations were found to be negatively correlated with reported employee relational obligations such as loyalty and extra work hours (Robinson, Kraatz & Rousseau, 1994). Thus, perceived violations may induce an employee to quit immediately or more readily in the future. Regardless, perceived obligations and violations of a psychological contract that affect quitting should be considered in future turnover models.

Constituent attachments

Reichers (1985) suggested that employees can become committed to constituencies within the organization (e.g. coworkers, supervisors, mentors, work teams, and unions), beyond commitment to the organization as a whole. If employees do not want to lose valued relationships with individuals and groups by leaving, they are more psychologically attached to the organization. Voluntary turnover models do not typically consider the impact of an employee's personal relationships, but constituent attachments to supervisors and coworkers have been linked empirically to quitting (Becker, 1992; Graen, Liden & Hoel, 1982; Hunt & Morgan, 1994; Krackhardt & Porter, 1985). These constituent attachments do not simply equate to facets of satisfaction. Following Meyer and Allen's (1991) conceptualization of organizational commitment, attachment to other referents may include calculative and normative components, as well as affective commitment (Meyer, Allen & Smith, 1993). These three psychological effects should be studied in the future to test if they are valid components of attachment for different organizational constituents.

Hunt and Morgan (1994) tested a mediated effects vs an independent effects model for constituent commitments. They claimed their findings support that constituent commitment effects are mediated by global organizational commitment. However, this conclusion is based not on statistical nested model comparisons, but only on numerical differences on several fit indices. Also, they did not test a partially mediated model at all, so the nature of constituent effects is still in question. One can easily imagine a situation where a person stays because of certain work relationships but dislikes the organization as a whole (Reichers, 1986), implying distinct effects. In any case, the number, directionality, and nature of constituent effects require more research in order to fully understand turnover decisions.

Conclusion

Even the most comprehensive turnover conceptualizations (e.g. Mobley et al., 1979; Price & Mueller, 1981; Steers & Mowday, 1981) exclude some of the antecedent categories in Figure 9.1. To increase understanding of different types of turnover decisions, future studies should simultaneously consider all the psychological forces that may impact the turnover decision. If this is not done, empirical studies of models risk estimation problems from omitting relevant causal variables (James, 1982). Researchers have bemoaned the lack of explained variance in turnover behavior by existing models (e.g. Hom, Griffeth & Sellaro, 1984; Hom et al., 1992; Peters & Sheridan, 1988). The exclusion of turnover antecedents may leave systematic variance in turnover behavior unexplained. Perhaps then turnover behavior can be better predicted and understood through a more comprehensive consideration of psychological antecedents.

Process Models

With the main antecedent forces in traditional models identified, the remaining variations primarily involve the different causal linkages among antecedents. Several other reviews focus on variations in multivariate models

(Baysinger & Mobley, 1983; Lee & Mitchell, 1994; Steers & Mowday, 1981), but none reviews all the major advances found in the process models of this period. Mobley's (1977) intermediate linkage model is the prototype of process models. Its variations have probably received the most research attention of all major conceptualizations. This section reviews process models in terms of their variation from and advancement beyond Mobley (1977). We also review the interaction of affect and alternatives in the decision process, the proposed adaptation–withdrawal process, and other key process developments.

Intermediate linkage models

Based on the assumption that intent to quit or stay is the cognitive event immediately preceding turnover behavior, Mobley's (1977) model proposed the intermediate linkages in the voluntary turnover decision between dissatisfaction and intention to quit. Following an evaluation of the job, experienced dissatisfaction leads to withdrawal cognitions, which lead to an evaluation of the utility of a job search. A positive utility yields an intent to search for a job followed by the search itself. Subsequently, an evaluation occurs of the alternative(s) found comparing it to the current job. An unfavorable comparison leads to an intention to quit, then leading to voluntary turnover. Mobley (1977) proposed feedback loops in which each construct can have a residual effect on preceding constructs. He recognized that not all employees follow the proposed progression to quitting but did not discuss specific alternative progressions. In addition, Mobley (1977) conceded that impulsive quitting may occur in an entirely different way than the proposed step-by-step process. Nevertheless, the basic linkages proposed are logical and compelling.

In their expanded model, Mobley et al. (1979) added that individual values, job perceptions, and labor market perceptions determine (a) expected utility of the current job, (b) expected utility of alternatives, and (c) current job satisfaction. These three elements combine to determine withdrawal intentions, presumably by way of linkages proposed in Mobley (1977). Mobley et al. (1979) also suggested that organizational level factors and economic factors influence quitting *indirectly* through their effects on job perceptions and labor market perceptions, respectively. In his integrative model, Bluedorn (1982) added organizational commitment between job satisfaction and job search in the Mobley, Horner and Hollingsworth (1978) version of the intermediate linkage model. Price and Mueller (1981) and Williams and Hazer (1986) also supported a causal path from job satisfaction to organizational commitment in turnover models. However, other effects have been proposed for the two variables as well.

In general, Mobley's (1977) model and its subsequent variations have received some empirical support (e.g. Hom, Griffeth & Sellaro, 1984; Hom et al., 1992; Miller, Katerberg & Hulin, 1979; Mobley, Horner & Hollingsworth,

1978; Youngblood, Mobley & Meglino, 1983). Using meta-analysis and structural equation modeling in combination, Hom et al. (1992) tested competing variations of intermediate linkages. These included Mobley, Horner and Hollingsworth (1978), Hom, Griffeth & Sellaro (1984), Bannister and Griffeth (1986), and Dalessio, Silverman and Schuck (1986). They concluded that the Dalessio, Silverman and Schuck (1986) model and the Hom, Griffeth and Sellaro (1984) model fit the meta-analytic data better than Mobley, Horner and Hollingsworth (1978), and much better than Bannister and Griffeth (1986). They supported all paths in both models except the path from search intention to turnover in Hom, Griffeth and Sellaro (1984). Even more consistent empirical support exists across studies for the reduced linkage model presented in Hom et al. (1992, p. 905): dissatisfaction → withdrawal cognitions → turnover. Although the integrative Mobley et al. (1979) model and other variations are more theoretically interesting, this reduced model is our most empirically defensible representation of the basic steps in the decision process. Future research should build on this reduced model when investigating additional linkages and their relative merits.

In summary, intermediate linkage research started to examine the steps in the turnover decision process. At the same time, models with variations in one or more linkages have received support as well. This has created confusion about which variation is most accurate. Moreover, the survey data used in past empirical studies do not directly examine how the decision process occurs. This approach only measures current standing on hypothetical psychological steps assumed to occur in the employee's mind. Studies then suggest that a relationship between these measures indicates that a certain psychological process occurred. This type of indirect evidence leaves uncertainty about which steps, if any, actually occur during the turnover decision process. Little research has actually attempted to directly assess the steps that employees go through during quit decisions, a deficiency that must be addressed in the future.

Alternatives, affect, and turnover

Models have made incremental conceptual contributions beyond intermediate linkages alone, including the relationships among alternatives, affect, and turnover. In Mobley (1977) negative affect causes thinking of quitting, while perceived alternatives seem to have two distinct effects. First, general perceptions of the labor market may influence search utility and search intentions (Hom, Griffeth & Sellaro, 1984; Mobley et al., 1979). Second, specific perceived alternatives may be compared with the current job to determine turnover intentions.

Muchinsky and Morrow (1980) proposed a model which includes individual factors, work-related factors, and economic opportunity factors as precursors to turnover. They proposed that alternative opportunities have the strongest *direct* impact on turnover behavior, and they deemphasized the behavioral intention construct as the single precursor to turnover. In addition, Muchinsky and morrow (1980) suggest that individual and work-related factors interact and have effects on turnover, mediated through opportunities. Michaels and Spector (1982) also posited that alternative opportunities have a direct positive influence on turnover behavior, not mediated through satisfaction or intention.

Work by Thibaut and Kelly (1959) on attitudes suggests that alternatives may be a determinant of job affect, namely that more and better job opportunities lead to greater dissatisfaction with the current job. The Hulin, Roznowski and Hachiya (1985) integrative model proposed that favorable market conditions increase the value of employee inputs and thus the opportunity costs for staying. Simultaneously, it also raises the frame of reference for evaluating the current job outcomes, resulting in relative devaluation of these outcomes. High alternatives may inflate the perceived value of inputs and decrease the perceived value of outcomes, lowering current satisfaction and encouraging termination. Bluedorn's (1982) model also proposed that the effect of alternative job opportunities on turnover is mediated through job satisfaction. Empirical research has also supported this effect of perceived alternatives through satisfaction (Dalessio, Silverman & Schuck, 1986; Martin, 1979; Price & Mueller, 1981).

Job alternatives have also been proposed to interact with satisfaction (Price, 1977) and with turnover intentions (Steers & Mowday, 1981) in causing turnover. Researchers have argued (a) that low perceived alternatives block the enacting of withdrawal intentions (Hom, Griffeth & Sellaro, 1984) or (b) that high unemployment 'discourages dissatisfied employees from developing firm decisions to seek alternatives or to resign' (Hom et al., 1992, p. 893). Conversely, when the perceived number or quality of alternatives is high, predictor relationships are stronger because attitudes and intentions can be enacted more easily. This perspective, if true, implies that people are generally risk averse in turnover decisions. This may be somewhat contrary to the finding that between 50% and 60% of employees reported quitting without having another job lined up (Matilla, 1974).

In conclusion, several relationships among alternatives, affect, and turnover have emerged in models, besides those based on Mobley (1977). Perceived alternatives may act directly on turnover behavior, they may influence turnover through satisfaction, or they may moderate the effects of affect or intentions on quitting. Competitive testing of these proposed relationships must be done in the future to accurately examine their relative validity.

In addition, general market perceptions vs crystallized expectations of specific work alternatives should be differentiated by their effects on the process (Griffeth & Hom, 1988). For instance, general perceptions of alternatives may influence search motivation and intention, while specific alternatives may be directly compared to the current job in an expectancy calculation. Low certainty in an alternative would cause calculation of outcomes for the specific alternative to drop (e.g. Vroom, 1964), and a generalized perception of alternatives may operate in place of a comparison between specific job opportunities. Number vs quality of perceived alternatives should also prove relevant (Price & Mueller, 1981). This suggests two dimensions for perceived alternatives: (a) general market perceptions vs uncertain specific alternatives vs certain specific alternatives (offers in hand) and (b) number of alternatives vs quality of alternatives. These dimensions of perceived alternatives may help to clarify the decision process.

Adaptation–withdrawal construct

Other process models in this period relate to the idea of a single withdrawal construct driving the turnover decision. Fishbein and Azjen (1975) stated that general attitudes should relate strongly to a class of behavioral responses, not to specific behaviors. Following this line of reasoning it was suggested that empirical research on work attitudes should relate them to a pattern or syndrome of withdrawal, rather than quitting or absenteeism behaviors alone (Hulin, 1991). Proponents have argued that behaviors such as quitting, absenteeism, lateness, and other dysfunctional behaviors are different manifestations of a single adaptation–withdrawal construct, serving to distance the employee from the organization.

In addition to traditional withdrawal behaviors, general adaptation–withdrawal responses may include input reduction and psychological withdrawal (daydreaming, shirking), behaviors to change job outcomes (stealing, moonlighting on the job), behaviors to change the work role itself (unionization, transfer attempts), retaliatory measures (sabotage, violence), or other cognitive adjustments. These behaviors purportedly stem from relative dissatisfaction and fulfill the same basic purpose—adapting to a dissatisfying work situation (Rosse & Hulin, 1985; Rosse & Miller, 1984). The choice of behaviors depends on a number of perceived opportunity constraints and personal factors (Rosse & Miller, 1984), and their future use depends on their success in improving relative satisfaction (Rosse & Hulin, 1985).

Several theoretical relations among the withdrawal behaviors have been suggested (e.g. Beehr & Gupta, 1978; Gupta & Jenkins, 1980; Hulin, 1991). These include (a) substitutability of behaviors, (b) compensatory relations, (c) spillover relations, and (d) a progression of withdrawal. The first two relations suggest that as one withdrawal behavior is enacted others are less likely to occur. They imply negative correlations among absence, lateness, and quitting. Such negative correlations have not been found. Spillover relations mean that the probability of one behavior increases in the presence of others, whereas a progression of withdrawal implies that withdrawal behaviors occur in a specific order over time. Some empirical evidence supports a progression of withdrawal (Mitra, Jenkins & Gupta, 1992; Rosse, 1988). For example, Rosse (1988) found evidence of a progression of lateness to absence, and from multiple absences to quitting. However, this study used a small sample ($n =$ 63) of hospital employees, and these findings should be replicated before they are generalized.

There has been some support for the validity of a withdrawal construct, primarily indirect evidence in the form of significant shared variance among withdrawal behaviors (e.g. Mitra, Jenkins & Gupta, 1992). In contrast, Steers and Mowday (1981) and others (e.g. Mobley, 1982; Price & Mueller, 1981) have argued that alternative withdrawal behaviors are separate and distinct behaviors from voluntary turnover and should be studied separately. In support, work affect has demonstrated different relationships with absenteeism, lateness, and turnover (Clegg, 1983; Porter & Steers, 1973). Also, variables such as company absence policy may significantly affect absence frequency, but not quit rates. Mobley (1982) argued that both absenteeism and turnover may result from attraction to alternatives, thus 'withdrawal' may not accurately describe the motivation behind these behaviors. Finally, possible third variable causes which may drive covariation between withdrawal behaviors have not been properly investigated in most studies (Clegg, 1983).

Despite some empirical support and significant conceptual development for the adaptation–withdrawal construct, these contrary arguments cannot be ignored. This suggests that fair competitive tests against alternative models should be conducted. Designing research to test the cyclical and progressive nature of adaptation–withdrawal is extremely challenging (Rosse & Hulin, 1985). Nevertheless, more creative research data and designs are needed to confirm, refute, or modify the general adaptation–withdrawal theory.

Other developments

The idea of multiple decision paths to voluntary turnover was introduced during this period. Steers and Mowday's (1981) model proposed that for some intention to quit leads directly to quitting. For others, intention to quit activates a search for and consideration of alternatives. They imply that turnover does not occur without an alternative, a view disputed by some (Lee & Mitchell, 1994). Regardless, Steers and Mowday (1981) introduced unprecedented complexity in their model by including two distinct decision paths.

In another conceptual advance, Sheridan and Abelson (1983) suggested that the turnover process may not be a linear progression of steadily decreasing satisfaction or increasing opportunities, as is assumed in most models. Instead, they suggested that there may be discontinuous changes in turnover propensity when threshold levels on antecedents are reached. For instance, a slight negative change in affect can become a catalyst that pushes the employee over the threshold, making turnover imminent. To test these ideas, Sheridan and Abelson (1983) and Sheridan (1985) fitted catastrophe models to antecedent data. They generally indicated support for their catastrophe models, implying a non-linear threshold relationship between control variables and withdrawal. However, the analyses that led to these conclusions involved some subjective placement of the bifurcation plane which directly impacts the results. Non-linear, threshold progression to quitting remains a provocative idea which needs to be tested more in the future.

Conclusion

Though no single process model achieved dominance empirically, variations of Mobley's (1977) model were most influential and most often studied. Intermediate linkages between affect and turnover, multiple proposed effects for perceived alternatives and affect, a general adaptation–withdrawal process, multiple decision paths, and discontinuous progressions toward quitting were each valuable conceptual advances which should be built on in the future. Despite these considerable contributions of multivariate models, a somewhat simplistic view of quitting was portrayed in most models. With few exceptions, traditional models have assumed a step-by-step, rational, decision process which has never been directly validated. The actual sequences of cognitive steps or linkages posited in variations of Mobley's (1977) model have not been tested directly, only indirectly by survey analyses. Moreover, Lee and Mitchell (1994) state: 'In short, over 17 years of research on traditional turnover models suggests that many employees may leave organizations in ways not specified by the traditional models' (p. 56). To help address this dilemma, we conclude that models of the quitting process must be integrated and expanded.

In addition, research on the quitting process could include more qualitative studies. Although this may seem remedial in such a well-studied area, qualitative methods have not been used much. For instance, diaries on thoughts about organization membership can be kept by employees during their tenure, and interviews can be conducted with those who are quitting regarding their decision process (e.g. Lee, Mitchell, Wise & Fireman, 1996). Without such studies we cannot uncover the full depth and complexity of the decision process.

RECENT STUDIES

Chronologically, we define recent studies roughly as those published during the late 1980s through the middle 1990s. This distinction conveys that recent research on voluntary turnover has moved in new directions. In this period research has focused primarily on moderators and macro factors, methodological issues, and further theoretical development. This research comes in the wake of several realizations about most turnover research prior to this period. First, 'box and line' models proposing antecedents of turnover are many, but coherent theories considering moderators and macro factors are few. Second, research methods for predictive turnover studies have been somewhat flawed or inappropriate, yielding limited knowledge and thwarting empirical prediction (Morita, Lee & Mowday, 1989; Peters & Sheridan, 1988). Third, existing models seem generally to underestimate the complexity of turnover decisions which occur in different populations of employees (Lee & Mitchell, 1994). These issues drive the major contributions in recent years, which are reviewed in the following sections. We also review some recent studies on how job search relates to the turnover process.

Moderators, Macro Factors, and Methodological Issues

Time lag and base rate

Early research (e.g. Mobley et al., 1979; Steel & Ovalle, 1984) recognized that the greater the time lag between predictor measurement and turnover occurrence and the more the base rate of quitting departs from 50%, the weaker the empirical prediction. Greater time lag may neutralize the effectiveness of short-term predictors such as intention (Steel & Ovalle, 1984). Base rates well below or well above 50% restrict range in criterion variance, reduce the effect sizes, and lower statistical power. Smaller relationships with greater time lags and lower base rates have been found for several turnover predictors and situations (Carsten & Spector, 1987; Hom et al., 1992; Steel & Ovalle, 1984). Moreover, if time lags are shortened to improve prediction, there is likely to be a low base rate of employees quitting, resulting once again in attenuated relationships. It seems that time lag and base rate considerations can act as a 'catch 22' in predictive studies. Until recently though, research has not focused specifically on how these interrelated factors jointly impact findings on voluntary turnover.

In their recent meta-analysis, Steel, Hendrix and Balogh (1990) examined the possible confounding effect of base rate on the time-lag moderation effect proposed by Steel and Ovalle (1984). As in this earlier meta-analysis, Steel, Hendrix and Balogh (1990) corrected for the effect size restriction of a point-biserial correlation (which has a maximum magnitude of 0.798). A significant positive correlation between study time lag and study base rate was detected, and base rate was found to have larger biasing effects in smaller samples (Steel, Hendrix & Balogh, 1990). They confirmed that greater time lag decreased the intentions–turnover and global satisfaction–turnover relationships, even after controlling for base rate. Evidently, confounding between base rate and time lag did not fully account for time lag moderation effects (e.g. Carsten & Spector, 1987; Steel & Ovalle, 1984). As a result, future research should consider both base rate and time-lag moderation in turnover prediction. In contrast, Steel, Hendrix and Balogh (1990) observed no time-lag moderation effect for organizational commitment and satisfaction with work itself, contrary to findings on global satisfaction and intentions. This finding offers hope of better prediction over considerable time lags, suggesting that certain predictors may be more or less effective depending on when they are measured with respect to subsequent turnover behavior.

Unemployment

Although effects of perceived alternatives were discussed earlier, it is useful to consider separately the moderating effects of the labor market, beyond their psychological impact on the decision process. As Steel and Griffeth (1989) point out, the labor market rates can have several effects, impacting predictive relationships. Predictors such as intentions and perceived alternatives should display greater variance in low unemployment environments, leading to better prediction. Also, marginal drifters, who may quit within a short time, may be differentially lured into the workplace during low unemployment, further increasing base rates overall (Hulin, Roznowski & Hachiya, 1985).

Empirically, there is considerable evidence that the intentions–turnover relationship is weaker with scarce job opportunities (Carsten & Spector, 1987; Gerhart, 1990). In their meta-analysis, Hom et al. (1992) found a more complex moderating effect for unemployment. Occupational unemployment (i.e. unemployment within job type) weakens the satisfaction–withdrawal cognitions relationship as expected, but contrary to prediction, it *strengthens:* (a) the satisfaction–turnover, (b) the probability of alternatives–withdrawal cognitions, and (c) the probability of alternatives–turnover relationships (see also, Steel & Griffeth, 1989). They demonstrated that national and regional unemployment moderate these latter relationships, but in the opposite direction from occupational unemployment. Also, occupational unemployment appears to be the stronger moderator in general than these other unemployment indicators (Carsten & Spector, 1987; Hom et al., 1992; Steel & Griffeth, 1989), suggesting that opportunities within job title are more relevant in turnover considerations than aggregated rates across occupations.

The large unemployment rate–aggregate turnover relationship (e.g. Eagly, 1965) and the small perceived alternatives–individual turnover relationship are well known findings. In explaining the discrepancy, Hulin, Roznowski and Hachiya (1985) suggested that low unemployment and the resulting availability of jobs may attract transient employees into the workforce who would be more likely to quit, regardless of their work perceptions. Thus, smaller predictive relationships for perceived alternatives could be partially explained by the failure of individual measures to capture this effect. Also, actual labor market conditions do not transfer directly into employee perceptions of their *personal* alternative opportunities (Gerhart, 1990). That is, employees may have inaccurate information or may feel that they are different from typical job seekers in the market. Therefore, labor market conditions may not be translated into psychological perceptions of alternatives. Steel and Griffeth (1989) proposed two other methodological problems which may also help to explain the discrepancy. First, in the typical one or two occupation studies interoccupational variance in labor market unemployment is untapped by perceptual measures of alternatives, while this variance is captured at the aggregate level. Second, differences across studies in measures of perceived alternatives may obscure relationships, while measures of unemployment are more consistent.

These arguments may suggest that labor market effects be explicitly considered in future predictive studies, even beyond the psychological effects of perceived alternatives. Types of unemployment also need to be differentiated (Steel & Griffeth, 1989). In particular, the apparently contrasting effects of occupational unemployment vs regional and national unemployment should be investigated further.

Organizational culture

Abelson and Baysinger (1984) generally called for a more organization-level perspective on turnover because the preponderance of models have been concerned with the individual level. Organization-level variables have been positively linked to turnover including high centralization, high routinization, low integration, low communication, and policy knowledge (Mobley, 1982; Price, 1977; Price & Mueller, 1981). However, these have typically been thought to influence turnover through individual satisfaction (Bluedorn, 1982; Price, 1977) or other psychological factors, not directly. One proposed explanation of direct organizational culture influences on turnover is that retention depends on some degree of employee fit with the organization's culture. Thus, findings on person–organization fit and retention are relevant to this perspective. For example, O'Reilly, Chatman, and Caldwell (1991) found that misfits on organization values terminated slightly faster than fits, but only after 20 months of tenure.

Alternatively, other researchers have suggested that organizational culture values influence turnover through determining human resource strategies and policies. These create an organizational environment either opposing or encouraging voluntary turnover (Kerr & Slocum, 1987; Kopelman, Brief & Guzzo, 1990). Kerr and Slocum (1987) proposed that cultural values of teamwork, security, and respect for individuals would foster loyalty and greater retention than values of initiative and individual rewards. Using accounting professionals, Sheridan (1992) confirmed that a culture emphasizing interpersonal relationships improved retention by an average of 14 months. However, he warns that the strong findings for cultural values may not generalize beyond relatively mobile occupations. Sheridan (1992) went on to question the relative efficacy of the fit perspective, citing smaller effects for value fit (i.e. O'Reilly, Chatman & Caldwell, 1991) than those discovered in his study.

Abelson (1993) proposed how a turnover culture may develop based on Schein's (1985) three-level model of organizational culture. According to Abelson (1993), turnover cultures exist where systematic patterns of shared cognitions influence turnover decisions. Briefly, these phenomena evolve through sense-making and social information processes. First, organization 'artifacts and creations' are interpreted by employees through sense-making cognitions and schemas. Interpretations are communicated and shared within and across organizational groups, leading to commonly held assumptions and higher order schemata relating to organizational movement. Finally, systematic patterns of these shared beliefs emerge, forming an organizational turnover culture which subsequently influences employee turnover decisions.

National culture

Theoretical models developed in English-speaking countries, as most turnover models are, can be ethnocentric (Boyacigiller & Adler, 1991) and may not apply abroad (Hofstede, 1983). With the overwhelming movement toward a global business environment, turnover models that may not transfer to other cultures could limit understanding and control of voluntary turnover in those cultures. Differences in values (Hofstede, 1980) and social norms (Triandis, 1989) across cultures may influence quitting in a number of ways. For example, some cultures may value loyalty to the organization more than others (Randall, 1993). Or, certain psychological forces may be more salient and therefore more highly weighted in their contribution to turnover decisions (Davidson, Jaccard, Triandis, Morales & Diaz-Guerrero, 1976). Specifically, normative forces are likely to be very important for turnover decisions in collectivist cultures, perhaps more than in individualist cultures such as the US (Triandis, 1989). In support, Maertz, Stevens, Campion, and Fernandez (1996) found that family-related pressures were the most frequently reported reasons for voluntary turnover among Mexican laborers. Unfortunately, existing turnover models do not include such direct or moderating effects of national culture. We must recognize cultural factors as potential influencers of voluntary turnover in our conceptual models, if these models are to be relevant in today's global organization.

Survival analysis

Peters and Sheridan (1988) partly attribute poor turnover prediction to the flawed, but typical, cross-sectional window design. In this design predictors are measured at time 1 and turnover instances that occur before time 2 are included. This design with its single antecedent measurement prevents causal inference or investigation of how the process unfolds. In addition to these obvious limitations, Peters and Sheridan's (1988) main criticisms involve three design limitations in the traditional predictive time 1 – time 2 measurement window design: arbitrary choice of the length of measurement window, right censorship of termination dates (i.e. some study participants quit after the study ends), and left censorship of hire dates (i.e. those hired after the study began may quit during the measurement window but are not included). Specifically, the arbitrary choices of time 1 predictor measurement and length of the measurement window (time 2 – time 1), as well as the company hiring rate just prior to time 1 measurement, directly influence the composition of the stayer and leaver groups. Thus, the significance and possibly the direction of predictive relationships can depend on arbitrary design choices often made based on convention or convenience. Consequently, Peters and Sheridan (1988) caution strongly against this traditional cross-sectional window design. Some adjustments within the design may help address low base rate problems and cohort effects. For instance, the measurement window should be long enough to allow for the turnover base rate to approach 50%, and employee tenure should be used as a covariate. However, to fully consider the flow of employees through organizations and the effects of time, survival analysis is needed.

Analysis of survival or wastage functions has been recognized for some time as a useful method for analyzing turnover (Price, 1976). Survival analysis, above all, allows for consideration of the time period during which an individual quits with respect to tenure stage and time of predictor measurement (Peters & Sheridan, 1988). Unlike other methods of integrating time, survival analysis has the unique advantage of using more available information through allowing estimation of survival functions on attenuated data (right or left censored). Time needs to be formally considered in our theories and research methods in order to understand causal relationships in the turnover process (Hom et al., 1992; Morita, Lee & Mowday, 1989). Survival analysis allows testing of hypotheses concerning the differential strength of various antecedents over time and the average length of time until turnover for various subgroups.

Morita, Lee and Mowday (1989) demonstrated an application of survival analysis in which, 'turnover may be viewed as a process whose intensity (rate) is allowed to vary over time rather than remain fixed' (p. 280). They explained the calculation of survivor or hazard functions which describe the unconditional probability of staying or turning over as of time t. Survival analysis allows study of situations where the fluctuations in turnover rate vary with time t. It also allows comparison of separate functions for subject groupings of interest using the log rank statistic (Morita, Lee & Mowday, 1989). For instance, the survival functions of high and low commitment groups of clerical employees (Kline & Peters, 1991) and of Air Force cadets (Lee, Ashford, Walsh & Mowday, 1992) have been found to differ significantly. Because of its ability to handle censored data and address temporal effects, survival analysis should be utilized in predictive research to test time-based hypotheses on turnover.

Lee and Mitchell's (1994) Unfolding Model

Departing from traditional process models (e.g. Mobley, 1977), Lee and Mitchell (1994) introduced a new decision-making perspective to the turnover research utilizing multiple decision paths and drawing on Image Theory (e.g. Beach, 1990; Beach & Mitchell, 1996). They proposed that turnover decisions may not involve extensive evaluation or even choice. Decisions may be automatic or script-driven and may be a product of any one of several decision strategies, most having different aims than expected utility maximization alone (Lee & Mitchell, 1994). Lee and Mitchell (1994) also develop the idea of 'shocks to the system' (p. 60) which are distinguishable events that jar employees to deliberate judgments about their employment. Five different decision paths are proposed which may be followed by an employee who is quitting. These paths vary on whether a shock to the system occurs, whether negative affect is present, and whether a consideration of alternatives occurs in the turnover decision process. Also, one path involves automatic enactment of a behavioral script for quitting. This represents a radical departure from previous rational economic perspectives.

Lee et al. (1996) attempted a preliminary test of the multi-path model. Using a qualitative interview methodology with nurses, they sought to assess whether the taxonomy of decision paths is consistent with reports about turnover decisions. The paths proposed by Lee and Mitchell (1994) were generally found to exist and thus received preliminary support, with several notable exceptions. Scripts, negative affect, and evaluation of alternatives seemed to be more prevalent and to occur in more decision paths than hypothesized. Lee et al. (1996) claimed their findings suggest that employees may switch paths during the turnover decision process. This may indicate that even more decision options exist than have been proposed in the Lee and Mitchell (1994) unfolding model.

In general, this area of research demonstrates that the turnover decision process may be considerably more complex than indicated in early models. In addition to multiple decision paths, Lee, Mitchell, and colleagues enumerated parameters of the turnover process that can no longer be ignored in efforts to understand the process. These include (a) the speed of the decision, (b) the presence or absence of shocks as catalysts, (c) the presence or absence of affect in the decision, (d) the presence or absence of consideration of job alternatives, and (e) automatic scripted decision processes. Future research is needed on these concepts and on Lee and Mitchell's (1994) model paths versus alternative path structures.

Job Search and Voluntary Turnover

Much research on job search has been linked with job choice (e.g. Schwab, Rynes & Aldag, 1987) and not specifically with turnover. However, job search has been included as a variable in some of the earliest turnover models (e.g. March & Simon, 1958) and was hypothesized as an intermediate link between dissatisfaction and turnover behavior (Mobley, 1977). In some studies, it has been superior as a predictor of turnover behavior even to turnover intentions

(Bretz, Boudreau & Judge, 1994). Although it has been widely held that job search precedes intentions to quit, turnover intentions can crystallize before search behavior occurs (Hom et al., 1992; Kirschenbaum & Weisberg, 1994; Steers & Mowday, 1981), and that search may have direct effects on turnover (Bretz, Boudreau & Judge, 1994). Because the ordering of job search both prior to intentions and following intentions has been supported, the role of job search in the turnover process is still largely unresolved. Fortunately, recent research has more fully addressed the antecedents, dimensions, and measurement of job search and its relation to quitting.

Bretz, Boudreau and Judge (1994) suggested that job search should be considered separately from turnover models alone because there are other purposes for job search besides turnover. For instance, search may be a tool for evaluating one's current situation with respect to the relevant market or for collecting bargaining information, and not necessarily an attempt to acquire another job (e.g. Hulin, 1991; Kirschenbaum & Weisberg, 1994). Bretz, Boudreau and Judge (1994) suggested that two types of antecedents to job search exist, 'pull' motivations external to the organization and 'push' motivations originating within the current organization. They found that push factors seem most influential on search motivation, consistent with the finding that job-motivated turnover is most predictable from job search measures (Blau, 1993).

Bretz, Boudreau and Judge (1994) also criticized past research for focusing on the unemployed who have relatively more motivation to search than the employed, and for focusing on low-level employees with relatively less human capital and opportunities. These weaknesses call into question the generalizability of past findings on employee job search. Among employed managers, human capital was negatively related to search but positively related to turnover (Bretz, Boudreau & Judge, 1994). This suggests that higher level employees may not need to engage in extensive search in order to find an alternative or to quit. Informal information gathering may take the place of formal search in some jobs. This implication is supported in the recruiting literature by findings on the pervasive use of informal sources of job information (e.g. Rynes, 1991). Moreover, different types and measures of job search with differential effects on the turnover process have been hypothesized (Blau, 1993; Kirschenbaum & Weisberg, 1994; Soelberg, 1967).

Two stages of search, preparatory and active, have been suggested previously (Bowen, 1982; Soelberg, 1967). Drawing on past measures of preparatory and active search behaviors (e.g. Kanfer & Hulin, 1985; Vinokur & Caplan, 1987), Blau (1993) created an overall search scale. Using nurses and insurance agents, he supported the proposed three-factor structure with preparatory job search behavior, active job search behavior, and general effort job search as the factors. Blau (1993) also confirmed the hypothesis that active job search behavior has the strongest relationship with voluntary turnover of the three types, and that it has incremental predictive validity beyond work attitudes and withdrawal cognitions. Presumably, this stronger relationship occurs because active search is measured as frequency of formal search behaviors, not as general attitudes or preparatory activities. Perhaps when formal search behaviors are performed rather than preparatory behaviors, more behavioral commitment to quitting is created (Salancik, 1977). In short, Blau (1993) suggested that his results point to a more lengthy two-stage job search process than that typically reflected in existing turnover models (cf Bowen, 1982; Soelberg, 1967). If true, management could potentially have more control by diagnosing preparatory stages of job search and offering inducements to discourage active search. Establishing the efficacy of such policies, the accuracy of a two-stage search model, and the validity of Blau's (1993) measures will require more research, however.

Kirschenbaum and Weisberg (1994) conceptualized active and passive search on a continuum rather than dichotomously and identified time and effort as distinct dimensions of search behaviors. They also called for greater refinement of traditional causal orderings of search intentions and turnover behavior. Findings on Israeli textile workers indicated that actual search was more frequent in employees with long tenure. This is consistent with the established negative relationship between tenure and turnover (e.g. Cotton & Tuttle, 1986). However, actual search behavior failed to add incrementally to prediction of turnover beyond attitudes and biodata variables (Kirschenbaum & Weisberg, 1994). The authors stated that this may have been a partial result of few concrete alternatives existing in the market for this sample.

Despite some equivocal findings, Kirschenbaum and Weisberg (1994) suggested a provocative causal ordering of proposed constructs: passive preparatory search activity leads to perceptions of alternatives, which contribute to formation of turnover intentions, which lead to active search behavior, which in turn identify actual alternatives and trigger turnover decisions. Also, this model challenges the widely held assumption that turnover intention alone is the only proximal cause of quitting behavior (e.g. Fishbein & Azjen, 1975; Mobley et al., 1979; Newman, 1974; Steel & Ovalle, 1984).

This recent research on job search and turnover suggests several important questions for the future study of voluntary turnover. First, this research and Steers and Mowday (1981) seem to assume that alternative opportunities are very important in the turnover process, contrary to models in which alternatives are not even considered. Are alternatives always considered in the process or not? Second, do organizational or job-related reasons lead to search more than 'pull' forces do? Third, are preparatory and active search behaviors distinct or do they exist on a continuum? Within these categories, the dimensions of amount of time spent and amount of effort exerted should be used to refine job search measures. Finally, does active job search occur with differential frequency or lead to turnover differentially depending on occupation, job level, or other factors?

CONCLUSIONS AND FUTURE RESEARCH

Organizational psychology has learned a great deal about voluntary employee turnover. However, turnover consequences, avoidability, and management control have been seriously understudied. These topics deserve further research attention because they are among the most important issues for organizations. Major categories of antecedents were reviewed, including some forgotten in most models such as non-work pressures, psychological contract obligations, and constituent attachments. To understand why some employees stay with an organization when they are dissatisfied with their job and when they have alternatives available, all relevant forces must be considered (Scholl, 1981). Despite the extensive research on models, empirical relationships with voluntary turnover behavior have been modest, with usually no more than 25% of variance explained. Overlooking macro influences and using suboptimal designs, often with low power, may help to explain some of the poor predictive results at the individual level. Regardless, even the best traditional models seem to inadequately reflect the complex nature of employee quit decisions. Lee and Mitchell's (1994) unfolding model moves beyond such traditional models by explicitly considering less rational decision-making processes and positing five different decision paths. Despite these valuable contributions, several questions remain regarding Lee and Mitchell (1994) and Lee et al. (1996) which need to be addressed in future modeling.

First, their model does not integrate psychological content specifically (i.e. what are the different motivations for quitting and how do they impact the various paths?), thereby failing to reflect the variety of distinct antecedents influencing turnover that have appeared in the literature. Until these different psychological forces are included in future models, the turnover decision cannot be fully understood. Perhaps the psychological forces could be integrated into Lee and Mitchell (1994) as different types of shocks experienced or as categories of images.

Second, their model holds that negative affect does not enter the decision to quit in combination with automatic, script-driven quitting. It also seems to classify inappropriately, in that script-driven path, both quitting which is simply planned in advance and quitting which is quick or reflexive in nature (Lee et al., 1996). We believe that these may represent distinct processes of quitting and both should be studied further. Also, affect (particularly negative affect) may potentially enter any turnover decision, automatic or not, depending on individual characteristics and situational factors.

Third, the distinction between general impressions of job opportunities and having an actual alternative in hand is ignored. This could be a crucial distinction to the employee's decision, possibly determining whether the process is speculative and based on an evaluation of general opportunities, or calculative and based on a comparison to a specific alternative job. In the current climate of uncertainty, we believe very few employees have never considered an alternative to their current job at some point. Yet Lee and Mitchell (1994) propose three out of five decision paths where no alternatives are evaluated, leading to the conclusion that the role of alternatives may need to be considered more carefully.

In addition to further development of Lee and Mitchell (1994), there are several other issues that need to be addressed in future turnover research.

1. Future models should consider Sheridan and Abelson's (1983) idea that there are threshold levels on antecedents and multiple equilibrium states with regard to turnover likelihood. This will add complexity to already complex models and such propositions are difficult to test. Nevertheless, non-linear progressions may reflect the reality of turnover decisions and should be investigated. Also, the adaptation–withdrawal process should be tested more competitively against alternative perspectives in the future.

2. Many theoretical and empirical research efforts have addressed the topics of how and why employees voluntarily decide to leave an organization. However, relatively less turnover research has focused specifically on how an employee decides to remain with an organization and what determines this attachment (c.f. Meyer & Allen, 1991; O'Reilly & Chatman, 1986). For instance, is there a different decision process to stay with an organization over a period of time or is it simply the absence of a quit decision? Attachment or retention processes should be studied along with quitting processes. These can be conceptualized as opposite ends of a continuum, from entrenched to ready-to-quit, suggesting that commitment and turnover research could be better integrated. An employee's current location on the attachment–withdrawal continuum could be a function of their standing on major psychological antecedent forces, see Figure 9.1.

3. Lee et a. (1996) departed from traditional methodologies by studying the quitting process using qualitative methods. We need to use more creative methods like these to investigate the many nuances and complexities of the decision. Qualitative methods should certainly be among them, but survival analysis on time-based hypotheses and competitive testing of structural equation models can also help to advance our knowledge.

In conclusion, there has been a great deal of progress in the area of voluntary turnover. However, many studies seem to have pursued their own research goals with little reference to what was required most to extend knowledge on voluntary turnover. It is hoped that this chapter has clarified the major subareas in voluntary turnover research and identified important issues for each, thereby providing direction for future research. If the area of voluntary turnover is to remain vital, future research must become more programmatic by concentrating on making incremental contributions that build systematically on past research.

REFERENCES

Abelson, M. A. (1987). Examination of avoidable and unavoidable turnover. *Journal of Applied Psychology*, **72**, 382–386.

Abelson, M. A. (1993). Turnover cultures. *Research in Personnel and Human Resource Management* (Vol. 11, pp. 339–376). Greenwich, CT: JAI Press.

Abelson, M. A. & Baysinger, B. D. (1984). Optimal and dysfunctional turnover: Toward an organizational level model. *Academy of Management Journal*, **9**, 331–341.

Bannister, B. D. & Griffeth, R. W. (1986). Applying a causal analytic framework to the Mobley, Horner, and Hollingsworth (1978) turnover model: A useful reexamination *Journal of Management*, **12**, 433–443.

Baysinger, B. D. & Mobley, W. H. (1983). Employee turnover: Individual and organizational analysis. *Research in Personnel and Human Research Management* (Vol. 1, pp. 269–319). Greenwich, CT: JAI.

Beach, L. R. (1990). *Image Theory: Decision Making in Personal and Organizational Contexts*. Chichester, UK: Wiley.

Beach, L. R. & Mitchell, T. R. (1996). Image theory, the unifying perspective. In L. R. Beach (Ed.), *Decision-making in the Workplace: A Unified Perspective* (pp. 1–19). Mawah, NJ: Lawrence Erlbaum.

Becker, H. (1960). Notes on the concept of commitment. *American Journal of Sociology*, **66**, 32–42.

Becker, T. E. (1992). Foci and bases of commitment: Are they distinctions worth making: *Academy of Management Journal*, **35**, 232–244.

Beehr, T. A. & Gupta, N. (1978). A note on the structure of employee withdrawal. *Organizational Behavior and Human Performance*, **21**, 73–79.

Blau, G. J. (1993). Further exploring the relationship between job search and voluntary turnover. *Personnel Psychology*, **46**, 313–330.

Bluedorn, A. C. (1982). A unified model of turnover from organizations. *Human Relations*, **35**, 135–153.

Boudreau, J. W. & Berger, C. J. (1985). Decision-theoretical utility analysis applied to employee separations and acquisitions. *Journal of Applied Psychology*, **70**, 581–612.

Bowen, D. (1982). Some unintended consequences of intention to quit. *Academy of Management Review*, **7**, 205–211.

Boyacigiller, N. A. & Adler, N. J. (1991). The parochial dinosaur: Organizational science in a global context. *Academy of Management Review*, **16**, 262–290.

Bretz, R. D., Boudreau, J. W. & Judge, T. A. (1994). Job search behavior of employed managers. *Personnel Psychology*, **47**, 275–301.

Campion, M. A. (1991). The meaning and measurement of turnover: A comparison of alternative measures and recommendations. *Journal of Applied Psychology*, **76**, 199–212.

Carsten, J. M. & Spector, P. E. (1987). Unemployment, job satisfaction, and employee turnover: A meta-analytic test of the Muchinsky model. *Journal of Applied Psychology*, **72**, 374–381.

Clegg, C. W. (1983). Psychology of employee lateness, absence, and turnover: A methodological critique and an empirical study. *Journal of Applied Psychology*, **68**, 88–101.

Cotton, J. L. & Tuttle, J. M. (1986). Employee turnover: A meta-analysis with implications for research. *Academy of Management Review*, **11**, 55–70.

Dalessio, A., Silverman, W. H. & Schuck, J. R. (1986). Paths to turnover: A re-analysis of existing data on the Mobley, Horner, and Hollingsworth turnover model. *Human Relations*, **39**, 245–264.

Dalton, D. R., Krackhardt, D. M. & Porter, L. W. (1981). Functional turnover: An empirical assessment. *Journal of Applied Psychology*, **66**, 716–721.

Dalton, D. R. & Todor, W. D. (1979). Turnover turned over: An expanded and positive perspective. *Academy of Management Journal*, **4**, 225–235.

Dalton, D. R. & Todor, W. D. (1982). Turnover: A lucrative hard dollar phenomenon. *Academy of Management Journal*, **7**, 212–218.

Dalton, D. R., Todor, W. D. & Krackhardt, D. M. (1982). Turnover overstated: The functional taxonomy. *Academy of Management Journal*, **7**, 117–123.

Davidson, A. R., Jaccard, J. J., Triandis, H. C., Morales, M. L. & Diaz-Guerrero, R. (1976). Cross-cultural model testing: Toward a solution of the etic-emic dilemma. *International Journal of Psychology*, **11**, 1–13.

Eagly, R. V. (1965). Market power as an intervening mechanism in Phillips curve analysis. *Economica*, **32**, 766–772.

Fishbein, M. (1967). Attitude and the prediction of behavior. In M. Fishbein (Ed.), *Readings in Attitude Theory and Measurement*. New York: Wiley.

Fishbein, M. & Azjen, I. (1975). *Belief, Attitude, Intention, and Behavior*. Reading, MA: Addison-Wesley.

Forrest, C. R., Cummings, L. L. & Johnson, A. C. (1977). Organizational participation: A critique and model. *Academy of Management Review*, **2**, 586–601.

Gerhart, B. (1990). Voluntary turnover and alternative job opportunities. *Journal of Applied Psychology*, **75**, 467–476.

Graen, G. B., Liden, R. C. & Hoel, W. (1982). Role of leadership in the employee withdrawal process. *Journal of Applied Psychology*, **67**, 868–872.

Greenhaus, J. & Beutell, N. (1985). Sources of conflict between work and family roles. *Academy of Management Review*, **10**, 76–88.

Griffeth, R. W. & Hom, P. W. (1988). A comparison of several conceptualizations of perceived alternatives in turnover research. *Journal of Organizational Behavior*, **9**, 103–111.

Gupta, N. & Jenkins, G. D. (1980). *The Structure of Withdrawal: Relationships among Estrangement, Tardiness, Absenteeism, and Turnover*. Springfield, VA: National Technical Information Service.

Gupta, N. & Jenkins, G. D. (1991). Rethinking dysfunctional employee behaviors. *Human Resource Management Review*, **1**, 39–59.

Hofstede, G. (1980). *Culture's Consequences*. Beverly Hills, CA: Sage.

Hofstede, G. (1983). The cultural relativity of organizational practices and theories. *Journal of International Business Studies*, **14**, 75–89.

Hom, P. W., Caranikas-Walker, F., Prussia, G. E. & Griffeth, R. W. (1992). A meta-analytical structural equations analysis of a model of employee turnover. *Journal of Applied Psychology*, **78**, 890–909.

Hom, P. W. & Griffeth, R. W. (1991). Structural equations modeling test of a turnover theory: Cross-sectional and longitudinal analysis. *Journal of Applied Psychology*, **76**, 350–366.

Hom, P. W., Griffeth, R. W. & Sellaro, C. L. (1984). The validity of Mobley's (1977) model of employee turnover. *Organizational Behavior and Human Performance*, **34**, 141–174.

Hom, P. W., Katerberg, R. & Hulin, C. L. (1979). Comparative examination of three approaches to the prediction of turnover. *Journal of Applied Psychology*, **68**, 280–290.

Hulin, C. L. (1991). Adaption, persistence, and commitment in organizations. In M. Dunnette & L. Hough (Eds), *Handbook of Industrial and Organizational Psychology*. (2nd edn, pp. 445–507). Palo Alto, CA: Consulting Psychologists Press.

Hulin, C. L., Roznowski, M. & Hachiya, D. (1985). Alternative opportunities and withdrawal decisions: Empirical and theoretical discrepancies and an integration. *Psychological Bulletin*, **97**, 233–250.

Hunt, S. & Morgan, R. (1994). Organizational Commitment: One of many commitments or key mediating construct? *Academy of Management Journal*, **37**, 57–79.

James, L. R. (1982). Aggregation bias in estimates of perceptual agreement. *Journal of Applied Psychology*, **67**, 219 229.

Jaros, S. J., Jermier, J. M., Koehler, J. W. & Sincich, T. (1993). Effects of continuance, affective, and moral commitment on the withdrawal process. *Academy of Management Journal*, **5**, 951–995.

Kanfer, R. & Hulin, C. (1985). Individual differences in successful job search after layoff. *Personnel Psychology*, **38**, 835–847.

Kerr, J. & Slocum, J. W. (1987). Managing corporate culture through reward systems. *Academy of Management Executive*, **1**(2), 99–108.

Kirschenbaum, A. & Weisberg, J. (1994). Job search, intentions, and turnover: The mismatched trilogy. *Journal of Vocational Behavior*, **44**, 17–31.

Kline, C. J. & Peters, L. H. (1991). Behavioral commitment and tenure of new employees: A replication and extension. *Academy of Management Journal*, **34**, 194–204.

Kopelman, R. E., Brief, A. P. & Guzzo, R. A. (1990). The role of culture and climate in productivity. In B. Schneider (Ed.), *Organizational Climate and Culture*, (pp. 282–318). San Francisco: Jossey-Bass.

Krackhardt, D. & Porter, L. W. (1985). When friends leave: A structural analysis of the relationship between turnover and stayers' attitudes. *Administrative Science Quarterly*, **30**, 242–261.

Kristoff, A. L. (1995). Person–organization fit: An integrative review of its conceptualizations, measurement and implications. *Personnel Psychology*, **48**, 1–49.

Lee, T. W., Ashford, S. J., Walsh, J. P. & Mowday, R. T. (1992). Commitment propensity, organizational commitment, and voluntary turnover: A longitudinal study of organizational entry processes. *Journal of Management*, **18**, 15–32.

Lee, T. W. & Mitchell, T. R. (1994). An alternative approach: The unfolding model of voluntary employee turnover. *Academy of Management Review*, **19**, 51–89.

Lee, T. W., Mitchell, T. R., Wise, L. & Fireman, S. (1996). An unfolding model of voluntary employee turnover. *Academy of Management Journal*, **39**, 5–36.

Maertz, C. P., Stevens, M. J., Campion, M. A. & Fernandez, A. (1996, August). *Worker turnover in Mexican factories: A qualitative investigation and model development*. Paper presented at the 56th annual meeting of the Academy of Management, Cincinnati, OH.

March, J. & Simon, H. A. (1958). *Organizations*. New York: Wiley.

Martin, T.N. (1979). A contextual model of employee turnover intentions. *Academy of Management Journal*, **22**, 313–324.

Matilla, J. P. (1974). Job quitting and frictional unemployment. *American Economic Review*, **64**, 235–239.

McEvoy, G. M. & Cascio, W. F. (1985). Strategies for reducing employee turnover: A meta-analysis. *Journal of Applied Psychology*, **70**, 342–353.

McEvoy, G. M. & Cascio, W. F. (1987). Do good or poor performers leave? A meta-analysis of the relationship between performance and turnover. *Academy of Management Journal*, **30**, 744–762.

Meyer, J. & Allen, N. (1991). A three-component conceptualization of organizational commitment. *Human Resource Management Review*, **1**, 61–98.

Meyer, J., Allen, N. & Smith, C. (1993). Commitment to organizations and occupations: Extension and test of a three-component conceptualization. *Journal of Applied Psychology*, **78**, 538–551.

Michaels, C. E. & Spector, P. E. (1982). Causes of employee turnover: A test of the Mobley, Griffeth, Hand and Meglino model. *Journal of Applied Psychology*, **67**, 53–59.

Miller, H. E., Katerberg, R. & Hulin, C.L. (1979). An evaluation of the Mobley, Horner, and Hollingsworth model of employee turnover. *Journal of Applied Psychology*, **64**, 509–517.

Mirvis, P. H. & Lawler, E. E. (1977). Measuring the functional impact of employee attitudes. *Journal of Applied Psychology*, **62**, 1–8.

Mitra, A., Jenkins, G. D. & Gupta, N. (1992). A meta-analytic review of the relationship between absence and turnover. *Journal of Applied Psychology*, **77**, 879–889.

Mobley, W. H. (1977). Intermediate linkages in the relationship between job satisfaction and employee turnover. *Journal of Applied Psychology*, **62**, 237–240.

Mobley, W. H. (1982). *Employee Turnover: Causes, Consequences and Control*. Reading, MA: Addison-Wesley.

Mobley, W. H., Griffeth, R., Hand, H. & Meglino, B. (1979). Review and conceptual analysis of the employee turnover process. *Psychological Bulletin*, **86**, 493–522.

Mobley, W. H., Horner, S. D. & Hollingsworth, A. T. (1978). An evaluation of precursors of hospital employee turnover. *Journal of Applied Psychology*, **63**, 408–414.

Morita, J. G., Lee, T. W. & Mowday, R. T. (1989). Introducing survival analysis to organizational researchers: A selected application to turnover research. *Journal of Applied Psychology*, **74**, 280–292.

Morrow, P. (1983). Concept redundancy in organizational research: The case of work commitment. *Academy of Management Review*, **8**, 486–500.

Mowday, R. T., Steers, R. M. & Porter, L. W. (1979). The measurement of organizational commitment. *Journal of Vocational Behavior*, **14**, 222–247.

Muchinsky, P. M. & Morrow, P. (1980). A multidisciplinary model of voluntary employee turnover. *Journal of Vocational Behavior*, **17**, 263–290.

Muchinsky, P. M. & Tuttle, M. L. (1979). Employee turnover: An empirical and methodological assessment. *Journal of Vocational Behavior*, **14**, 43–77.

Newman, J. (1974). Predicting absenteeism and turnover: A field comparison of Fishbein's model and traditional job attitude measures. *Journal of Applied Psychology*, **59**, 610–615.

O'Reilly, C. A. & Chatman, J. (1986). Organizational commitment and psychological attachment: The effects of compliance, identification, and internalization on prosocial behavior. *Journal of Applied Psychology*, **71**, 492–499.

O'Reilly, C. A., Chatman, J. & Caldwell, D. F. (1991). People and organizational culture: A profile comparison approach to person–organization fit. *Academy of Management Journal*, **34**, 487–516.

Peters, L. & Sheridan, J. (1988). Turnover research methodology: A critique of traditional designs and a suggested survival model alternative. *Theoretical and Methodological Issues in Human Resource Management* (pp. 201–232). Greenwich, CT: JAI Press.

Porter, L. W. & Steers, R. M. (1973). Organizational, work, and personal factors in employee turnover and absenteeism. *Psychological Bulletin*, **80**, 151–176.

Prestholdt, P. H., Lane, I. M. & Mathews, R. C. (1987). Nurse turnover as reasoned action: Development of a process model. *Journal of Applied Psychology*, **72**, 221–227.

Price, J. L. (1976). The measurement of turnover. *Industrial Relations Journal*, **6**, 33–46.

Price, J. L. (1977). *The Study of Turnover*. Ames: Iowa State University Press.

Price, J. L. & Mueller, C. W. (1981). A causal model of turnover for nurses. *Academy of Management Journal*, **24**, 543–565.

Randall, D. (1993). Cross-cultural research on organizational commitment. A review and application of Hofstede's value survey module. *Journal of Business Research*, **26**, 91–110.

Reichers, A. (1985). A review and reconceptualization of organizational commitment. *Academy of Management Review*, **10**, 465–476.

Reichers, A. (1986). Conflict and organizational commitments. *Journal of Applied Psychology*, **71**, 508–514.

Robinson, S. L., Kraatz, M. S. & Rousseau, D. M. (1994). Changing obligations and the psychological contract: A longitudinal study. *Academy of Management Journal*, **37**, 137–152.

Rosse, J. G. (1988). Relations among lateness, absence, and turnover: Is there a progression of withdrawal? *Human Relations*, **41**, 517–531.

Rosse, J. G. & Hulin, C. L. (1985). Adaption to work: An analysis of employee health, withdrawal, and change. *Organizational Behavior and Human Decision Processes*, **36**, 324–347.

Rosse, J. G. & Miller, H. (1984). An adaption cycle interpretation of absence and withdrawal. In P. Goodman & R. S. Atkin (Eds), *Absenteeism: New Approaches to Understanding, Measuring, and Managing Employee Absence* (pp. 194–228). San Francisco: Jossey-Bass.

Rousseau, D. M. (1989). Psychological and implied contracts in organizations. *Employee Rights and Responsibilities Journal*, **2**, 121–139.

Rousseau, D. M. & Parks, J. M. (1992). Contracts of individuals and organizations. *Research in Organizational Behavior*, **15**, 1–43.

Rynes, S. L. (1991). Recruitment, job choice, and post-hire consequences: A call for new research directions. In M. D. Dunnette (Ed.), *Handbook of Industrial and Organizational Psychology*, (2nd edn, pp. 399–444). Chicago: Rand McNally.

Salancik, G. (1977). Commitment and the control of organizational behavior and belief. In B. Staw and G. Salancik (Eds), *New Directions in Organizational Behavior* (pp. 1–54). Chicago: St Clair.

Schein, E. H. (1985). *Organizational Culture and Leadership*. San Francisco: Jossey-Bass.

Scholl, R. (1981). Differentiating organizational commitment from expectancy as a motivating force. *Academy of Management Review*, **6**, 589–599.

Schuh, A. J. (1967). The predictability of employee turnover: A review of the literature. *Personnel Psychology*, **20**, 133–152.

Schwab, D. P., Rynes, S. L. & Aldag, R. J. (1987). Theories and research on job search and choice. In G. R. Ferris & K. M. Rowlands (Eds), *Research in Personnel and Human Resources*, (Vol. 5, pp. 129–166). Greenwich, CT: JAI Press.

Sheridan, J. E. (1985). A catastrophe model of employee withdrawal leading to low job performance, high absenteeism, and job turnover during the first year of employment. *Academy of Management Journal*, **28**, 88–109.

Sheridan, J. E. (1992). Organizational culture and employee retention. *Academy of Management Journal*, **35**, 1036–1056.

Sheridan, J. E. & Abelson, M. A. (1983). Cusp catastrophe model of employee turnover. *Academy of Management Journal*, **26**, 418–436.

Soelberg, P. (1967). Unprogrammed decision making. *Industrial Management Review*, **8**, 19–29.

Staw, B. M. (1980). The consequences of turnover. *Journal of Occupational Behaviour*, **1**, 253–273.

Steel, R. P. & Griffeth, R. W. (1989). The elusive relationship between perceived employment opportunity and turnover behavior: A methodological or conceptual artifact? *Journal of Applied Psychology*, **74**, 846–854.

Steel, R. P., Hendrix, W. H. & Balogh, S. P. (1990). Confounding effects of the turnover base rate on relations between time lag and turnover study outcomes: An extension of meta-analysis findings and conclusions. *Journal of Organizational Behavior*, **11**, 237–242.

Steel, R. P. & Ovalle, N. (1984). A review and meta-analysis of research on the relationship between behavioral intentions and employee turnover. *Journal of Applied Psychology*, **69**, 673–686.

Steers, R. M. & Mowday, R. T. (1981). Employee turnover and post-decision accommodation processes. In L. L. Cummings & B. M. Staw (Eds), *Research in Organizational Behavior* (Vol. 1, pp. 235–281). Greenwich, CT: JAI Press.

Tett, R. & Meyer, J. (1993). Job satisfaction, organizational commitment, turnover intention and turnover: Path analyses based on meta-analytic findings. *Personnel Psychology*, **46**, 259–293.

Thibaut, J. W. & Kelley, H. H. (1959). *The Social Psychology of Groups*. New York: Wiley.

Triandis, H. C. (1975). Culture training, cognitive complexity, and interpersonal attitudes. In R. Brislin, S. Bochner & W. Lonner (Eds), *Cross-cultural Perspectives on Learning* (pp. 39–77). Beverly Hills, CA and New York: Sage and Wiley/Halsted.

Triandis, H. C. (1989). The self and social behavior in differing cultural contexts. *Psychological Review*, **96**, 506–520.

Vinokur, A. & Caplan, R. (1987). Attitudes and social support: Determinants of job seeking and well-being for the unemployed. *Journal of Applied Social Psychology*, **17**, 1007–1024.

Vroom, V. (1964). *Work and Motivation*. New York: Wiley.

Wiener, Y. (1982). Commitment in organizations: A normative view. *Academy of Management Review*, 7, 418–428.

Williams, L. & Hazer, J. (1986). Antecedents and consequences of satisfaction and commitment in turnover models: A re-analysis using latent variable structural equation methods. *Journal of Applied Psychology*, 71, 219–231.

Youngblood, S. A., Mobley, W. H. & Meglino, B. M. (1983). A longitudinal analysis of the turnover process. *Journal of Applied Psychology*, **68**, 507–516.

Chapter 10

PSYCHOLOGICAL CONTRACTS: EMPLOYEE RELATIONS FOR THE TWENTY-FIRST CENTURY?

Lynne J. Millward and Paul M. Brewerton
University of Surrey, UK

the most complex organizational issue since the industrial revolution: the fundamental and irrevocable shift in the psychological contract between employee and organization. (Noer, 1993)

The employment contract is basic to organizational membership. It constitutes the mainstay of employment relations, establishing an exchange of promises and contributions between two parties: employer and employee (Rousseau, 1989, p. 121). Whilst the employment contract can be viewed from many angles—psychological, political, economic, organizational, sociological and legal—none of these provides a complete picture. Moreover there is often difficulty in defining disciplinary boundaries due to much conceptual and empirical overlap. In this review, we are concerned with what Rousseau (1995, p. 1) calls the 'organizational, social and psychological meaning of contracts'.

It has long been recognized that 'subjectivity is inherent in all contracts' (Rousseau, 1989, p. 121), whether in written or unwritten form. This concerns the way the contract of employment is lived and breathed; the way it is interpreted, understood and enacted on a daily basis as employees interface with their workplace. Argyris (1960) was the first to undertake a formal study of the subjective aspects of contracts and the first to introduce the term 'psychological contract'. He described the psychological contract as an *underwritten agreement* that exists between an individual and the organization when undertaking terms of employment (Argyris, 1960). Others followed suit (e.g. Kotter, 1973; Levinson, 1962) but it was not until the 1980s that the concept began to enter the vocabulary of writers on organizational life and behaviour (Schein, 1980; Farnsworth, 1982; MacNeil, 1985). Farnsworth (1982) for example, used the term psychological contract to

Psychological Contracts: Employee Relations for the Twenty-First Century? by Lynne J. Millward and Paul M. Brewerton taken from IRIOP 2000 v15, Edited by Cary L. Cooper and Ivan T. Robertson: © 2000 John Wiley & Sons, Ltd

denote issues of exchange and of mutual expectation in the link between individuals and their employing organization. Thus, the concept of psychological contract emerged as a tool for describing and explaining what was *implicit* to the agreements made between employee and employer, and in particular the role played by *reciprocity and exchange* in the process of forming such agreements.

Until the last decade, the term psychological contract was used mainly as a framework or backdrop (rather than a scientific construct) in which to talk about what is 'implicit' to the exchange relationship between employee and employer. Little formal research had been undertaken at this stage. Since the early 1990s, however, the psychological contract has acquired construct status and in so doing has taken a major conceptual and empirical turn. It has been transposed from being a term used to refer to what is nebulous and difficult to access in connection with the *quality of the exchange relationship*, into a *cognitive-perceptual entity*. In this form it has been deemed to be *measurable* and *owned solely by the individual*, as opposed to being a property of the relationship between two parties. This was facilitated in part by the publication of a thesis by Rousseau (1989) on the distinction between psychological and implied contracts, which was later to form part of a more formal system of thinking about the psychology of the employment contract.

This thinking is presented in Rousseau's 1995 book *Psychological Contracts in Organizations* in which she defines the psychological contract as 'an individual's belief in paid for promises, or a reciprocal obligation between the individual and the organization' (pp. 16–17). An implicit contract however, is described as one that can be inferred by others as pertaining to the unwritten aspects of the employment contract. The psychological contract then became a reference to the 'beliefs' held by individuals pertaining to reciprocal obligations (not the reciprocal obligations themselves), and might be implicit or explicit to the agreements the individual perceives that he or she is party to. It became something specific and internal to the individual and the way they perceived the world. Beliefs in reciprocal obligations, notes Rousseau (1995), can arise from overt promises (e.g. bonus systems discussed in the recruitment process), interpretations of patterns of past exchange, vicarious learning (e.g. witnessing other employees' experiences), as well as through various factors which each party may take for granted (e.g. good faith or fairness). By contrast, the implicit contract (which used to pertain to what was 'psychological' about contracts) became instead the property of an observer, looking in from the outside (i.e. using behaviour as the basis through which to infer the unwritten aspects of contracts).

Since then, the psychological contract literature has grown in complexity, with some writers operating ostensibly in the cognitive-perceptual field, while others try to retain some of the more dynamic and relational aspects of the interface between individuals and organizations, as intimated by people like Barnard (1938), Argyris (1960) and also Levinson (1962) and Schein (1980).

Confusing the picture even further is the use of the term psychological contract as a metaphor for describing the current state of employment relations. In particular, the term has been harnessed by researchers and practitioners alike, as a means of analysing the nature and impact of transformation in the character of the contemporary workplace. It took the breakdown in traditional contracts of employment (which guaranteed a job-for-life and career prospects in return for loyalty and hard work), in parallel with a major increase in the centrality of contracting (i.e. short-term, task-specific, monetary contracts), to bring the psychological side of contracts and contracting into stark relief.

Changes in economic and political life, with the attendant collapse of traditional organizational designs and structures (through mass downsizing, streamlining and the contracting-out of peripheral functions) severely undermined conventional forms of employee-employer exchange (e.g. job security and career prospects offered in exchange for loyalty and commitment). Thus, organizational behaviour researchers began to concern themselves with the violation of 'old' contracts of employment, and its consequences for employee performance and morale. More general questions were also being asked about the character of the psychological contract, its conceptualization, measurement and more recently, and perhaps more urgently, its management (e.g. Herriot, Hirsch & Reilly, 1998; Sparrow, 1998, in the UK; Rousseau, 1995, in the US).

The concept of psychological contract is now of worldwide interest and significance (Schalk & Rousseau, 1999, in press) though it has as yet generated perhaps more questions than answers (see for example, Guest, 1999). This, coupled with multiple conceptualizations and measurement attempts, has generated an abundant literature. To some this is merely 'old wine in new bottles' (i.e. subjective regulation of employees by another name, or organizational commitment in a more fashionable guise); to others it offers a valuable means of reauthoring our old ways of construing the employee–employer interface. Reauthoring affords new insights and as such may provide the impetus and vision required to pull the employment world, and our understanding and management of it, into the new millennium.

This review assumes that the psychological contract pertains to a construct with theoretical substance, empirical validity and practical significance. Whilst the term has been used by some writers and practitioners as mere rhetoric, this review aims to separate the hyperbole from the researched reality of the construct. It is undoubtedly true that the psychological contract is a metaphor (at least one of many other potential metaphors) for describing the employee relations scene in the 1990s, given the burgeoning interest in the language and ideology of contracts among the British and American workforces. This, however, does not necessarily undermine the viability of the term 'psychological contract' as a scientific construct. The question is one of being able to agree on a definition, and making a case for the added value of the construct as a means of conceptualizing, investigating and managing employee relations. It is to this end that the current review is geared.

CHANGING NATURE OF EMPLOYMENT AND EMPLOYEE RELATIONS

For a period following World War II, there was stability, predictability and growth in both the US and the UK economies. Since the 1970s, however, an increase in the magnitude and frequency of economic booms and busts (Herriot & Pemberton, 1995b) has meant that it is harder for organizations to predict and survive change. Globalization and deregulation of emerging markets has increased competition, forcing US and UK organizations to compete against cheaper labour costs and large economies of scale. Organizations have thus reacted by becoming 'leaner and meaner', operating as smaller, semi-autonomous businesses, better equipped to be responsive and flexible to change. Enforced redundancies have resulted, with a corresponding growth in part-time and contracted-in labour markets to keep labour costs down. Organizations have delayered, with originally bureaucratic, hierarchical structures undergoing flattening through the stripping out of executive layers. The Royal Bank of Scotland, for example, has compressed its corporate structure from twenty grades to five (Hiltrop, 1995). In many organizations, this has reduced the opportunity for promotion with movement now being primarily lateral, or even downward. Performance-related pay schemes have been introduced and roles and responsibilities are no longer well defined. Employees are expected to be multi-skilled and willing to relocate at the employer's whim. Many factors contributing to work-related psychological well-being such as job security, opportunity for promotion, status and increased salary are now no longer guaranteed. Organizations have tried to justify these changes but employees have not been fooled (Herriot & Pemberton, 1995b).

New Ways of Working

The changing context of the workplace in the 1990s derives from a variety of economic, technological and sociological phenomena, too complex to be fully explored here. The point is that these changes have had significant implications for the majority of the full-time workforce within the industrialized world. Handy (1990) in *The Age of Unreason*, summarizes the implications of such changes for workers: 'many will work temporary or part-time— sometimes because that's the way they want it, sometimes because that's all that's available'. Pritchett (1994) opines, 'less than half the workforce in the industrial world will be holding conventional full-time jobs in organizations by the beginning of the 21st century. Those full-timers or insiders will be the new minority.' Other workplace commentators have suggested that 'constant training, retraining, job-hopping and even career-hopping will become the norm' (O'Hara-Devereux & Johansen, in Pritchett, 1994).

In mid-1996, demand for temporary staff in the UK had risen by 23% on the previous year and stood at its highest level since 1982 (Tooher, 1996). Companies now outsource many of their non-core, peripheral activities to external agencies, with many workers consequently employed on short-term or part-time contracts, with resultant reduced job security and continuously changing work environments. In the Survey of Long Term Employment Strategies 1996, one company executive was quoted as saying:

> Increasing rationalisation and economies of scale will lead to narrower margins and a considerable reduction in the number of providers in the world-wide market. Only the fittest, most innovative and flexible employers will survive.

It is clear from these comments that the world of work is fast becoming a very different one from that familiar a few decades ago. Management experts are now predicting a shift from traditional working patterns to a core/complementary structure by the turn of the century; that is organizations employing core long-term contract based and complementary short-term contract based employees. This has major implications for 'core' staff within organizations who are likely to become employed on fixed-term, rather than permanent, contracts and will become increasingly required to contemplate alternative forms of working, including teleworking, part-time working and job sharing (Millward & Hopkins, 1998). Short-term complementary staff must accept even more fully the change in contractual terms with employing organizations, and will be obliged to become proactive in seeking and retaining work while expecting little in return from employers other than financial recompense.

The New Deal

So, the trend away from the 'traditional' working relationship with the employee offering loyalty, conformity, commitment and trust to the employing organization in return for job security, promotional prospects, training and development opportunities and support (see Table 10.1) is becoming increasingly evident. The contractual norm is shifting increasingly towards the individual accepting long hours, more responsibility, a requirement for a broader rang of skills and tolerance of change and role ambiguity, with the organization providing returns of high pay, rewards for performance and, in the simplest terms, a job (Arnold, 1996).

These changes are having, and will continue to have, wide-ranging implications for the workforce, regardless of the forms of work adopted in the future. Long-established organizational, professional and occupational identities are being eroded in order that organizations may multi-skill, rebrand, downsize,

Table 10.1   Old to new deals

Old deal	New deal
• Long-term security	• No security
• Fair pay for good performance	• High pay for high performance
• Structured, predictable employment scenario	• Flexible and ambiguous employment scenario
• Career managed by organization	• Career managed by individual
• Time and effort rewarded	• Performance/results expected
• Income related to experience/status	• Income related to performance— performance-related pay
• Offered promotion prospects and supported in return for 'going the extra mile'	• Transactional attitudes 'tit for tat' mentality
• Mutual trust and investment	• Little trust, much cynicism

delayer and refocus. The potential impact on the individual worker is immense. Employees will be required to adopt multiple coping strategies in order to deal with this fast-moving and demanding new environment, with their various identities coming under fire from all directions, as new ways of working are introduced, mass redundancies and restructuring into teams erode the established social network, the focus of work shifts from production to service and stable 'jobs for life' are replaced with self-managed regular career 'hops' (Herriot, Hirsch & Reilly, 1998).

Diversity and the Mutlicultural Working World

Recognition of diversity and its systematic management is, according to many scholars of organizations, the key to future organizational survival and success (e.g. Herriot, 1992). Diversity is introduced into organizations insofar as:

- An increasing number of females are entering the employment world with different value priorities and many varied orientations to work.
- An increasing number of 'older' workers are represented in the workforce, meaning that there are intergenerational differences in value priority and orientation to work.
- An increasingly multicultured employment world is appearing as more and more organizations are operating on a global scale (i.e. multinational or even transnational).
- The practice of equal opportunity is becoming more prevalent with more minority group members entering the employment world (although some would say, not enough!).

- The proliferation of different types of employment contracts (e.g. part-time, flexi-time, job-share, annual hours, temporary, fixed-term) is increasing within a flexible, core/peripheral employment structure. In addition, many organizations are moving towards outsourcing and strategic alliance (with employees working alongside people from different organizations with differing business cultures and skill sets).

Diversity has major implications for how people work together and in particular for what work means to them, and thus provides an essential backdrop against which to investigate contractual issues. However, in undertaking the review which follows, it is important to point out that no direct correspondence between economic or structural and psychological realities is assumed (see for example, Herriot, Hirsch & Reilly, 1998; Millward & Herriot, 1999).

THE ORGANIZATION AS A 'COOPERATIVE SYSTEM' OF EXCHANGE

Whilst often regarded as a relatively fresh concept in the literature, the psychological contract can be said to have originated from the work of Barnard (1938), in his 'Cooperative Systems View' of organizational behaviour. Barnard argued that the 'natural cooperation' inherent in human nature was largely responsible for the success or failure of business ventures. He argued that an investment or input by both employee and employer was crucial to an organization's success—in return for good treatment, he suggested, employees could be persuaded to 'pledge allegiance' to a common organizational goal or purpose, placing this above all else in organizational life, and leading to increased productivity within the workplace.

Barnard (1938, p. 139) argues that 'the individual is always the basic strategic factor in organizations. Regardless of his history or his obligations he must be induced to cooperate or there will be no cooperation . . . inadequate incentives mean dissolution'. This thesis is based on a conceptualization of the organization as 'a system of cooperation' (p. 3) and that its survival depends on individual 'cooperative' contributions. These contributions, he argues, are not automatically afforded; instead, the organization has to actively 'elicit' them. Whilst organizational effectiveness is defined as the extent to which the organization achieves its goals, this depends, he says, very heavily on organizational efficiency. Efficiency in turn can only be ensured to the extent that individual motives are satisfied. The test of efficiency then is the ability to 'elicit sufficient individual wills to cooperate' (Barnard, 1938, p. 60). Without cooperation the organization will fail in its purpose.

Barnard (1938, p. 141) points out that an organization can secure the efforts necessary to its existence by either providing objective inducements and/or 'changing states of mind'. The provision of objective inducement may involve: material inducements such as money or other financial compensation; personal non-material opportunity such as status or power; communion (e.g. social support, comradeship); increased participation; fulfilment of personal ideals; associational attractiveness (e.g. desire to belong); and desirable physical conditions. By contrast, changing states of mind in the workforce may require the 'method of persuasion' (Barnard, 1938, p. 149) either by rationalization (e.g. propaganda, rhetoric/argument) and/or the 'inculcation of motives', in addition to occasional coercion. Barnard (1938, p. 158) argues that 'every type of organization, for whatever purpose' will need to provide 'several incentives' and 'some degree of persuasion . . . in order to maintain the contributions required.

Barnard (1938, p. 230) describes the critical function of the executive as one of 'eliciting . . . the quantity and quality of efforts' required of organizational contributors. In his description of what exactly the executive can do to 'elicit' effort, it is clear that the executive role is about managing the 'exchange of utilities' (p. 240). Barnard also reminds us that the nature of the exchange will need to undergo continual adjustment and change due to changing individual requirements and states of mind (including employees' appraisal and reappraisal of existing exchange utilities).

Barnard's view of the 'exchange' process between individuals and organizations is echoed in various historical definitions of the psychological contract, and continues to form the backbone of psychological contract research and debate in the 1990s as the following examples illustrate:

> An implicit contract between individual and organization which specifies *what each expects to give and receive from each other in their relationship.* (Kotter, 1973)

> An unwritten set of *expectations operating at all times between every member of an organization* and the various managers and others in that organization. (Schein, 1980)

> An individual's beliefs regarding the terms and conditions of a *reciprocal exchange agreement* between that person and another party. (Robinson & Rousseau, 1994).

This cooperative systems view of organizational life assumes that the interface between employer and employee cannot be taken for granted; it must be conceptualized, studied and more importantly, systematically managed. The notion of *interface* can thus be considered crucial to our understanding of the psychological contract, since it:

- Signals a *process of exchange* between the individual and the organization.
- Requires that questions are asked about the *character* of the interface (*i.e. content or type of contractual deal*) as well as its *dynamics* (*i.e. the process of contracting*).
- Requires consideration of the *needs of both individual and organization.*

- Presents questions about the nature of the exchange at *individual, group and intergroup levels of analysis.*

Until recently however, the focus of interest has been less in what the organization can offer the employee in exchange for their loyalty and commitment, and more in terms of what the employee can offer (or be made or persuaded to offer) the organization. Moreover, it would seem that what the employee might offer in terms of performance potential, has typically been regarded as something that can be conceptualized and measured independently of what is afforded them in return by the organization. Pet constructs such as commitment and satisfaction, which have generated volumes of research over the last century, are prime examples of the *single-sided employee-only* stance adopted by researchers on workplace motivation. This may in part be attributable to the reductionist nature of much psychological research on organizational life, insofar as the organizational side of the equation might be deemed the jurisdiction of management science and/or sociological analysis. Here is not the place to enter into a debate about levels of analysis or into philosophical discussion about the dialectic at work in connecting individuals with organizational entities. Such complexities are currently being addressed in postmodernist debates on the nature and workings of organizational life (see, for example, Alvesson, 1998). It is clear nonetheless that the behaviour of individuals in organizations cannot be understood in a social vacuum. The topic of motivation, for instance, pertains to a regulatory issue that is inextricably linked with how the individual is located within the organization as a whole.

Psychological contracts, then, can be described in terms of both content (the perceived terms of the employment contract) and process (how the contract was arrived at) (Millward & Herriot, 1999). To date, the majority of research on the psychological contract has been conducted in the 'content' rather than 'process' vein, and until recently, has been investigated somewhat single-sidedly as something owned and held by the individual, consistent with the conceptualization offered by Rousseau (1989).

THE CONTENT AND CHARACTER OF THE PSYCHOLOGICAL CONTRACT

The Psychological Contract as a Cognitive-perceptual Entity

As indicated earlier, Rousseau and colleagues have adopted a primarily cognitive-perceptual stance on the psychological contract. In the words of Rousseau (1995, p. 6), 'contracts are stable and enduring mental models', and accessing the model used by people will reveal how they come to understand the employment contract as it evolves through experience. The notion of 'belief' is pivotal to the particular way in which Rousseau conceptualizes and investigates the interface between employer and employee. In particular, this perspective holds that the psychological contract is characterized by *beliefs pertaining to reciprocal obligations* (i.e. beliefs about what each party in the relationship is 'obliged' to contribute to that relationship) (Rousseau, 1995, pp. 20–22), and 'promissory exchange' (i.e. beliefs about the exact nature of the exchange agreement) (Rousseau, 1995, pp. 16–18) as formed by individuals upon undertaking terms of employment (Argyris, 1960; Kaufman & Stern, 1988; Levinson, 1962; MacNeil, 1985; Schein, 1980). More formally stipulated, Rousseau (1995) defines the psychological contract as follows:

1. An individual's belief(s) in reciprocal obligations between that individual and another party.
2. Where one party has paid for, or offered consideration in exchange for, a promise that the other party will reciprocate (i.e. fulfil the promise).
3. Where both the promise and the consideration are highly subjective (i.e. exist 'in the eye of the beholder'). Parties to a contract, whether written or unwritten, can hold different perceptions regarding its terms (e.g. different people might focus on different elements of the contract in creating their understanding of it, depending on cognitive limits and frames of reference).
4. The individual holding the belief in a psychological contract attaches to that belief assumptions of good faith, fair dealing and trust, which results in the contract becoming part of the mainstay of the relationship between the parties.

The Psychological Contract as an Implicit, Relationship-based Agreement

Drawing on the work of MacNeil (1985), Rousseau (1989) argues that the employment contract signals far more than simple economic forms of exchange (i.e. market-oriented, monetary, competitive). It can involve relationship-based agreements which denote the commitment of parties to maintaining the relationship (i.e. to stay together, continuing employment), providing some form of exchange (such as loyalty and hard work) indefinitely. Where interactions occur over time, and continued interaction is expected, beliefs about what is owed can arise from overt promises and other factors more likely to be taken for granted (e.g. assumptions of fairness and of good faith). Relationship-based agreements compensate for the inability to draw up economic contracts of sufficient coverage and scope to frame the employment relationship over the long term. The more taken for granted the 'considerations' exchanged, the greater the potential for *personal idiosyncrasies in the way the employment contract is interpreted and enacted* (Rousseau, 1989, p. 124)— that is people 'fill in the blanks . . . in somewhat unpredictable ways' (Rousseau, 1995, p. 1).

Even agreements in writing are open to different interpretations, which often only become evident when the contract is violated. The longer the relationship endures, the broader the array of considerations involved in the exchange and the deeper the relationship becomes. The psychological contract then, pertains to the subjectivity inherent to all employment contracts. 'When an individual perceives that contributions he or she makes obligate the organization to reciprocity (or vice versa), a psychological contract emerges' (Rousseau, 1989, p. 124). To this extent, contracts are 'constructions' created by the interpretation of what a promise or obligation means to each individual.

The Psychological Contract as Perceived 'Obligations of Reciprocity'

Psychological contracts are distinct from norms of reciprocity (i.e. they denote more than simply the endorsement of a norm, they involve '*obligations* of reciprocity' established a priori and also from what Rousseau (1989) terms *implied contracts*, that is those that can be inferred by an observer as to the patterns of obligation arising from the interaction between the two parties in an exchange relationship. An example of this might be an organization's reputation as a 'good employer' (e.g. affording job security and career prospects in exchange for loyalty and hard work) (Kiriakodou & Millward, 1999). Psychological contracts also denote more than simple considerations of equity (i.e. whether expectations have been met); they involve *socio-emotional considerations of trust and identification* and it is these which are not so easily restored when contracts are violated. In the words of Rousseau (1989, p. 127) psychological contracts 'interject a deeper emotional component to the experience of inequity' within a relationship.

Failed expectations can result in disappointment, whereas contract violation (i.e. perceived failure to meet contractual terms) can induce feelings of betrayal, anger, outrage, injustice and so on. Whilst all psychological contracts entail expectations, not all expectations are in themselves invested with a promissory interpretation. It is this promissory element that differentiates expectations from psychological contracts (see e.g., research by Robinson, 1995). Violation can fundamentally change the way the relationship is viewed (e.g. because of damage to self-respect as well as the basic sense of entitlement). The longer the duration of the psychological contract, the higher the investment and promissory element of both parties.

Robinson (1995) measured seven features of employment (e.g. pay, promotion, etc.) in two ways: as obligations (beliefs regarding extent of each specific obligation) and as expectations (descriptions of relative presence or absence of each feature). Psychological contract (promissory) beliefs contributed independently and more substantially to the prediction of trust, commitment and satisfaction than non-promissory expectations. Beliefs formed in the context of the psychological contract entail a special subset of expectations based on one party conveying a promise to another. The distinction between psychological contracts and expectations is of great practical significance since failure to meet contract-based expectations can engender more intense and emotionally salient reactions than failure to meet non-contract-based expectations (Rousseau, 1989; Robinson, 1995).

'Individuals Hold Psychological Contracts, Organizations Do Not'

It is important to point out that within this conceptualization, *the psychological contract is held unilaterally by the employee*: 'individuals have psychological contracts, organizations do not' (Rousseau, 1989, p. 126). The organization provides the 'context' for the creation of psychological contracts. However, psychological contracts can also be shared. Whilst individual contract holders may rely on their own experience to understand the contract, group members may 'share' a contract and to this extent can develop a reality about it. To this extent, psychological contracts become 'normative' where members 'identify themselves in similar ways with it' and believe they are party to the same contract (e.g. part-timers) (Rousseau, 1995, pp. 10–11). Normative contracts can create pressures to adhere to commitments (e.g. absence contracts which denote entitlement to use up sick leave) (Nicholson & Johns, 1985), and thus create a degree of homogeneity in values and behaviours (which then become self-perpetuating through selection, adaptation and attrition processes) (Herriot, 1989).

The Psychological Contract as a Driver of Behaviour

How individual employees each view their contract is assumed to have a powerful effect on their behaviour. Rousseau (1995) argues that we can predict behaviour from the creation, change, or violation of contracts. Contracts operate like goals and to this extent are both self-organizing and self-fulfilling. They are promissory to the extent that they are formed on the basis of warranties and communications of future intent. Thinking contractually means believing one has made a commitment and is therefore bound to some future action in return for the promise (which is believed, accepted and relied upon) of future benefits. It should be noted, however, that promise-keeping per se is not the central theme of contracting, it is instead the reduced likelihood of loss that is fundamental.

The fuzziness and ambiguity that is such an integral part of the psychological contract might well afford flexibility in the way the contractual relationship is enacted by an individual, but it also means that conflict over the kinds of agreements and promises made is inevitable. It is also important to point out that several psychological contracts can occur simultaneously (e.g. with the team, with the department or division, with the profession or occupation of which one is a part, and with organization) (see Millward & Hopkins, 1998, for more on this), affording multiple contractual possibilities and realities lived and breathed by each and every employee. The prediction of behaviour is thus a complex issue, that requires simultaneous consideration of organizational, social (normative) and personal (idiosyncratic) factors, and assumes that the psychological contract is a precisely quantifiable entity, a point on which some might disagree (e.g. Guest, 1998; Herriot & Pemberton, 1997).

The Process of Contract-making or Psychological Contracting

Rousseau (1995, pp. 34–44) outlines a model of psychological contracting in which she presents two sets of factors as critical to the formation of promissory contracts: *external messages* which may be in the form of overt statements (e.g. during the recruitment and/or organizational induction process), observations of the treatment and behaviour of others with the same kind of deal, and expressions of organizational policy and *personal interpretations and dispositions* (e.g. career motives and aspirations). Contracts can be formed by anyone who conveys (and is perceived to have the authority to convey) some form of future commitment to another, that is organizational representatives such as managers and recruiters (Rousseau, 1995, p. 60). Contracts are not imposed on people; they are made voluntarily. This requires acknowledgement of the active role that employees have in the contracting process (which is part and parcel of managing one's own socialization).

Rousseau (1990) conducted a survey on newly recruited MBAs to an organization, examining the development of psychological contracts. She found that employees developed their contractual orientation to the organization during the recruitment process. In particular, it was found that the content of the contract—that is transactional or relational orientation—was related to the *type of relationship the employee sought with the employer*. It was discovered that those individuals perceiving their current position as a stepping stone to another, and who emphasized short-term monetizable benefits in exchange for hard work, demonstrated a more transactionally oriented short-term view of their commitment to the organization. By contrast, those seeking a long-term relationship with their employer felt party to a contract exchanging job security for their loyalty, indicative of a more relational contractual orientation.

Types of Psychological Contract

Whilst it is clear that psychological contracts can take on a potentially infinite number of cognitive-perceptual forms (Rousseau, 1995, pp. 91–97), certain contractual terms (e.g. an attractive benefits package, pay tied to performance, relatively secure job, good opportunities for promotion, competitive salary versus fair treatment, career development, support, open communication, collaborative work environment) are assumed to cluster together along dimensions of focus (economic, relational), inclusion (scope and flexibility), time-frame (duration of the relationship), formalization (specification of performance requirements), and tangibility (implicit, explicit). At the most aggregated level, Rousseau conceptualizes (and has also operationalized) the psychological contract in two forms, defined by the type of relationship perceived to predominate between employee and employer: 'transactional' and 'relational' (Robinson, Kraatz & Rousseau, 1994; Robinson & Rousseau, 1994; Rousseau, 1990, 1995; Rousseau & Parks, 1993; see also Herriot, Manning & Kidd, 1997; Millward & Hopkins, 1998; Stiles, Gratton, Truss, Hope-Hailey & McGovern, 1996). These two types of contractual relationship have been described as follows (Rousseau, 1995, pp. 90–95):

Transactional
- Short-term monetizable exchanges
- Specific economic conditions as primary incentive (wage rate)
- Limited personal involvement in job
- Specified time-frame
- Commitments limited to well-specified conditions
- Limited flexibility
- Use of existing skills
- Unambiguous terms

Relational
- Open-ended relationship and time-frame
- Considerable investment by employees (company skills, career development) and employers (training)
- High degree of mutual interdependence and barriers to exit
- Emotional involvement as well as economic exchange
- Whole-person relations
- Dynamic and subject to change
- Pervasive conditions (affects personal life)
- Subjective and implicitly understood

In short, the relational psychological contract can be regarded as being akin to the traditional working 'partnership' between employee and employer. A relational-type employee–employer relationship can engender feelings of affective involvement or attachment in the employee, and can commit the employer to providing more than purely remunerative support to the individual with investments such as training, personal and career development, and provision of job security. In contrast, the transactional contract denotes an attitude of 'money comes first': employees are more concerned with remuneration and personal benefit than with being good 'organizational citizens', or 'going the extra mile'. This type of contract may also include employees bending organizational rules to meet personal ends.

Rousseau (1995, p. 97) argues that 'transactional and relational terms are basic elements in most employment contracts', but that how long the relationship is expected to last will usually differentiate contracts that are largely transactional from more relational ones. In practice, however, this is not quite as simple as it sounds. Many short-term contractual relationships can be highly relational (e.g. student/mentor). Also specific performance requirements (which are most typical of transactional contracts) can be built into long-term contracts through appraisal and performance-related pay systems. Thus, transactional and relational terms are not mutually exclusive, although of course, extreme scenarios can be presented (e.g. employment agencies mostly operate with purely 'transactional' contracts). Transactional type psychological contracts may be sought out by those who prefer low-investment roles, perhaps because they have investments elsewhere (e.g. family and home, activities and interests outside the workplace), or because they have personal goals and agendas to fulfil (e.g. developing a career portfolio, the desire to simply earn some money) (Hall, 1993). Rousseau (1995, p. 104) does point out however that 'over a period of time . . . relational elements can drift into the contract' that might otherwise have been purely transactional at the outset (e.g. contractors whose short-term contracts are continually renewed over time) (for evidence that this can indeed be the case, see Williamson, 1991; Millward & Brewerton, 1999).

Evidence from both US (Robinson, Kraatz & Rousseau, 1994) and UK research (e.g. Millward & Hopkins, 1998; Millward & Brewerton, 1999) has confirmed the viability of the transactional and relational distinction. For example, using a 50-item bank derived from focus group discussion with employees, Millward and Hopkins (1998) constructed a 32-item scale to measure 'relational' and 'transactional' aspects of the contractual relationship. Scale construction was informed by the conceptualization provided by Rousseau (1995, pp. 91–97) using the following analytical dimensions: focus (emotional/economic); inclusion (extent of individual integration in an organization); time-frame (short term/long term); formalization (degree of performance specification); stability (stasis/dynamic); scope (job-specific versus whole-person implications); and tangibility (subjective/objective). Factor analysis yielded a two-factor solution which was then used to produce two reliable subscales.

Millward and Hopkins (1998) also obtained substantial preliminary evidence for the construct validity of these subscales. Specifically, the 'relational' subscale was significantly more strongly linked with permanent than temporary contracts, with full-time than with part-time working patterns, and with long-term than short-term employment relationships (as indicated by organizational and job tenure). In contrast, the transactional subscale was significantly more strongly associated with a temporary workplace relationship (i.e. temporary employment contracts, short-term organizational and job tenure). Moreover, the relational subscale was significantly positively correlated with job and organizational commitment, and also with the expressed willingness to work overtime without pay (i.e. go the extra mile for the organization). The transactional subscale, on the other hand, was significantly negatively correlated with each of these three measures.

Taken together, these findings indicate the validity of considering a relational psychological contract that comprises a tendency towards a promissory contract based on trust for the exchange party, a high degree of affective commitment, a high degree of integration and identification with the exchange partner, expectations of stability and long-term commitment, and a self-reported contribution to reciprocal exchange with the employing organization (Rousseau, 1995). Likewise, the findings add support to the idea of a transactional psychological contract characterized by a short time-frame and an attitude of limited organizational contribution, low commitment, weak organizational integration/identification, attitudes of limited flexibility, and easy exit.

Although current wisdom contends that the psychological contract should be conceptualized in terms of a bipolar continuum, ranging from relational (emotional involvement and 'extra mile' behaviours) to transactional (emotional distance, and contractually defined behaviours) (Herriot, Manning & Kidd, 1997; Millward & Hopkins, 1998; Robinson, Kraatz & Rousseau, 1994; Robinson & Rousseau, 1994; Rousseau, 1990, 1995; Rousseau & Parks, 1993; Stiles et al. 1996), researchers such as Arnold (1996) have pointed out that in order for this conceptualization to be robust, the various elements of transactional and relational contracts should be identified.

Robinson, Kraatz and Rousseau (1994) were the first researchers to attempt this, developing a series of items which study respondents were asked to report whether they believed *their employing organization* was obliged to provide (employer obligations) and another series of items which they were asked to report whether they believed *they* were obliged to provide (employee obligations). Their findings provided suggestive evidence for subcomponents of relational and transactional contracts, although some confused factor structures, a sample-specific result and no other forms of validation suggest that their conclusions were based more on intuitive reasoning than on psychometric or experimental rigour.

Current research by Millward and Brewerton (1998), building on work undertaken by Millward and Hopkins (1998) in developing and validating the Psychological Contract Scale (PCS), found evidence for a number of distinct subcomponents for each of the transactional and relational subscales contained within the instrument. These are listed below:

Transactional Subscale

Transactional orientation	Focus on financial gain, and on sole fulfilment of contractual and job requirements
Long-term future	Not envisaging the organization as a long-term employer
Absence of extra mile	Lack of involvement in work; unwillingness to exceed specified work requirements

Relational Subscale

Emotional affinity	Feelings of organizational membership, identification with the organization's stated goals
Professional development	Opportunities and expectations for training, promotion and professional growth
Equitability	Perceptions of fair and just reward from the organization for employee inputs

Each of these subfactors has been shown to achieve simple structure using a forced-factor oblique rotation under principal components factor analysis, with internal consistency reliability of alpha = 0.70 and above obtained for each subfactor ($n > 2000$). However, it should be noted that these factors and subfactors were derived from the clustering of attitudes concerning contract terms as opposed to perception of contract terms per se (which is the focus of the work conducted by Robinson, Kraatz & Rousseau, 1994) and are thus not directly comparable (see the section below on Operationalizing the Psychological Contract which focuses more specifically on measurement issues).

Are Relational and Transactional Contracts Independently or Inversely Related?

It has been proposed by Rousseau (1995) that transactional and relational components of the psychological contract denote opposite ends of a bipolar continuum linked respectively to the notions of economic and social exchange. These contractual 'types' are seen as extremes, anchoring either end of a single continuum, describing the full range of both organizational types, and individual contracts, perceived by employees. Transactional, or 'buy', organizations (according to the definition offered by Miles & Snow, 1980) include contract and recruitment agencies whose approach to employment in many cases epitomises the transactional contractual orientation—employees expect nothing more than monetary reward for their efforts at work, and organizations expect little commitment or emotional involvement in return. Alternatively, relational, or 'make' organizations will continue to provide support for employees, and expect commitment and good citizenship in return.

Individuals expected to fall along the proposed contractual continuum in terms of their *beliefs* or orientations are said to range from purely temporary workers who tend to adopt transactional psychological contracts, through to core staff with secure 'jobs for life' whose contracts tend to be more relational in nature. Indeed, there is some evidence that this is the case (Millward & Hopkins, 1998). However, as pointed out above, temporary staff continuously assigned to the same company on relatively long-term contracts *may* begin to develop a relational contract with the long-term host organization even though the nature of their job demands a transactional relationship with the employer (see e.g. Millward & Brewerton, 1999). Moreover, as Arnold (1996) points out in his concise and critical review of the psychological contract construct, it is yet to be made clear which specific aspects of the workplace are related to which type of contract and whether each aspect is exclusive to one or other of the contract types.

If we are to assume that the relational-transactional continuum is, indeed, bipolar, that is those employees displaying highly relational contracts fall at one end of a spectrum and those employees displaying highly transactional contracts fall at the other end, we would expect to find a strong inverse relationship between measures of the two components. On examination of data from well over 2000 employees across various organizations (where respondents have completed the Psychological Contract Scale as presented in Millward & Hopkins, 1998) it becomes apparent, however, that the *moderate* inverse relationship (generally −0.2 to −0.3) between relational and transactional orientation may be masking some more complex responses (Millward & Brewerton, 1998). Some respondents report both relatively high relational *and* transactional orientation and some respondents show the opposite pattern, in addition to the recognized high relational-low transactionals and low relational-high transactionals. Is this pattern describing something more than simply high relational or high transactional individuals? If we conceptualize high-highs as 'careerists' and low-lows as 'indifferent', we may unmask some of the apparent anomalies in response.

Some further pilot work on this topic has identified that the incidence of careerists and indifferent employees may differ according to sociological or organizational group membership (Brewerton, 1999). For example, careerists are more often to be found among younger age groups, and among those groups who have only been with the organization for a short period. As age and organizational tenure increase, so the incidence of careerism decreases and employees become more relationally oriented towards their employer. Of course, this makes sense intuitively—young, dynamic, recently acculturated organizational members will retain a drive and ambition which may lead to a self-managed career, or these employees may develop a less transactional relationship over time, as they become comfortable with their employer and lose the desire to move on in order to further their careers elsewhere.

Rousseau (1995, pp. 104–105) likewise describes a slightly more complex model than that suggested by the bipolar relational-transactional continuum, based on a four-way conceptualization of contract duration and on the level of stated specificity of employee performance. This model and its essential features are described below in Figure 10.1.

Summary, Conclusions and Outstanding Issues

It has been the cognitive-perceptual view of the psychological contract that has underpinned most of the research pursued to date. However, various criticisms have also been levelled. Arnold (1996) for instance, closely scrutinized the concept, pointing out areas of confusion (e.g. concerning the role

PERFORMANCE TERMS

	Specified	Not specified
DURATION		
Short-term	**Transactional** (e.g. shop assistants hired during Christmas season): • Low ambiguity • Easy exit/high turnover • Low member commitment • Freedom to enter new contracts • Little learning • Weak integration/ identification	**Transitional** (e.g. employee experiences during organizational retrenchment or following merger or acquisition) • Ambiguity/uncertainty • High turnover/termination • Instability
Long-term	**Balanced** (e.g. high-involvement team): • High member commitment • High integration/ identification • Ongoing development • Mutual support • Dynamic	**Relational** (e.g. family business members) • High member commitment • High affective commitment • High integration/ identification • Stability

Figure 10.1 Rousseau's (1995) psychological contract typology

Adapted from D.M. Rosseau (1995). *Psychological Contracts in Organizations: Understanding Written and Unwritten Agreements.* London & New York: Sage Publications

of promises versus expectations in contract formation and operationalization, and also the validity of the distinction between transactional and relational terms) and inconsistency in the way it has been modelled (e.g. as an employee-only psychological construct as opposed to a relationship of exchange and its relationship with other psychological constructs such as commitment) and operationalized (e.g. lack of close attention to psychometric considerations).

Guest (1999) has also pointed out inconsistencies and confusions in the conceptualization and use of the term psychological contract. He notes the lack of precision in the conceptualization, and how too much attention has been paid to 'types' of contract (transactional, relational) with little consideration for other dimensions such as implicit/explicit, time-span, scope and so on. Such dimensions (as originally proposed by MacNeil, 1985, and since taken up by Rousseau, 1995) are theoretical rather than empirical, and so far, says Guest (1999) no one has questioned their validity or utility. Guest also highlights the confusion over the use of terms 'implicit/explicit' in connection with the psychological contract. In early definitions, the psychological contract was synonymous with all that was implicit (i.e. unwritten) about contracts. In subsequent work, the psychological contract has taken on both explicit (transactional, usually in written form) and implicit (relational, usually in unwritten form) aspects, which has clouded the issue somewhat, particularly given the use by Rousseau (1989, 1995) of the term 'implicit contract' to refer to what others (i.e. observers) might infer about the psychological contract.

Herriot and Pemberton (1997) have pointed out the limitations of the content-focused approach to psychological contract research. They note that the concept has become reified into something fixed and substantive, as if it exists other than in a hypothetical or analytical form. They point to the term's original use as a backdrop for discussing the employee–employer exchange process, and argue that a process view on the psychological contract may be more fruitfully adopted in exploring this operationalization, particularly in terms of perceived breaches in the employment relationship.

Finally, the question of 'who is the other party in the contractual exchange?' has been raised by several commentators. In the words of Guest (1999) 'Who is the nebulous "other party" called the "organization"?' Until recently, the 'other party' was taken for granted as the anthropomorphized organization. However, it has since been realized that this is not satisfactory: even if we were to hold onto the single-sided view of the psychological contract as a cognitive-perceptual idiographic entity we still need to reckon with the issue of with whom the individual sees him or herself as holding the contract. In the next section—the process of contracting—the question of 'with whom the contract is held' is addressed as a central issue.

THE PROCESS OF CONTRACTING

'Contracting' versus 'Contracts'

In light of criticisms of single-sided research approaches to the psychological contract, it has been argued (e.g. by Herriot & Pemberton, 1997) that rather than address the question of the psychological contract as content, it may be more fruitful to recapture what was originally quite distinctive about the construct, as defined by Argyris (1960) and others (e.g. Schein, 1980). This distinctiveness concerns the potential of the construct to describe and explain the *exchange relationship* between employer and employee. It has been argued above that the term psychological contract has its roots in the notion of cooperative contribution described by Barnard (1938), whereby the individual is persuaded to pledge allegiance to an organization (to cooperate with it) in exchange for appropriate incentives. To this extent, the psychological contract can be said to be *located in the relationship between two parties*—the organization and the individual. To facilitate the analysis of the 'exchange relationship', it is perhaps useful to think in terms of a *process* of contracting.

The process or dialectical perspective on the psychological contract takes the view that content can only be examined in a snapshot fashion. This view is best exemplified in the work of Herriot and his colleagues (Herriot & Pemberton, 1997; Herriot, Hirsch & Reilly, 1998; Millward & Herriot, 1999). Questions about content, Herriot and Pemberton (1997) argue, enable us to describe a current relationship between employer and employee, and hence can point us to the product of the contractual process. Central to the ideas of those in the process tradition is the fundamentally two-way nature of the employer–employee exchange relationship. This is a critical consideration: as a mere snapshot of what the employment deal consists of, the content of the psychological contract can pertain to something so uniquely personal, context-bound, and fluid as to render it impossible to envisage making statements of any generic kind (Herriot, Hirsch & Reilly, 1998). Taking the contract as a process, however, questions arise such as 'With whom is the contract made?', 'How is the contract made?', 'What constitutes a breach in the contract?' and 'What are the consequences of such a breach?' (Millward & Herriot, 1999).

With Whom is the Contract Made?

It is often assumed within the psychological contract literature that a psychological contract is held by individuals and that questions about the other party to the exchange are either irrelevant or non-problematic (Coyle-Shapiro & Kessler, 1998; Sparrow, 1998). But who is the employer? In a small organization, there is likely to be little doubt. In a large and highly complex multinational or transnational organization, however, the question is less likely to be so straightforward. With the devolution of responsibility to divisions, departments or even teams, the employer may be more appropriately construed in local day-to-day terms (e.g. Divisional Manager, Department Manager, Team Leader).

In the contracted-out employment scenario now becoming increasingly prevalent in the UK, in legal and technical terms at least, the employer is the recruitment or contracts agency. At a more psychological level though, the employer is likely to be more meaningfully located in the host organization or division in which an employee actually works. Many contractors also belong to professional institutions to which they feel first and foremost obligated, and in which they strongly invest their identify and self-esteem. It is even feasible to contemplate multiple exchange scenarios in operation at any one moment in time (e.g. with the agency and with the host organization, with the profession, with the division, department or team in which one also invests time and energy) (Millward & Hopkins, 1998). There is indeed some evidence to show that 'deals' can be forged at all these levels (Millward & Brewerton, 1998).

The complexity of the contemporary workplace, in its devolved and deregulated state, coupled with its increasingly matrix-managed and 'virtual' form, strongly suggests the need for caution in assuming that the employer side of the exchange relationship can be neatly sewn up in terms of one homogeneous category of 'employer'. If we take the term 'employer' to mean organization, thus denoting the need to adopt an 'organizational' level of analysis, it becomes equally clear that what the organization constitutes is not obvious either. To equate the employer with the organization as a whole, is to anthropomorphize the latter. As Rousseau (1995) stipulates, organizations cannot hold psychological contracts. Rather, she says, we need to think in terms of 'organizational representatives'.

Despite the heterogeneous character of large and also of many medium-sized enterprises within the UK workplace, and despite the large number of potential 'representatives' who might take on the persona of 'employer', research has nonetheless tended to be pursued largely without questioning who, exactly, the 'other party' might be in the exchange relationship. Millward and Hopkins (1998) found that *commitment to the job* was a far stronger mediator of the psychological contract than *commitment to the organization*. They took this to suggest that contracting is more appropriately construed at a more concrete and day-to-day level of reality than that signalled by the abstract term 'organization'. In many cases, 'organization' is little more than an umbrella term to denote a bundle of activities all pursued in its name but with little substantive meaning beyond that comprised by the activities themselves. This is increasingly the case in today's economic climate of outsourcing and the devolution of project management to small-scale teams. Very little is actually known about who the employer is, in the eyes of employees, or at what level of analysis it is appropriate to talk about the kinds of contracts that are made (Millward & Herriot, 1999).

The Organization as a Framework for Contracting—the Drive to Develop 'New Deals'

The analysis above perhaps takes a rather extreme view on the 'organization', construing it in terms of Handy's (1994) empty raincoat image. The distinction made earlier between 'make' and 'buy' organizations (Miles & Snow, 1980) may be useful to revisit at this stage. A 'buy' organization is one that literally buys in labour on a just-in-time basis and as such is highly cost-driven. Employee regulation strategies in such organizations are largely economic in flavour. A 'make' organization on the other hand, is one that seeks to forge a lasting relationship with an employee; one that provides the employee with an important source of social identification and self-esteem as well as developing their skills and knowledge. Employee regulation strategies in this kind of organization are likely to be more concerned with winning over the hearts and minds of the employee. That is, subjective regulation strategies strive to harness a deeper social and emotional level of investment of the employee in the organization and its interests, than that possible within a purely economic exchange relationship. Handy (1994), however, predicted an employment scenario whereby organizations would transform from 'make' into 'buy' strategies.

It is indeed the case that in recent years both the US and the UK have witnessed a major growth in the contracts industry. Cost/economy driven restructuring of the workplace has not only involved mass downsizing but also the introduction of contractualization as the primary means by which to enhance numerical and financial flexibility (IES, 1998). In mid-1996, demand for temporary staff in the UK had risen by 23% on the previous year and stood at its highest level since 1982 (Tooher, 1996). Underpinning this movement is a shift from traditional working patterns to a core/complementary employment structure—that is organizations employing core long-term contract-based and complementary short-term contract-based employees (IES, 1998).

Large organizations now outsource many of their non-core, peripheral activities to external agencies, with many workers consequently employed on short-term or part-time contracts, with resultant reduced job security and continuously changing work environments (Brown, 1997). In the UK, it is estimated that the average number of functions outsourced by organizations has risen 225% (from 1.2 to 3.9 functions) in the last five years, an area set to show continued growth into the new millennium. As part of this growth, it is anticipated that core activities will also be strategically put out to tender as a means of in-house value creation (Brown, 1997). Where 'employment relations' at one time prevailed over 'labour contracting' the opposite is now increasingly the case (Williamson, 1991).

This move to 'externalization' of employees reflects a shift by organizations away from a reliance on social exchange considerations to a reliance on economic exchange considerations, with employees taken on as calculated risks (i.e. a 'buy' employment model) rather than as people with needs, concerns and interests of their own. The Human Resource metaphor is a prime example of how employees are construed as 'resources' to be harnessed in pursuit of economic ends. Whilst it is undoubtedly clear that economic concerns do reign supreme, and that cost-cutting has been pursued in the majority of cases with little regard for its human costs, evidence suggests that many organizations are now urgently trying to remake themselves, along with other 'survivors' of the storm.

There have always been those organizations in which both 'make' and 'buy' strategies comfortably coexist. This is still very much the case even in organizations that have contracted out most of their more peripheral functions to agency regulation and control (Millward & Brewerton, 1999), a UK finding consistent with that obtained by Pearce (1993) in the US. There is also a major increase in Human Resource Management (HRM) interest in organizational culture, culture change and culture management, partly due to the fear of potential cultural dilution or confusion resulting from merger, acquisition, or major reorganization. All of this suggests that organizations are still very much intent on 'making' rather than simply 'buying' at least some of their employees, whilst adopting a more transactional approach with others (Hirsh & Jackson, 1996).

Yet we must question whether employees can be 'remade' in the image of the new organization. This may have been feasible in the days when the employment deal comprised an organizational guarantee of a job-for-life in return for employee loyalty and commitment. The flexible, amoebic organization of the cost-conscious 1990s is no longer the entity it once was for the employee. Security of tenure—with its concomitant predictability of payment for services rendered, life/workplace routine and sense of belonging—has been largely replaced with insecurity over employment prospects, concern over promotional prospects, and hesitation in taking on long-term financial burdens such as mortgages, loans, and so on. The substitution of fixed-term for permanent contracts even for 'core' employees (i.e. employees with primary organizational responsibilities), coupled with mass redundancy of friends and colleagues, has exacerbated the feelings of insecurity felt by otherwise 'secure' employees in the contemporary marketplace.

This picture of widespread employee insecurity is the context in which organizations are attempting to reconstitute themselves and prepare themselves for the future. It is commonly noted that whilst clearly the 'old' employment deal is dead, 'new' deals through which the time, energy and commitment of employees can be harnessed have yet to be coherently formulated and articulated within organizational contexts. The 'deal' that exists at the social level of analysis (i.e. the social contract) is primarily economic in character. This makes for an insecure anchorage of the individual within the organization, one that does not bode well for organizations in the long term.

Herriot, Hirsch and Reilly (1998) note that those organizations which now seek to reanchor and reintegrate employees on a more 'make' than 'buy' basis, may face the fundamental challenge of rebuilding lost trust. Breach of the 'old' employment deal or social contract, it is argued, has undermined trust to the point where social capital (denoting the willingness of people to trust in and collaborate with others) within organizations is at an all time low and is being further undermined by management rhetoric which, more often than not, does not tally with the realities of organizational life. The absence of reserve social capital within the stock of UK society generally (due to the large-scale disintegration of institutions like the family and the education system), has made it less and less likely that 'trust' will be effectively secured.

Thus, organizations face the immediate challenge of rebuilding social capital on the basis of which more integrative deals can be forged with employees. This is the context within which new psychological contracts can emerge. It may therefore be appropriate to construe the organization as affording a normative framework in which shared psychological contracts (Rousseau, 1995) can be developed between the organization and its employees. It is feasible to contemplate a process of contracting at a normative level, which in turn provides the interpretative backdrop within which contracting can be pursued at the more psychological level.

Most organizations, it seems, have not yet reinvented themselves at the normative level, let alone at the more individuated level of the psychological contract. Many employees have turned to their professions or occupations as suitable vehicles within which to anchor their identity and self-esteem (Millward & Hopkins, 1998). Many perceive organizations as merely employment zones rather than as meaningful institutions in which to carve themselves out a viable niche in society. Many organizations are still fumbling about with 'buy' and 'make' considerations in a disorganized fashion, having yet to articulate any basis for the employment relationship beyond the purely financial.

It is important however, in thinking about the normative context in which deals are forged, not to lapse into advocating that one new deal will provide the ultimate collaborative solution. As stipulated by the process view on the psychological contract, a deal is a two-way affair that by definition has to be negotiated before it can be said to truly exist. Whilst many different types of deal scenarios are currently being envisaged (Sparrow, 1998), many organizations have been inclined to *impose* new 'deals' on their employees (Noon & Blyton, 1997). In their simultaneous efforts to change structurally and culturally, and also to enhance performance, organizations may encourage employees to accept new 'deals' that do not address their personal interests and needs. For the sake of anchorage, and of sheer survival on a financial level, many employees may find it difficult to resist the offer of a deal that provides them with the promise of a secure footage at least in the short term.

The Dynamics of Contracting—the Need for Individuated Deals

Herriot, Hirsch and Reilly (1998) describe the dynamics of psychological contracting as an interplay of 'wants' and 'offers' on the part of both employees and organization alike. A psychological contract is said to be afforded by a match between what is wanted and what is on offer, for both parties in the exchange. It is unlikely that a perfect match will simply occur naturally. The process of contracting requires negotiation of wants and offers, and as such cannot take either for granted. Potentially, what an employee wants from a relationship with the organization is much more variable than what the organization wants in return (e.g. Guest, 1998). In the contemporary economic climate, the organization is likely to want investment in optimal performance, flexibility and the ability to adapt quickly and effectively to rapid change. On the other hand, each employee's wants are likely to be as idiosyncratic and subjective as ever.

Because the types of things that individuals might want from an organization are potentially infinite, the idea is obviously too unwieldy to contemplate without some means of organizing needs and wants into viable categories. To this end, Schein's (1993) model of 'career anchors' (or work value) is used by Herriot, Hirsch and Reilly (1998) as a way of unpacking individual differences in the kinds of things that an employee might be looking for in their relationship with an employer. According to Schein there are eight different categories of work value: security; autonomy/independence; technical/functional; managerial; entrepreneurship; service/dedication; challenge; and lifestyle integration. It should be noted that there are many sections of the UK workforce for whom security needs are so predominant (because of financial crisis), that anything beyond this basic transactional requirement is purely academic (Herriot, Manning & Kidd, 1997). There are also those for whom work is not the 'lived in' reality that it is for those who live to work. Some employees work to live. Yet research has tended to focus primarily on the former: employees who seek relational contracts with their employing organization rather than transactional ones.

It would be tempting at this stage to attempt segmentation of the workforce in terms of predominant work values. It is likely, for instance, that professionals will be looking primarily for autonomy and independence in their relationship with an employer, and that female employees with families will be more interested in lifestyle integration. However, such simplistic divisions must be avoided for risk of stereotyping particular groups of employees—such a practice would not be consistent with the process of contracting which addresses *individual* needs and interests. Moreover, conventional divisions such as age, sex and occupation for instance, are no longer viable ways of segmenting the UK workforce; diversity has been reconfigured and is potentially infinitely variable (Sparrow, 1998).

It is generally agreed by HRM experts that the diverse character of the workforce, coupled with the demand on organizations for innovation and adaptation to change in order to survive, requires highly individuated strategies of psychological contract management (Guest 1998; Herriot, Hirsch & Reilly, 1998; Sparrow, 1998). Organizations tend to underestimate the diversity of their employees' needs, assuming homogeneity of cultural values and thus personal values therein. Thus, norm structures can obscure individual needs and interests to the point of neglect. This is particularly true of employees lower down the organizational hierarchy and/or in peripheral roles.

There is evidence for some attempts by organizations in the UK to establish individuated deals with employees in all types of jobs and at all levels of status. Vauxhall Motors, for instance (as cited by Parsons & Strickland, 1996), has established a development scheme in which all employees are afforded the opportunity to identify and pursue their personal development needs both within and outside the employing organization. Since its introduction, there has been a 60% take up of the 'offer' of personal development, and a notable reduction in employee turnover. Other examples in the UK include First Direct and also Lloyds TSB, both of whom afford supervisors the autonomy to offer their telesales staff work patterns to suit their individual lifestyle needs (Herriot, Hirsch & Reilly, 1998).

VIOLATION OF THE CONTRACT: PROMISES OR EXPECTATIONS?

The old psychological contract is dead! (Hall, 1993)

As the above statement illustrates, a major theme to be found within the literature is that of contract violation. It is this, it is argued, which is most likely to result in negative outcomes for the organization and for the individual (Herriot, Manning & Kidd, 1997; McLean Parks & Kidder, 1994; Robinson & Rousseau, 1994). It has been stipulated that in order for a breach to constitute a violation of a contract, the contract must comprise a promissory element, as opposed to merely carrying the expectations of *both parties*. According to Rousseau (1995, p. 111) contract violation can range from subtle misperceptions to stark breaches of good faith. She says that violation is commonplace (e.g. due to unfamiliarity with the job), often inadvertent (e.g. 'over-promise', say one thing—do another) and difficult to articulate, although this need not be fatal. Not all discrepancies are noticed and not all that are noticed are perceived as violations. Often, inadvertent contract violation occurs because of failure to communicate (see also Herriot, Hirsch & Reilly, 1998). Strongly felt experiences of violation, however, tend to occur when a failure to keep a commitment injures or causes damages that the contract was designed to avoid (Rousseau, 1995, pp. 112–113). Such outright failure can arise from opportunism (i.e. self-serving at the expense of other) or sheer negligence (i.e. non-fulfilment) (see also Robinson & Rousseau, 1994).

As already pointed out, Rousseau (1990), in one of the first major empirical studies of the psychological contract, emphasized that violated promises were at the core of the construct, arguing that this differentiated the psychological contract from the concept of unmet expectations (Wanous, Poland, Premack & Davis, 1992). She also suggested that this lent more weight (in terms of accounting for increased variance) to the prediction of work-related outcomes such as satisfaction and intention to leave. Violation, then, is a failure to comply with the promissory terms of a contract: how people interpret the circumstances of this failure determines whether they experience a violation (Rousseau, 1995, p. 112). Robinson and Rousseau (1994) addressed the contract violation theme with a longitudinal study of graduates over their first two years of employment. They found that over this period, 55% of the sample reported that reciprocal obligations had been violated by the employing organization and that reported occurrence of violation correlated positively with turnover and negatively with trust, satisfaction and intention to stay with the organization.

However, in practice, contract violation has not always been conceptualized solely in terms of this promissory element. Guzzo, Noonan and Elron (1994), for example, questioned expatriate managers about the support they felt they *should* receive from their employing organization, compared with the support they did receive, thereby eliminating the promissory element from the manager–organization contract. Similarly, Baker (1985) cites work role, social, economic and cultural employee *expectations* as underpinning the psychological contract with an employing organization, suggesting that violation of these expectations alone, whether or not they contain a promissory element, will ultimately result in dissatisfaction and be instrumental in a decision to quit.

Other researchers have focused on potential mediators of perceived contract violation, including Shore and Tetrick (1994), who discussed causal attribution in this context, arguing that reactions to violation may depend in part on the *type* of violation and the *extent to which the organization is perceived as being responsible* for it. They suggest that 'action-oriented' individuals (Kuhl, 1992) may be most likely to attempt to reinstate or renegotiate the contract, whereas 'state-oriented' individuals may be more inclined to avoid/withdraw from the situation. This assertion clearly has implications for individual-level management of the psychological contract by the employing organization. It has also been suggested that the relational-transactional contract distinction may be fundamental in predicting worker reaction to perceived violation. For example, McLean Parks and Kidder (1994) linked the psychological contract concept with that of procedural versus distributive justice. They argued that perceptions of procedural justice following a violation may be most salient to employees holding a relational contract, whereas distributive justice may be most significant to those with a transactional one. Intuitively, and as has been suggested by other researchers (e.g. Robinson & Rousseau, 1994), it could be argued that violation of a relational contract is likely to have more significant *affective* outcomes for the individual holding the contract, since the relationship between individual and organization is based more on trust, loyalty and commitment than a transactional contract. In short, relationship strength is likely to mediate perceived violation. Transactional employees may adopt a more pragmatic stance to a perceived violation, and are perhaps less likely to experience personal disillusionment and other affective responses (feeling 'cheated', becoming less trusting of the organization, etc.).

Noer (1993) describes the effects of downsizing on organizations' remaining employees, and the importance of negotiating new contracts with these staff. Goffee and Scase (1992) and Brockner, Grover, Reed and DeWitt (1992) have also provided evidence of alienated 'shell-shocked' survivors of organizational trauma, responding by either 'getting out', 'getting safe' (keeping their heads down) or 'getting even' (by psychological withdrawal or sabotage) (Arnold, 1996). Clearly, any of these outcomes will impact negatively on the organization. Evidence suggests that violation can promote distrust, anger, attrition (Robinson & Rousseau, 1994), can change behaviour (Rousseau et al, 1992) engineer declines in loyalty (Griffin, O'Leary-Kelly & Collins, 1998) and prompt an increase in litigation (Tyler & Bies, 1979).

It is clear that in many cases 'violation is a trauma for a relationship and undermines good faith'—once lost it is not easily restored. In the words of Rousseau (1995, p. 120), 'troubled relationships often go from bad to worse'. This is because the experience of violation can make people more alert to future potential violations, which can be self-fulfilling. Violation is said to be most likely to occur when there is:

- A history of conflict and low trust
- Social distance—parties do not understand the perspective of the other
- External pattern of violation (e.g. during an era of business retrenchment)
- Incentives to breach contracts are high
- One party perceives little value in the relationship

In summary, the issue of contract violation is a fashionable one given the change in contractual tone within the contemporary marketplace. However, some are wondering whether the issue simply rejuvenates (in the language of contracts) long-standing, almost century-old concerns about job dissatisfaction and its impact on workforce morale and performance (Guest, 1999). Until we know more about what the psychological contract is and how it can be most appropriately investigated, the notion of violation begs the question of what exactly it is that is being breached and in particular, on what basis can a breach be said to have occurred?

OPERATIONALIZING THE PSYCHOLOGICAL CONTRACT

Types of Contract Measurement

Early research on the psychological contract was primarily interview-driven (e.g. Argyris, 1962; Levinson, 1962). Attempts to quantify the psychological contract have only been fairly recently developed, although there is now a plethora of different approaches. Most of these measurement attempts are underpinned by the assumption that psychological contracts are cognitive-perceptual constructs, as espoused by Rousseau (1989, 1995) which means that (a) the self-report method is deemed the most valid way of accessing them (see for example, Pearce, 1997) and (b) that they are held by employees (not the employer) which means that they can be investigated form one viewpoint alone. As will be demonstrated, there are exceptions to the second of these principles, particularly in contemporary ways of exploring psychological contracts.

Measurement attempts can be divided into two main approaches: *content* (identifying the obligations and terms that employees hold themselves to be party to in the employment relationship, describing the types of relationship which predominate) (e.g. Robinson, Kraatz & Rousseau, 1994; Hutton & Cummins, 1997), and *process measures* (pertaining to the dynamic aspects of contract fulfilment and violation, such as whether an obligation has or has not been met) (e.g. Robinson & Rousseau, 1994; Robinson, 1996). The majority of published research is content-oriented, focusing on contractual obligations, although process research is on the increase. It should be noted, however, that process research is concerned with contract violation and not the psychological contract per se, which means that questions concerning the contracting process itself have yet to be formally addressed.

Content-focused Measures

Content-focused research can be divided into studies which have attempted to elicit idiosyncratic information and those which aim at psychometric standardization (Robinson & Wolfe-Morrison, 1995). If, as it can be argued, psychological contracts comprise both idiosyncratic (usually obtained in qualitative form) and generalizable (usually obtained in quantitative form) aspects, then both types of measurement are likely to be viable (Rousseau, 1990).

Efforts at standardization

Standardization was first attempted by Robinson, Kraatz and Rousseau (1994) who developed a psychometric tool to measure the psychological contract from the employee's perspective. On the basis of extensive pilot work, they developed a series of items which respondents were asked to report whether they believed *their employing organization* was obliged to provide (employer obligations) and another series of items which they were asked to report whether they believed *they* were obliged to provide (employee obligations). The aim of the tool was not only to ascertain contract content but to enable the tracking of contracts over time. Robinson, Kraatz and Rousseau (1994) reported a test-retest reliability item mean of 0.80 across a two-week time gap. However, some differences in the factor structure between administrations of the items suggested instability of some items, leading some researchers to suggest the need for further work to confirm the most appropriate scale for each work aspect (e.g. Arnold, 1996).

The vast number of obligation terms that could be potentially incorporated in a tool like this (with different obligations relevant for particular populations of respondent) can undermine the scope for generalization (e.g. what the employer is obliged to offer may cover working conditions, benefits, intrinsic job characteristics, good faith and so on, and what the employee is obliged to offer in return may cover things such as professionalism, loyalty and commitment, hard work, etc.). In a longitudinal study of MBA students (Rousseau, 1990; Robinson & Rousseau, 1994), the relational and transactional dimensions identified at time 1, also revealed themselves at time 2, suggesting relative stability across a period of 2½ years (see also Robinson & Wolfe-Morrison, 1995 and 1997). Although the factor structures derived from research on MBA students have not been replicated across other samples (Barksdale & McFarlane Shore, in press; Freese & Schalk, 1996), some obligation terms appear to be relatively valid and stable indicators of the relational psychological contract (i.e. the provision of job security and development opportunity in exchange for loyalty and commitment) and likewise the transactional contract (i.e. high monetary reward in exchange for efficient and effective performance).

Two other psychometric instruments geared to eliciting data on the psychological contract are worthy of note, both of which take an employee-only stance on the issue. Hutton and Cummins (1997) published a measure termed the Psychological Contract Inventory (PsyCon) in the *Australian Journal of Career Development*. Drawing on the qualitative work of Herriot, Manning and Kidd (1997) (as described below) coupled with the quantitative work of Robinson and Wolfe-Morrison (1995), Hutton and Cummins (1997) derived 44 items for inclusion in their scale. The response options ranged across a five-point scale from 1 (not at all obligated) through to 5 (completely obligated). Employee obligations were defined as 'anything you believe you owe your employer or workplace even though there may be no written or clearly spoken agreement between you'. Employer obligations were defined as 'anything you believe your employer should provide even though . . .' Responses were derived from a sample of 114 employees (in technical and professional jobs), both male and female in approximately equal numbers.

Factor analysis of employee obligations yielded three factors:

- 'Good will towards work including positive presence, effort, involvement and personal integrity'
- 'Doing more than required including intention to stay and flexibility'
- 'Loyalty including protecting the interests of the organization'

Factor analysis of perceived employer obligations yielded two factors:

- 'Support for the individual including opportunities for advancement and development, and recognition for needs and circumstances'
- 'Respect and fair practice including appropriate rewards, justice, resources and training'

The scale demonstrates potential but has as yet only been investigated on a limited sample. The scale was evolved on exploratory grounds, although as indicated above it was informed by previous research. The authors argue that the construct is in need of theoretical development, and agree that much more theoretical and empirical work is needed before the PsyCon Inventory can be considered to be the tool of choice in this regard.

In 1998, Millward and Hopkins published the Psychological Contract Scale (PCS), which was evolved on a priori grounds (to enable the identification of relational and transactional psychological contracts) (see also Millward & Brewerton, 1999). A 50-item bank initially derived from focus group discussions was subsequently reduced to a 37-item questionnaire, comprising 22 'relational' and 15 'transactional' items (reporting stable factor structure and internal consistency reliability). This tool has subsequently been validated on a sample of over 5000 employees across a wide range of industries and organizations, and has also been slightly shortened (Millward & Brewerton, 1998). The PCS now comprises 20 items for the transactional subscale and 12 items for the relational subscale, with the following internal consistency reliabilities: transactional (alpha = 0.79); and relational (alpha = 0.80). Consistent with the advice of Arnold (1996) in his incisive critique of the psychological contract, the possibility of subfactors within contractual types was explored and these results were discussed in an earlier section of this chapter. Interestingly, there is overlap with these factors and those identified by Hutton and Cummins (1997) described above, suggesting that through triangulation of methods it may be possible to identify some generic components of the psychological contract. However, as they themselves stipulated, much more work is needed before any definitive conclusions can be drawn.

Moving on from the employee-only stance on the psychological contract, Barksdale and McFarlane Shore (in press) used Robinson, Kraatz and Rousseau's (1994) 15-item measure to look at whether particular types of interrelations between employer and employee obligations could be identified. To this end, they cluster analysed the obligation terms to identify people with different kinds of contracts. From this, four types of interrelation were identified and defined in terms of scope (i.e. covering a broad or limited array of contract terms) and the balance of the exchange of obligations (high-high, low-low, high-low, low-high). This approach is consistent with the definition of a psychological contract as a process involving reciprocal exchanges and agreements (Herriot & Pemberton, 1997; Herriot, Hirsch & Reilly, 1998). The findings showed that where mutual obligations are perceived to be high, and where the contracts are of broad rather than limited scope, there was significantly higher employee commitment, and intention to stay. The findings also demonstrate the potential of investigating the relevance of the notion of exchange to the way that psychological contracts operate.

Using a different approach altogether, Wade-Benzoni and Rousseau (1997) tested out the viability of using a very simple classification task involving doctoral students and faculty members in choosing 'the description which most closely fits the collaborative research relationship':

- *Transactional*—structured project with specified time-frame; clear and explicit performance terms
- *Relational*—mentoring relationship; open-ended time-frame, implicit performance standards
- *Balanced/Hybrid*—involved a mentoring relationship and at least one structured project; long-term time-frame, well-specified performance terms
- *Transitional/Uncertain*—no specified time-frame or performance requirements

Findings confirmed the viability of using typologies of this kind to elicit data on psychological contracts as a relationship of reciprocity and exchange. In this research, there was much agreement between students and faculty members on the contract types they saw as relevant to them.

The qualitative approach

Attempts to explore the idiosyncratic nature of the psychological contract construct have been pursued in several ways, one of which is psychodynamic. Rousseau and Tijoriwala (1996) found that the psychological contract may be underpinned by a parent–child dynamic—for example nurses in relation to their seniors. On a different note, Herriot and Pemberton (1995b) looked at divergence in how the employment relationship was construed by managers and employees, divergence of the kind that can generate overt conflict. They used the focus group method to elicit both management's and employees' views of the 'new' psychological contract (following years of escalating competitiveness and pressures created by mass downsizing). In a similar vein, Herriot, Manning and Kidd (1997) utilised Critical Incidents technique to explore the psychological contract construct, deriving data from two samples: representatives from management, and employees. Both samples were asked to report specific instances when:

1. The organization offered more than it was obligated to.
2. An employee/employees offered more than they were obligated to.
3. The organization offered less than it was obligated to.
4. An employee/employees offered less than obligated to.

The elicited themes derived from content analysis of over 1000 incidents elicited from participants are summarized below:

Organizational obligations	Employee obligations
• Training	• Hours
• Fairness	• Work

Organizational obligations	Employee obligations
• Needs	• Honesty
• Consultation	• Loyalty
• Discretion	• Property
• Humanity	• Self-presentation
• Recognition	• Flexibility
• Environment	
• Justice	
• Pay	
• Benefits	
• Security	

By content and chi-square analysing these contractual themes within each group of participants, it was found that in terms of organizational obligations, management representatives focused on relational aspects of the workplace, and employees more on 'hygiene' aspects. In terms of employee obligations, again, a relational view was adopted by management (e.g. loyalty), with a more transactional view taken by employees (e.g. self-presentation, property). No group differences appeared, however, for the themes 'hours', 'work' and 'honesty'.

The principal rationale for using idiosyncratic measurement is that in times of radical change, structural features of one organization may not carry the same meaning in another (nor indeed within the same organization over time). In such circumstances, it could be argued that idiosyncratic measures are not only appropriate but are the only realistic source of information on psychological contracts (Herriot, Hirsch & Reilly, 1998). Moreover, given that employment relations are undergoing dramatic change, the particular practices that once characterized relational or transactional type contracts may also change (e.g. some employers may no longer offer career advancement but may instead offer more lifestyle type contracts with built-in flexibility to suit both parties and/or alternative types of development opportunities). It is feasible that many different combinations of 'offers' might nonetheless produce a similar employment relationship (e.g. for some employees, a relational contract is forged by offering them flexible contracts in exchange for their loyalty and commitment). In addition, it is becoming evident that a hybrid form of psychological contract is emerging which reconciles the precisely specified performance requirements of the conventional transactional contract with traditional relational agreements between employee and employer (Rousseau & Tijoriwala, 1996). The idiosyncratic approach to measurement is also characterized by an assumption of the psychological contract as a two-way rather than a one-way affair, thereby taking the construct out of the head of the individual and into the relationship characterized by a two-party exchange.

In summary, there is as yet little evidence for stable composites of obligation characterizing the employment relationship in the way predicted by the cognitive-perceptual model of the psychological contract. However, investigated in the form of an attitude, there is growing evidence for the viability of the relational and transactional distinction within the psychological contract model. The distinction holds strong across different organizational settings and samples. Whether the elements of which these 'types of relationship' are comprised will remain stable over time is yet to be ascertained, although this seems highly unlikely due to changes in the meaning of particular contractual terms with time. Moreover, this approach locates the psychological contract still very firmly in the head of the employee, thereby neglecting the two-party nature of the contractual exchange. To investigate the dynamics of contracting, its two-way nature as well as changes in meaning, a more idiosyncratic qualitative approach might be appropriate, although some attempts have already been made to quantify the relationship using classification as well as adapted versions of existing questionnaire methods. The use of employee-only measures of the psychological contract do not preclude the possibility of investigating the employer side of the equation, though the viability of this has yet to be systematically ascertained.

Process-focused Measures

Process-focused measures aim to assess how well or otherwise a party to the contract has performed against promises and obligations—that is they aim to measure contract violation, rather than the psychological contract per se. Process measures can be divided into two main types: *direct* and *indirect*. Of the direct measures that have been used, the two most commonly cited are: (a) contract fulfilment (1–5 'not at all' to a 'very great extent') and (b) a dichotomous index of violation (yes/no) (see, for example, Robinson & Rousseau, 1994).

Using the continuous index, fulfilment and violation are found to be negatively related (−0.53). However, in reality, argues Rousseau (1995) violation and fulfilment can coexist within the same psychological contract—that is people can perceive some aspects of their contract to be fulfilled and other aspects to be violated. To this extent, she advocates that the dichotomous 'yes'/'no' measure is a more valid indicator of contract fulfilment/violation, enabling particular domains of fulfilment or violation to be more discretely ascertained. Likewise, Robinson and Wolfe-Morrison (1997) investigated obligation fulfilment using 25 obligation terms at time 1 and then traced how well each obligation had been fulfilled at time 2. These 25 obligation fulfilment items fell into 6 factors: enriched job; fair pay; opportunity for growth and advancement; sufficient tools and resources; supportive work environment; and attractive benefits.

An example of a more *indirect* measure of contract fulfilment is 'perceived organizational support' (POS) (which measures the perceived quality of support (Eisenberger et al, 1986) as used by Barksdale and Renn (in press), and

Barksdale and McFarlane-Shore (in press), Barksdale and Renn (in press) confirmed the validity of using the POS to investigate contract violation in the context of an organization in which radical changes in compensation policy had been experienced (i.e. from annual merit increases to lump sum bonuses). Existing employees tended to be low on POS and were especially prone to absenteeism whereas employees contracted in under the new scheme were largely unaffected.

One of the problems with the notion of contract violation is that it assumes that we know exactly what it is that has been violated (or fulfilled), when in fact (as the above discussion reveals) we are still not really sure what the psychological contract is or how in itself it should be measured. Moreover, some have pondered whether contract violation is no more than simply a surrogate term for job dissatisfaction particularly insofar as it is defined as a primarily affective construct (Guest, 1999).

In summary, contract fulfilment appears to be conceptually and empirically distinct from contract violation, thus confirming the inclination to measure these as discrete constructs rather than via a continuous scale. Surrogate variables of contract fulfilment such as perceived organizational support also appear to have some viability. In general, considerable caution is needed in the use of indicators of both contract violation and fulfilment, insofar as (a) it is not clear what exactly it is that is being violated or fulfilled and (b) it is not clear that the terms contract fulfilment and contract violation add any conceptual or empirical value over and above the more straightforward concepts of satisfaction and dissatisfaction, respectively.

Performance Implications

Whilst affective outcomes to contract violation, such as commitment levels and job satisfaction, have been well documented (Robinson & Rousseau, 1994; Rousseau, 1990; Wanous et al. 1992), behavioural implications of contract violation and contract type are also of interest in that it is these behaviours which are most likely to impact *directly* on an organization's performance. A variety of behavioural indicators have been studied within the literature, most notably organizational citizenship behaviour (OCB), absenteeism, staff turnover and intent, and workplace violence. Robinson and Wolfe-Morrison (1995), in a longitudinal study of MBA alumni, found that if employees perceived organizational obligations to have been unfulfilled after 18 months within the company, they were significantly less likely to engage in organizational citizenship behaviour at 30 months tenure (although they noted that this relationship was mediated, in part, by trust). McLean Parks and Kidder (1994) also discussed the relationship between contract violation and employee engagement in anti-OCB behaviours, including theft and sabotage.

Nicholson and Johns (1985) attempted to link the psychological contract construct with the concept of 'absence cultures', arguing the contract to be the surface manifestation of communicated corporate values which may result in the production of one of four absence cultural 'types'. Geurts (1995) also suggested that absence from work may derive in part from the nature of an employee's psychological contract with the workplace. Work by Brewerton and Millward (1997) confirmed this assertion, reporting a significant relationship between relational psychological contractual orientation (as quantified using an abridged version of Millward and Hopkins' 1998 'Psychological Contract Scale') and worker absenteeism over a three-month period within a UK-based telemarketing call centre.

Staff turnover and intention to stay with or leave an organization has been explored by various researchers. Robinson and Rousseau (1994) found that perceived contract violation correlated positively with staff turnover and negatively with intention to remain. Guzzo, Noonan and Elron (1994) developed a model which maintained that the psychological contract held by expatriate managers could act as a mediator of organizational practices in predicting retention-relevant outcomes, including intention to leave the organization, and intention to return early to a domestic assignment. Research by Millward and Brewerton (1998) reports the following highly significant relationships between the psychological contract (as quantified by the Psychological Contract Scale) and intention to leave, across three major UK-based organizations: relational with intent to leave ($r = -0.31$, $n = 1561$) and transactional with intent to leave ($r = 0.20$, $n = 1542$).

Evaluation

Research on the psychological contract which until recently has been largely content-focused, is becoming attuned to the need to investigate the two-party nature of contracting. In the early 1990s, the focus was principally on the employee as the holder of the psychological contract. More recently, however, the reciprocal nature of the exchange agreements involved in the process of contracting has been acknowledged and taken up. To this extent, it is now being argued that it is critical to look at the *interplay between employer and employee* terms as the definitive characteristic of the psychological contract in an organizational setting (Barksdale & McFarlane Shore, in press; Herriot, Hirsch & Reilly, 1998; Millward & Herriot, 1999). Reciprocity cannot be investigated solely from employee-derived data.

It is also clear from the above review that there is a strong case for using a combination of measures: content-focused as well as process-focused, qualitative (idiosyncratic) and quantitative (standardized, generic). There is evidence that the psychological contract comprises both stable and dynamic (i.e. continually in transition) elements (see Herriot, Hirsch & Reilly, 1998), as well as both generic and idiosyncratic aspects (which in turn are a function of person-specific, organization-specific, economic and political factors). To this extent, there is unlikely to be such a thing as a 'pure' contract in the absolute and substantive sense, and we are perhaps in danger of reifying the concept if we assume that there is. This criticism extends to research on contract fulfilment and violation which assumes that there is something fixed and stable to fulfil and violate, which masks the reality of a dynamic process of negotiation and adaptation to circumstances denoting a breach of contract (Sparrow, 1998). The discussion below on contemporary contracts takes up the issue of adaptation in connection with breached or changing contracts in more detail.

RELATIONSHIPS WITH OTHER PSYCHOLOGICAL CONSTRUCTS: OLD WINE IN NEW BOTTLES?

Arnold (1996) has argued that if the psychological contract construct is to be of use, at least in its employee-only, idiosyncratic form, then it needs to be systematically differentiated (conceptually and empirically) from closely related constructs such as commitment. Many of the pet constructs researched by organizational psychologists, for example, report alarmingly strong relationships with supposedly conceptually and empirically distinct concepts, for example organizational commitment, job satisfaction, job involvement, and so on. Many conflated relationships are believed to exist due to method covariance and other statistical biases. It is possible however, one one level, to argue that such relationships are also descriptive of the complex and interdependent nature of workplace reactions. It is with these caveats in mind that we can explore the relationships found between the psychological contract and other measures of workplace perception and reaction, thereby attempting to identify or clarify what is distinct about the psychological contract.

Organizational Commitment

It might be argued that the psychological contract as a cognitive-perceptual construct holds little explanatory or predictive significance over and above the concept of organizational commitment (e.g. Somers, 1995). Argyle (1989), citing Etzioni (1961), proposed that commitment can be thought of in two ways: calculative and affective. Calculative commitment corresponds to Etzioni's notion of 'utilitarian exchange', signalling an instrumental attachment to an organization, whilst affective commitment corresponds to Etzioni's notion of 'moral involvement', signalling a non-instrumental 'emotional' attachment to the organization through internalizing its values. This conceptualization of commitment echoes with the idea of a 'transactional' (i.e. calculative) and 'relational' (i.e. affective) organizational orientation.

Likewise, Becker's (1960) 'side-bet' *behavioural* theory of commitment pictures an individual bound to the organization through instrumental interests (e.g. salary, benefits, seniority/status) (also underpinning the work of McGee

& Ford, 1987) indicating, perhaps, a kind of transactional organizational orientation. Similarly, the affective/attitudinal view of commitment parallels the idea of a relational organizational orientation insofar as it is defined as 'the strength of an individual's identification and involvement with an organization' (Porter, Steers, Mowday & Boullian, 1974, p. 12; see also Mowday, Steers & Porter, 1979).[1] It might be argued, then, that the psychological contract is merely another way of operationalizing organizational commitment: the transactional orientation is similar to the calculative type of commitment proposed by Etzioni (1961) with the relational orientation corresponding to Etzioni's idea of an affective/attitudinal type of commitment.

Unlike the psychological contract, however, organizational commitment is construed to comprise employee attitudes towards an entire organization, rather than specific aspects or facets of that organization. As such, the commitment construct is believed to be less influenced by daily events (Angle & Perry, 1981; Dipboye, Smith & Howell, 1994), and to be more indicative of a relatively stable employee attribute (Porter et al., 1974; Koch & Steers, 1978). However, the conceptual and empirical overlap between the two models is difficult to ascertain from the existing literature. The concept of organizational commitment used by contemporary researchers is anchored one-sidedly in the affective/attitudinal tradition of Porter et al. (1974).

As pointed out by Rousseau (1995), the concept of the psychological contract is most definitely tied to that of organizational commitment; however, it does not address beliefs about reciprocity and obligation. Together, findings show that, even as a cognitive-perceptual employee-only construct, the psychological contract (operationalized in transactional and relational terms) explains substantially more variance than either organizational or job commitment, in organizational behaviour including extra-role activity, intention to stay or leave, and absenteeism (Millward & Hopkins, 1998; Millward & Brewerton, 1999; Coyle-Shapiro & Kessler, 1998). The added value of the psychological contract construct as an explanatory tool is also illustrated by evidence (to be described below in the section on the links with organized culture) demonstrating its fundamentally two-way, as opposed to one-way, character. Whereas organizational commitment pertains to the degree of emotional investment in, and identification with, an organization and its goals, the psychological contract can be said to operate in a more multifaceted and dynamic fashion. Organizational commitment can thus be said to denote an 'input', whereas the psychological contract distinctly denotes a 'relationship of exchange' (Millward & Hopkins, 1998; Millward & Herriot, 1999).

Links with Organizational Culture

The potential relationship between the psychological contract and concepts such as organizational culture are clearly largely reliant on the way in which these concepts are conceptualized and measured. Rousseau (1995) has noted how psychological contracts are informed by social contracts in the form of particular cultural norms and values (e.g. assumptions of good faith, fair dealing and trust). In short, she says that the psychological contract is a product of culture not a cause, and to this extent will reflect it without being synonymous with it.

Taking a distinctly psychometric line on the topic of organizational culture, Millward and Brewerton's (1998) research into the measurement of organizational culture has identified 12 distinct dimensions of the construct which may be rated by employees within any organization. In order to explore the relationship between employees' perceptions of their organization's culture and their own psychological contracts, regression models were built for both relational and transactional psychological contract ratings, regressing each of the 12 dimensions onto transactional/relational contract rating in order to identify which cultural dimensions were most closely related to the psychological contract. Utilizing a sample size of over 5000, which comprised employees from a wide range of different organizations, both common (cross-organization) and distinguishing (organization-specific) patterns emerged from the data.

Specifically, it was found that perceptions of opportunity to develop, to belong, and to obtain recognition were cultural dimensions that predicted a high score on the relational subscale. It is the perceived absence of development opportunity, of organizational coherence and direction, and of loyalty and commitment demonstrated by employee and employer alike, that predicted a heightened score on the transactional subscale. Whilst causal links should not be assumed between what the organization is perceived to 'offer' and what the employee might then 'offer' in return, the evidence does suggest that the psychological contract is inextricably bound up with considerations of *employer–employee exchange*. Importantly, the findings also show clearly that relational and transactional contracts are unlikely to be part of a single bipolar construct (since different elements of culture were found to differentially predict relational and transactional contract formation).

Similar findings are reported by Coyle-Shapiro and Kessler (1998) for whom exchange was operationalized as the extent to which various obligations (on the part of the organization) of both a relational and transactional kind, were deemed fulfilled (Robinson & Rousseau, 1994). Their evidence, derived from public sector employees such as teachers and firefighters, demonstrated that the character of the exchange relationship is driven by the extent to which employees perceive themselves to be valued and supported.

Other researchers have also attempted to link the psychological contract and organizational culture constructs. Nicholson and Johns (1985) suggest that since the psychological contract is said to emerge from employee interaction and communication, it thereby effectively dictates how culture is 'acted out' at the *behavioural* level of analysis. The researchers go on to discuss the transmission of culture through the social context, reinforcing the social order of the organization via this medium and leading to formation of an appropriate psychological contract.

Borrill and Kidd (1994) discussed the experience of return to work following the birth of a child for samples of men and women, suggesting that for women at least, who were generally shown to shift from full-time to part-time work following pregnancy, the renegotiation of the psychological contract with their employing organization was problematic, if not impossible, if a truly mutually acceptable contract was to be arrived at. The researchers pointed to the alteration and change of various cultural practices and values within the organization as a possible mediator of this negotiation problem. Stiles et al. (1996) focus on the potential problems of renegotiating employee contracts following major organizational change programmes. Cultural changes within the workplace were found to result in violations of the old psychological contract for employees of three major UK-based firms, resulting in lowered morale, commitment and satisfaction at work. Finally, Rousseau (1995), in her introductory text concerning the psychological contract paradigm, links her conceptualization of the psychological contract with a Schein-esque (1980) 'layered' view of organizational culture.

CONTEMPORARY CONTRACTS

A Shift from Relational to Transactional Contracts?

It is commonly argued by commentators on organizational life that employees (in the US and UK alike) are experiencing a breach in the psychological contracts which they have evolved with their employers (e.g. Handy, 1994). In particular, breaches are said to have occurred in the 'relational' aspects of the psychological contract, to the point where an exchange relationship based on mutual loyalty and commitment can no longer be guaranteed (Herriot & Pemberton, 1995b). Economic pressures have created a workplace characterized by transactional forms of dealing. This, it is argued, will fashion a calculating, self-interested and opportunistic workforce, working within the 'limits' of the contract and no more, in return for high compensation or remuneration.

This analysis, however, presupposes a direct correspondence between economic and psychological reality. It also assumes that transactional contracts are intrinsically bad. There is, as yet, little actual evidence (at least within the UK) for a greater prevalence of 'transactional' than 'relational' psychological contracts (Millward & Hopkins, 1998; Millward & Brewerton, 1999). So, although many employees may feel that their psychological contracts have been breached (Herriot, Hirsch & Reilly, 1998; Coyle-Shapiro & Kessler, 1998), this has not necessarily led them into becoming more transactional in their exchange relationships with organizations (Guest & Conway, 1997; Guest,

1998). Whilst there is some suggestion that many employees have been forced into a situation whereby short-term survival or 'hygiene' needs do prevail, this does not necessarily equate with transactional contractual orientation. Instead, the issue may be a rather more complex one of employees seeking assurances that basic transactional requirements are met, before relational aspects of the contract can be considered (Herriot, Manning & Kidd, 1997, p. 161).

Herriot and Pemberton (1997) point out that 'transactional' deals may be appropriate, in some instances, for both parties in the exchange. More crucially, it can be argued that transactional deals need not preclude loyalty. Defined in terms of content, it might be difficult to reconcile transactional deals with relational-type content. However, defined in terms of process, transactional deals denote a strictly defined exchange of goods (i.e. one good is exchanged for another), indicating nothing about the actual content of the exchange (such as short-termism or preoccupation with pay and benefits). Instead, an employee operating primarily within a transactional deal is likely to value distributive equity (i.e. fair exchange of goods). Likewise, what differentiates the relational contract is not its content (of long-term loyalty, commitment, identification and so on) but reciprocity on a broader scale and over a longer time-frame. In this case, an employee is more likely to value procedural equity (i.e. fair decision-making procedures). An employee operating primarily within a relational deal is thus more likely to tolerate distributive inequity at one point in time, with view to justice in the long term.

It would seem from UK evidence that the exchange relationship is much more appropriately characterized as comprising both relational and transactional aspects in uniquely complex combinations (Millward & Brewerton, 1999a). Evidence from the US suggests that a similar pattern is emerging in the form of so-called 'hybrid contracts' (Rousseau, 1997). As such, an employee may choose to invest a great deal of effort or trust in a company with a view to obtaining a high personal return (financial, developmental) whilst retaining a practical (i.e. circumscribed) transactional attitude should their contract be terminated. This picture in fact may describe the classic 'entrepreneur', highly motivated to obtain the highest return for their input. In this sense, loyalty and commitment may result from fulfilment of transactional needs and interests (i.e. commitment of a calculative kind) (Meyer, Allen & Smith, 1993).

It is in the notion that relational deals signal reciprocity of a general (i.e. organizational level) rather than job or task-specific kind that the term 'social capital', used earlier in this review, can be most readily understood. If social capital describes the build-up of trust and willingness to collaborate in the long term (i.e. general reciprocity), then it is a short step to realizing that a breach of reciprocity at this level could have serious costs in terms of organizational survival (Herriot, Hirsch & Reilly, 1998). When it is perceived by employees that their long-term expectations for personal growth, increased pay and/or autonomy, for example, have not been honoured, they may react with anger, exit or withdrawal of organizational-level investment (Goffee & Scase, 1992; Robinson, Kraatz & Rousseau, 1994). For many employees, compulsory relocation, demotion or job change, threats of redundancy, and intensified workloads will have been construed as fundamental violations of long-term reciprocity deals (i.e. contractual elements encapsulated by the term relational contract).

Self-correcting Contracts

We must be careful, however, not to assume that it is all doom and gloom with the contemporary psychological contract. Some UK commentators within the HRM field have suggested that we have overstated the case for the violation of relational contracts (e.g. Guest, 1998; Sparrow, 1998), with similar findings being documented in the US (Rousseau, 1997). Guest (1998) reports on findings from a recent telephone survey of 1000 UK employees (Guest & Conway, 1997) which indicate that feelings of security and trust in the employer are much higher than had been forecast, and that in the main, employees seem to hold a fairly optimistic view of their future. Levels of trust, commitment and satisfaction are reported to be slowly recovering, with 79% of employees saying they trust their management 'a lot'. Although 25% of the sample had experienced redundancy, expectations of future redundancy are low. Whilst 53% say they are working harder, most of these (42%) say it is because they want to. Moreover, those on temporary/fixed-term contracts are on average more satisfied than those on full-time contracts. It could be argued, then, that there is only limited evidence of any overt employee reaction to contractual violation within the UK (at least within this sample).

Whilst media stories in the UK document mass insecurity and opinion polls suggest universal reduction in job security, more detailed investigation shows that deterioration in the psychological contract is restricted to around 20% of employees, of whom most are less well-educated employees in peripheral jobs (Guest, Conway, Briner & Dickmann, 1996).

This, it is argued, may constitute evidence for 'self-correction' (i.e. an adjustment process) amongst those who have survived structural changes and job dislocation. On the other hand, it may be that HRM strategies designed to re-engage employees and rebuild their commitment have paid off. Moreover, many young employees will be entering the labour market today with expectations moderated by encounters with the increasing individualization of the employment experience and by their awareness of uncertain employment futures with a diminishing likelihood of full-time employment. For such employees, little other than this experience will be known or anticipated.

Thus, young employees will have entered the current situation as the only employment reality they know. What are perceived as 'new rules of the game' by older employees are merely accepted as the norm by younger ones. This would suggest a change in the psychological make-up of employees (e.g. a heightened importance of personal rather than organizational identity), and thus an imperative to evolve new strategies for HRM. Moreover, many older employees for whom the job-for-life scenario was their reality in the past, may have nonetheless adapted to the new employment scene (Sparrow, 1998). Many may find satisfaction in the autonomy and flexibility of transactional deals; others may simply have reinvested, but on new, more explicit and highly circumscribed contractual terms (i.e. more transactionally oriented commitment and trust). It is in the explicit nature of contractual terms that many may have derived satisfaction from new deals. The old employment deal was largely implicit and unquestioned, assuming homogeneity of employee requirements (i.e. a job-for-life, a prescribed career and so on). The new deal, however, affords opportunity for a diversity of different psychological deals to be made, within an employment world in which the language and ideology of 'contracts' and 'contracting' are becoming the norm.

There is of course, the likelihood that some employees will have little capacity or resilience for change, and will have found adjustment difficult (Sparrow, 1998). It is these employees for whom violation of old relational contracts may have hit the hardest. Such employees are unlikely to respond to conventional attempts to raise their levels of organizational trust and commitment to previous levels. These are the employees whose identity and self-esteem have been profoundly threatened or undermined by organizational change, and for whom the language of contract negotiation is not yet meaningful.

In short, the evidence strongly suggests that there is much more dynamism within the contracting and recontracting process than has hitherto been assumed. It is clear that there are likely to be some aspects of psychological contracts that resist change: some individuals will invest in their particular contract more than others and to this extent we can say that the individual is the 'holder' of the contract. However, there are aspects of the psychological contract that exist in the relationship or interface itself which are perhaps rather more nebulous and daunting to grapple with but which can be fruitfully explored by focusing on the contracting *process*. Perhaps the stability attributed to the psychological contract is era-specific. The old contract or deal may well have been fixed for a time, but now we are clearly moving into an era of continual adjustment and change, and to this extent the language of process is more appropriate. As researchers, we should also be mindful that the language we ourselves use to define and measure the psychological contract is also a product of the age.

DE-GENDERING THE PSYCHOLOGICAL CONTRACT

It is commonly assumed that women are fundamentally different from men in their interface with the workplace (e.g. Gallos, 1989). Traditional assumptions hold that if women interface with the 'market world' they do so in largely 'transactional' terms (i.e. to short-term, temporary, secondary or supplementary ends) deriving their social identity from other, more primary, sectors of their lives (e.g. motherhood). They are also often construed as 'employment liabilities' whose priorities lie elsewhere, and who in the main do not depend on the organization as a source of identity or primary income. Whereas the relational contract can be taken as an indicator of the extent to which an individual identifies with the goals of the organization and the degree to which they intend to work to attain those goals (Mowday, Steers & Porter, 1979), a transactional contractual orientation on the other hand is predictive of turnover, absenteeism, and the pre-eminence of personal over social identity considerations (Millward & Hopkins, 1998; Millward & Brewerton, 1999). It is indeed the case that until recently, work and organizational life has—in the main—been more central to male than female identity (e.g. Hearn & Parkin, 1992; Wilson, 1996).

These predictions, however, are derived from traditional assumptions about male and female identity and their differential routes to social validation and self-worth. Whilst it cannot be denied that males and females interface 'from different directions and with recognition of opposite truths' (Gallos, 1989), this does not preclude the possibility that females may seek to fulfil their identity needs primarily through employment (Breakwell, 1985). Indeed, the 'male breadwinner' understanding of gender location and identity has been criticized as 'becoming increasingly less viable in the face of new employment realities' (Bradley, 1997, p. 89). The European employment scene is said to have undergone feminization[2] (Jensen, Hagen & Reddy, 1988; se ealso Furedi, 1995), referring to the increasing presence of women (i.e. the distribution of women in employment) and also 'women's work' (i.e. service work) in contemporary Western society. The notion of part-time, low paid, low status, semi-skilled 'secondary' work is increasingly confined to older women (e.g. 52% of 55–59 year olds versus 13% of 21–24 year olds) (Waldby, 1997). Likewise, rapid changes in educational policy and practice mean that young educated women are benefiting in relation to the careers they are entering, being much more likely than their female seniors to have a profile in skilled, professional work (Bradley, 1997; Waldby, 1997). Moreover, the blurring of boundaries between home and work (e.g. with the widespread introduction of teleworking), between economic and non-economic spheres, and between male and female roles generally, seriously calls into question 'old' assumptions about the relative insignificance (or peripheral significance) of 'market work' for the identity of adult women.

There is as yet scant research in the area of gender and the psychological contract. Mathieu and Zajac (1990) purport nonetheless that gender considerations are highly likely to interact with the way employees construe their interface with the workplace (see also Scandura & Lankau, 1997). Thus despite evidence for fundamental agreement between males and females in beliefs about employee–employer obligations (Herriot, Manning & Kidd, 1997), differences in the salience and importance of these 'obligations' are likely to arise as a function of whether work is an important source of identification and self-worth. Although women generally retain a primary responsibility for family and domestic duties, in addition to being full-time employed (Bielby & Bielby, 1984), this does not mean to say that work is not also important to their identity.

Research conducted by Millward and Brewerton (1999), demonstrates variation between males and females particularly in terms of their transactional orientation. Specifically, females (*n* = 906) came across as significantly more transactional than males (*n* = 1635) on all relevant components within the subscale—that is less inclined to be willing to go the extra mile, less oriented to a future within the company, and more oriented to financial gain. Crucially, however, it was also found that these differences were in part an artefact of the differing hierarchical levels and disciplines taken up by men and women in the organizations sampled. Moreover, the sample comprised a mix of both part-time and full-time working women, populations which can be extremely 'polarized' in the way they interface with the workplace (Hakim, 1996).

In a more focused investigation, Millward and Brewerton (in press) explored differences in full-time male and female contractual beliefs and orientations, as a function of their status in the organizational hierarchy. The findings clearly demonstrated that there is no such thing as the 'average' female employee. Whilst various predictable patterns were discernible in the way full-time female employees interface with their workplace, they demonstrated more in common with their male counterparts than ordinarily given credit for. Popular assumption fuelled by lack of knowledge about full-time (as opposed to part-time) female employees, perhaps leads us to expect that females will be largely 'transactional' in the way they connect with the workplace—that is maintaining a certain 'emotional distance from it and oriented to short-term financial gain. However, females (*n* = 666) were found to be no more 'transactional' in their interface with the workplace than their male counterparts. This finding held true within each of five different organizations (representing five different professional disciplines/occupations): two male-dominated (numerically more male than female employees), two female-dominated (numerically more female than male employees) and one in which males and females were fairly equally represented. In absolute terms, both male and female employees were found to be more 'relational' than 'transactional' in their contractual beliefs overall (again, across all five organizations and professional/ occupational disciplines), despite the increasingly transactional nature of working life (see for example, Herriot & Pemberton, 1995a). Males and females reportedly felt equally strong in terms of their degree of emotional connection with the organization and in terms of how equitably they felt they were treated by it. Moreover, full-time female employees were actually significantly more oriented to professional development than males.

These preliminary findings throw into question commonly held assumptions and beliefs about differences in males' and females' interfaces with the workplace. In many cases, male and female employees, when matched for grade, age and industry, were found to exhibit almost identical orientations towards the workplace, with women demonstrating 'relational' investment comparable to that of their counterparts, while at the same time showing a suppressed 'transactional' orientation inconsistent with the traditional view of women at work. Whilst the findings pertain to full-time employees and cannot be generalized to other subpopulations within the female community, they do present an interesting picture of sex differences (and similarities) in the contemporary workplace. Full-time male and female employees in lower grade organizational positions were found to be almost identical in the way they interface with the workplace. Differentials—in instances where they did emerge—were only evident higher up the organizational scale and were largely context-specific. This calls into question the viability of studying sex differences in contextual isolation (Aries, 1996; Osterberg, 1996). Whilst clearly there remains a need for issues of gender 'to figure more loudly in organizational analysis' (Wilson, 1996), the study of sex differences should not be pursued to the point of clouding over the common features of the male and female work experience.

CONCLUSIONS: CONSENSUAL AND CONTENTIOUS ASPECTS

Areas of Agreement and Debate

In summary, then, the literature presents a number of elements of the psychological contract construct which have gained wide agreement and consensus, whilst others remain open to considerable discussion and debate. Areas that have gained consensual agreement include the following:

- The psychological contract comprises promises made and held by individuals and organizations. These promises are not necessarily mutual but can be understood to be reciprocal in nature.
- Understanding of the same contract may differ between individuals and between parties.
- Contract violations are significantly related to job performance, organizational commitment, job satisfaction, intent to leave, staff turnover and organizational citizenship behaviours.
- Psychological contracts can, and do, change over time.
- Contracts are shifting wholesale from traditional to dynamic and, in some cases, from relational to transactional in nature and content.
- Shifts such as these are resulting in mixed signals being transmitted from organizations to employees, with a consequent need for the negotiation of 'new' contracts.

- Contracts can be managed by both employees and employers.
- Multiple methods of measurement (generic, idiosyncratic, qualitative, quantitative) are required to investigate the psychological contracts and in particular the dynamics of contracting.

Areas touched on in the literature requiring further exploration and which continue to attract debate and contention include the following:

- Debate as to the precise content of the psychological contract, and the level of commonality of this content across organizations.
- Whether the construct incorporates only promises which may be violated, or expectations, which may be unmet, and whether contract violation simply denotes job dissatisfaction by another name. The frequency of contract violation may be overstated and hence also the dynamic aspects of contract negotiation and renegotiation (and repair) risk being understated.
- Whether the construct exists from an organization's perspective, or should be regarded at individual-level only—that is whether it exists only 'in the head' of the employee or whether it is more appropriately located within the employer–employee relationship.
- Whether transactional and relational contracts lie at opposite ends of a single continuum or whether they form discrete constructs which are conceptually and empirically distinct, and which can produce 'hybrid' forms.
- Whether the psychological contract is a valid analytic or scientific construct or simply a metaphor for describing contemporary organizational life.
- With whom the deal is made. Is this the organization, the division, the team, or the profession? To whom are breaches in the contract attributed? How are organizational responsibilities construed or represented? If the psychological contract is a two-way affair, who constitutes the nebulous 'other' (Guest, 1999)?
- The extent to which psychological contracts form normative contracts, and the ways in which these might be conceptualized and measured. Preliminary research involving nurses by Rousseau and Tijoriwala (1996) on this issue suggests that contracts are individual-level phenomena with little in common with coworkers, even within the same hospital subunit. What might be the conditions under which individuals share common elements in their psychological contract?
- The impact of cross-cultural differences in psychological contract formation and maintenance. Contracts may emerge differently across cultures with differential importance associated with facets of contracts themselves, especially explicitness and stability (Rousseau & Tinsley, 1997).

- Conceptualization and measurement of the *dynamics of contracting* including issues of contract formation, mutuality/reciprocity and contract negotiation and renegotiation, in the strict sense of the concept of psychological contract as pertaining to a relationship of exchange.
- Different ways in which individuals actively cope with, and adapt to, contract violation and change (e.g. Sparrow, 1998).

Exploding Assumptions

It should be noted that, as the body of psychological contract literature grows, the concept is becoming increasingly widely used in a variety of organizational contexts as a neat and useful explicator or metaphor for understanding organizational changes and their impact on employees (Millward & Herriot, 1999). Whilst this widespread acceptance and adoption of the construct is to be encouraged, researchers should be vigilant that the term does not become an 'umbrella' descriptor of all to do with organizations. It seems that the construct is salient to so many areas of organizational behaviour, including career development and management, organizational performance, the political nature of downsizing and restructuring decisions, the changing relationship between employee and employer, and the management of that changing relationship, that it is at risk of becoming diluted in meaning and in its explicative power.

Many recent papers have been keen to incorporate the idea of organizations' 'short run myopic focus', resulting in 'a decade of downsizing and layoffs, more palatably termed "rightsizing" (McLean Parks & Kidder, 1994), which has supposedly led directly to the development of a transactional relationship between employees and employers. Whilst the metaphorical use of the psychological contract construct in this way seems appealing, it is clear that substantially more research is required into the content and meaning of the construct before such politicized comment can be lent any conceptual (or empirical) weight. Unfortunately, many organizations have latched onto the term psychological contract as useful rhetoric, one that hides the reality of imposed deals and ill-thought out attempts to reharmonize an insecure workforce.

The assumption is commonly made that 'commitment' is good for an organization: the more the better. Similarly, an implicit assumption is often made in the literature that the loss of the old relational contract is unfortunate and that we should aim to recreate new ones. Like commitment however, the issue of relational contracts is a two-edged sword. For instance, high relational contracts can lead to insufficient turnover (and thus organizational stagnancy) and also to too much conformity/rigidity and inability to either innovate or adapt, as personal considerations are sacrificed for organizational ones (Randall, 1988). On the other side of the coin, transactional contracts might in some instances be good for an organization, insofar as they afford the opportunity for personal contributions of the creative and innovative kind. Moreover, such a climate could perpetuate a 'natural' system for the turnover of disruptive/poor performers.

From the individual point of view, relational contracts might well afford career advancement and compensation opportunities but may also foster resistance to change, stress and tension with employees having to juggle family/personal responsibilities with work and limited time for non-work activity. In a fast changing workforce, Meyer (1997) wonders whether a highly committed workforce might be a 'liability'. Alternatively, as organizations become leaner, they may rely more heavily on the commitment of just the core workers. Likewise, Rousseau (1995, p. 106) is eager to emphasize that the relational contract is by no means the 'best' or most 'appropriate'. Transactional contracts (as held by many 'careerists', for example) can afford 'flexibility' to an organization in which the dominant contract is relational. Moreover, transactional contracts increase the lifestyle options for individuals.

Conclusions

In conclusion, this review has illustrated that the term psychological contract has potential utility as a scientific and analytic construct over and above constructs such as commitment. However, much work remains to be done in clarifying our use of the term, both theoretically and empirically. We need to decide whether a content- or process-focused view of the construct is likely to bear more analytical fruit or whether it is possible to integrate the content and process literature into a single analytical framework. The latter is a possibility that is already being contemplated by researchers in the UK (e.g. Guest, 1998; Herriot & Pemberton, 1997), and it is clear that many US writers on the topic are beginning to introduce 'process' considerations into their research efforts.

It is agreed by most researchers and commentators, that the term psychological contract is in need of a theory. Some have suggested that Equity Theory is the most obvious candidate here (e.g. Herriot & Pemberton, 1997; Hutton & Cummins, 1997) but others have argued that this itself is in need of theoretical clarification and elaboration (e.g. Guest, 1999). Perhaps an attempt to integrate considerations of equity with those pertaining to the psychological contract would aid the task of theoretical clarification on both fronts. Terms such as procedural and distributive justice, which are in the process of being knitted into Equity Theory may also help to provide some theoretical substance to the notion of contract violation (see, e.g., Herriot & Pemberton, 1997).

There are always problems in keeping analytic concepts that are taken up and used as management rhetoric and metaphor, within scientific bounds. Whilst the scientific nature of a construct should not preclude its application to real issues, there are dangers in the construct becoming reified. There is a sense in which the concept is being used to dress up established issues and constructs—that is to address the issue of subjective regulation of employee behaviour. Employee relations began its life in the form of a preoccupation with increasing job satisfaction. Later, the focus changed to one of how to heighten organizational commitment. Most recently, this has been replaced by the language of psychological contracts. All of these constructs have been used with a view to understanding how to alter the 'inputs' of an individual to the organization, in ways which optimize their performance contributions. However, the difference with the psychological contract construct is that it has the potential to be conceptualized and applied in a genuinely two-way fashion, taking into consideration the wants and offers of both individual and organization (Herriot, Hirsch & Reilly, 1998) in the way originally envisaged by Barnard in 1938.

NOTES

1. It should be noted that this brief tour of commitment concepts is a simplified version of what is truly a very complex and multifaceted area (Meyer, Allen & Smith, 1993). Morrow (1983) for example, noted that there are more than 25 different commitment related-concepts in the literature.
2. Some have argued that 'feminization' of the workplace is more of a vision of the way things should be (i.e. equality of work distribution and reward in paid and unpaid working environments) as opposed to what they actually are (i.e. largely segregated from men in low-paid, low-status, insecure part-time or temporary jobs with few career prospects) (Bradley, 1997; Crompton, 1997; ILO, 1993). For instance, the ILO (1993) noted that women's earnings had only risen 2% since 1985 and were still only 71% of those of men. Others have since pointed to the persistence of male dominance and positional power in the contemporary workplace operating at both macro- (e.g. employment strategy) and micro-levels (e.g. masculine cultures of exclusion, discourses of masculinity and femininity) (Crompton, 1997). Most would agree however with the description of the contemporary employment scene as 'feminized' at least in the *numerical sense* (i.e. increased numbers of women in paid employment, new job creation particularly in fields traditionally described as 'women's work') (Bradley, 1997, p. 87).

REFERENCES

Abramson, J. & Franklin, B. (1986). *Where Are They Now?*. New York: Doubleday.

Acker, J. (1992). Gendering organizational theory. In A. J. Mills & P. Tancred (Eds), *Gendering Organizational Analysis* (pp. 248–260). London: Sage.

Alvesson, M. (1998). Gender relations and identity at work: A case study of masculinities and femininities in an advertising agency. *Human Relations*, **51**(8), 969–1005.

Angle, H. L. & Perry, J. L. (1981). An empirical assessment of organizational commitment and organizational effectiveness. *Administrative Science Quarterly*, **26**, 1–14.

Argyle, M. (1989) *The Social Psychology of Work*. London: Penguin.

Argyris, C. (1960). *Understanding Organizational Behavior*. Homewood, Ill: Dorsey.

Aries, E. (1996). *Men and Women in Interaction: Reconsidering the Differences*. New York: Oxford University Press.

Arnold, J. (1996). The psychological contract: A concept in need of close scrutiny? *European Journal of Work and Organizational Psychology*, 5(4), 511–520.

Astin, H. S. (1984). The meaning of work in women's lives: A socio-psychological model of career choice and work behaviour. *Counselling Psychologist*, 12, 117–126.

Bakan, D. (1966). *The Duality of Human Existence*. Chicago: Rand McNally.

Baker, H. G. (1985). The unwritten contract: Job perceptions. *Personnel Journal*, 64(7), 37–41.

Baker, H. G. & Berry, V. M. (1987). Processes and advantages of entry-level career-counselling. *Personnel Journal*, 66(4), 111–121.

Bardwick, J. (1980). The seasons of a woman's life. In D. McGuigan (Ed.), *Women's Lives: New Theory, Research and Policy*. Ann Arbor: University of Michigan Center for Continuing Education for Women.

Barksdale, K. & McFarlane Shore, L. (in press). A typological approach to examine psychological contracts. *Journal of Organizational Behavior*.

Barksdale, K. & Renn, R. W. (in press). A field study of the effects of a new pay-for-performance compensation plan on perceived organizational support and attendance: a psychological contract and justice perspective. *Group and Organizational Management*.

Barnard, C. (1938). *The Functions of the Executive*. Cambridge, MA: Harvard University Press.

Becker, G. S. (1960). Notes on the concept of commitment. *American Journal of Sociology*, 66, 32–40.

Becker, G. S. (1985). Human capital, effort and the sexual division of labour. *Journal of Labour Economics*, 3, S33–S38.

Becker, G. S. (1991). *A Treatise on the Family*. Cambridge MA: Harvard University Press.

Bell, C. S. & Chase, S. E. (1996). The gendered character of women superintendent's professional relationships. In Arnold, K. D. et al. (Eds), *Remarkable Women: Perspectives on Female Talent Development*. New Jersey: Cresskill.

Betz, N. (1993). Women's career development. In F. L. Denmark & M. A. Paludi (Eds), *The Psychology of Women: Handbook of Issues/Theory*, pp. 627–684, Westport, CT: Greenwood Press.

Beutel, A. M. & Marini, M. M. (1995). Gender and values. *American Sociological Review*, 60, 436–448.

Bielby, D. D. & Baron, J. N. (1984). A woman's place is with other women: Sex segregation within organisations. In G. F. Reskin (Ed.), *Sex Segregation in the Workplace: Trends, Explanations, Remedies*, pp. 27–55. Washington DC: National Academy Press.

Bielby, D. D. & Bielby, W. T. (1984). Work commitment, sex-role attitudes and women's employment. *American Sociological Review*, 49, 234–247.

Bierema, L. L. (1996). How executive women learn corporate culture. *Human Resource Development Quarterly*, 7(2), 145–164.

Blau, P. M. (1964). *On the Nature of Organizations*. New York: Wiley.

Bochner, S. & Hesketh, B. (1994). Power distance, individualism/collectivism, and job-related attitudes in a culturally-diverse work group. *Journal of Cross Cultural Psychology*, 25(2), 233–257.

Borrill, C. & Kidd, J. M. (1994). New parents at work: Jobs, families and the psychological contract. *British Journal of Guidance and Counselling*, 22(2), 219–231.

Boss, R. W. (1985). The psychological contract: A key to effective organization development consultation. *Consultation—An International Journal*, 4(4), 284–304.

Bradley, H. (1989). *Men's Work. Women's Work: A Sociological History of the Sexual Division of Labour in Employment*. Cambridge: Polity Press.

Bradley, H. (1997). Gender and change in employment: Feminization and its effects. In R. Brown (Ed.), *The Changing Shape of Work* (pp. 87–102). Macmillan: Basingstoke.

Breakwell, G. (1985). *The Quiet Rebel: Women at Work in a Man's World*. London: Century Publishing.

Brett, J. M. & Stroh, L. K. (1997). Jumping ship: Who benefits from an external labour market career strategy? *Journal of Applied Psychology*, **82**(3), 331–341.

Brewerton, P. M. (1999). Exploring the Psychological Contract: Combining relational and transactional. Unpublished Phd Thesis, University of Surrey, UK.

Brewerton, P. M. & Millward, L. J. (1997). Predicting performance at work: Organizational culture, person–culture 'misfit' and affective workplace attitudes. Unpublished MSc thesis, University of Surrey, UK.

Brockner, J., Grover, M. S., Reed, T. S. & DeWitt, R. L. (1992). Layoffs, job insecurity and survivor work effort: Evidence of an inverted U relationship. *Academy of Management Journal*, **35**, 413–425.

Brown, M. (1997). Outsourcery. *Management Today*, January, 56–58.

Burack, E. (1993). *Corporate Resurgence and the New Employment Relationship*. Westport, CT: Quorum.

Carrier, S. (1995). Family status and career situation for professional women. *Work, Employment and Society*, **9**, 343–358.

Carsten, J. M. & Spector, P. E. (1987). Unemployment, job satisfaction and employee turnover: A meta-analytic test of the Muchinsky model. *Journal of Applied Psychology*, **72**, 374–381.

Cassell, C. & Walsh, S. (1997). Organisational cultures, gender management strategies and women's experience of work. *Feminism and Psychology*, **7**(2), 224–230.

Chodorow, N. (1978). *The Reproduction of Mothering*. Berkeley, CA: University of California Press.

Cook, C. (1996). Gender differences in commitment. In A. L. Kalleberg, D. Knoke, P. V. Masden & J. L. Spaeth (Eds), *Organizations in America: Analysing their Structures and Human Resource Practices*. Beverly Hills, CA: Sage.

Coyle-Shapiro, J. & Kessler, I. (1998). Consequences of the psychological contract for the employment relationship: A large scale survey. Paper presented at the Academy of Management Conference.

Crompton, R. (1997). *Women and Work in Modern Britain*. Oxford: Oxford University Press.

Davidow, W. & Malone, M. (1992). *The Virtual Corporation*. New York: Harper.

De Meuse, K. P. & Tornow, W. W. (1997). Leadership and the changing psychological contract between employee and employer. Available from http://deming.eng.clemson.edu/pub/tqmbbs/prin.pract/psycon.txt. [accessed 6 June 1997].

de Vaus, D. & McAllister, I. (1991). Gender and work orientation: Values and satisfaction in Western Europe. *Work and Occupations*, **18**, 72–93.

Deaux, K. & Kite, M. (1993). Gender stereotypes. In F. L. Denmark & M. A. Paludi (Eds), *The Psychology of Women: Handbook of Issues/Theory* (pp. 107–140). Westpoint, CT: Greenwood Press.

Derr, C. B. (1986). *Managing the new Careerists: The Diverse Career Success Orientations of Today's Workers*. San Francisco: Jossey-Bass.

Diamond, E. E. (1987). Theories of career development and the reality of women at work. In B. A. Gutek & L. Larwood (Eds), *Women's Career Development*. Beverly Hills, CA: Sage.

Dipboye, R. L., Smith, C. S. & Howell, W. C. (1994). *Understanding Industrial and Organizational Psychology: An Integrated Approach*. Fort Worth, TX: Harcourt Brace.

Dodd-McCue, D. & Wright, G. B. (1996). Men, women, and commitment: The effects of workplace experiences and socialization. *Human Relations*, **49**(8), 1065–1091.

Doise, W., Clement, A. & Lorenzi-Cioldi, F. (1993). *The Quantitative Analysis of Social Representations*. European Monographs in Social Psychology. London & New York: Harvester Wheatsheaf.

Dunahee, M. H. & Wangler, L. A. (1974). The psychological contract: A conceptual structure for management/employee relations. *Personnel Journal*, **53**(7), 518–526.

Eichenbaum, L. & Orbach, S. (1988). *Between Women*. New York: Viking.

Eisenberger, R., Huntington, R., Hutchinson, S. & Sowa, D. (1986). Perceived organizational support. *Journal of Applied Psychology*, **71**, 500–507.

Etzioni, A. (1961). *A Comparative Analysis of Complex Organizations*. New York: Free Press.

Evatts, J. (1996). *Gender and Career in Science and Engineering*. London: Taylor & Francis.

Farmer, H. S. (1997a). Women's motivation related to mastery, career salience and career aspirations: a multivariate model focusing on the effects of sex role socialisation. *Journal of Career Assessment*. 5(4) 355–381.

Farmer, H. S. (1997b). Gender differences in career development. In H. S. Farmer et al. (Eds), *Diversity and Women's Career Development: From Adolescence to Adulthood*, Vol. 2 (pp. 127–158). Thousand Oaks, CA: Sage.

Farnsworth, E. A. (1982). *Contracts*. Boston, MA: Little Brown.

Feller, R. W. (1995). Action Planning for personal competitiveness in the 'Broken Workplace'. Special Issue: Action Planning. *Journal of Employment Counselling*, **32**(4), 254–263.

Fitzgerald, L. F. & Crites, J. O. (1980). Toward a career psychology of women: What do we know? What do we need to know? *Journal of Counselling Psychology*, **27**, 44–62.

Freese, C. & Schalk, R. M. (1996). The dynamics of psychological contracts. Paper presented at Changes in Psychological Contracts Conference, University of Tilberg, December.

Furedi, F. (1995). Is it a girls' world? *Living Marxism*, **79**, 10–13.

Gallos, J. V. (1989). Exploring women's development: Implications for career theory, practice and research. In M. B. Arthur, D. T. Hall & B. S. Lawrence (Eds), *Handbook of Career Theory* (pp. 110–132). Cambridge: Cambridge University Press.

Gilbert, L. A. (1984). Comments on the meaning of work in women's lives. *Counselling Psychologist*, **12**, 129–130.

Gilligan, C. (1977). In a different voice: Women's conceptions of self and of morality. *Harvard Education Review*, **47**, 4.

Gilligan, C. (1980). Restoring the missing text of women's developments to life-cycle theories. In D. McGuigan (Ed.), *Women's Lives: New Theory, Research and Policy*. Ann Arbor: University of Michigan Center for Continuing Education for Women.

Gilligan, C. (1982). *In a Different Voice: Psychological Theory and Women's Development*. Cambridge, MA: Harvard University Press.

Goffee, R. & Scase, R. (1992). Organizational change and the corporate career: The restructuring of managers' job aspirations. *Human Relations*, **45**, 363–385.

Golembiewsky, R., Billingsley, K. & Yeager, S. (1976). Measuring change and persistence in human affairs: Types of change generated by OD designs. *Journal of Applied Behavioural Science*, **12**, 133–157.

Granrose, C. S. & Skromme, E. E. (1996). *Work-Family Role Choices of Women in their 20–30s: From College Plans to Life Experiences*. New York: Greenwood.

Griffin, R., O'Leary-Kelly, A. & Collins, J. (1998). Dysfunctional work behaviours in organizations. In Cooper, C. L. & Rousseau, D. (Eds), *Trends in Organizational Behaviour*, Vol. 5 (pp. 65–82). Chichester: Wiley.

Guerts, S. A. (1995). Employee absenteeism: In defense of theory-based studies: Development in occupational psychology and organizational psychology. *Psychology*, **30**(9), 363–368.

Guest, D. (1998). The role of the psychological contract. In S. Perkins & St John Sandringham (Eds), *Trust, Commitment & Motivation*. Oxford: Strategic Remuneration Research Centre.

Guest, D. (1999) Is the psychological contract worth taking seriously? *Journal of Organizational Behaviour*, **19**, 649–664.

Guest, D. & Conway, N. (1997). *Employee Motivation and the Psychological Contract*. Issues in People Management. Institute of Personnel Directors, London, Report No. 21.

Guest, D. E., Conway, R., Briner, R. & Dickmann, M. (1996). *The State of the Psychological Contract in Employment*. Issues in People Management. Institute of Personnel Directors, London, Report No. 16.

Guzzo, R. A. & Berman, L. M. (1995). At what level of generality is psychological contract fulfillment best measured? Paper presented at the Academy of Management meetings, Vancouver.

Guzzo, R. A. & Noonan, K. (1994). Human resource practices as communications and the psychological contract. *Human Resource Management*, **33**, 447–462.

Guzzo, R. A., Noonan, K. A. & Elron, E. (1994). Expatriate managers and the psychological contract. *Journal of Applied Psychology*, **79**(4), 617–626.

Hakim, C. (1991). Grateful slaves and self-made women: Fact and fantasy in women's work orientations. *European Sociological Review*, 7, 101–121.

Hakim, C. (1993). The myth of rising female employment. *Work, Employment and Society*, 7, 97–120.

Hakim, C. (1995). Five feminist myths about women's employment. *British Journal of Sociology*, **46**, 429–455.

Hakim, C. (1996). *Key Issues in Women's Work: Female Heterogeneity and the Polarisation of Women's Employment*. London: Athlone Press.

Hall, D. T. (1993). *The new career contract: Alternative career paths*. Paper presented at the Fourth German Bsuiness Conference on Human Resources, Cologne.

Hall, D. T. & Mirvis, P. H. (1995). Careers as lifelong learning. In A. Howeard (Ed.), *The Changing Nature of Work*. The Jossey-Bass social and behavioral science series. San Francisco, CA: Jossey-Bass.

Handy, C. B. (1990). *The Age of Unreason*. London: Business Books.

Handy, C. B. (1994). *The Empty Raincoat*. London: Hutchinson.

Hardesty, S. & Jacobs, N. (1986). *Success and Betrayal: The Crisis of Women in Corporate America*. New York: Franklin Watts.

Hartley, J. & Mackenzie-Davey, K. (1997). The gender agenda in organisations: A review of research about women and organisational psychology. *Feminism and Psychology*, 7(2), 214–223.

Hearn, J. & Parkin, P. W. (1992). Gender and organizations: A selective review and critique of a neglected area. In A. J. Mills & P. Tancred (Eds), *Gendering Organizational Analysis* (pp. 46–66). London: Sage.

Hennig, M. & Jardim, A. (1978). *The Managerial Woman*. New York: Pocket.

Herriot, P. (1989). Selection as a social process. In M. Smith & I. Robertson (Eds), *Advances in Selection and Assessment*. London: Wiley.

Herriot, P. (1992). *The Career Management Challenge. Balancing Individual and Organizational Needs*, London: Sage.

Herriot, P. & Pemberton, C. (1995a). Contracting Careers. *Human Relations*, **49**(6), 757–790.

Herriot, P. & Pemberton, C. (1995b). *New Deals*. Chichester: Wiley.

Herriot, P. & Pemberton, C. (1997). Facilitating new deals. *Human Resource Management*, 7(1), 45–56.

Herriot, P., Hirsch, W. & Reilly, P. (1998). *Trust and Transition: Managing Today's Employment Relationship*. Chichester: Wiley.

Herriot, P., Manning, W. E. G. & Kidd, J. M. (1997). The content of the psychological contract. *British Journal of Management*, **8**, 151–162.

Hiltrop, J.-M. (1995). The changing psychological contract: The human resource challenge of the 1990s. *European Management Journal*, **13**, 286–294.

Hirsch, W. & Jackson, C. (1996). Strategies for career development: Promise, practice, and pretence. Brighton: Institute of Employment Studies, Report 280.

Hofstede, G. (1980, 1994). *Cultures Consequences: International Differences in Work Related Values*. Beverly Hills and New York: Sage.

Hunt, A. (1968). A survey of women's employemnt. London: HMSO.

Hutton, D. & Cummins, R. (1997). Development of the Psychological Inventory. *Australian Journal of Career Development*, **6**(3), 35–41.

Institute of Employment Studies (IES) (1998). Long Term Survey of Employment Trends. Report.

ILO (International Labour Office) (1993). *Job Evaluation*. Geneva: Author.

Irving, P. G. & Meyer, J. P. (1994). Reexamination of the Met-Expectations Hypothesis: A longitudinal analysis. *Journal of Applied Psychology*, **79**(6), 937–949.

Jackson, S. E. & Schuler, R. S. (1985). A meta-analysis and conceptual critique of research on role ambiguity and role conflict in work settings. *Organizational Behavior and Human Decision Processes*, **36**, 16–28.

Jensen, J., Hagen, E. & Reddy, C. (Eds) (1988). *Feminization of the Labour Force: Paradoxes and Promises*. New York: Oxford University Press.

Johnson, P. R. & Indvik, J. (1994). Workplace violence: An issue of the nineties. *Public Personnel Management*, **23**(4), 515–523.

Josselson, R. (1987). *Finding Herself: Pathways to Identify Development in Women*. San Francisco: Jossey-Bass.

Kanfer, F. H., Cox, L. E., Griner, J. M. & Karoly, P. (1974). Contracts, demand characteristics and self-control. *Journal of Personality and Social Psychology*, **30**, 605–619.

Katz, D. & Kahn, R. I. (1966). *The Social Psychology of Organizations*. New York: Wiley.

Kaufman, P. J. & Stern, L. W. (1988). Relational exchange norms, perceptions of unfairness, and retained hostility in commercial litigation. *Journal of Conflict Resolution*, **32**, 534–552.

Klenke, K. (1996). *Women and Leadership: A Contextual Perspective*. New York: Springer.

Kiriakodou, O. & Millward, L. (1999). The nature of corporate identity: Relations between culture, identitiy and image. Sixth European Congress of Psychology, 4–9 July 1999, Rome.

Koch, J. L. & Steers, R. M. (1978). Job attachment, satisfaction and turnover among public sector employees. *Journal of Vocational Behavior*, **12**, 119–128.

Kobasa, S. C. (1979). Stressful life events, personality and health: An inquiry into hardiness. *Journal of Personality and Soical Psychology*, **37**, 1–11.

Kolb, J. A. (1997). Are we still stereotyping leadership: A look at gender and other predictors of leader emergence. *Small Group Research*, **28**(3), 370–393.

Kotter, J. P. (1973). The psychological contract: Managing the joining-up process. *California Management Review*, **15**, 91–99.

Kuhl, J. (1992). A theory of self-regulation: Action versus state orientation, self-discrimination and some applications. *Applied Psychology: An International Review*, **10**, 397–407.

Larwood, L. & Gutek, B. A. (1987). Working towards a theory of women's career development. In B. A. Gutek & L. Larwood (Eds), *Women's Career Development*. Beverly Hills, CA: Sage.

Levinson, D. (1978). *The Seasons of a Man's Life*. New York: Knopf.

Levinson, H. (1962). *Organizational Diagnosis*. Cambridge, MA: Harvard University Press.

Levinson, H., Price, C. R., Munden, K. J. & Solley, C. M. (1962) *Men Management and Mental Health*. Cambridge, MA: Harvard University Press.

Lind, E. A. & Tyler, T. R. (1988). *The Social Psychology of Procedural Justice*. New York: Plenum.

Loden, M. (1985). *Feminine Leadership or How to Succeed in Business Without Becoming One of the Boys*. New York: Times Books.

London, M. & Stumpf, S. (1986). Individual and organizational career development in changing times. In D. Hall & Associates, *Career Development in Organizations*. San Francisco: Jossey-Bass.

Lucero, M. A. & Allen, R. E. (1994). Employee benefits: A growing source of psychological contract violations. *Human Resource Management*, **33**, 425–446.

Lynn, S. A., Cao, L. T. & Horn, B. C. (1996). The influence of career stage on the work attitudes of male and female accounting professionals. *Journal of Organizational Behaviour*, **17**(2), 135–149.

Macaulay, S. (1963). Noncontractual relations in business: A preliminary study. *American Sociological Review*, **28**, 55–69.

MacNeil, I. R. (1985). Relational Contract: What we do and do not know. *Wisconsin Law Review*, pp. 483–525.

Maddock, S. & Parkin, D. (1996). Gender cultures: Women's choices and strategies at work. Billsbury, J. et al. (Eds), *The Effective Manager: Perspectives and Illustrations*. London: Sage.

Marini, M. M. & Fan, P. L. (1997). The gender gap in earnings at career entry. *American Sociological Review*, **62**(4), 588–604.

Marshall, J. (1984). *Women Managers: Travellers in a Male World*. Chichester: Wiley.

Marshall, J. (1989). Revisioning career concepts: A feminist invitation. In M. B. Arthur, D. T. Hall & B. S. Lawrence (Eds), *Handbook of Career Theory* (pp. 275–291). Cambridge: Cambridge University Press.

Mathieu, J. E. & Zajac, D. M. (1990). A review and meta-analysis of the antecedents, correlates and consequences of organizational commitment. *Psychological Bulletin*, **108**(2), 171–194.

McFarlane Shore, L. & Tetrick, L. E. (1994). The psychological contract as an exploratory framework in the employment relationship. In C. L. Cooper & D. M. Rousseau (Eds), *Trends in Organizational Behavior*, Vol. 1. Chichester: Wiley.

McGee, G. W. & Ford, R. C. (1987). Two (or more?) dimensions of organizational commitment: Reexamination of the effective and continuance commitment scales. *Journal of Applied Psychology*, **72**, 638–642.

McLean Parks, J. & Kidder, D. L. (1994). 'Till death us do part . . .': Changing work relationships in the 1990s. In C. L. Cooper and D. M. Rousseau (Eds), *Trends in Organizational Behavior*, Vol. 1. Chichester: Wiley.

Melamed, T. (1996). Career success: An assessment of a gender specific model. *Journal of Occupational and Organizational Psychology*, **69**(3), 217–242.

Meyer, J. P. (1997). Organizational commitment. In C. L. Cooper & I. T. Robertson (Eds), *International Review of Industrial and Organizational Psychology*, Vol. 12. Chichester: Wiley.

Meyer, J. P., Allen, N. & Smith, C. A. (1993). Commitment to organisations and occupations: Extension and test of the three-component conceptualisation. *Journal of Applied Psychology*, **78**, 538–551.

Miles, R. E. & Snow, C. C. (1980). Designing strategic human resource systems. *Organizational Dynamics*, **8**, 36–52.

Mills, A. J. (1992). Organization, gender and culture. In A. J. Mills & P. Tancred (Eds), *Gendering Organizational Analysis* (pp. 93–111). London: Sage.

Millward, L. J. (1995). Contextualizing social identity in considerations of what it means to be a nurse. *European Journal of Social Psychology*, **25**, 303–324.

Millward, L. J. & Brewerton, P. (1998) Validation of the Psychological Contract Scale in an organisational context. SPERI Publication, University of Surrey, Guildford, UK.

Millward, L. J. & Brewerton, P. (1999). Contractors and their Psychological Contract. *British Journal of Management*, **10**, 253–274.

Millward, L. J. & Brewerton, P. M. Gender and exchange stance: a psychological contract approach. *Journal of Organizational Behavior*.

Millward, L. J. & Hopkins, L. J. (1998). Psychological contracts, organizational and job commitment. *Journal of Applied Social Psychology*, **28**(16), 16–31.

Millward, L. J. & Herriot, P. (1999). Psychological contracts in the UK. In R. Schalk & D. Rousseau (Eds), *International Psychological Contracts*. London: Sage.

Morey, N. C. & Luthans, F. (1984). An emic perspective and ethnoscience methods for organizational research. *Academy of Management Review*, **9**, 27–36.

Moray, N. (1997). Models of models of . . . mental models. In T. B. Sheridan & T. Van Luntern (Eds), *Perspectives on the Human Controller: Essays in Honor of Henk G. Stassen* (pp. 271–285). Mahwah, NJ: Lawrence Erlbaum.

Morris, L. (1990). The workings of the household. Cambridge: Polity Press.

Morris, L. (1997). Economic change and domestic work. In R. Brown (Ed.), *The Changing Shape of Work* (pp. 125–149). Basingstoke Macmillan.

Morrow, P. C. (1983). Concept redundancy in organizational research: The case of work commitment. *Academy of Management Review*, **8**, 486–500.

Mowday, R. T., Steers, R. M. & Porter, L. W. (1979). The measurement of organizational commitment. *Journal of Vocational Behavior*, **14**, 224–247.

Murrell, A. J., Frieze, I.-H. & Olson, J. E. (1996). Mobility strategies and career outcomes: A longitudinal study of MBAs. *Journal of Vocational Behaviour*, **49**(3), 324–335.

Nelson, D. L., Quick, J. C. & Joplin, J. R. (1991). Psychological contracting and newcomer socialization: An attachment theory foundation. Special Issue: Handbook on job stress. *Journal of Social Behavior and Personality*, **6**(7), 55–72.

Nicholson, N. & Johns, G. (1985). The absence culture and the psychological contract: Who's in control of absence? *Academy of Management Review*, **10**(3), 397–407.

Nicholson, N. & West, M. (1996). Men and women in transition. In Billsbury, J. et al. (Eds), *The Effective Manager: Perspectives and Illustrations*. London: Sage.

Nicolson, P. (1996). *Gender, Power and Organisation*. London: Routledge.

Noer, D. M. (1993). *Healing the Wounds: Overcoming the Trauma of Layoffs and Revitalizing Downsized Organizations*. San Francisco, CA: Jossey-Bass.

Noon, M. & Blyton, P. (1997). *The Realities of Work*. London: Macmillan.

Nordhaug, O. (1989). Reward functions of personnel training. *Human Relations*, **42**, 373–388.

Northouse, P. G. (1997). *Leadership: Theory and Practice*. Thousand Oaks, CA: Sage.

O'Hara-Devereux, M. & Johansen, R. (1994). Global Work: Bridging Distance, Culture and Time. In P. Pritchett (Ed.), *New Work Habits for a Radically Changing World*. Dallas, TX: Pritchett & Associates.

Osterberg, M. J. (1996). Gender in supervision: Exaggerating the differences between men and women. *Clinical Supervisor*, **14**(2), 69–83.

Parks, J. & Van Dyne, L. (1995). An idiosyncratic measure of contracts. Paper presented at the Academy of Management meetings. Vancouver.

Parsons, G. & Strickland, E. (1996). How Vauxhall Motors is getting its employees on the road to life-long learning. *European Journal of Work and Organizational Psychology*, **5**(4), 597–608.

Payne, K. E. & Cangemi, J. (1997). Gender differences in leadership. *IFE Psychologia. An International Journal*, **5**(1), 22–43.

Pearce, J. L. (1993). Towards an organisational behavior of contract laborers: Their psychological involvement and effects on employee co-workers. *Academy of Management Review*, **36**, 1082–1096.

Poole, M-E. & Langan-Fox, J. (1997). Australian women and careers: Psychological and contextual influences over the life course. Melbourne (longitudinal study). Cambridge University Press.

Porter, L. W., Pearce, J. L., Tripoli, A. & Lewis, K. (1996). The psychological contract: An empirical assessment. Paper presented at Changes in Psychological Contracts Conference, University of Tilberg, December.

Porter, L. W., Steers, R. M., Mowday, R. T. & Boullian, P. V. (1974). Organizational commitment, job satisfaction and turnover among psychiatric technicians. *Journal of Applied Psychology*, **59**(5), 603–609.

Post, P., Williams, M. & Brubaker, L. (1996). Career and life-style expectations of rural eighth grade students: A second look. *Career Development Quarterly*, **44**(3), 250–257.

Prasad, P., Mills, A. J., Elmes, M. & Prasad, A. (Eds) (1997). *Managing the Organizational Melting Pot*. Thousand Oaks, CA: Sage.

Pratch, L. & Jacobowitz, J. (1996). Gender, motivation and coping in the evaluation of leadership effectiveness. *Consulting Psychology Journal: Practice and Research*, **48**(4), 203–220.

Pritchard (1969). Equity theory: A review and critique. *Organizational Behavior and Human Performance*, **4**, 176–211.

Pritchett, P. (1994). *New Work Habits for a Radically Changing World*. Dallas, TX: Pritchett & Associates.

Radford, L. M. & Larwood, L. (1982). A field study of conflict in psychological exchange: The California taxpayers' revolt. *Journal of Applied Social Psychology*, **12**(1), 60–69.

Ragins, B. R. & Sundstrom, E. (1989). Gender and power in organisations: A longitudinal perspective. *Psychological Bulletin*, **105**, 52–88.

Randall, D. M. (1988). Multiple roles and organizational commitment. *Journal of Organizational Behavior*, **9**(4), 309–317.

Rawls, J. (1971). *A Theory of Justice*. Cambridge, MA: Bleknap.

Rizzo, J. R., House, R. & Lirtzman, S. (1970). Role conflict and role ambiguity in complex organizations. *Administrative Science Quarterly*, **15**, 150–163.

Robinson, S. L. (1995). Violation of PC: Impact on employee attitudes. In L. E. Tetrick & J. Barling (Eds), *Changing Employment Relations: Behavior and Social Perspectives*. Washington, DC: American Psychiatric Association.

Robinson, S. L. (1996). Trust and breach of the psychological contract. *Administrative Science Quarterly*, **41**, 574–599.

Robinson, S. L., Kraatz, M. S. & Rousseau, D. M. (1994). Changing obligations and the psychological contract: A longitudinal study. *Academy of Management Journal*, **37**, 137–152.

Robinson, S. L. & Rousseau, D. M. (1994). Violating the psychological contract: Not the exception but the norm. *Journal of Organizational Behaviour*, **15**, 245–259.

Robinson, S. L. & Wolfe-Morrison, E. (1995). Psychological contracts and OCB: The effect of unfulfilled obligations on civic virtue behaviour. *Journal of Organizational Behavior*, **16**, 289–298.

Robinson, S. L. & Wolfe-Morrison, E. (1997). The development of psychological contract breach and violation: A longitudinal study. *Academy of Management Review* (under review).

Roehling, M. (1996). The origins and early development of the psychological contract construct. Paper presented at the Academy of Management meetings, Cincinnati.

Rosin, H. M. & Korabik, K. (1991). Workplace variables, effective responses and intention to leave among women managers. *Journal of Occupational Psychology*, **64**, 317–330.

Rousseau, D. M. (1989). Psychological and implied contracts in organizations. *Employee Rights & Responsibilities Journal*, **2**, 121–139.

Rousseau, D. M. (1990). New hire perception of their own and their employees' obligations: A study of psychological contracts. *Journal of Organizational Behaviour*, **11**, 389–400.

Rousseau, D. M. (1995). *Psychological Contracts in Organizations: Understanding Written and Unwritten Agreements*. London & New York: Sage.

Rousseau, D. M. (1996). Changing the deal while keeping the people. *Academy of Management Executive*, **10**, 50–61.

Rousseau, D. (1997). Organizational behaviour in the new organizational era. *Annual Review of Psychology*, **48**, 515–546.

Rousseau, D. M. & Parks, J. M. (1993). The contracts of individuals and organizations. In L. L. Cummings & B. M. Staw (Eds), *Research in Organizational Behavior*. Greenwich, CT: JAI Press.

Rousseau, D. M., Robinson, S. L. & Kraatz, M. S. (1992). Renegotiating the psychological contract. Paper presented at the Society for Industrial/Organizational Psychology meeting, Montreal.

Rousseau, D. M. & Tijoriwala, S. (1996). It takes a good reason to change a psychological contract. Presented at Society for Industrial Organizational Psychology, April, San Diego.

Rousseau, D. M. & Tinsley, K. (1997). Human Resources are local: Society and social contracts in a global economy. In N. Anderson & P. Herriot (Eds), *Handbook of Selection and Appraisal*. London: Wiley.

Rousseau, D. M. & Wade-Benzoni, K. A. (1995). Changing individual–organization attachments: A two-way street. In A. Howard (Ed.), *The Changing Nature of Work*. The Jossey-Bass social and behavioral science series. San Francisco, CA: Jossey-Bass.

Sackmann, S. A. (1997). *Cultural Complexity in Organizations: Inherent Contrasts and Contradictions*. Thousand Oaks, CA: Sage.

Salminen, E. O. (1994). Career development anchors: A follow-up study of managerial success form the point of view of the individual and the organization. *Psykologica*, **29**(3), 173–175.

Scandura, T. A. & Lankau, M. J. (1997). Relationships of gender, family responsibility and flexible hours to organizational commitment and job satisfaction. *Journal of Organizational Behaviour*, **18**(4), 377–391.

Schalk, R. & Rousseau, D. (Eds) (1999). *International Psychological Contracts*. New York: Sage.

Schein, E. H. (1980). *Organizational Psychology*. Englewood Cliffs, NJ: Prentice-Hall.

Schein, E. H. (1993). *Career Anchors: Discovering your Real Values*. Revised Edn. London: Pfeiffer.

Sheppard, D. (1992). Women managers' perceptions of gender and organizational life. In A. J. Mills & P. Tancred (Eds), *Gendering Organizational Analysis* (pp. 151–166). London: Sage.

Shore, L. & Tetrick, L. E. (1994). The psychological contract as an exploratory framework in the employment relationship. In C. L. Cooper and D. M. Rousseau (Eds), *Trends in Organizational Behavior*, Vol. 1. Chichester: Wiley.

Shortell, S. M. & Zajac, E. J. (1990). Perceived and archival measures of Miles & Snow's strategic types: A comprehensive assessment of reliability and validity. *Academy of Management Journal*, **33**, 817–832.

Sims, R. R. (1992). Developing the learning climate in public sector training programs. *Public Personnel Management*, **21**(3), 335–346.

Smith, C. A., Organ, D. W. & Near, J. P. (1983). Organizational citizenship behaviour: Its nature and antecedents. *Journal of Applied Psychology*, **68**, 653–663.

Snow, C. C., Miles, R. E. & Coleman, H. J. (1992). Managing 21st century network organisations. *Organizational Dynamics*, Winter, 5–21.

Somers, M. J. (1995) Organizational commitment, turnover and absenteeism: An examination of direct and interaction effects. *Journal of Organizational Behavior*, **16**, 49–58.

Sparrow, P. R. (1996). Careers and the psychological contract: Understanding the European context. *European Journal of Work and Organizational Psychology*, **5**(4), 479–500.

Sparrow, P. R. (1998). New organisational forms, processes, jobs and psychological contracts: resolving the issues. In P. Sparrow & M. Marchington (Eds), *Human Resource Management: the New Agenda*. London: Pitman.

Spence, J. T. (1984). Masculinity, femininity, and gender-related traits: A conceptual analysis and critique of current research. *Progress in Experimental Personality Research*, **13**, 1–97.

Stiles, P., Gratton, L., Truss, C., Hope-Hailey, V. & McGovern, P. (1996). Performance management and the psychological contract. *Human Resource Management Journal*, **7**(1), 57–66.

Stroh, L. K., Brett, J. M. & Reilly, A. H. (1996). Family structure, glass ceiling and traditional explanations for the differential rate of turnover of female and male managers. *Journal of Vocational Behaviour*, **49**(1), 99–118.

Stroh, L. K. & Reilly, A. H. (1997). Rekindling organizational loyalty: The role of career mobility. *Journal of Career Development*, **24**(1), 39–54.

Tooher, P. (1996). Temps take over the British workplace. *The Independent*, 15/7/96.

Tornow, W. W. & De Meuse, K. P. (1994). 'New paradigm approaches in strategic human resource management': Comment. *Group and Organization Management*, **19**(2), 165–170.

Tyler, T. R. & Bies, R. J. (1990). Interpersonal aspects of procedural justice. In J.S. Carroll (Ed.), *Applied Social Psychology and Organizational Settings* (pp. 77–98). Hillsdale, NJ: Erlbaum.

Wade-Benzoni, K. A. & Rousseau, D. M. (1997). Psychological contracts in the faculty-doctoral student relationship (under review).

Waldby, S. (1997). *Gender Transformations*. London: Routledge.

Wanous, J. P., Poland, T., Premack, S. L. and Davis, K. S. (1992). The effects of met expectations on newcomer attitudes and behaviors: A review and meta-analysis. *Journal of Applied Psychology*, **77**(3), 288–297.

Wanous, J. P. & Reichers, A. E. (1996). Estimating the reliability of a single-item measure. *Psychologiucal Reports*, **78**, 631–634.

Wickwire, K. S. & Kruper, J. C. (1996). The glass ceiling effect: An approach to assessment. *Consulting Psychology Journal: Practice and Research*, **49**(1), 32–39.

Williamson, O. E. (1991). Comparative economic organization. The analysis of discrete structural alternatives. *Administrative Science Quarterly*, **36**, 269–296.

Wilson, F. (1996). Organizational theory: blind and deaf to gender? *Organization Studies*, **17**(5), 825–842.

INDEX